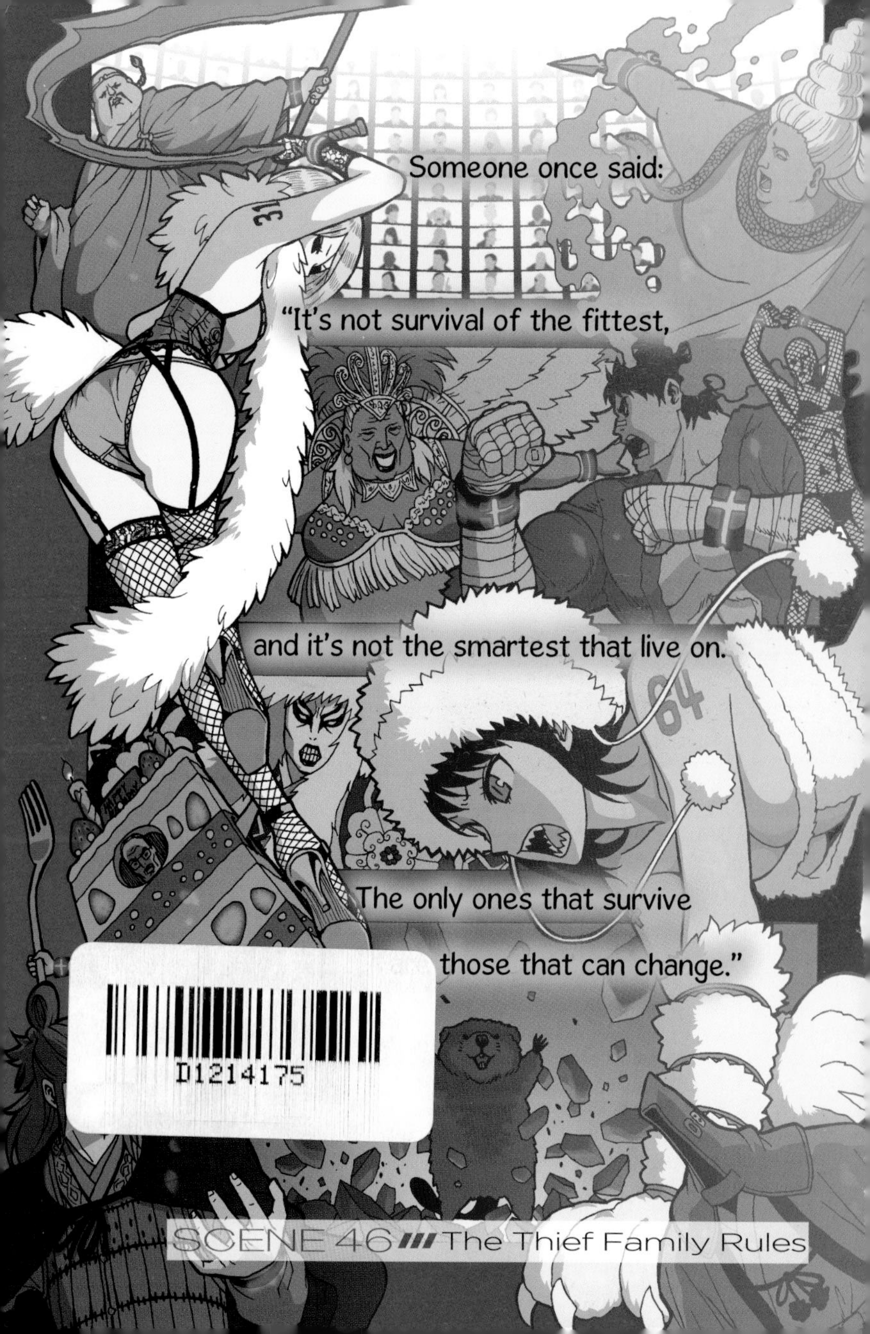
Someone once said:
"It's not survival of the fittest,
and it's not the smartest that live on.
The only ones that survive
those that can change."
31
64
SCENE 46 /// The Thief Family Rules

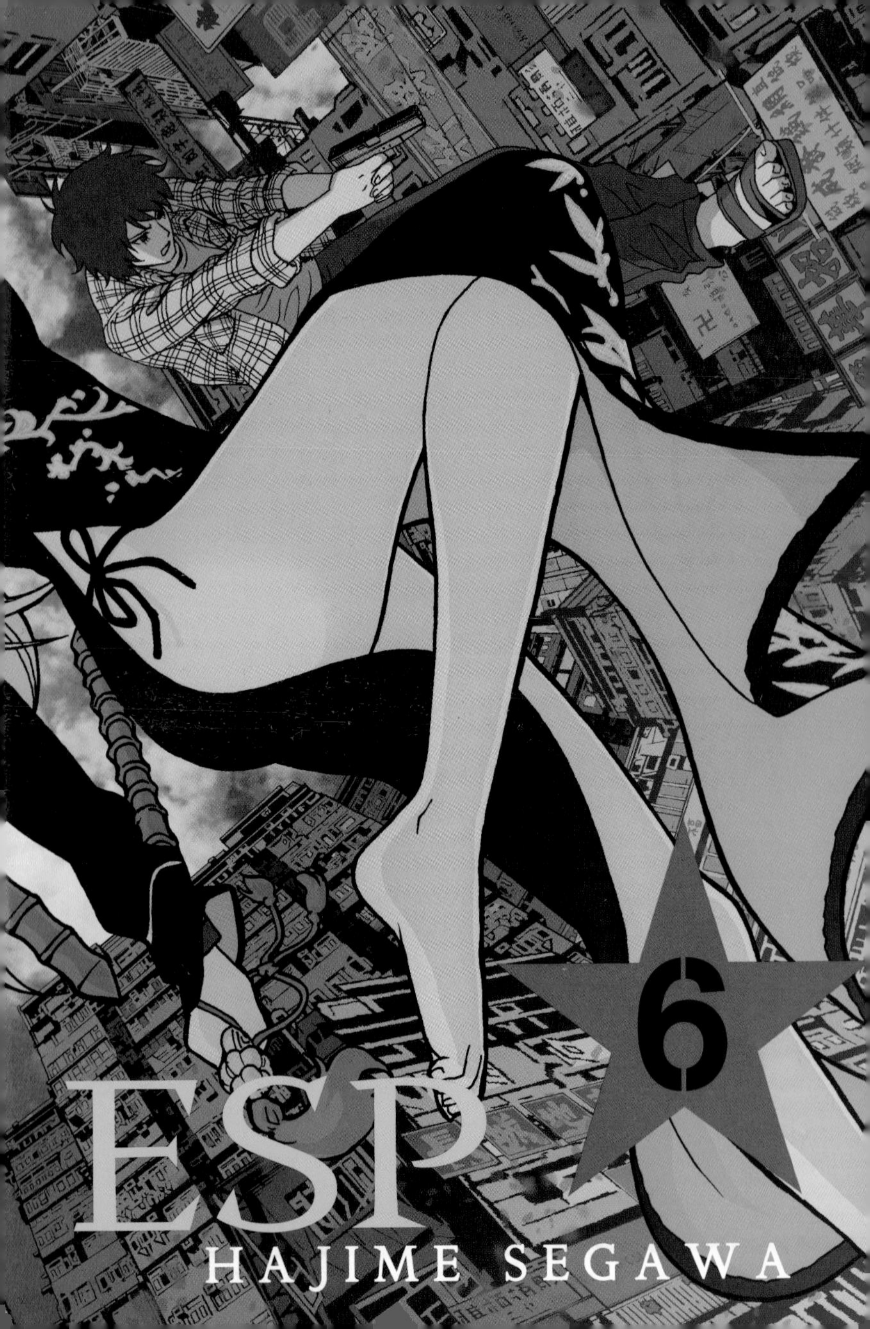
ESP
6
HAJIME SEGAWA

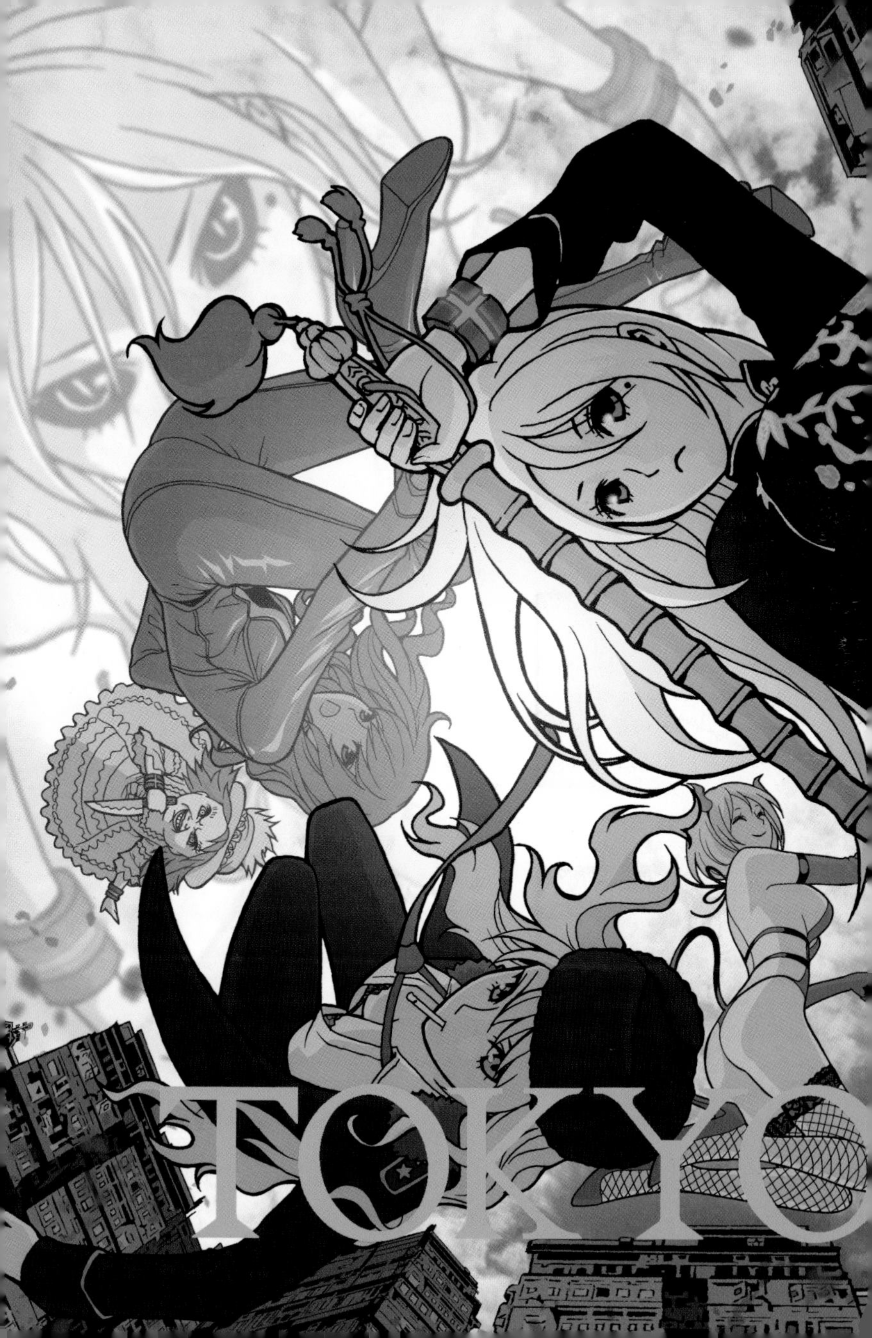
TOKYO

CONTENTS 6

Hajime Segawa Presents

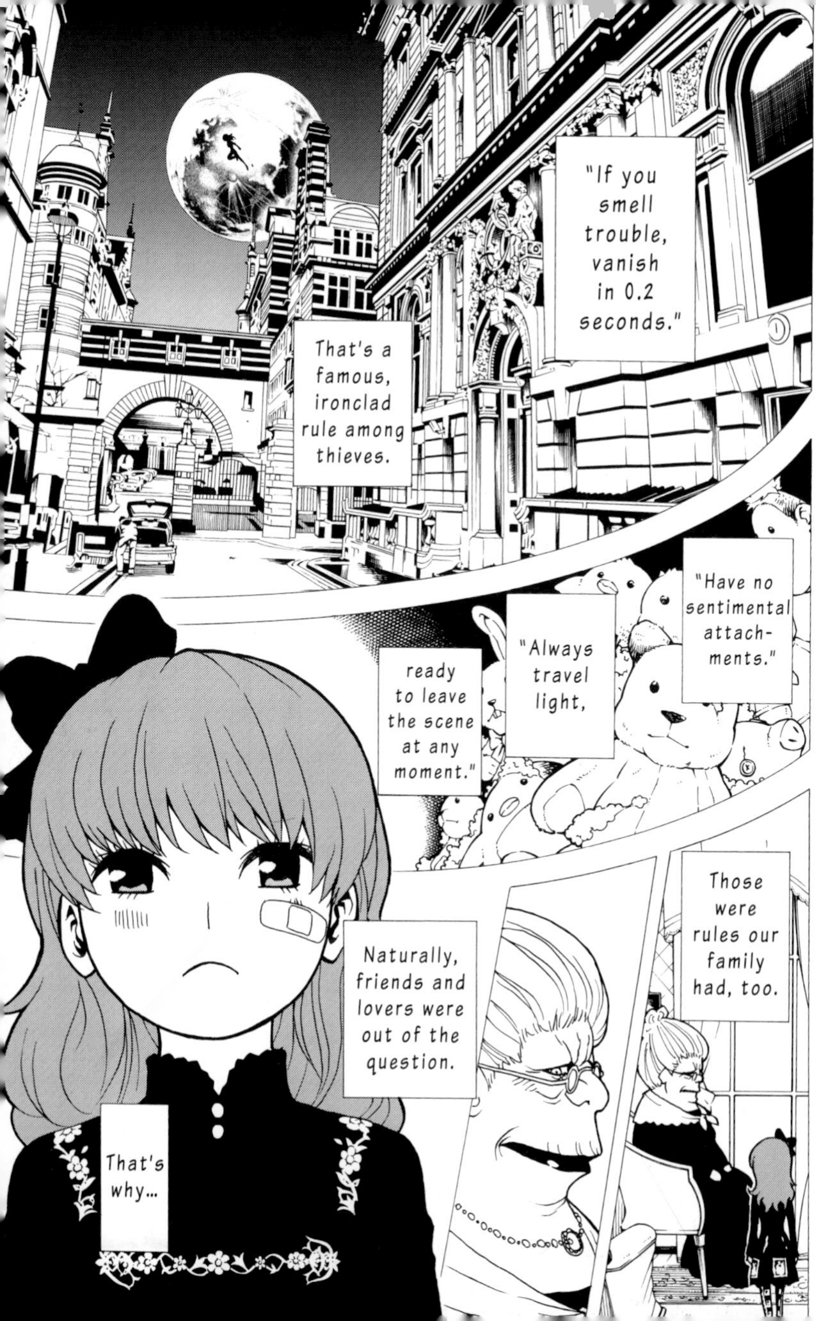
"If you smell trouble, vanish in 0.2 seconds."
That's a famous, ironclad rule among thieves.
"Have no sentimental attachments."
"Always travel light,
ready to leave the scene at any moment."
Those were rules our family had, too.
Naturally, friends and lovers were out of the question.
That's why...

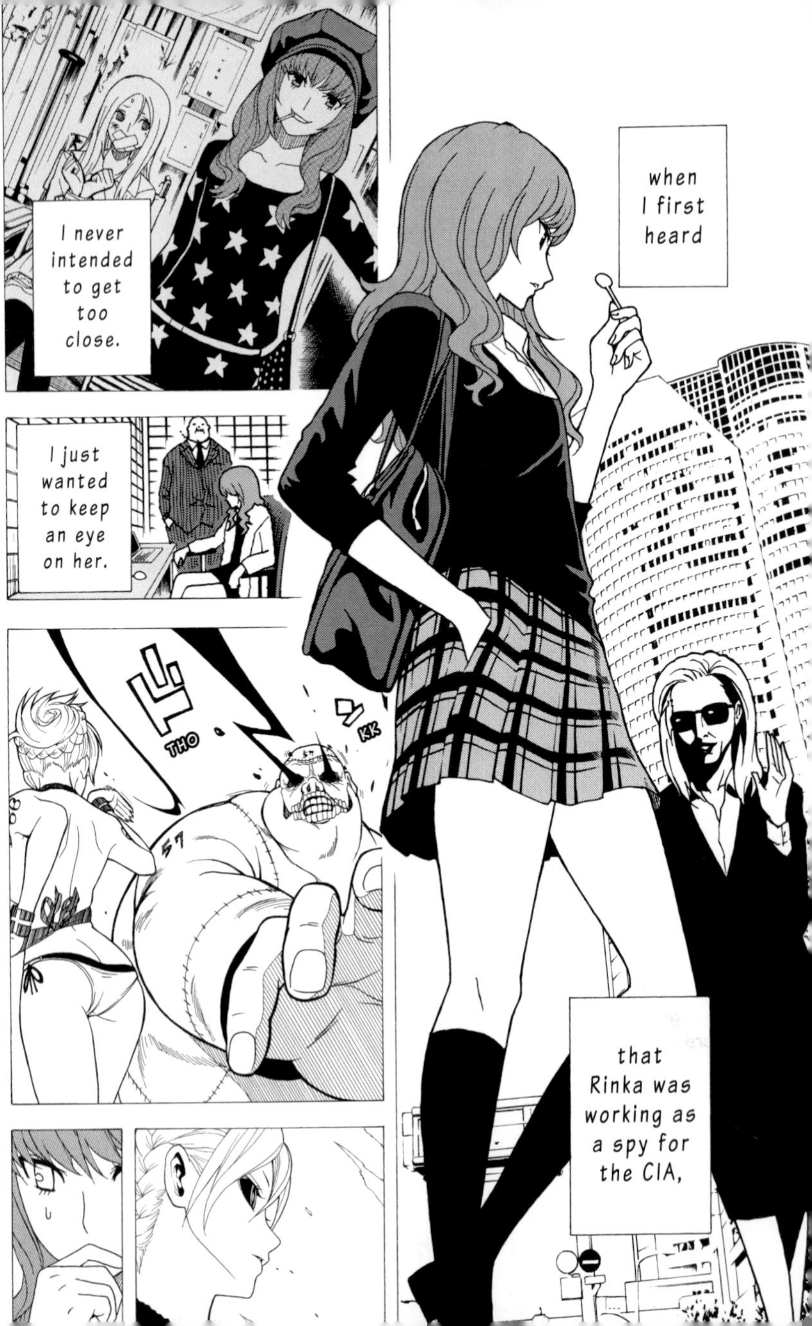
when I first heard
that Rinka was working as a spy for the CIA,
I never intended to get too close.
I just wanted to keep an eye on her.
KK
THO

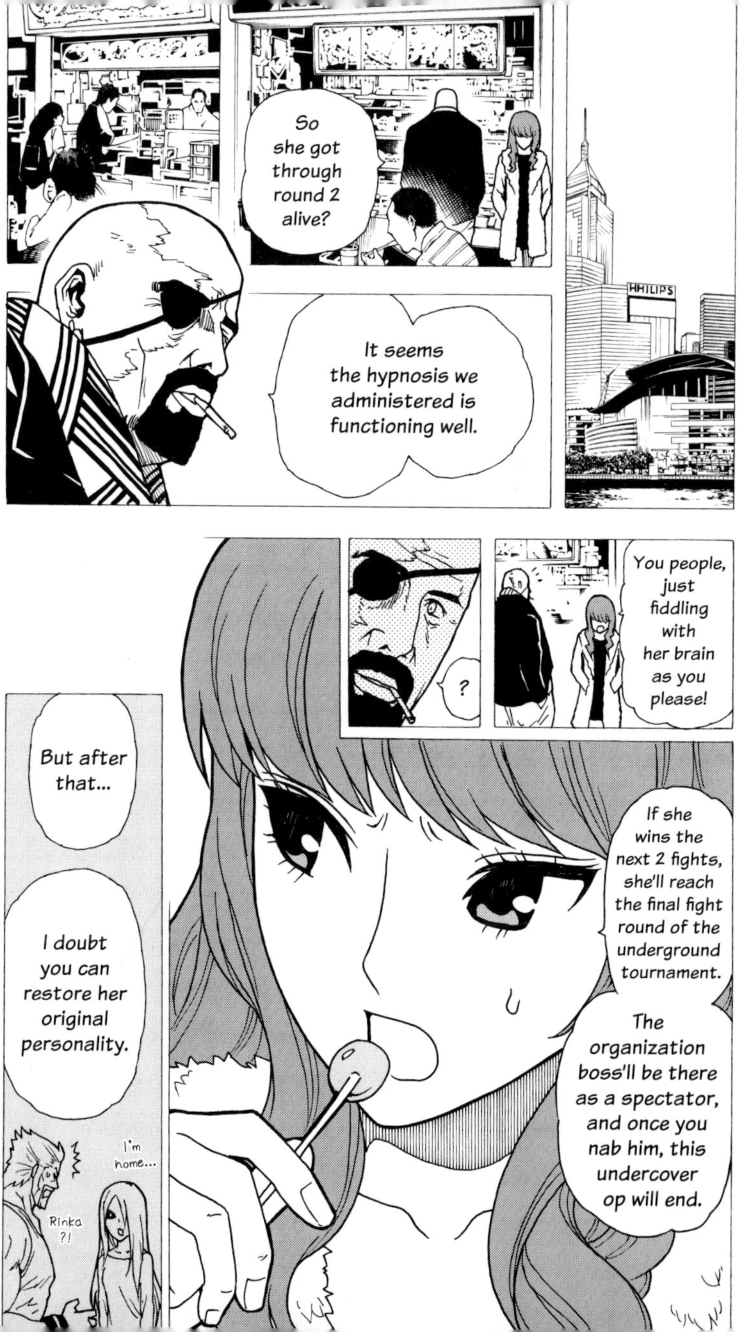
So she got through round 2 alive?
It seems the hypnosis we administered is functioning well.
You people, just fiddling with her brain as you please!
?
If she wins the next 2 fights, she'll reach the final fight round of the underground tournament.
The organization boss'll be there as a spectator, and once you nab him, this undercover op will end.
But after that...
I doubt you can restore her original personality.
I'm home...
Rinka ?!

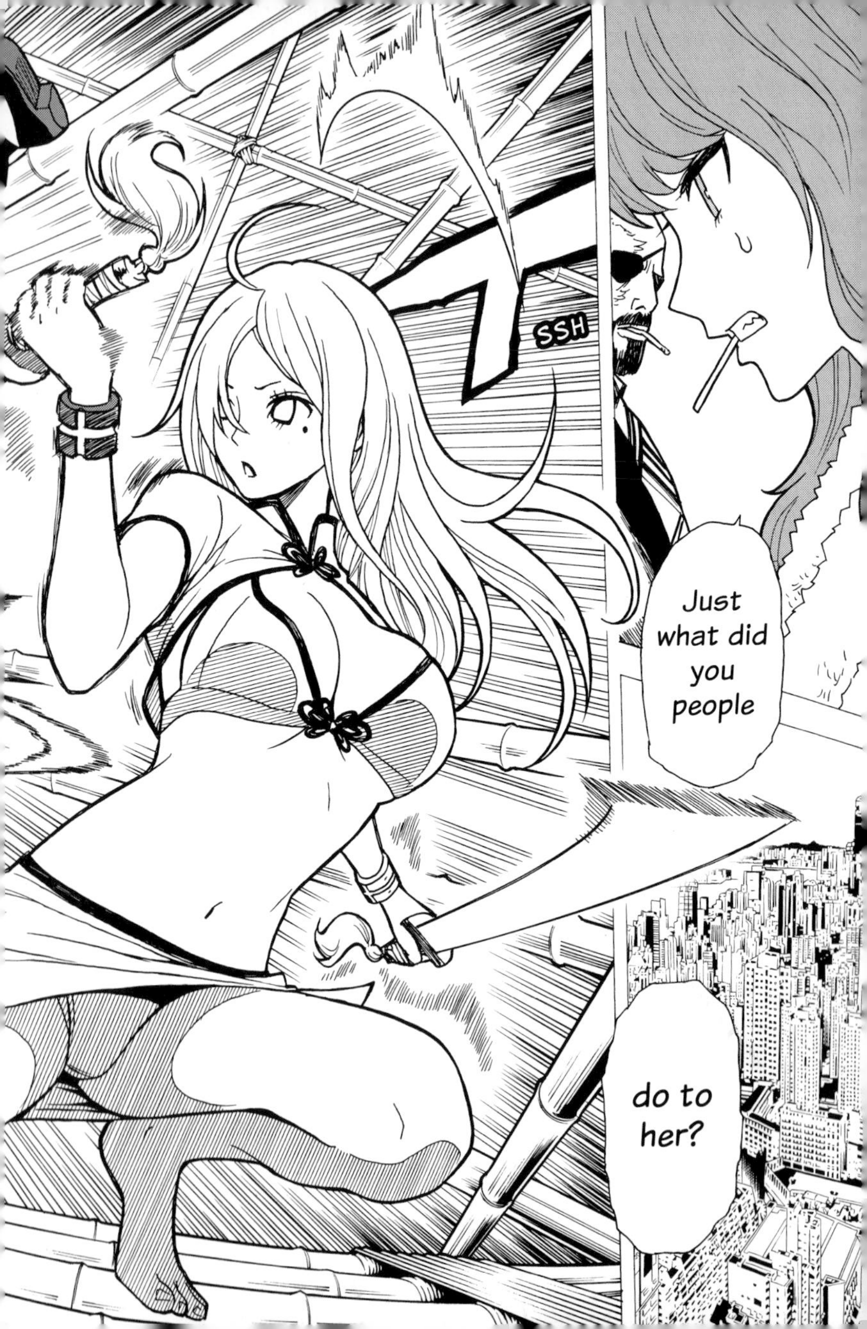
Just what did you people
do to her?
SSH

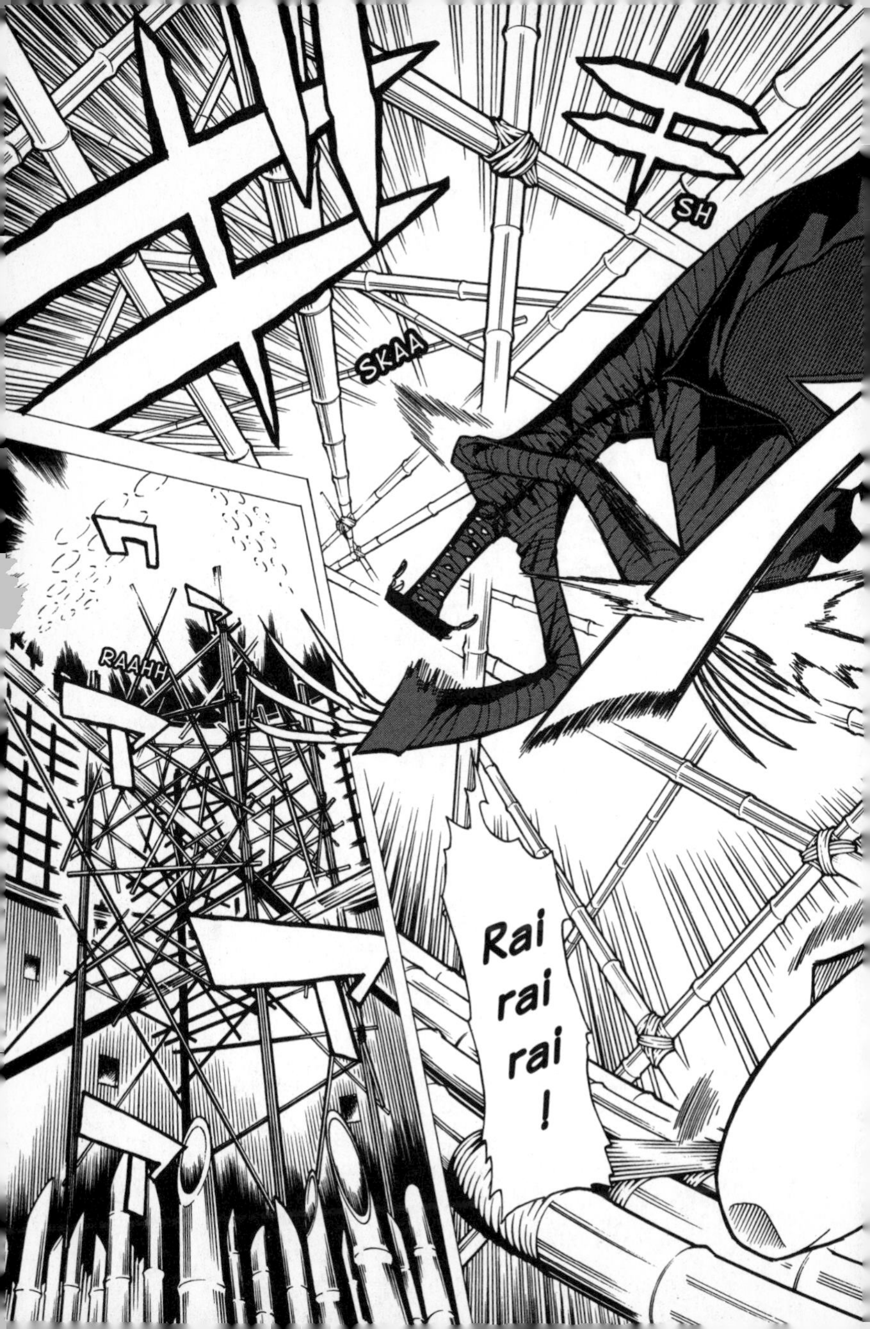
SH
SKAA
Rai rai rai!
RAAHH

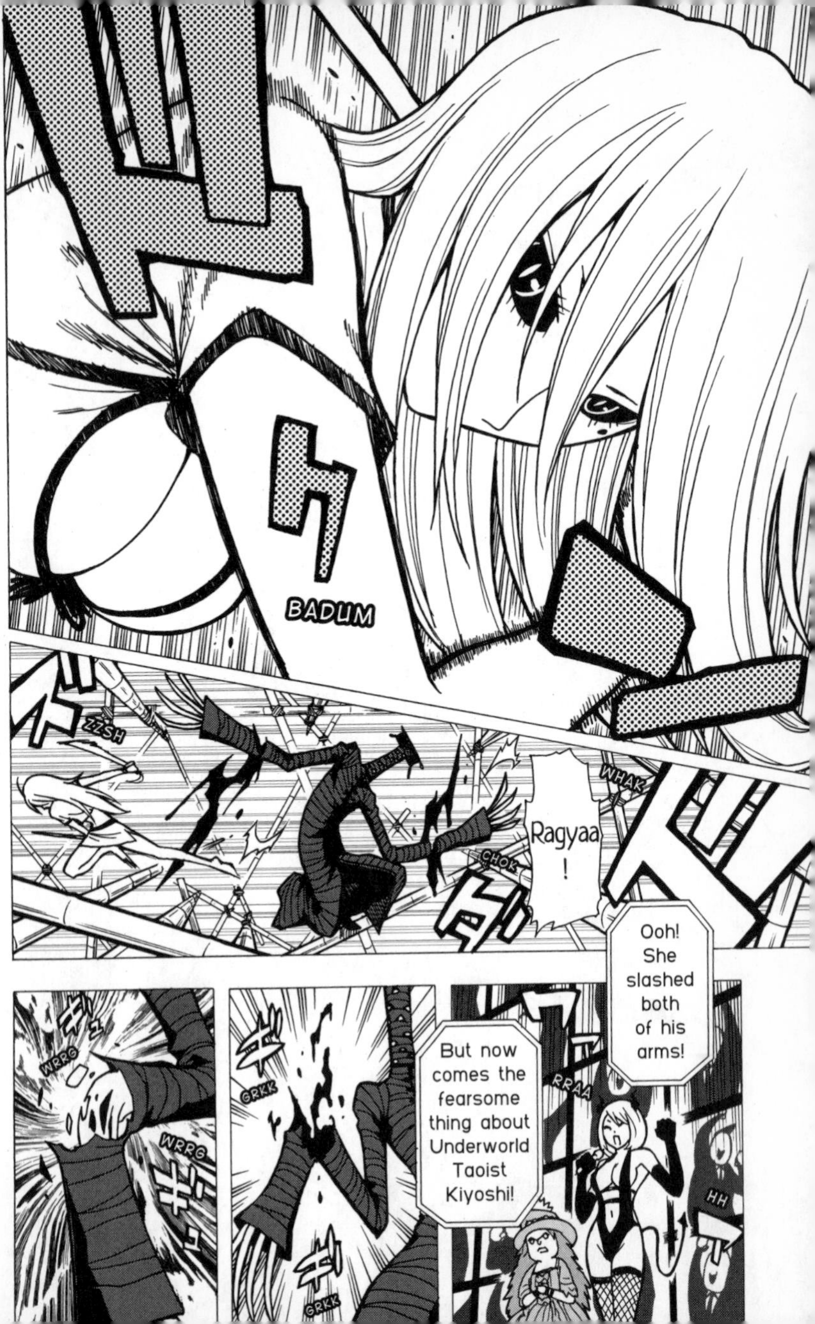
BADUM
WHAK
Ragyaa!
CHOK
ZZSH
Ooh! She slashed both of his arms!
But now comes the fearsome thing about Underworld Taoist Kiyoshi!
RRAA
HH
GRKK
GRKK
WRRG
WRRG

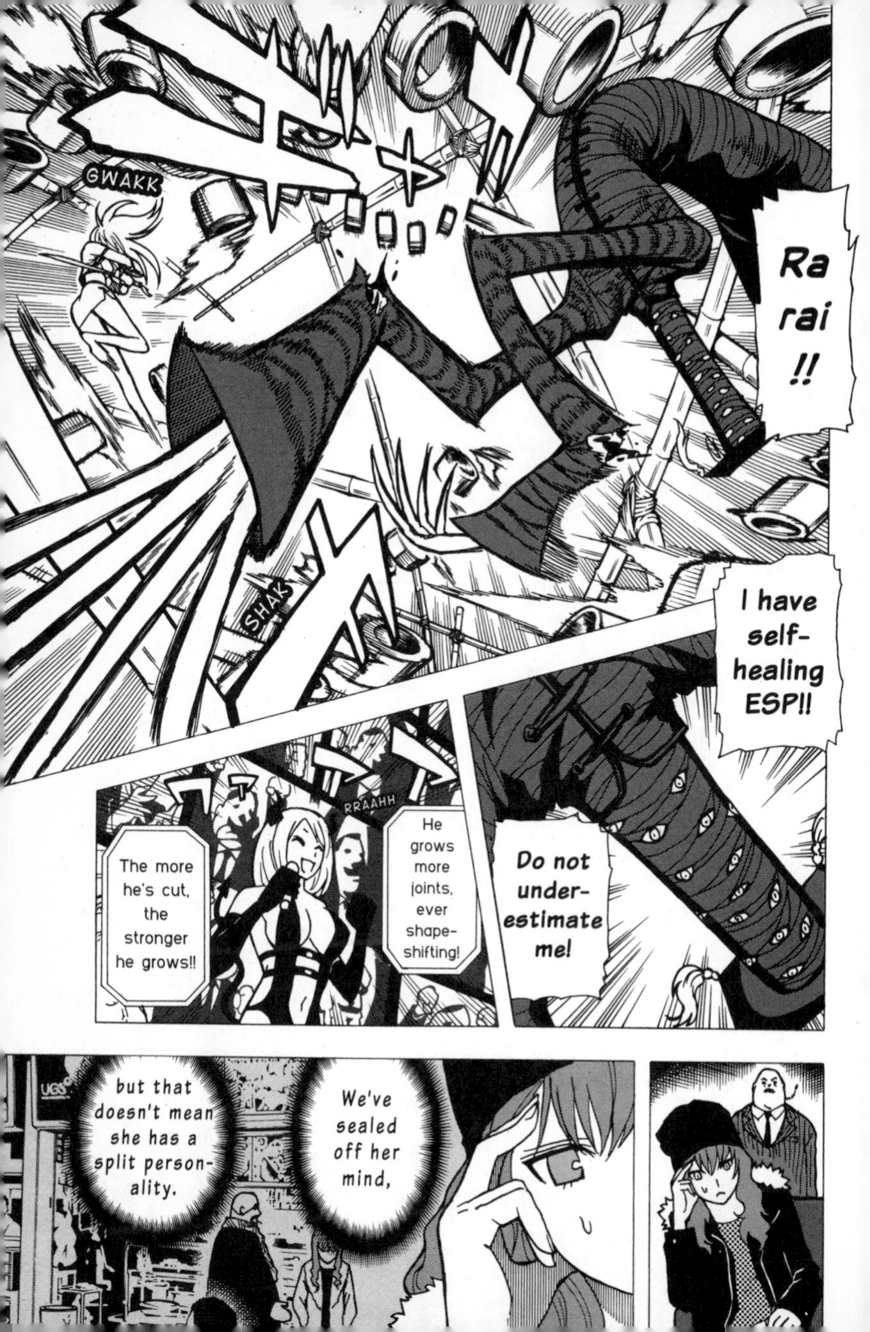

Ra rai!!
GWAKK
SHAK
I have self-healing ESP!!
Do not under-estimate me!
RRAAHH
He grows more joints, ever shape-shifting!
The more he's cut, the stronger he grows!!
We've sealed off her mind,
but that doesn't mean she has a split person-ality.
UGS

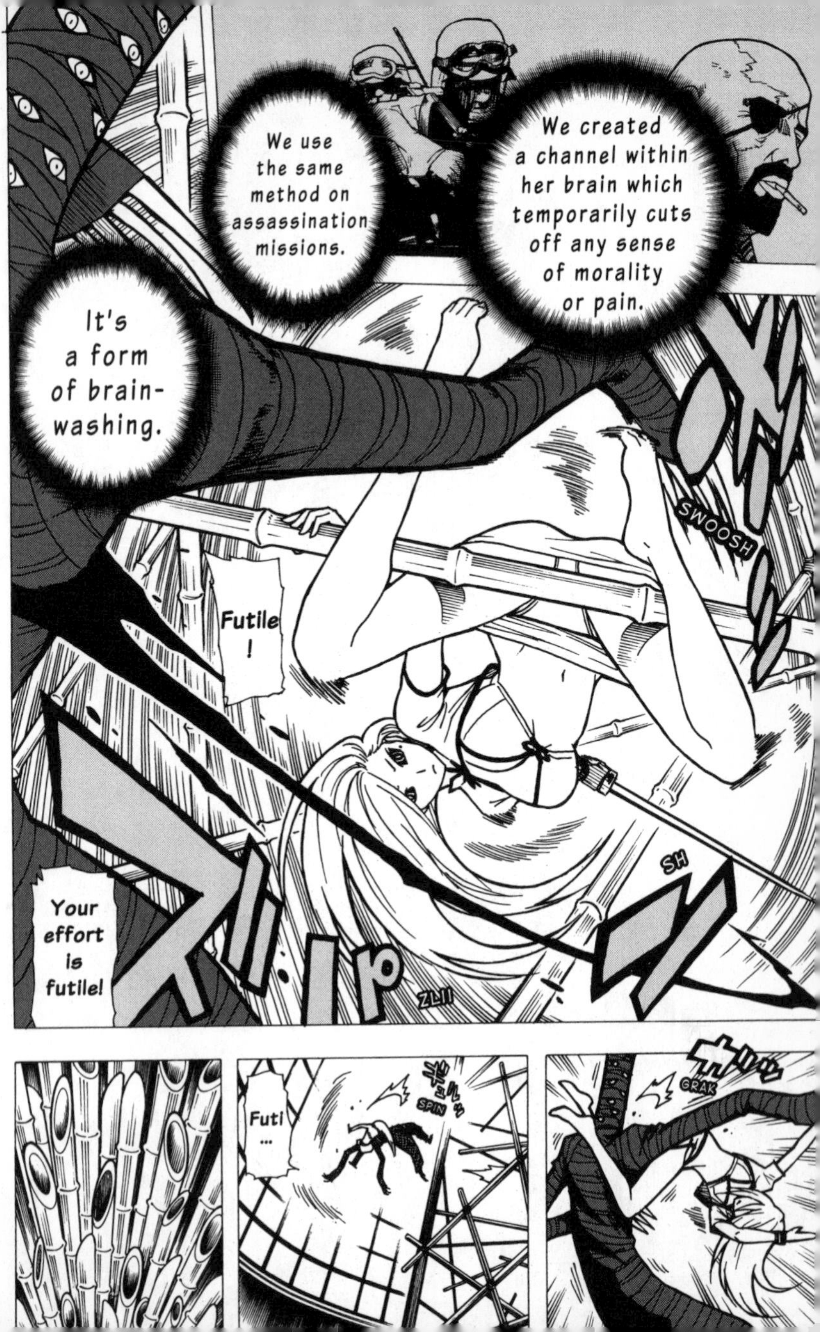
We created a channel within her brain which temporarily cuts off any sense of morality or pain.
We use the same method on assassination missions.
It's a form of brain-washing.
SWOOSH
Futile!
SH
Your effort is futile!
ZLII
GRAK
SPIN
Futi...

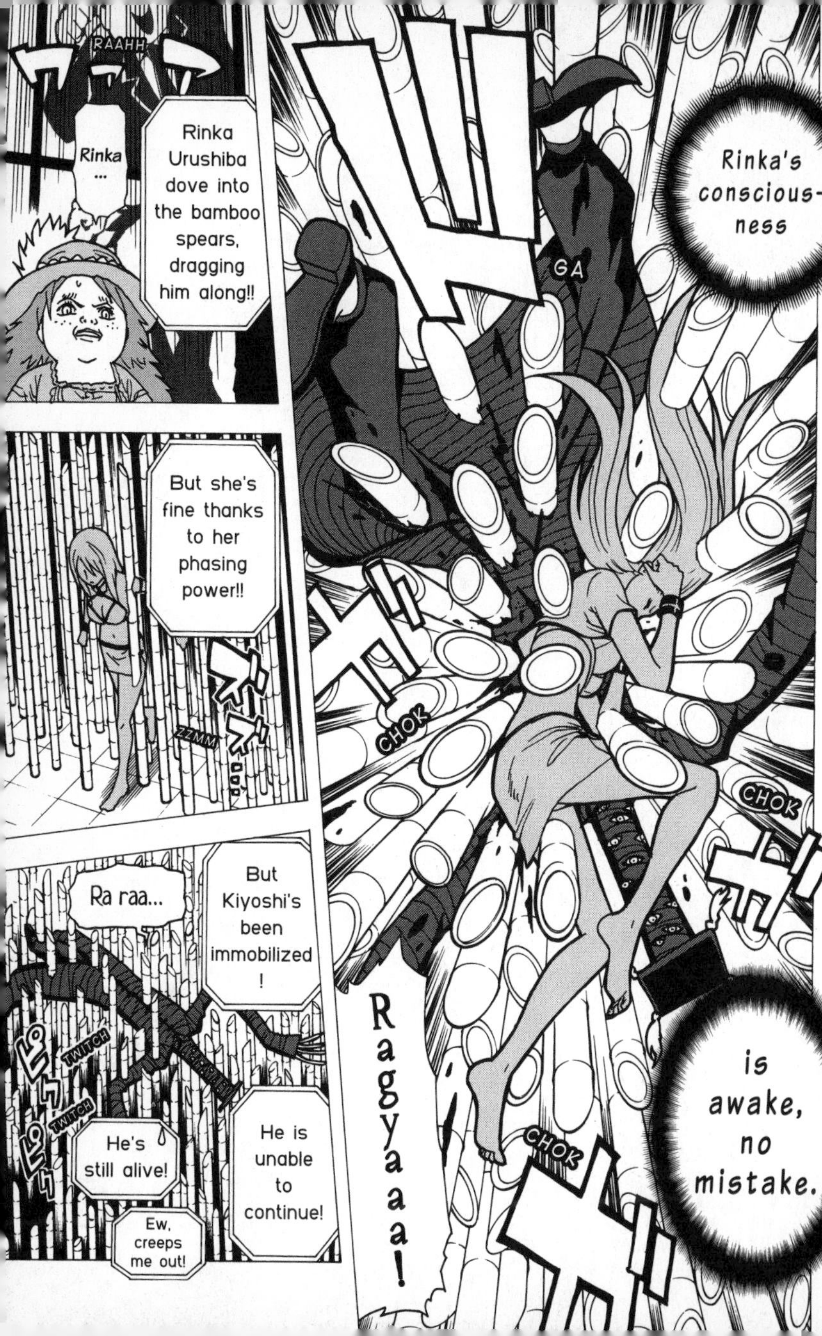
Rinka's consciousness
GA
CHOK
CHOK
is awake, no mistake.
CHOK
Ragyaaa!
RAAHH
Rinka Urushiba dove into the bamboo spears, dragging him along!!
Rinka ...
But she's fine thanks to her phasing power!!
ZZMM
But Kiyoshi's been immobilized!
Ra raa...
He is unable to continue!
He's still alive!
TWITCH
TWITCH
Ew, creeps me out!

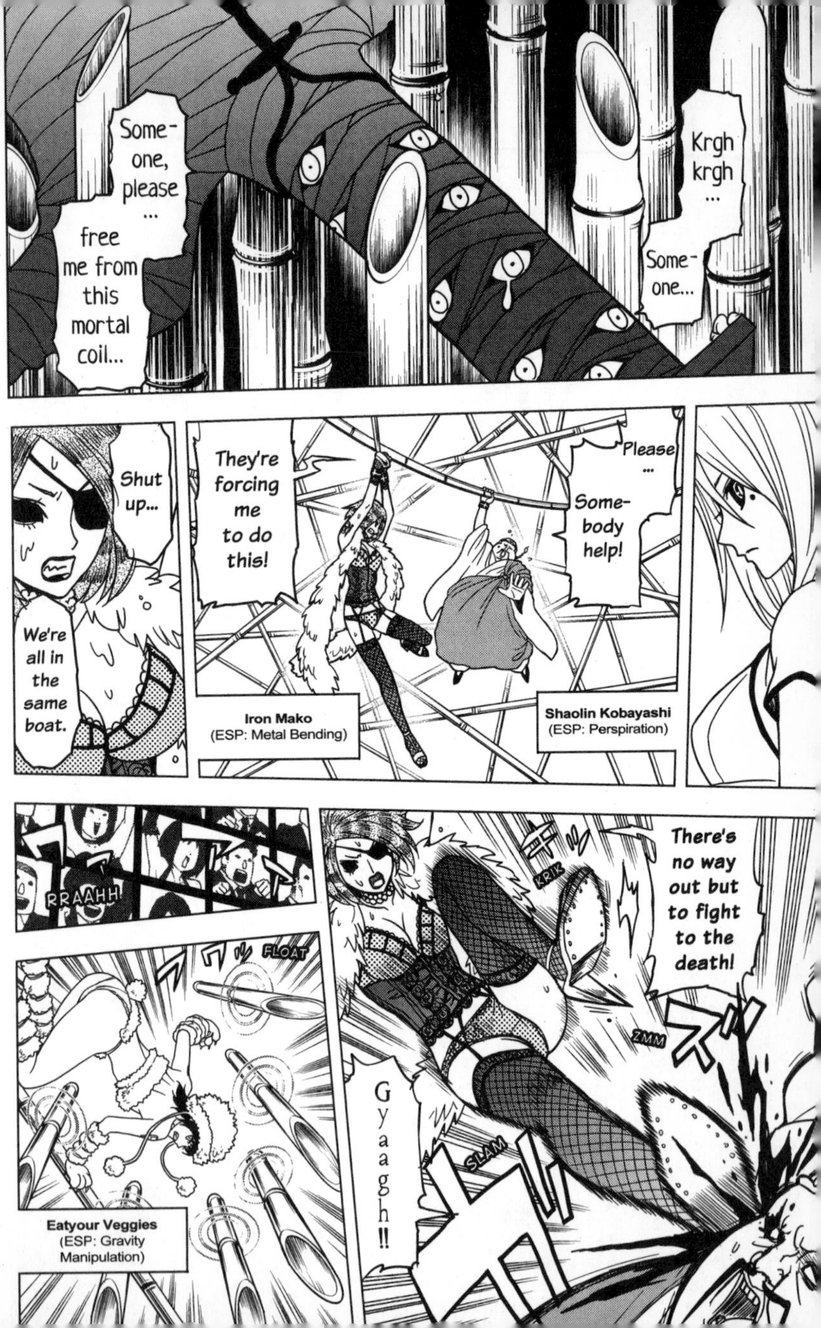
Krgh krgh ...
Some-one...
Some-one, please ... free me from this mortal coil...
Please ... Some-body help!
They're forcing me to do this!
Shaolin Kobayashi (ESP: Perspiration)
Iron Mako (ESP: Metal Bending)
Shut up...
We're all in the same boat.
There's no way out but to fight to the death!
KRIK
ZMM
SLAM
Gyaagh!!
RRAAHH
FLOAT
Eatyour Veggies (ESP: Gravity Manipulation)

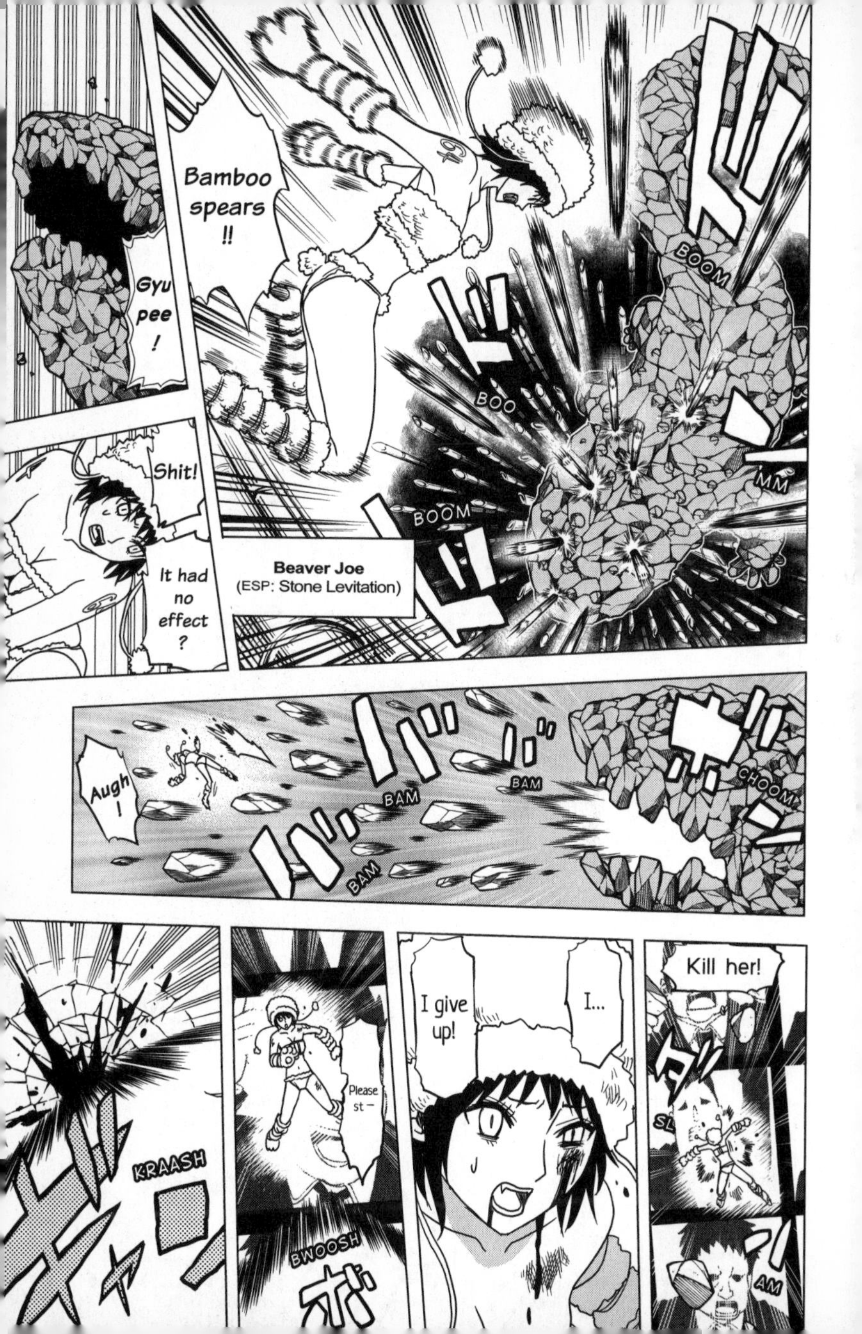

BOOM
Bamboo spears !!
BOO
MM
BOOM
Beaver Joe
(ESP: Stone Levitation)
Gyu pee !
Shit!
It had no effect ?
CHOOM
BAM
BAM
BAM
Augh !
Kill her!
SL
AM
I...
I give up!
Please st –
BWOOSH
KRAASH

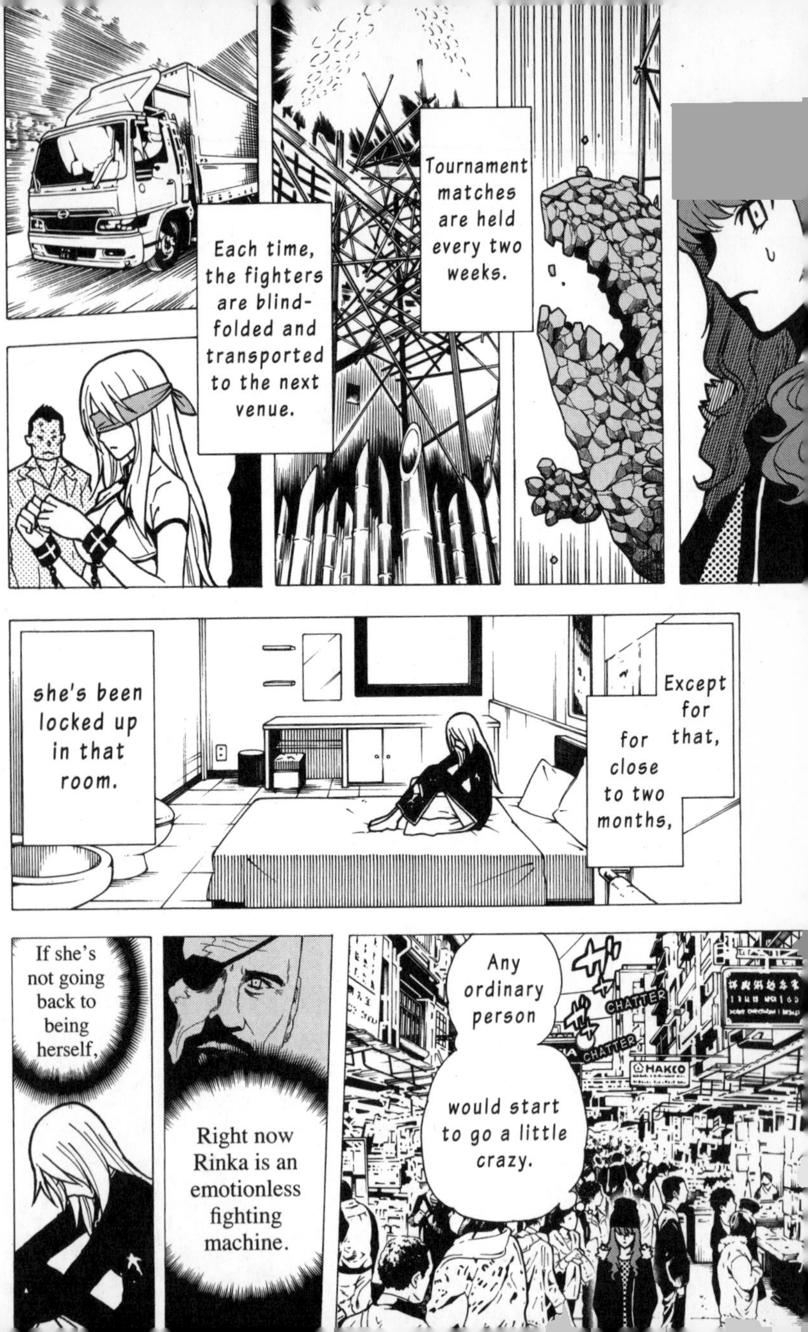
Tournament matches are held every two weeks.
Each time, the fighters are blind-folded and transported to the next venue.
Except for that, for close to two months,
she's been locked up in that room.
Any ordinary person
CHATTER
CHATTER
HAKCO
would start to go a little crazy.
Right now Rinka is an emotionless fighting machine.
If she's not going back to being herself,

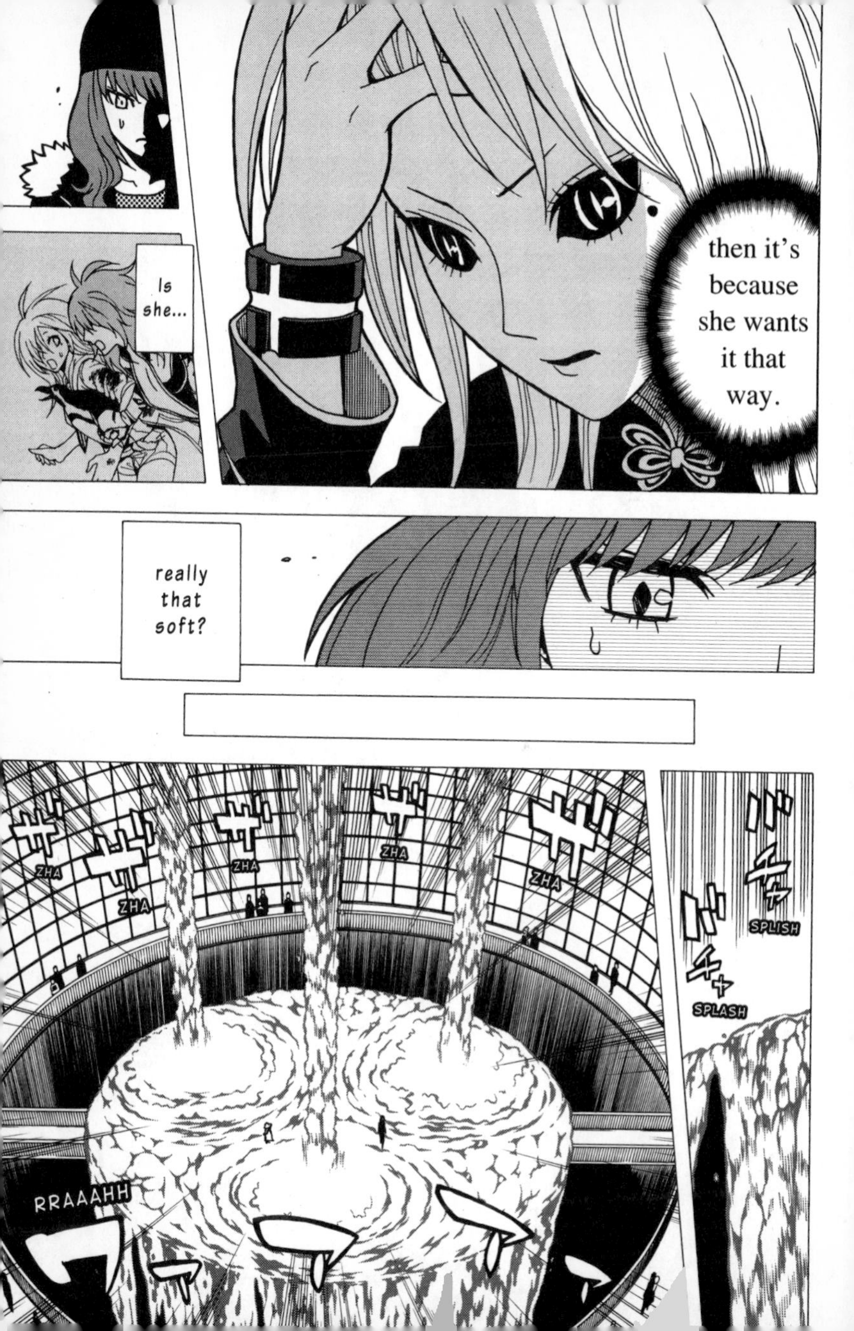
then it's because she wants it that way.
Is she...
really that soft?
SPLISH
SPLASH
ZHA
ZHA
ZHA
ZHA
ZHA
RRAAAHH

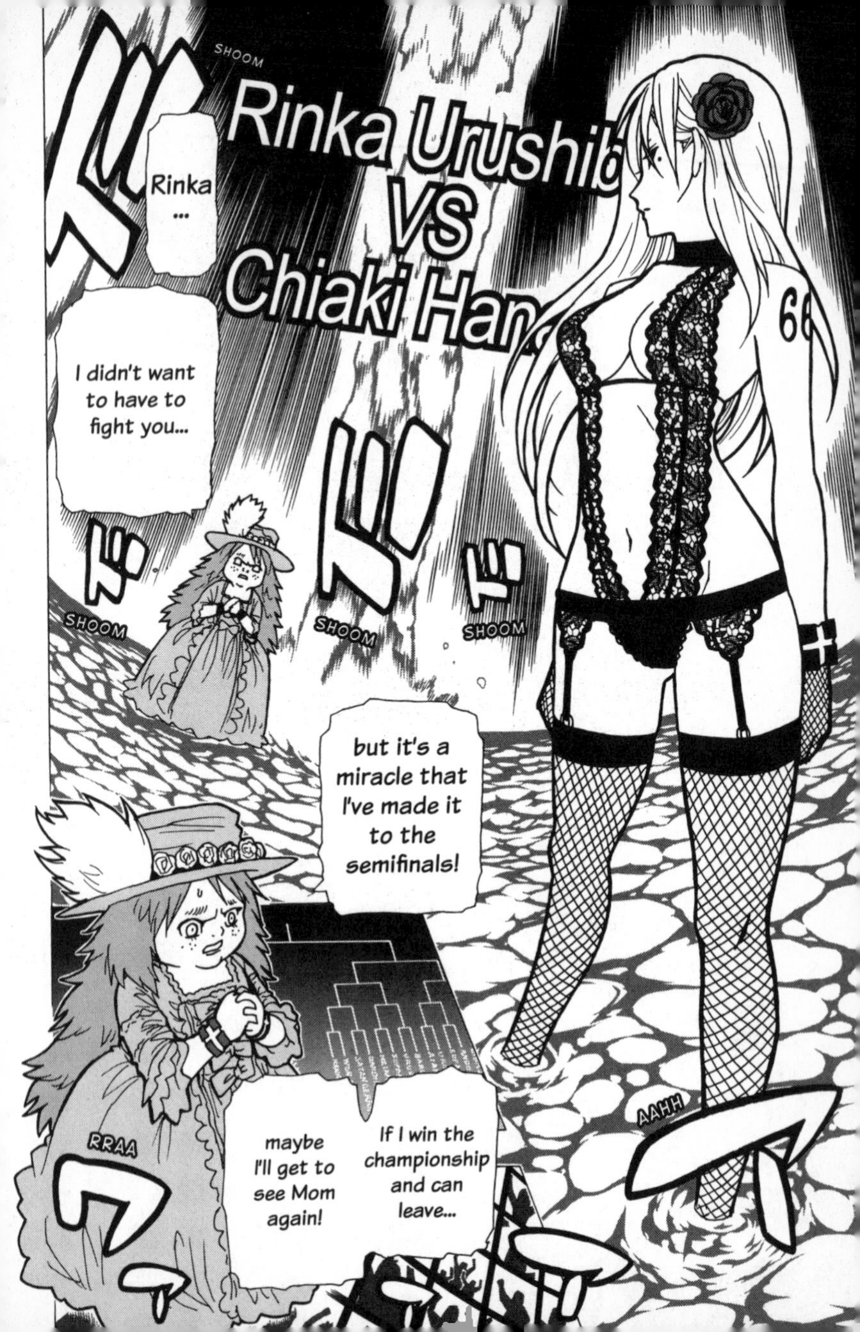

SHOOM
Rinka Urushib
VS
Chiaki Han
66
Rinka ...
I didn't want to have to fight you...
SHOOM
SHOOM
SHOOM
but it's a miracle that I've made it to the semifinals!
If I win the championship and can leave...
maybe I'll get to see Mom again!
AAHH
RRAA

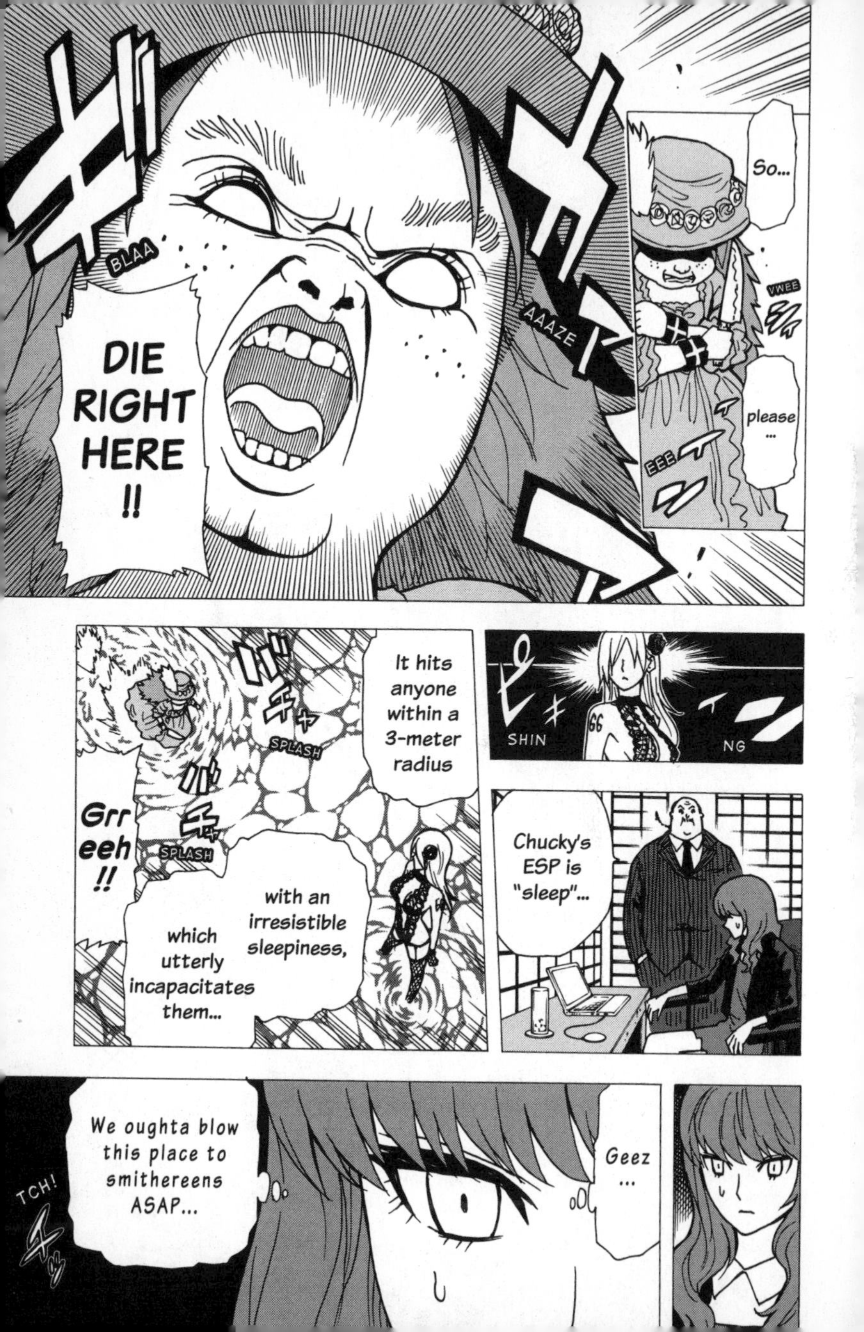
So...
VWEE
please ...
EEE
AAAZE
BLAA
DIE RIGHT HERE !!
SHIN
NG
Chucky's ESP is "sleep"...
It hits anyone within a 3-meter radius
SPLASH
SPLASH
with an irresistible sleepiness,
which utterly incapacitates them...
Grr eeh !!
Geez ...
We oughta blow this place to smithereens ASAP...
TCH!

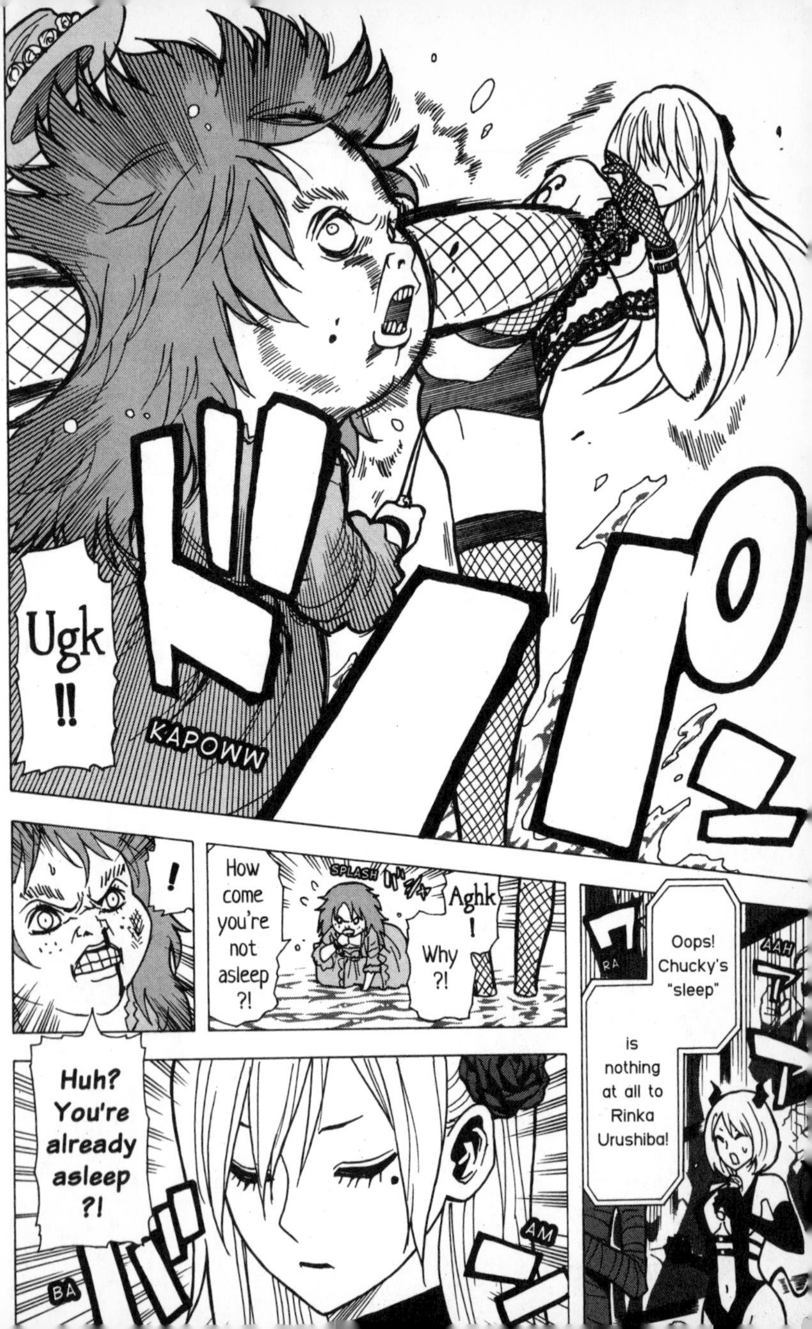
Ugk !!
KAPOWW
Oops! Chucky's "sleep" is nothing at all to Rinka Urushiba!
RA
AAH
Aghk !
SPLASH
Why ?!
How come you're not asleep ?!
!
Huh? You're already asleep ?!
AM
BA

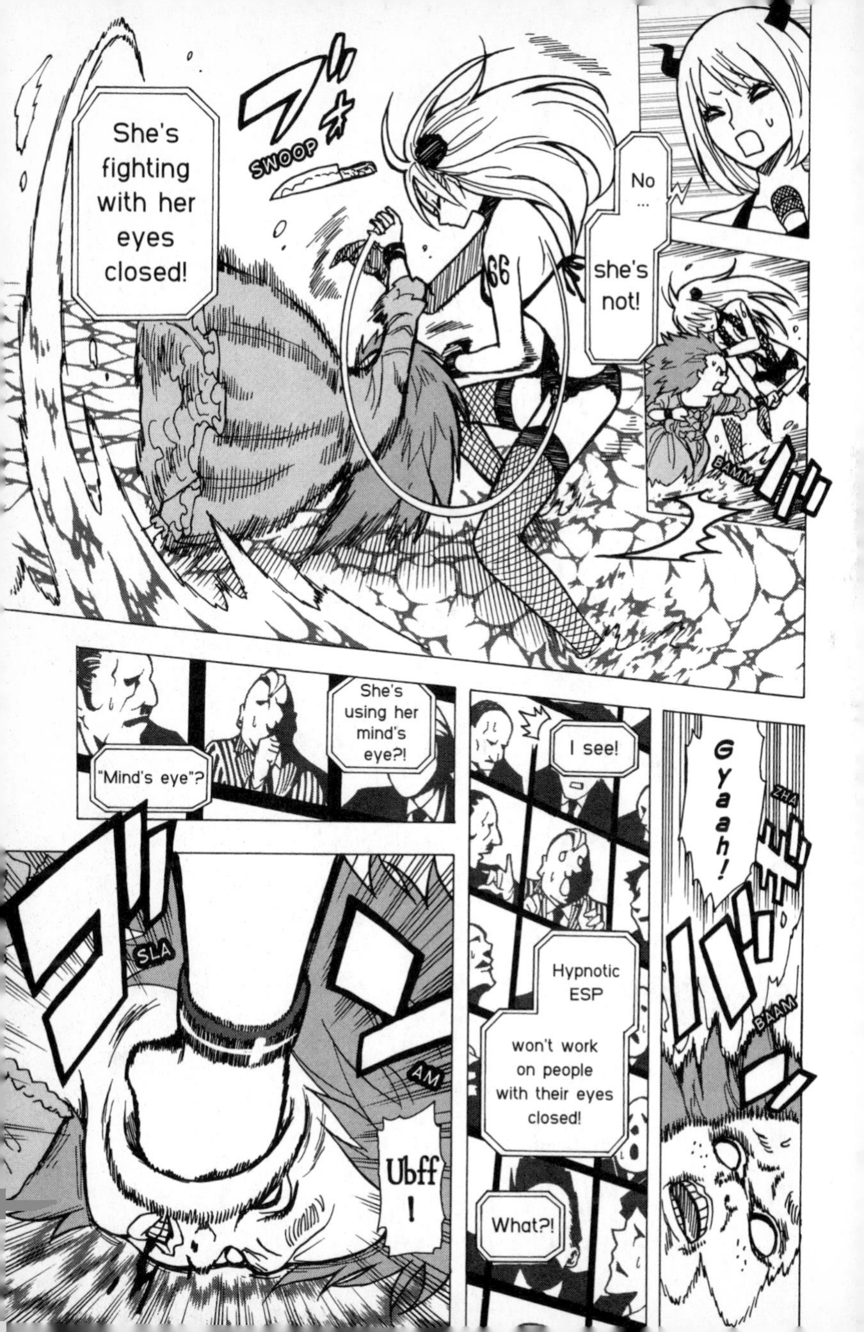
No ...
she's not!
BAMM
SWOOP
She's fighting with her eyes closed!
Gyaah!
ZHA
BAAM
I see!
Hypnotic ESP
won't work on people with their eyes closed!
What?!
She's using her mind's eye?!
"Mind's eye"?
SLA
AM
Ubff!

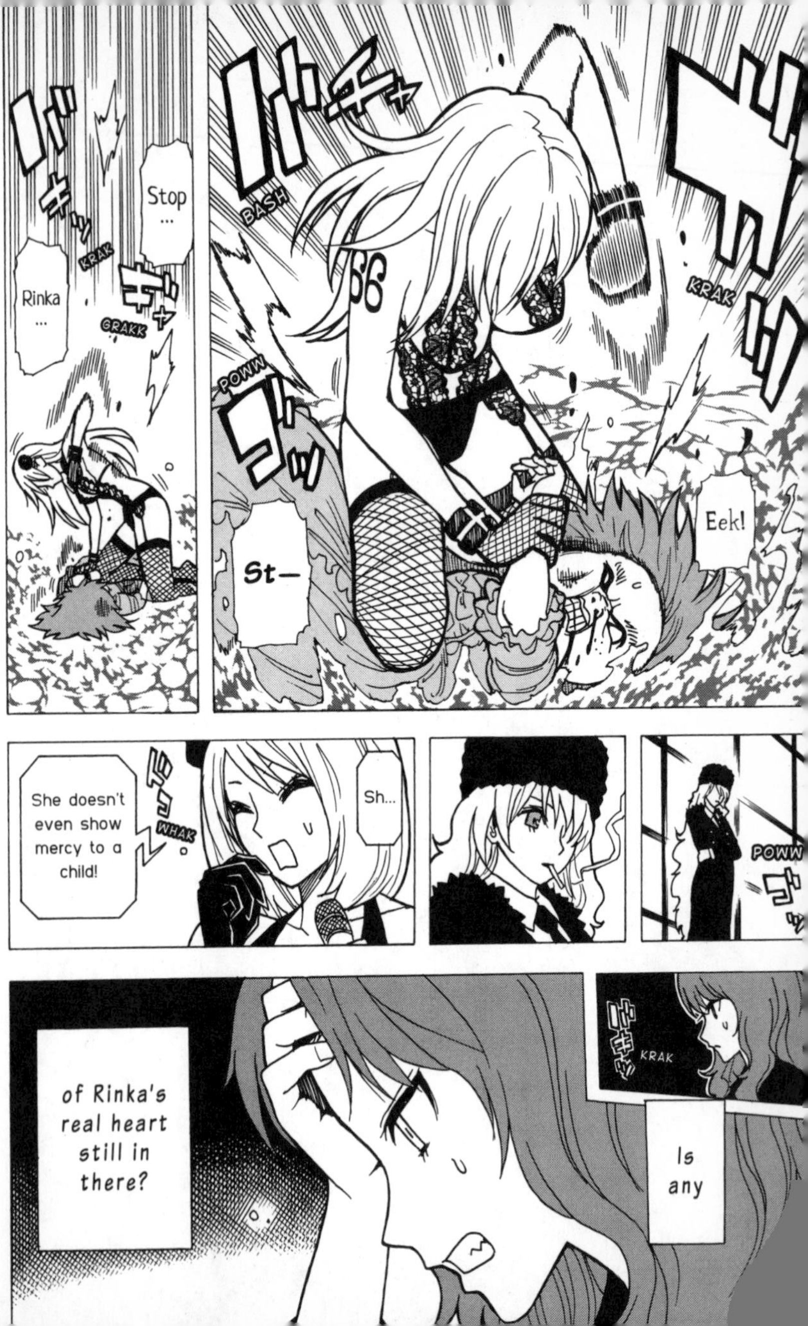

KRAK
BASH
Eek!
POWW
St—
Stop ...
KRAK
Rinka ...
GRAKK
POWW
Sh...
WHAK
She doesn't even show mercy to a child!
KRAK
Is any
of Rinka's real heart still in there?

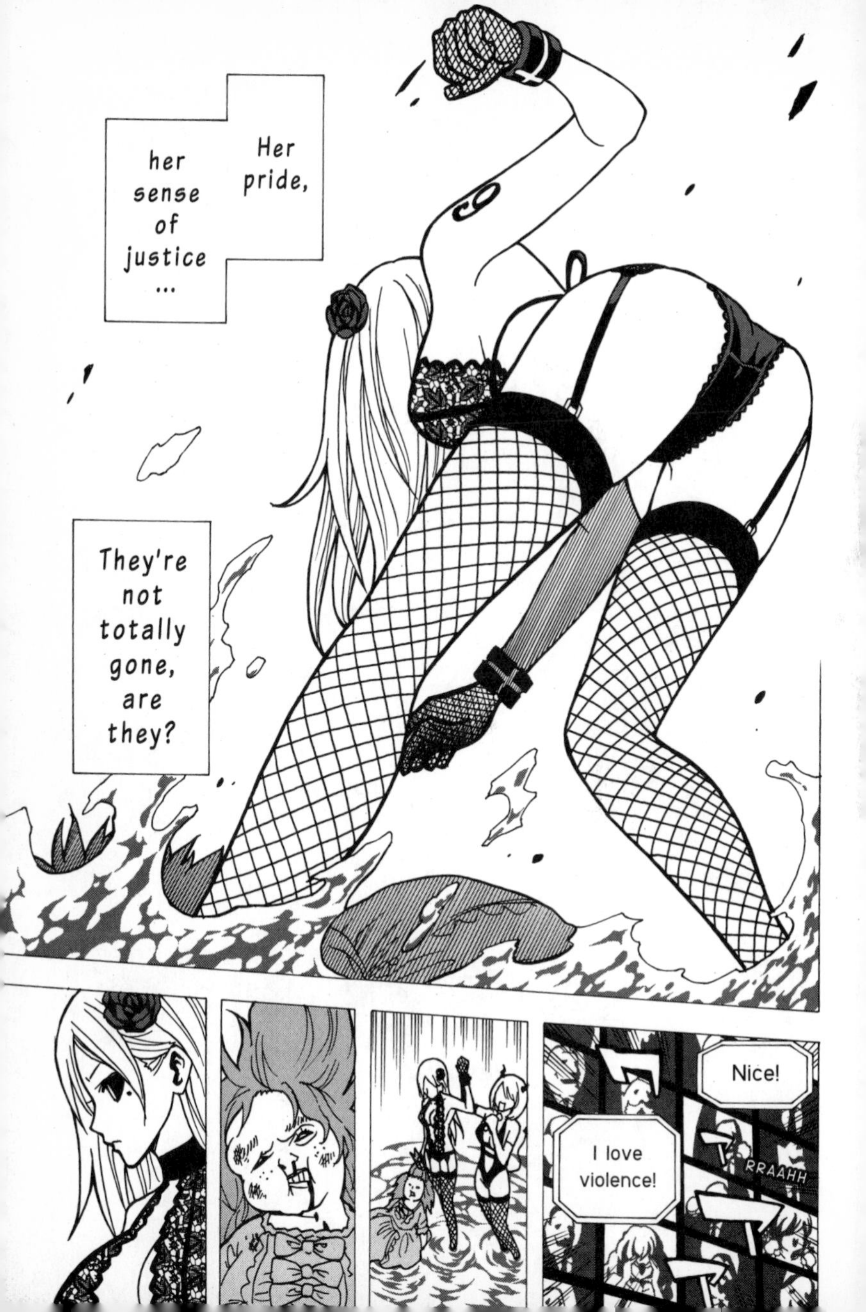
Her pride, her sense of justice...
They're not totally gone, are they?
Nice!
I love violence!
RRAAHH

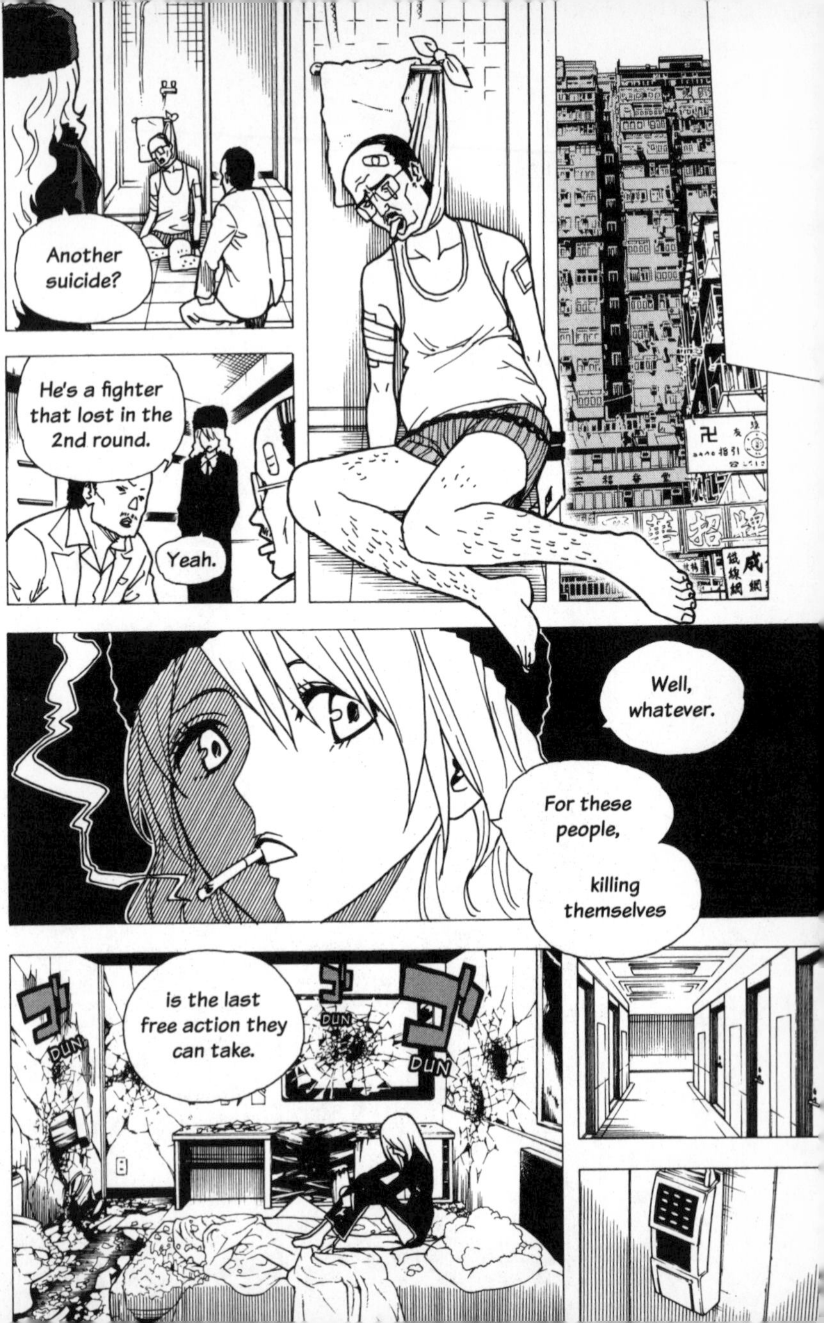

Another suicide?
He's a fighter that lost in the 2nd round.
Yeah.
Well, whatever.
For these people,
killing themselves
DUN
DUN
is the last free action they can take.
DUN

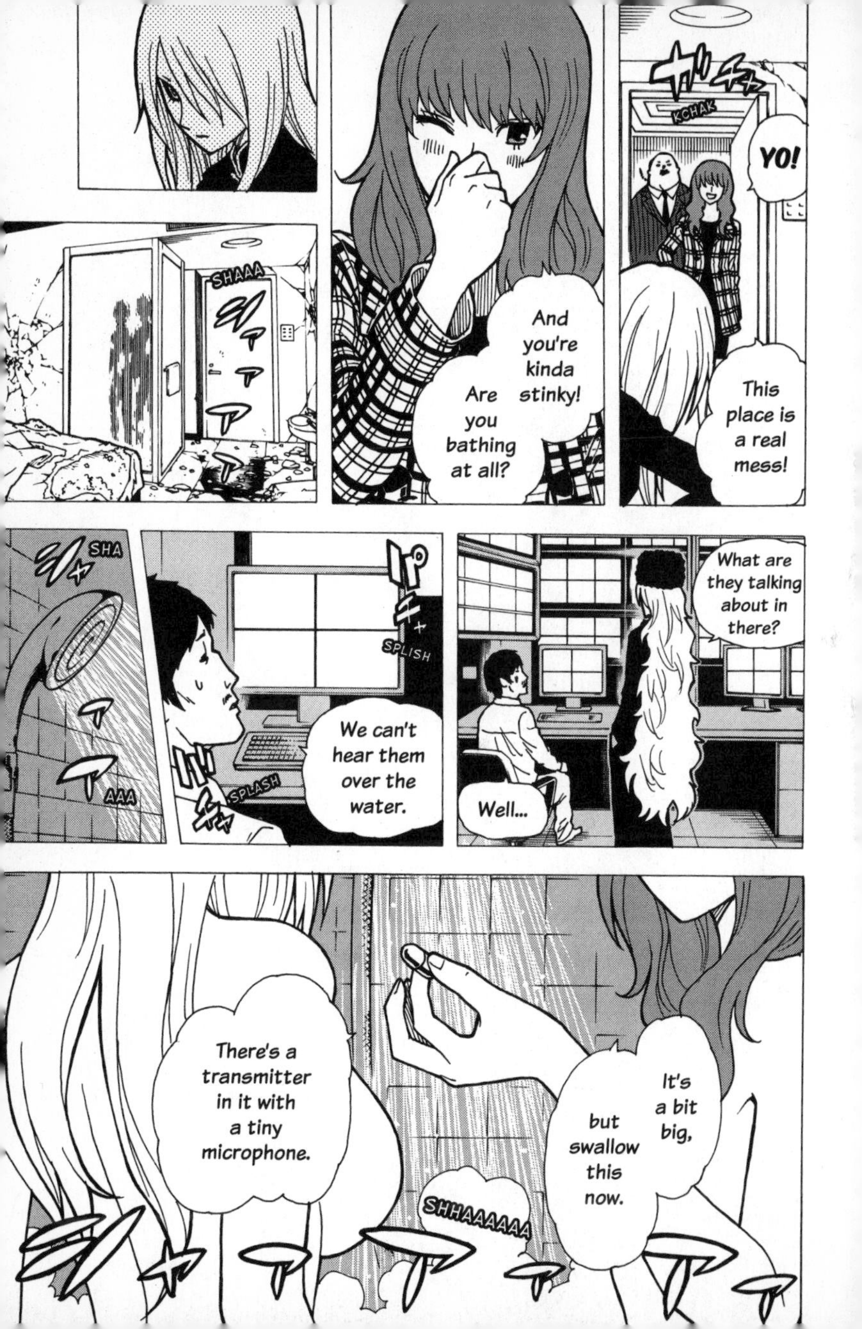
KCHAK
YO!
This place is a real mess!
And you're kinda stinky!
Are you bathing at all?
SHAAA
What are they talking about in there?
Well...
SPLISH
We can't hear them over the water.
SPLASH
SHA
AAA
It's a bit big, but swallow this now.
SHHAAAAAAA
There's a transmitter in it with a tiny microphone.

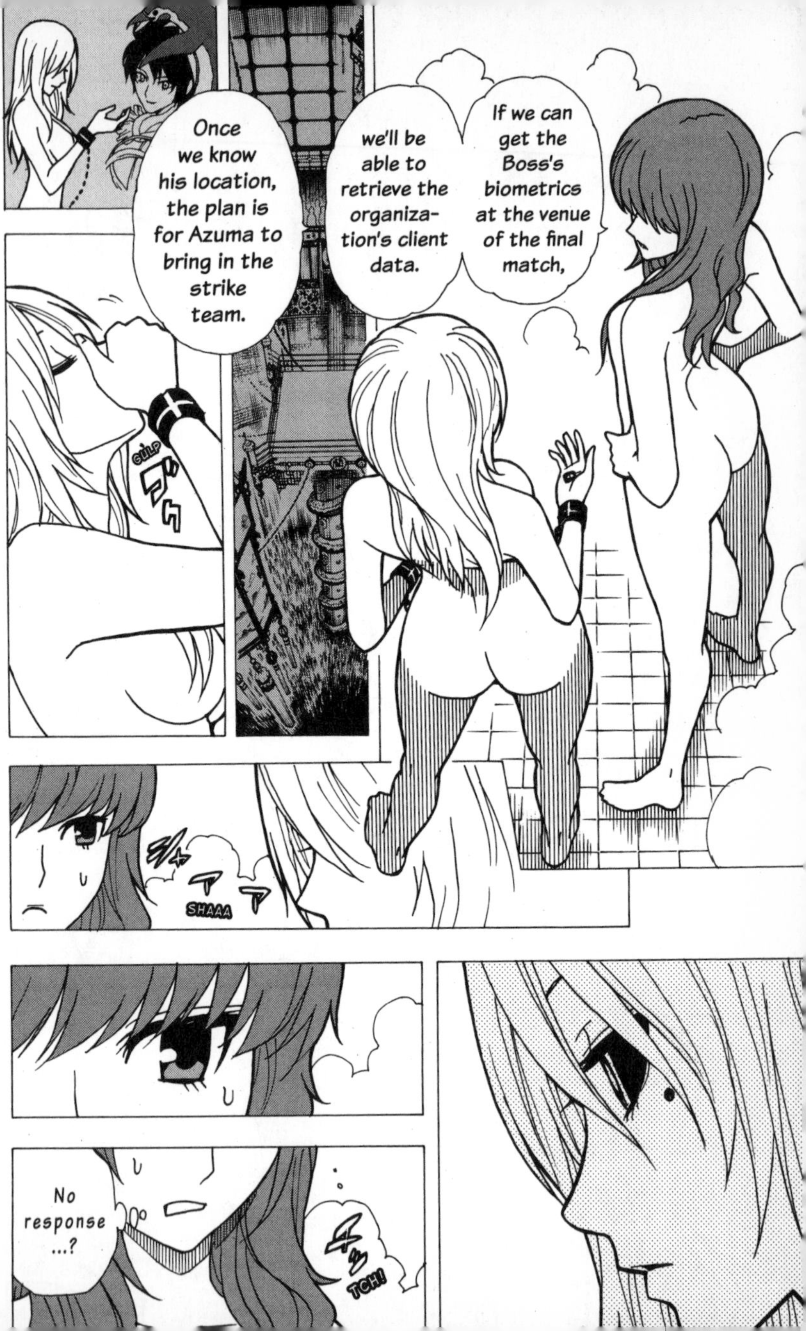
If we can get the Boss's biometrics at the venue of the final match,
we'll be able to retrieve the organiza-tion's client data.
Once we know his location, the plan is for Azuma to bring in the strike team.
GULP
SHAAA
TCH!
No response ...?

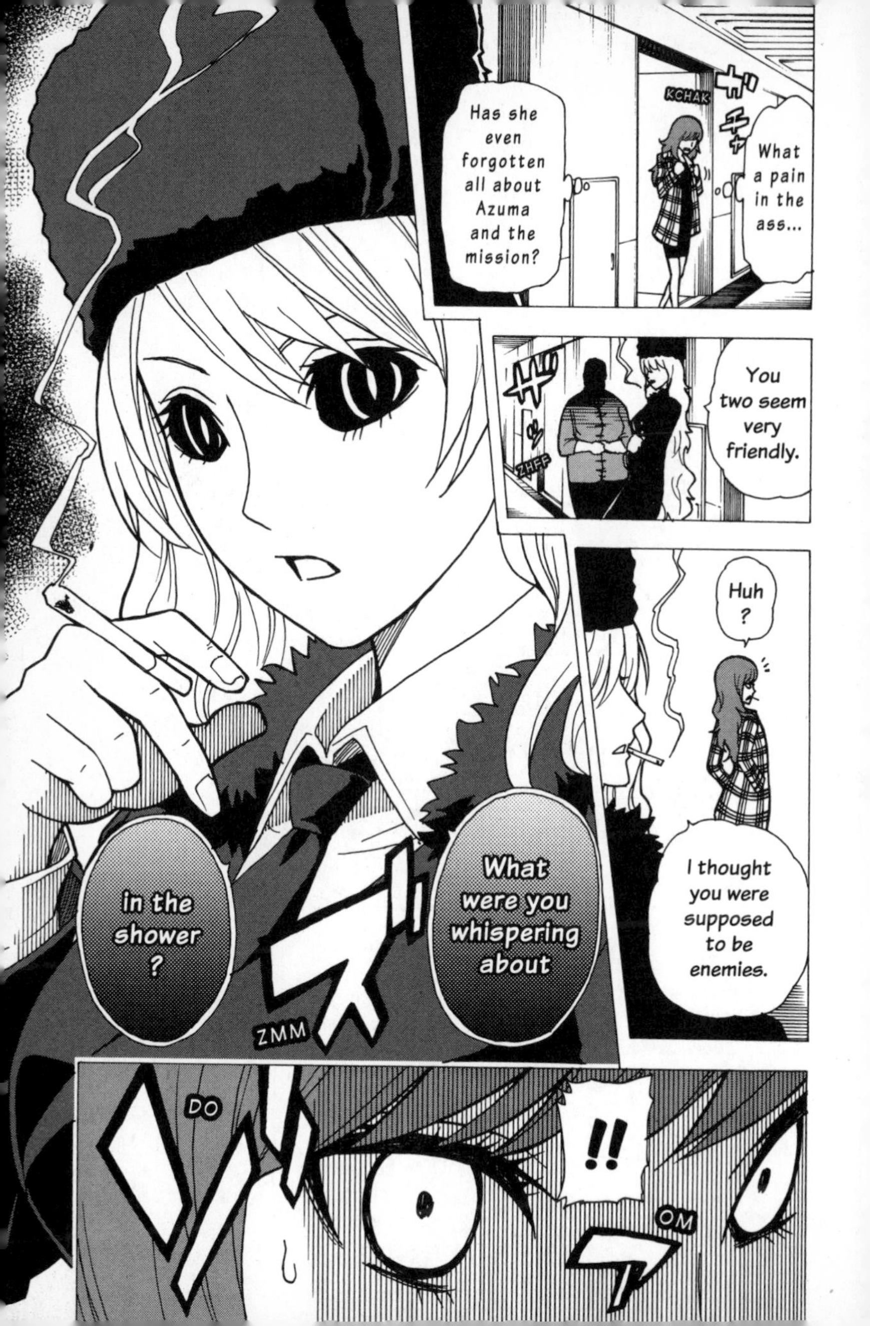
KCHAK
What a pain in the ass...
Has she even forgotten all about Azuma and the mission?
ZHFF
You two seem very friendly.
Huh?
I thought you were supposed to be enemies.
What were you whispering about
in the shower?
ZMM
DO
!!
OM

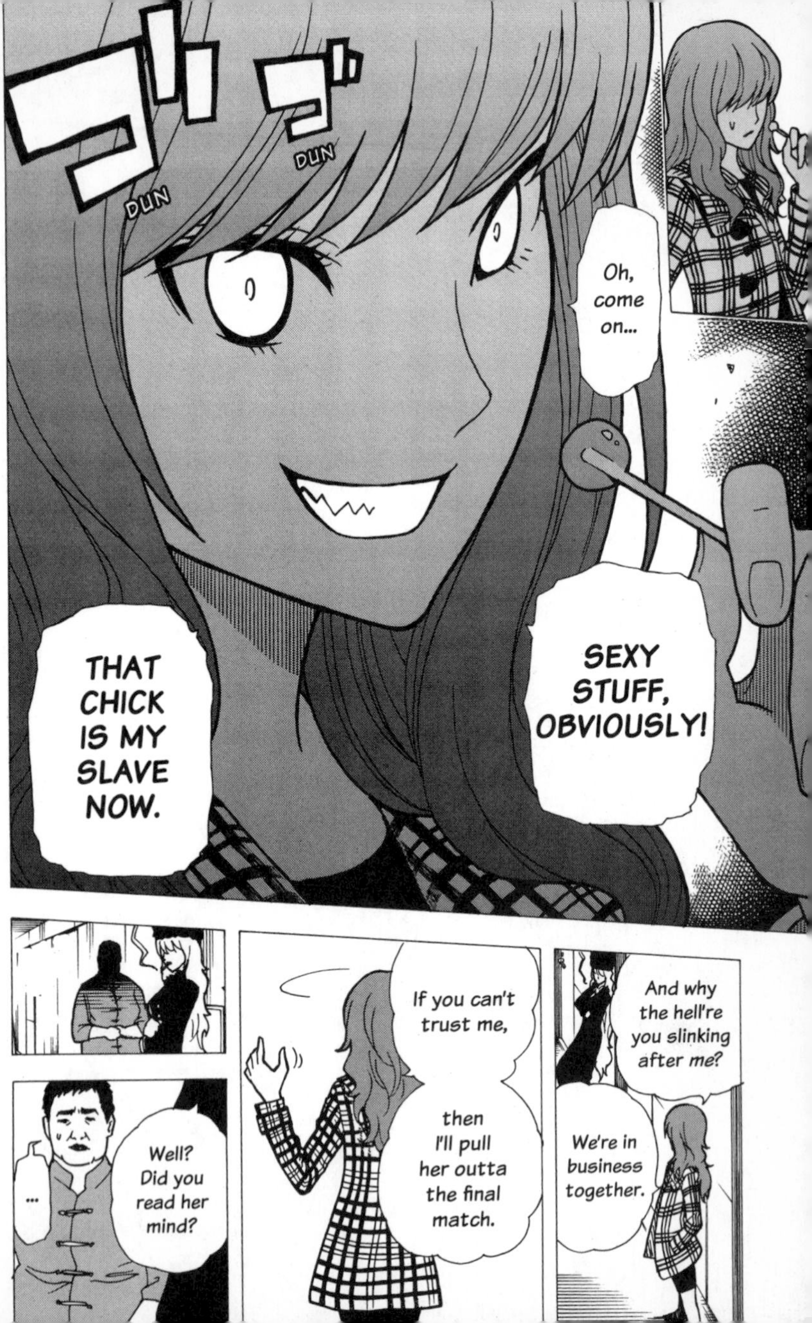
Oh, come on...
SEXY STUFF, OBVIOUSLY!
THAT CHICK IS MY SLAVE NOW.
DUN
DUN
And why the hell're you slinking after me?
We're in business together.
If you can't trust me,
then I'll pull her outta the final match.
Well? Did you read her mind?
...

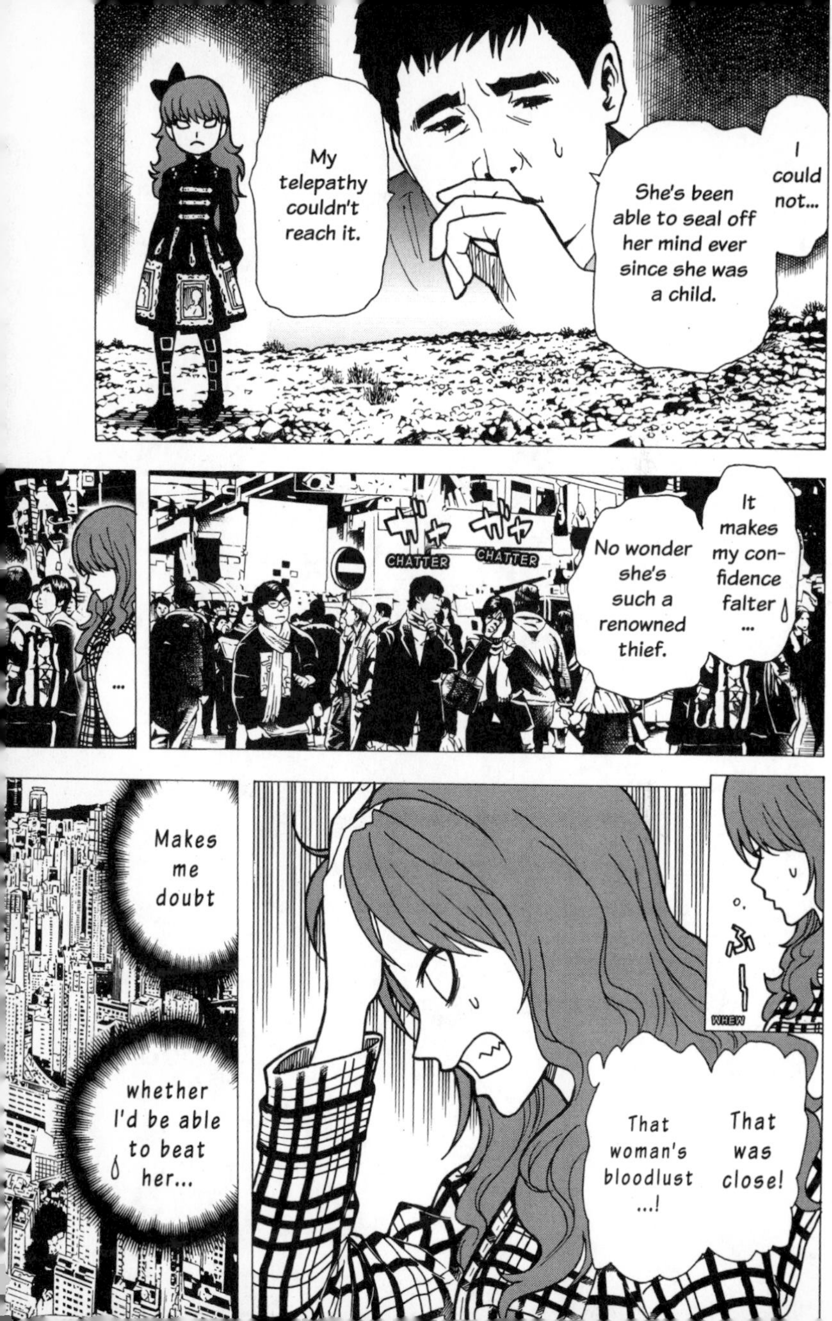
I could not...
She's been able to seal off her mind ever since she was a child.
My telepathy couldn't reach it.
It makes my confidence falter...
No wonder she's such a renowned thief.
ガヤ
CHATTER
ガヤ
CHATTER
...
ふー
WHEW
That was close!
That woman's bloodlust...!
Makes me doubt
whether I'd be able to beat her...

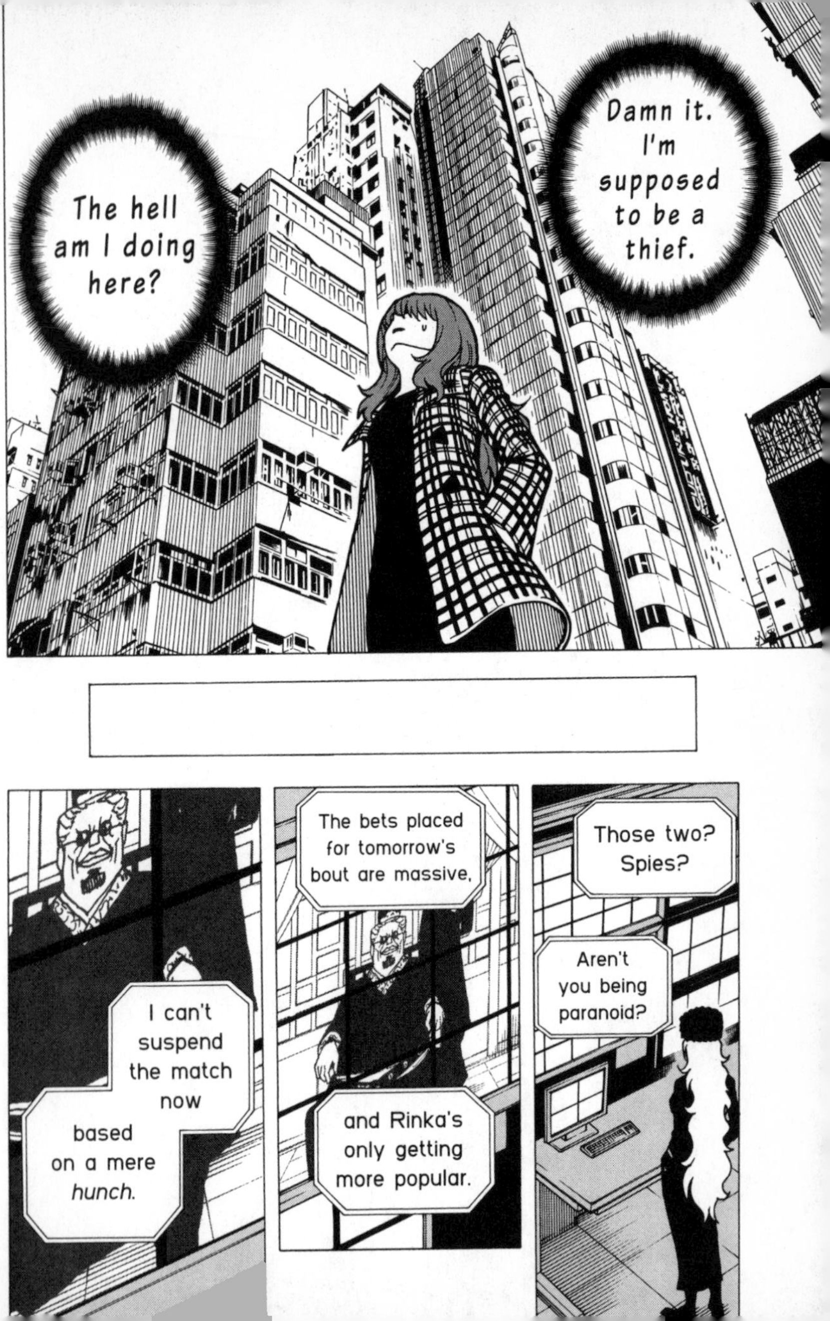
Damn it. I'm supposed to be a thief.
The hell am I doing here?
Those two? Spies?
Aren't you being paranoid?
The bets placed for tomorrow's bout are massive,
and Rinka's only getting more popular.
I can't suspend the match now
based on a mere *hunch.*

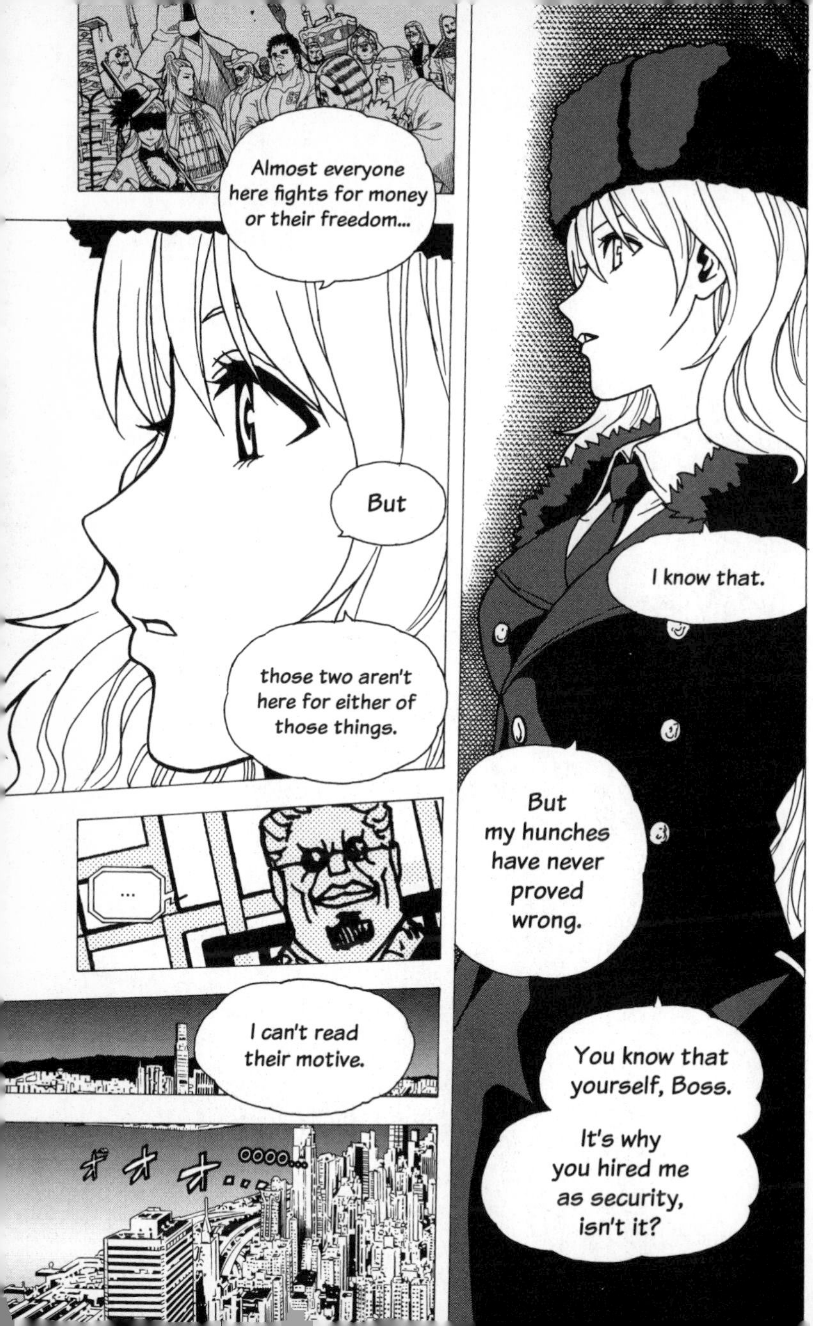
I know that.
But my hunches have never proved wrong.
You know that yourself, Boss.
It's why you hired me as security, isn't it?
Almost everyone here fights for money or their freedom...
But
those two aren't here for either of those things.
...
I can't read their motive.
オオオ
oooo...

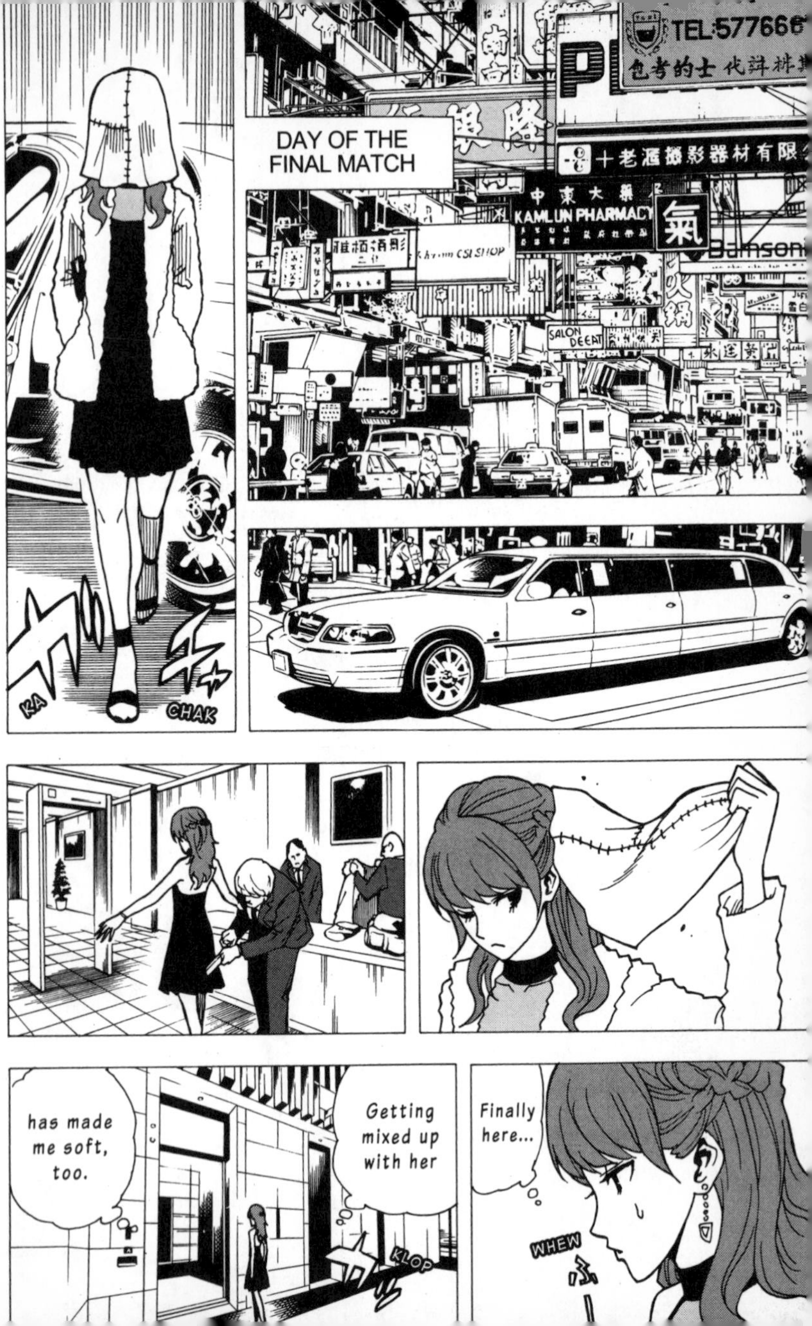
DAY OF THE FINAL MATCH
KAMLUN PHARMACY
KA
CHAK
Finally here...
WHEW
Getting mixed up with her
has made me soft, too.
KLOP

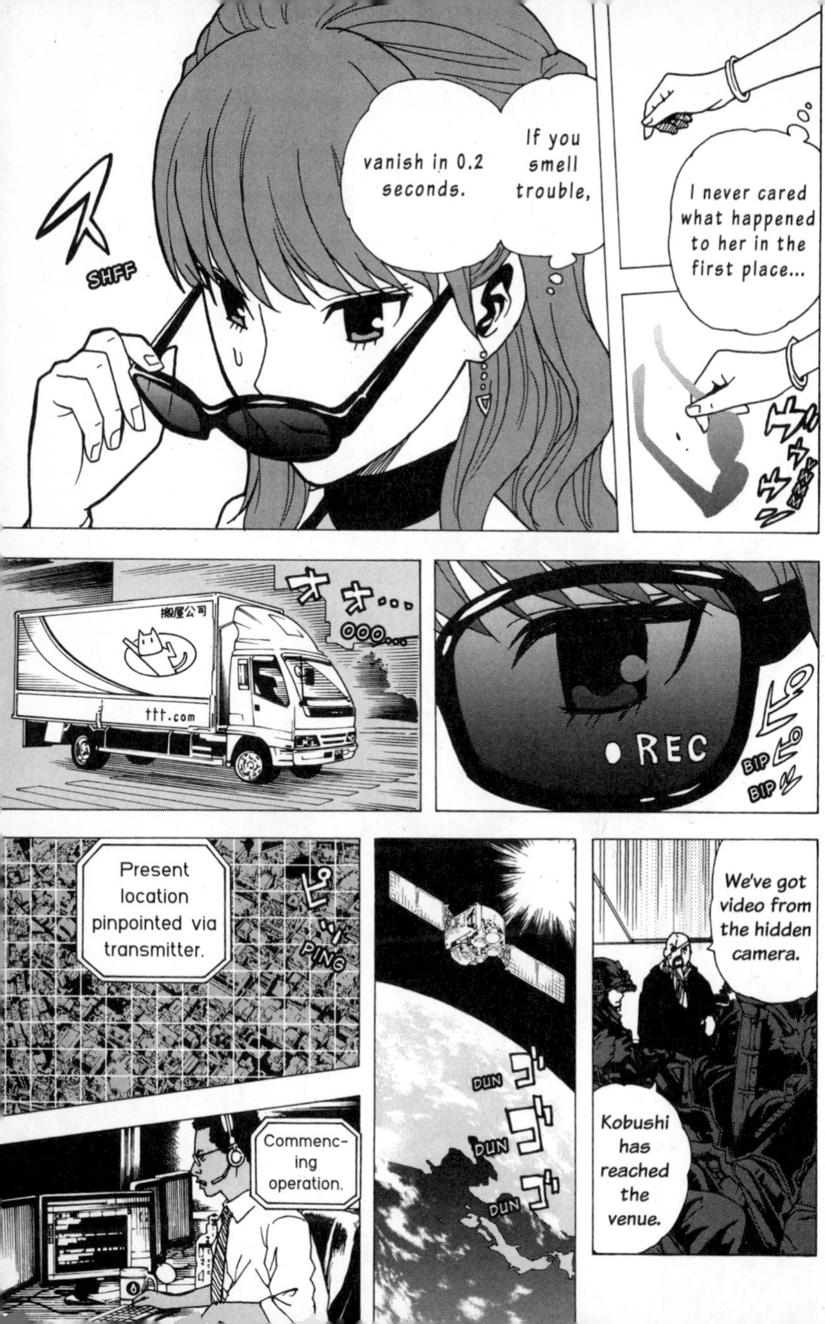

I never cared what happened to her in the first place...
VWWW
If you smell trouble,
vanish in 0.2 seconds.
SHFF
REC
BIP
BIP
搬屋公司
ttt.com
OOO...
We've got video from the hidden camera.
Kobushi has reached the venue.
DUN
DUN
DUN
Present location pinpointed via transmitter.
PING
Commencing operation.

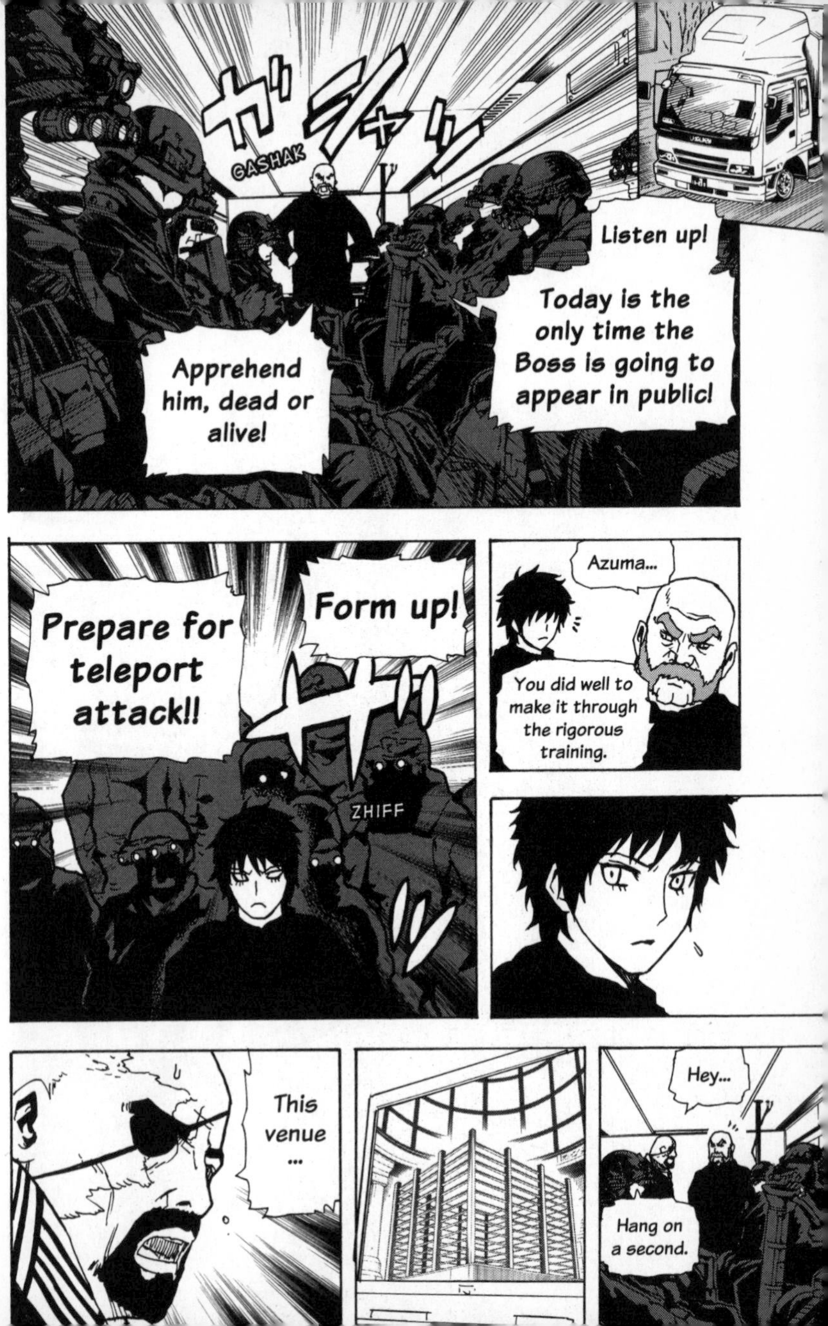
GASHAK
Listen up!
Today is the only time the Boss is going to appear in public!
Apprehend him, dead or alive!
Azuma...
You did well to make it through the rigorous training.
Form up!
Prepare for teleport attack!!
ZHIFF
Hey...
Hang on a second.
This venue ...

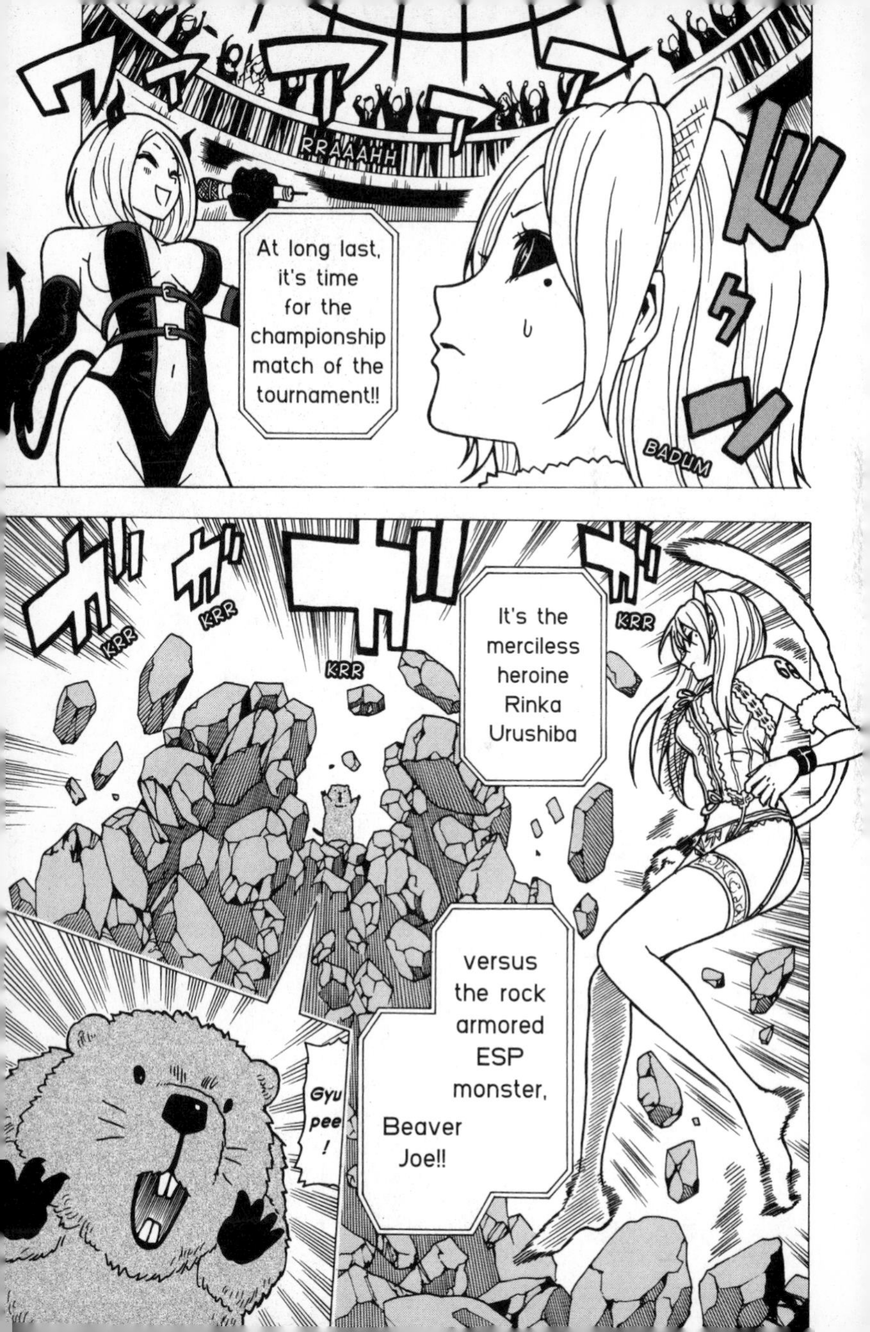
RRAAAHH
BADUM
At long last, it's time for the championship match of the tournament!!
KRR
It's the merciless heroine Rinka Urushiba
KRR
KRR
KRR
versus the rock armored ESP monster, Beaver Joe!!
Gyu pee!

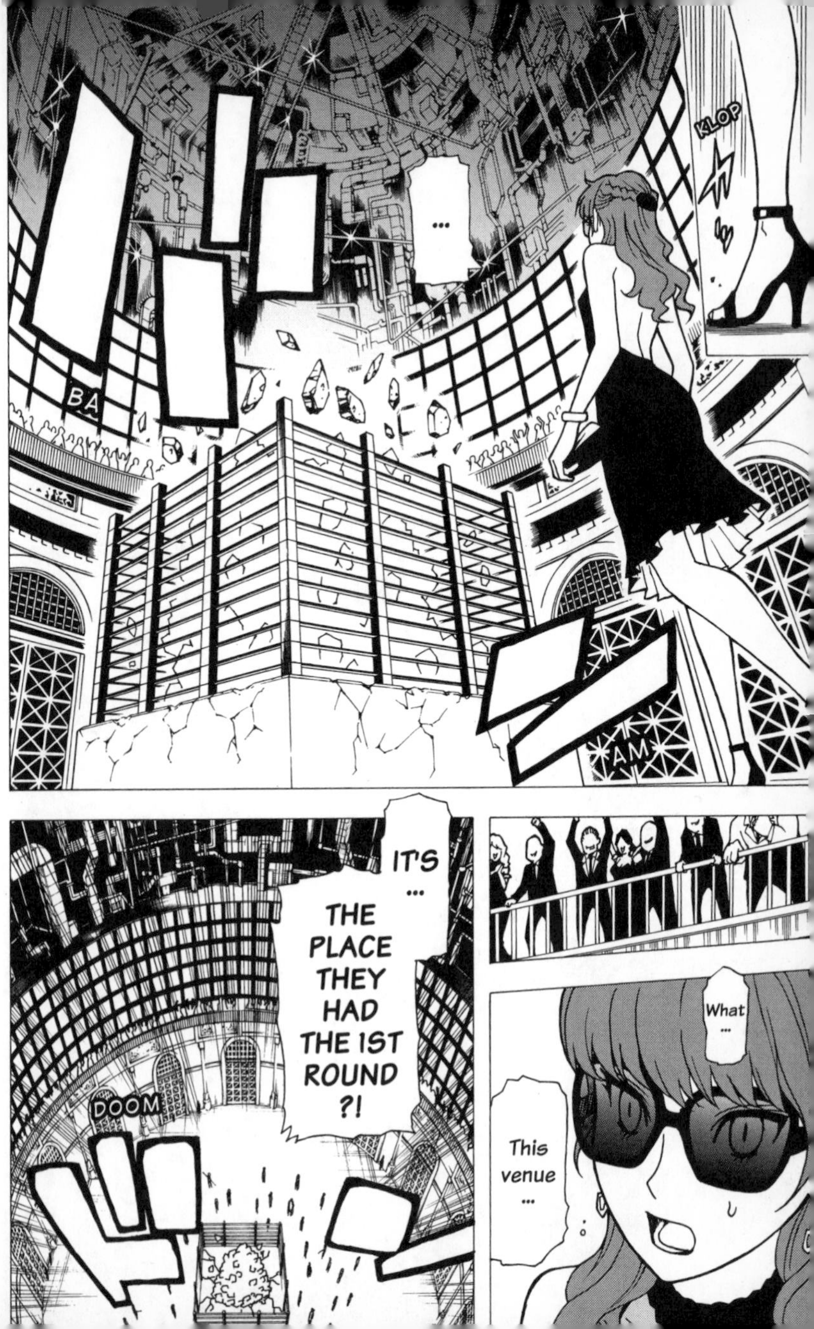
KLOP
...
BA
AM
What ...
This venue ...
IT'S ...
THE PLACE THEY HAD THE 1ST ROUND ?!
DOOM

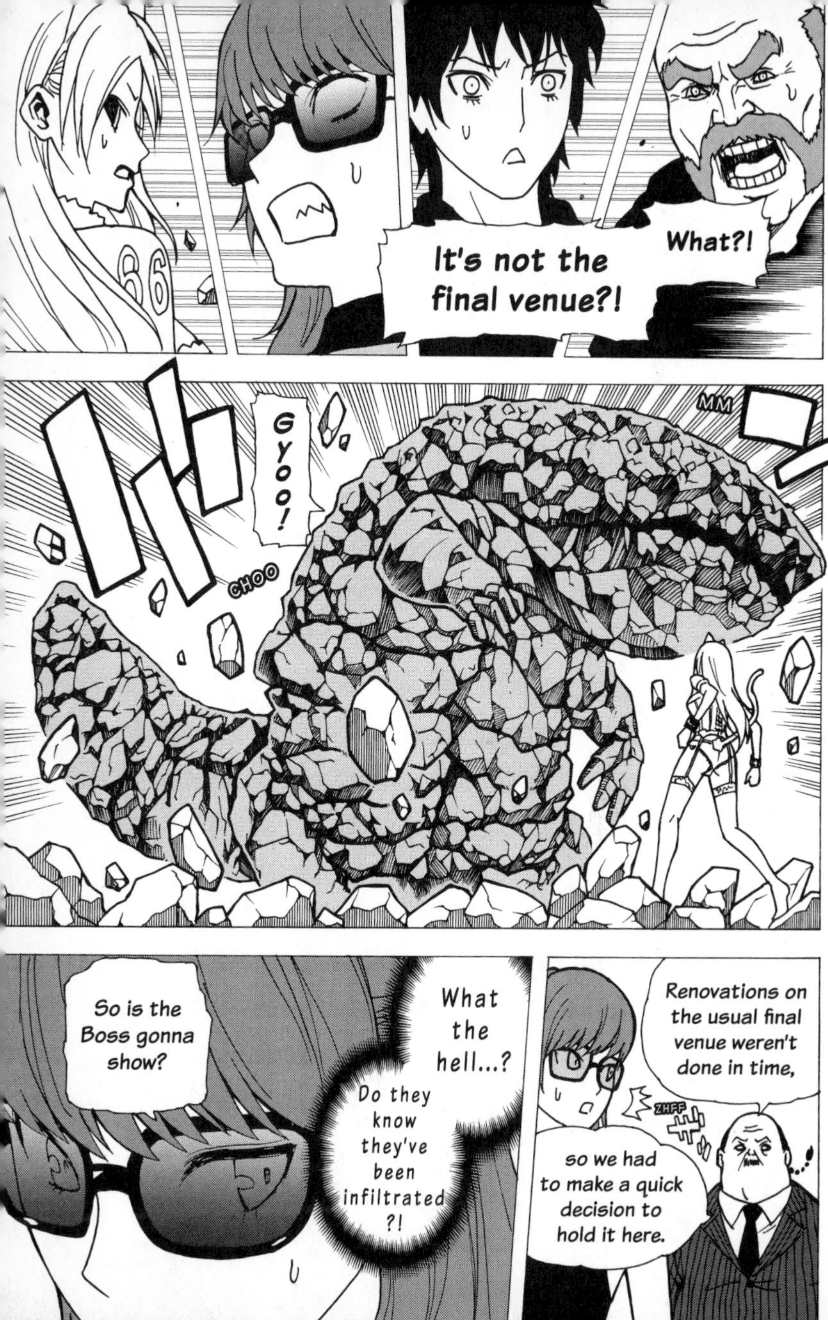
What?!
It's not the final venue?!
MM
Gyooo!
CHOO
Renovations on the usual final venue weren't done in time,
ZHFF
so we had to make a quick decision to hold it here.
What the hell...?
So is the Boss gonna show?
Do they know they've been infiltrated?!

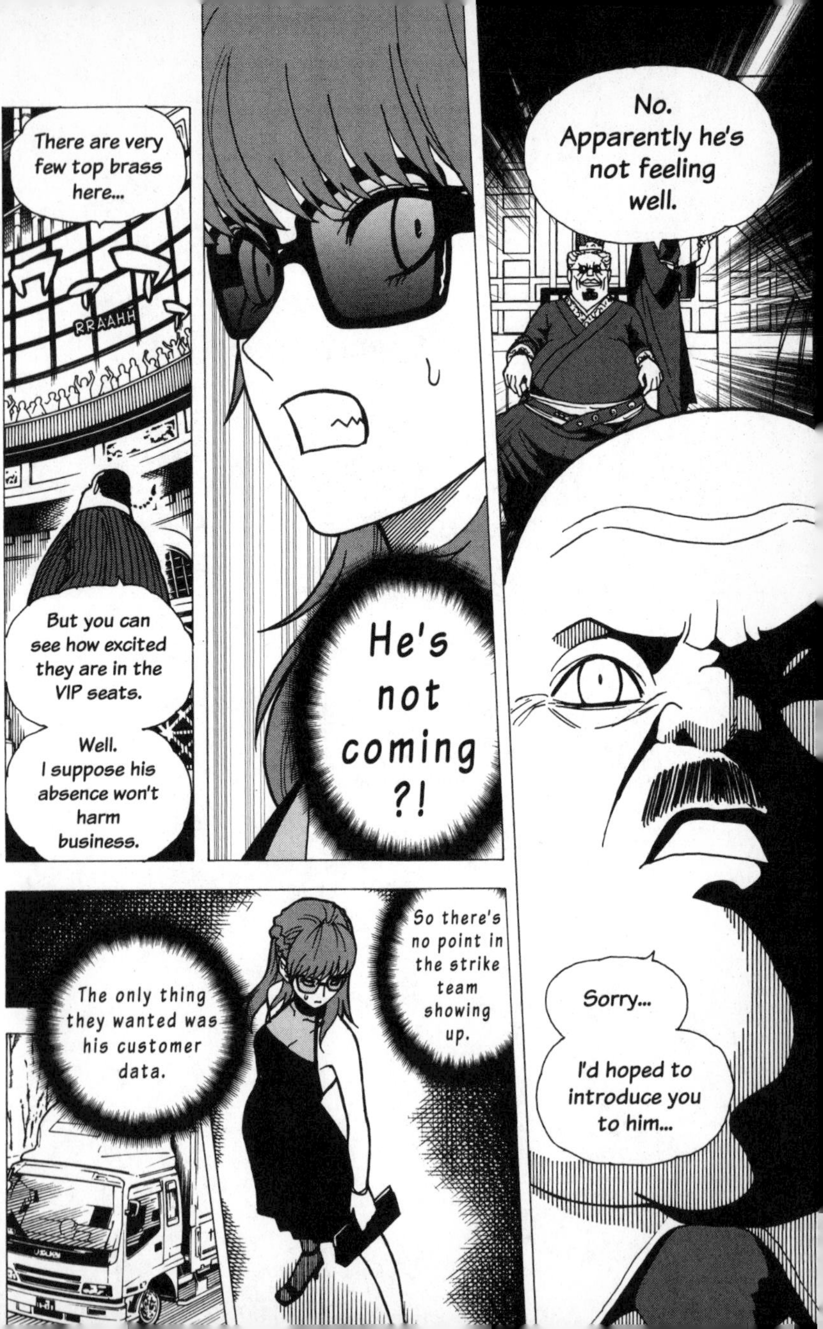
No. Apparently he's not feeling well.
Sorry...
I'd hoped to introduce you to him...
He's not coming ?!
There are very few top brass here...
RRAAHH
But you can see how excited they are in the VIP seats.
Well. I suppose his absence won't harm business.
So there's no point in the strike team showing up.
The only thing they wanted was his customer data.

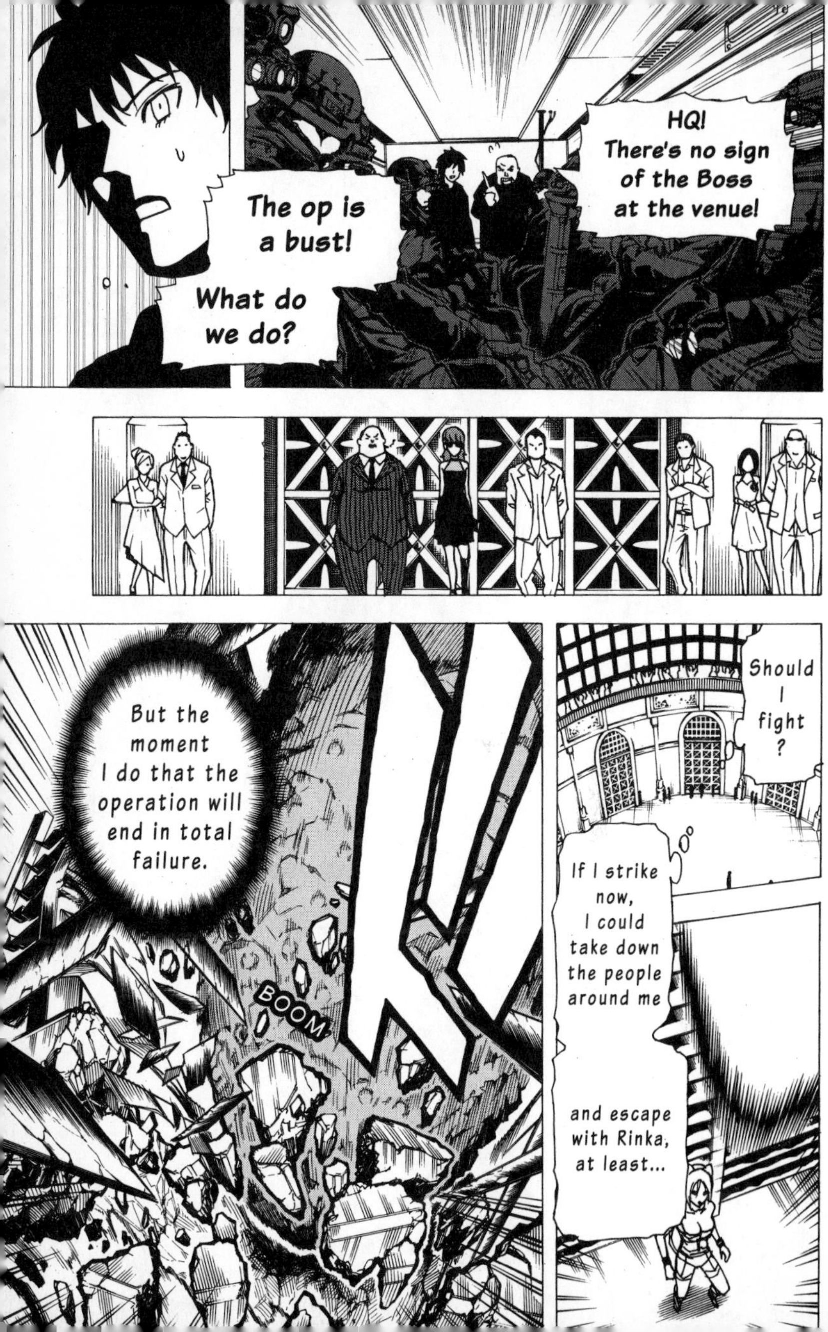
HQ! There's no sign of the Boss at the venue!
The op is a bust!
What do we do?
Should I fight?
If I strike now, I could take down the people around me
and escape with Rinka, at least...
But the moment I do that the operation will end in total failure.
BOOM

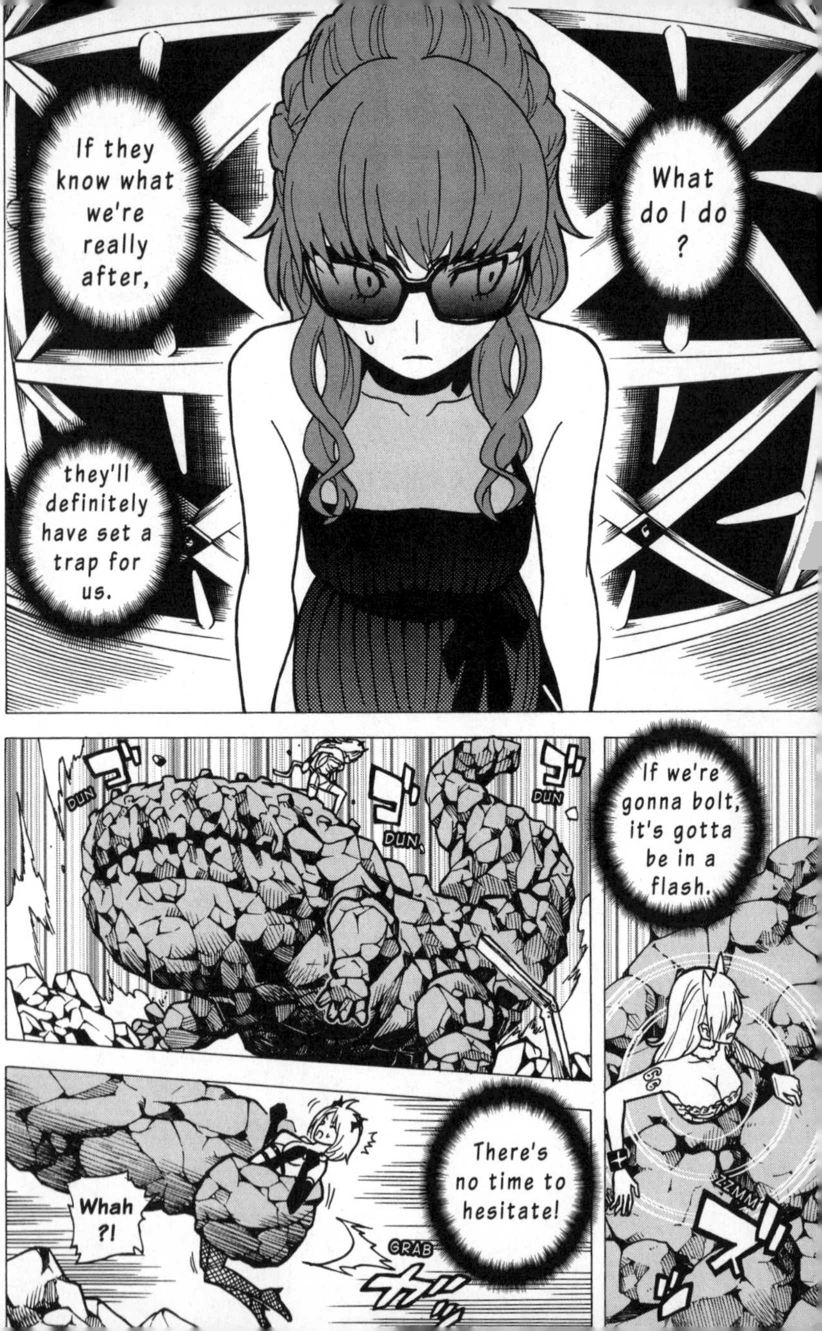
What do I do ?
If they know what we're really after,
they'll definitely have set a trap for us.
If we're gonna bolt, it's gotta be in a flash.
ZZMM
DUN
DUN
DUN
There's no time to hesitate!
Whah ?!
GRAB

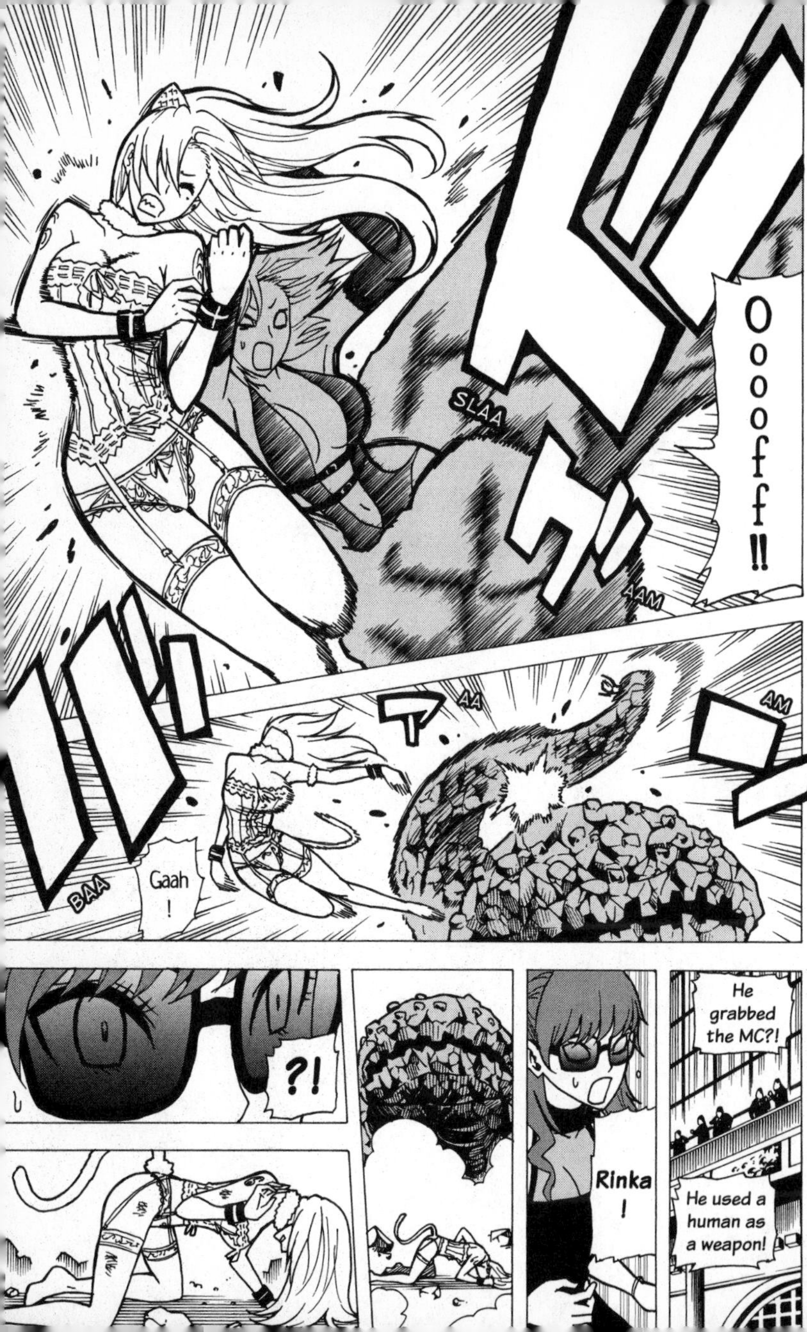
Ooooff!!
SLAA
AAM
AM
AA
Gaah!
BAA
He grabbed the MC?!
He used a human as a weapon!
Rinka!
?!

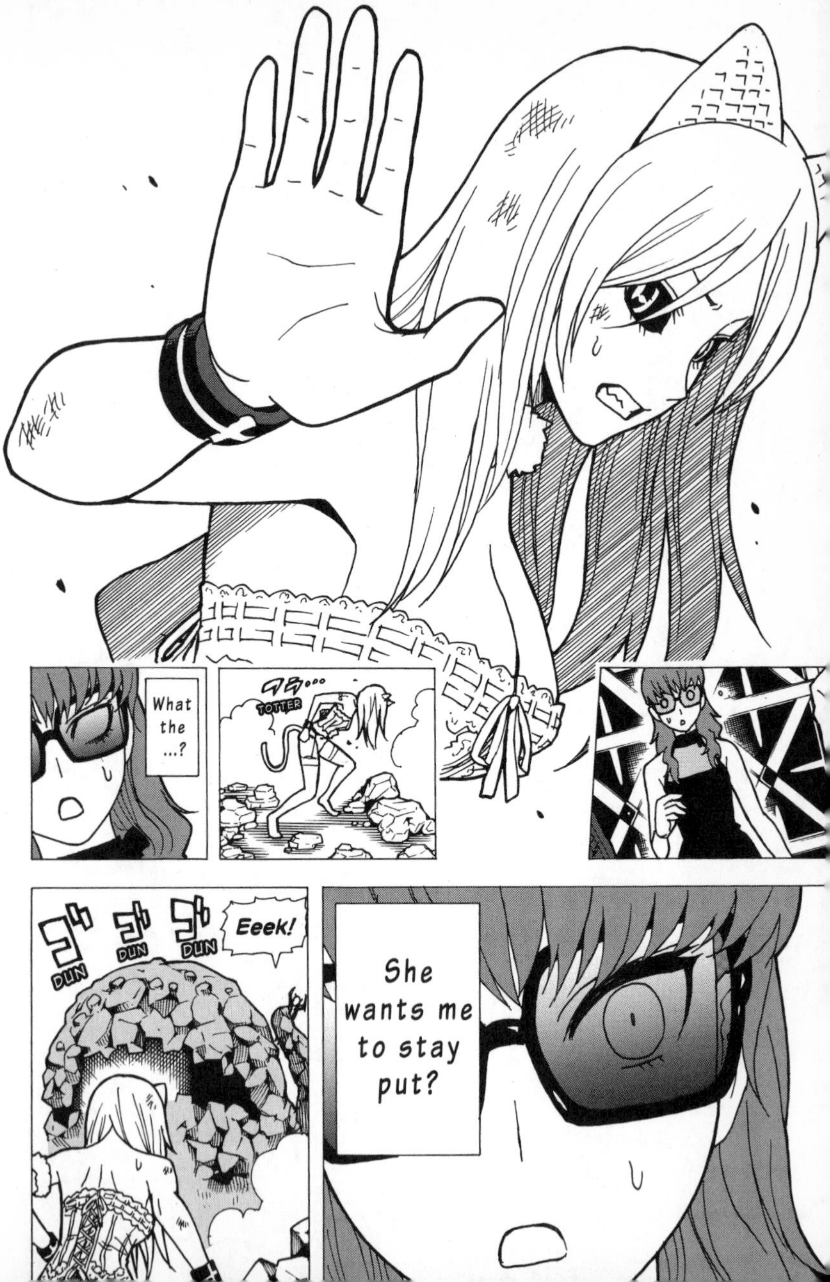
TOTTER
What the ...?
She wants me to stay put?
DUN
DUN
DUN
Eeek!

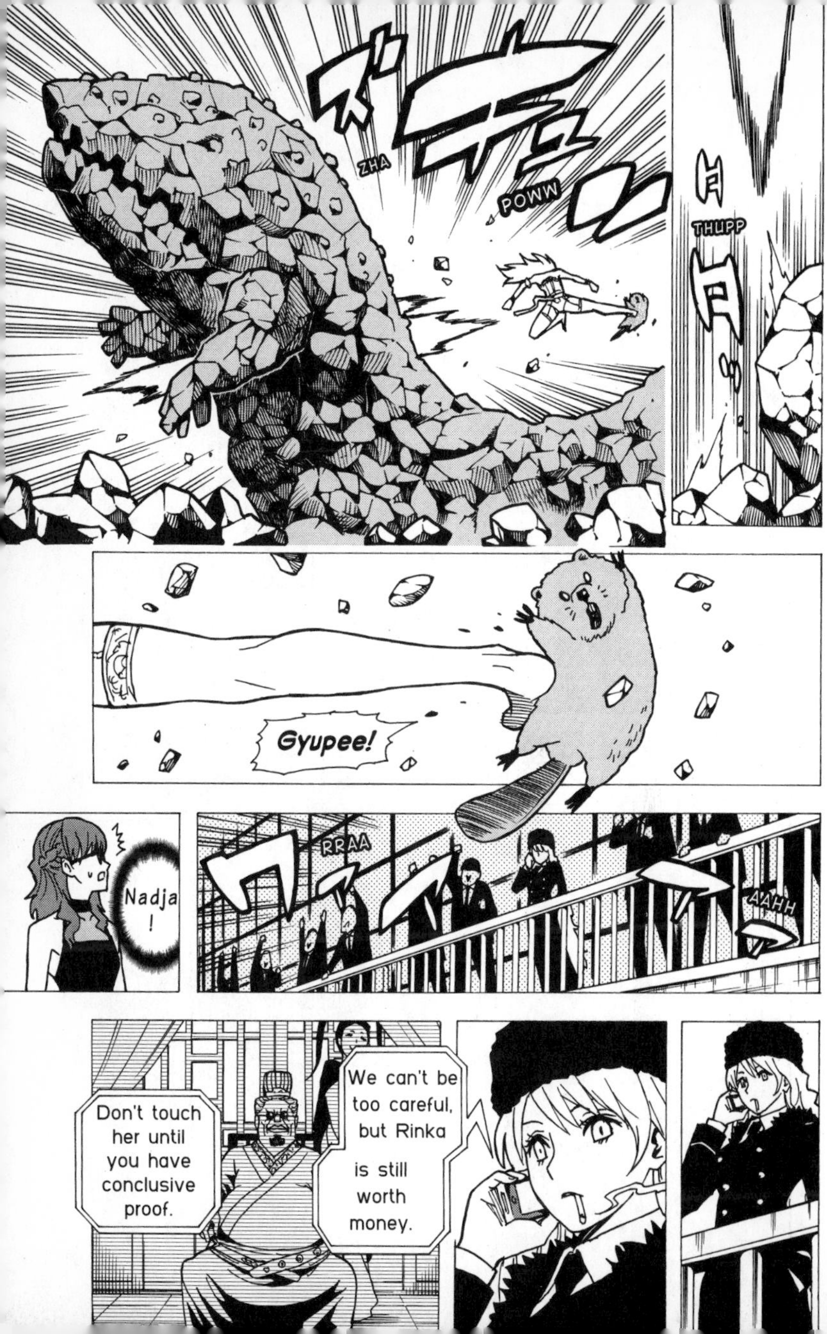
THUPP
ZHA
POWW
Gyupee!
RRAA
AAHH
Nadja!
We can't be too careful, but Rinka
is still worth money.
Don't touch her until you have conclusive proof.

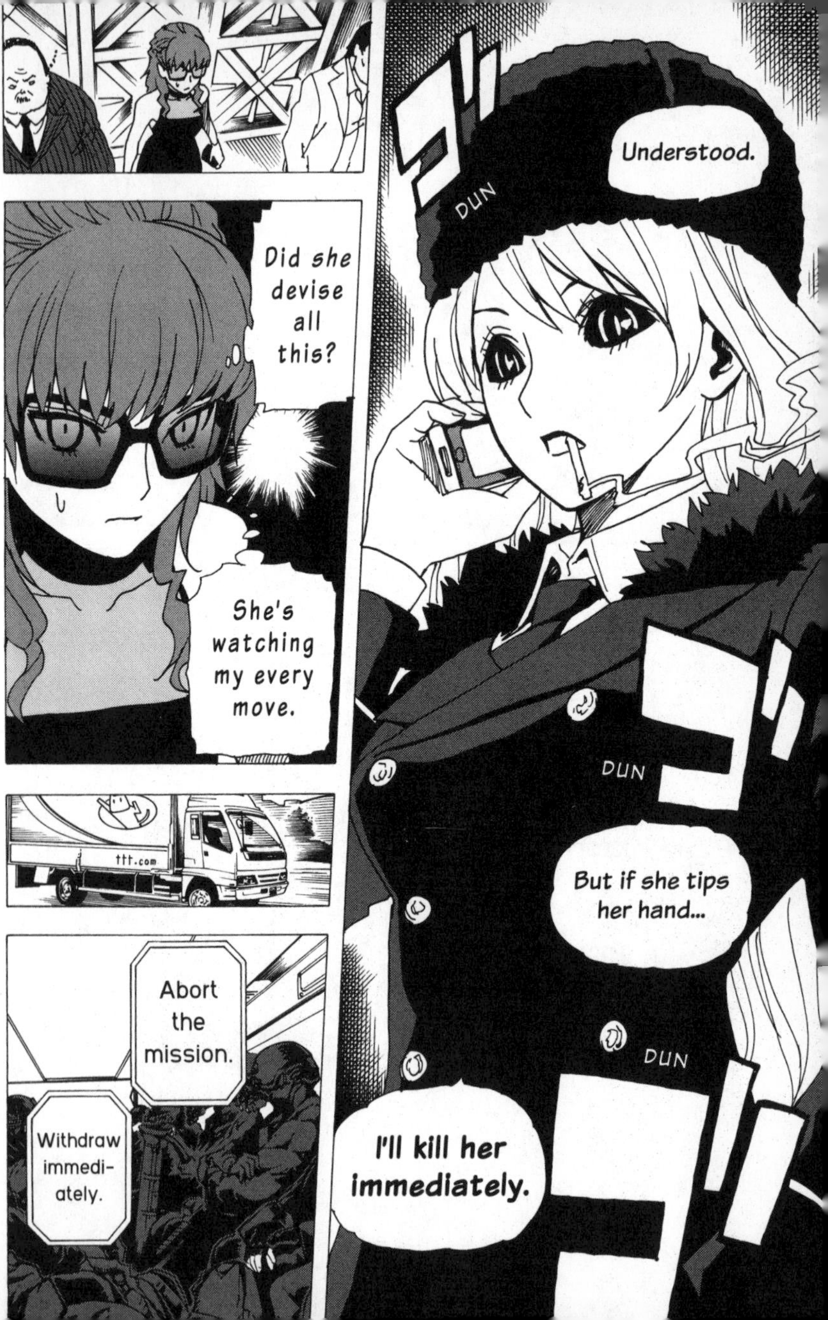
DUN
Understood.
DUN
But if she tips her hand...
DUN
I'll kill her immediately.
Did she devise all this?
She's watching my every move.
ttt.com
Abort the mission.
Withdraw immediately.

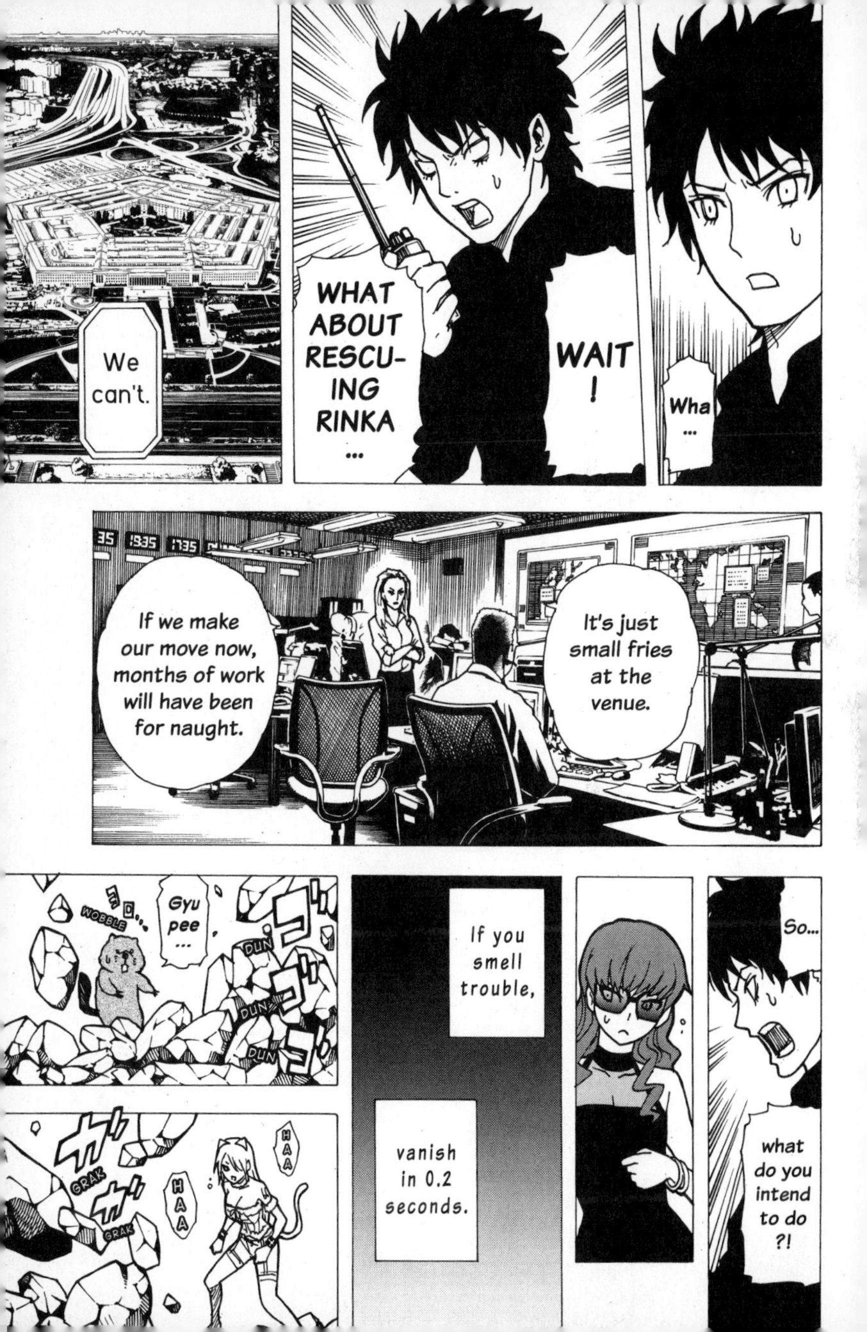
Wha ...
WAIT !
WHAT ABOUT RESCU-ING RINKA ...
We can't.
It's just small fries at the venue.
If we make our move now, months of work will have been for naught.
So...
what do you intend to do ?!
If you smell trouble,
vanish in 0.2 seconds.
Gyu pee ...
WOBBLE
DUN
DUN
DUN
HAA
HAA
GRAK
GRAK

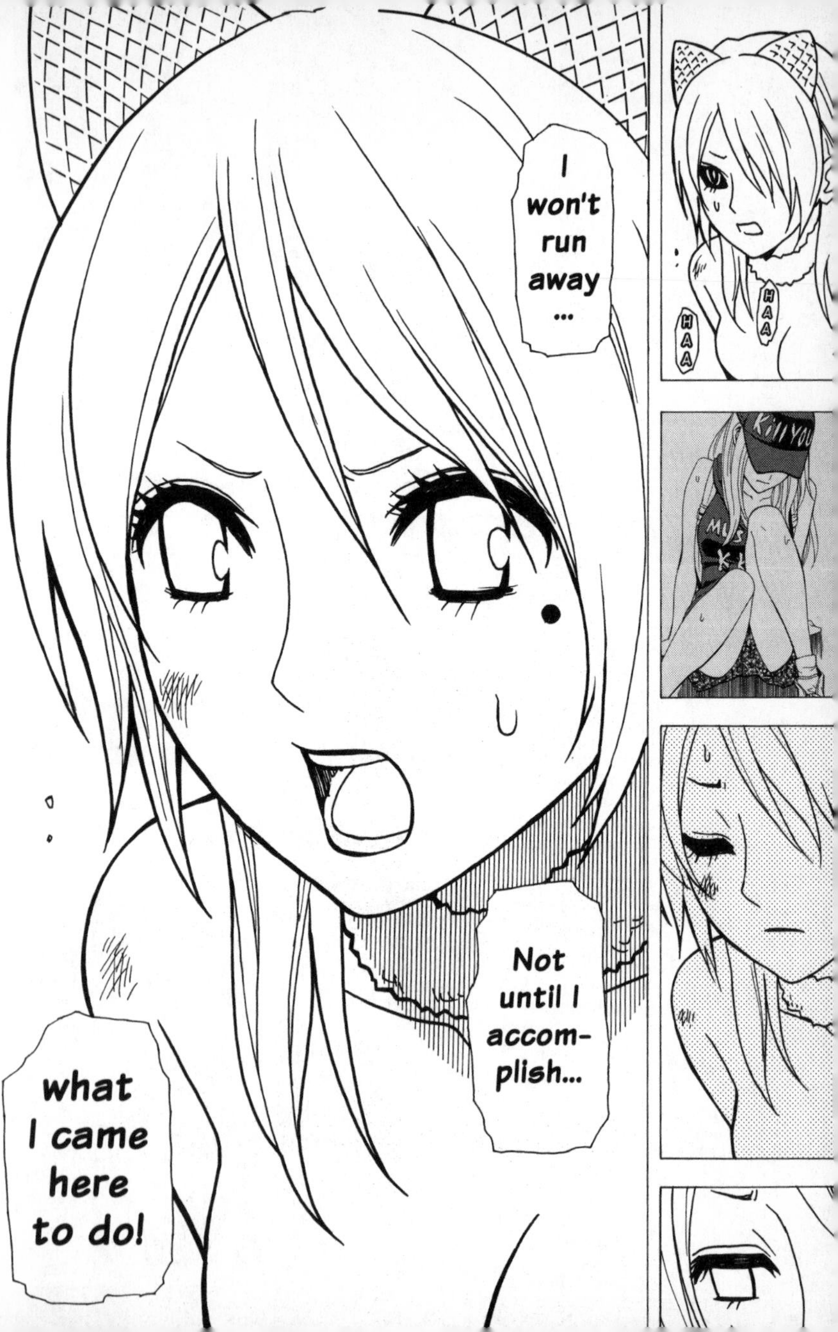
HAA
HAA
I won't run away...
Not until I accom-plish...
what I came here to do!

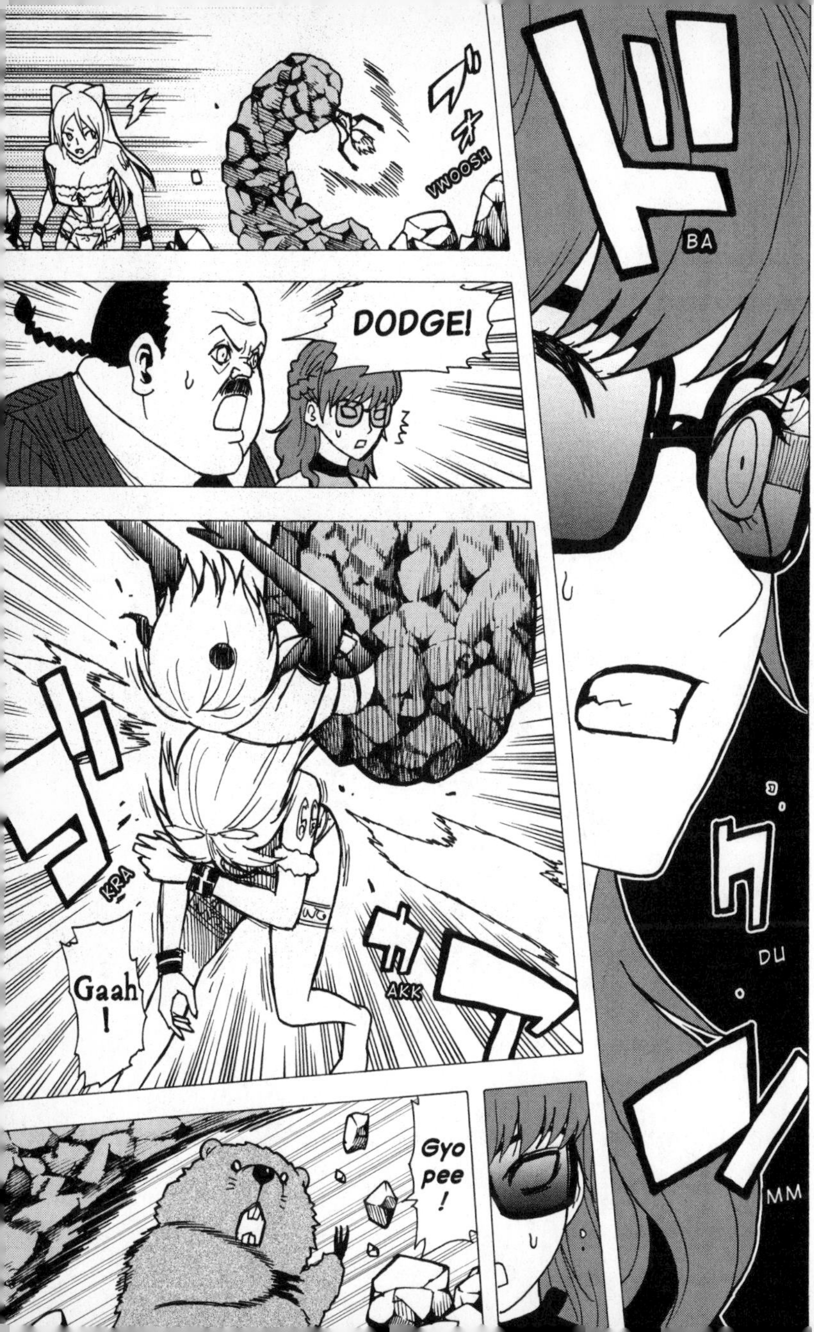
BA
DU
MM
VWOOSH
DODGE!
KRA
AKK
Gaah!
Gyo pee!

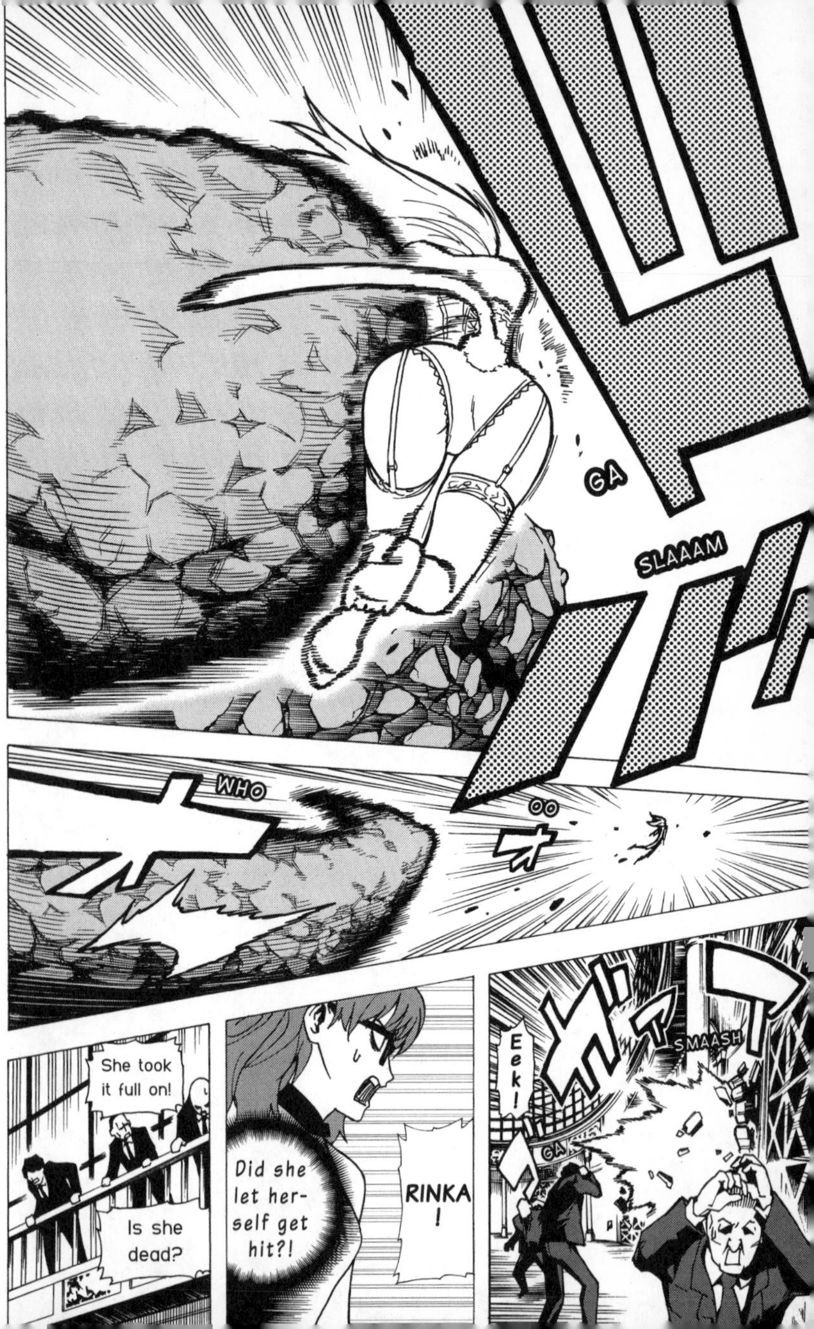
GA
SLAAAM
WHO
OO
Eek!
SMAASH
GA
RINKA!
Did she let her-self get hit?!
She took it full on!
Is she dead?

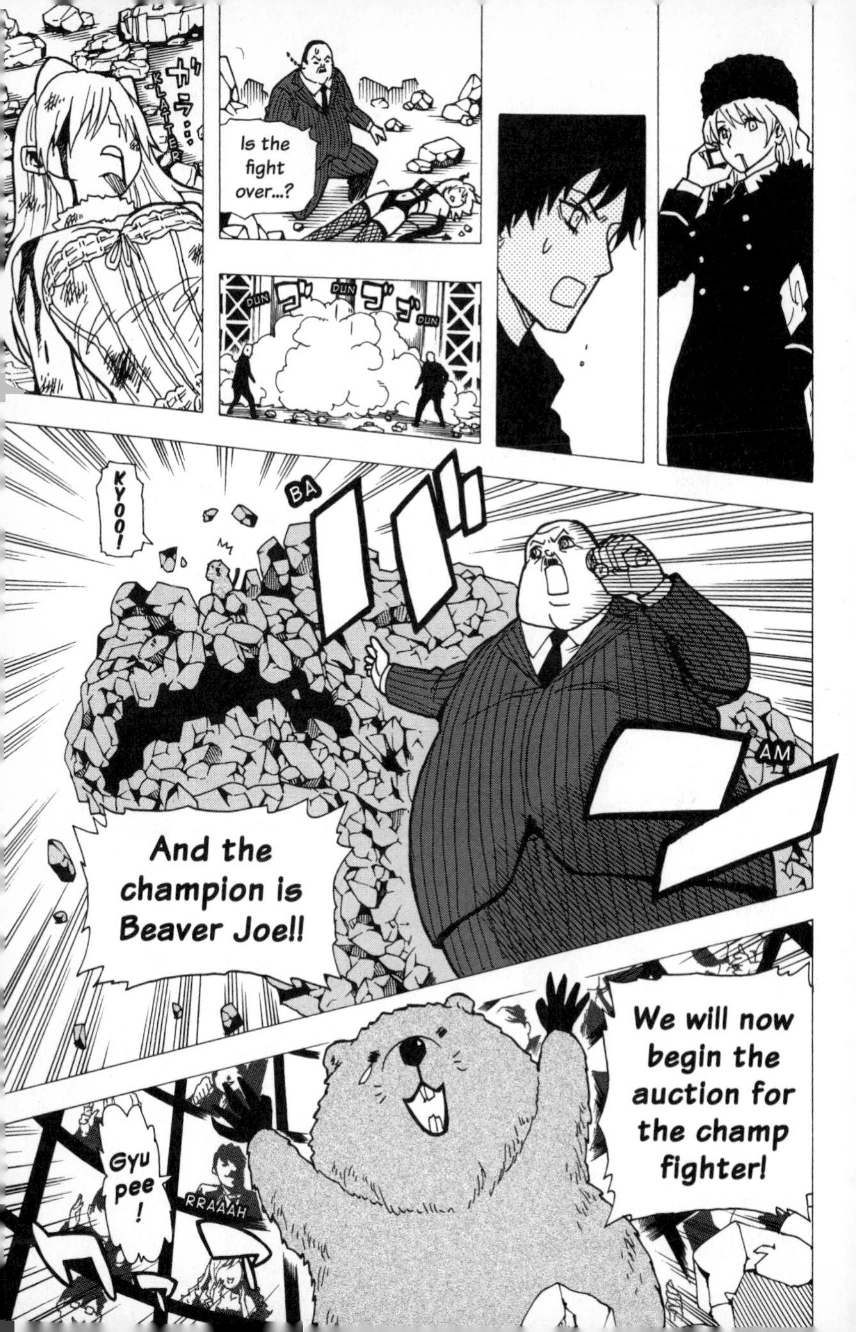
Is the fight over...?
DUN
DUN
DUN
KLATTER
BA
KYOOO!
AM
And the champion is Beaver Joe!!
We will now begin the auction for the champ fighter!
RRAAAH
Gyu pee !

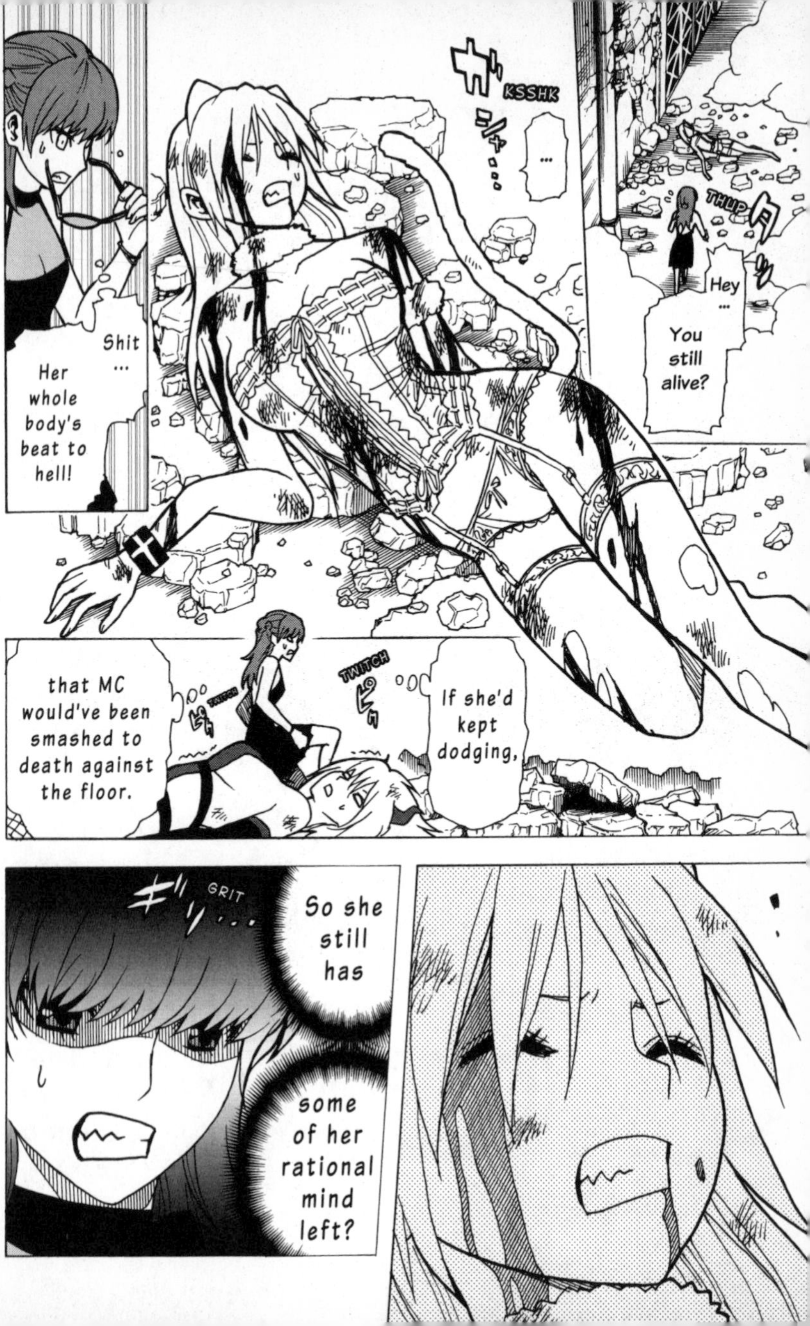
KSSHK
...
THUP
Hey... You still alive?
Shit... Her whole body's beat to hell!
If she'd kept dodging,
TWITCH
TWITCH
that MC would've been smashed to death against the floor.
GRIT
So she still has some of her rational mind left?

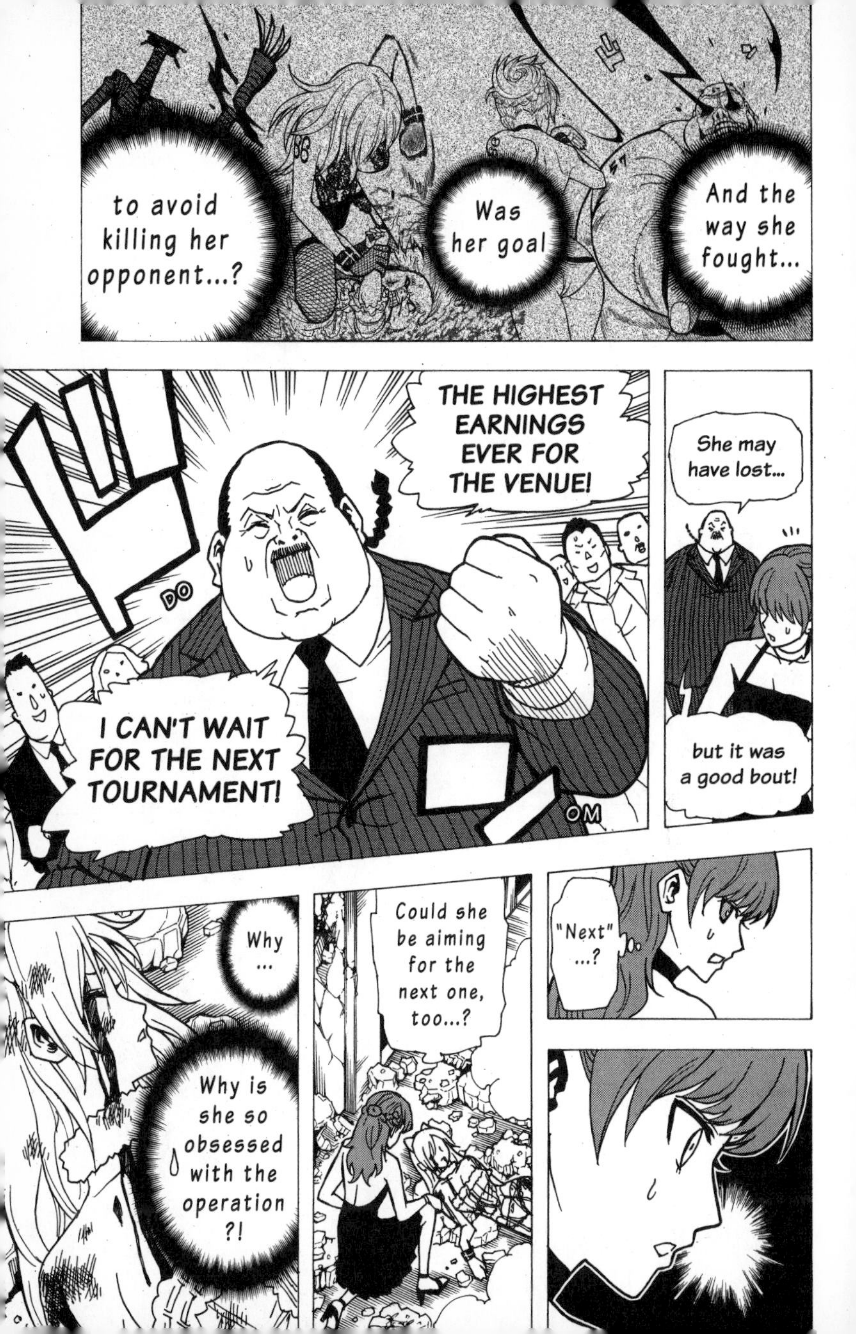
And the way she fought...
Was her goal
to avoid killing her opponent...?
She may have lost...
but it was a good bout!
THE HIGHEST EARNINGS EVER FOR THE VENUE!
DO
OM
I CAN'T WAIT FOR THE NEXT TOURNAMENT!
"Next" ...?
Could she be aiming for the next one, too...?
Why ...
Why is she so obsessed with the operation ?!

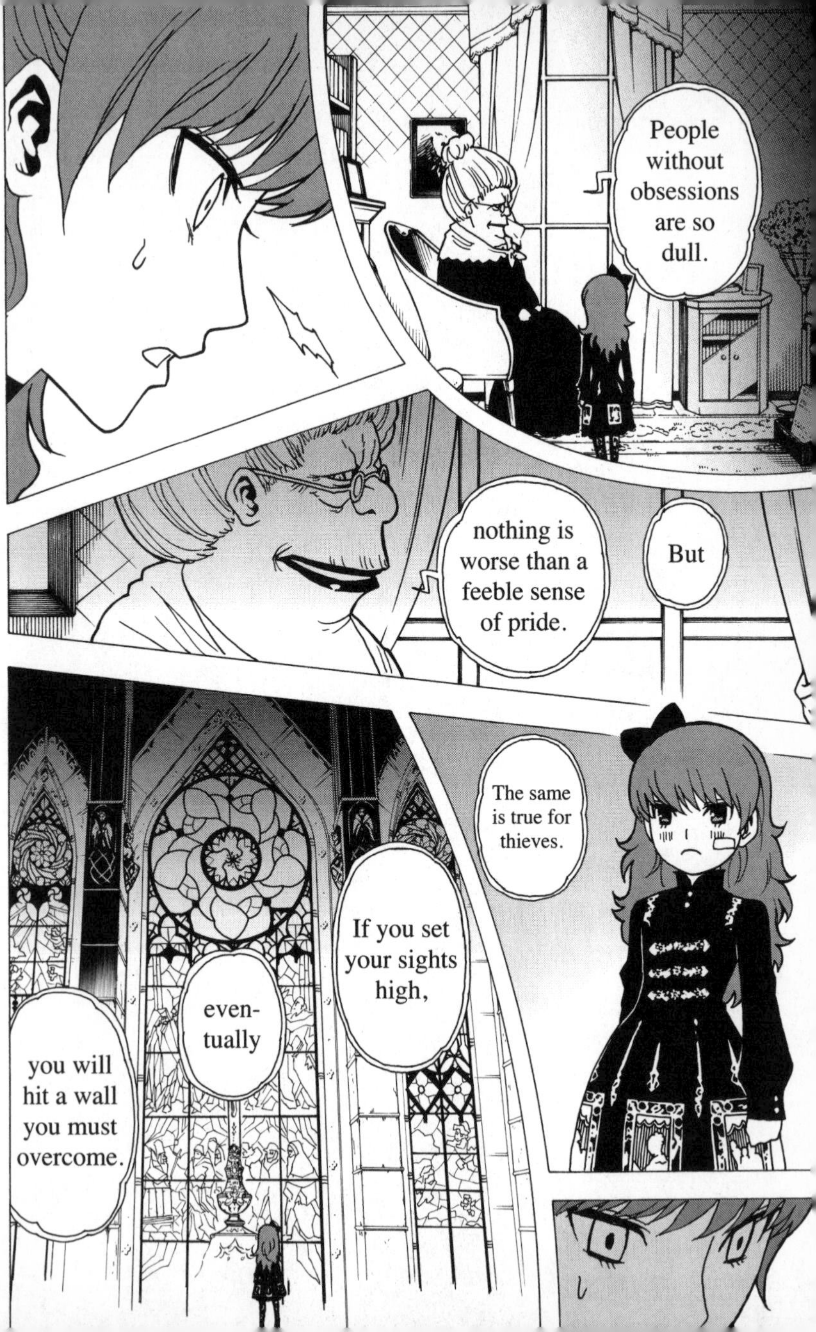
People without obsessions are so dull.
But
nothing is worse than a feeble sense of pride.
The same is true for thieves.
If you set your sights high,
even-tually
you will hit a wall you must overcome.

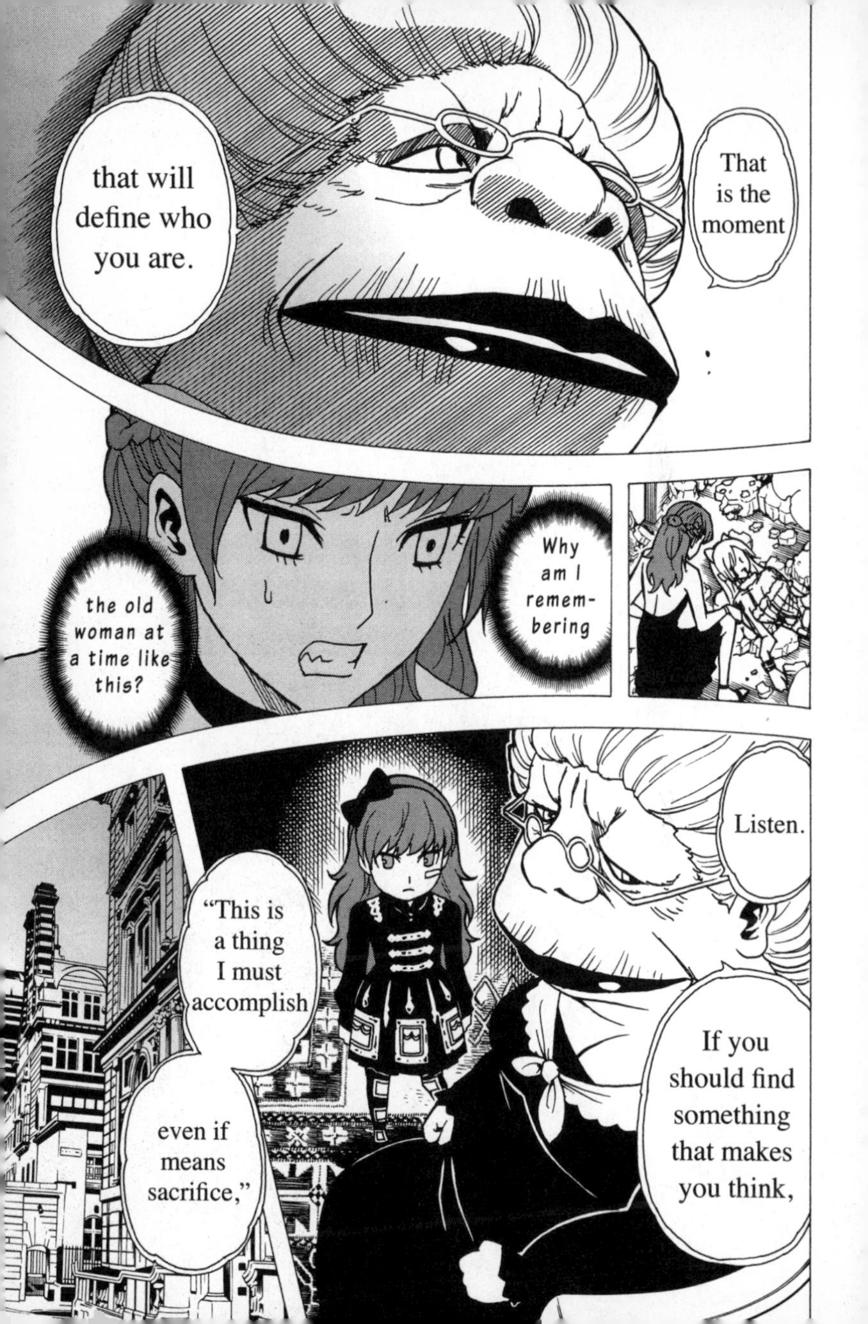
That is the moment
that will define who you are.
Why am I remembering
the old woman at a time like this?
Listen.
If you should find something that makes you think,
"This is a thing I must accomplish
even if means sacrifice,"

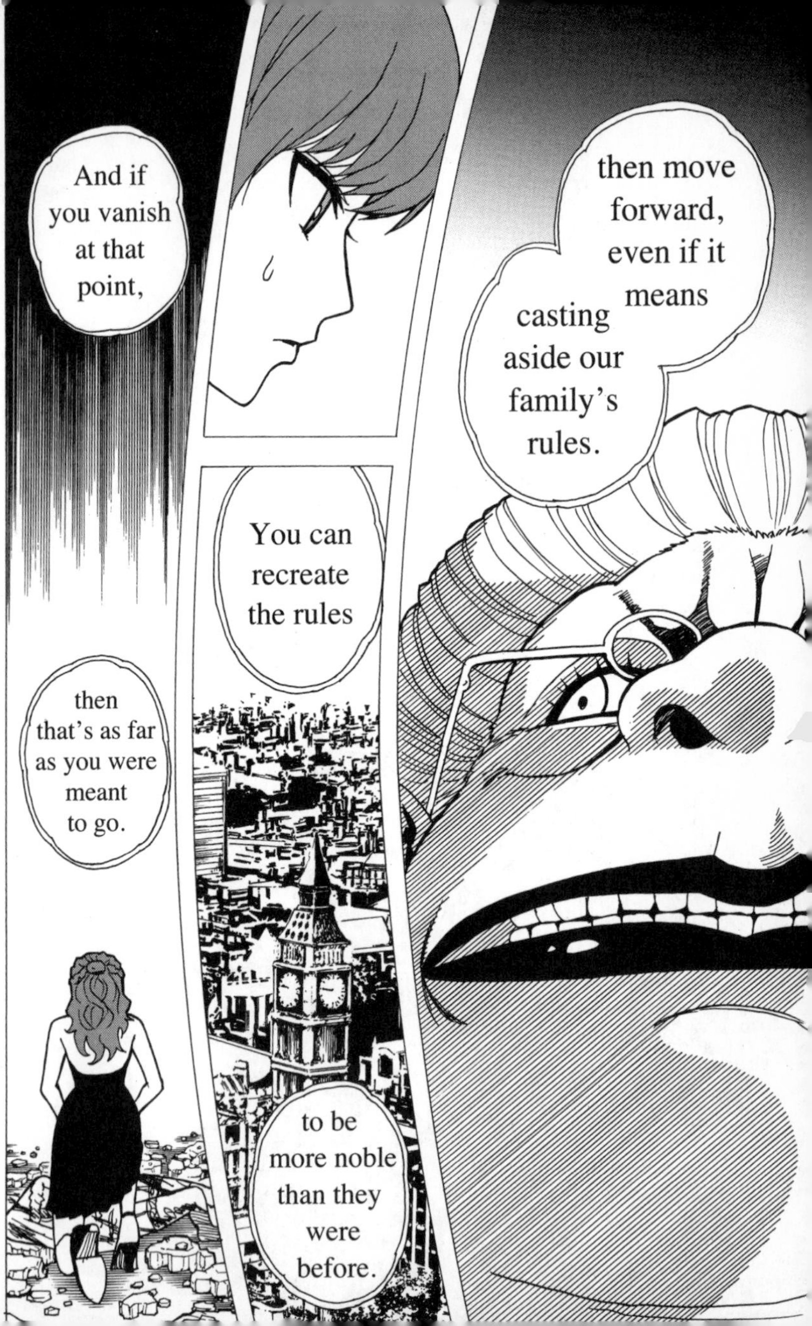
then move forward, even if it means casting aside our family's rules.
You can recreate the rules
to be more noble than they were before.
And if you vanish at that point,
then that's as far as you were meant to go.

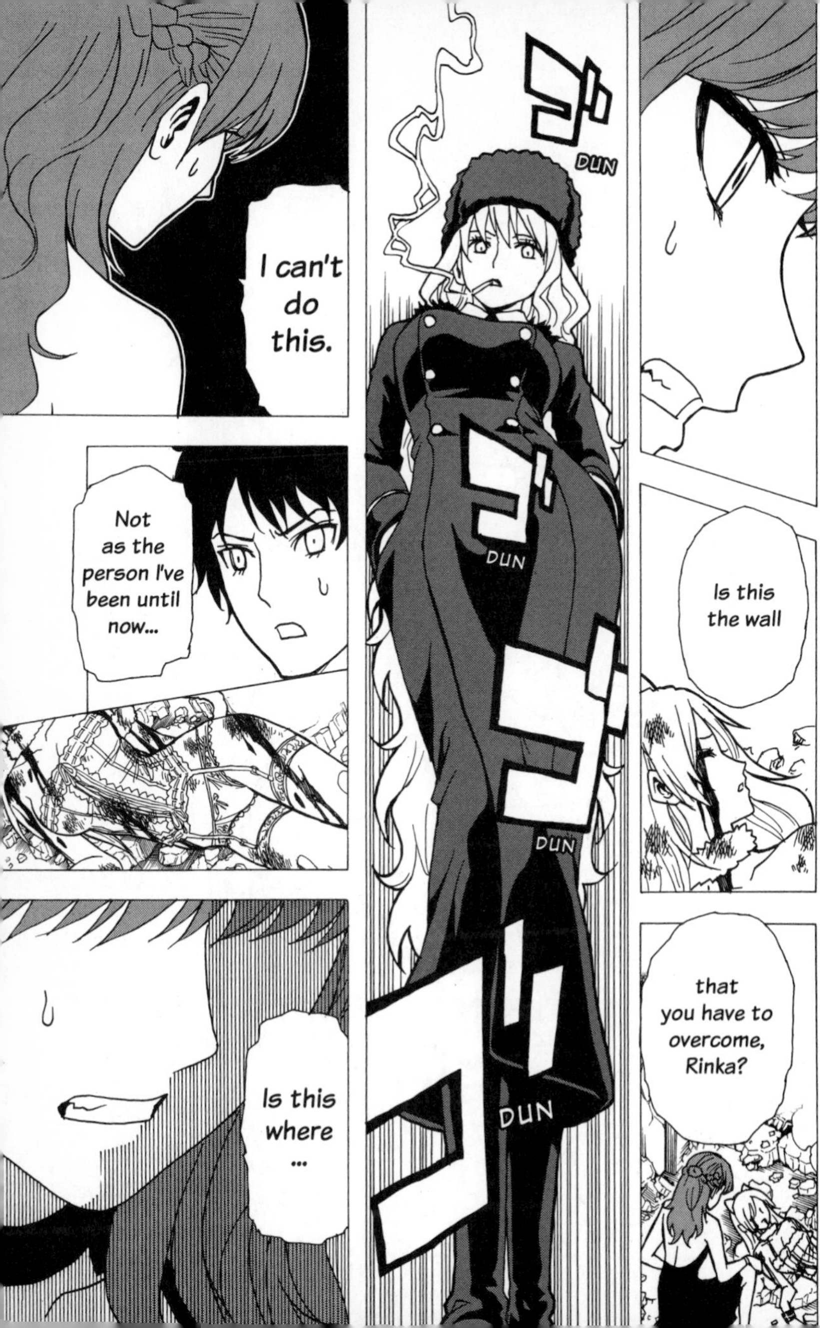
Is this the wall
that you have to overcome, Rinka?
DUN
DUN
DUN
DUN
I can't do this.
Not as the person I've been until now...
Is this where ...

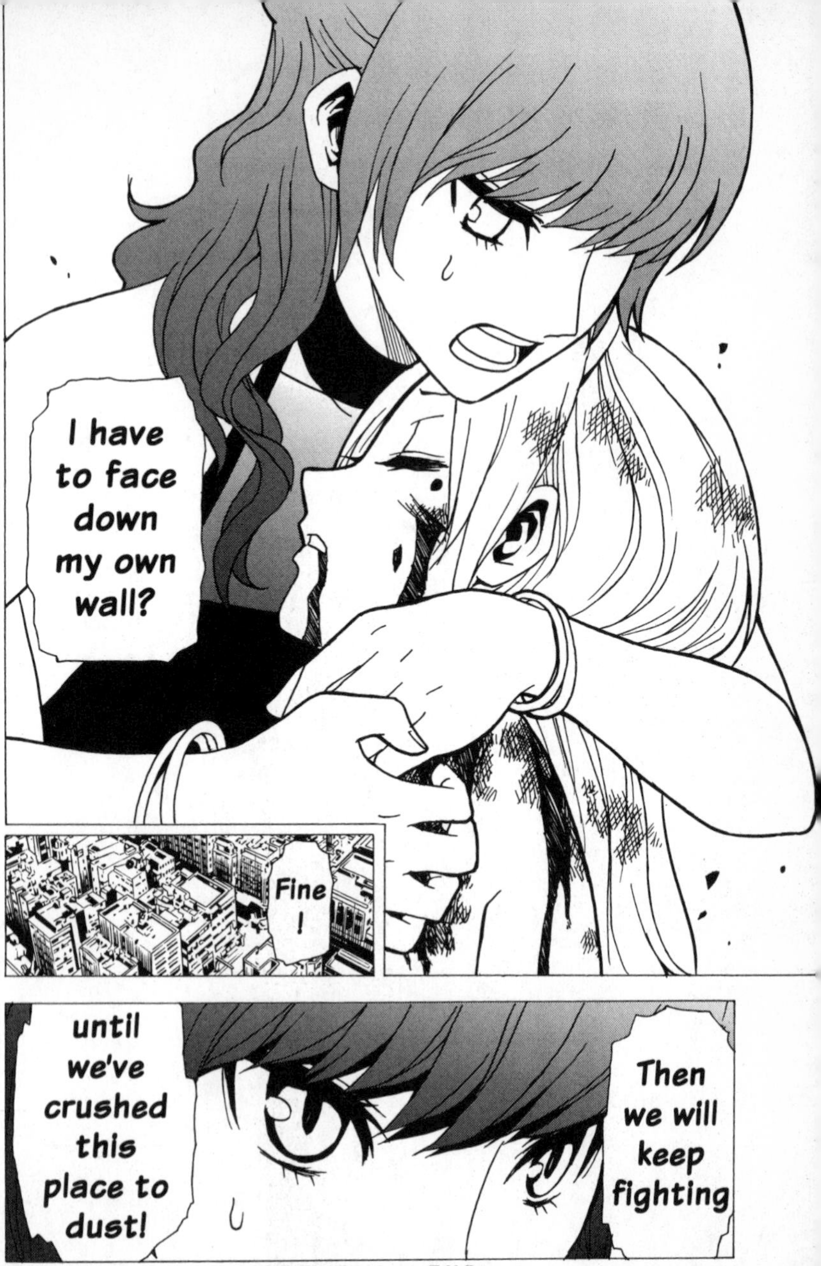
I have to face down my own wall?
Fine!
Then we will keep fighting
until we've crushed this place to dust!

SCENE 46 /// END

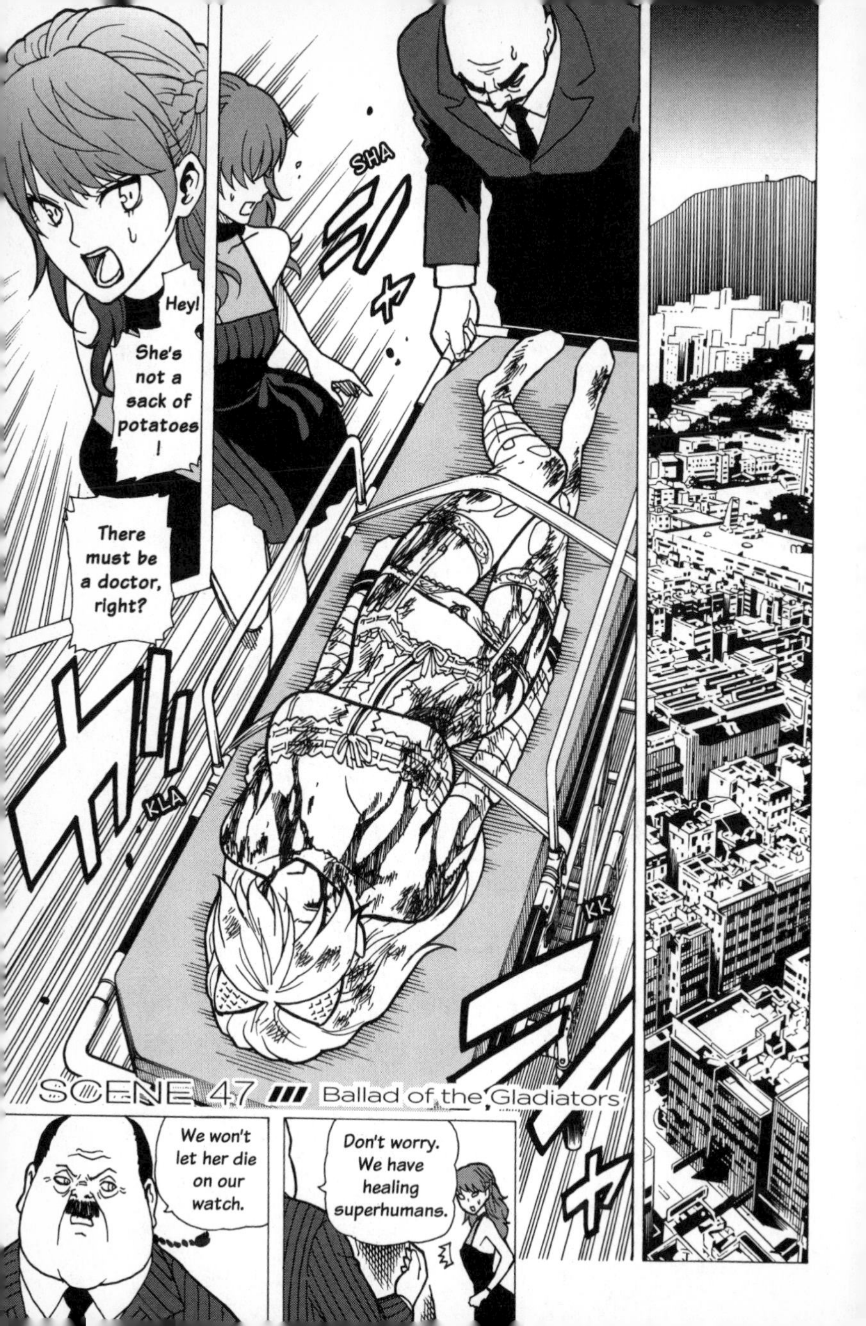
SHA
Hey!
She's not a sack of potatoes!
There must be a doctor, right?
KLA
KK
SCENE 47 /// Ballad of the Gladiators
Don't worry. We have healing superhumans.
We won't let her die on our watch.

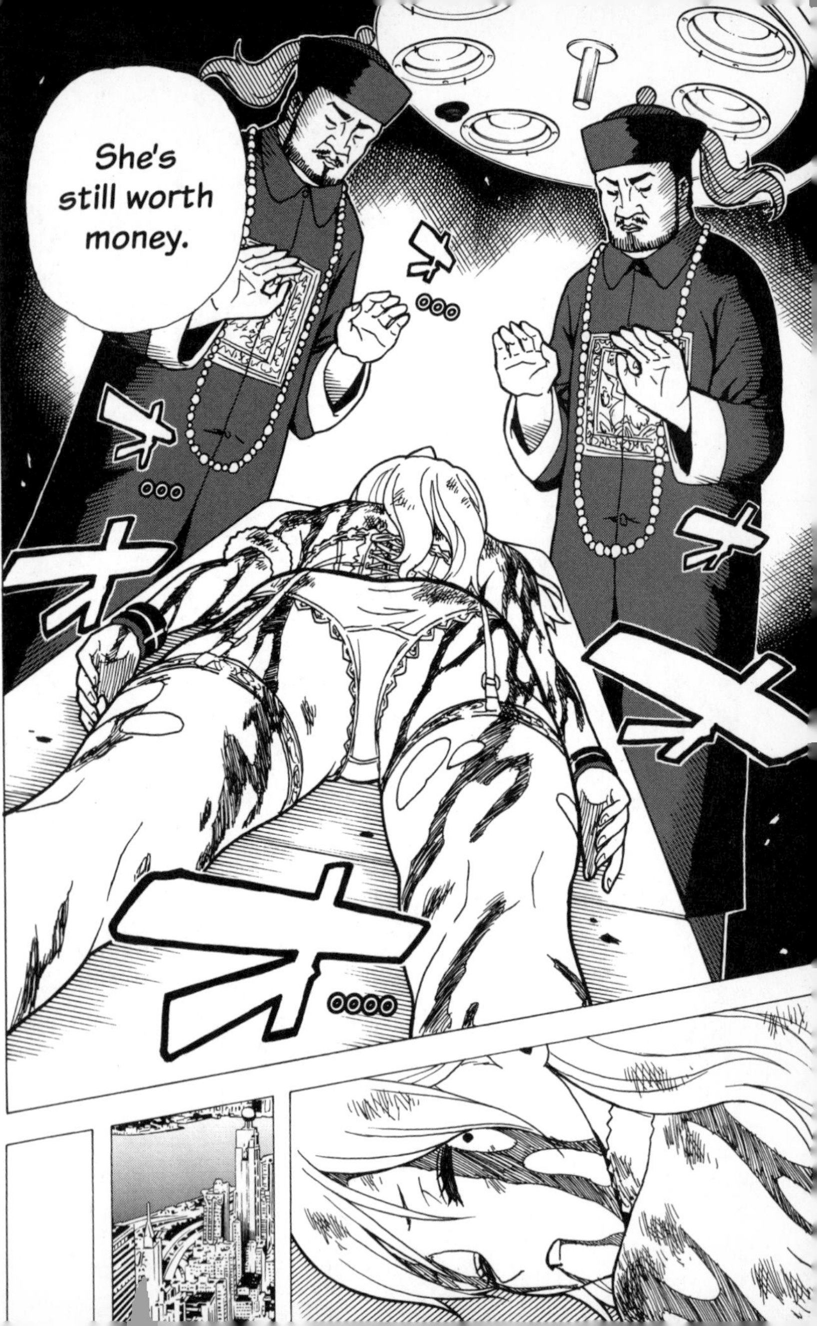
She's still worth money.

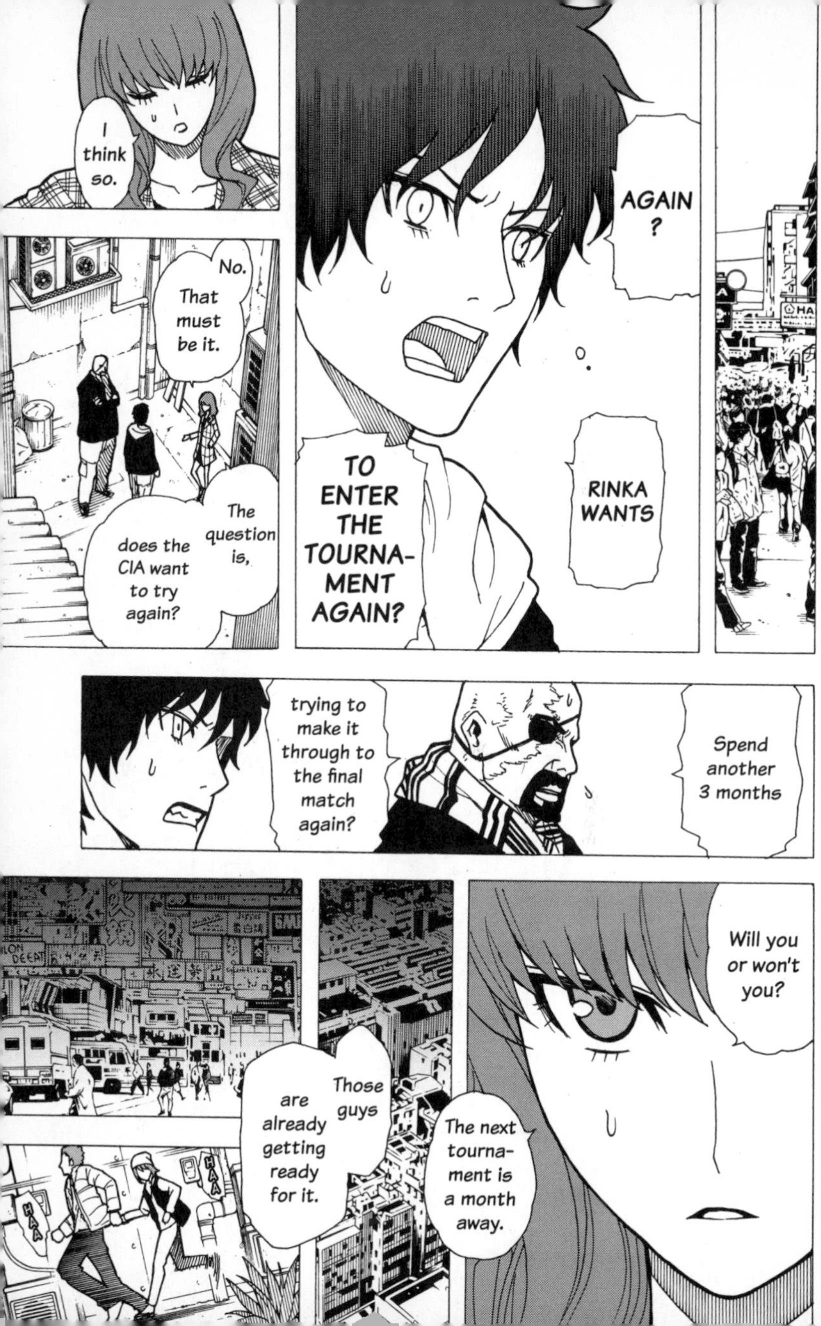
AGAIN?
RINKA WANTS
TO ENTER THE TOURNAMENT AGAIN?
I think so.
No. That must be it.
The question is, does the CIA want to try again?
Spend another 3 months
trying to make it through to the final match again?
Will you or won't you?
The next tournament is a month away.
Those guys are already getting ready for it.
HAA
HAA

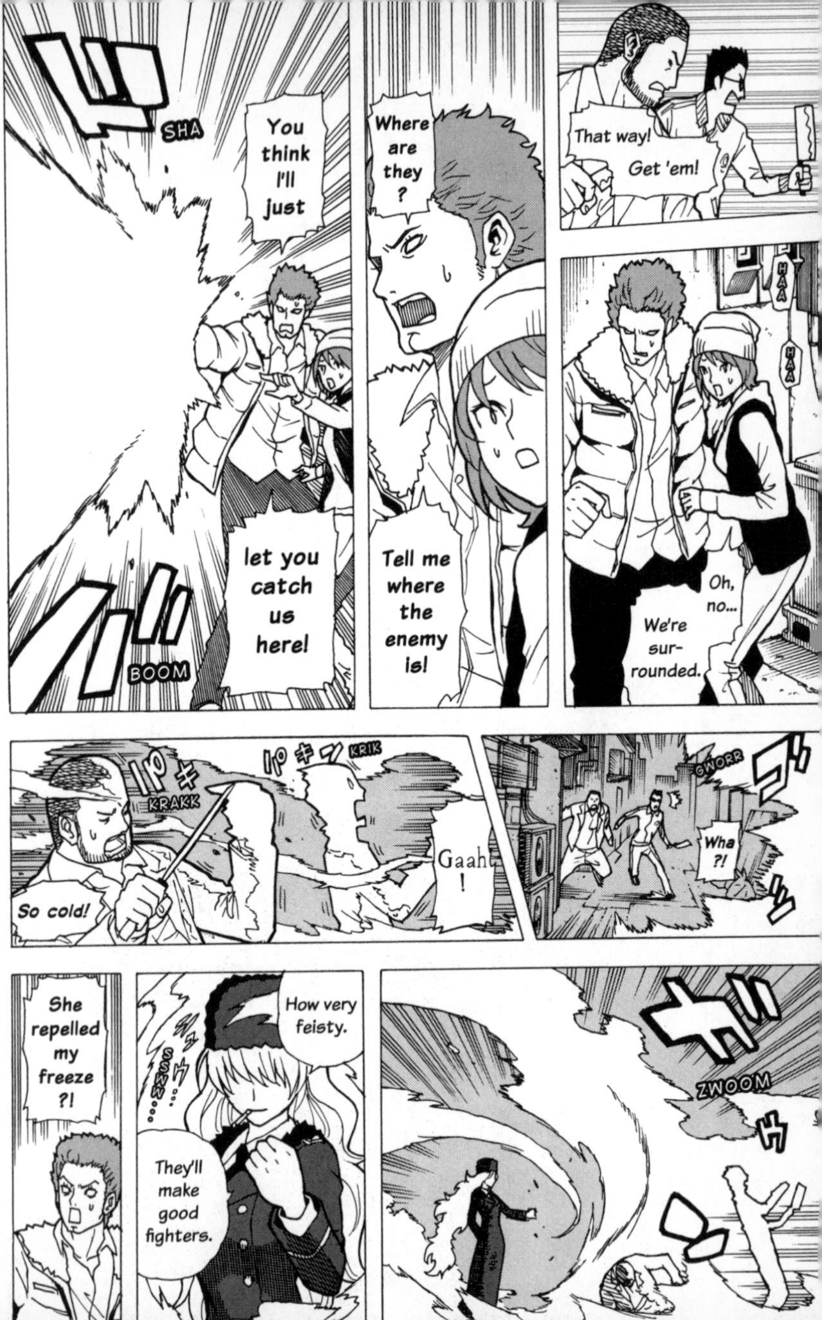
That way!
Get 'em!
HAA
HAA
Oh, no...
We're surrounded.
Where are they?
Tell me where the enemy is!
SHA
You think I'll just
let you catch us here!
BOOM
GWORR
Wha?!
KRIK
KRAKK
Gaah!
So cold!
ZWOOM
How very feisty.
SSWW...
They'll make good fighters.
She repelled my freeze?!

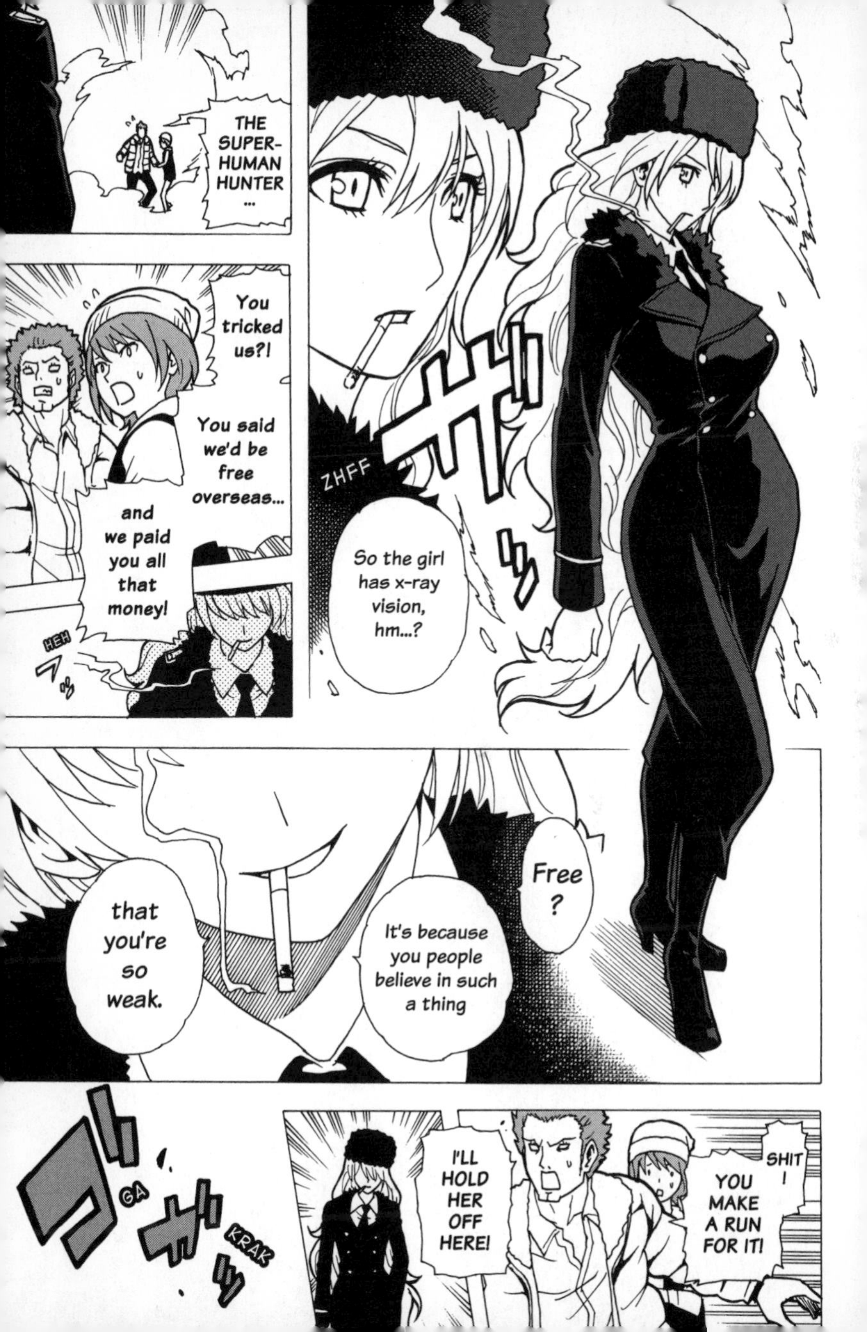
ZHFF
So the girl has x-ray vision, hm...?
THE SUPER-HUMAN HUNTER ...
You tricked us?!
You said we'd be free overseas...
and we paid you all that money!
HEH
Free?
It's because you people believe in such a thing
that you're so weak.
SHIT!
YOU MAKE A RUN FOR IT!
I'LL HOLD HER OFF HERE!
GA
KRAK

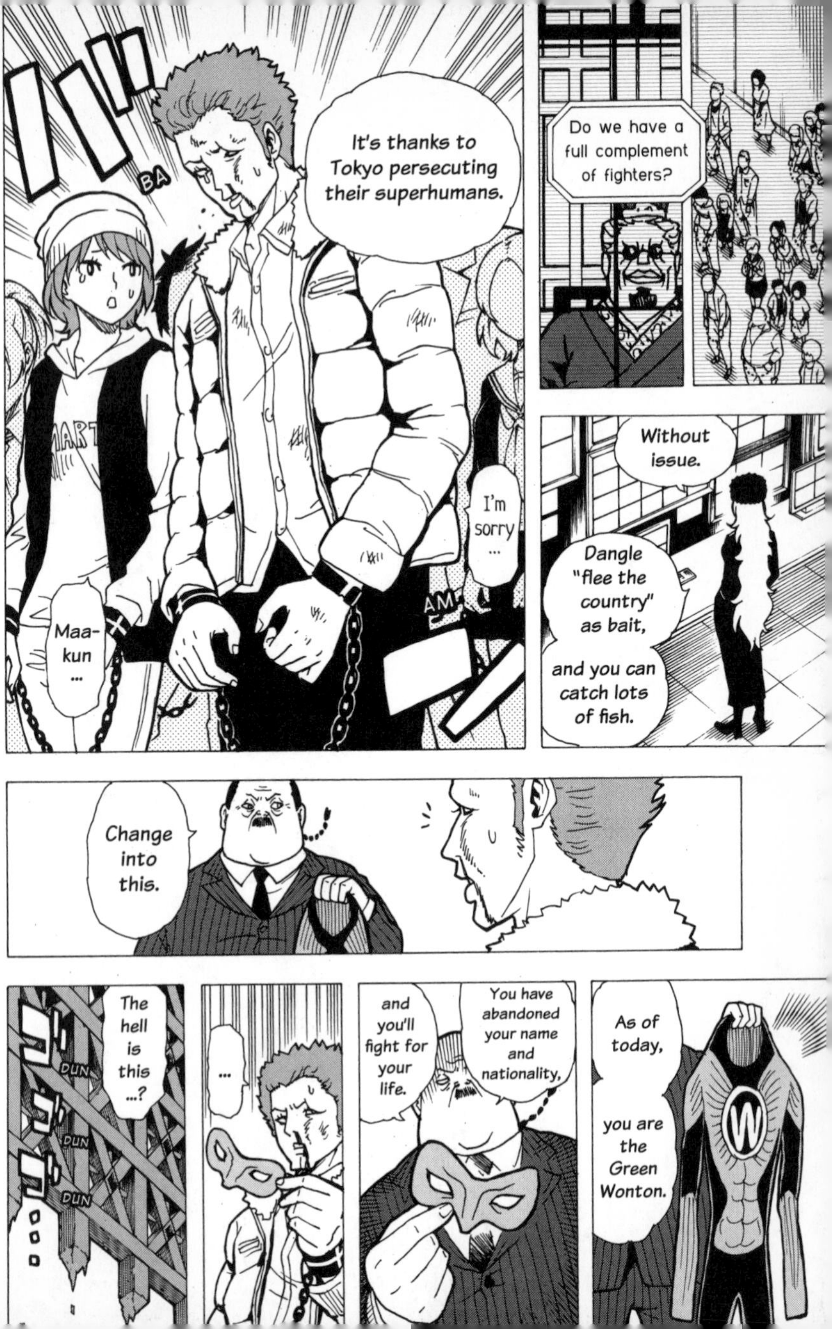

Do we have a full complement of fighters?
Without issue.
Dangle "flee the country" as bait,
and you can catch lots of fish.
BA
It's thanks to Tokyo persecuting their superhumans.
I'm sorry ...
AM
Maa-kun ...
Change into this.
As of today,
you are the Green Wonton.
You have abandoned your name and nationality,
and you'll fight for your life.
...
The hell is this ...?
DUN
DUN
DUN

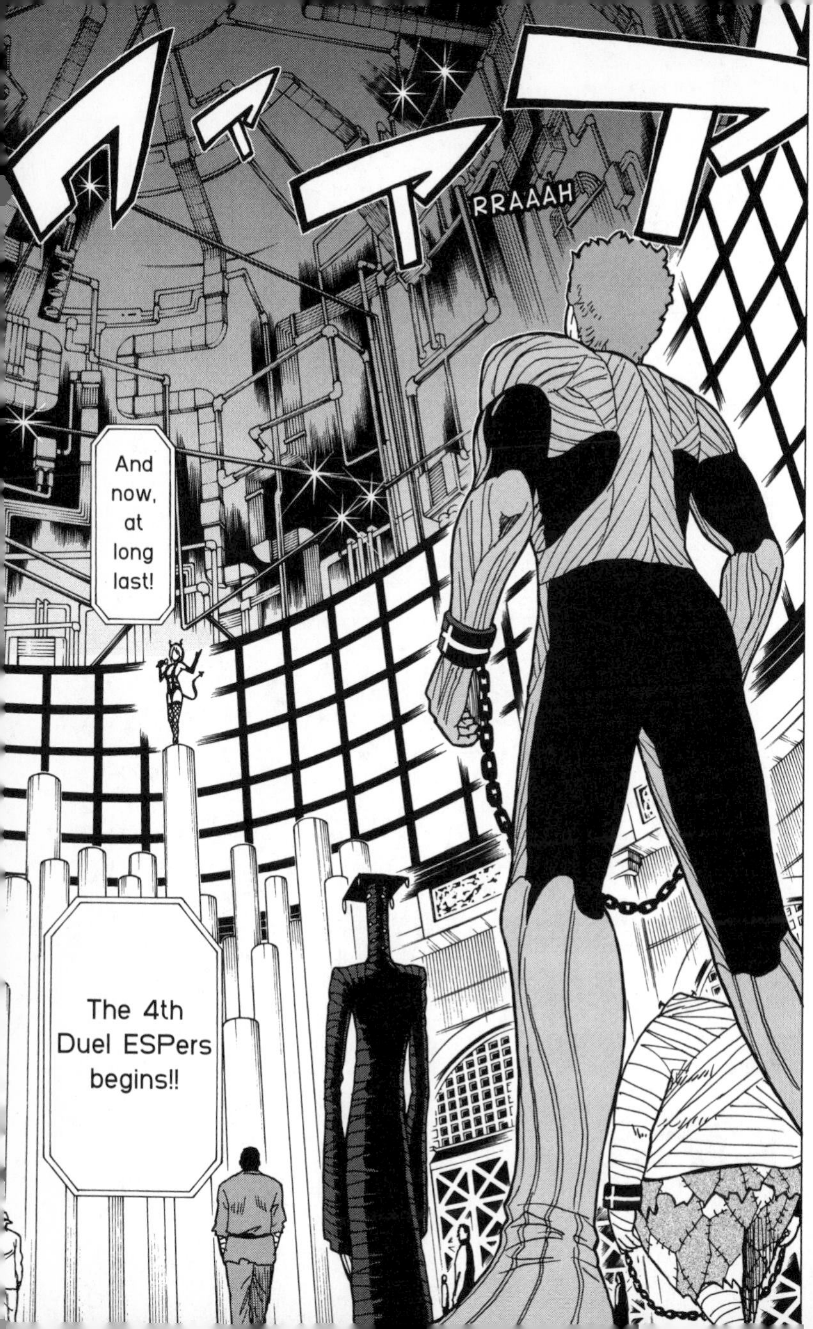
RRAAAH
And now, at long last!
The 4th Duel ESPers begins!!

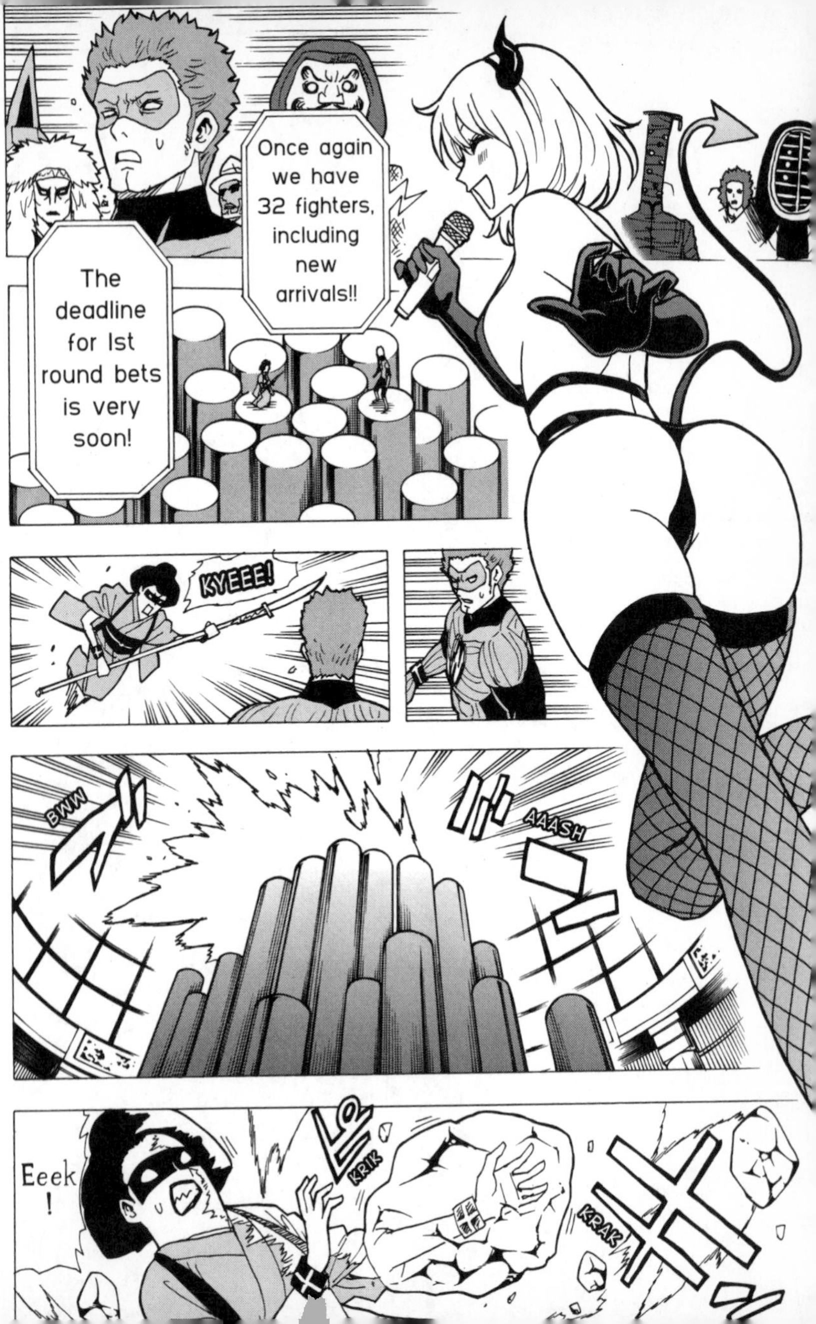
Once again we have 32 fighters, including new arrivals!!
The deadline for 1st round bets is very soon!
KYEEE!
BWW
AAASH
KRAK
KRIK
Eeek!

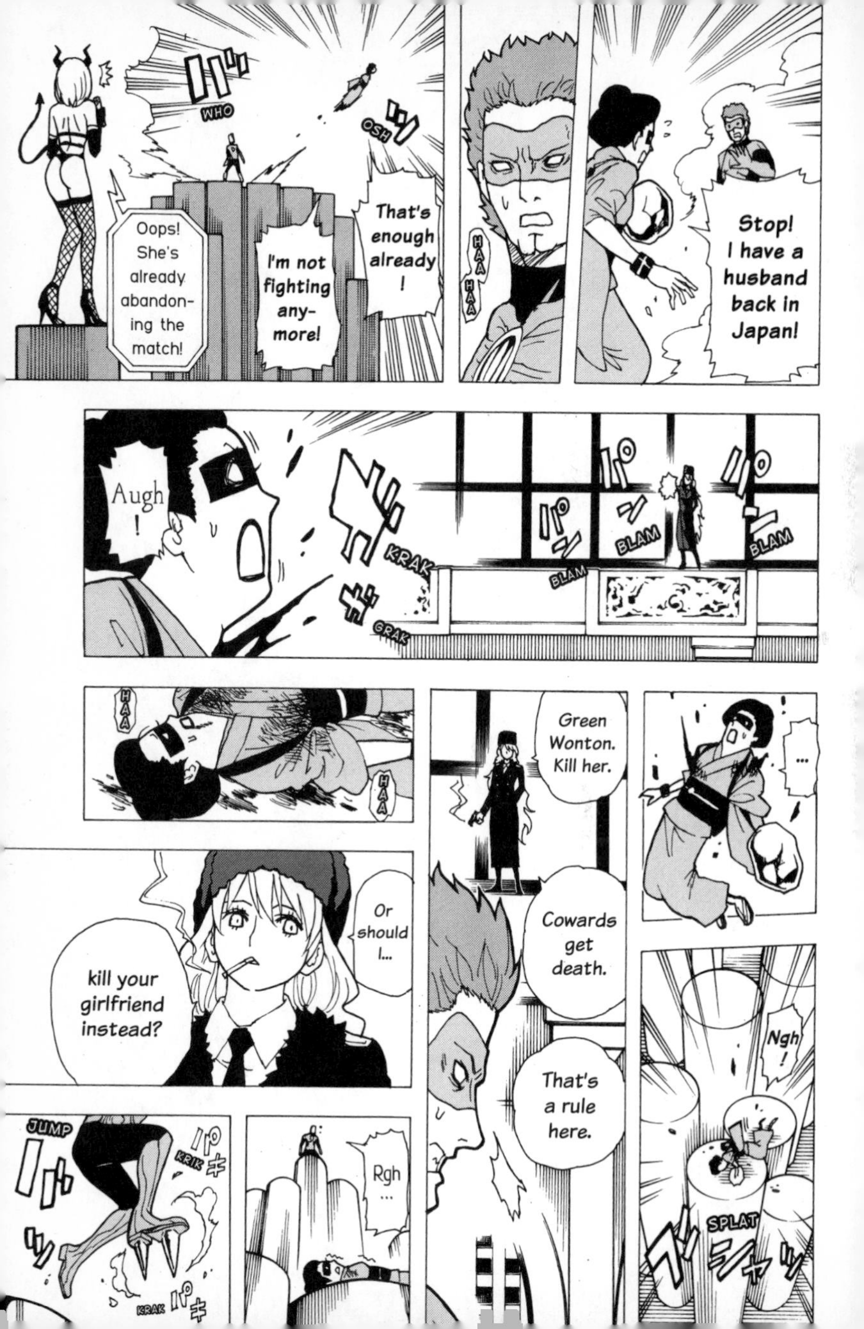

Stop! I have a husband back in Japan!
HAA HAA
OSH
That's enough already!
WHO
I'm not fighting anymore!
Oops! She's already abandoning the match!
BLAM
BLAM
BLAM
KRAK
GRAK
Augh!
...
Green Wonton. Kill her.
HAA
HAA
Ngh!
SPLAT
Cowards get death.
That's a rule here.
Or should I...
kill your girlfriend instead?
Rgh...
JUMP
KRIK
KRAK

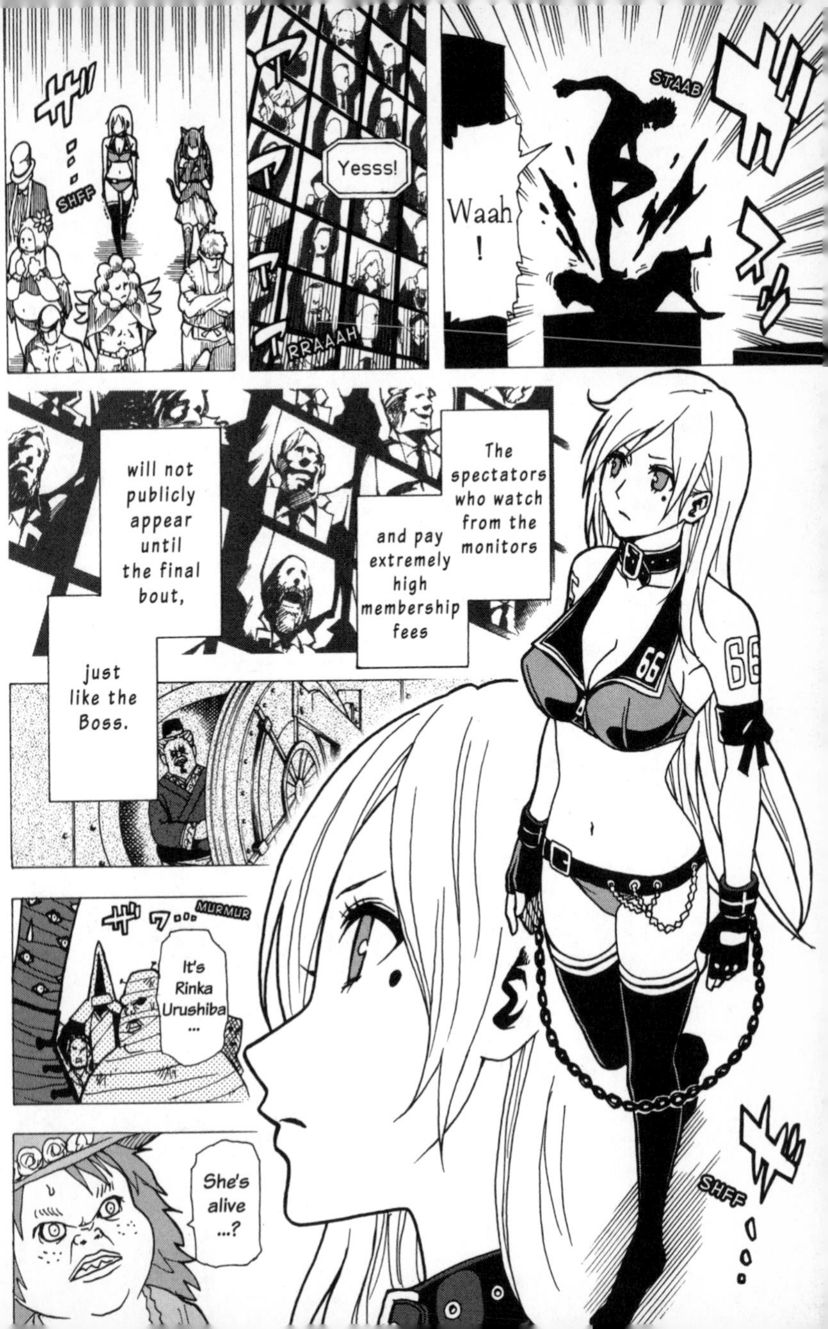
STAAB
Waah!
Yesss!
RRAAAH
SHFF
The spectators who watch from the monitors
and pay extremely high membership fees
will not publicly appear until the final bout,
just like the Boss.
SHFF
MURMUR
It's Rinka Urushiba...
She's alive...?

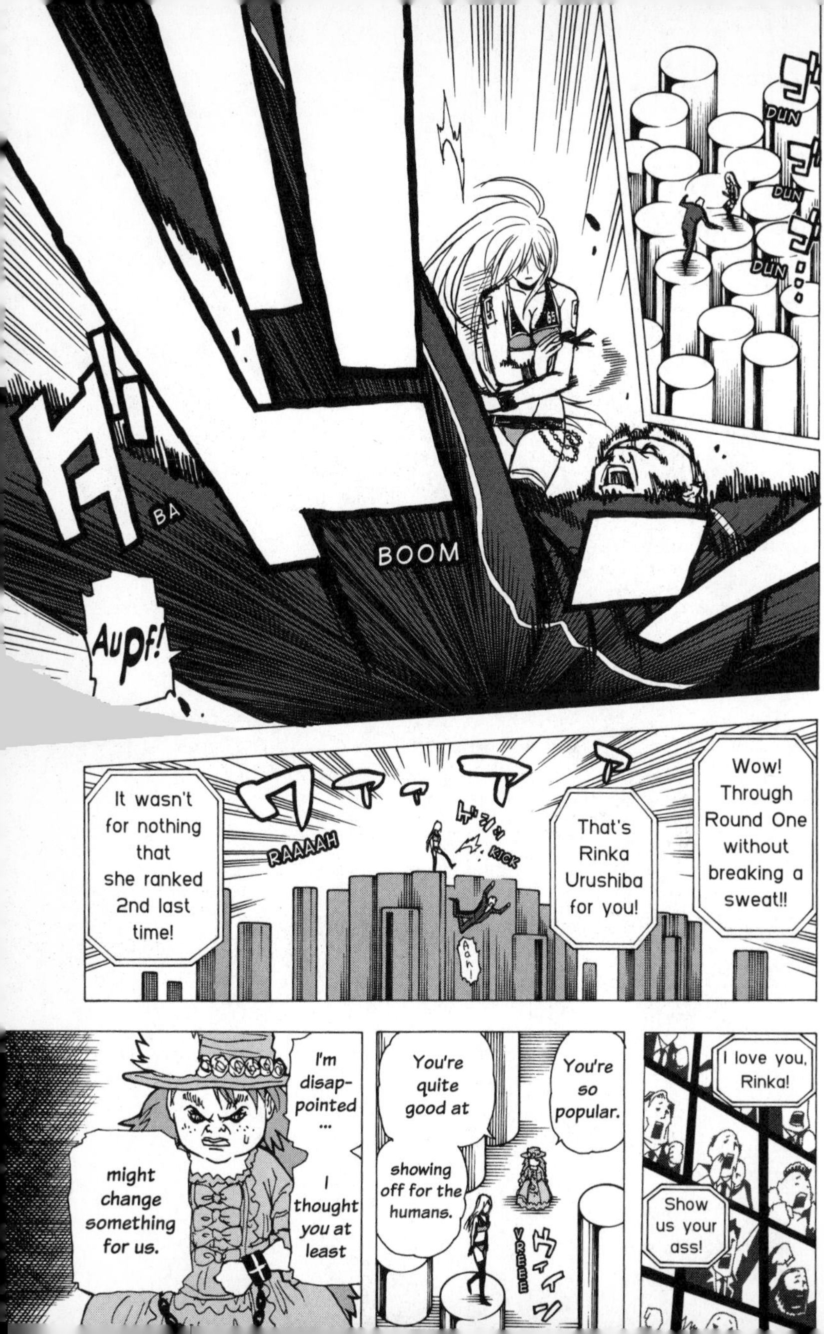
DUN
DUN
DUN
BA
BOOM
AUPF!
Wow! Through Round One without breaking a sweat!!
That's Rinka Urushiba for you!
KICK
Aah!
RAAAAH
It wasn't for nothing that she ranked 2nd last time!
I love you, Rinka!
Show us your ass!
You're so popular.
You're quite good at
showing off for the humans.
VREEE
I'm disappointed...
I thought you at least
might change something for us.

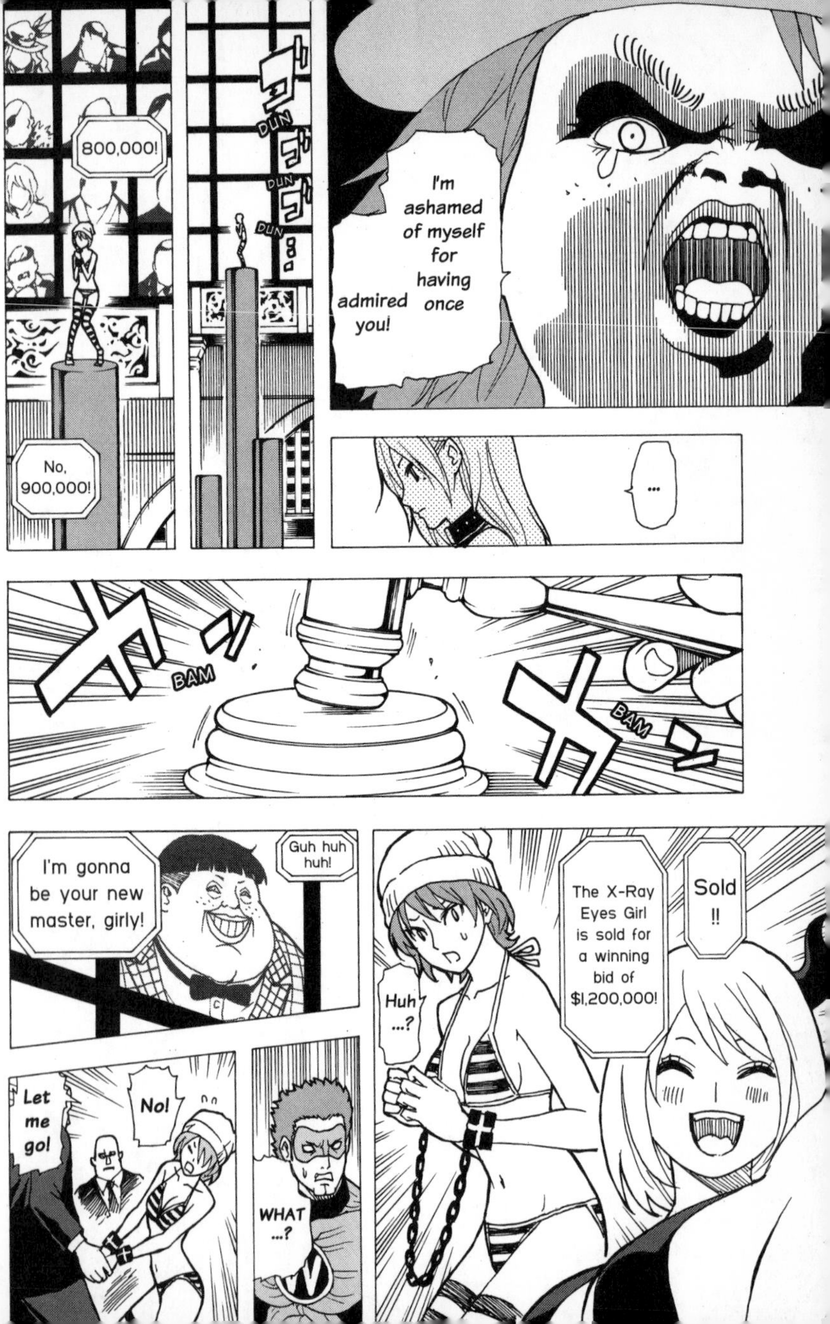
I'm ashamed of myself for having once admired you!
...
DUN
DUN
DUN
800,000!
No, 900,000!
BAM
BAM
Sold!!
The X-Ray Eyes Girl is sold for a winning bid of $1,200,000!
Huh...?
Guh huh huh!
I'm gonna be your new master, girly!
WHAT...?
No!
Let me go!

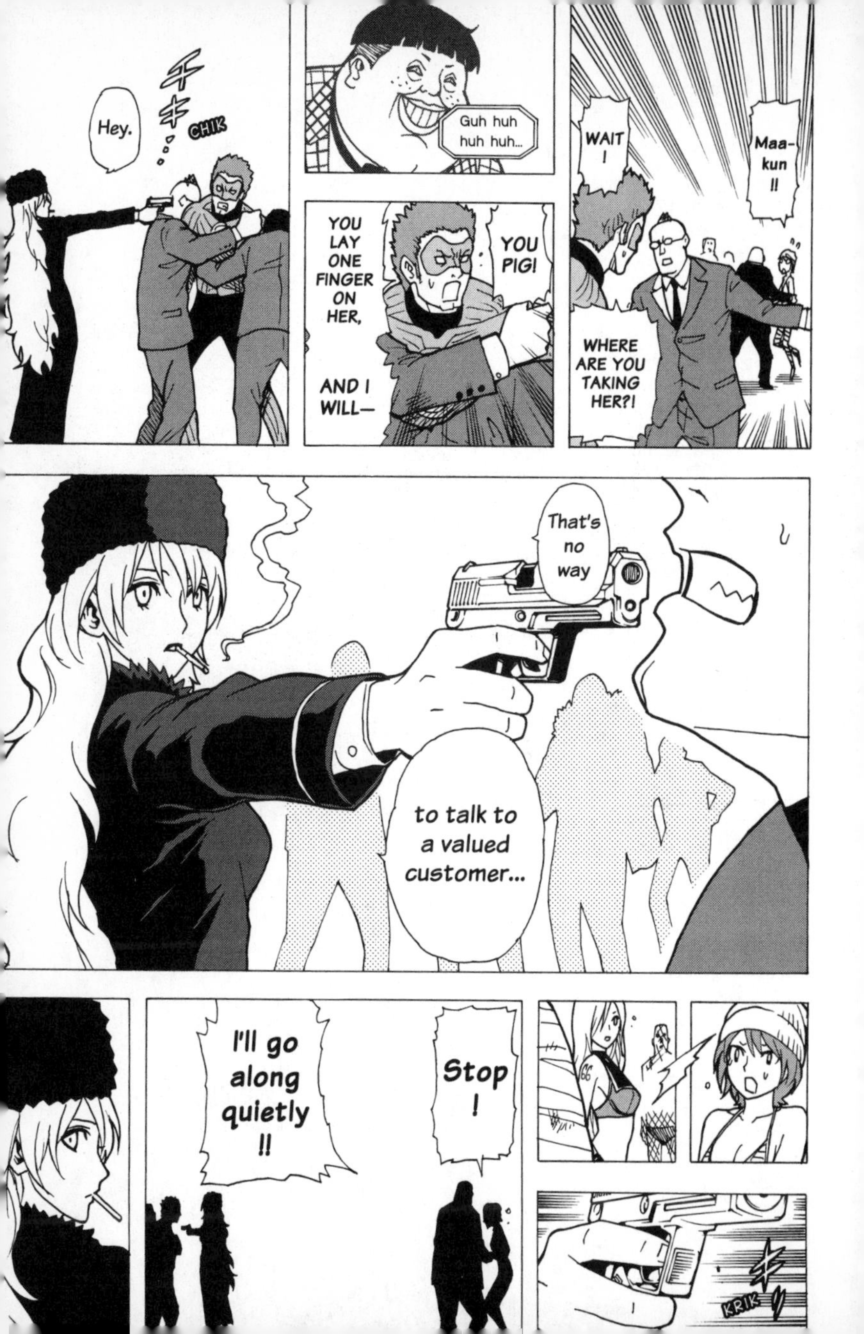
Maa-kun !!
WAIT !
WHERE ARE YOU TAKING HER?!
Guh huh huh huh...
YOU PIG!
YOU LAY ONE FINGER ON HER,
AND I WILL—
CHIK
Hey.
That's no way
to talk to a valued customer...
KRIK
Stop !
I'll go along quietly !!

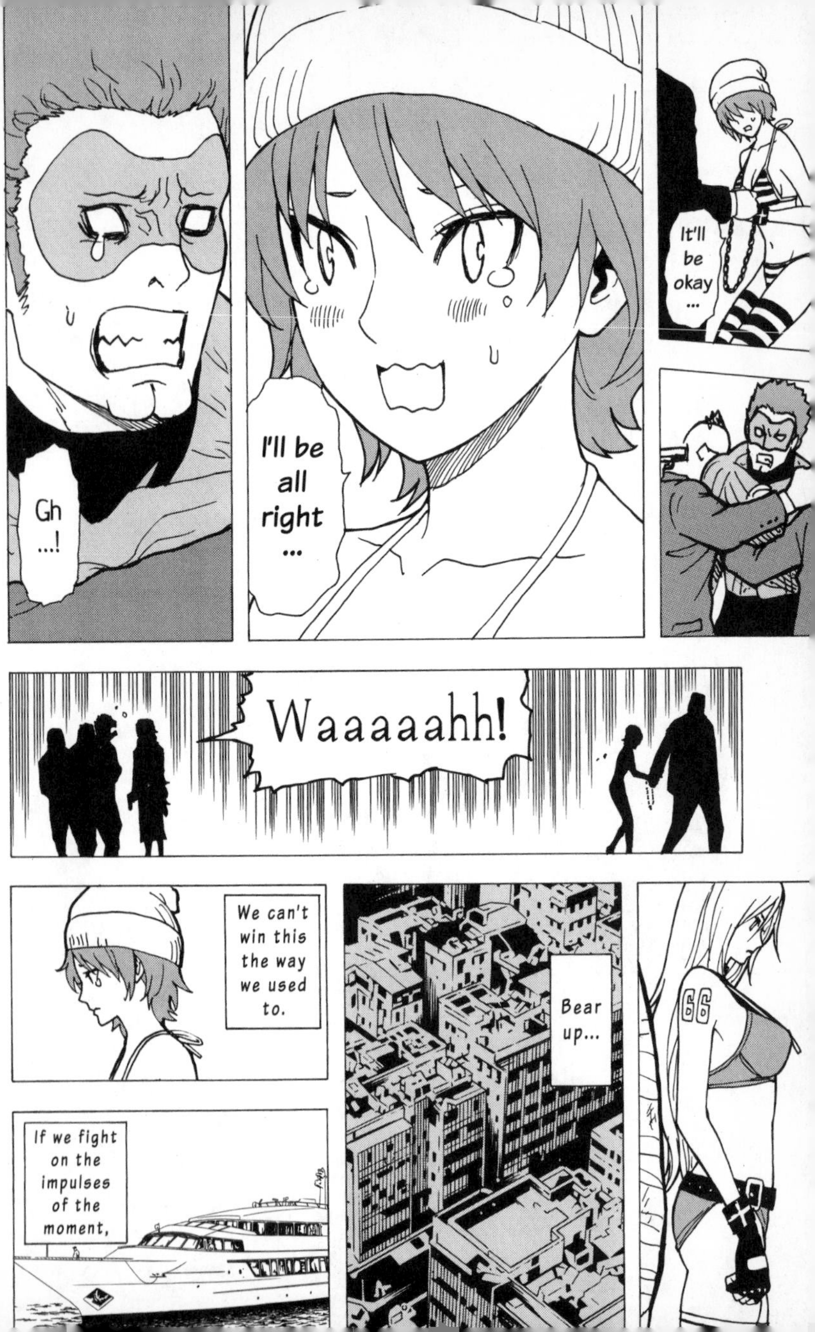
It'll be okay ...
I'll be all right ...
Gh ...!
Waaaaahh!
Bear up...
We can't win this the way we used to.
If we fight on the impulses of the moment,

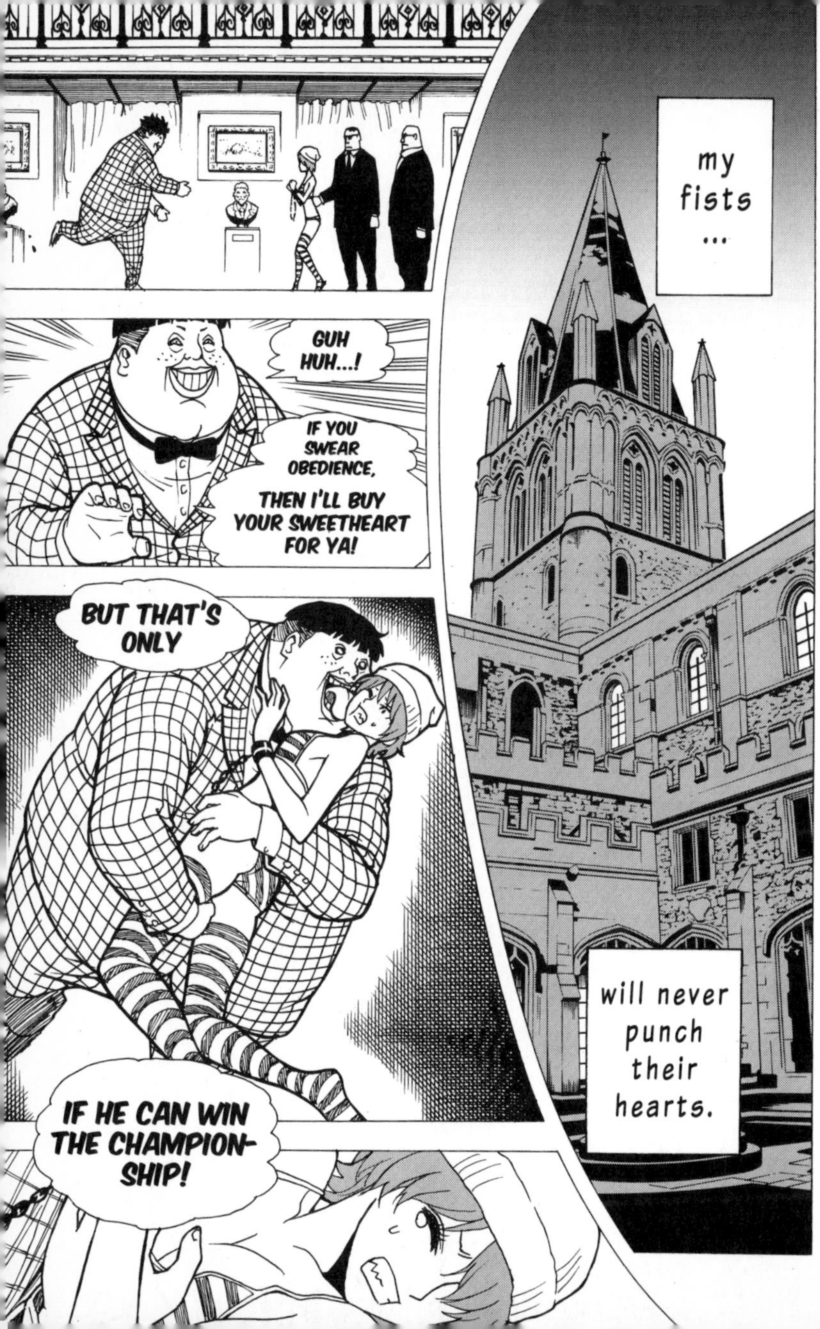
my fists ...
will never punch their hearts.
GUH HUH...!
IF YOU SWEAR OBEDIENCE,
THEN I'LL BUY YOUR SWEETHEART FOR YA!
BUT THAT'S ONLY
IF HE CAN WIN THE CHAMPIONSHIP!

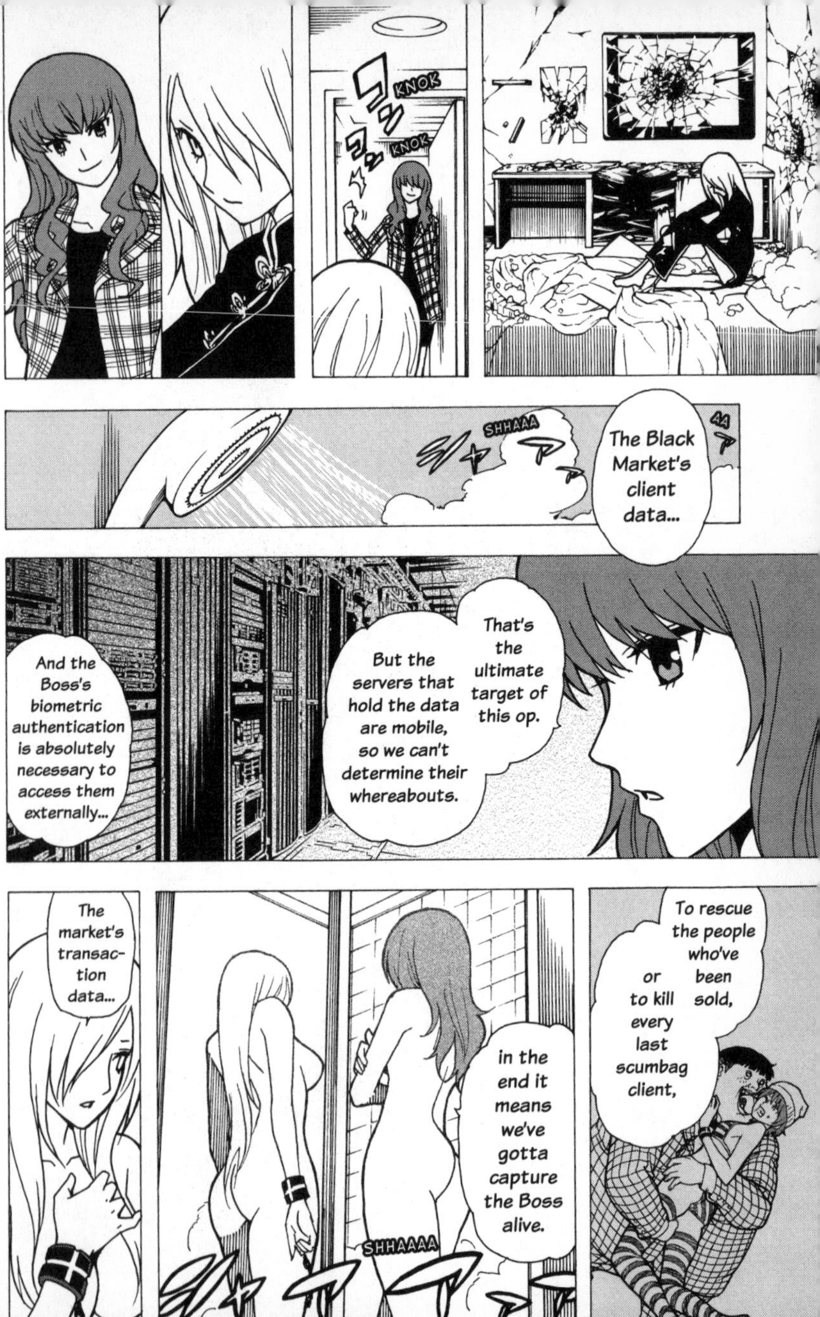
KNOK
KNOK
SHHAAA
The Black Market's client data...
That's the ultimate target of this op.
But the servers that hold the data are mobile, so we can't determine their whereabouts.
And the Boss's biometric authentication is absolutely necessary to access them externally...
To rescue the people who've been sold,
or to kill every last scumbag client,
in the end it means we've gotta capture the Boss alive.
SHHAAAA
The market's transaction data...

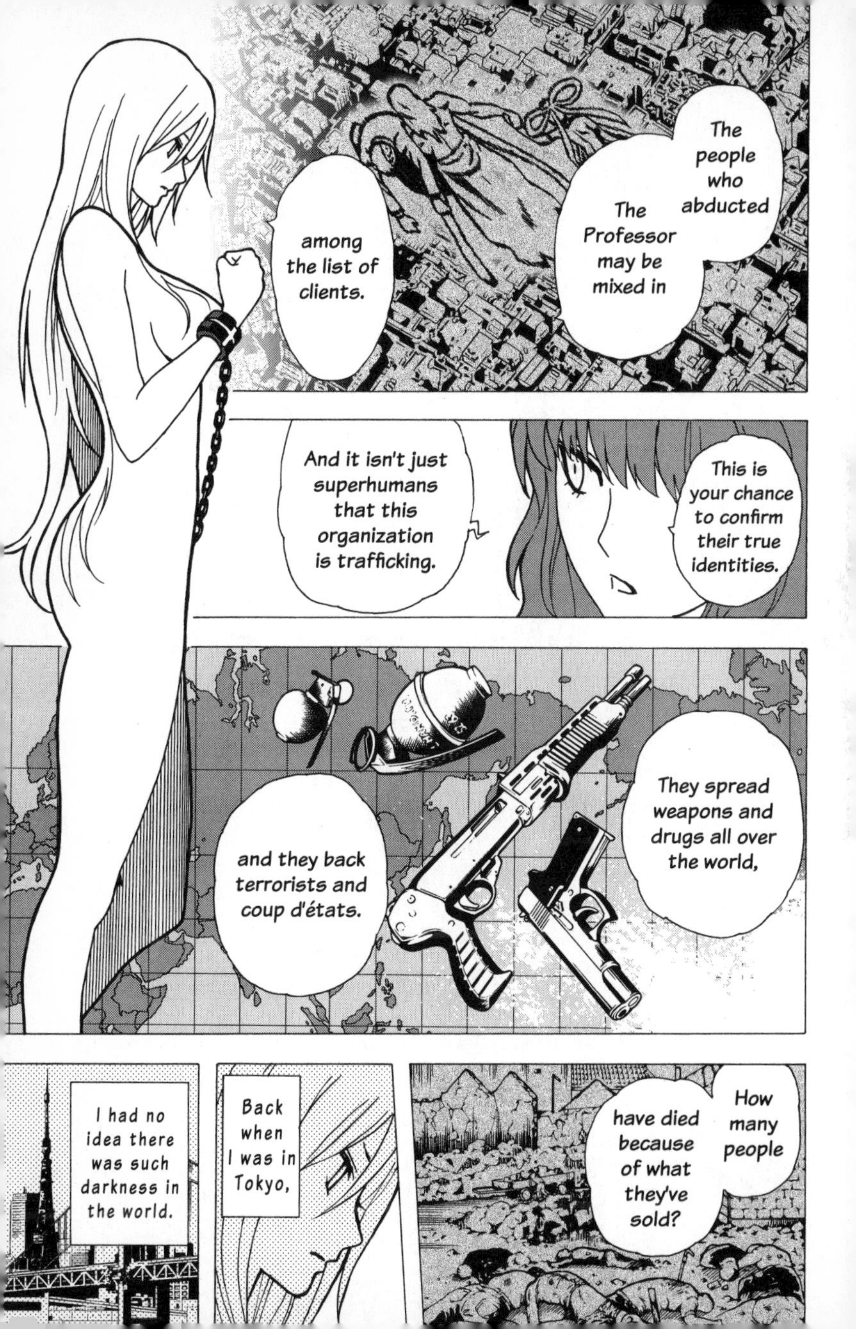
The people who abducted
The Professor may be mixed in
among the list of clients.
This is your chance to confirm their true identities.
And it isn't just superhumans that this organization is trafficking.
They spread weapons and drugs all over the world,
and they back terrorists and coup d'états.
How many people
have died because of what they've sold?
Back when I was in Tokyo,
I had no idea there was such darkness in the world.

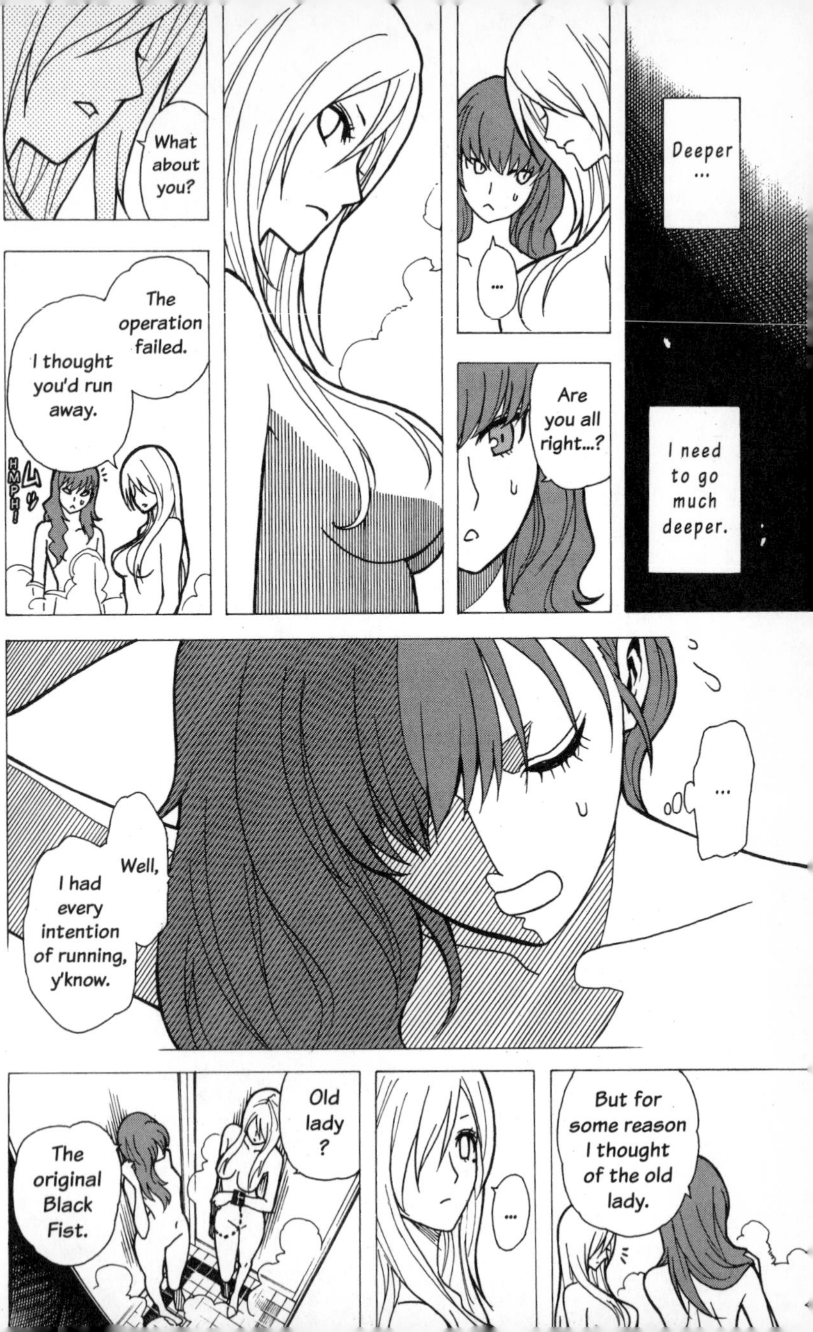

Deeper ...
I need to go much deeper.
...
Are you all right...?
What about you?
The operation failed.
I thought you'd run away.
HMPH!
...
Well, I had every intention of running, y'know.
But for some reason I thought of the old lady.
...
Old lady?
The original Black Fist.

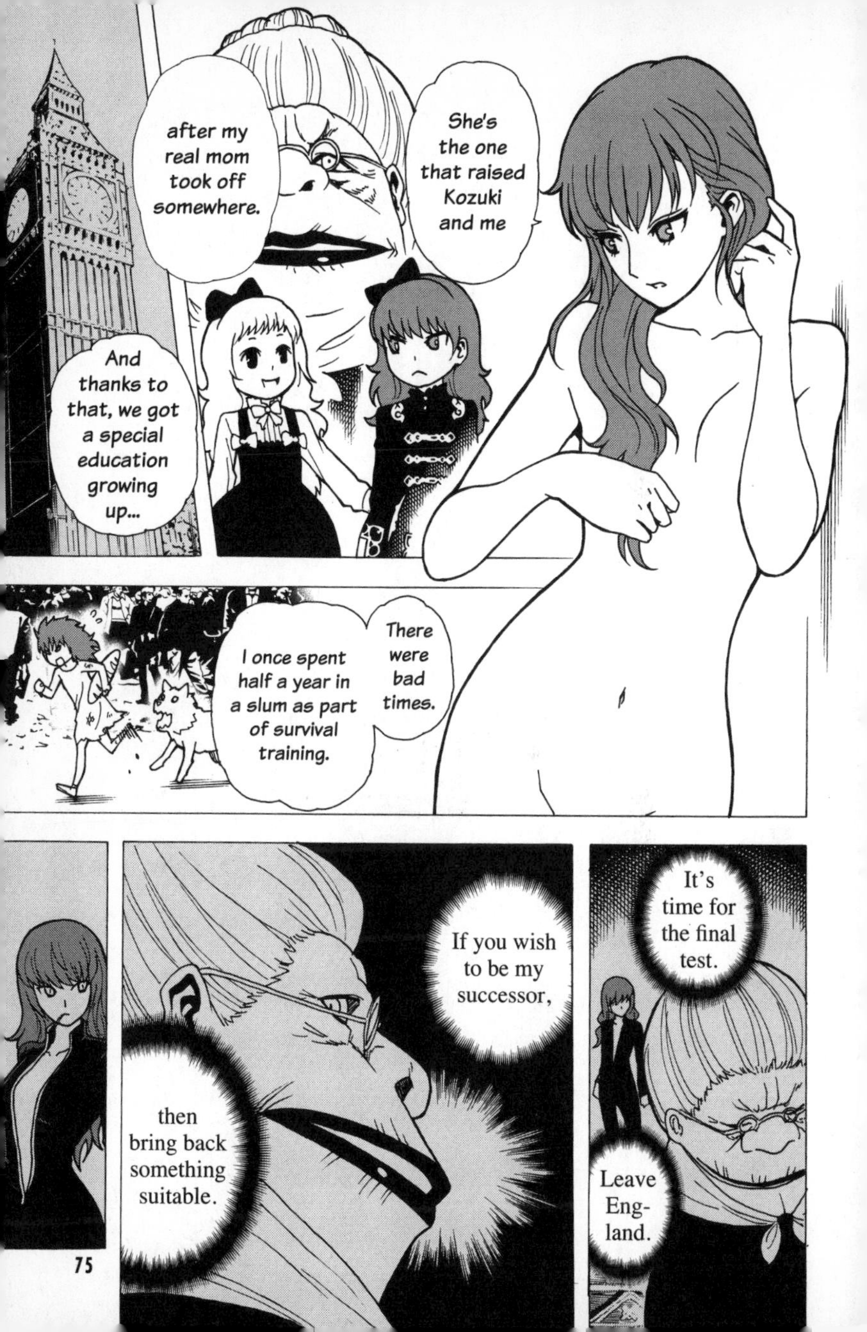

She's the one that raised Kozuki and me
after my real mom took off somewhere.
And thanks to that, we got a special education growing up...
There were bad times.
I once spent half a year in a slum as part of survival training.
It's time for the final test.
Leave Eng-land.
If you wish to be my successor,
then bring back something suitable.

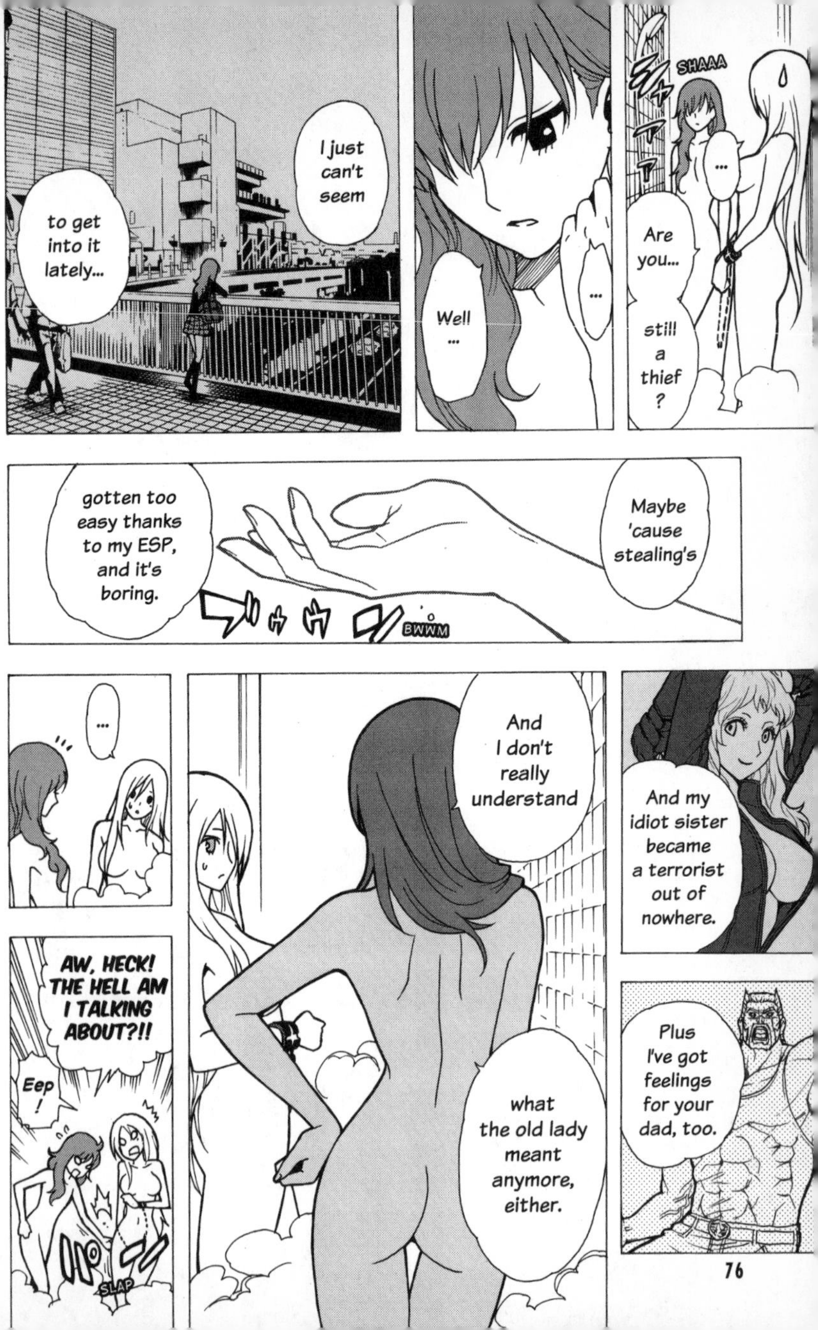
SHAAA
...
Are you...
still a thief?
...
Well ...
I just can't seem
to get into it lately...
Maybe 'cause stealing's
gotten too easy thanks to my ESP, and it's boring.
BWWM
And my idiot sister became a terrorist out of nowhere.
Plus I've got feelings for your dad, too.
And I don't really understand
what the old lady meant anymore, either.
...
AW, HECK! THE HELL AM I TALKING ABOUT?!!
Eep!
SLAP

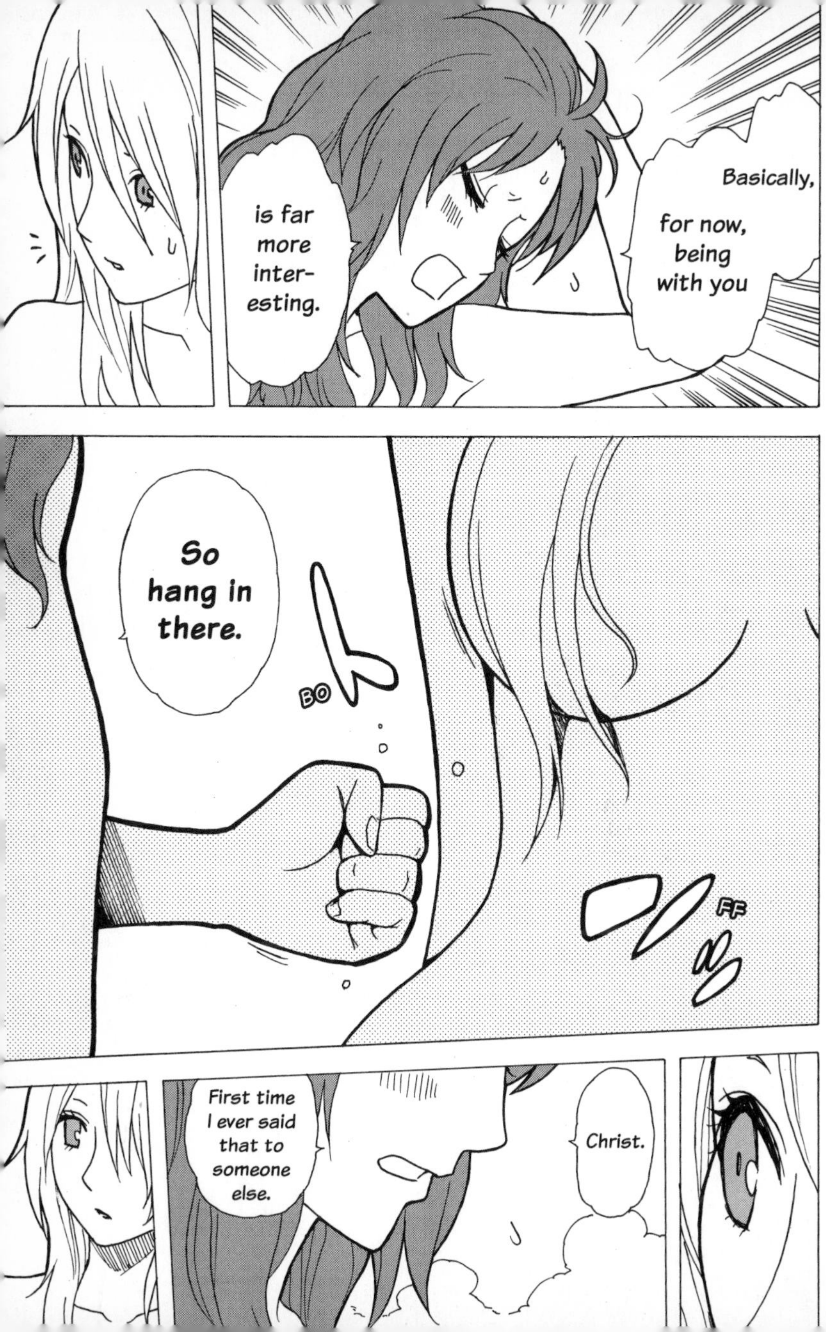
Basically, for now, being with you
is far more inter-esting.
So hang in there.
BO
FF
Christ.
First time I ever said that to someone else.

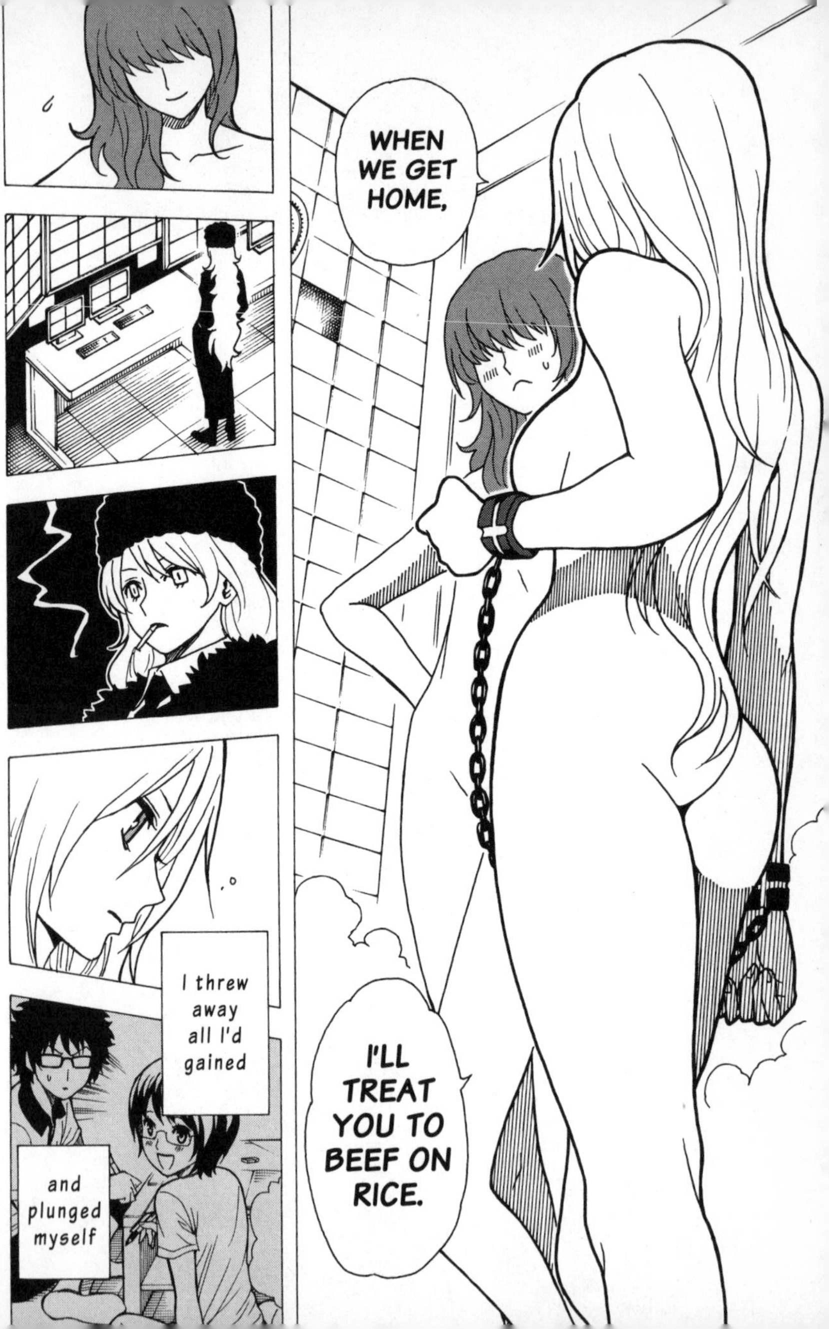
WHEN WE GET HOME,
I'LL TREAT YOU TO BEEF ON RICE.
I threw away all I'd gained
and plunged myself

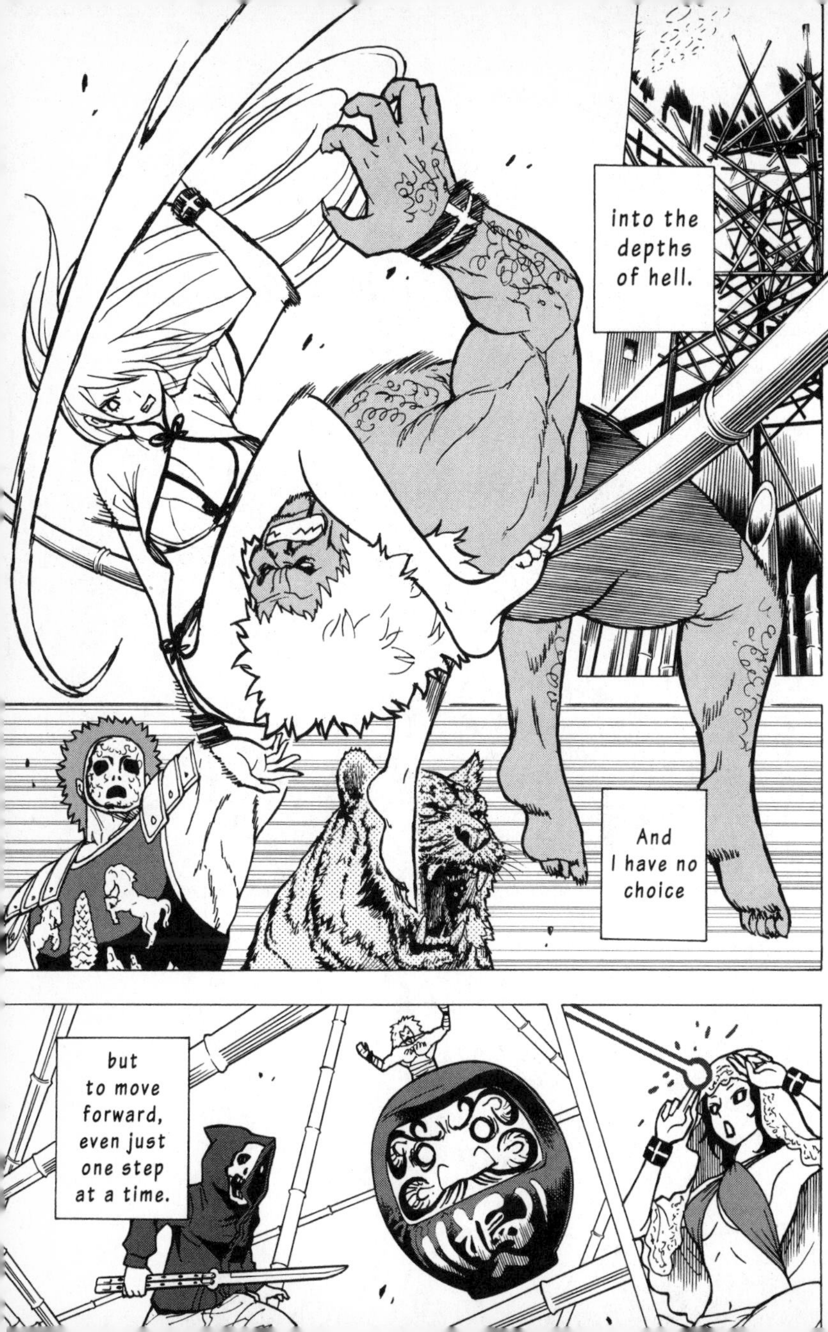
into the depths of hell.
And I have no choice
but to move forward, even just one step at a time.

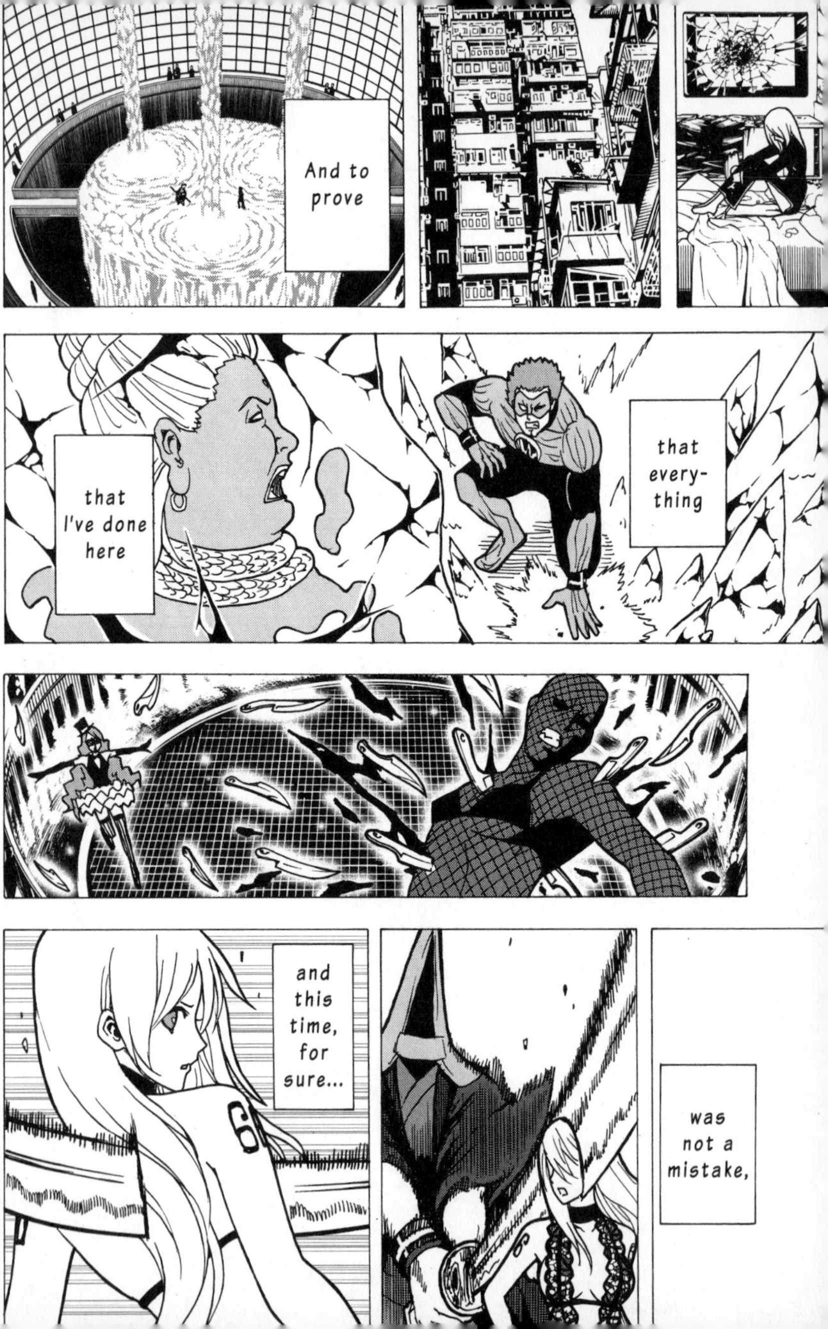
And to prove
that every-thing
that I've done here
was not a mistake,
and this time, for sure...

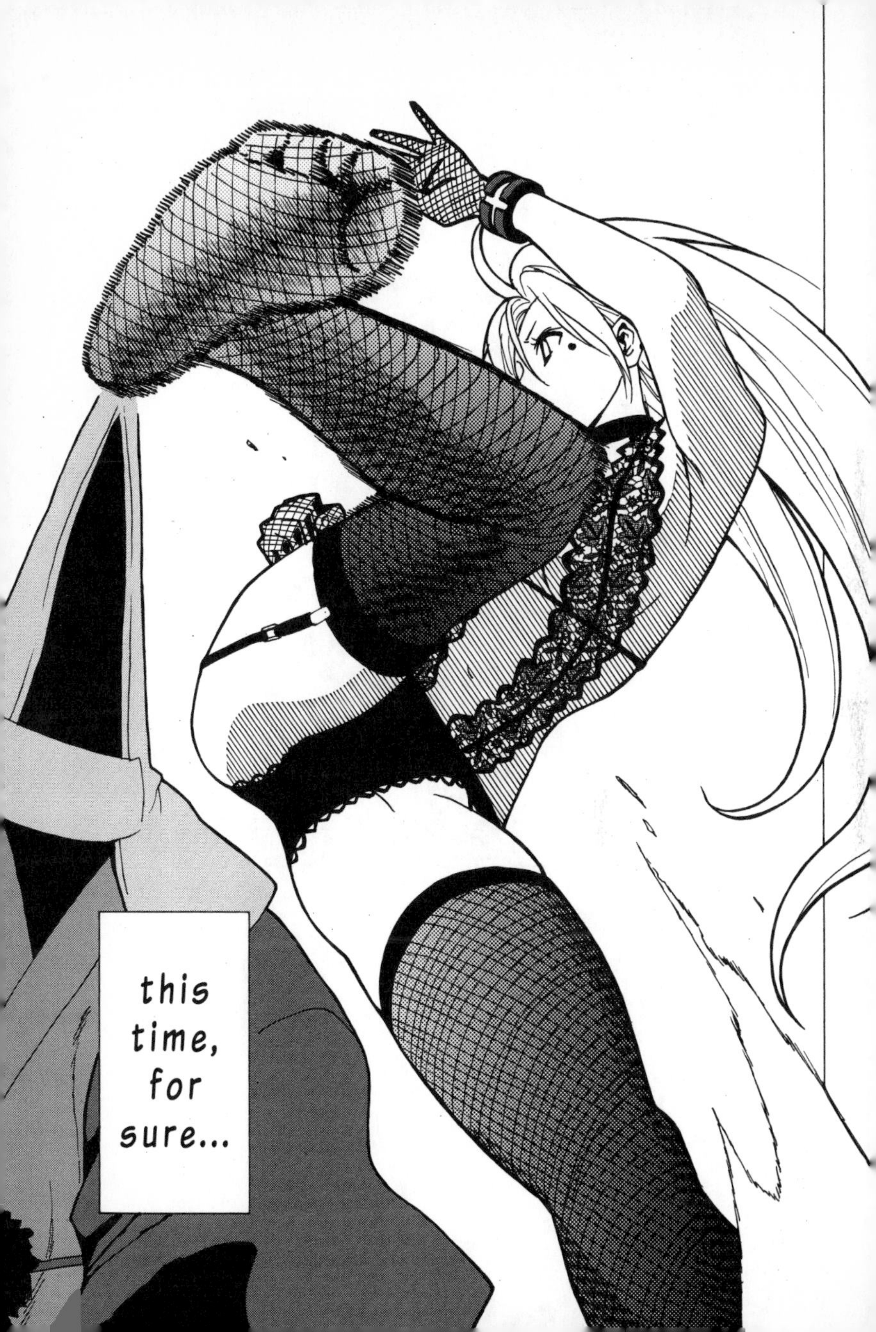
this time, for sure...

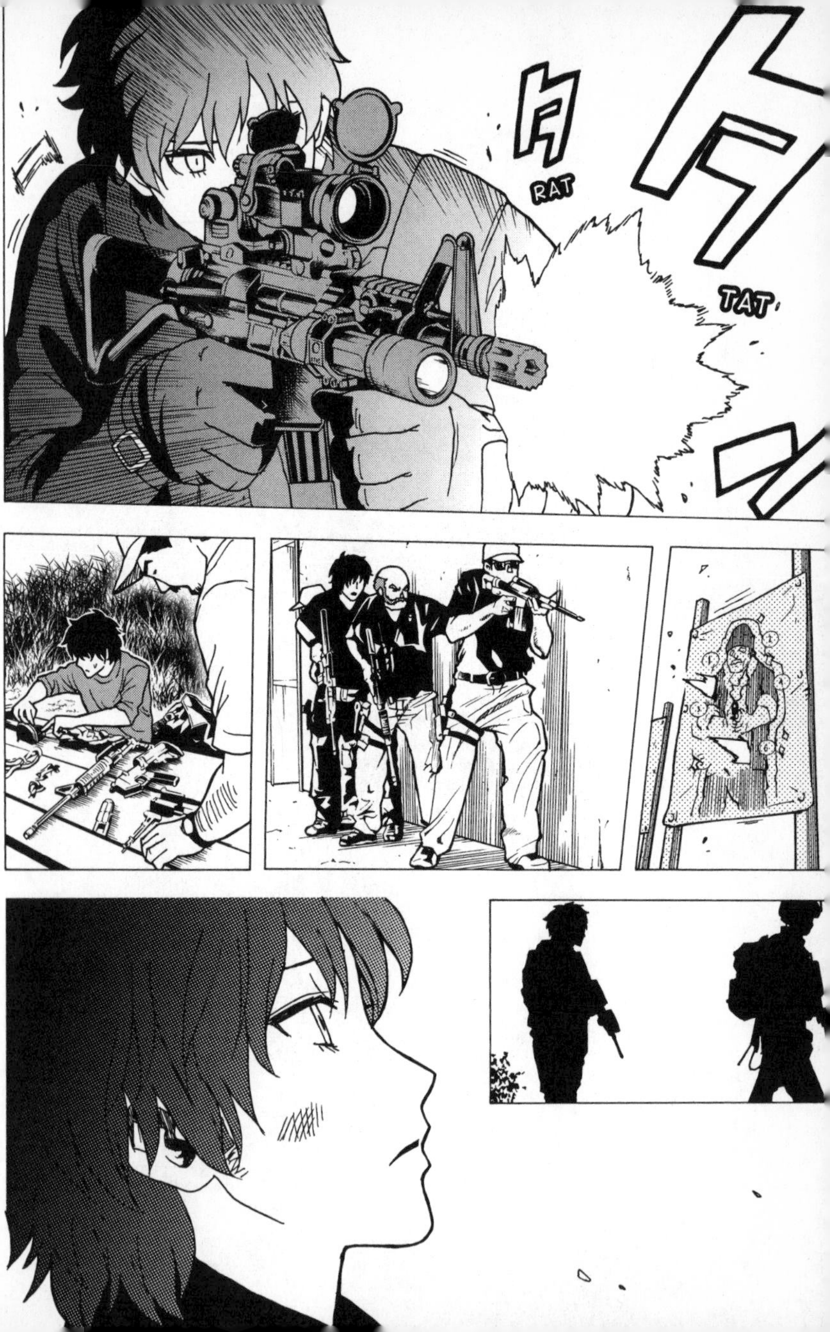
RAT
TAT

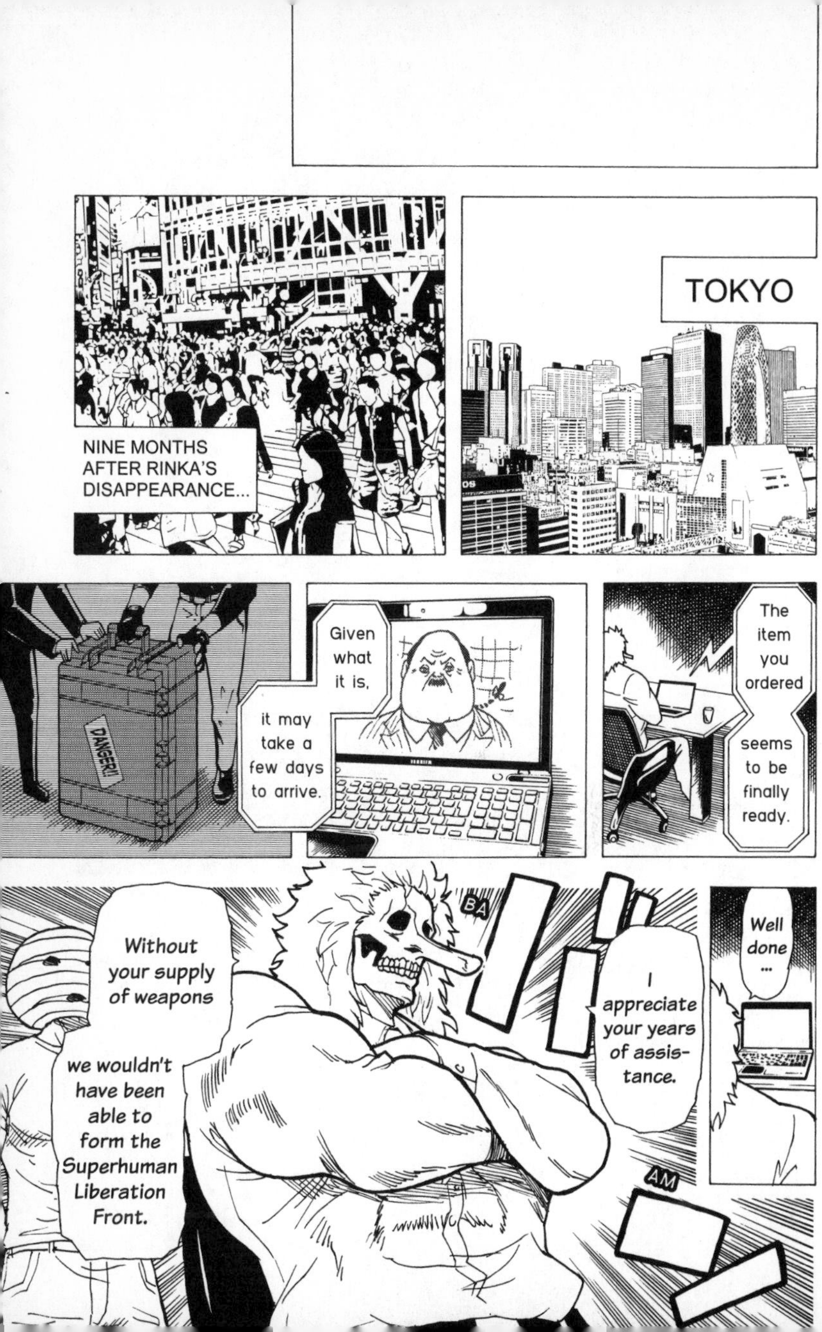
TOKYO
NINE MONTHS AFTER RINKA'S DISAPPEARANCE...
The item you ordered seems to be finally ready.
Given what it is, it may take a few days to arrive.
DANGER!!
Well done...
I appreciate your years of assistance.
Without your supply of weapons we wouldn't have been able to form the Superhuman Liberation Front.
BA
AM

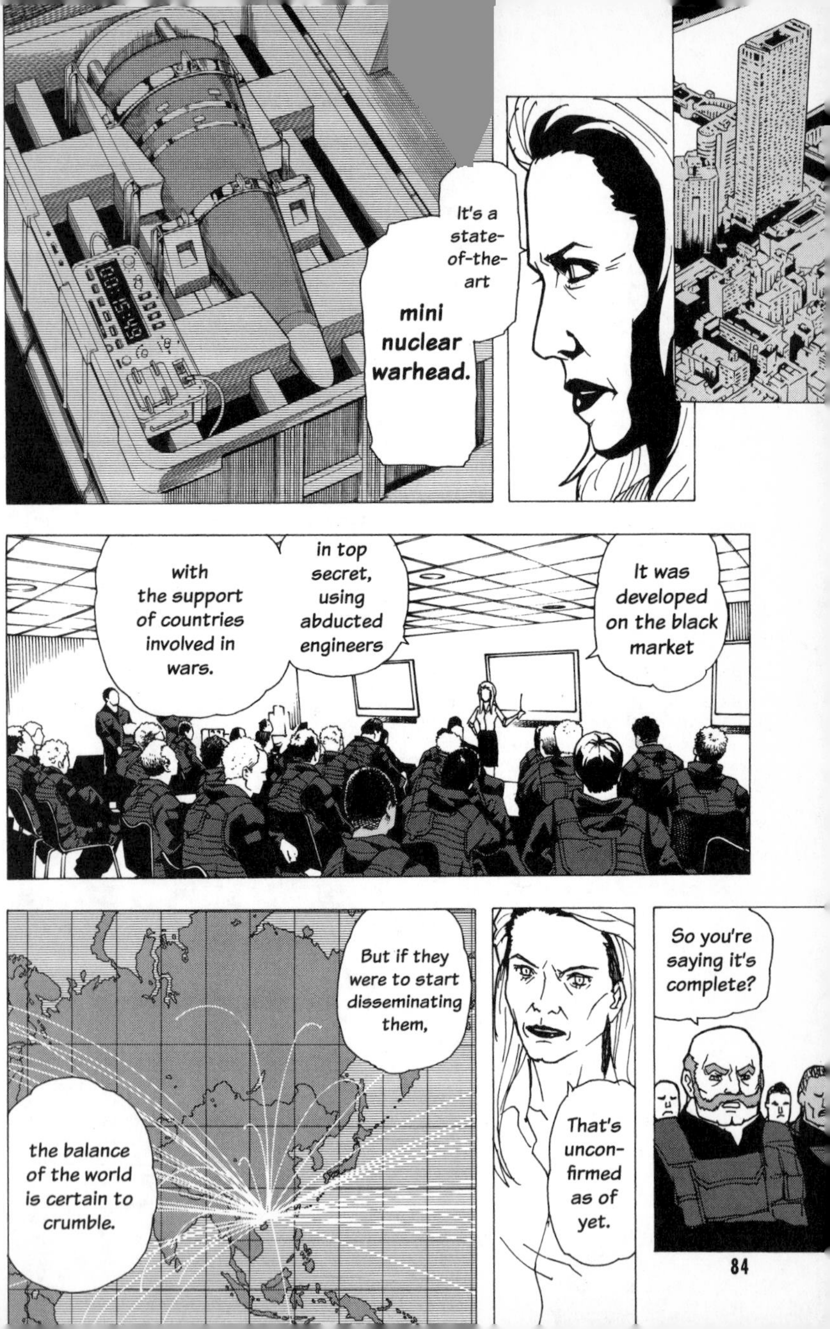

It's a state-of-the-art mini nuclear warhead.
It was developed on the black market
in top secret, using abducted engineers
with the support of countries involved in wars.
So you're saying it's complete?
That's unconfirmed as of yet.
But if they were to start disseminating them,
the balance of the world is certain to crumble.

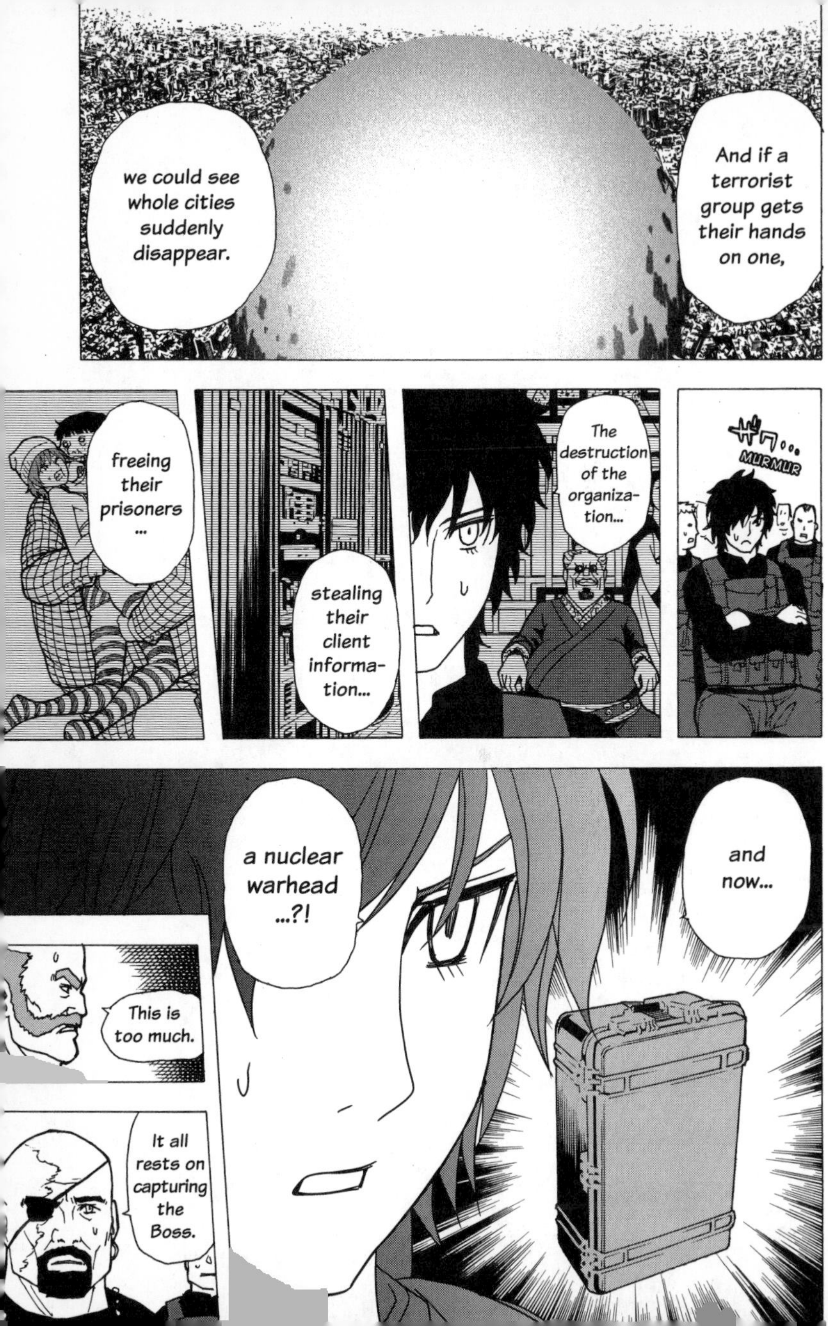
And if a terrorist group gets their hands on one,
we could see whole cities suddenly disappear.
MURMUR
The destruction of the organization...
stealing their client information...
freeing their prisoners ...
and now...
a nuclear warhead ...?!
This is too much.
It all rests on capturing the Boss.

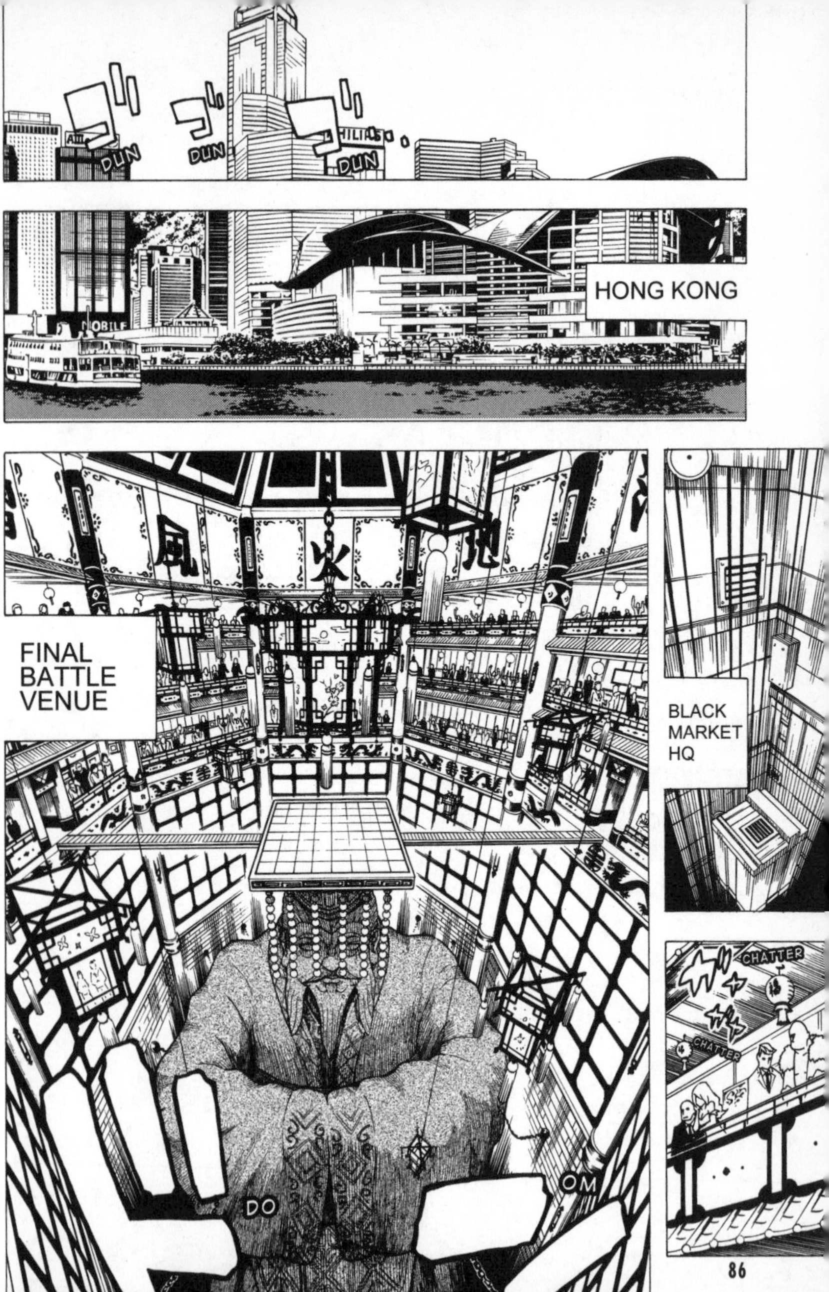
DUN
DUN
DUN
HONG KONG
BLACK
MARKET
HQ
CHATTER
CHATTER
FINAL
BATTLE
VENUE
DO
OM

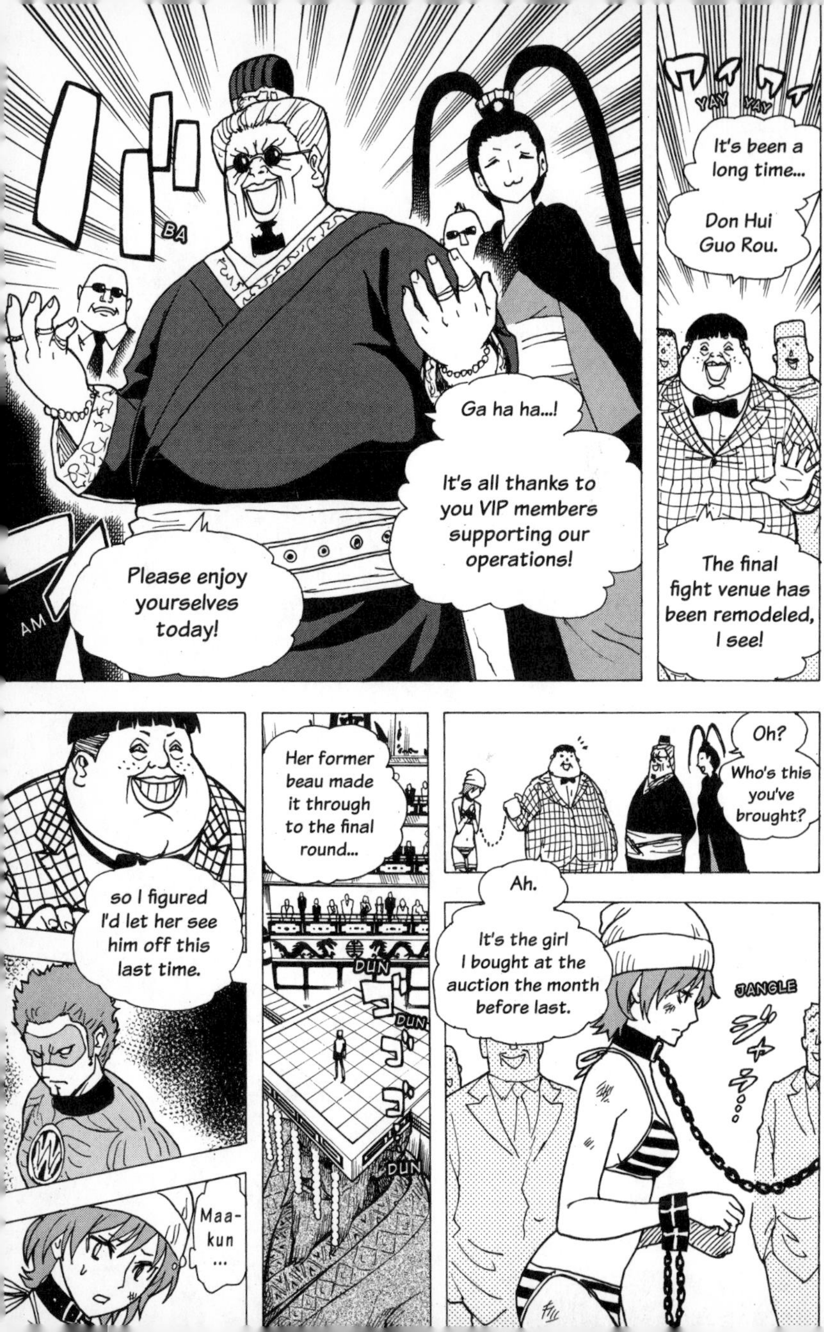
YAY YAY
It's been a long time...
Don Hui Guo Rou.
The final fight venue has been remodeled, I see!
BA
Ga ha ha...!
It's all thanks to you VIP members supporting our operations!
Please enjoy yourselves today!
AM
Oh?
Who's this you've brought?
Ah.
It's the girl I bought at the auction the month before last.
JANGLE
Her former beau made it through to the final round...
DUN
DUN
DUN
so I figured I'd let her see him off this last time.
Maa-kun ...

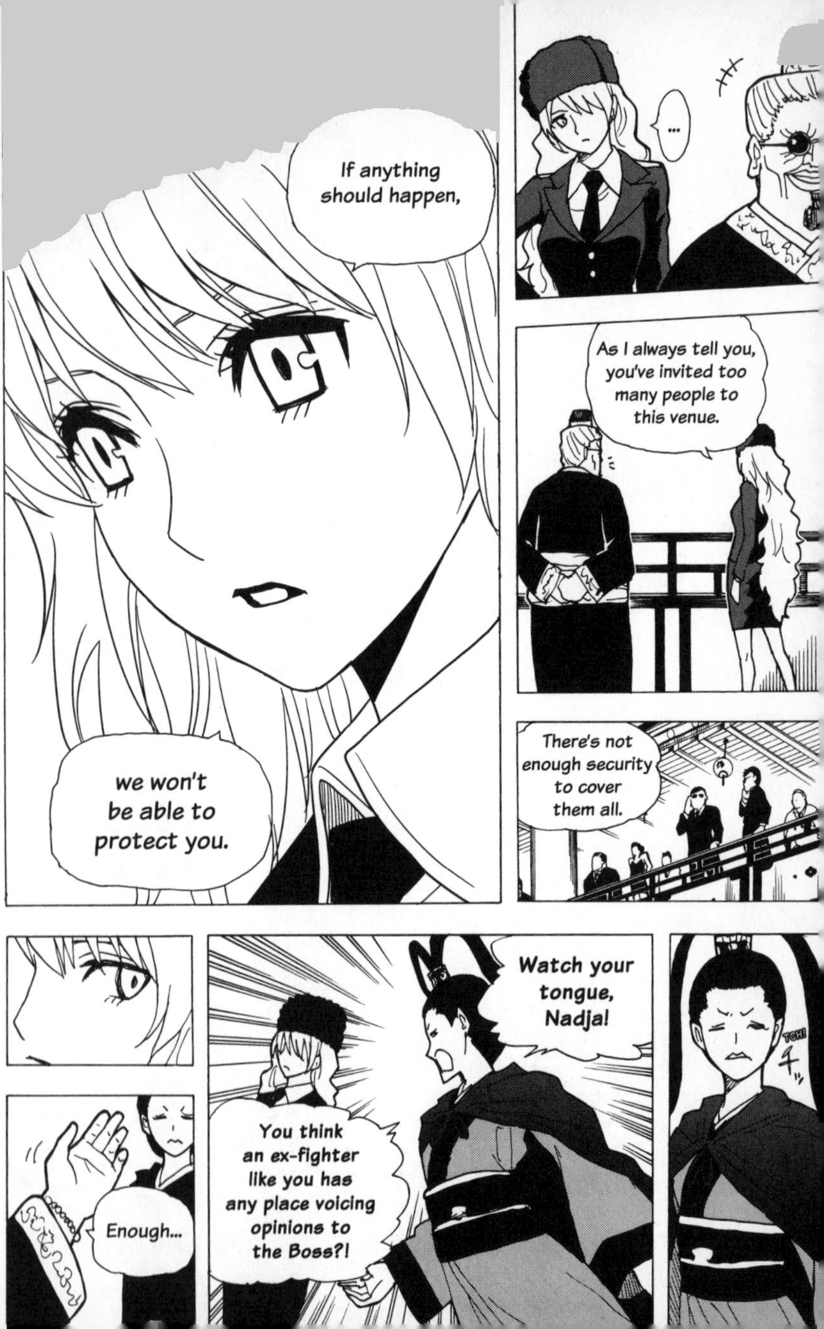
...
As I always tell you, you've invited too many people to this venue.
There's not enough security to cover them all.
If anything should happen,
we won't be able to protect you.
TCH!
Watch your tongue, Nadja!
You think an ex-fighter like you has any place voicing opinions to the Boss?!
Enough...

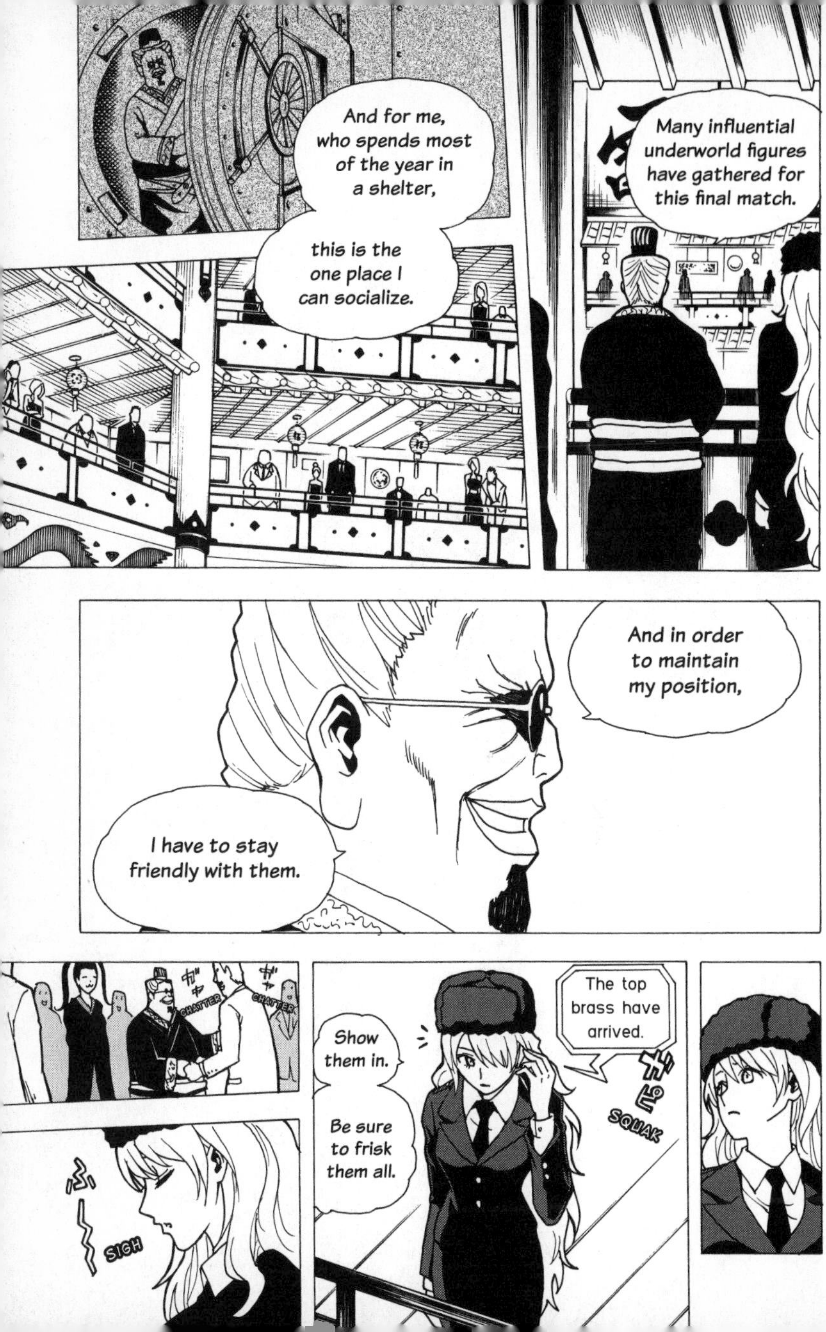
Many influential underworld figures have gathered for this final match.
And for me, who spends most of the year in a shelter,
this is the one place I can socialize.
And in order to maintain my position,
I have to stay friendly with them.
The top brass have arrived.
SQUAK
Show them in.
Be sure to frisk them all.
CHATTER
CHATTER
SIGH

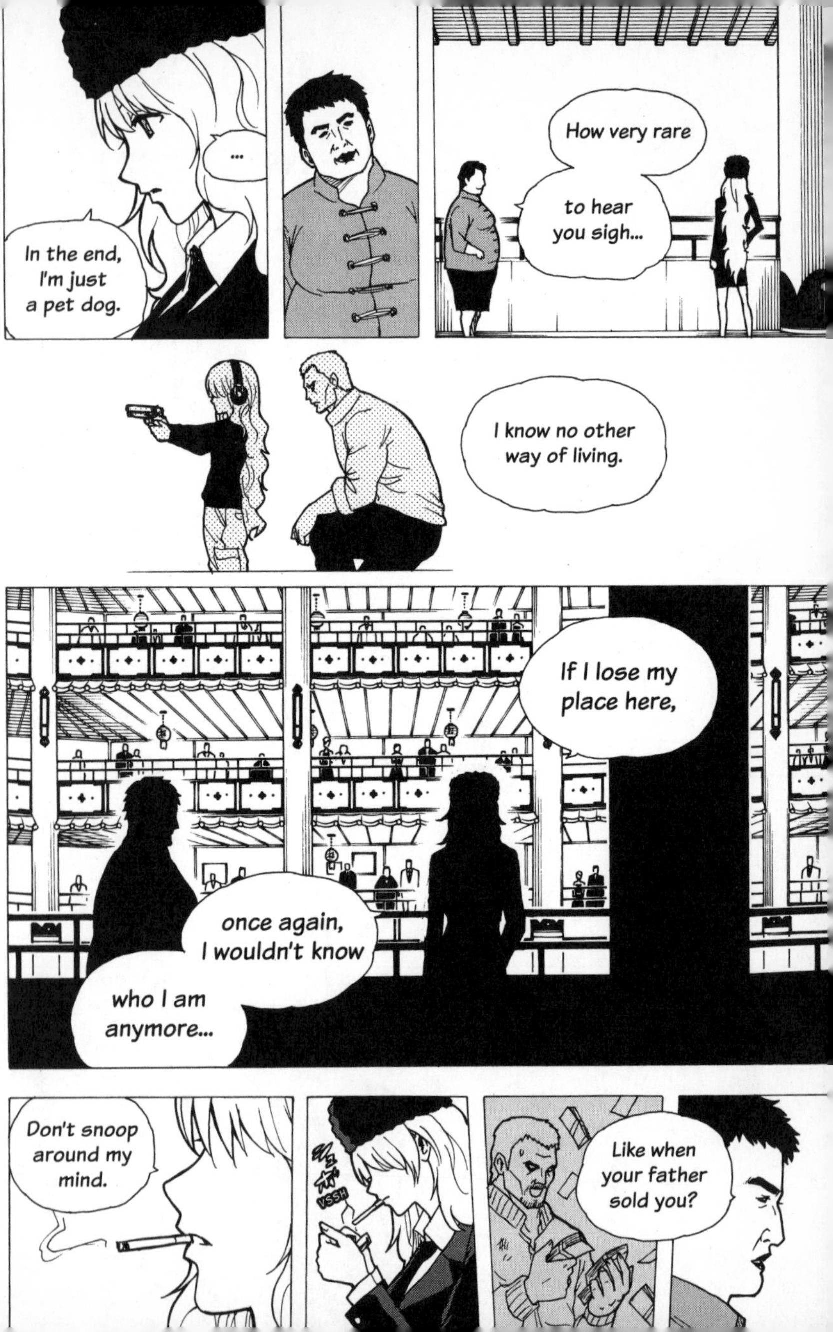
How very rare
to hear you sigh...
...
In the end, I'm just a pet dog.
I know no other way of living.
If I lose my place here,
once again, I wouldn't know
who I am anymore...
Like when your father sold you?
VSSH
Don't snoop around my mind.

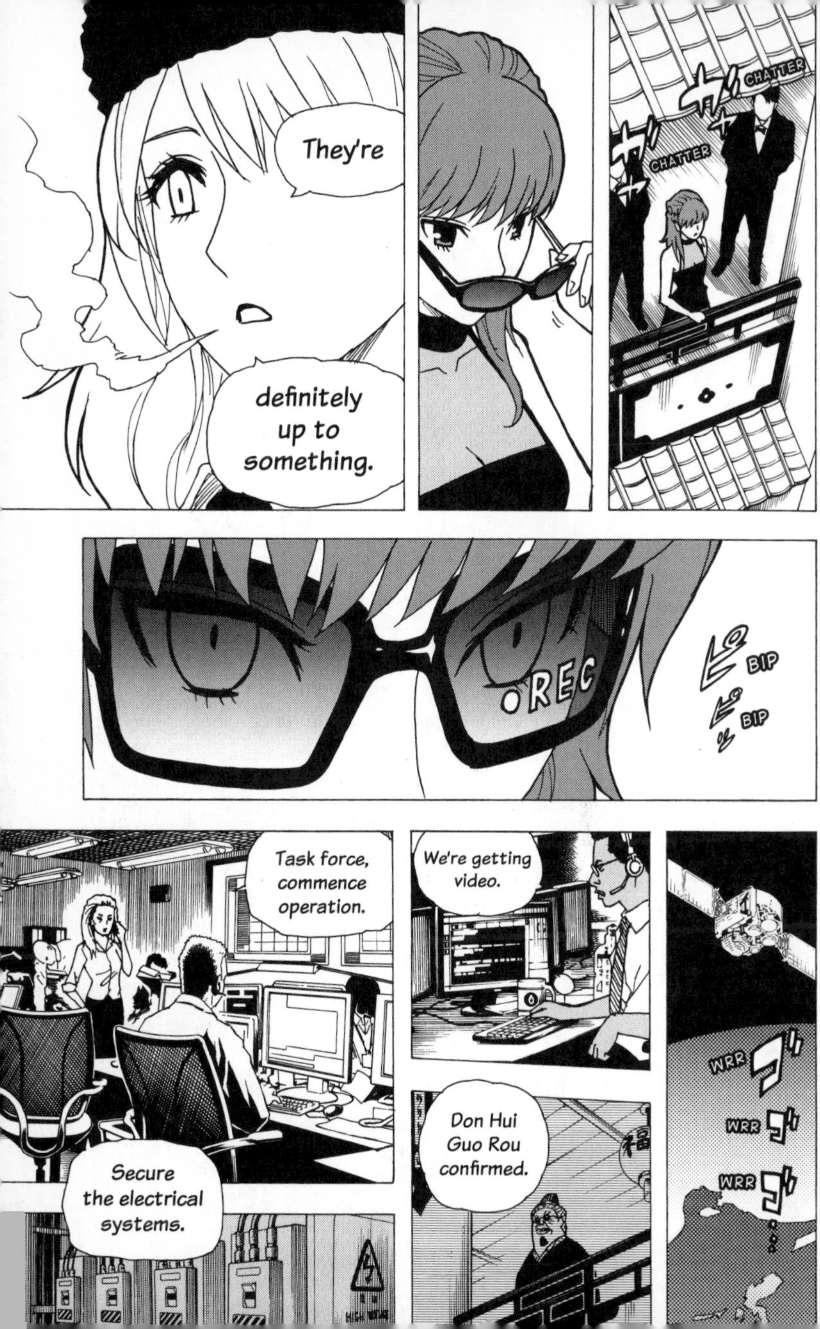
CHATTER
CHATTER
They're
definitely up to something.
BIP
BIP
REC
WRR
WRR
WRR
We're getting video.
Don Hui Guo Rou confirmed.
Task force, commence operation.
Secure the electrical systems.

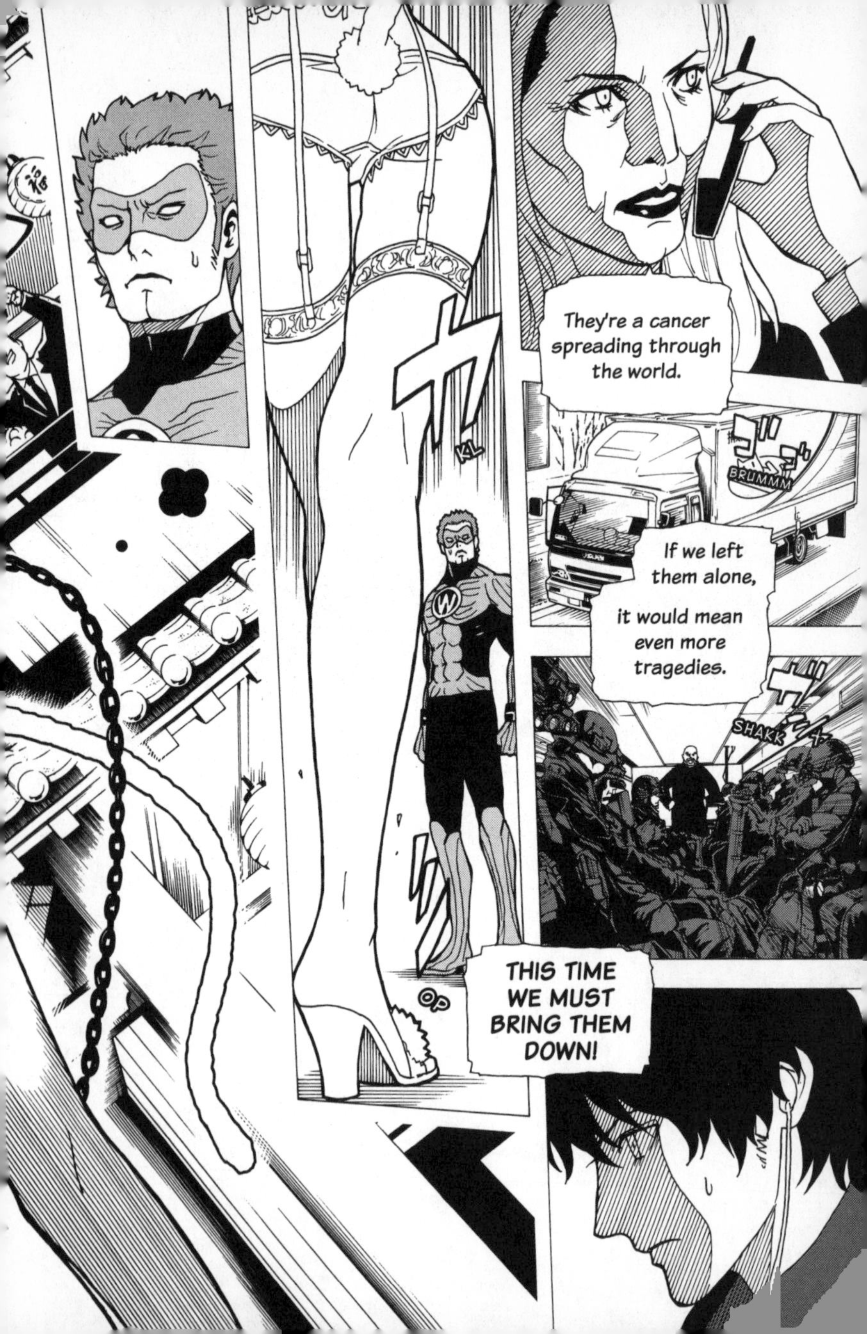
They're a cancer spreading through the world.
BRUMMM
If we left them alone,
it would mean even more tragedies.
SHAKK
KL
OP
THIS TIME WE MUST BRING THEM DOWN!

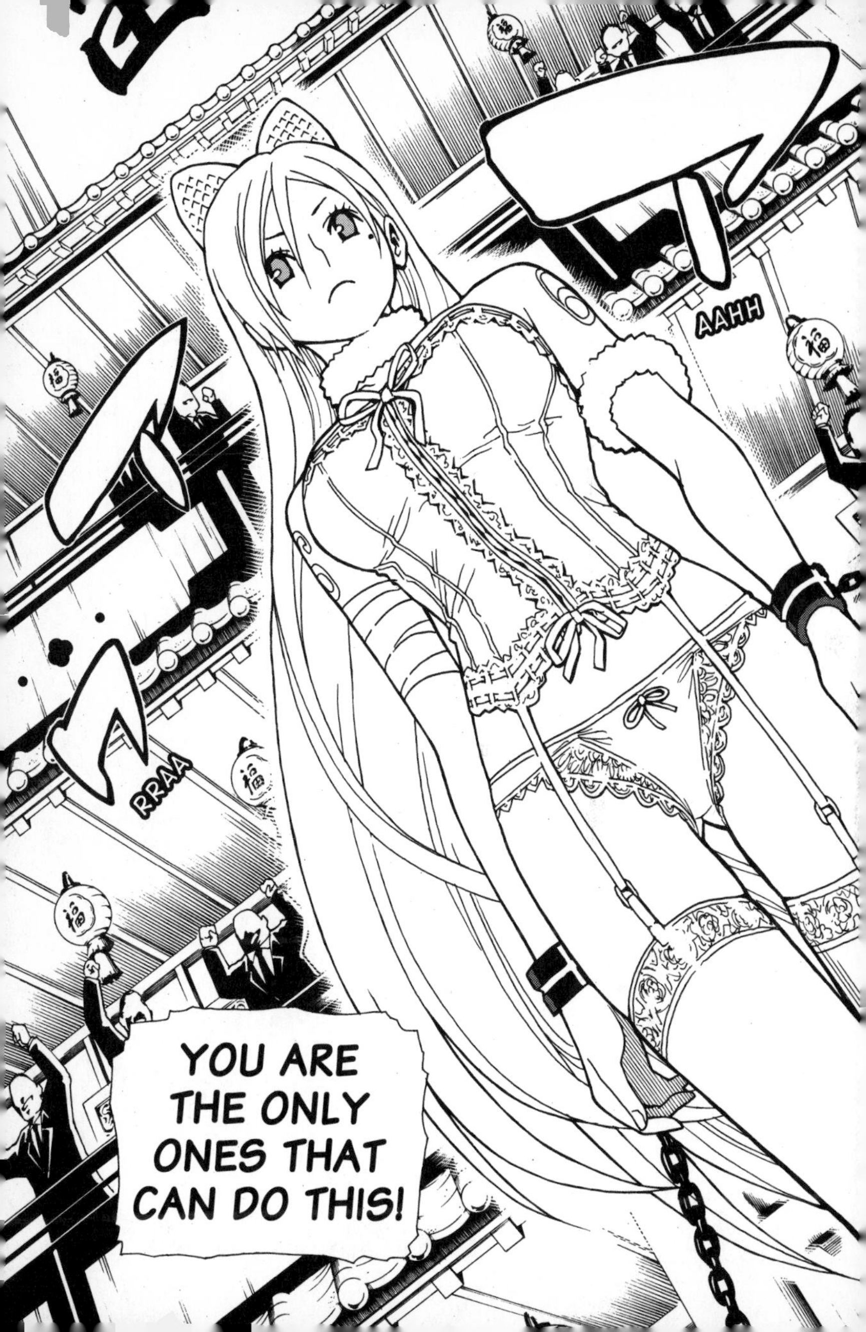
AAHH
RRAA
YOU ARE THE ONLY ONES THAT CAN DO THIS!

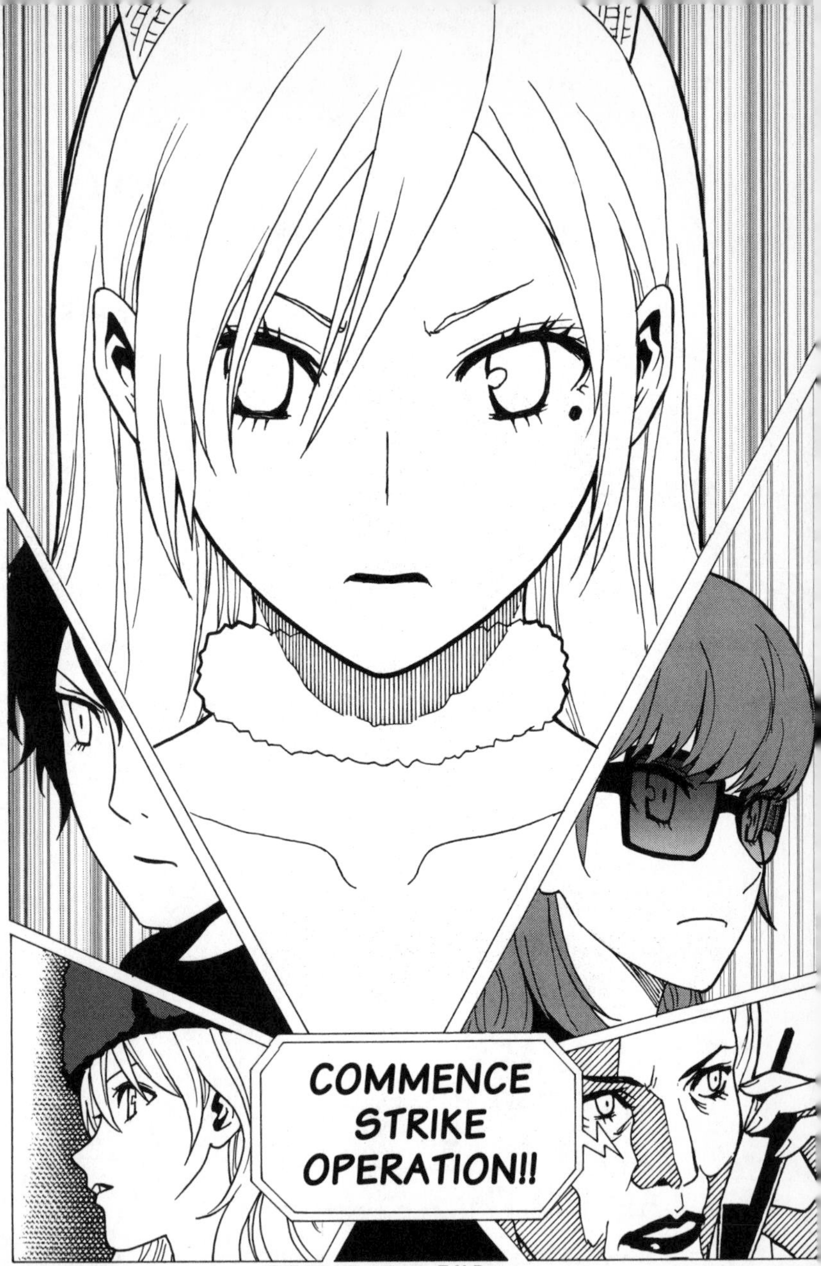
COMMENCE STRIKE OPERATION!!

SCENE 47 /// END

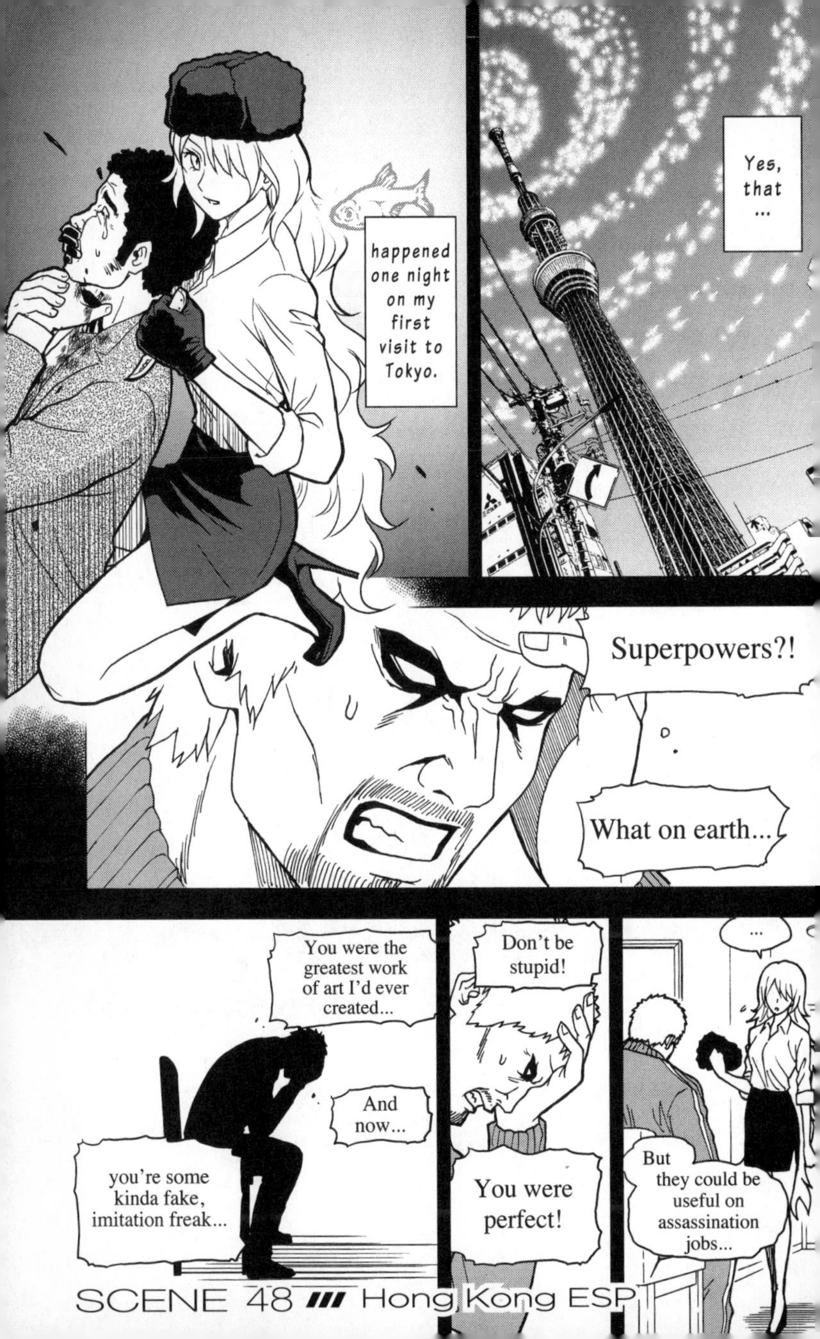

Yes, that ...
happened one night on my first visit to Tokyo.
Superpowers?!
What on earth...
...
But they could be useful on assassination jobs...
Don't be stupid!
You were perfect!
You were the greatest work of art I'd ever created...
And now...
you're some kinda fake, imitation freak...

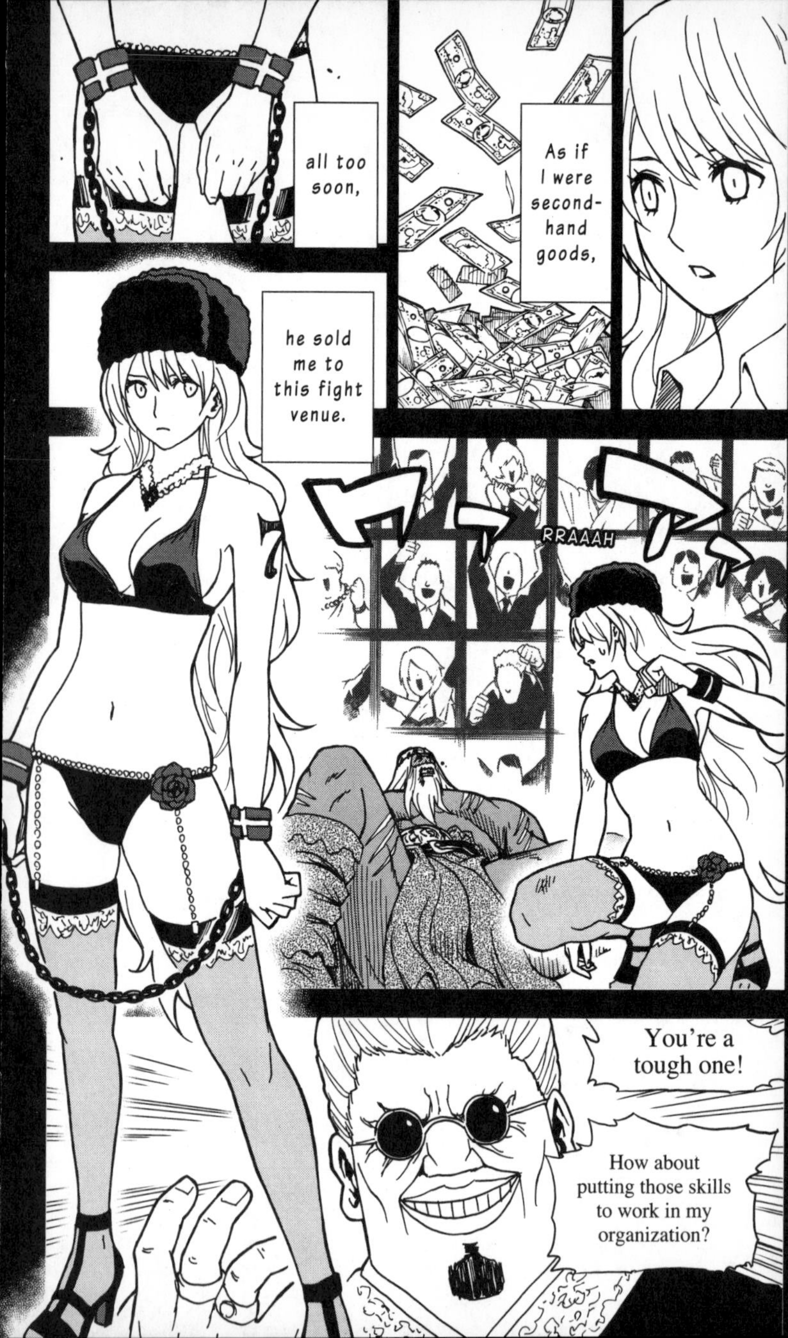
As if I were second-hand goods,
all too soon,
he sold me to this fight venue.
RRAAAH
You're a tough one!
How about putting those skills to work in my organization?

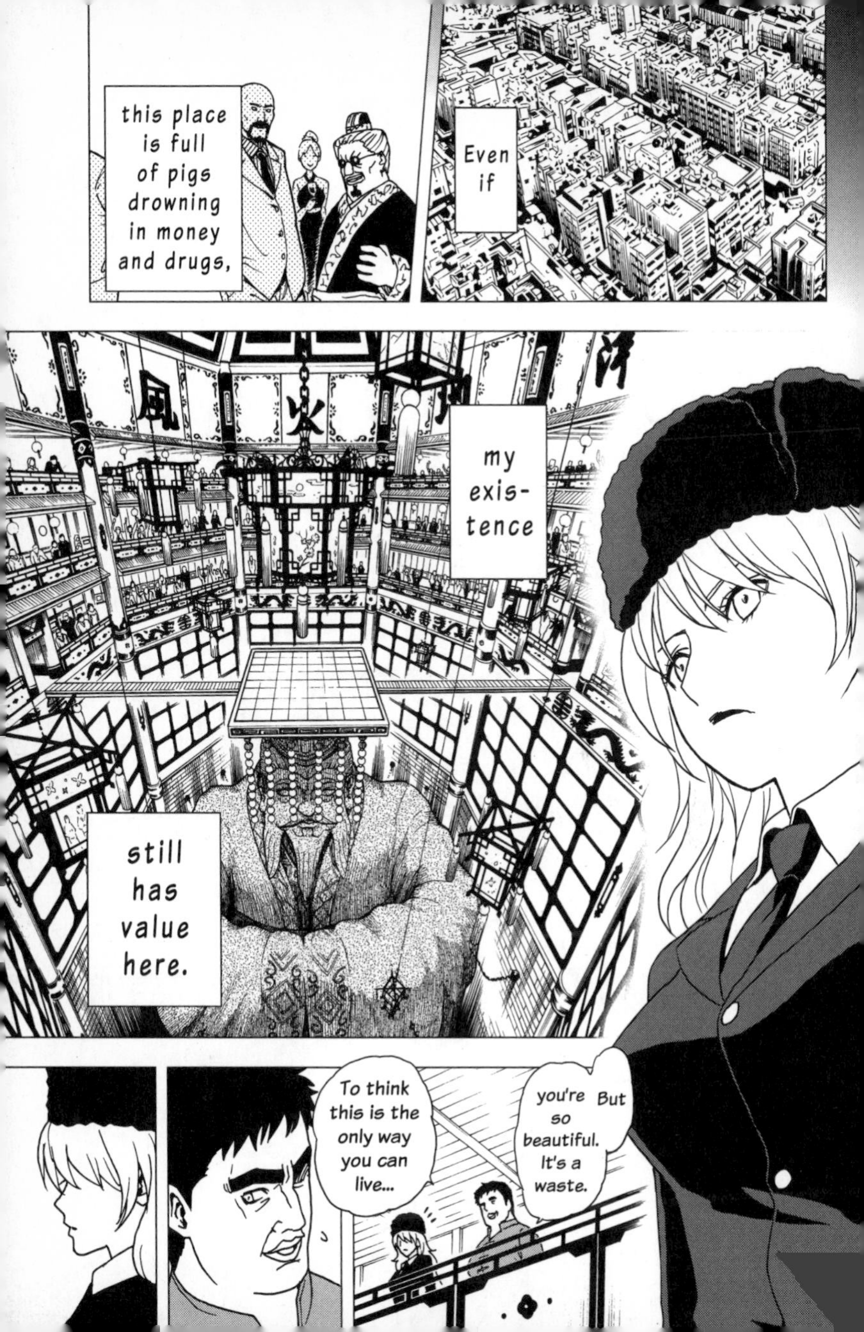
Even if
this place is full of pigs drowning in money and drugs,
my existence
still has value here.
But you're so beautiful. It's a waste.
To think this is the only way you can live...

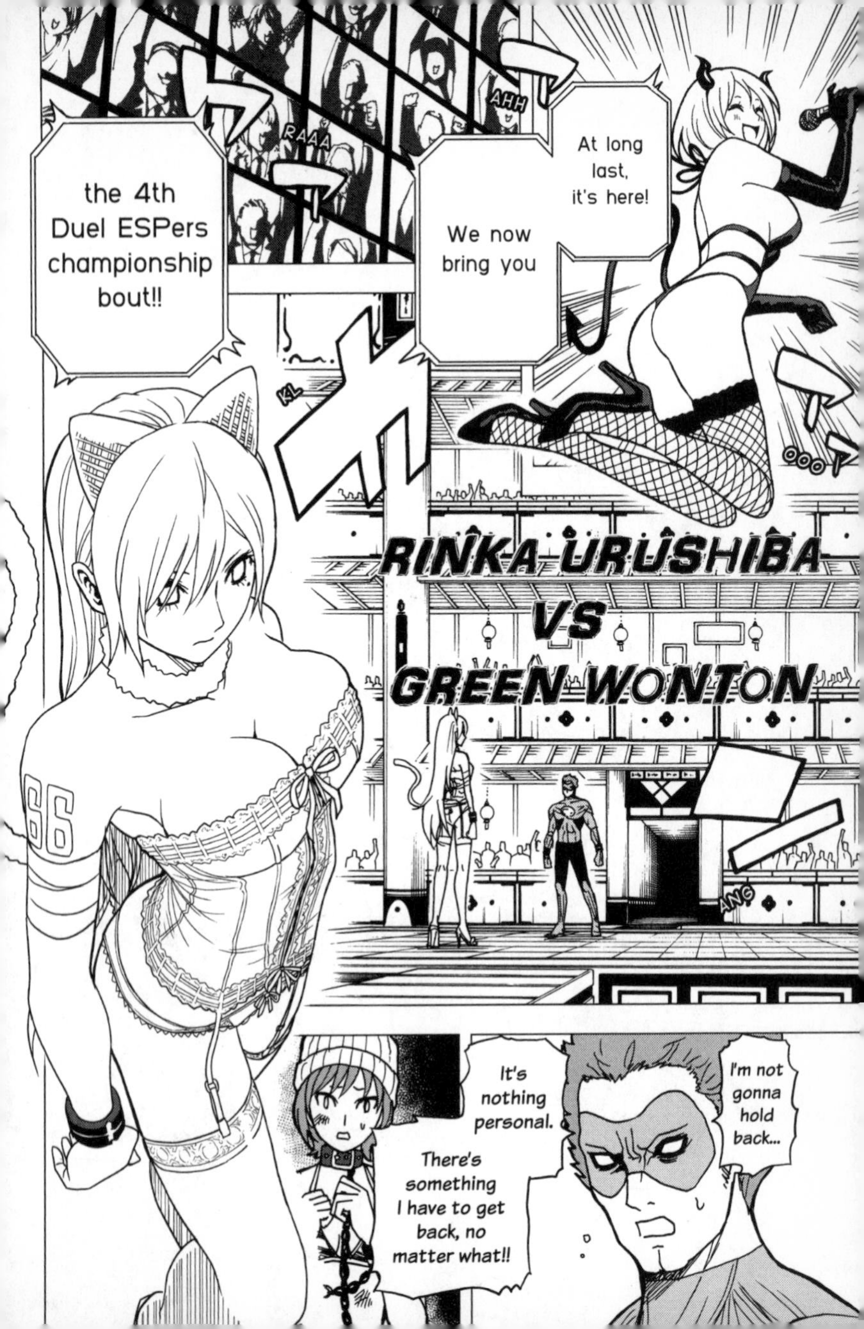
AHH
RAAA
At long last, it's here!
We now bring you
the 4th Duel ESPers championship bout!!
ooo
KL
RINKA URUSHIBA VS GREEN WONTON
ANG
I'm not gonna hold back...
It's nothing personal.
There's something I have to get back, no matter what!!

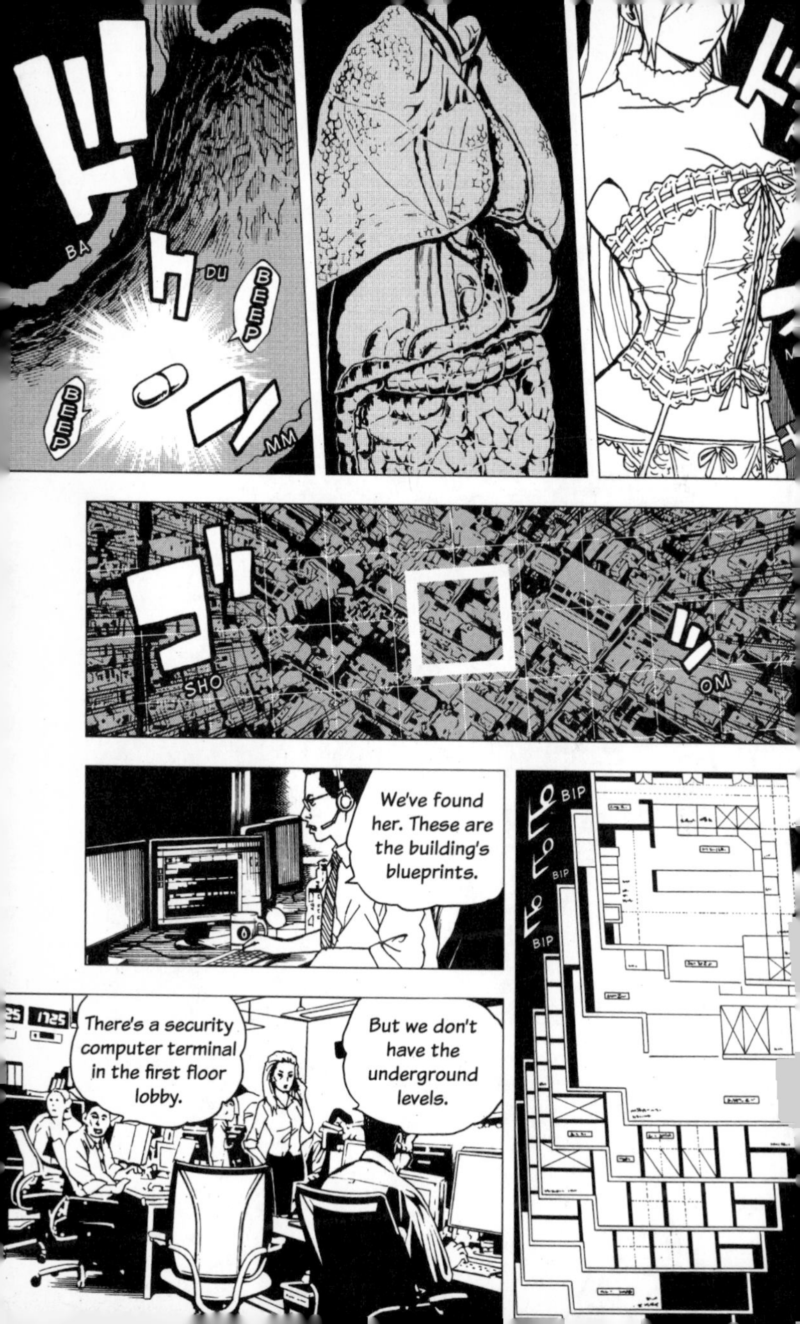
DU
BEEP
BA
BEEP
MM
OM
SHO
BIP
BIP
BIP
We've found her. These are the building's blueprints.
But we don't have the underground levels.
There's a security computer terminal in the first floor lobby.
1725

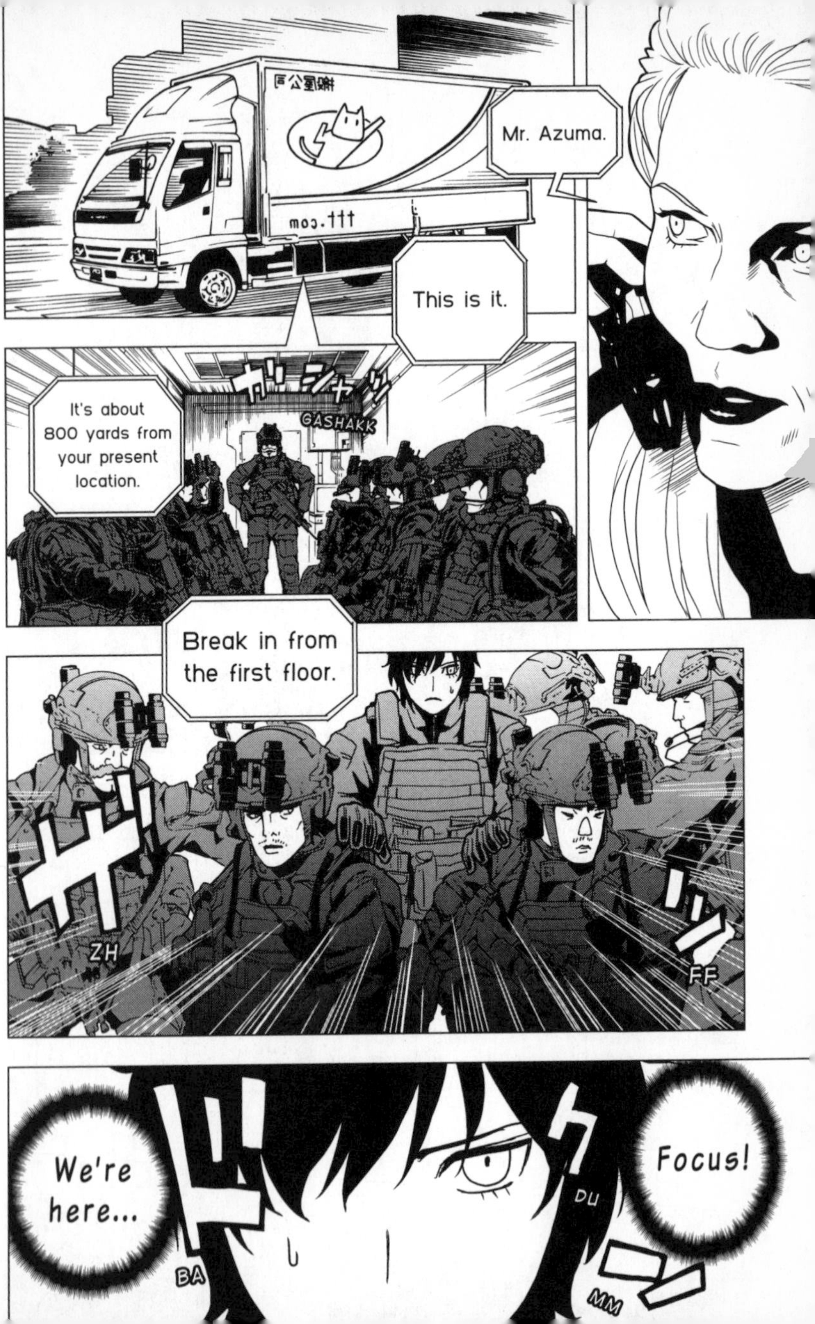
Mr. Azuma.
This is it.
It's about 800 yards from your present location.
GASHAKK
Break in from the first floor.
FF
ZH
Focus!
DU
MM
We're here...
BA

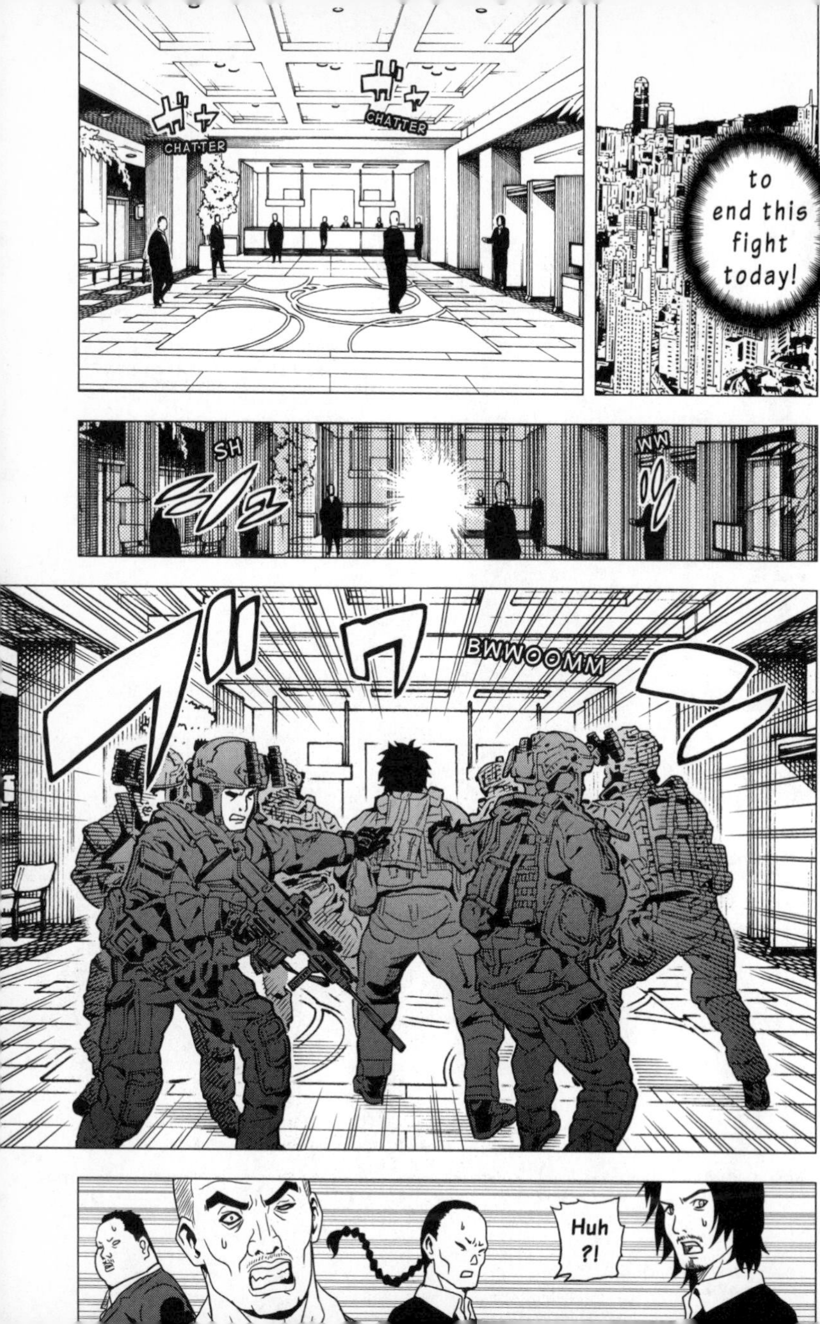
to end this fight today!
CHATTER
CHATTER
WW
SH
BWWOOMM
Huh ?!

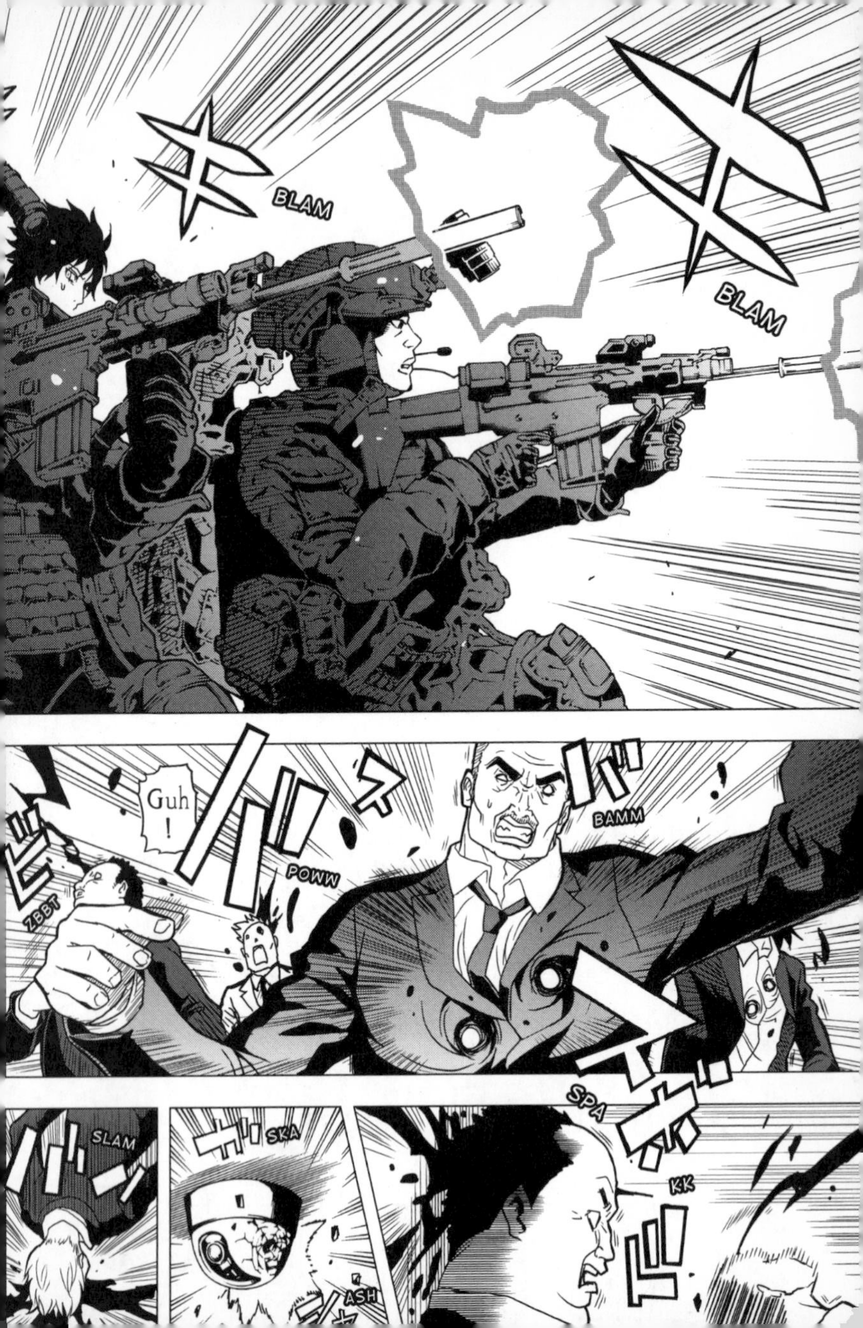
BLAM
BLAM
BAMM
POWW
Guh!
ZBBT
SPA
KK
SKA
ASH
SLAM

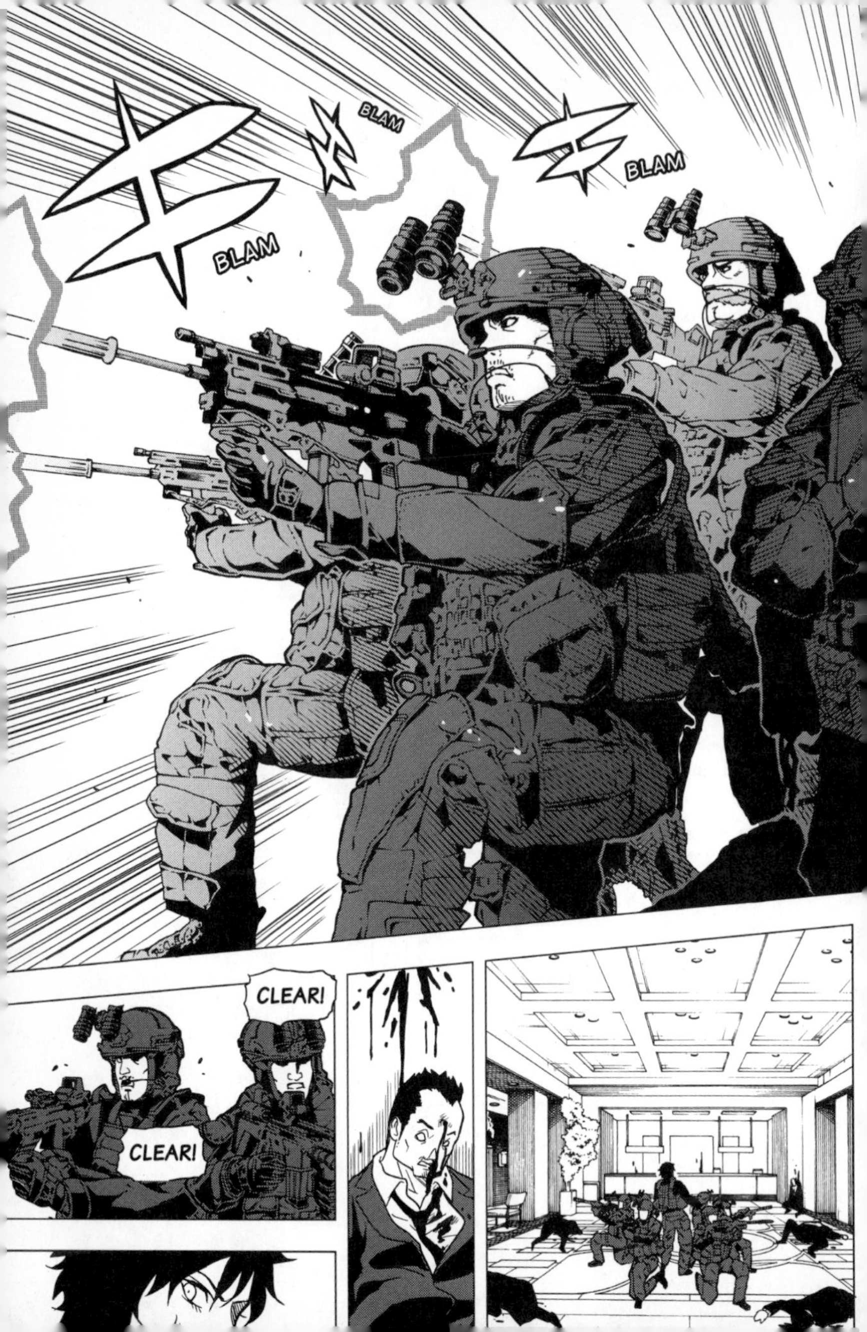
BLAM
BLAM
BLAM
CLEAR!
CLEAR!

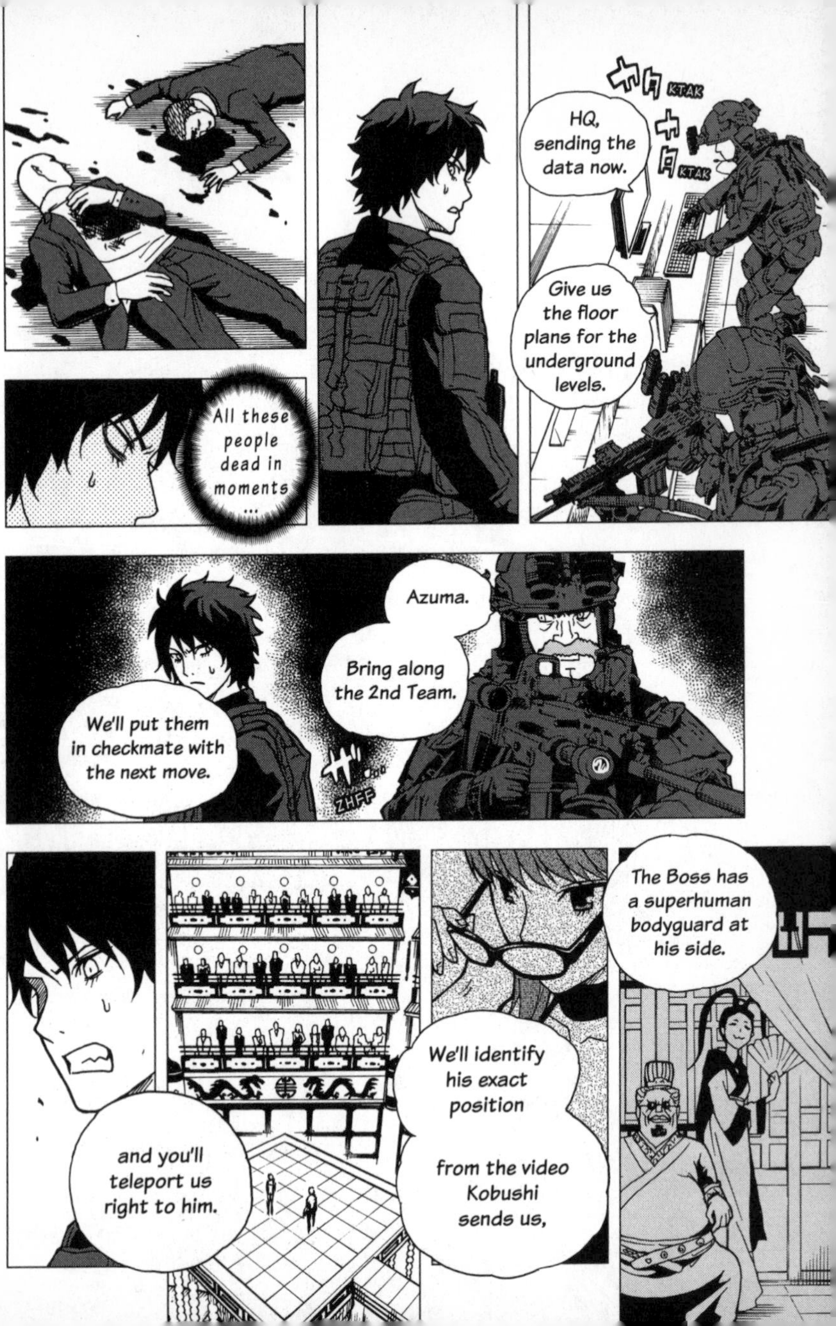

KTAK
KTAK
HQ, sending the data now.
Give us the floor plans for the underground levels.
All these people dead in moments ...
Azuma.
Bring along the 2nd Team.
ZHFF
We'll put them in checkmate with the next move.
The Boss has a superhuman bodyguard at his side.
We'll identify his exact position
from the video Kobushi sends us,
and you'll teleport us right to him.

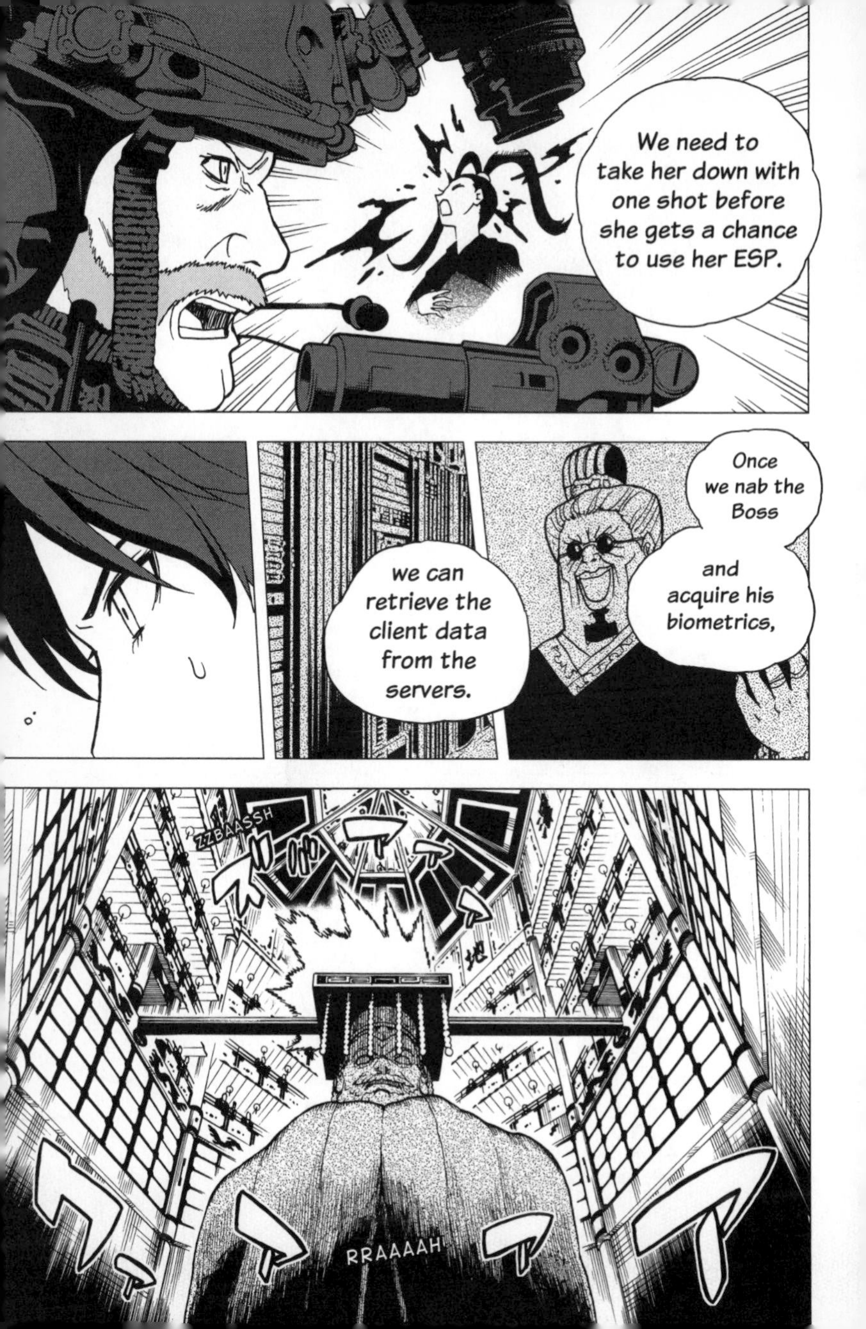
We need to take her down with one shot before she gets a chance to use her ESP.
Once we nab the Boss
and acquire his biometrics,
we can retrieve the client data from the servers.
ZZBAASSH
RRAAAAH

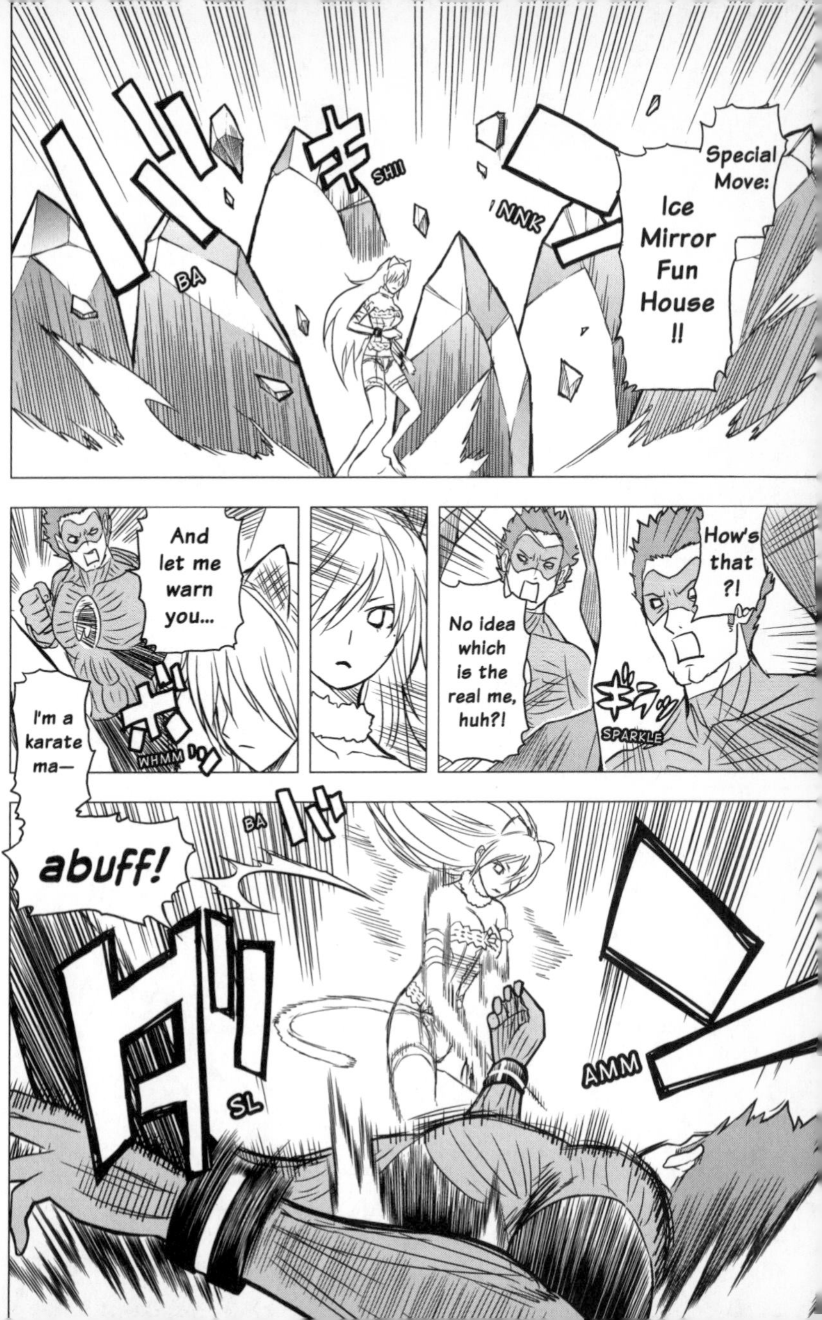
Special Move: Ice Mirror Fun House!!
SHIINNK
BA
How's that?!
No idea which is the real me, huh?!
SPARKLE
And let me warn you...
I'm a karate ma—
WHMM
BA
abuff!
AMM
SL

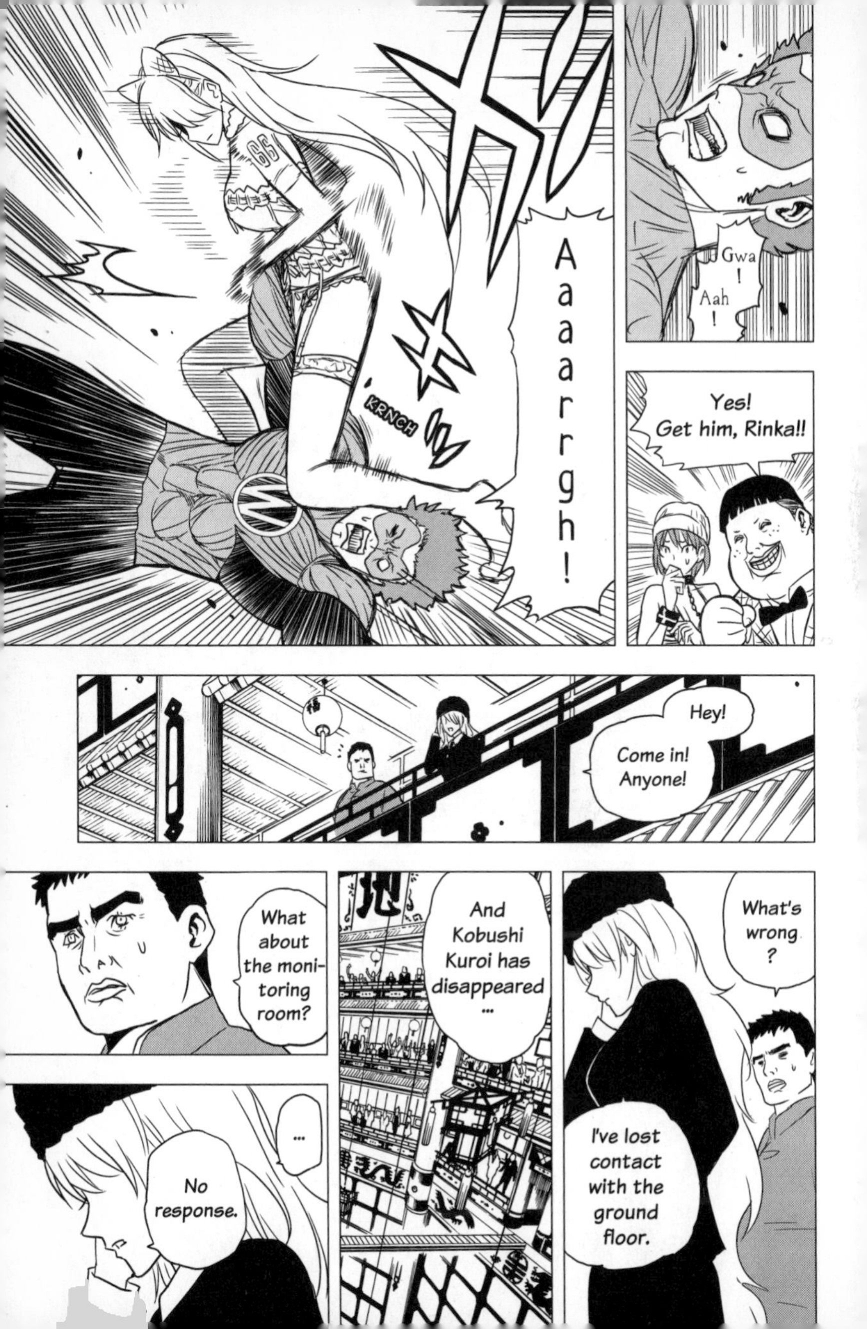
Gwa!
Aah!
Yes! Get him, Rinka!!
Aaaarrgh!
KRNCH
Hey!
Come in! Anyone!
What's wrong?
I've lost contact with the ground floor.
And Kobushi Kuroi has disappeared...
What about the moni-toring room?
...
No response.

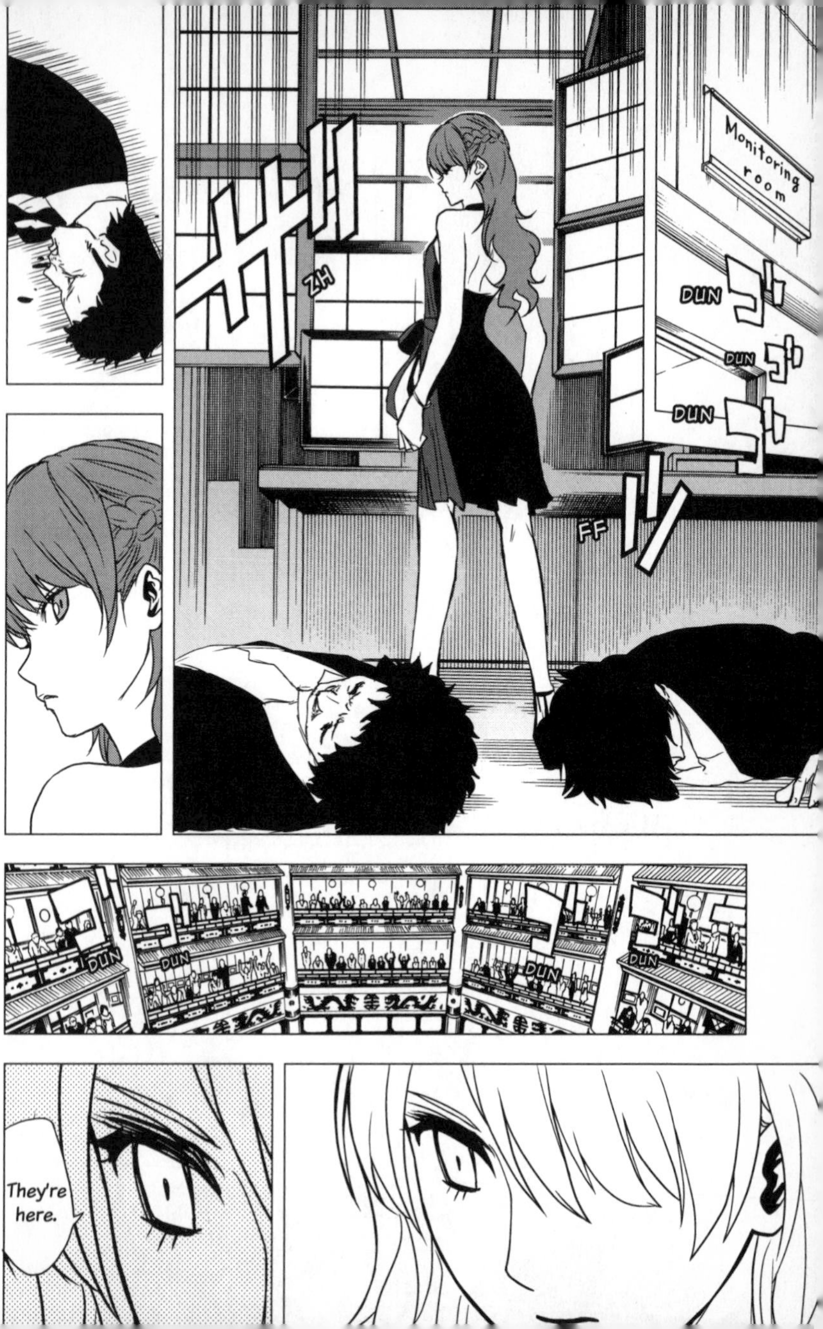
Monitoring room
DUN
DUN
DUN
ZH
FF
DUN
DUN
DUN
DUN
DUN
They're here.

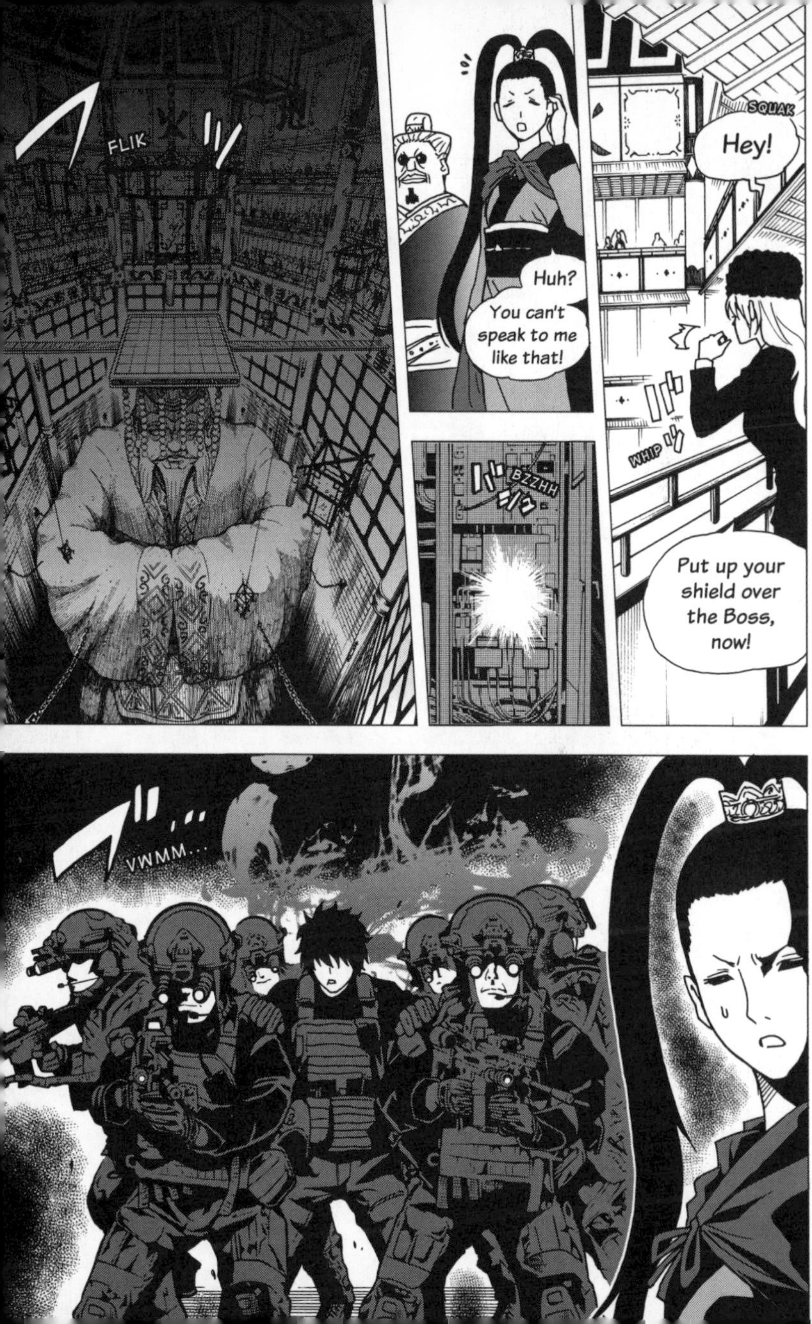
SQUAK
Hey!
WHIP
Put up your shield over the Boss, now!
Huh?
You can't speak to me like that!
BZZHH
FLIK
VWMM...

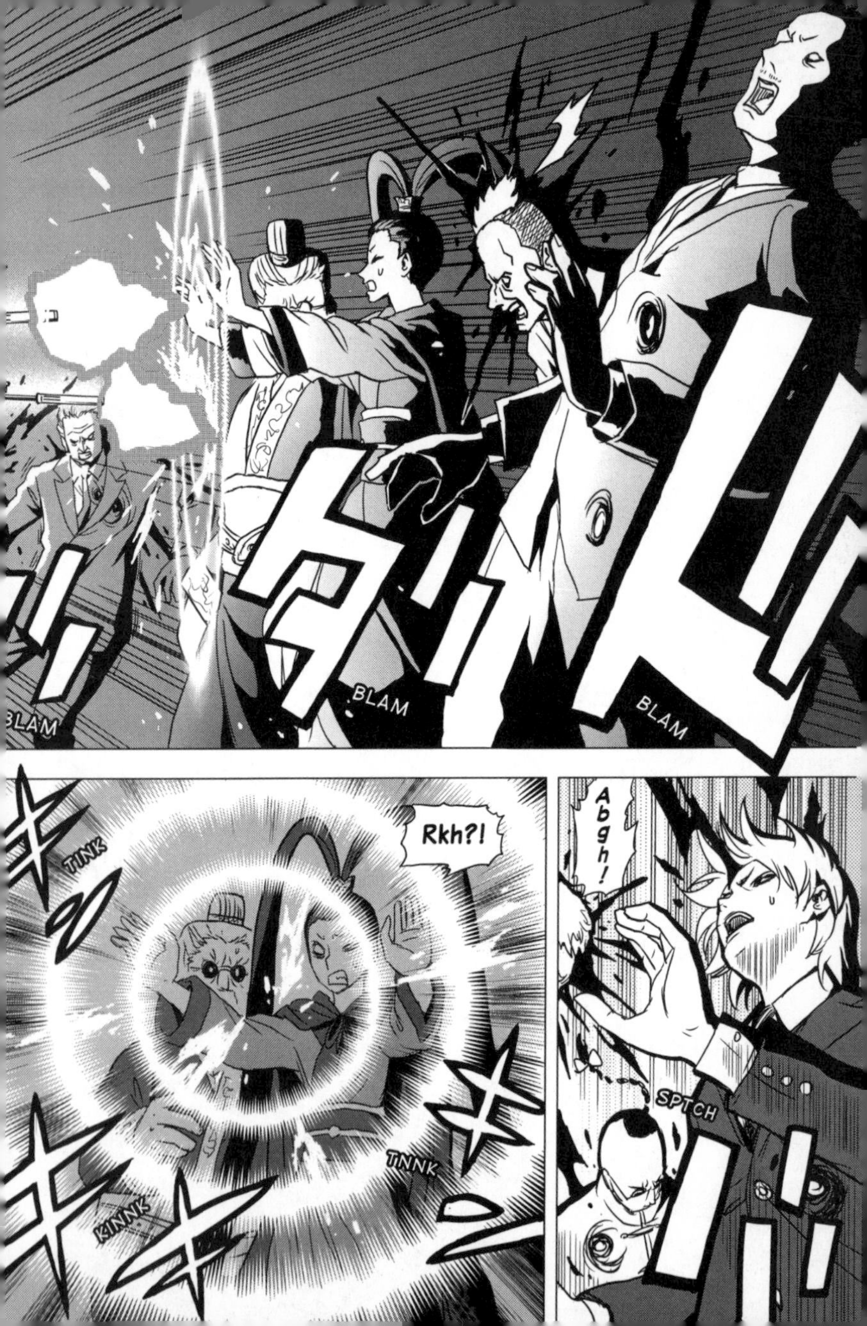
BLAM
BLAM
BLAM
Abgh!
SPTCH
Rkh?!
TINK
TNNK
KINNK

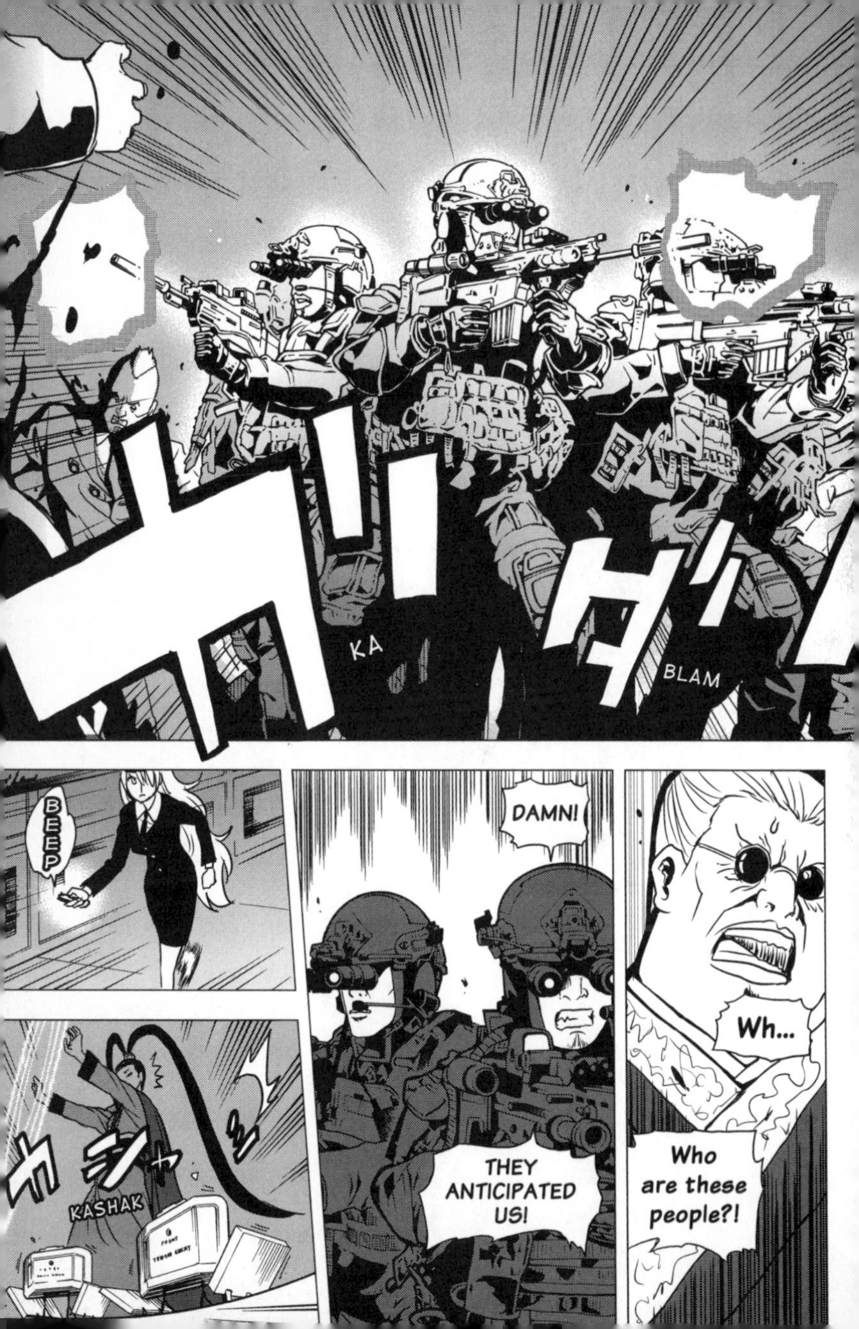
KA
BLAM
Wh...
Who are these people?!
DAMN!
THEY ANTICIPATED US!
BEEP
KASHAK

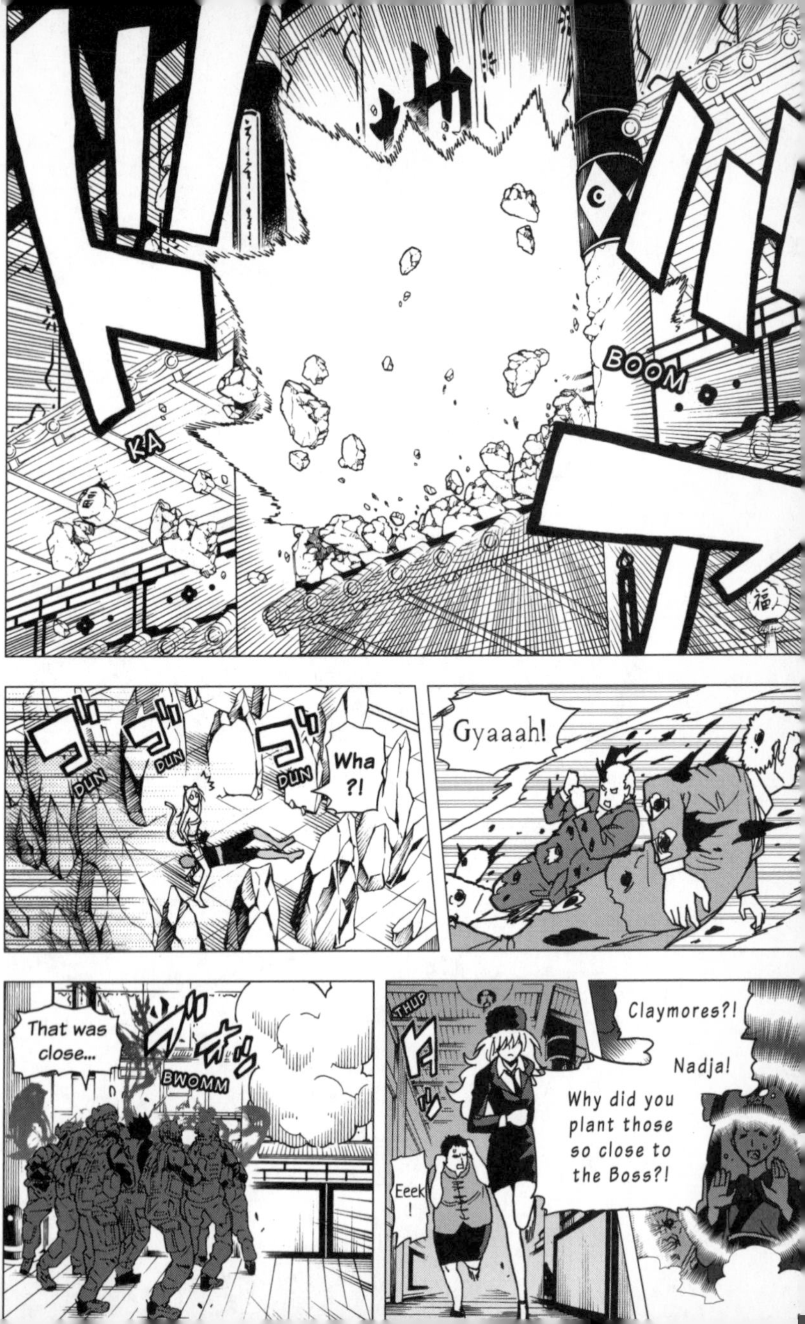
BOOM
KA
Gyaaah!
DUN
DUN
DUN
Wha ?!
THUP
Claymores?!
Nadja!
Why did you plant those so close to the Boss?!
Eeek !
That was close...
BWOMM

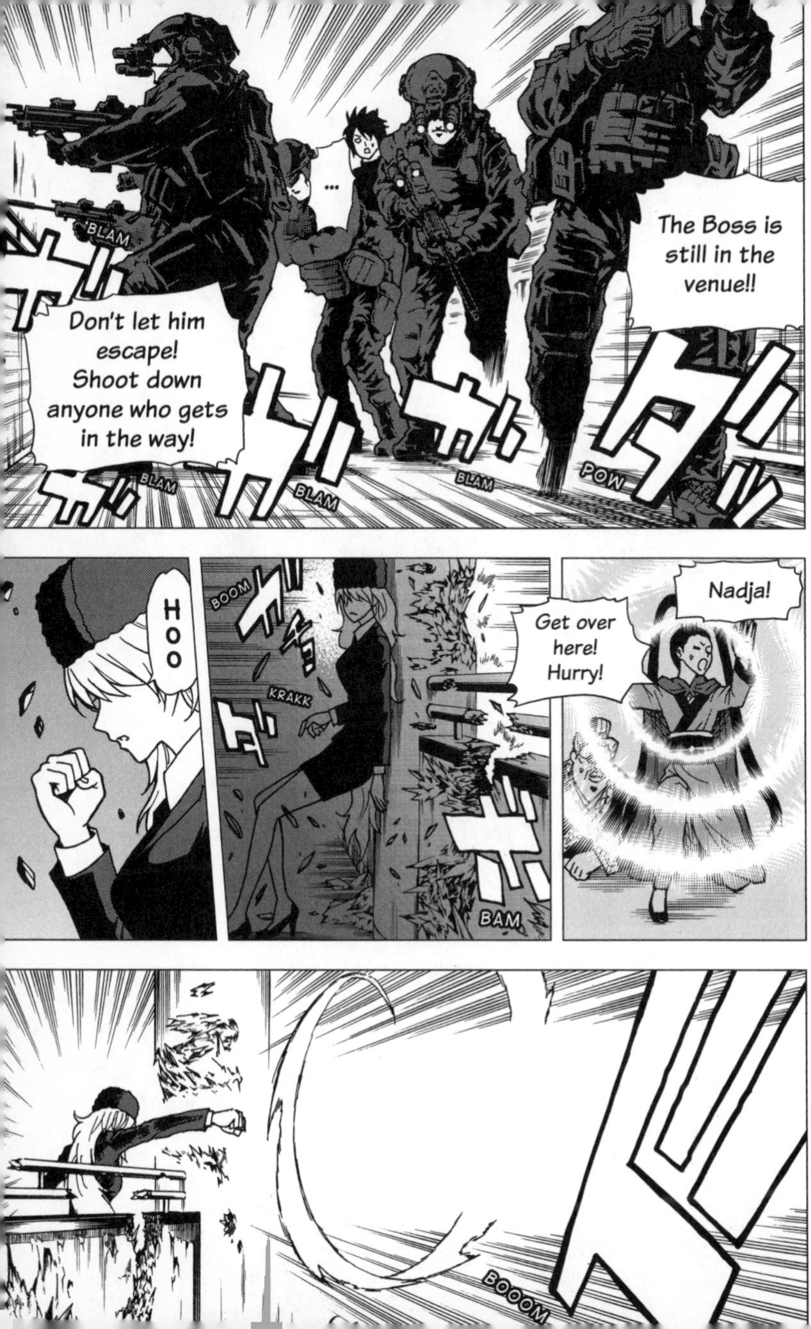
The Boss is still in the venue!!
...
BLAM
Don't let him escape! Shoot down anyone who gets in the way!
POW
BLAM
BLAM
BLAM
Nadja!
Get over here! Hurry!
BOOM
KRAKK
BAM
HOO
BOOOM

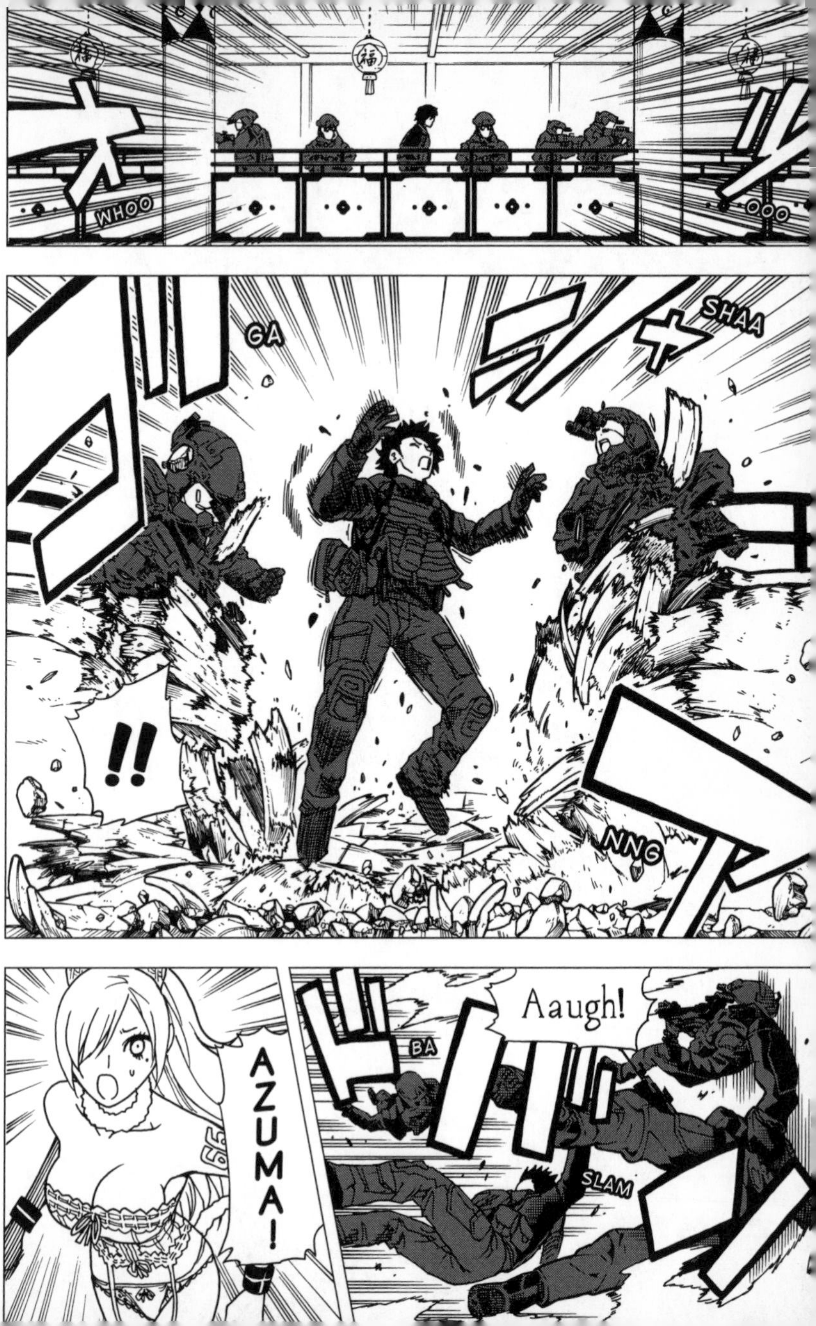
OOO
WHOO
SHAA
GA
!!
NNG
Aaugh!
BA
SLAM
AZUMA!

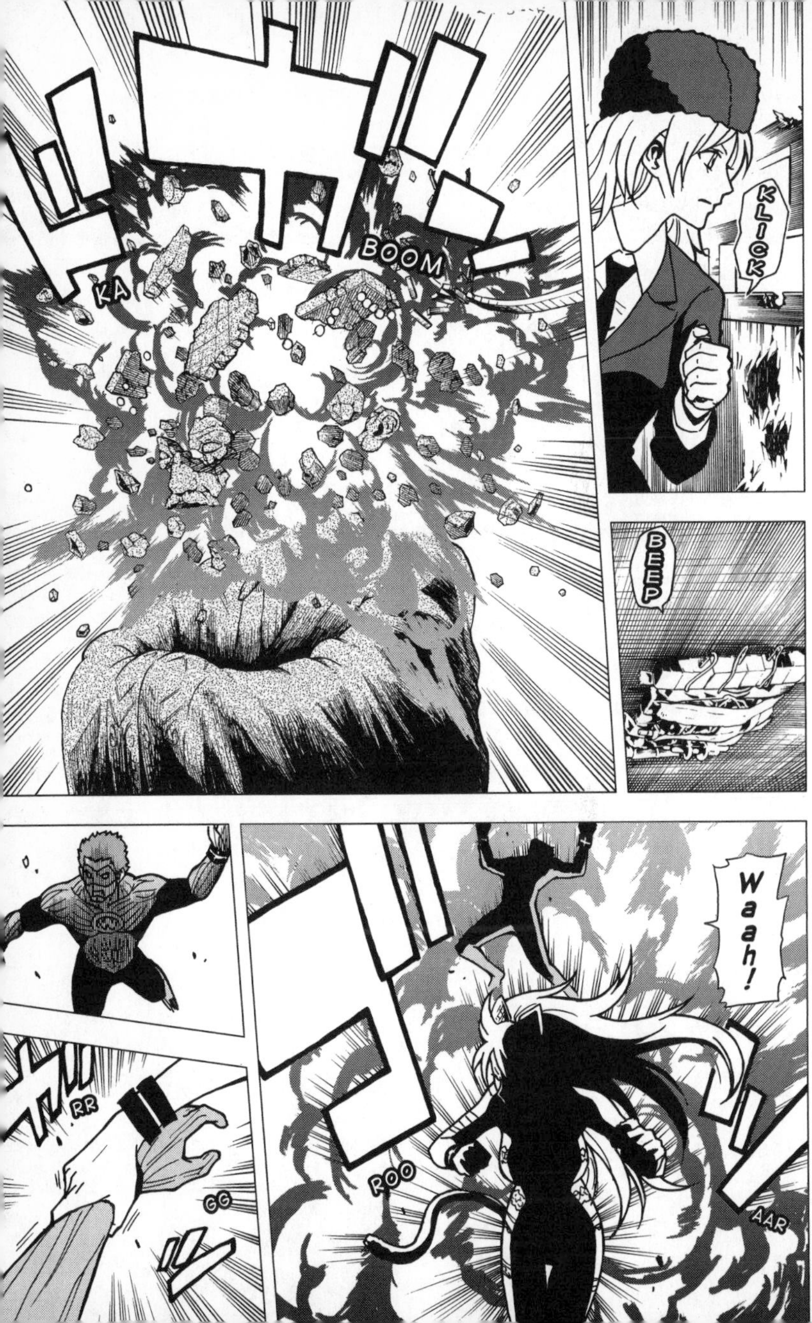
KLICK
BEEP
KA
BOOM
Waaah!
ROO
AAR
RR
GG

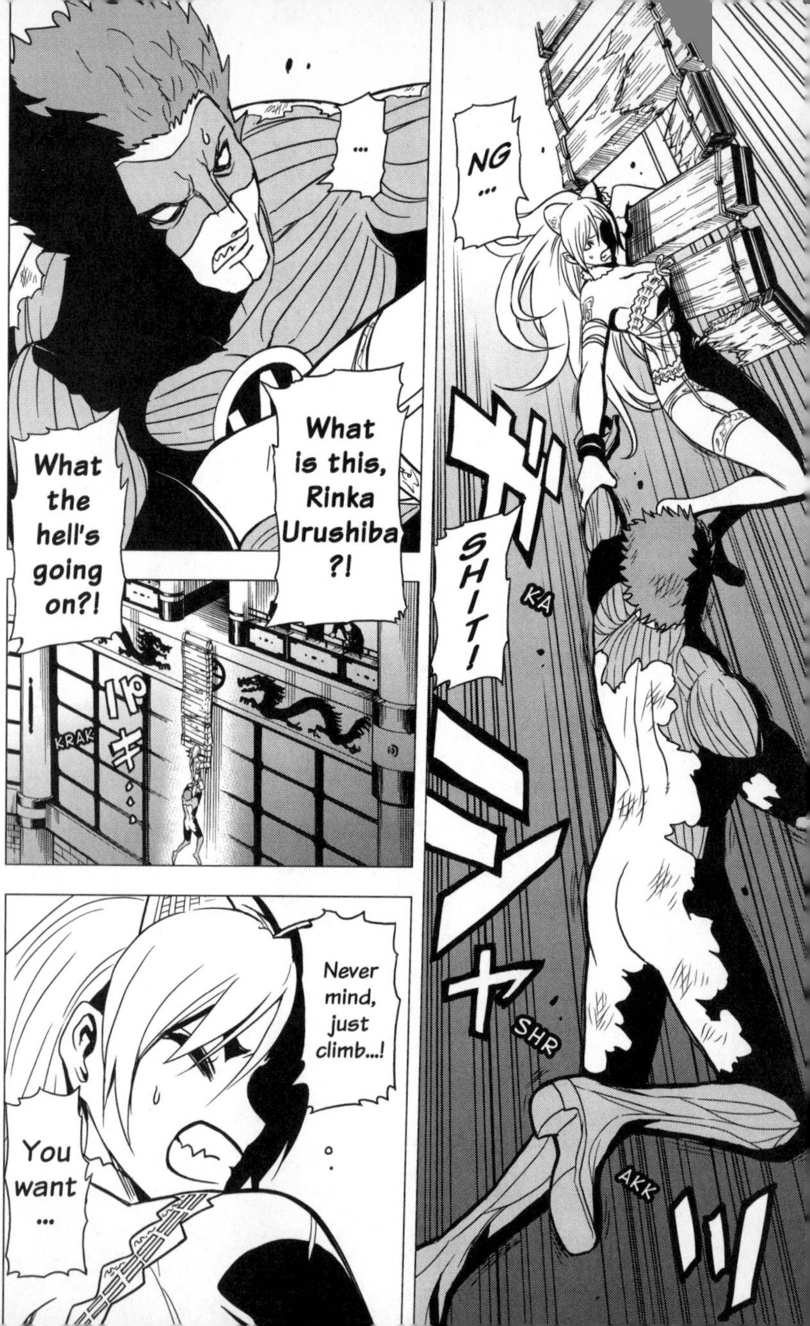
NG ...
SHIT!
KA
SHR
AKK
...
What is this, Rinka Urushiba?!
What the hell's going on?!
KRAK
Never mind, just climb...!
You want ...

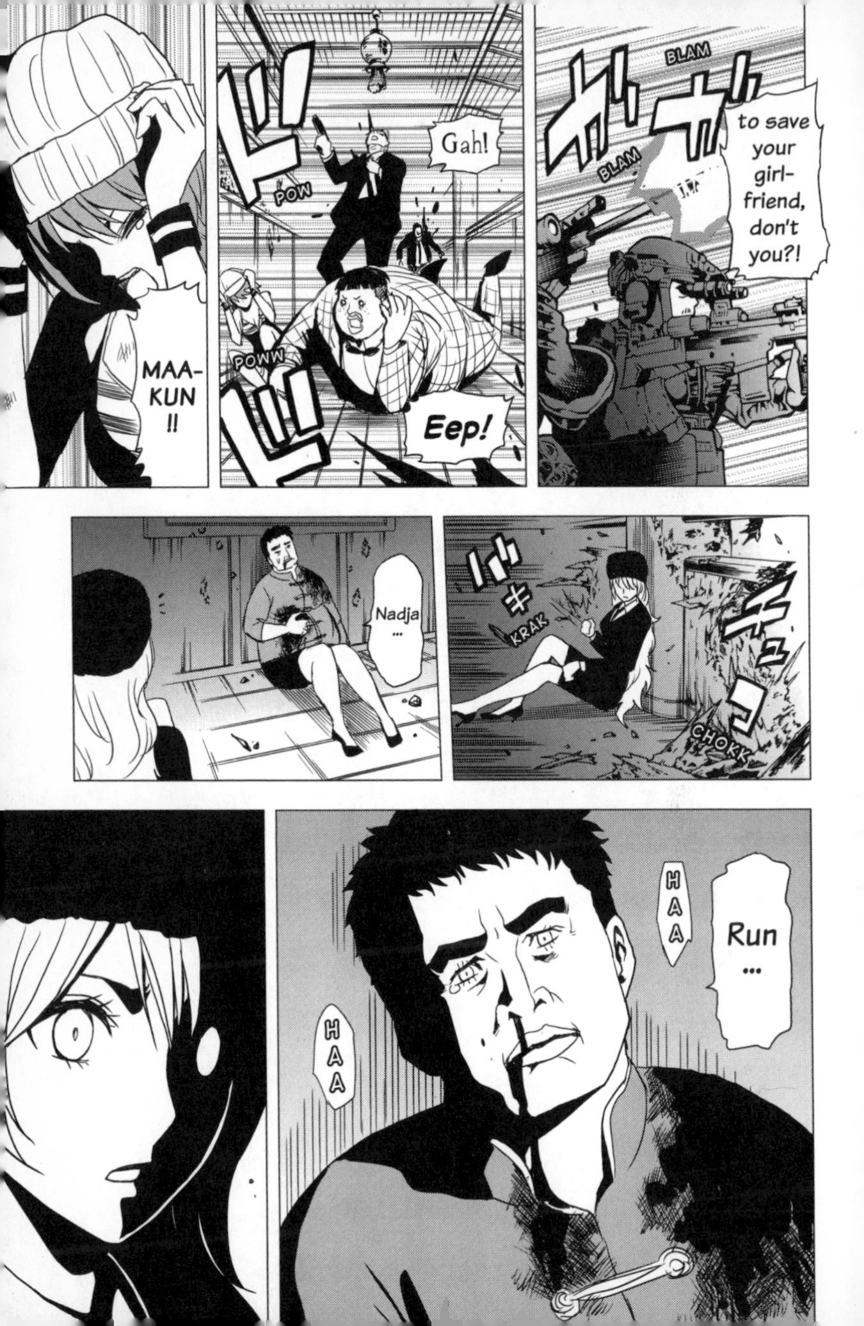
BLAM
BLAM
to save your girl-friend, don't you?!
Gah!
POW
POWW
Eep!
MAA-KUN !!
KRAK
CHOKK
Nadja ...
HAA
Run ...
HAA

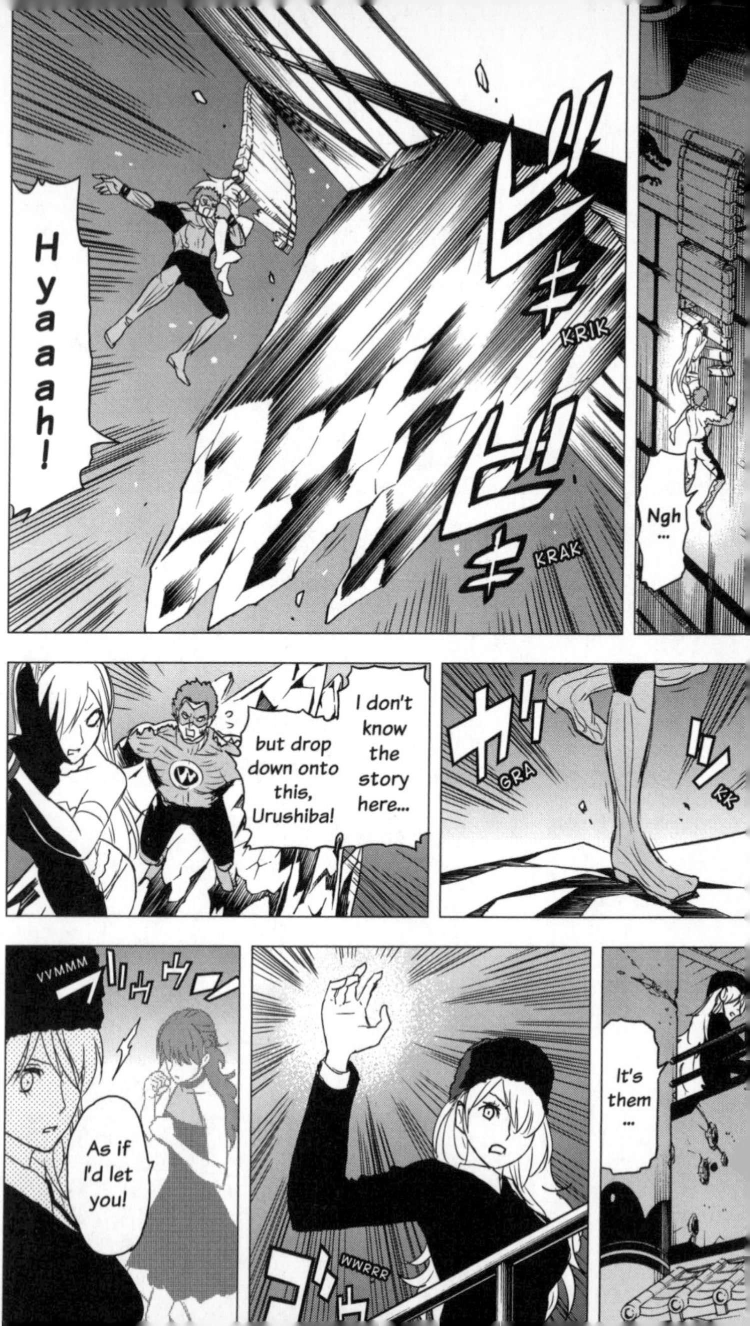
Ngh ...
KRIK
KRAK
Hyaaaah!
GRA
KK
I don't know the story here...
but drop down onto this, Urushiba!
It's them ...
WWRRR
VVMMM
As if I'd let you!

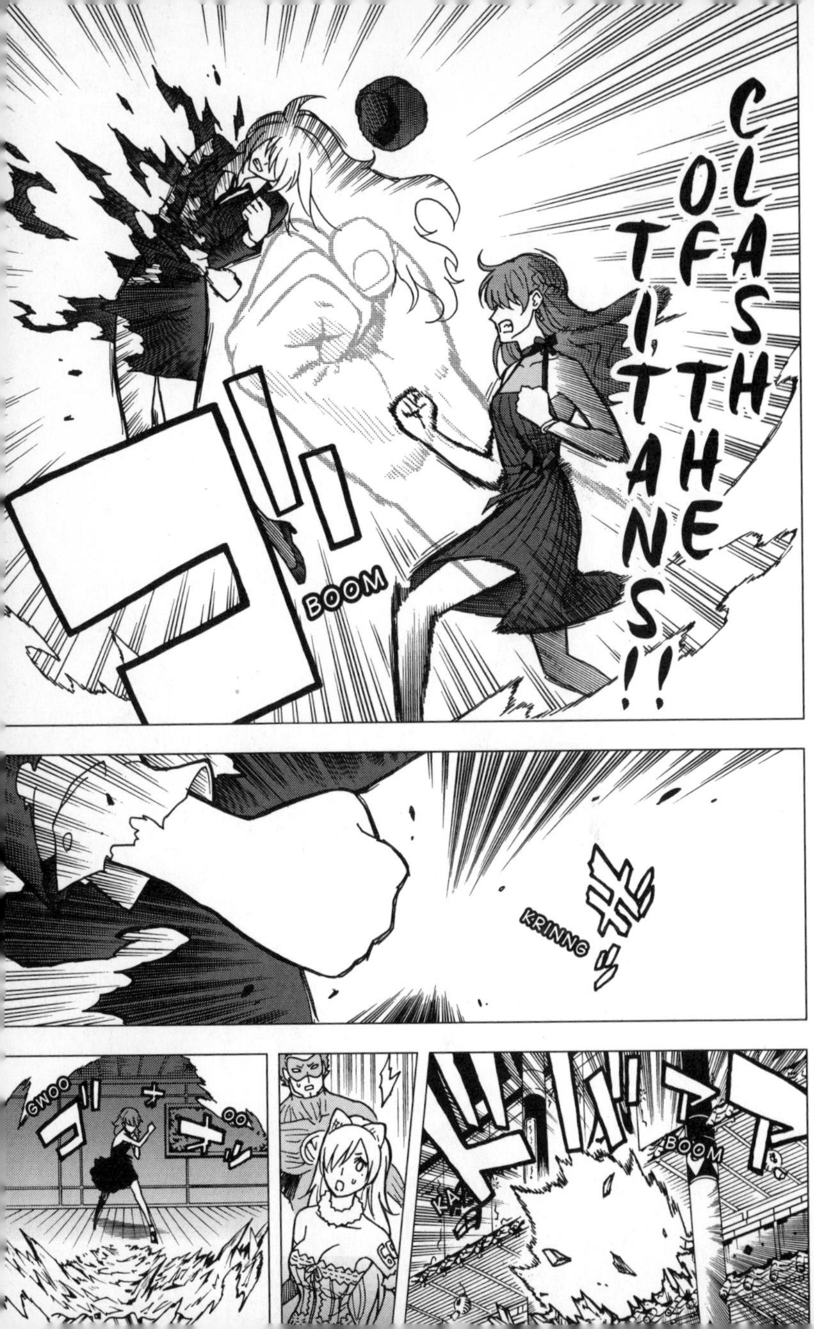
CLASH OF THE TITANS!!
BOOM
KRINNG
BOOM
KA
GWOO
O.O

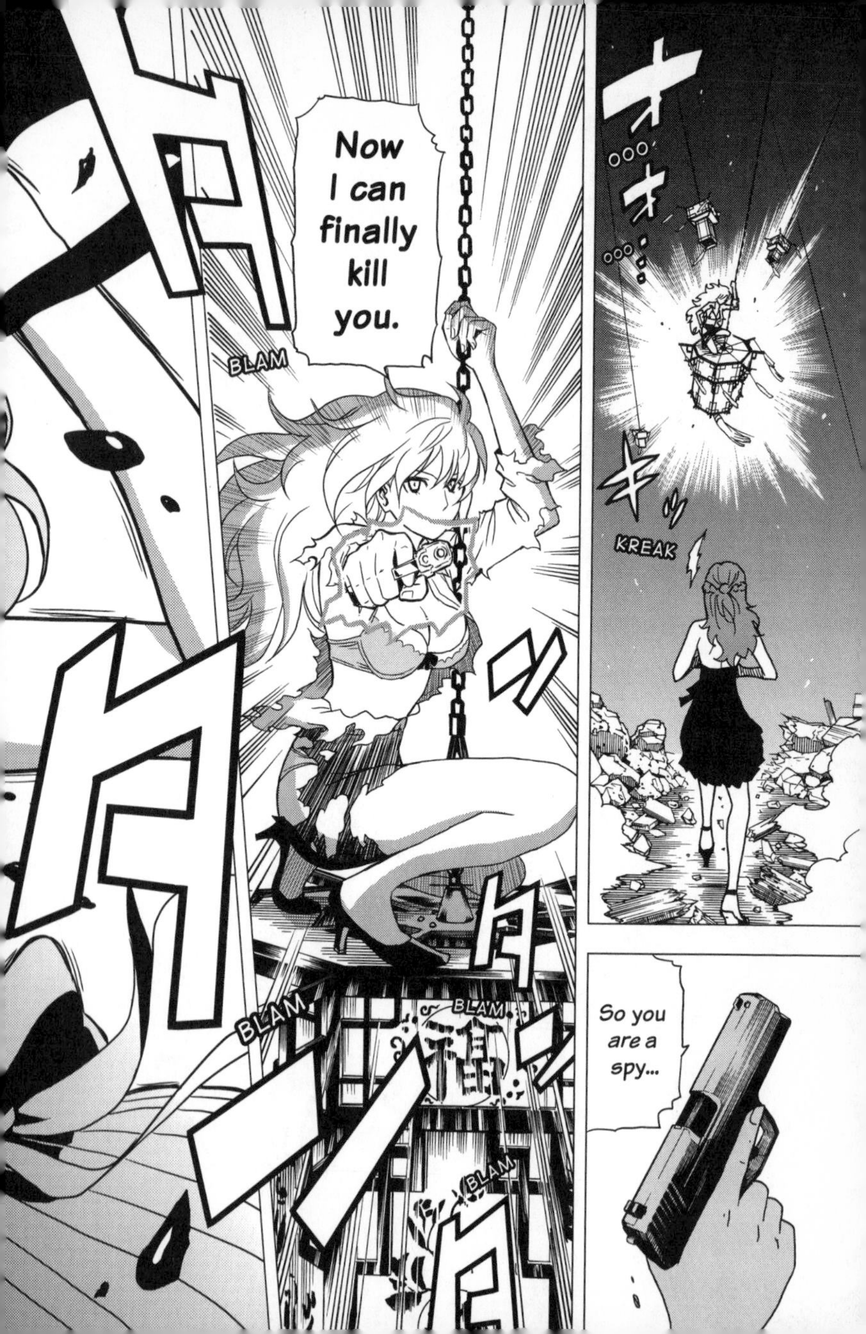
ooo
ooo
KREAK
So you are a spy...
Now I can finally kill you.
BLAM
BLAM
BLAM
BLAM

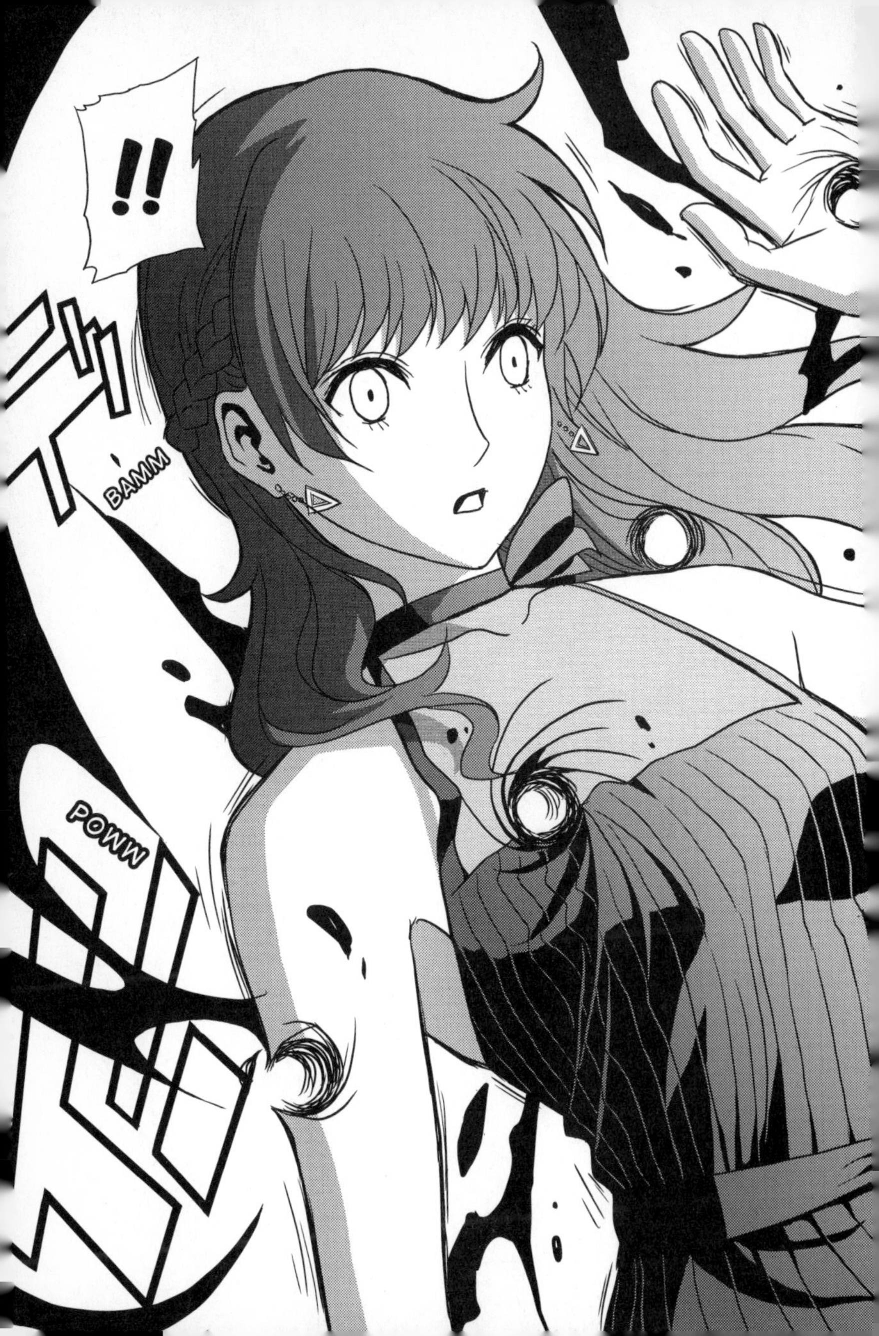
!!
BAMM
POWW

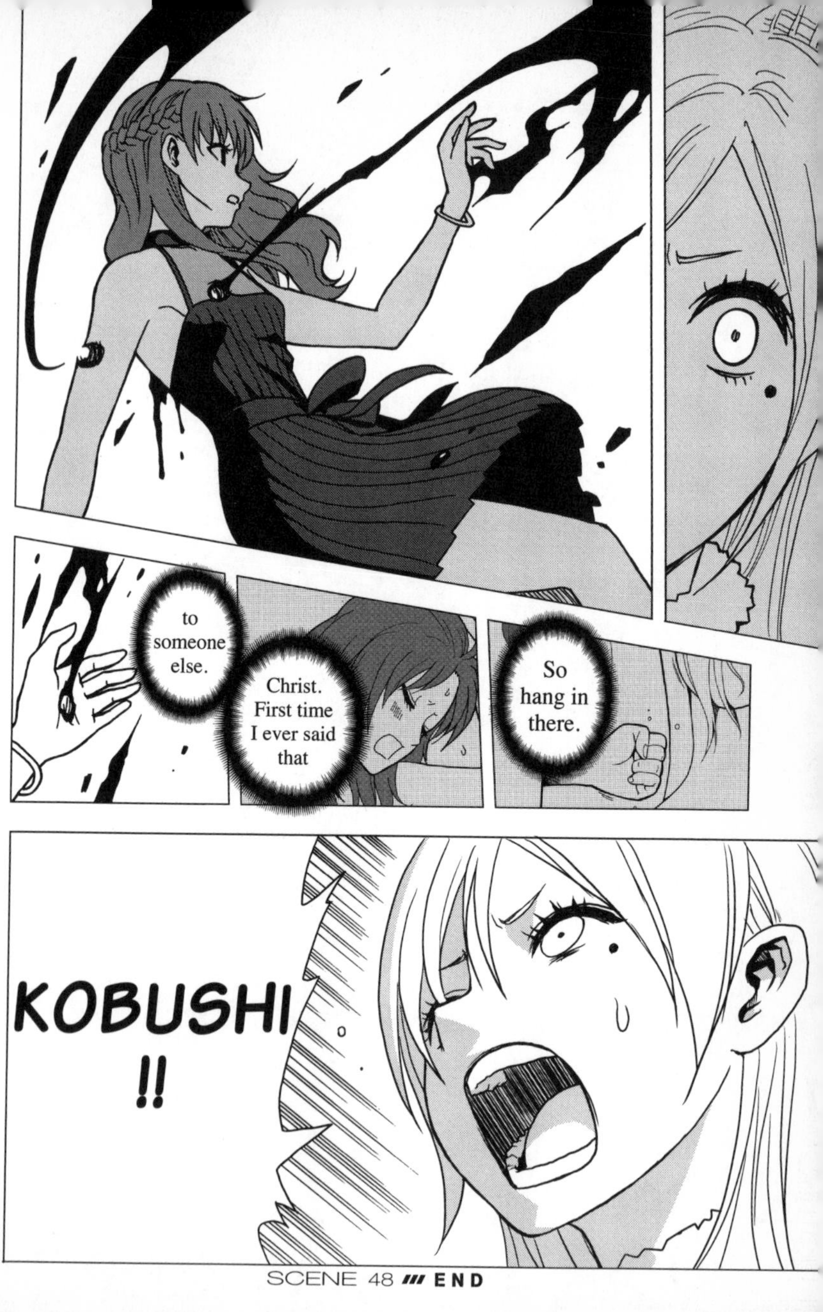
So hang in there.
Christ. First time I ever said that
to someone else.
KOBUSHI !!

SCENE 48 /// END

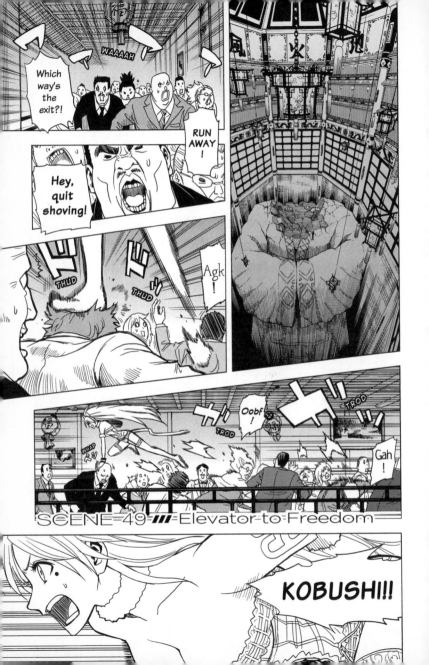

WAAAAH

Which way's the exit?!

RUN AWAY!

Hey, quit shoving!

THUD

THUD

Agk!

Oobf!

TROD

WHAP

TROD

Gah!

SCENE 49 /// Elevator to Freedom

KOBUSHI!!!

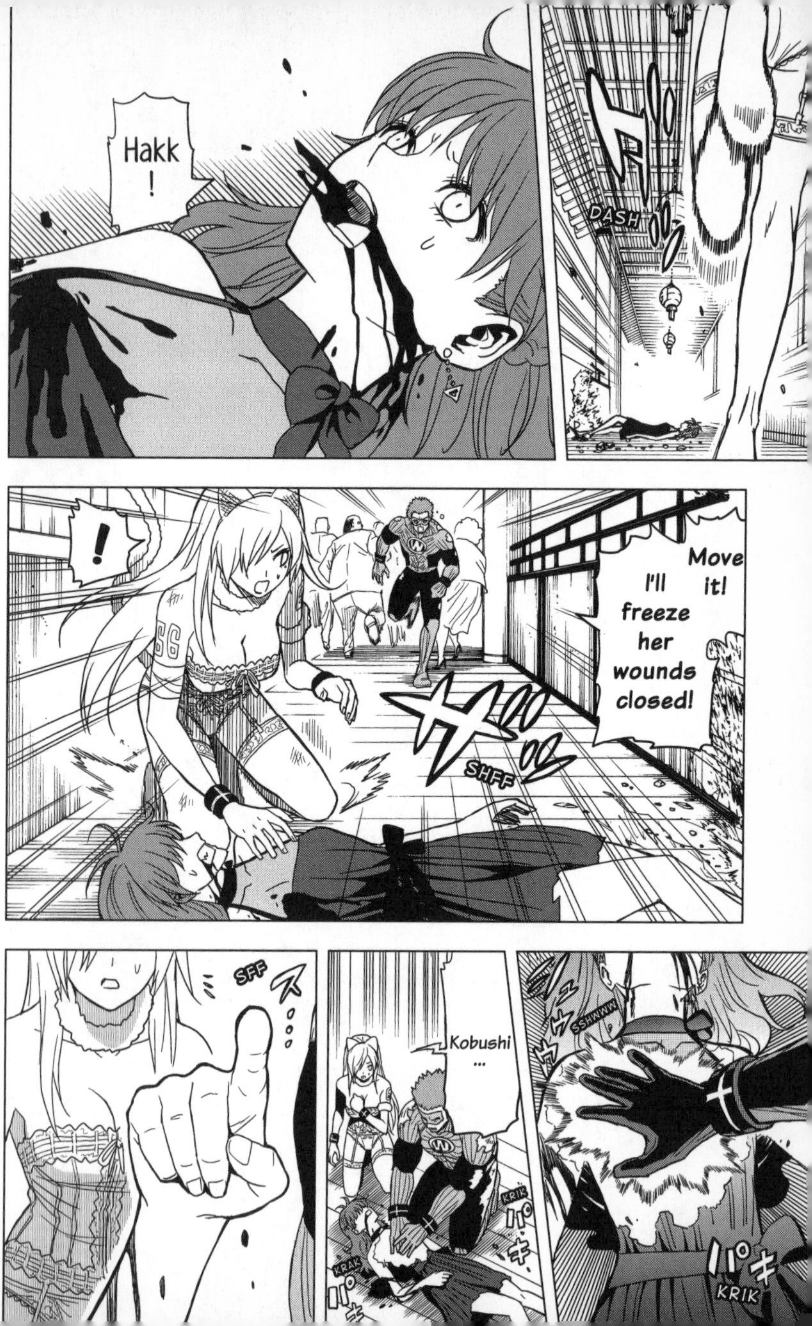
DASH
Hakk!
Move it!
I'll freeze her wounds closed!
!
SHFF
SSHWWN
KRIK
Kobushi...
KRIK
KRAK
SFF

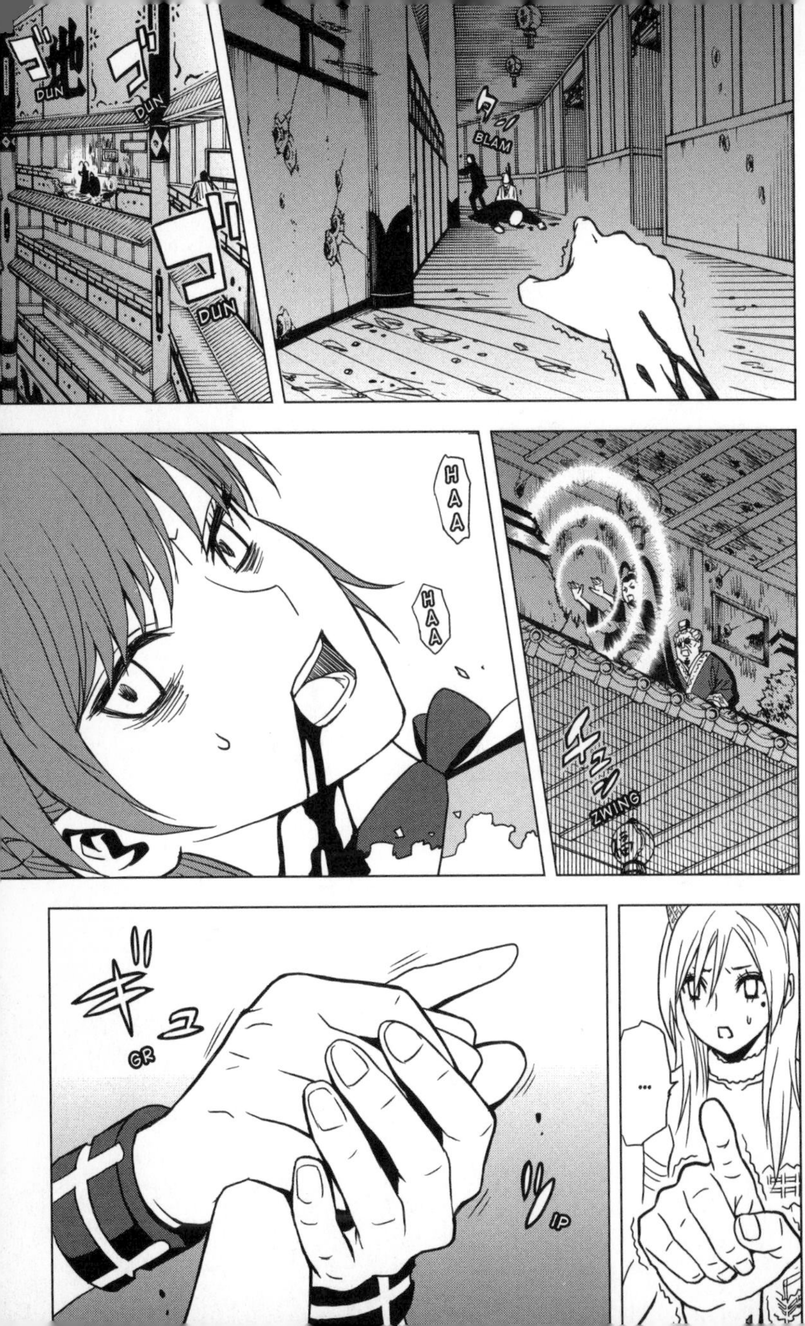
BLAM
DUN
DUN
DUN
ZWING
HAA
HAA
...
GR
IP

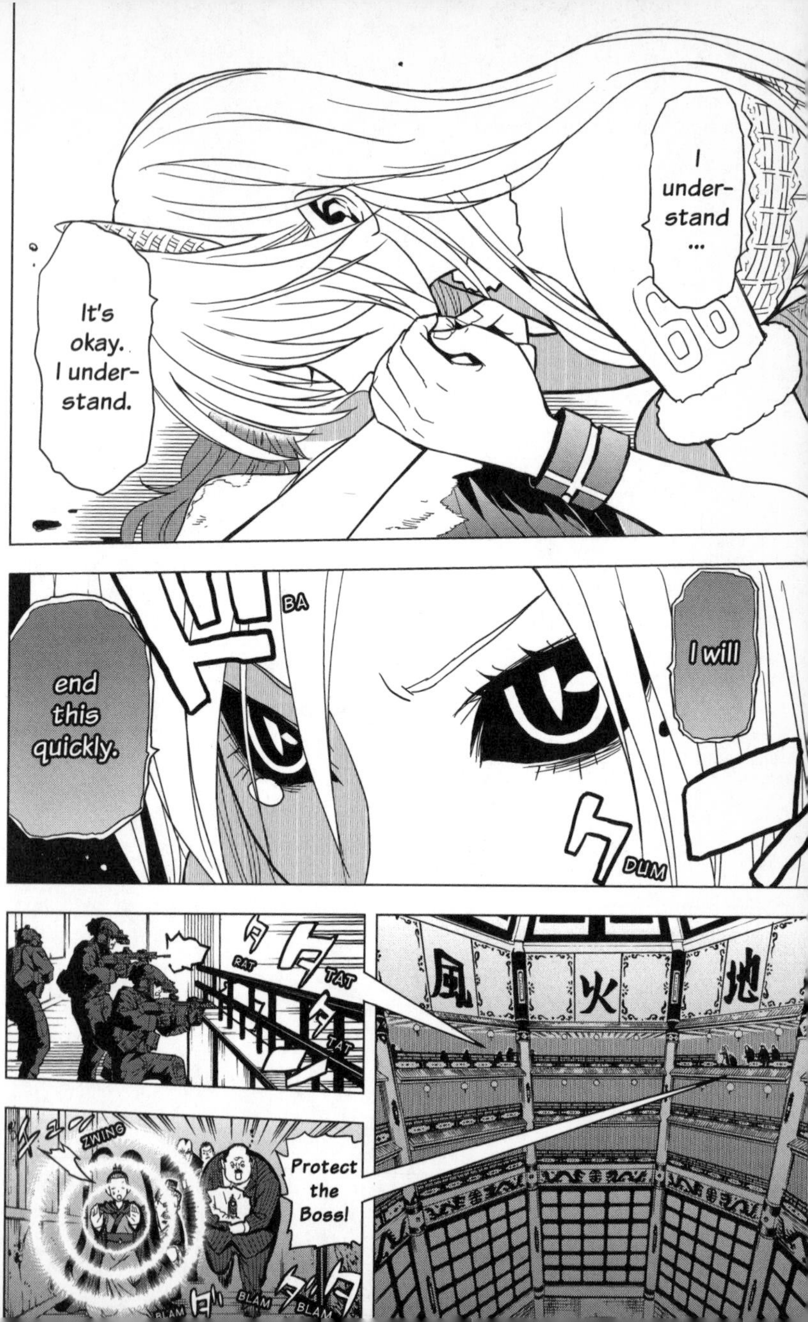
I understand...
It's okay. I understand.
BA
I will
end this quickly.
DUM
RAT
TAT
TAT
ZWING
Protect the Boss!
BLAM
BLAM
BLAM
BLAM

GASHAK
Can you stand, Azuma ...?
Time for the final push!
HAA
HAA
CHAK
VWASH
SH
WW
WHA!
MM
BWOO
Rngh!
BLAM
BLAM
KA
BLAM

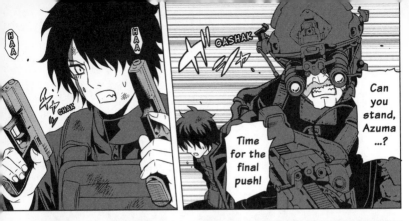

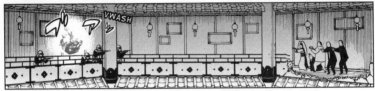

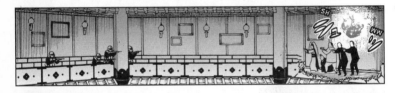

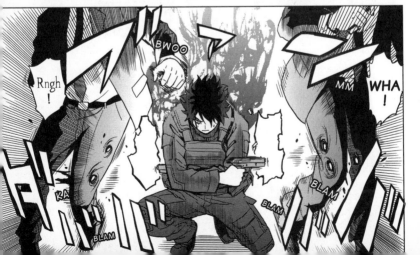

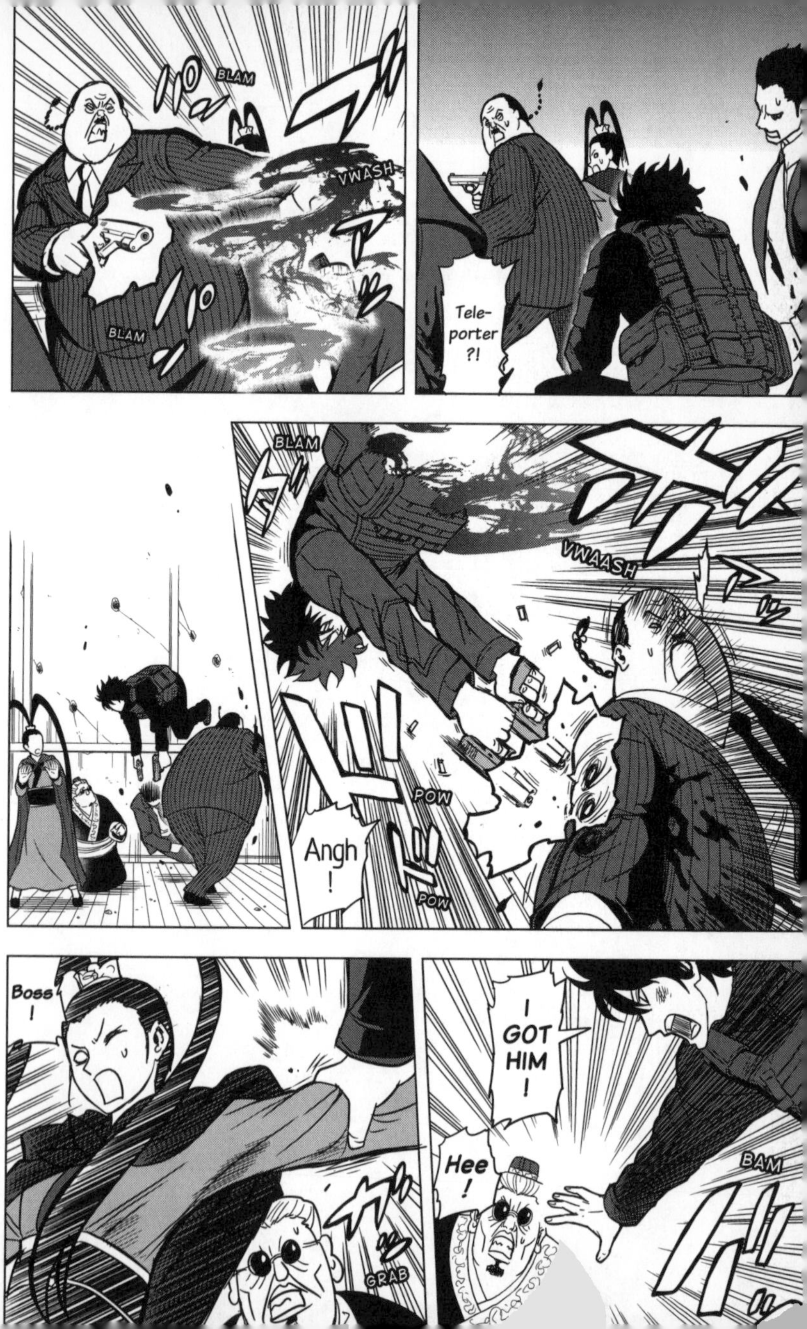
Tele-
porter
?!
BLAM
VWASH
BLAM
BLAM
VWAASH
POW
Angh
!
POW
I GOT HIM!
BAM
Hee!
Boss!
GRAB

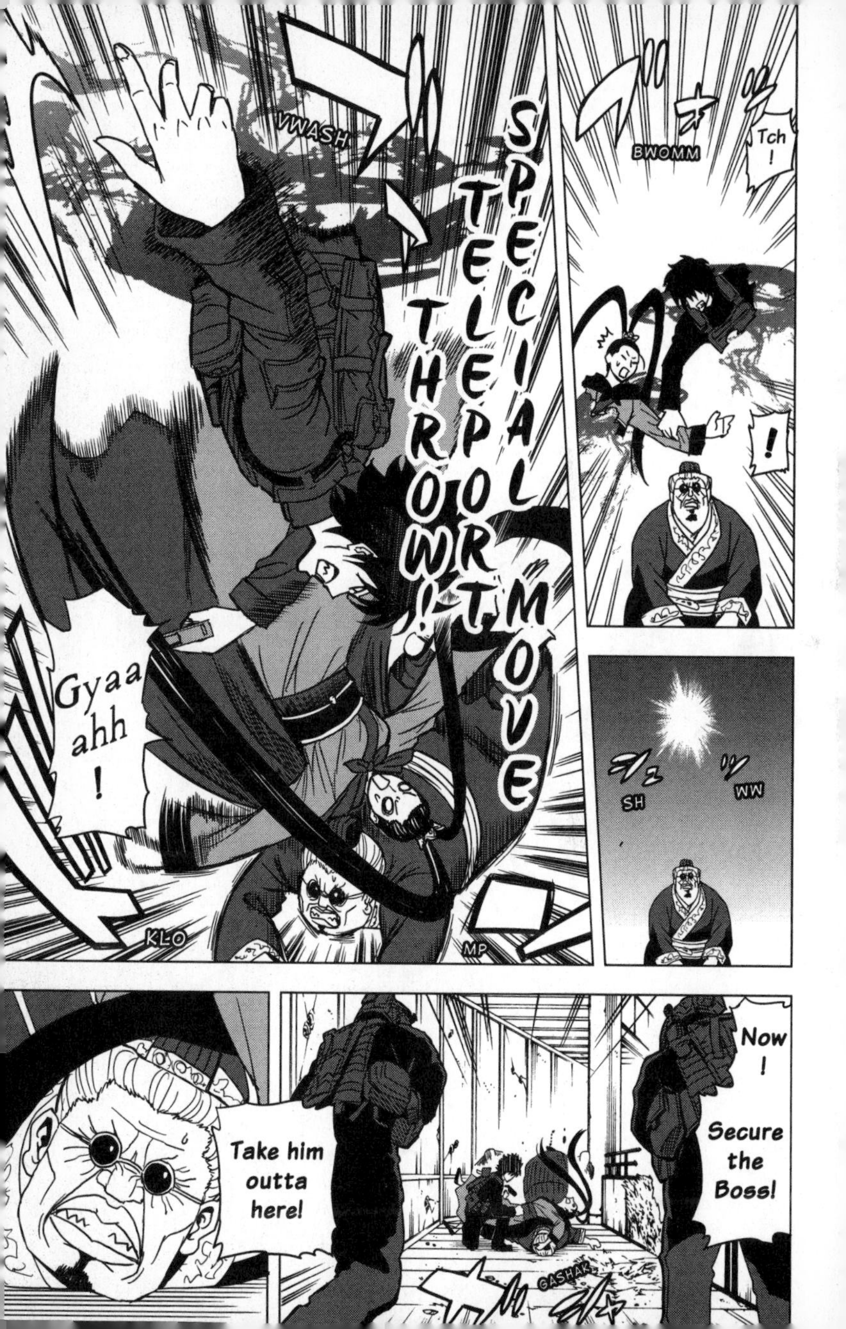
BWOMM
Tch!
!
SH WW
VWASH
SPECIAL MOVE
TELEPORT
THROW!
Gyaa ahh!
KLO MP
Now!
Secure the Boss!
GASHAK
Take him outta here!

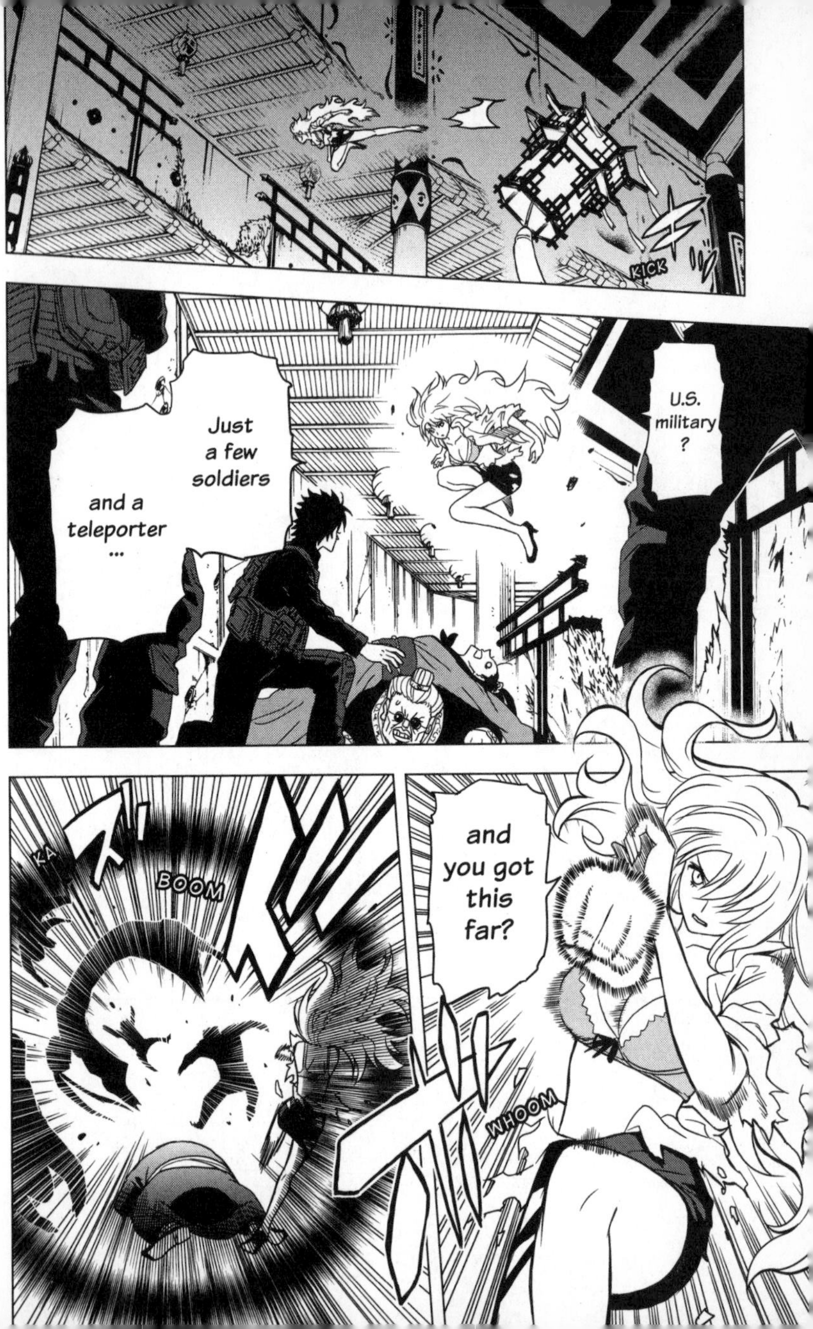
KICK
U.S. military ?
Just a few soldiers
and a teleporter ...
and you got this far?
WHOOM
KA
BOOM

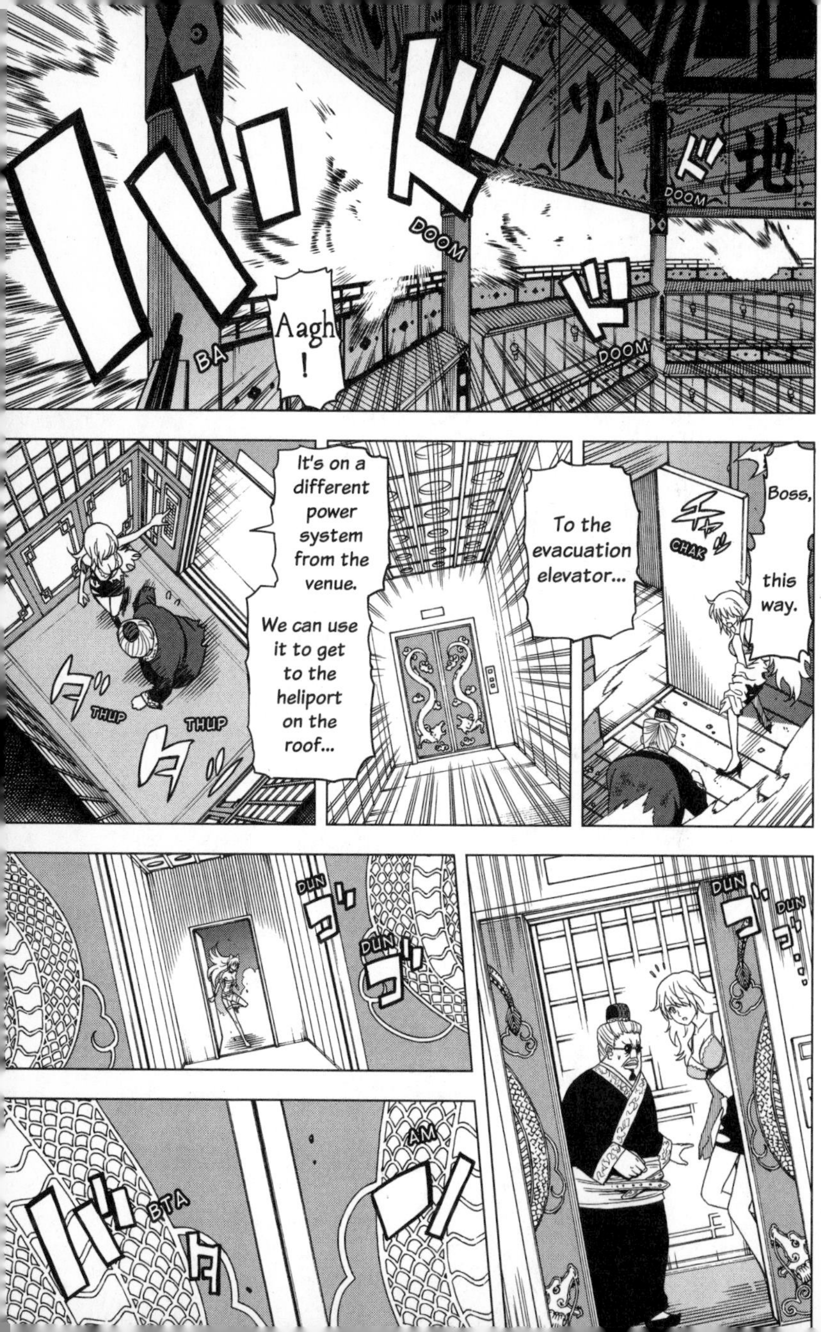

DOOM
DOOM
DOOM
Aagh!
BA
Boss, this way.
CHAK
To the evacuation elevator...
It's on a different power system from the venue.
We can use it to get to the heliport on the roof...
THUP
THUP
DUN
DUN
DUN
DUN
AM
BTA

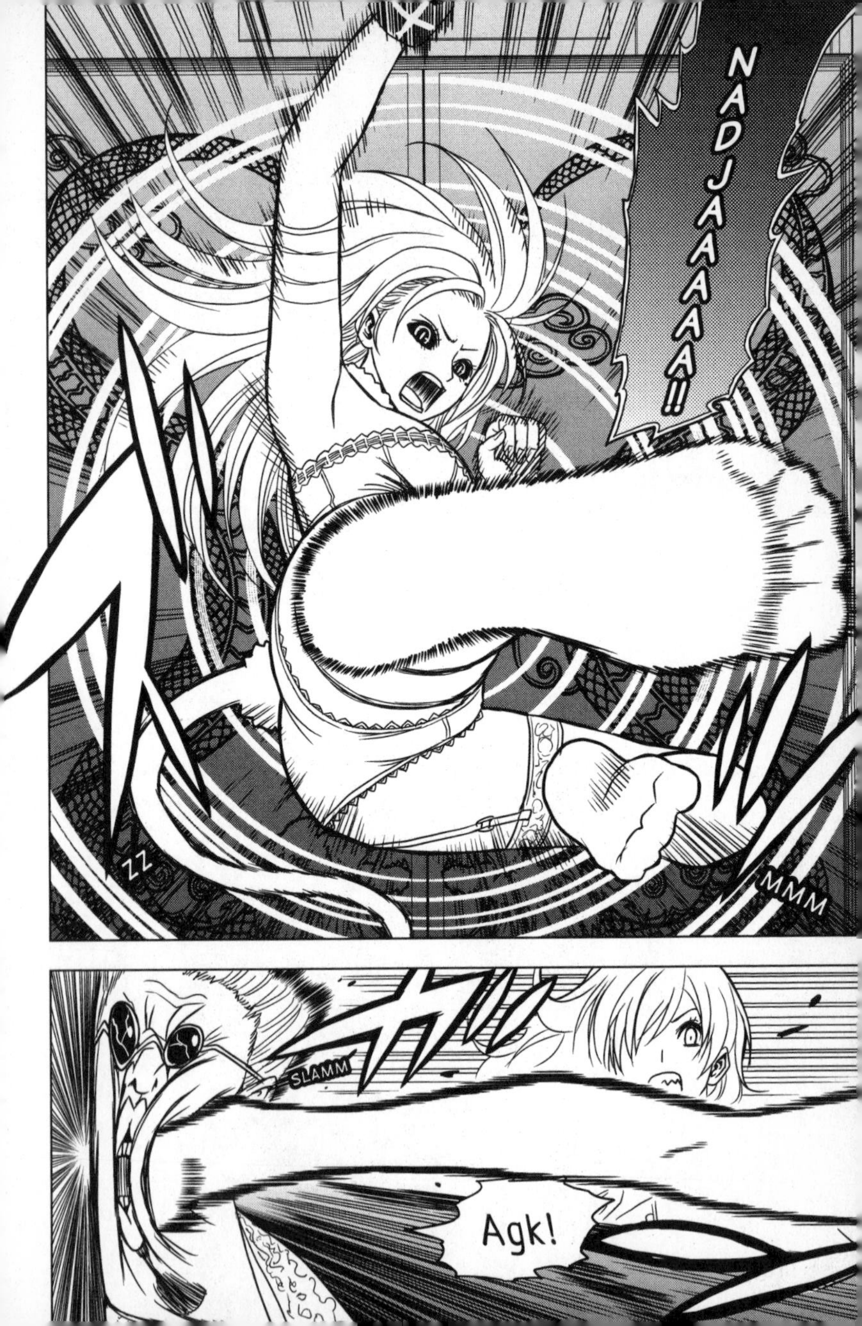
NADJAAAAAAA!!
MMM
ZZ
SLAMM
Agk!

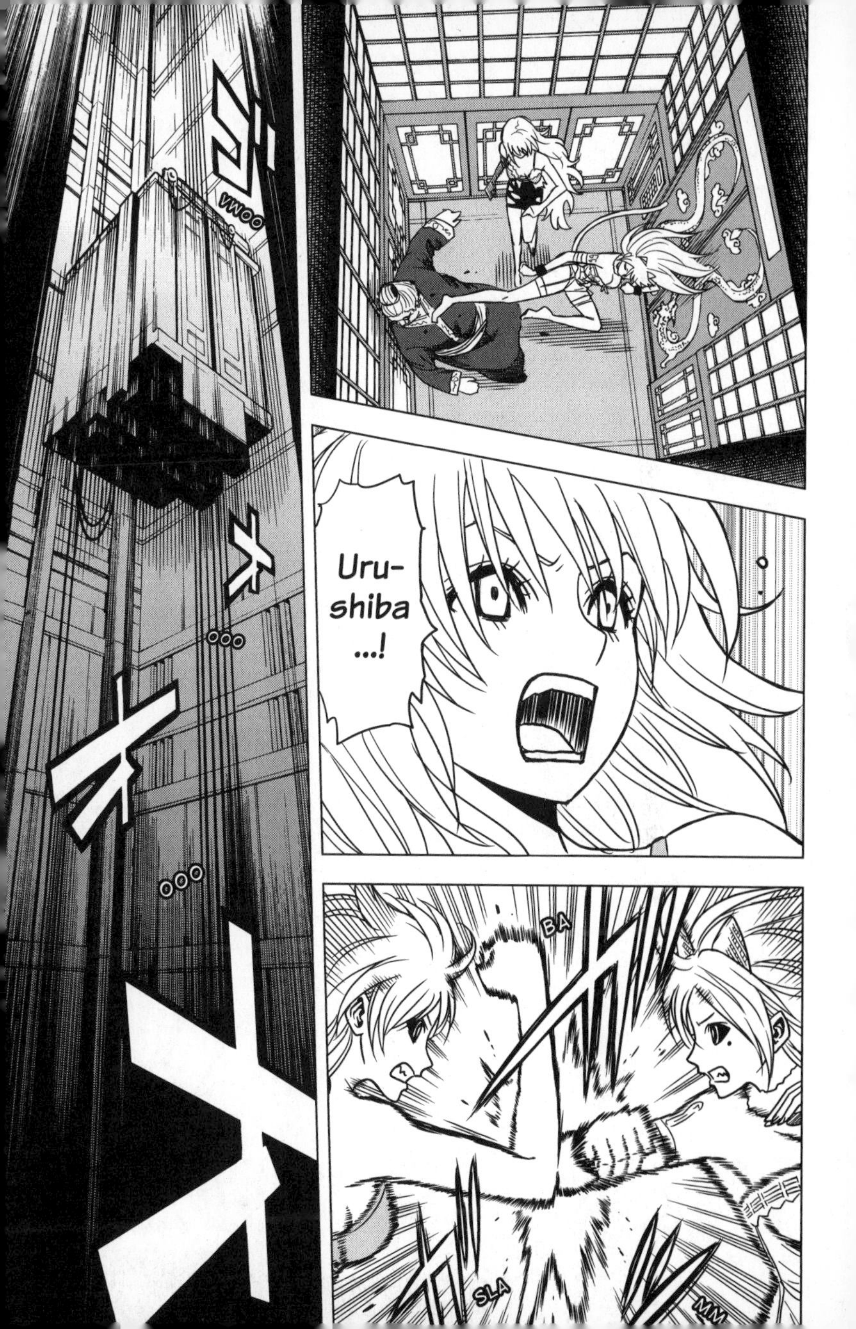
Uru-
shiba
...!
BA
SLA
MM
VWOO
ooo
ooo

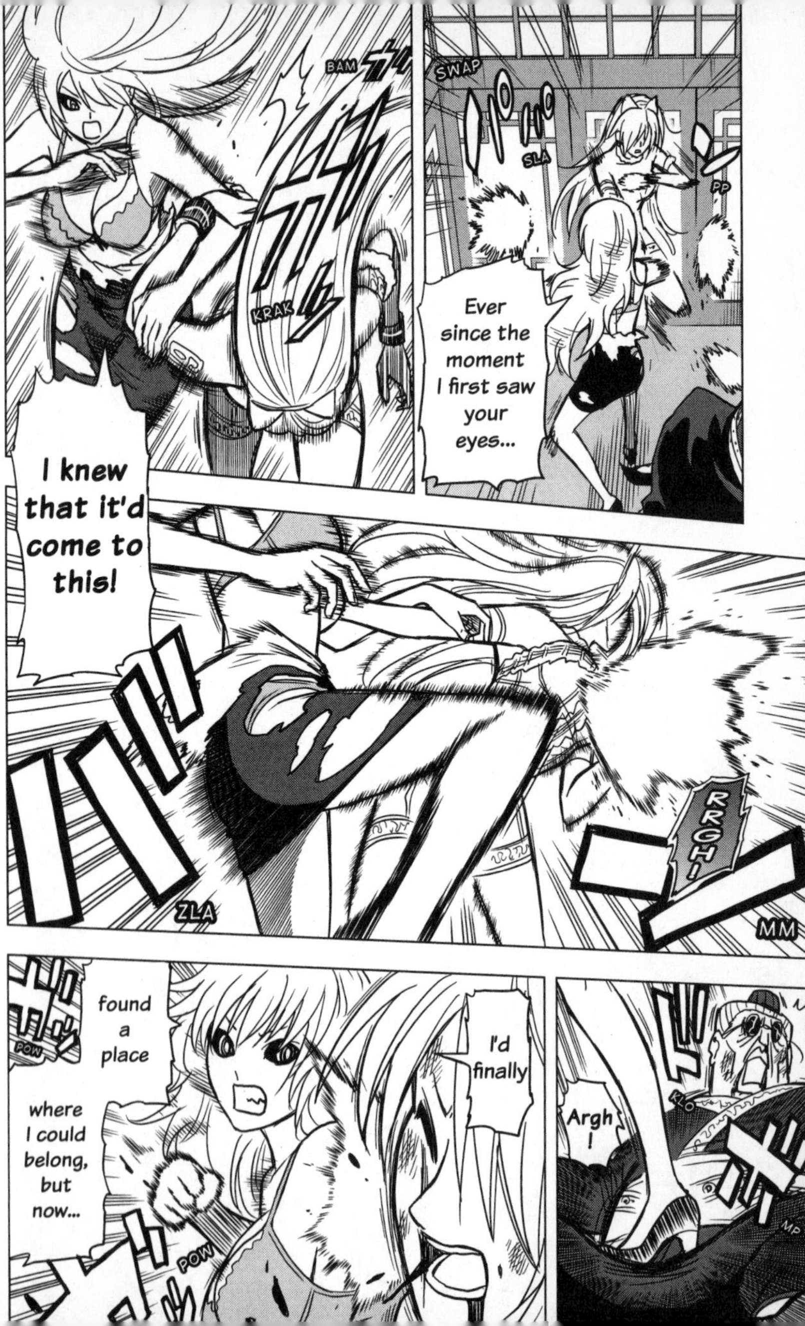
SWAP
SLA
PP
Ever since the moment I first saw your eyes...
BAM
KRAK
I knew that it'd come to this!
RRGH!
MM
ZLA
KLO
Argh!
MP
I'd finally
found a place
POW
where I could belong, but now...
POW

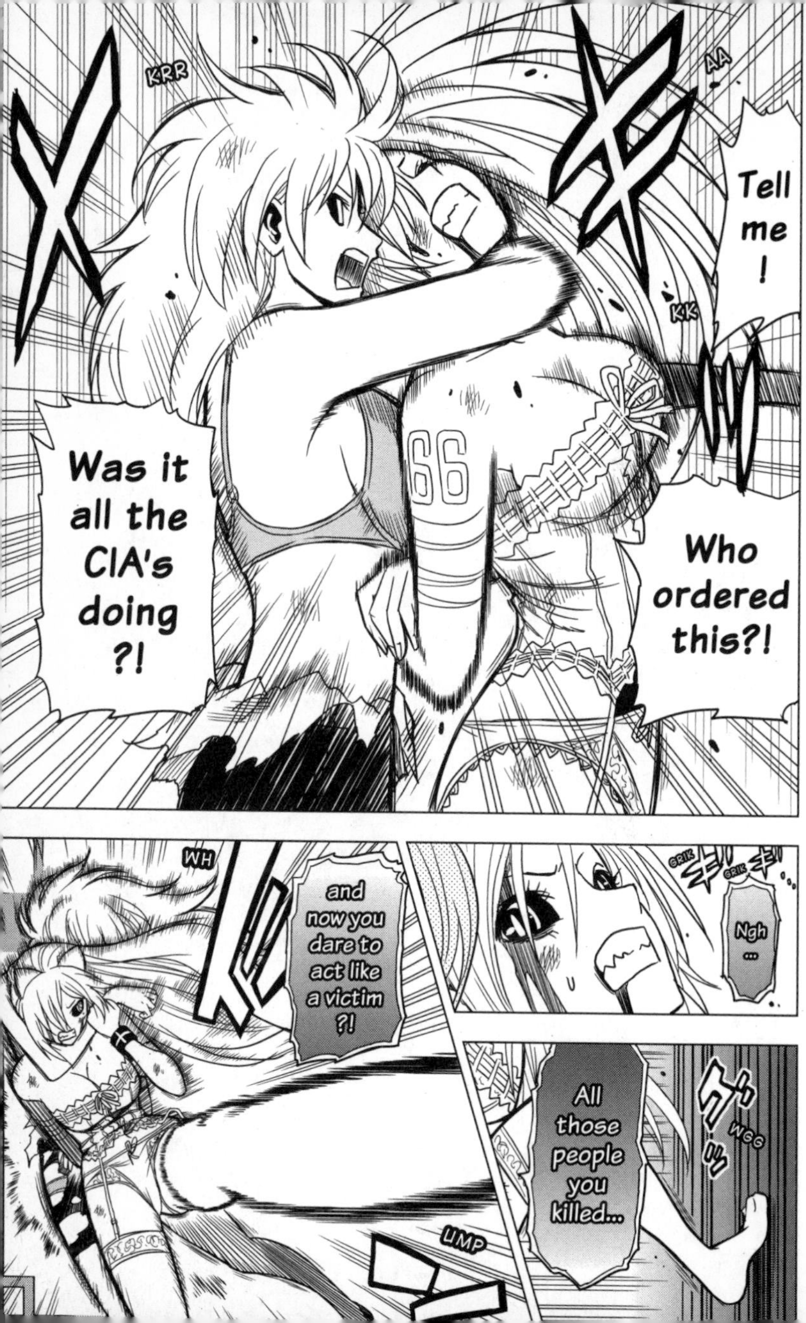
AA
Tell me
!
KK
Who ordered this?!
KRR
Was it all the CIA's doing
?!
GRIK
GRIK
Ngh
...
WGG
All those people you killed...
WH
and now you dare to act like a victim
?!
UMP

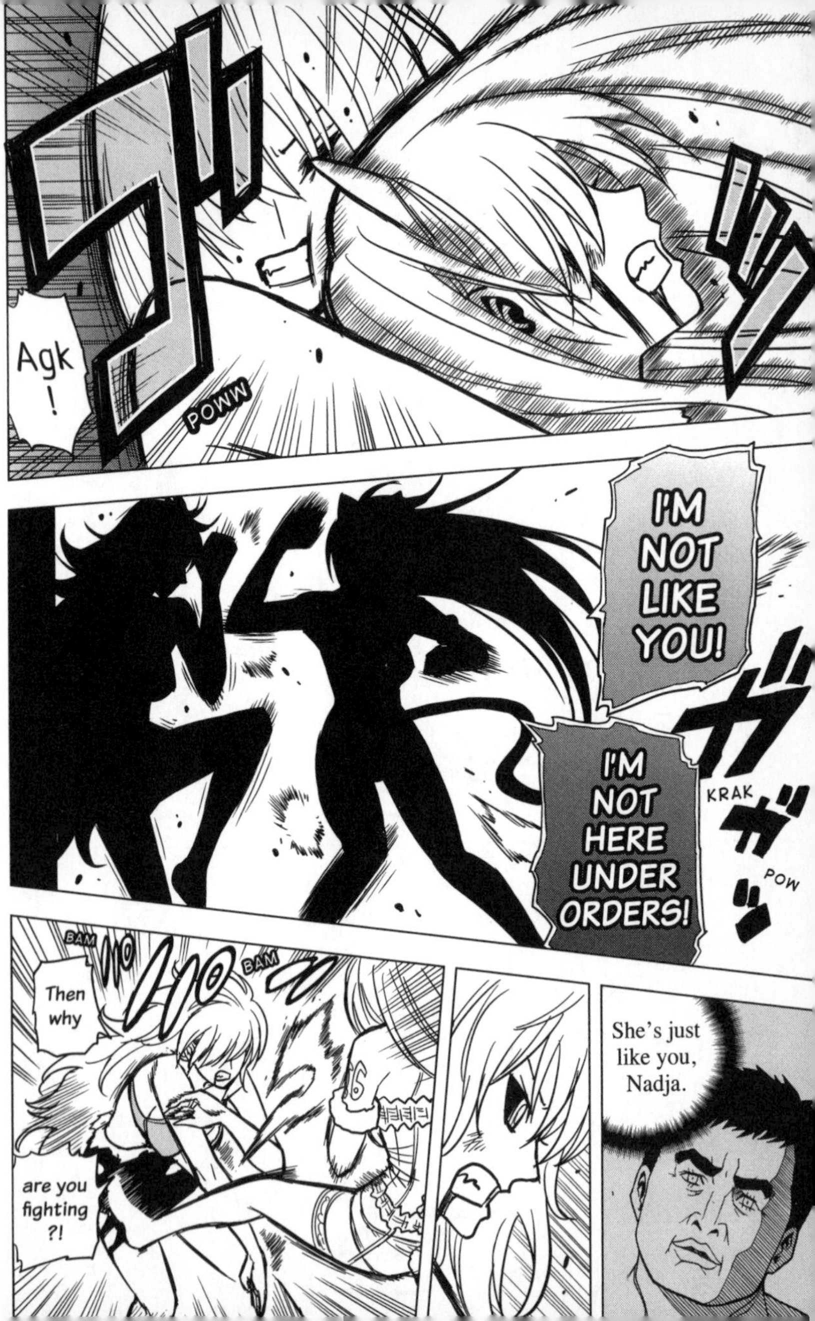
Agk
!
POWW
I'M NOT LIKE YOU!
I'M NOT HERE UNDER ORDERS!
KRAK
POW
She's just like you, Nadja.
BAM
BAM
Then why
are you fighting ?!

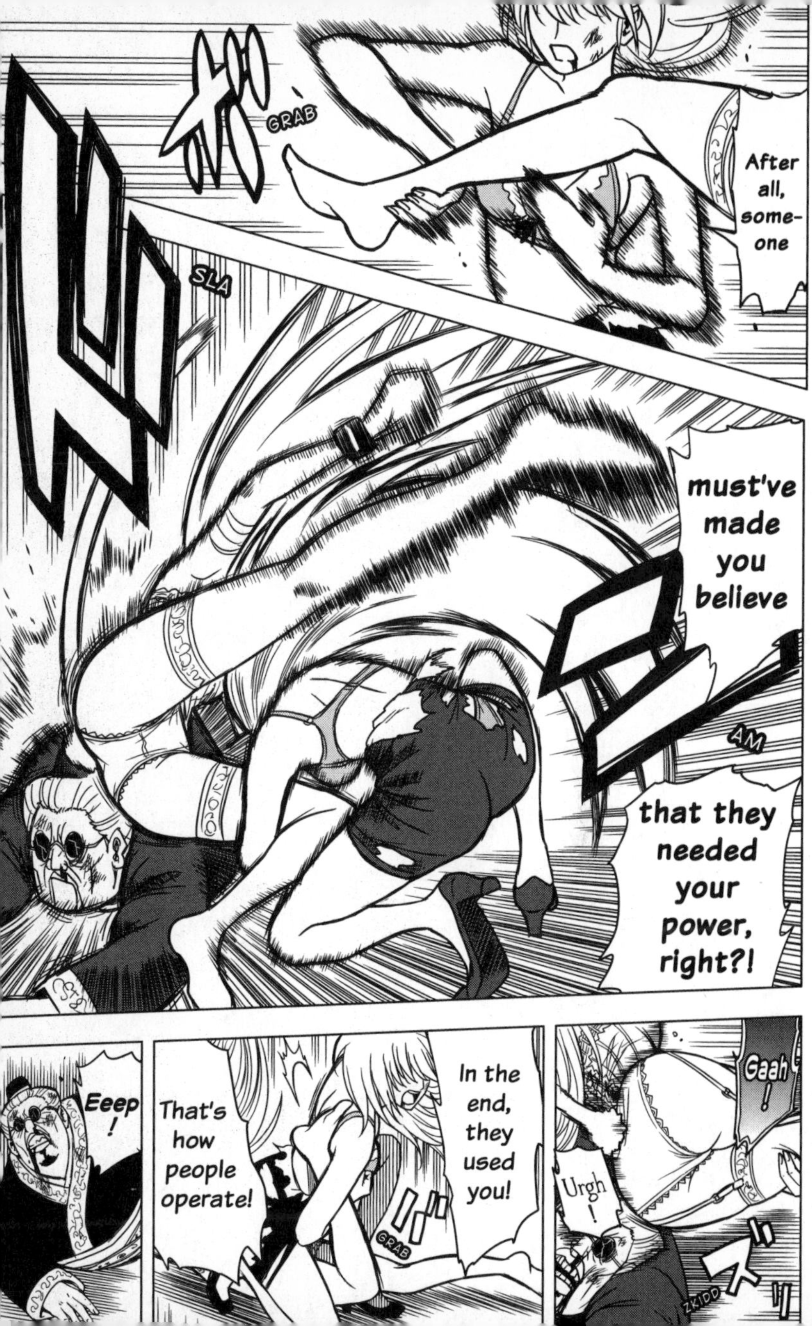
After all, someone
GRAB
must've made you believe
that they needed your power, right?!
AM
SLA
Gaah!
Urgh!
ZKIDD
In the end, they used you!
That's how people operate!
GRAB
Eeep!

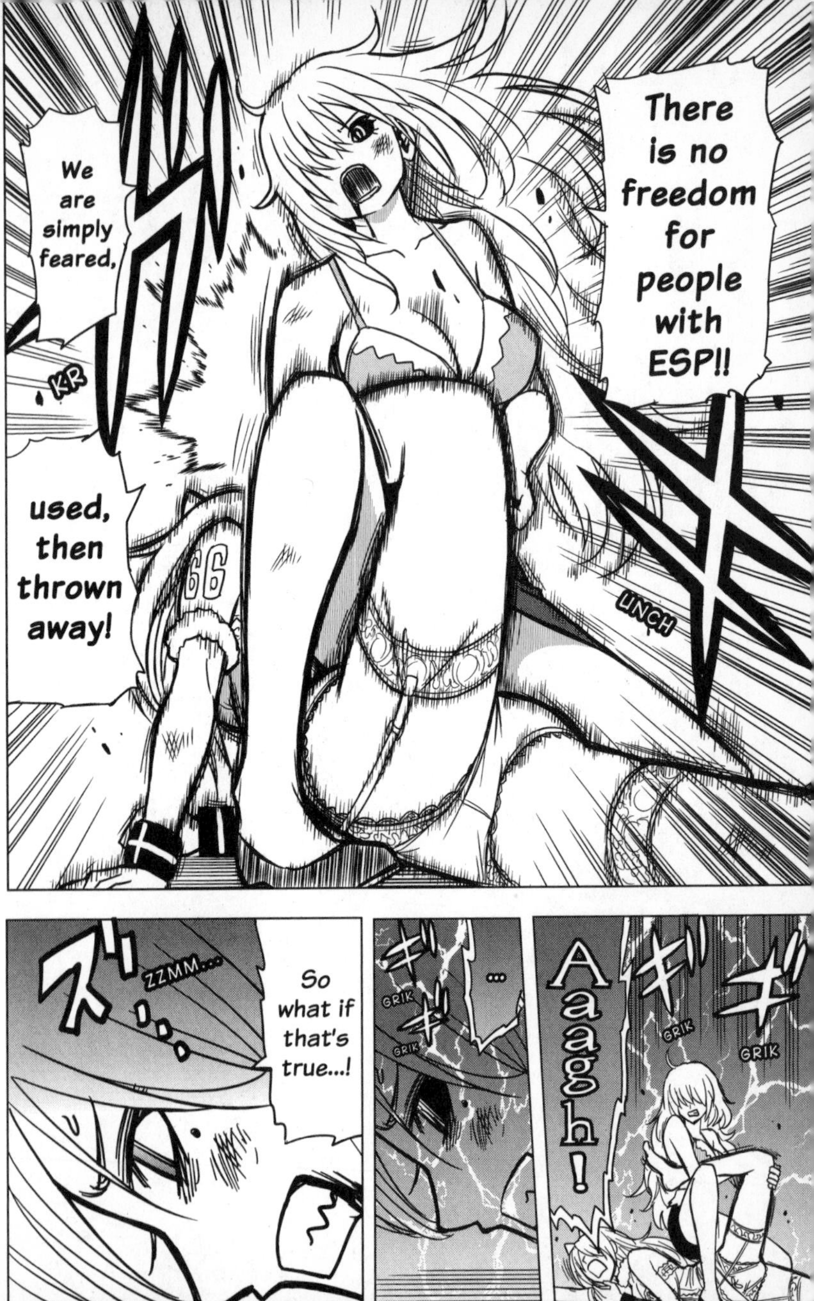
There is no freedom for people with ESP!!
We are simply feared,
KR
used, then thrown away!
LINCH
Aaagh!
GRIK
GRIK
...
GRIK
GRIK
ZZMM...
So what if that's true...!

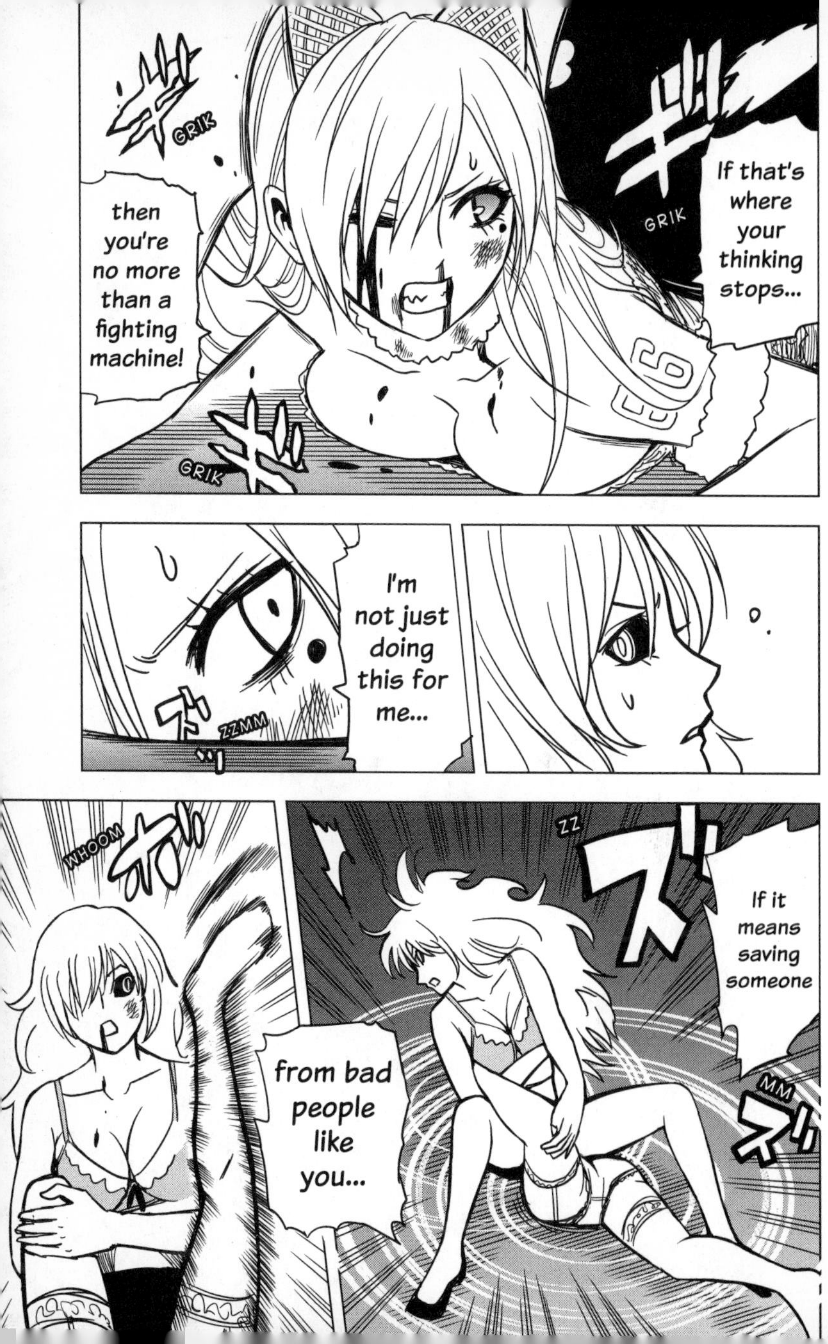
GRIK
If that's where your thinking stops...
GRIK
then you're no more than a fighting machine!
GRIK
I'm not just doing this for me...
ZZMM
ZZ
If it means saving someone
MM
WHOOM
from bad people like you...

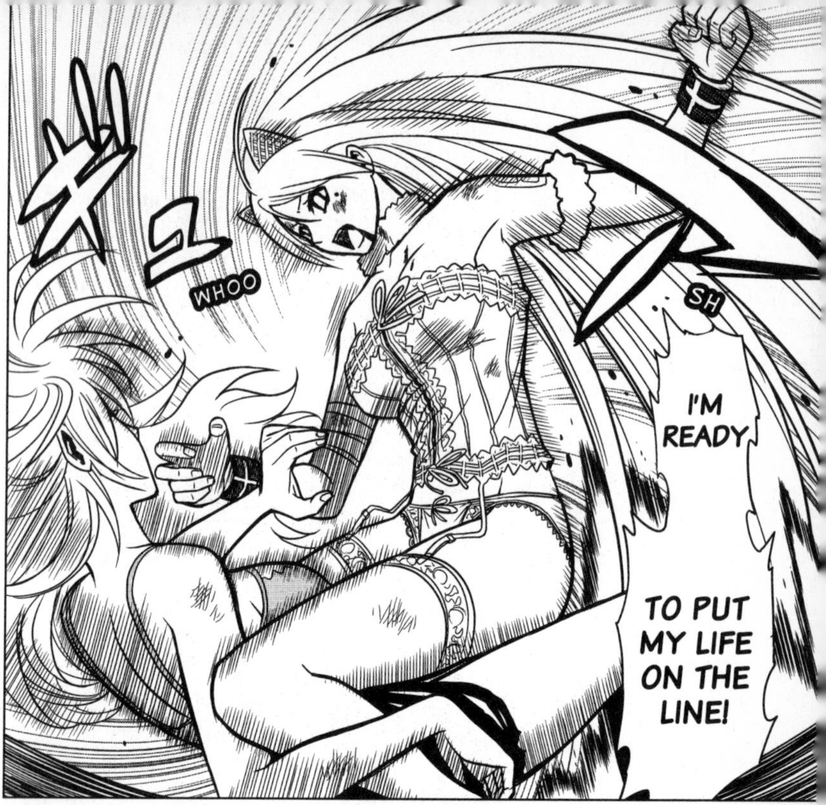
SH
I'M READY
TO PUT MY LIFE ON THE LINE!
WHOO

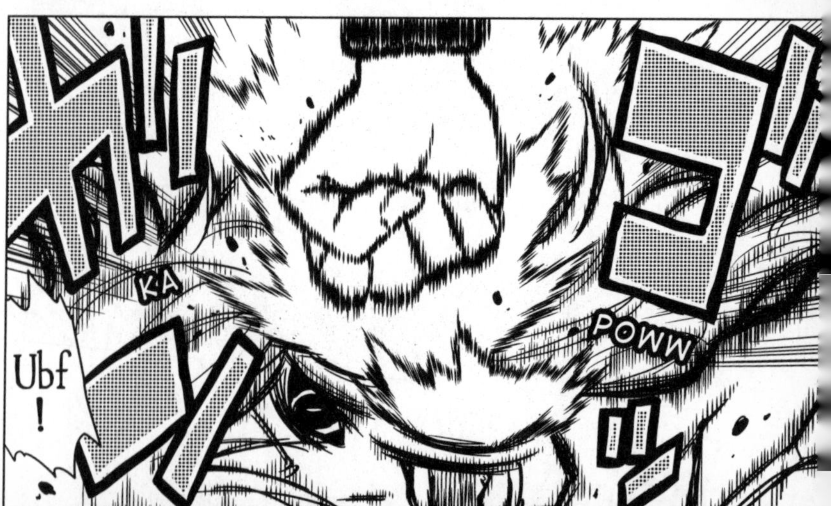
POWW
KA
Ubf!

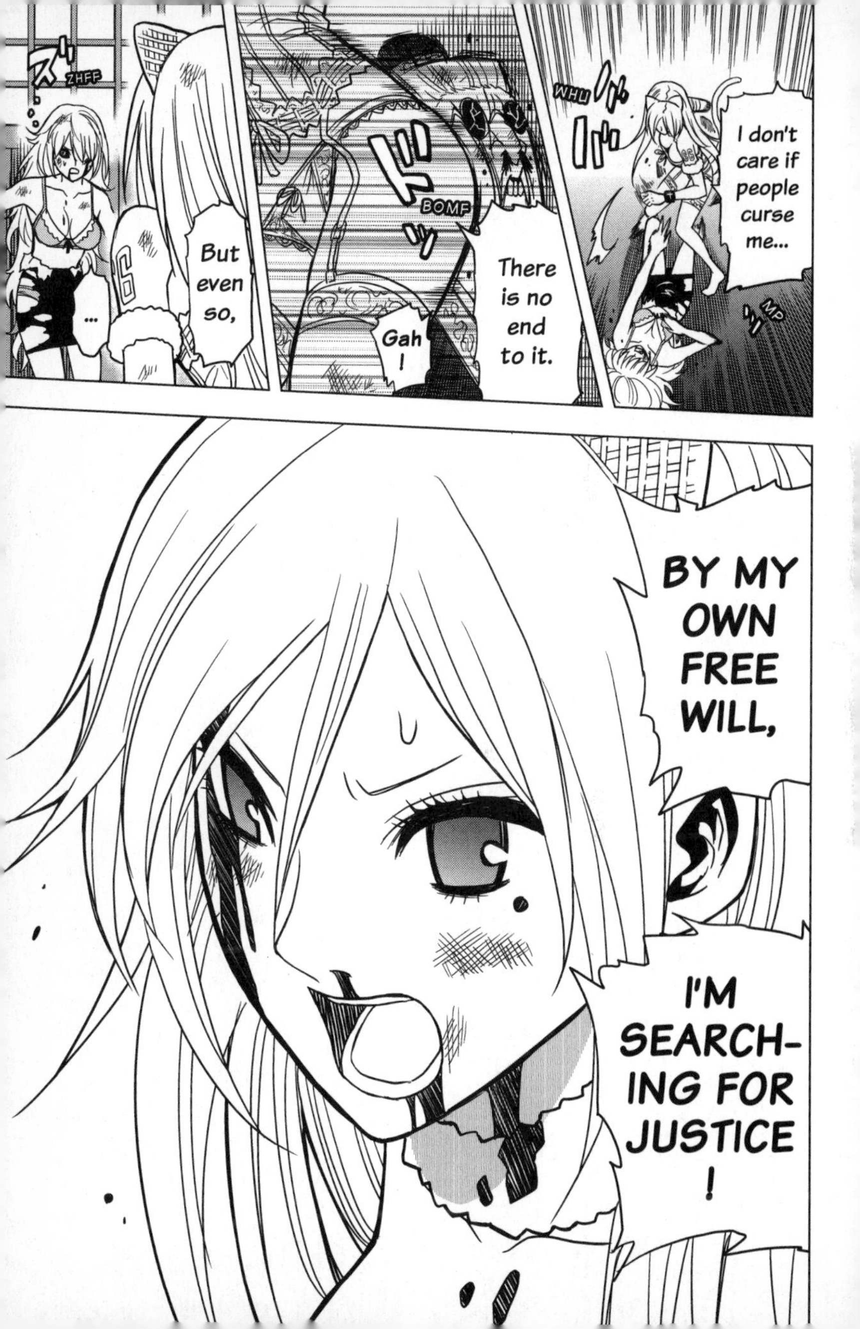
WHU
I don't care if people curse me...
MP
BOMF
There is no end to it.
Gah!
ZHFF
But even so,
...
BY MY OWN FREE WILL,
I'M SEARCHING FOR JUSTICE!

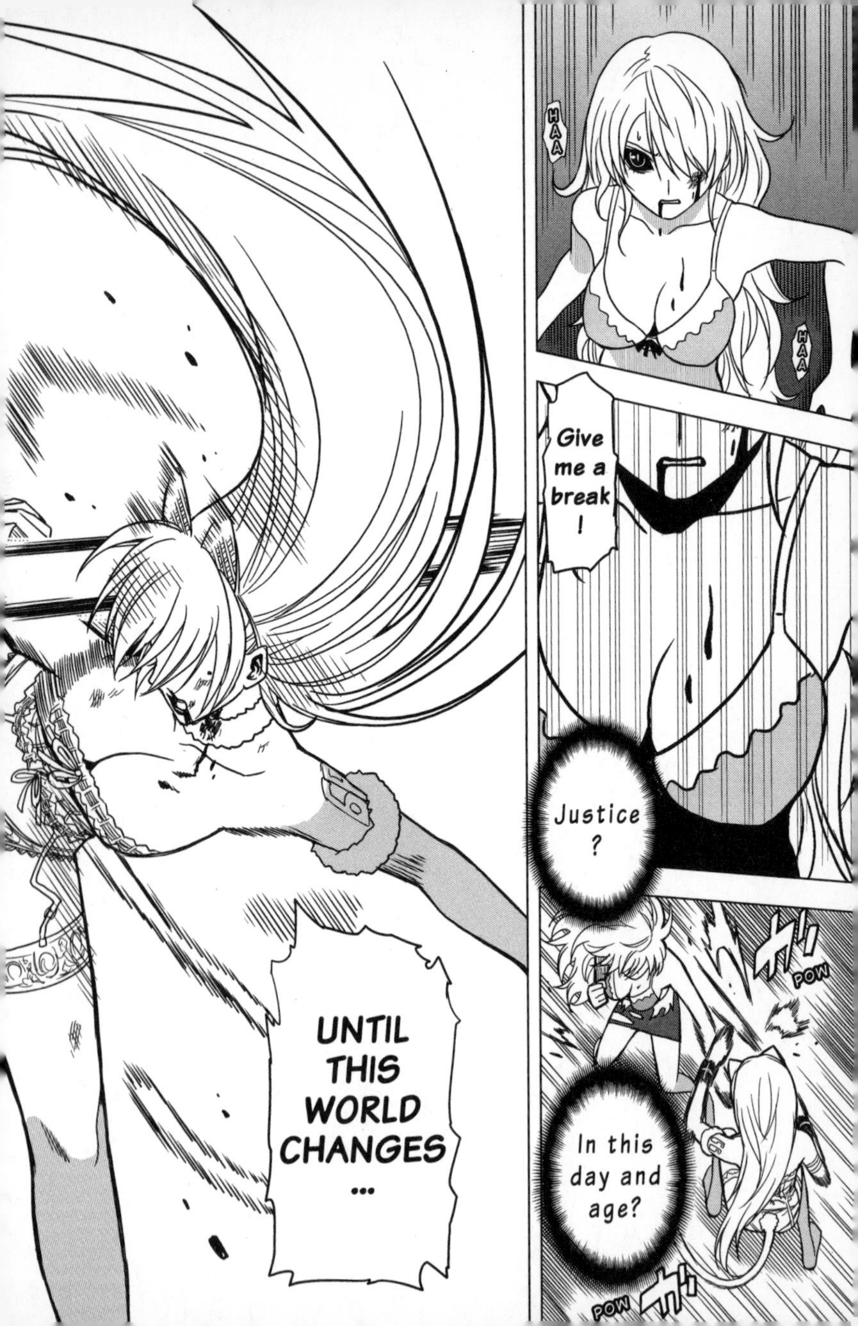
HAA
HAA
Give me a break!
Justice?
POW
In this day and age?
POW
UNTIL THIS WORLD CHANGES...

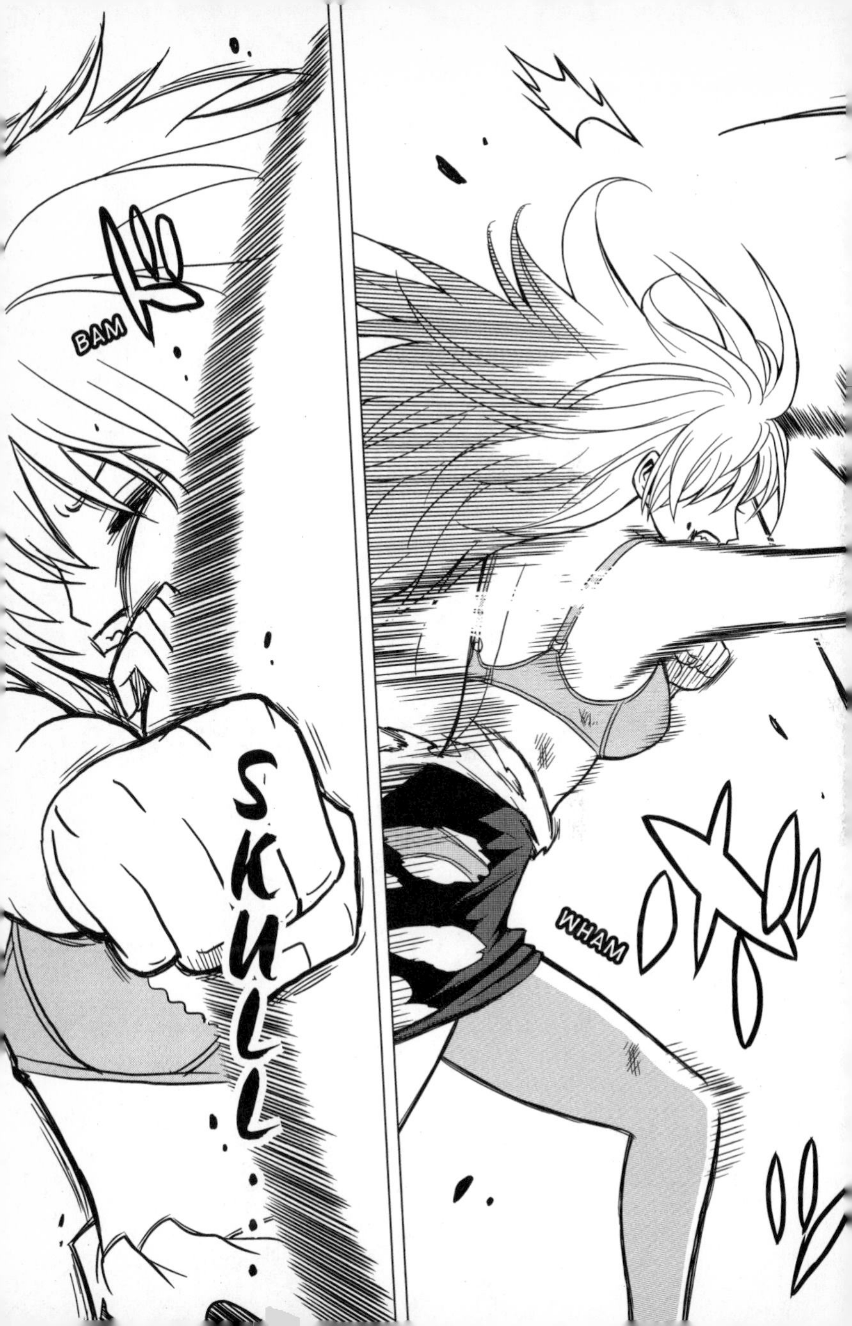
WHAM
BAM
SKULL

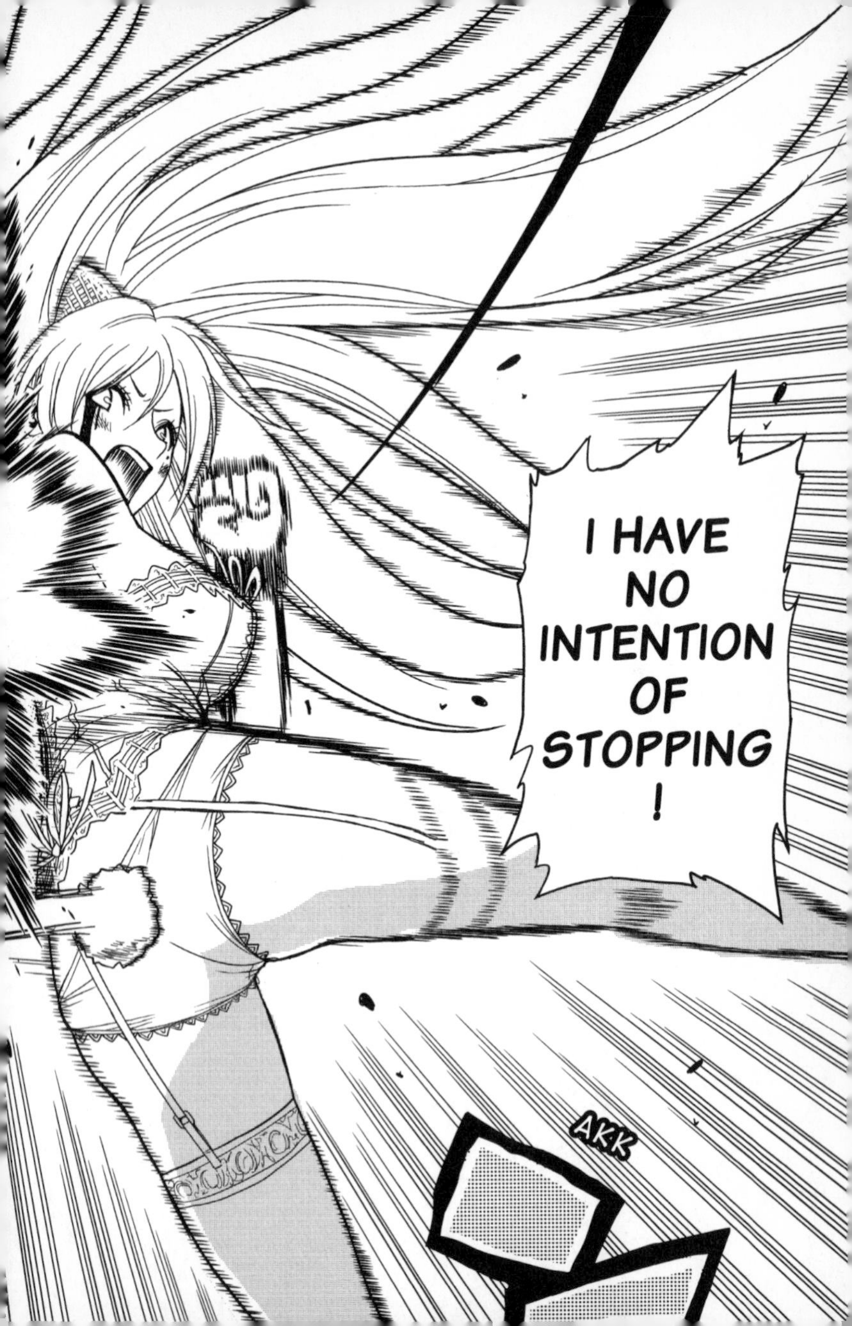
I HAVE NO INTENTION OF STOPPING!
AKK

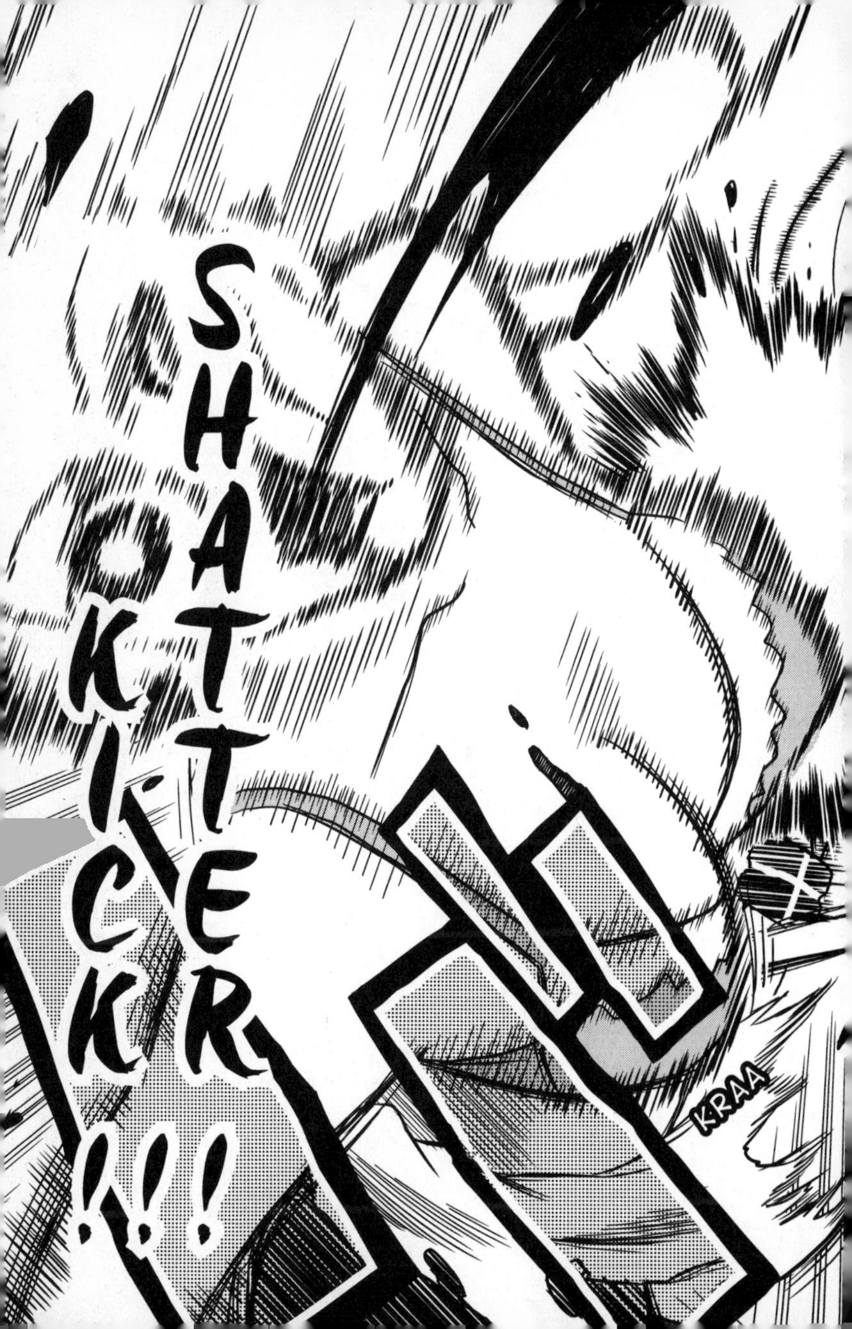
SHATTER
KRAA
CRACK!!!

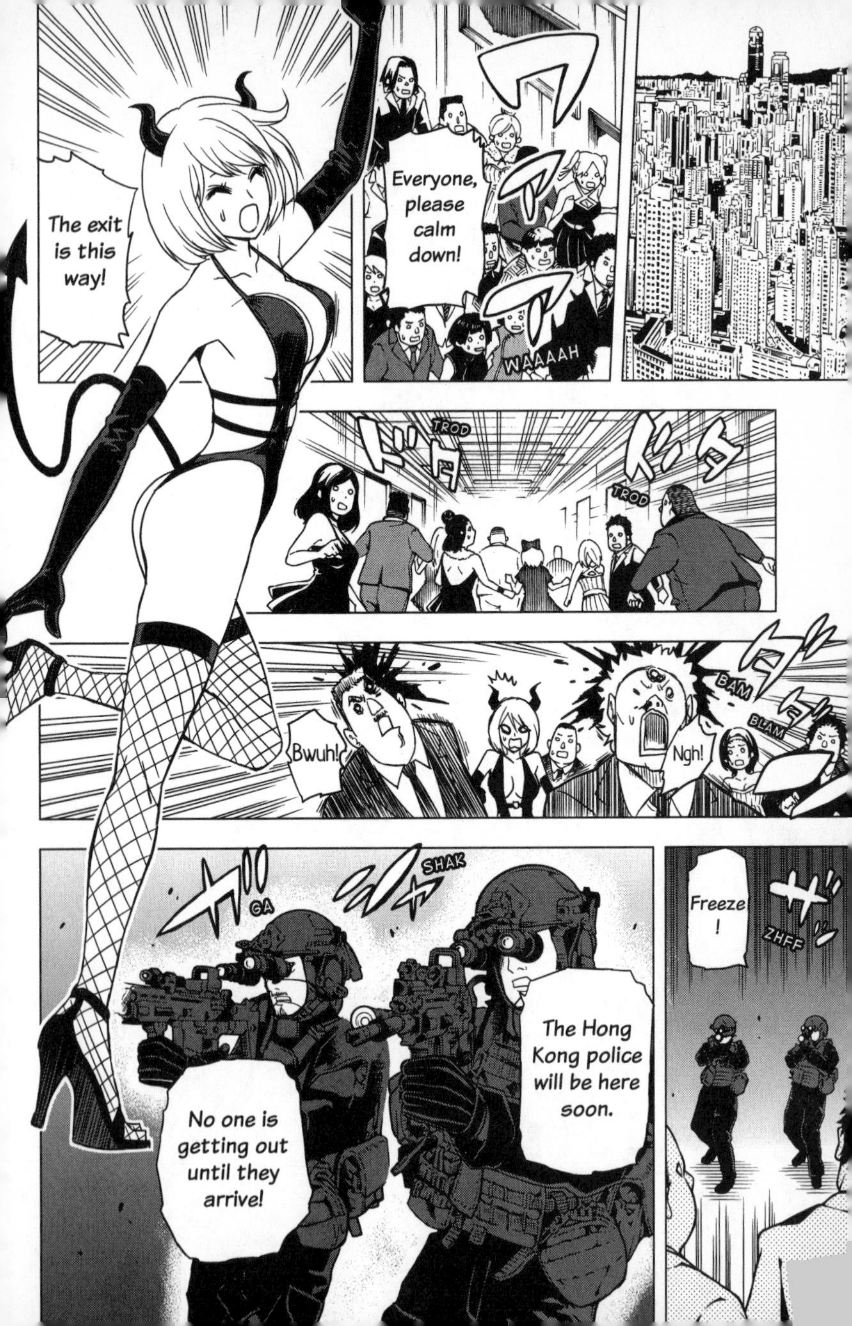
Everyone, please calm down!
WAAAAH
The exit is this way!
TROD
TROD
BAM
BLAM
Ngh!
Bwuh!
Freeze!
ZHFF
SHAK
GA
The Hong Kong police will be here soon.
No one is getting out until they arrive!

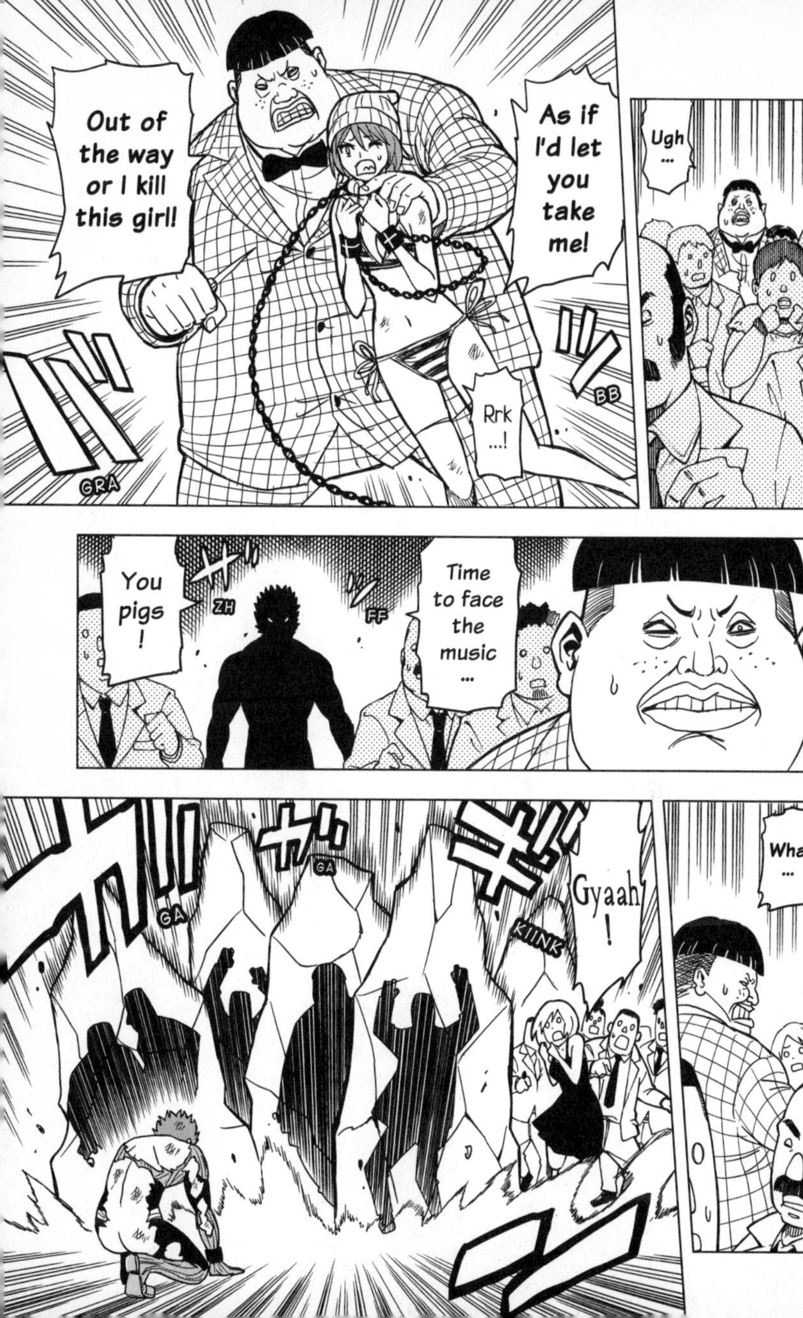
Ugh ...
As if I'd let you take me!
BB
Rrk ...!
Out of the way or I kill this girl!
GRA
Time to face the music ...
FF
ZH
You pigs !
Wha ...
Gyaah !
KIINK
GA
GA

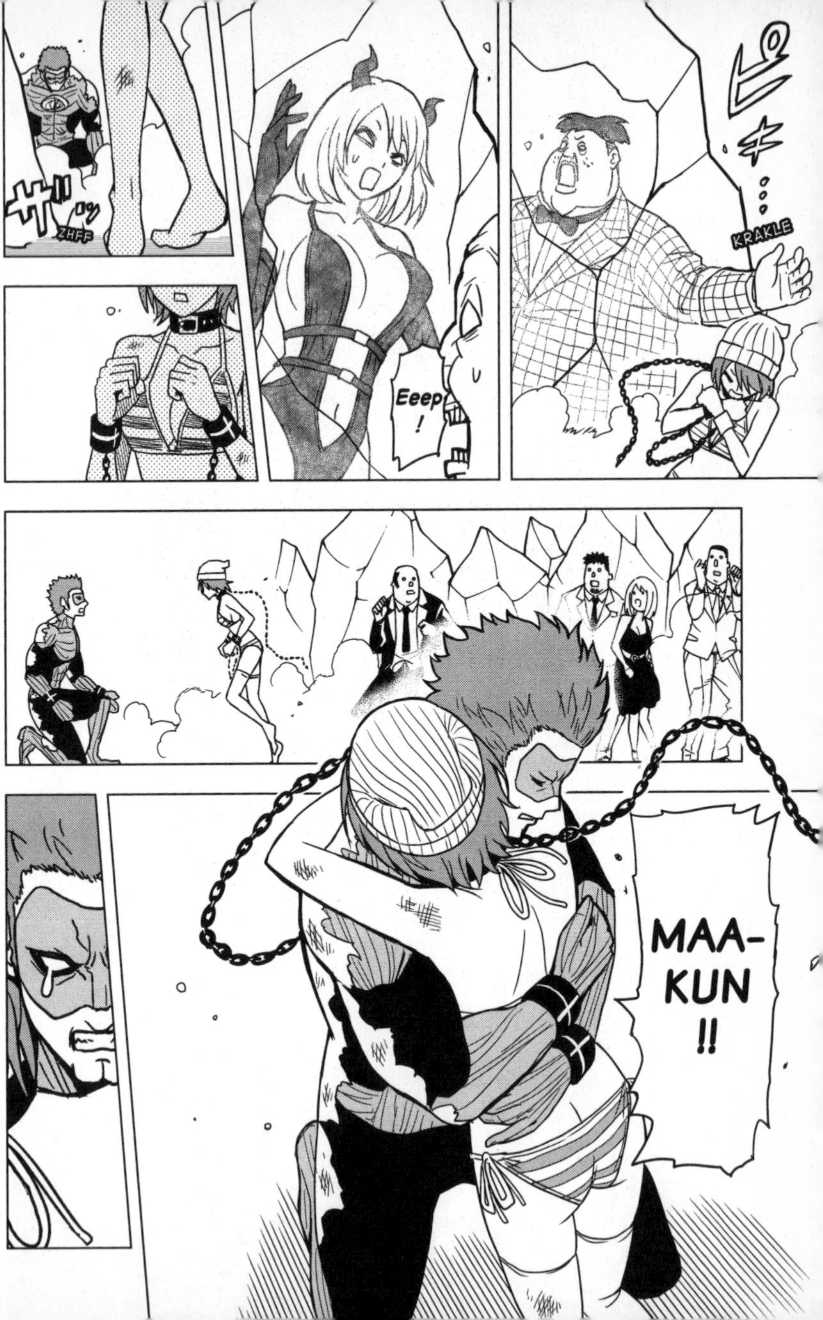
KRAKLE
Eeep!
ZHFF
MAA-KUN!!

You both... have healing powers, right?

You two... Hey!

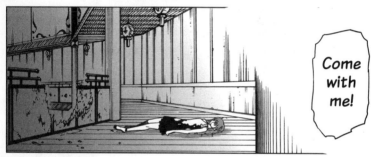

Come with me!

It's an emergency!

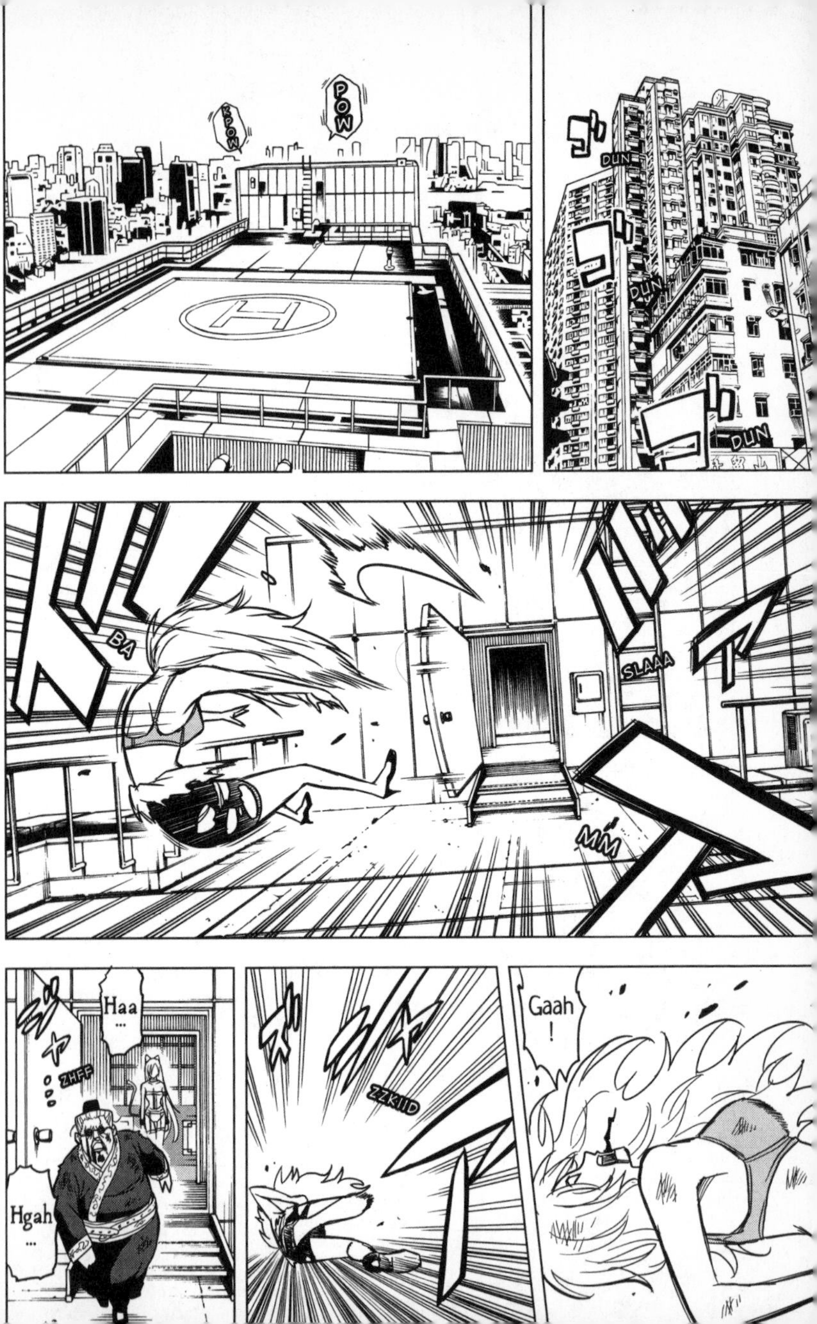
DUN
DUN
DUN
POW
KPOW
SLAAA
BA
MM
Gaah!
ZZKIID
Haa...
ZHFF
Hgah...

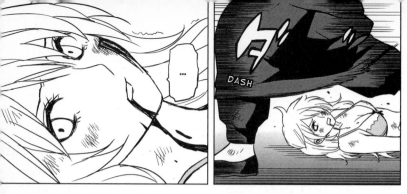

...

DASH

No way.

TWITCH

Aieee!

ZHFF

lose ...?

How did I

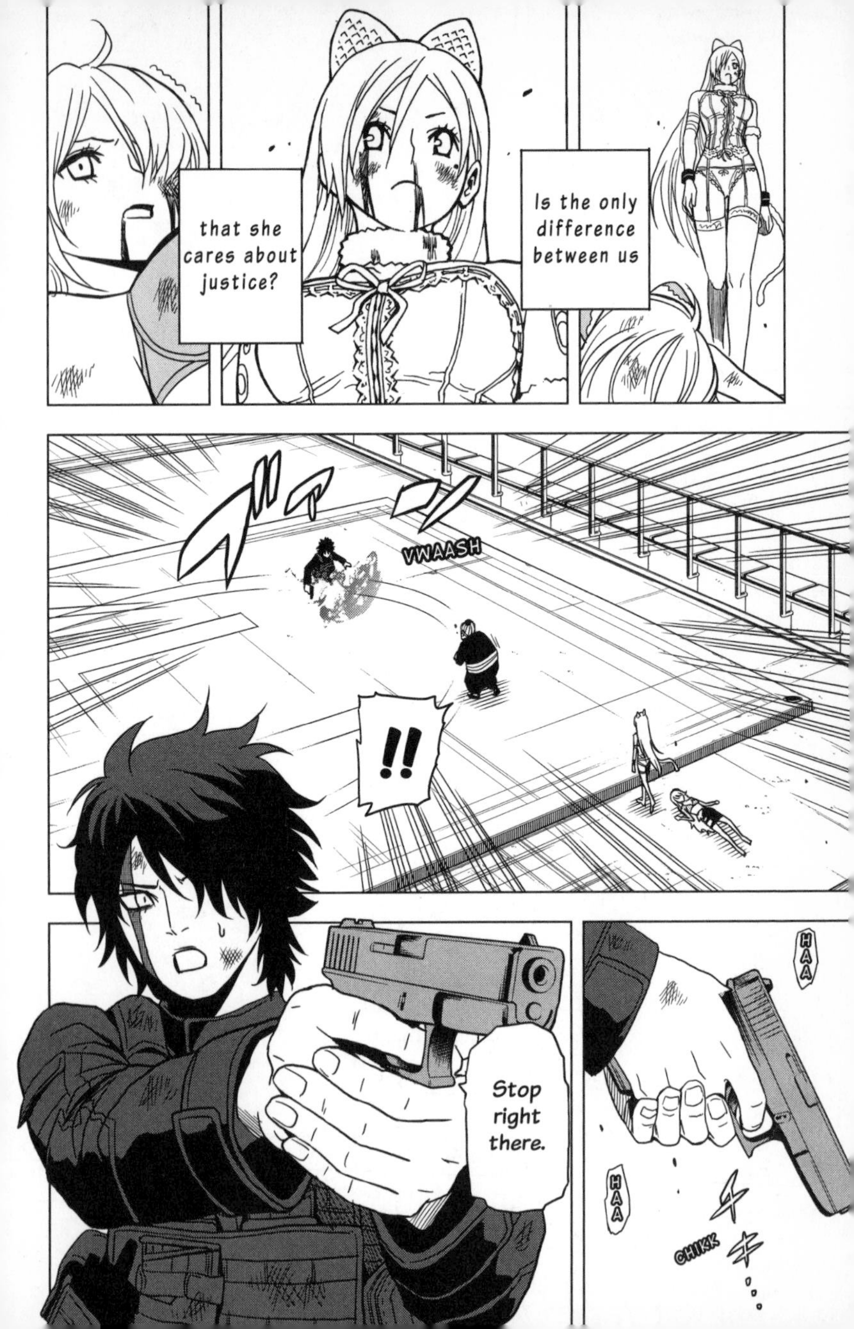
Is the only difference between us
that she cares about justice?
ブァン
VWAASH
!!
HAA
HAA
CHIKK
Stop right there.

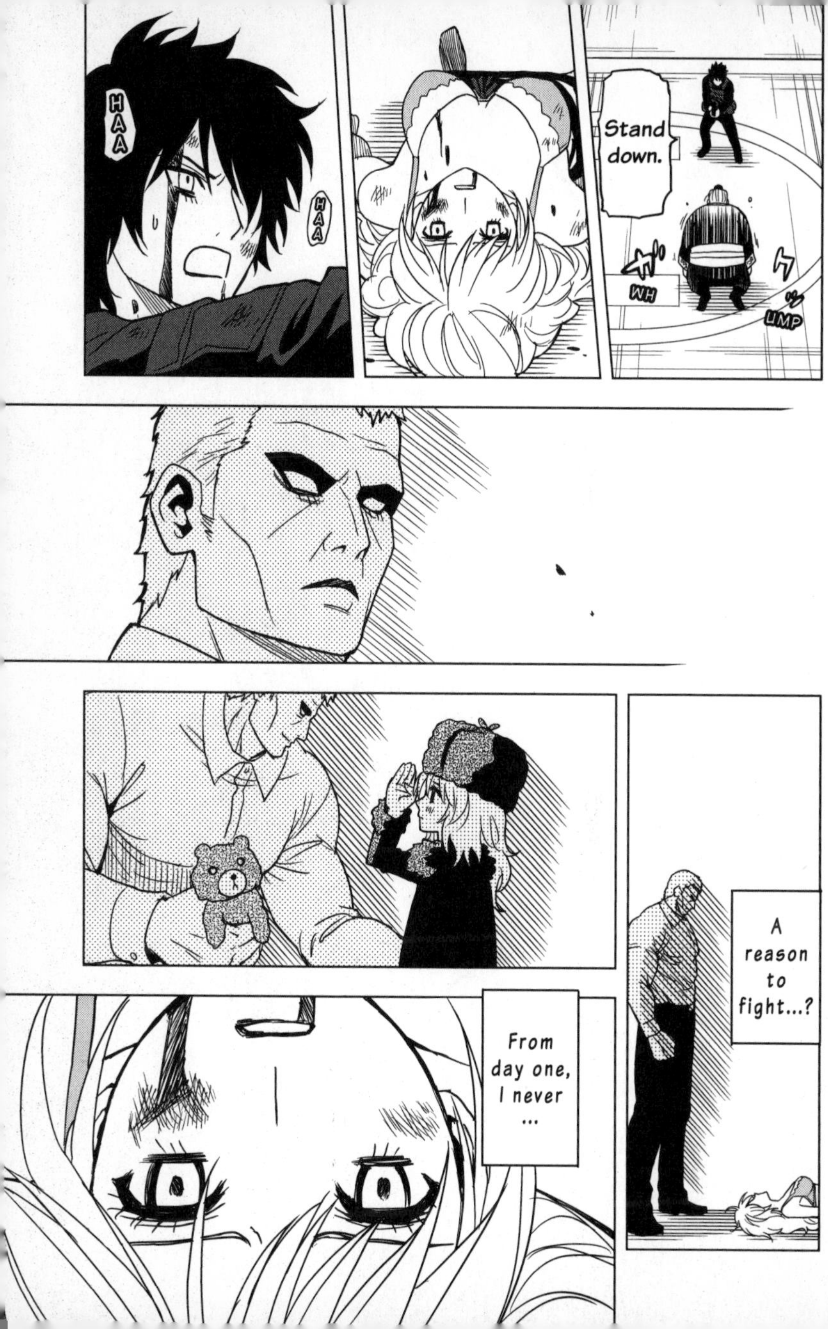

Stand down.
WH
UMP
HAA
HAA
A reason to fight...?
From day one, I never ...

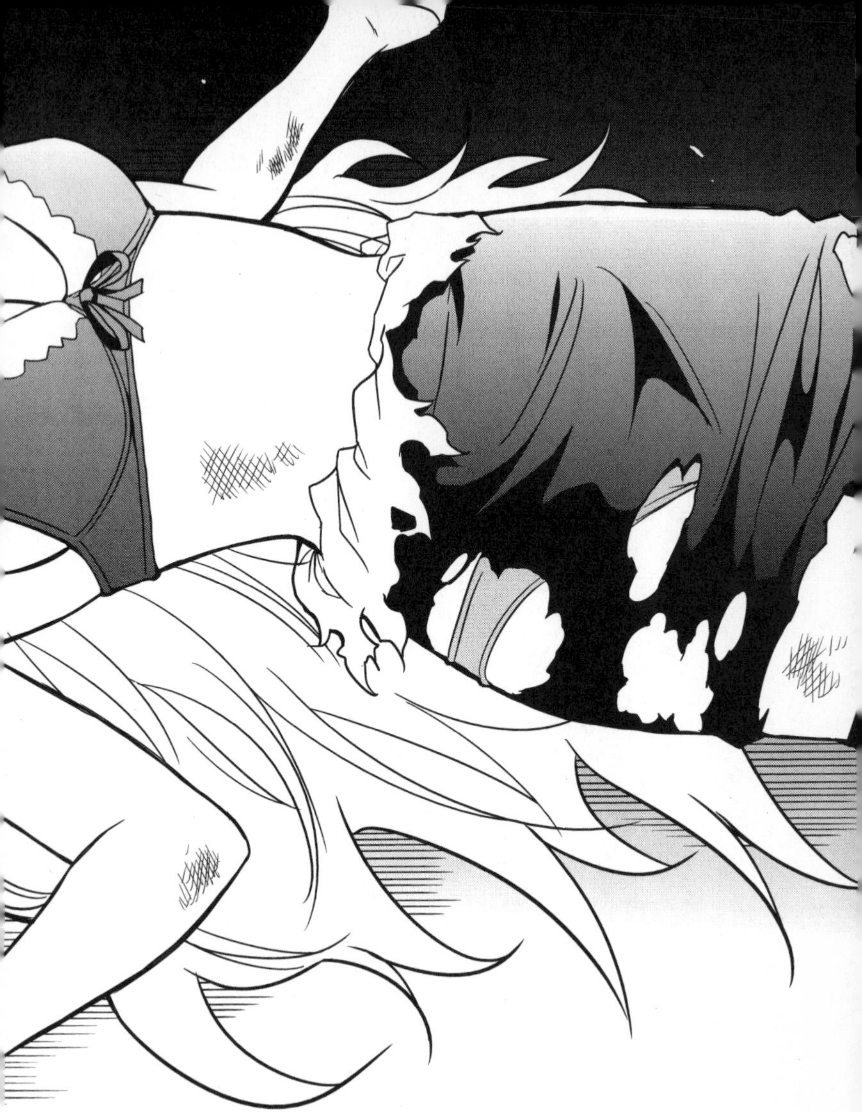

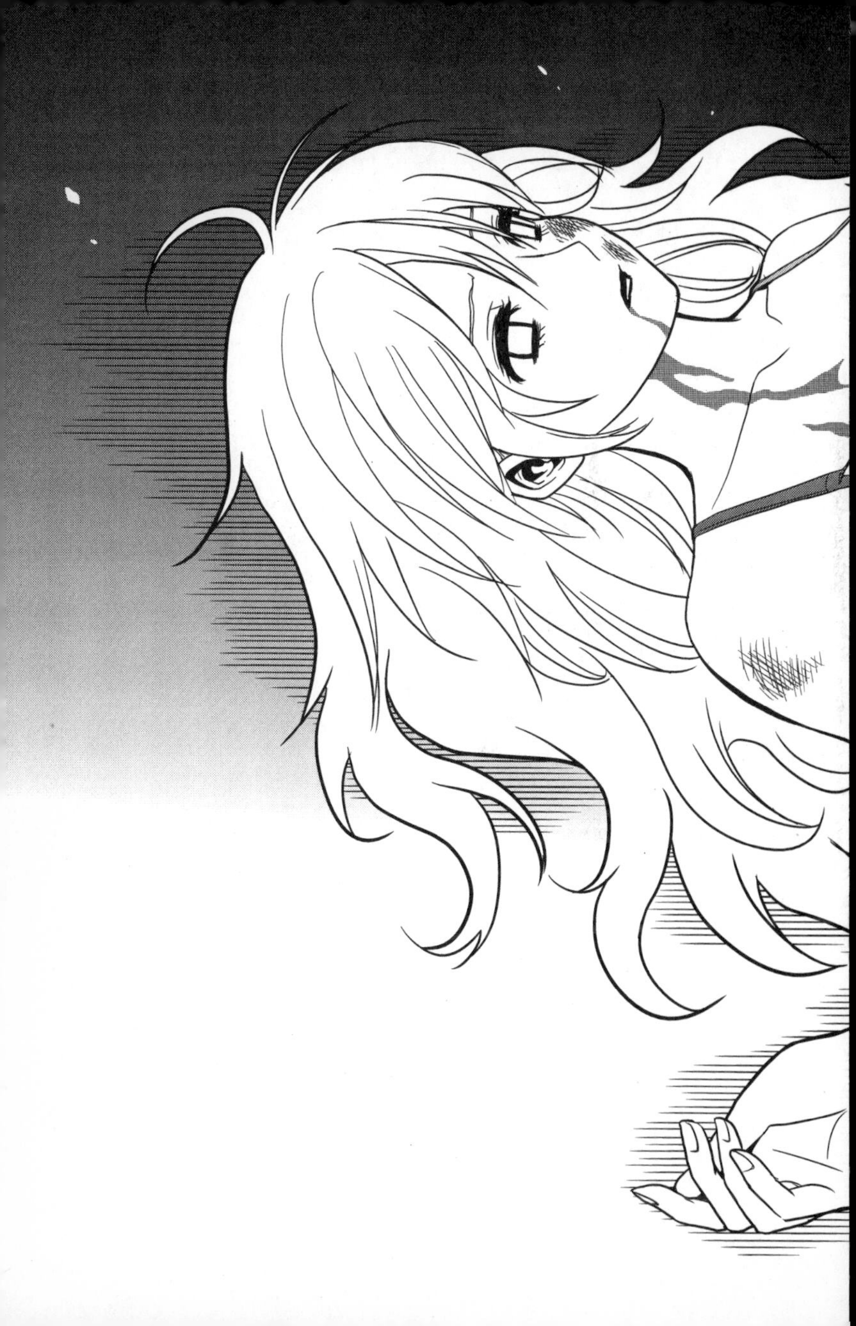

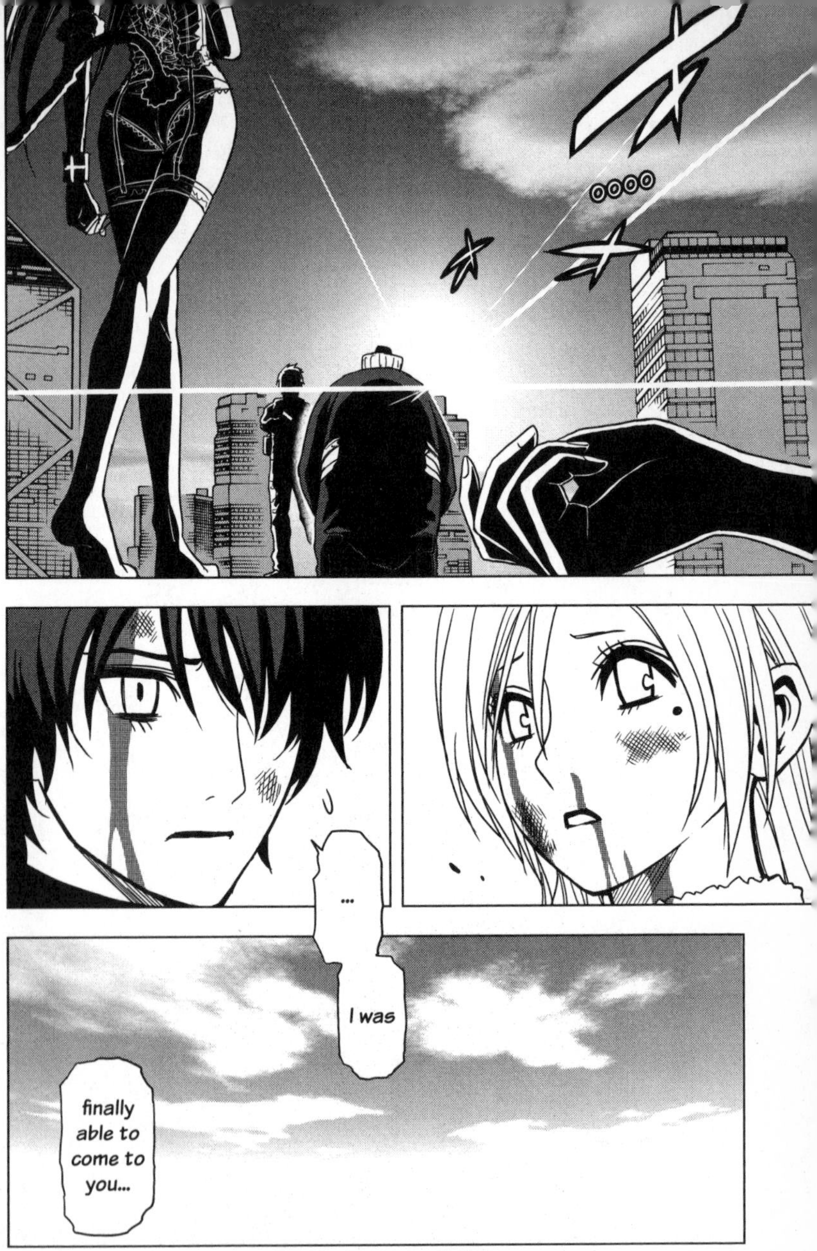
...
I was
finally able to come to you...

SCENE 49 /// END

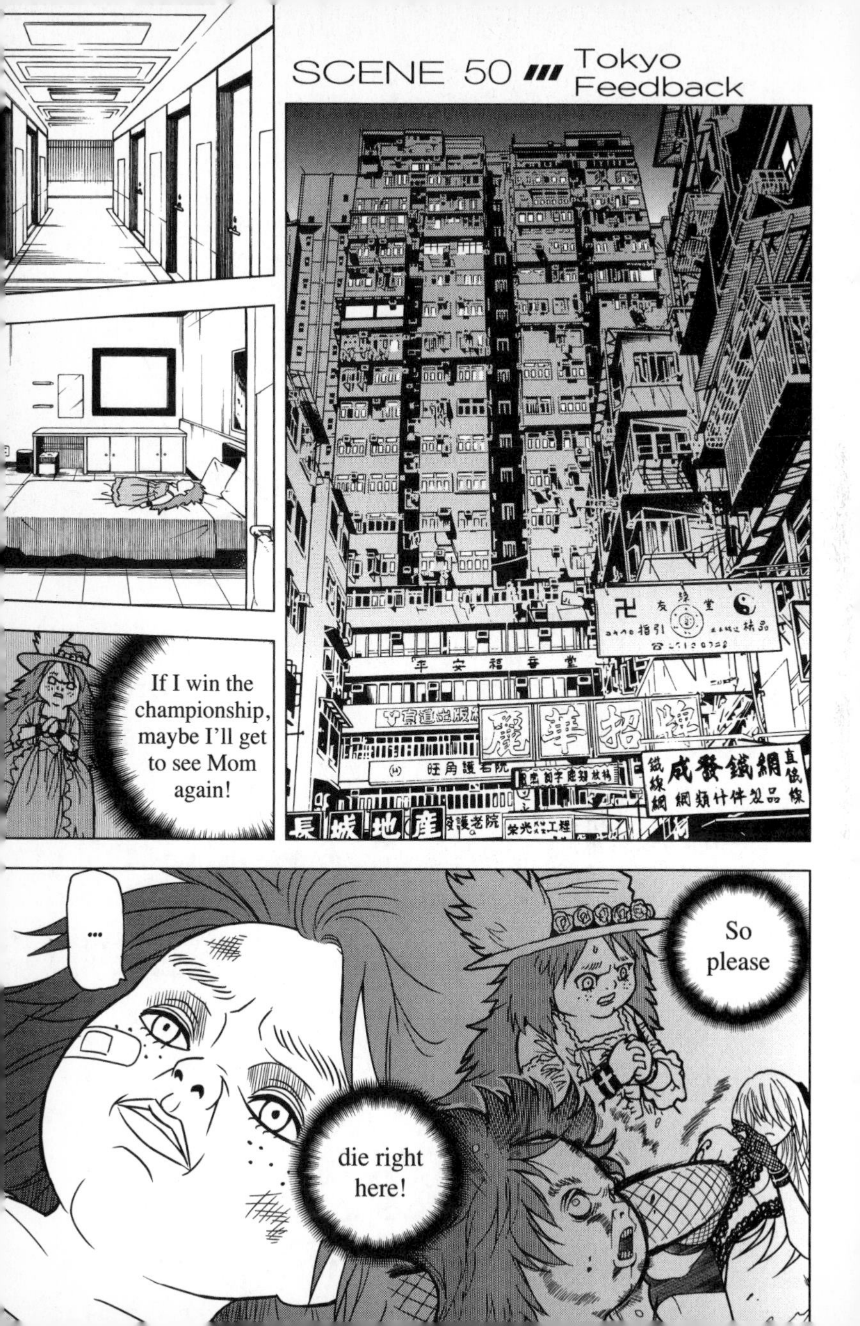
SCENE 50 /// Tokyo Feedback
If I win the championship, maybe I'll get to see Mom again!
So please
...
die right here!

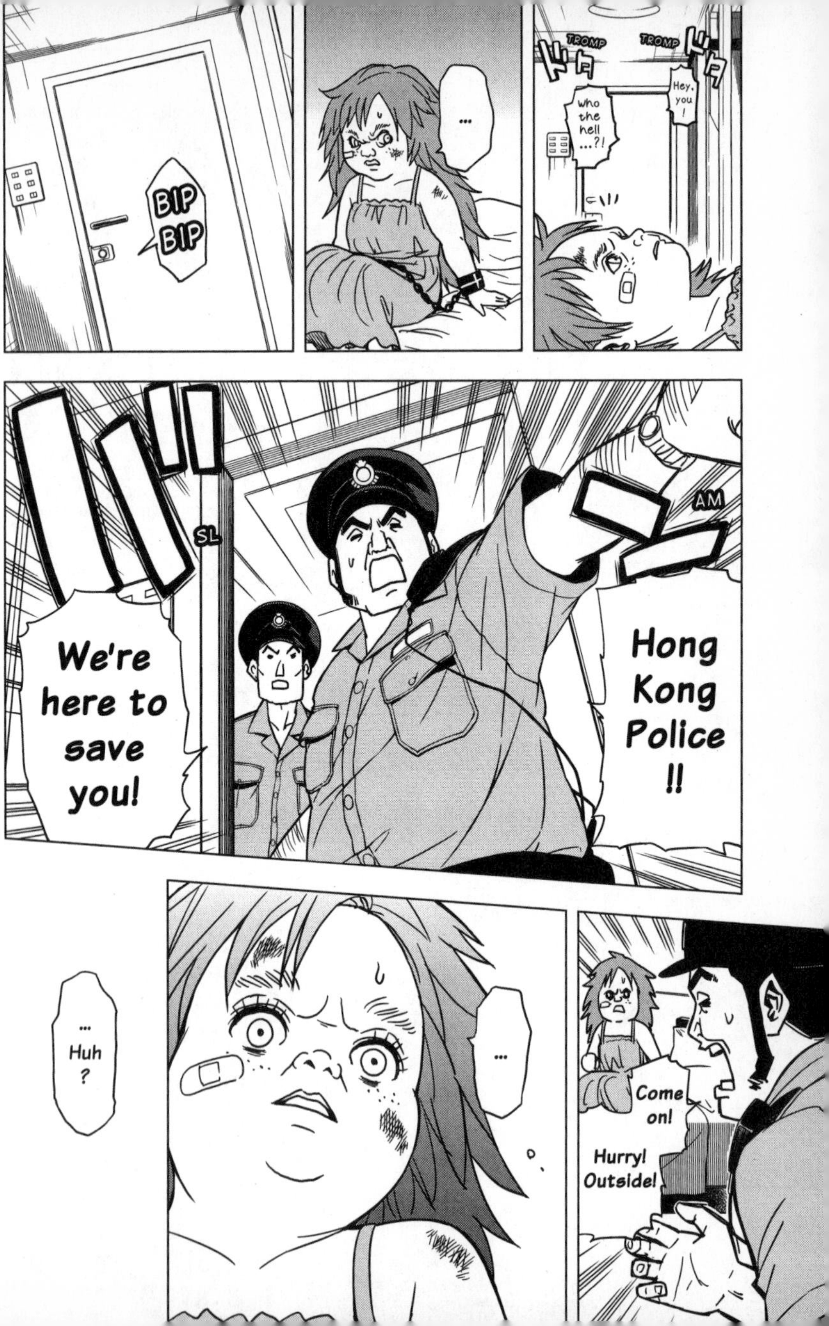
TROMP
Hey, you!
TROMP
who the hell ...?!
...
BIP BIP
Hong Kong Police!!
AM
SL
We're here to save you!
Come on!
Hurry! Outside!
...
... Huh?

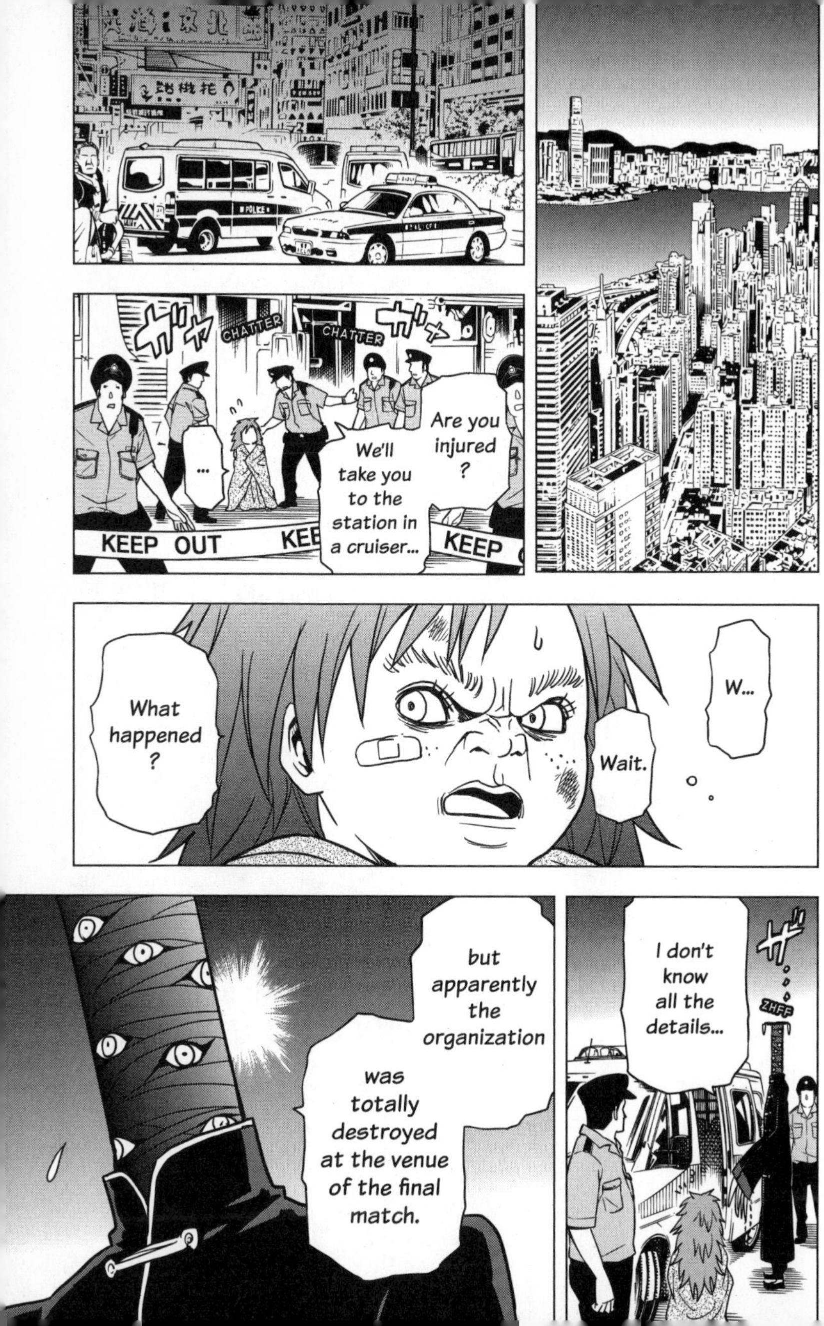

ガヤ
CHATTER
ガヤ
CHATTER
Are you injured?
We'll take you to the station in a cruiser...
...
KEEP OUT
KEE
KEEP
W...
Wait.
What happened?
I don't know all the details...
ZHFF
but apparently the organization
was totally destroyed at the venue of the final match.

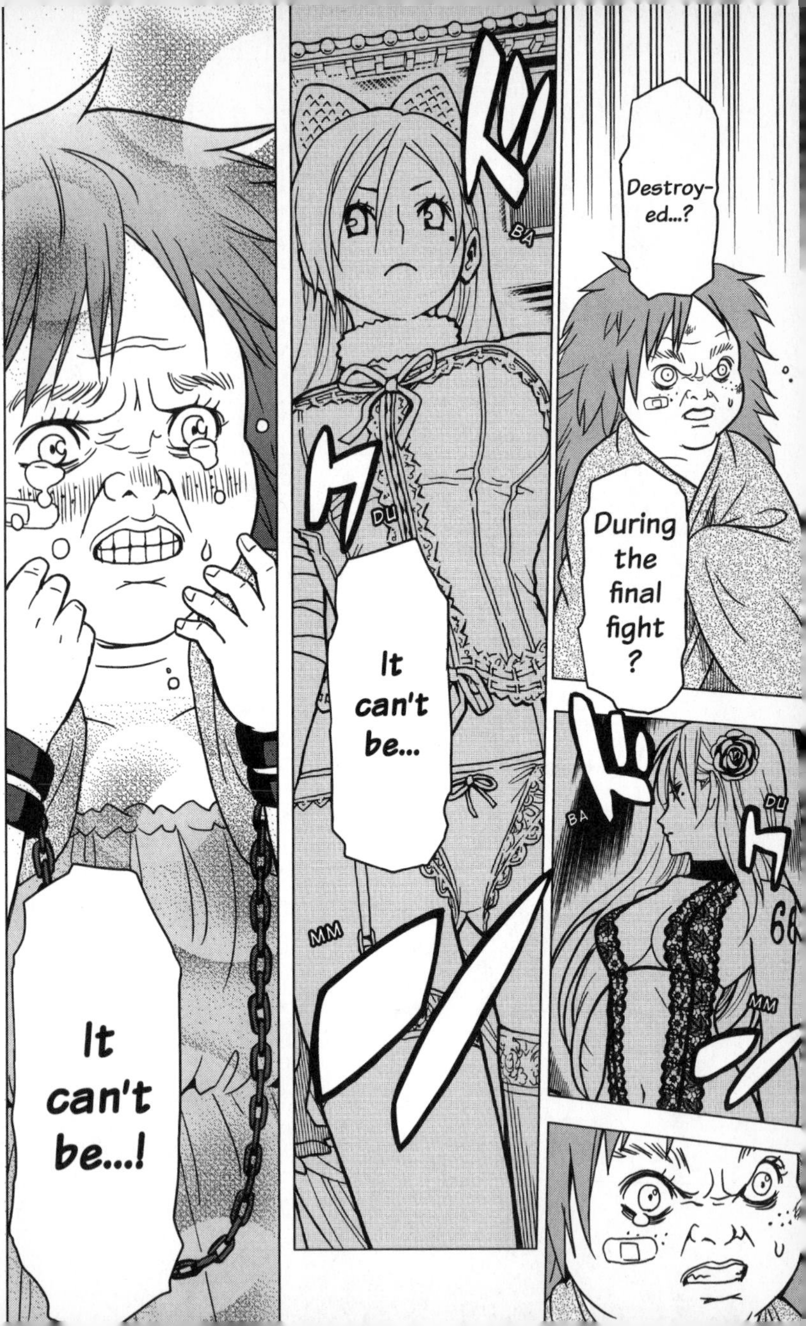
Destroy-ed...?
During the final fight?
DU
BA
MM
BA
DU
It can't be...
MM
It can't be...!

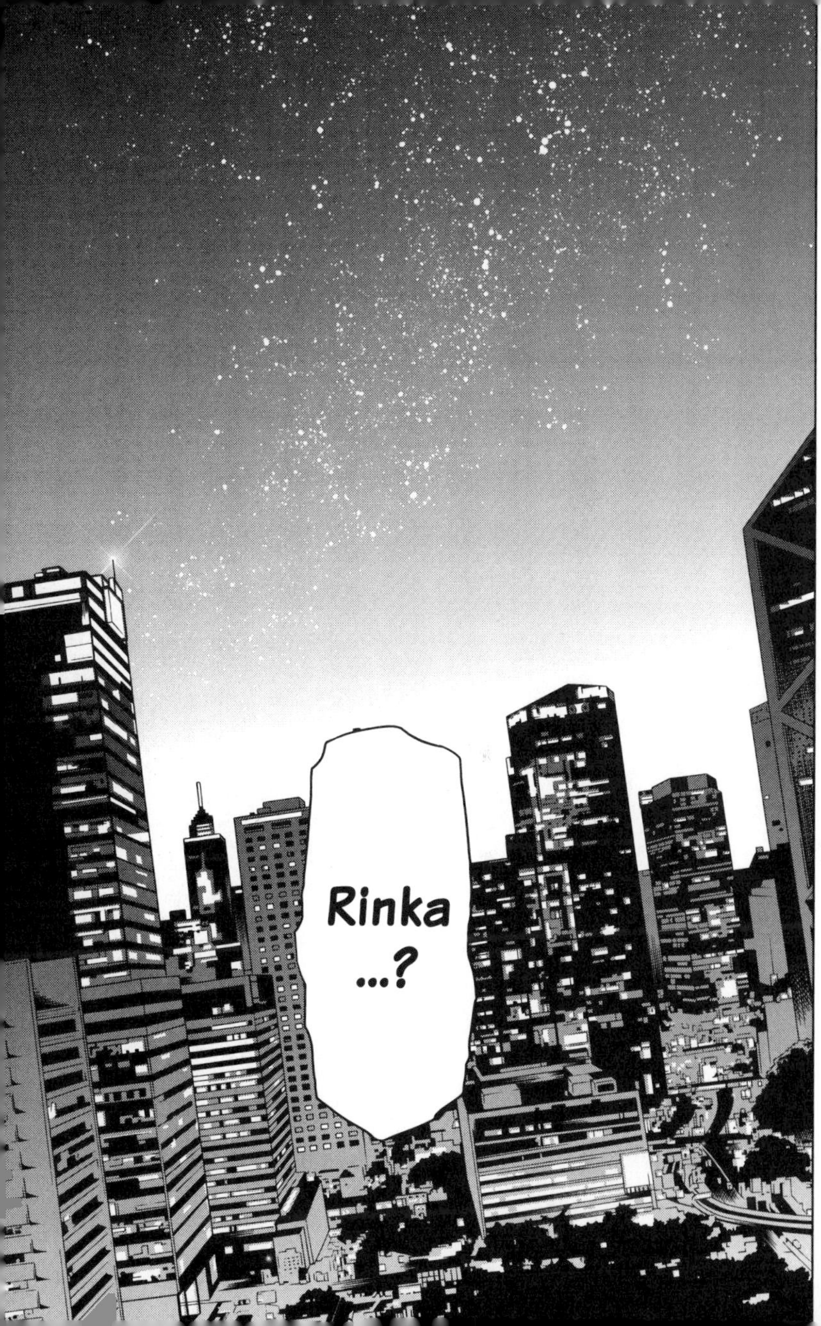
Rinka ...?

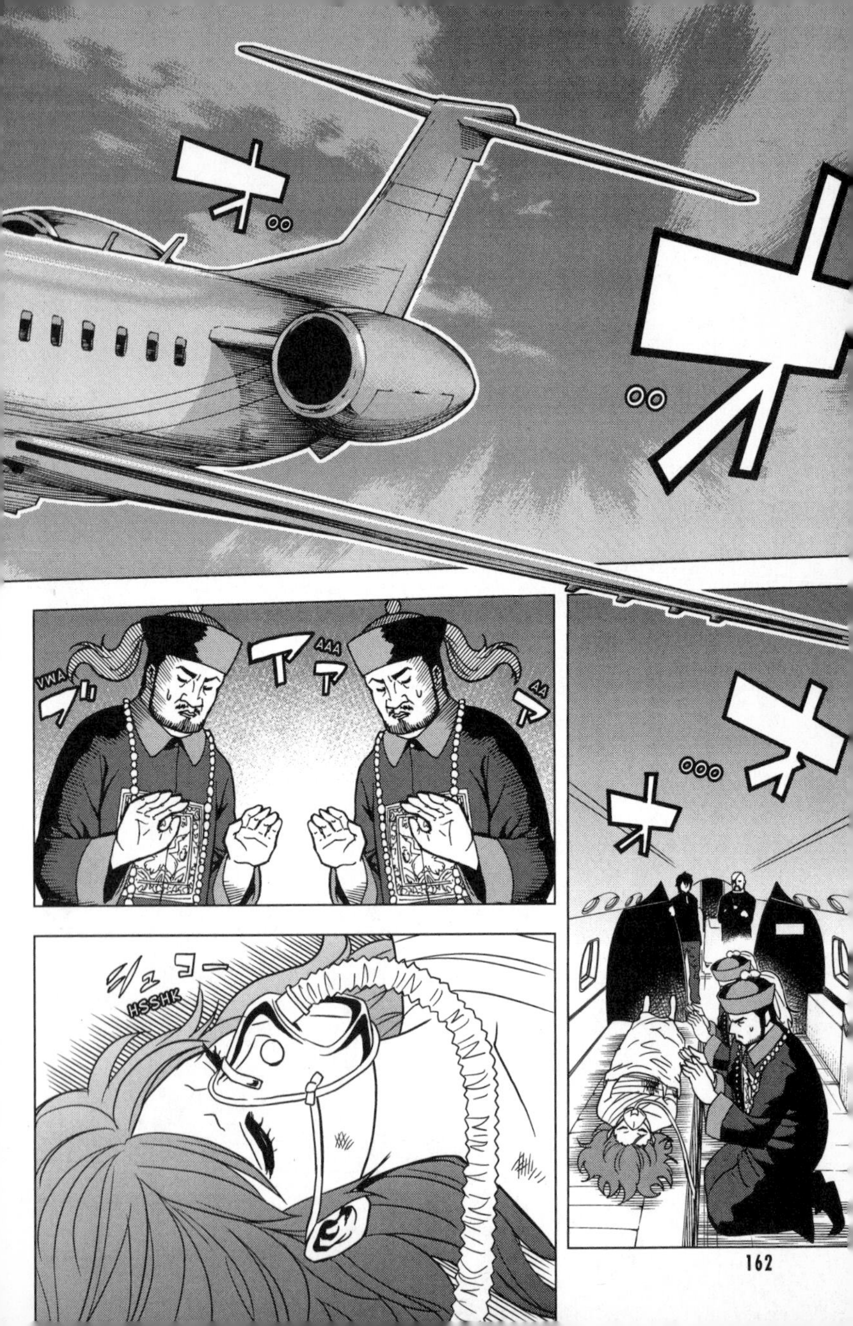
オ
オ
オ
オ
ア
AA
ア
AAA
ア
ヴァ
VWA
シュコー
HSSHK

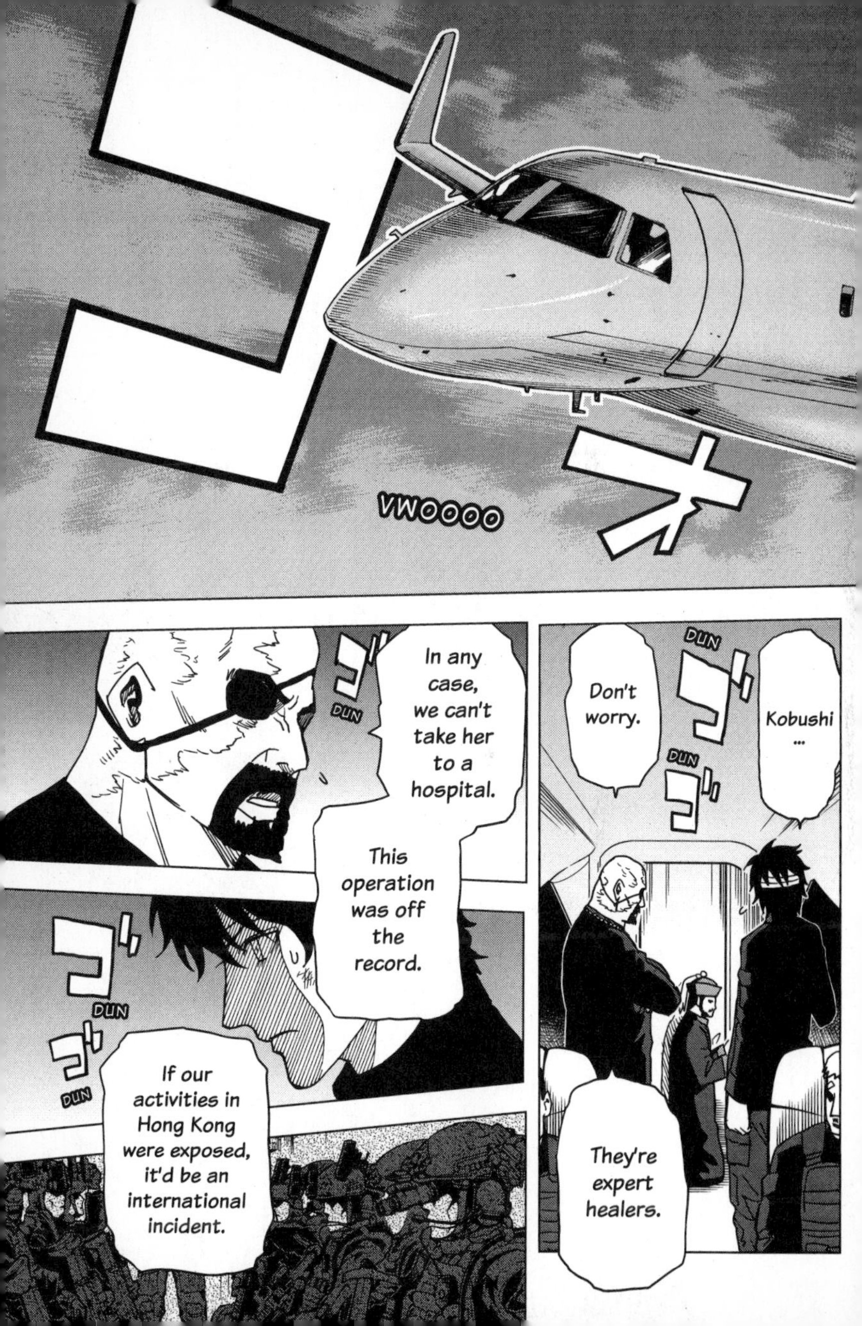
VWOOOO
Kobushi...
DUN
DUN
Don't worry.
They're expert healers.
DUN
In any case, we can't take her to a hospital.
This operation was off the record.
DUN
DUN
If our activities in Hong Kong were exposed, it'd be an international incident.

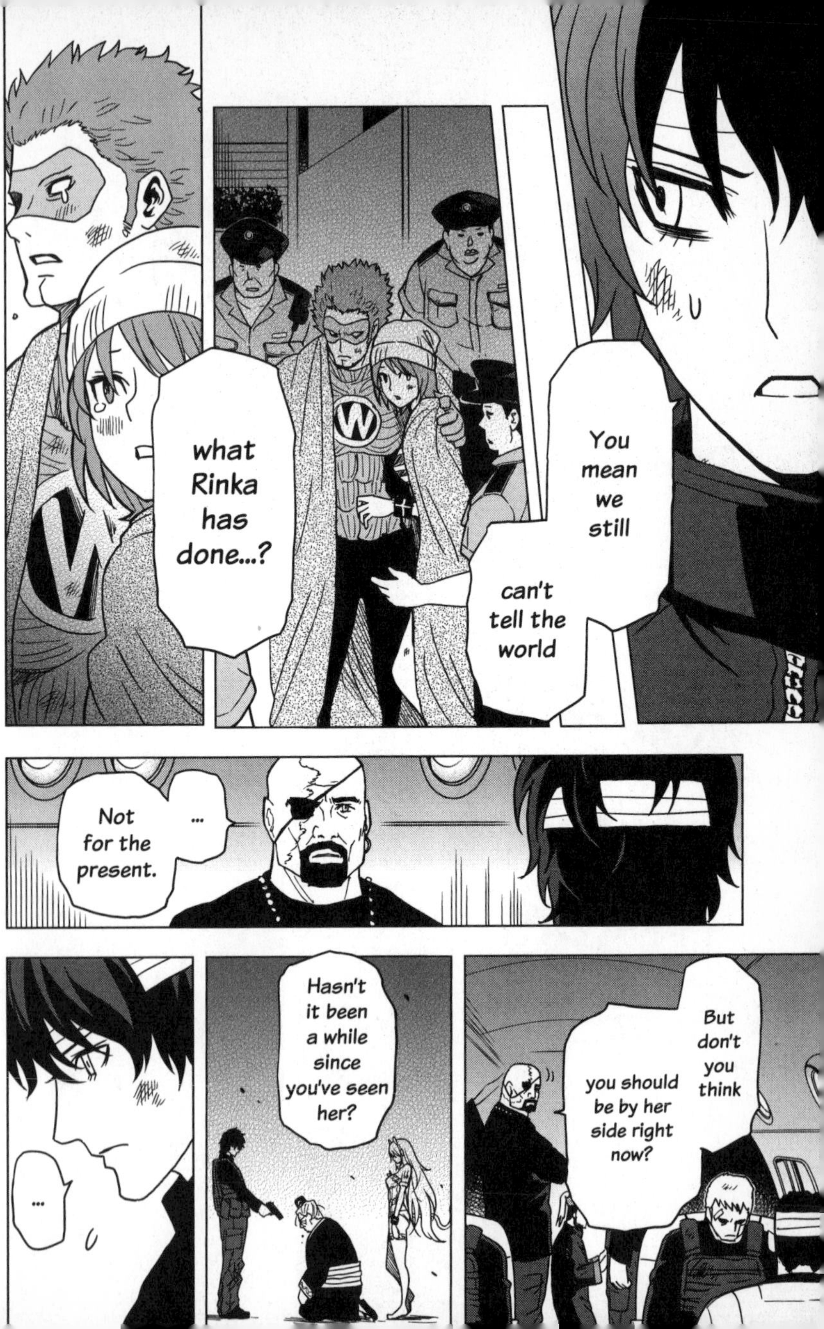
You mean we still
can't tell the world
what Rinka has done...?
... Not for the present.
But don't you think
you should be by her side right now?
Hasn't it been a while since you've seen her?
...

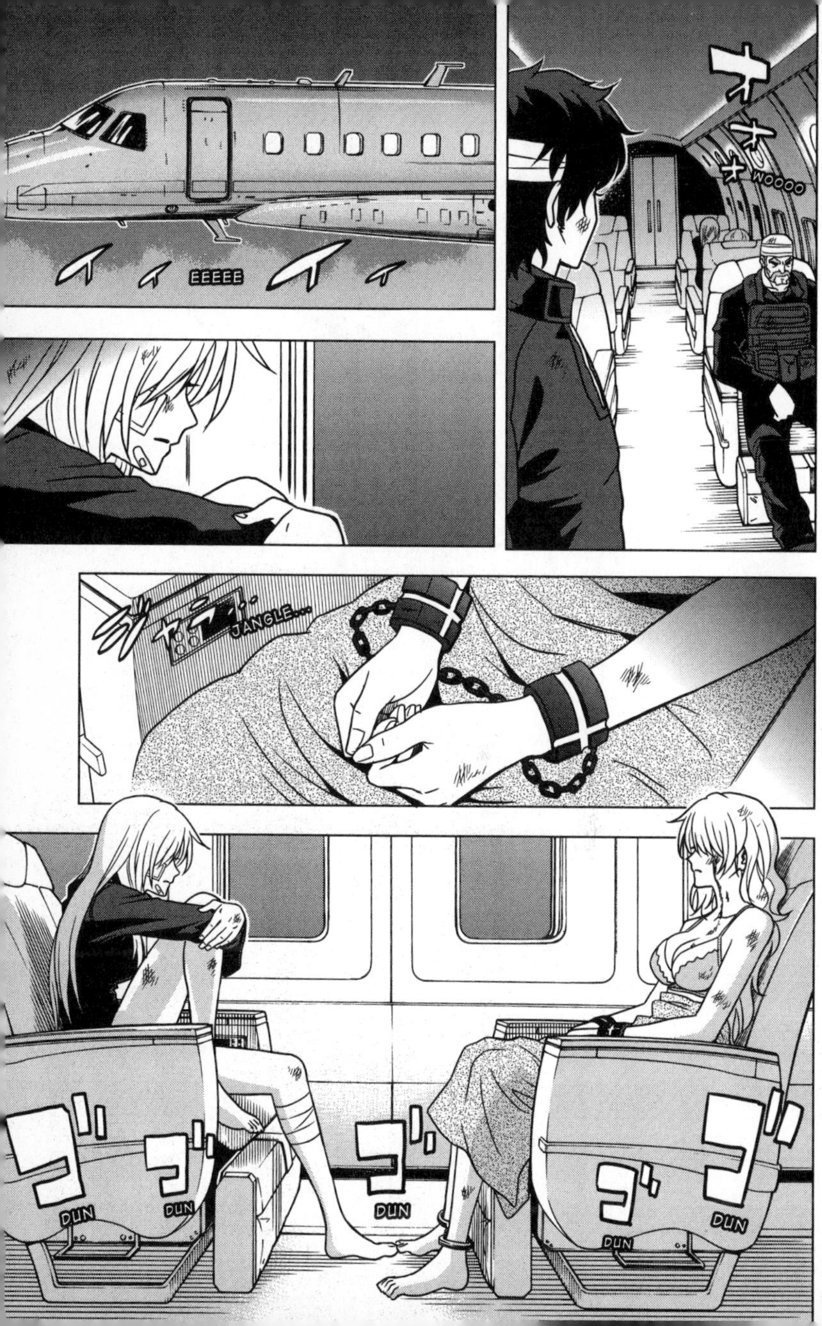

オォォ
WOOOO
イィ
EEEEE
イィ
JANGLE...
ゴ
DUN
ゴ
DUN
ゴ
DUN
ゴ
DUN
ゴ
DUN

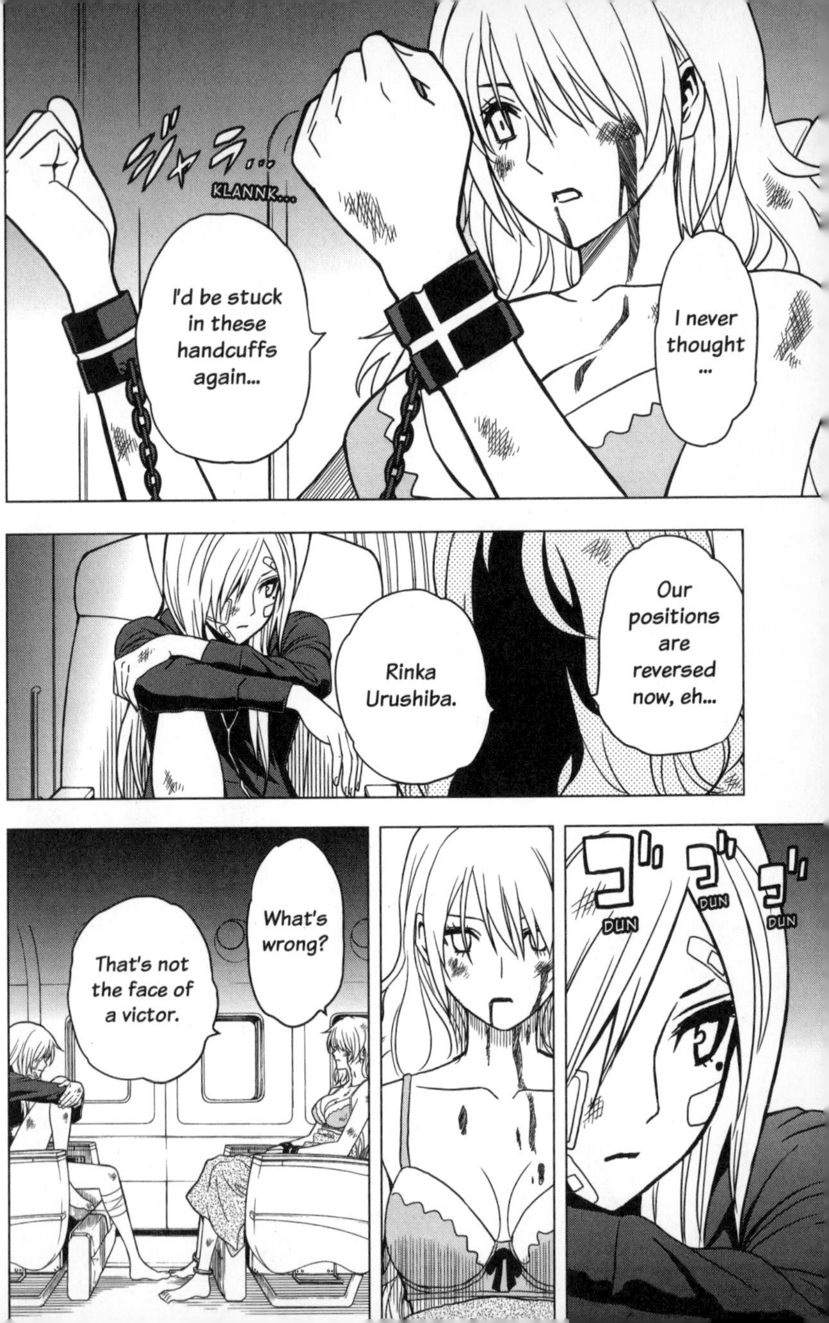
ジャラ...
KLANNK...
I never thought...
I'd be stuck in these handcuffs again...
Our positions are reversed now, eh...
Rinka Urushiba.
ゴゴゴ
DUN DUN DUN
What's wrong?
That's not the face of a victor.

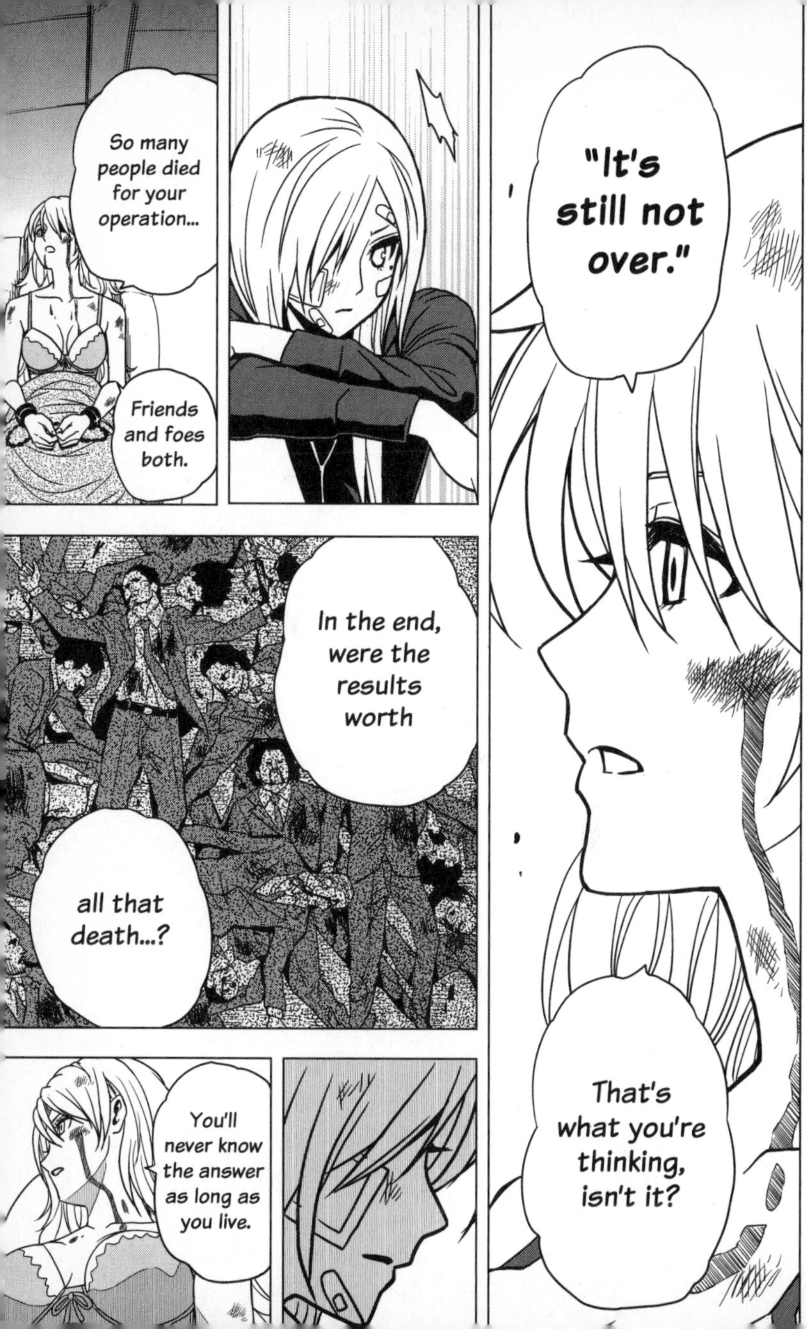
"It's still not over."
That's what you're thinking, isn't it?
So many people died for your operation...
Friends and foes both.
In the end, were the results worth
all that death...?
You'll never know the answer as long as you live.

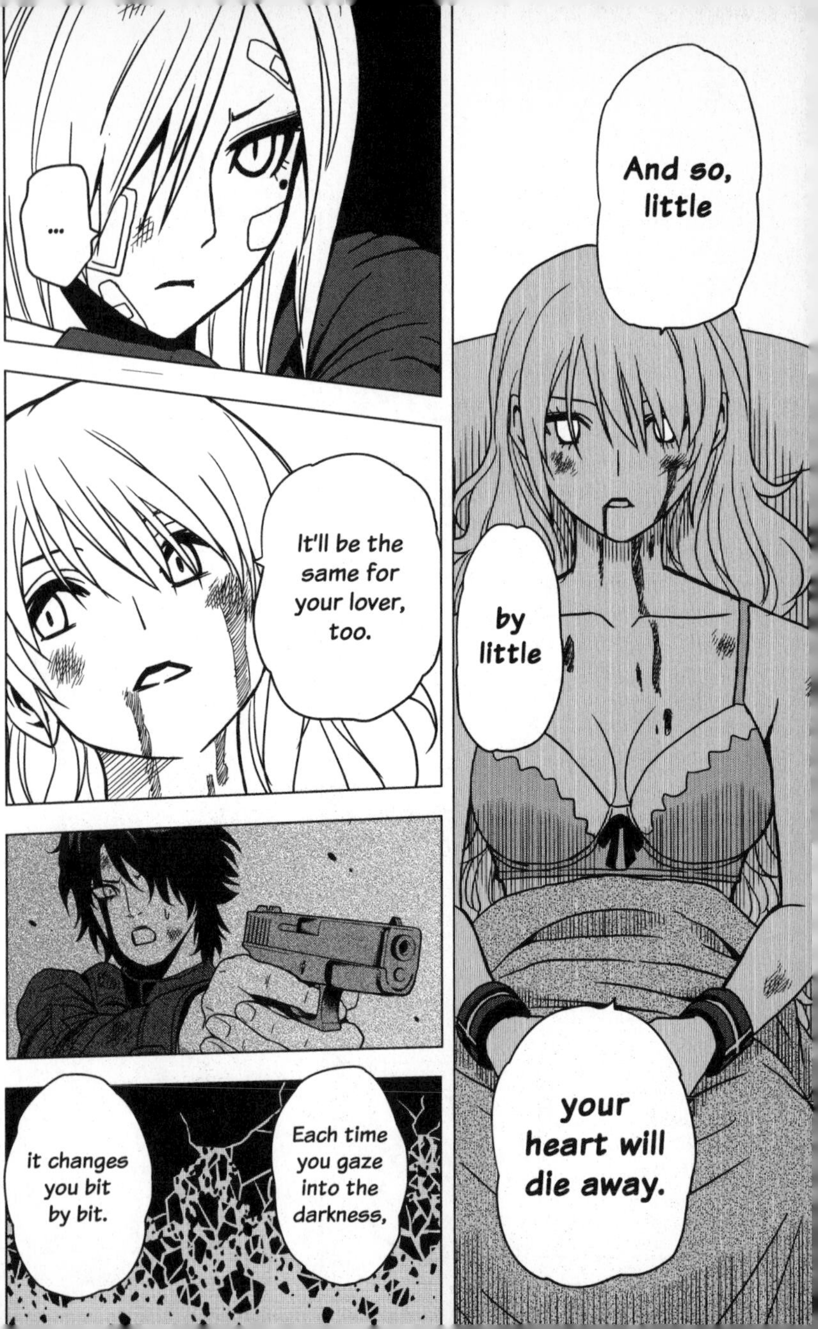
And so, little
by little
your heart will die away.
...
It'll be the same for your lover, too.
Each time you gaze into the darkness,
it changes you bit by bit.

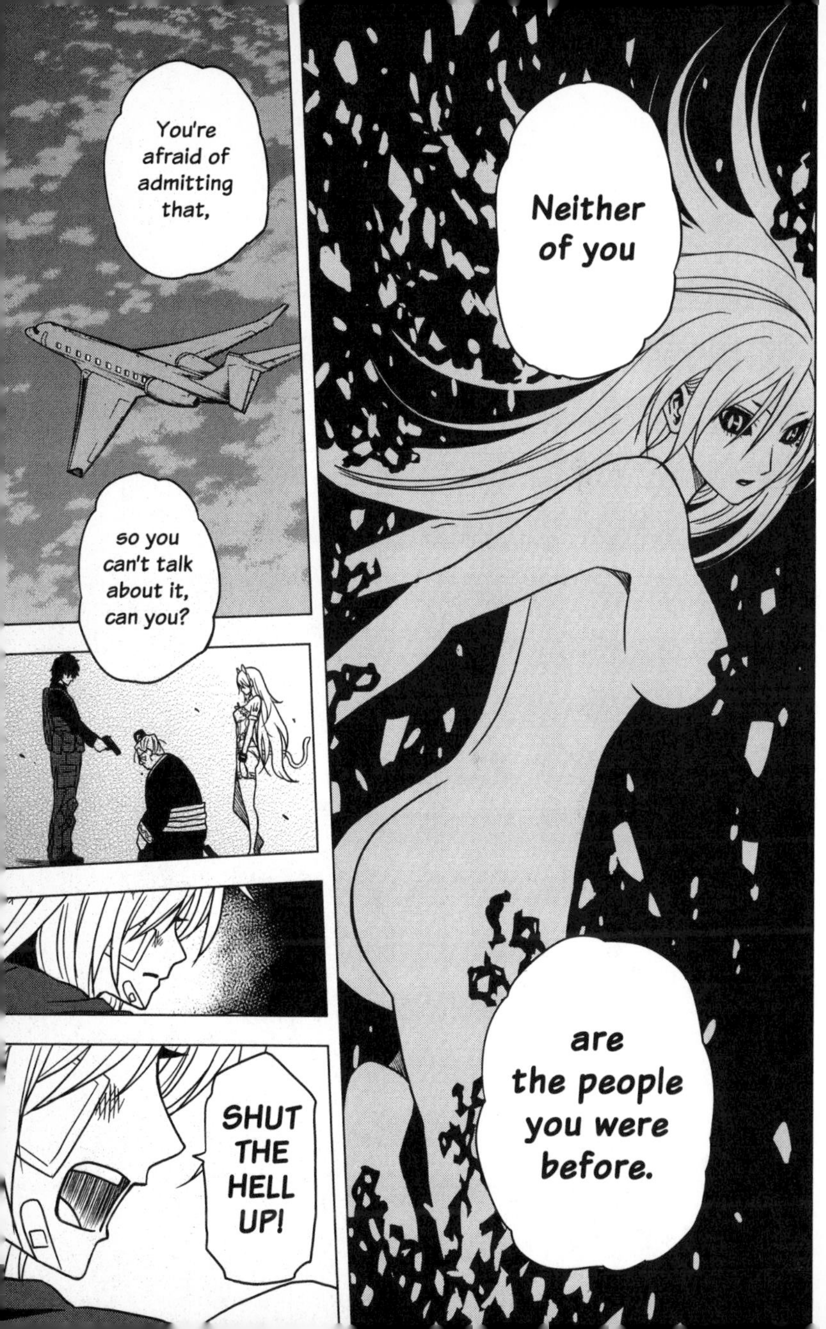
Neither of you
are the people you were before.
You're afraid of admitting that,
so you can't talk about it, can you?
SHUT THE HELL UP!

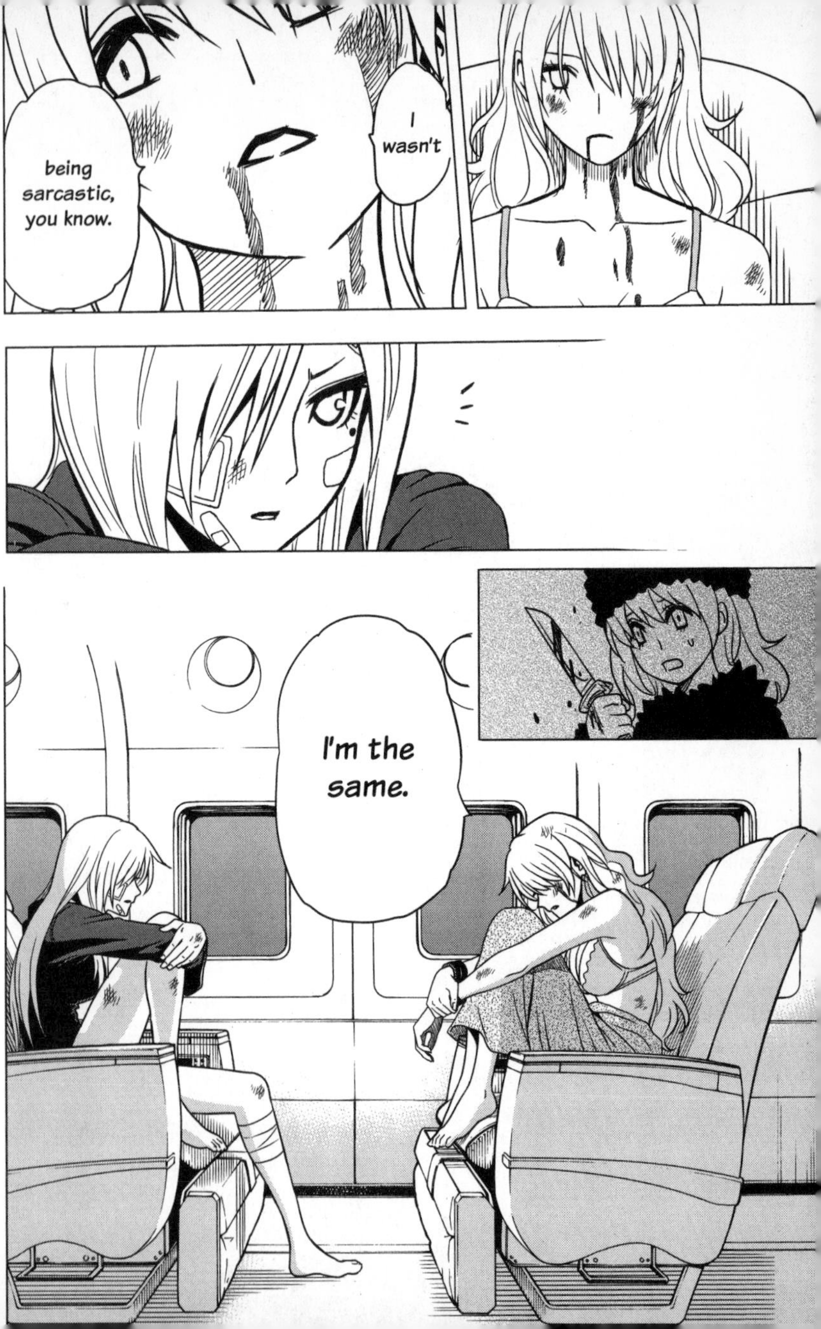
I wasn't
being sarcastic, you know.
I'm the same.

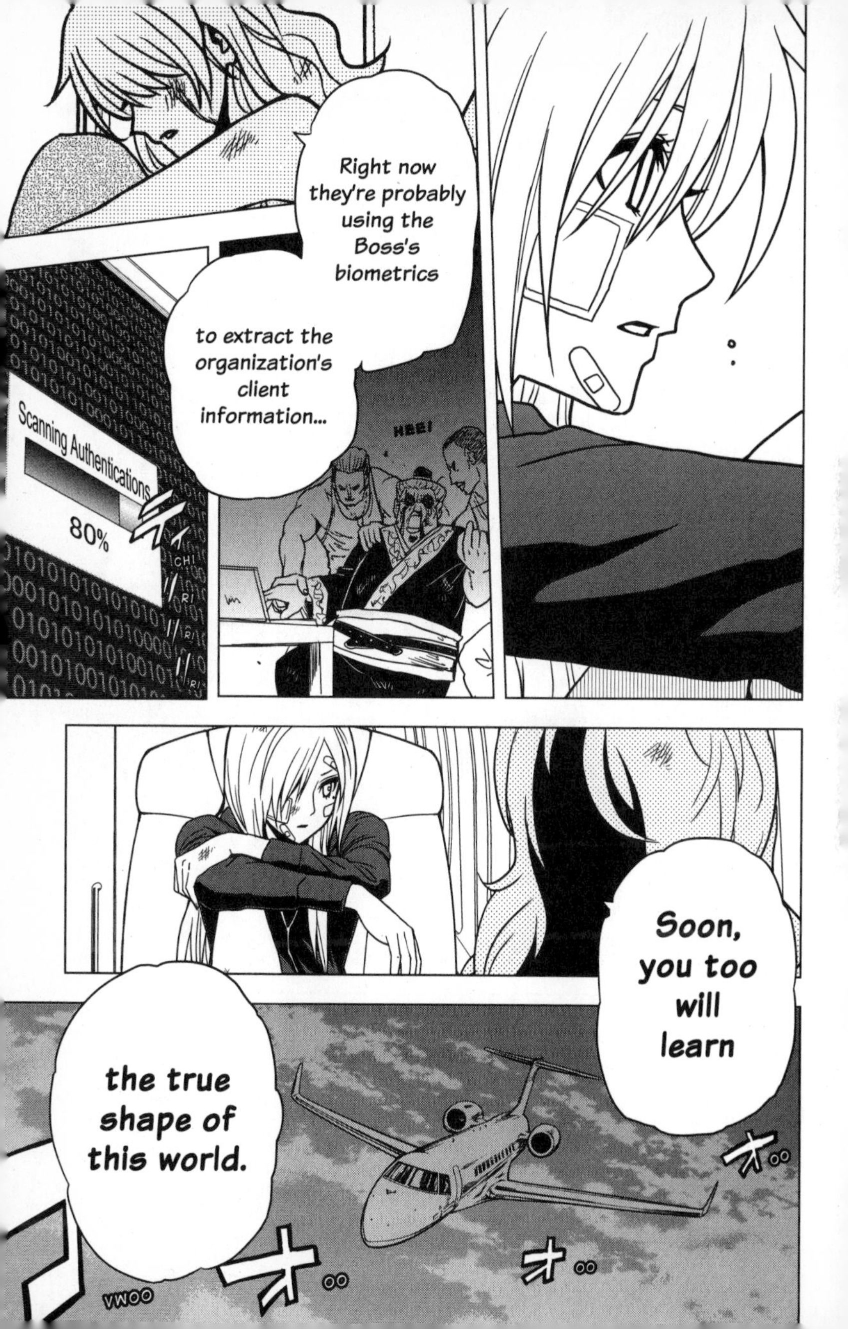
Right now they're probably using the Boss's biometrics
to extract the organization's client information...
HBE!
Scanning Authentications
80%
CHI
RI
RI
RI
Soon, you too will learn
the true shape of this world.
VWOO

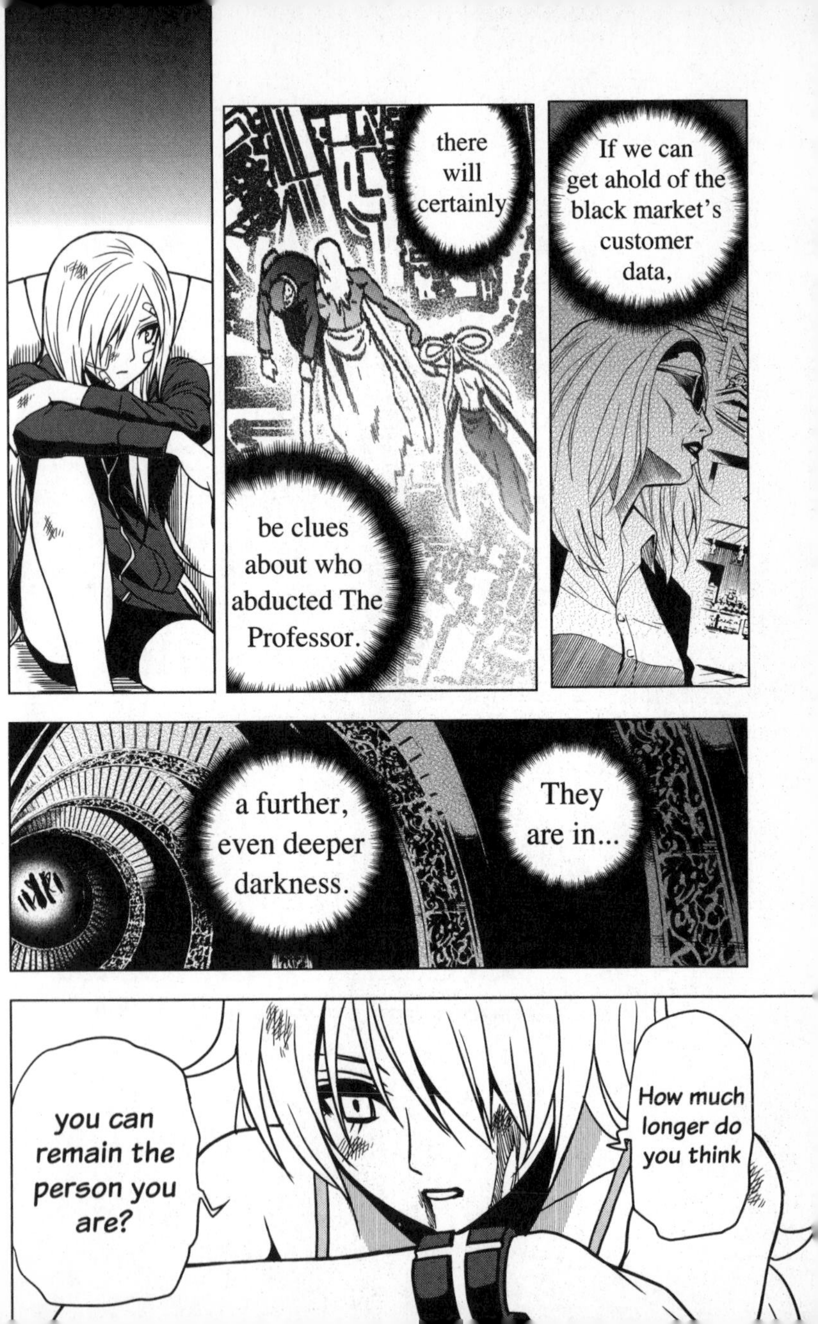
If we can get ahold of the black market's customer data,
there will certainly
be clues about who abducted The Professor.
They are in...
a further, even deeper darkness.
How much longer do you think
you can remain the person you are?

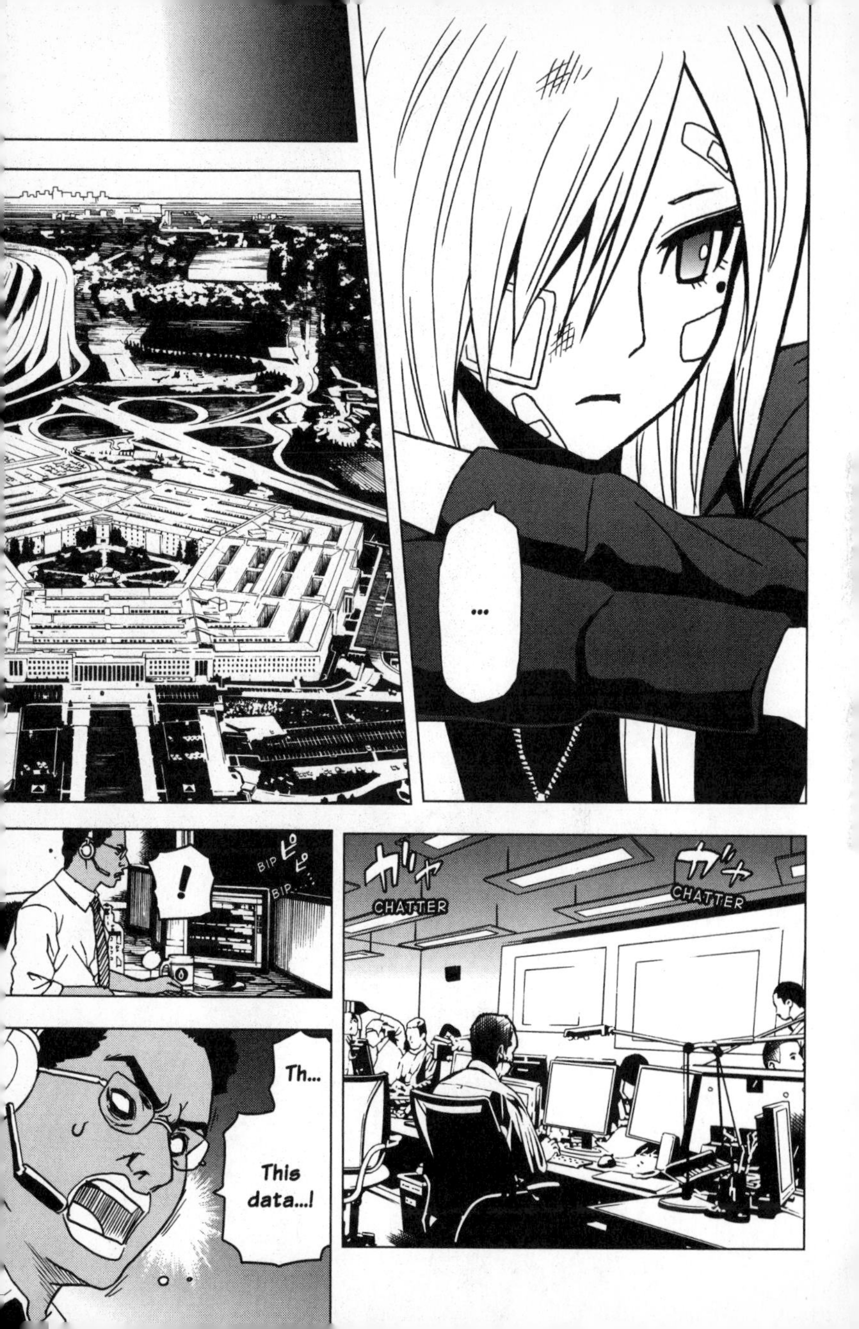
...
ガヤ
CHATTER
ガヤ
CHATTER
ピピ
BIP
BIP...
!
Th...
This data...!

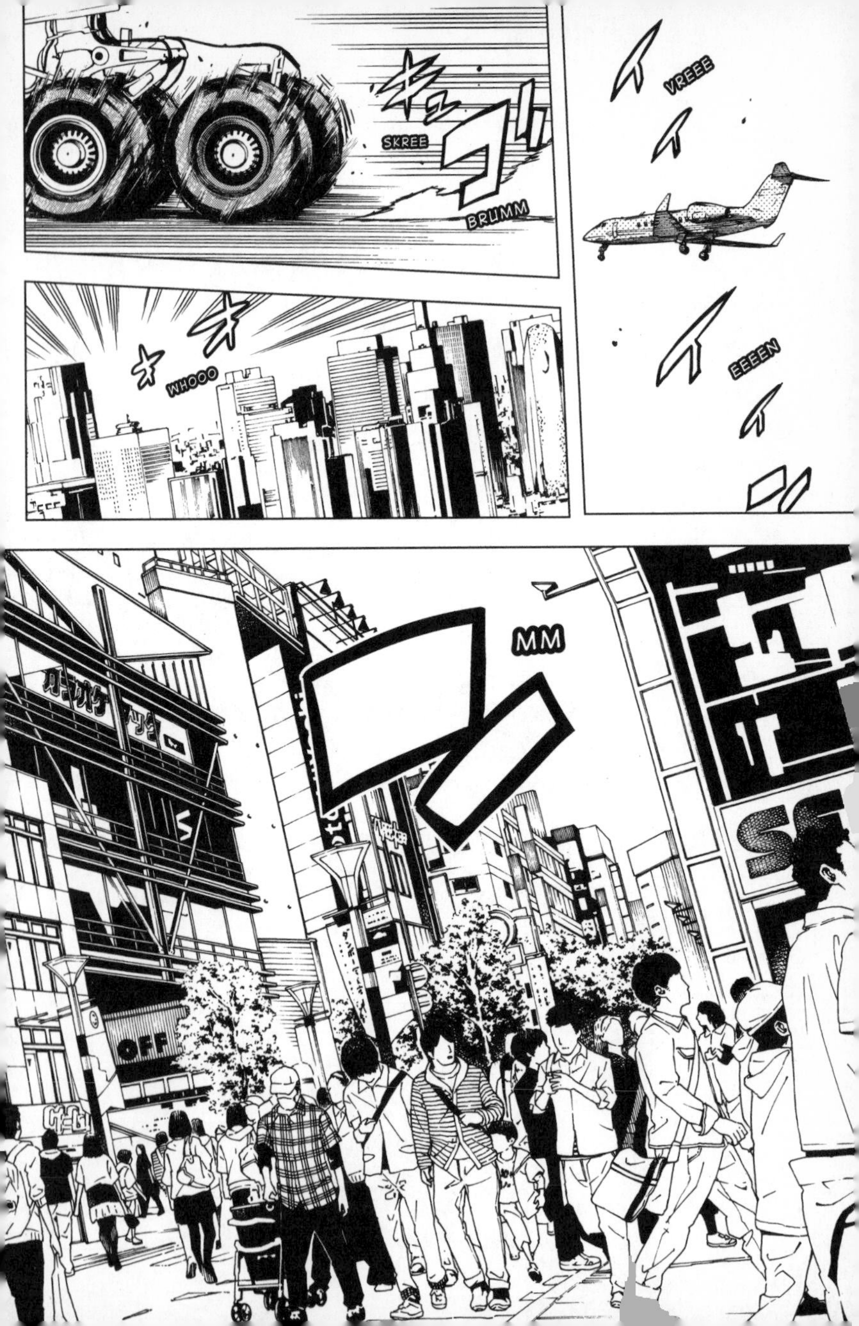
VREEE
EEEEN
SKREE
BRUMM
WHOOO
MM
OFF

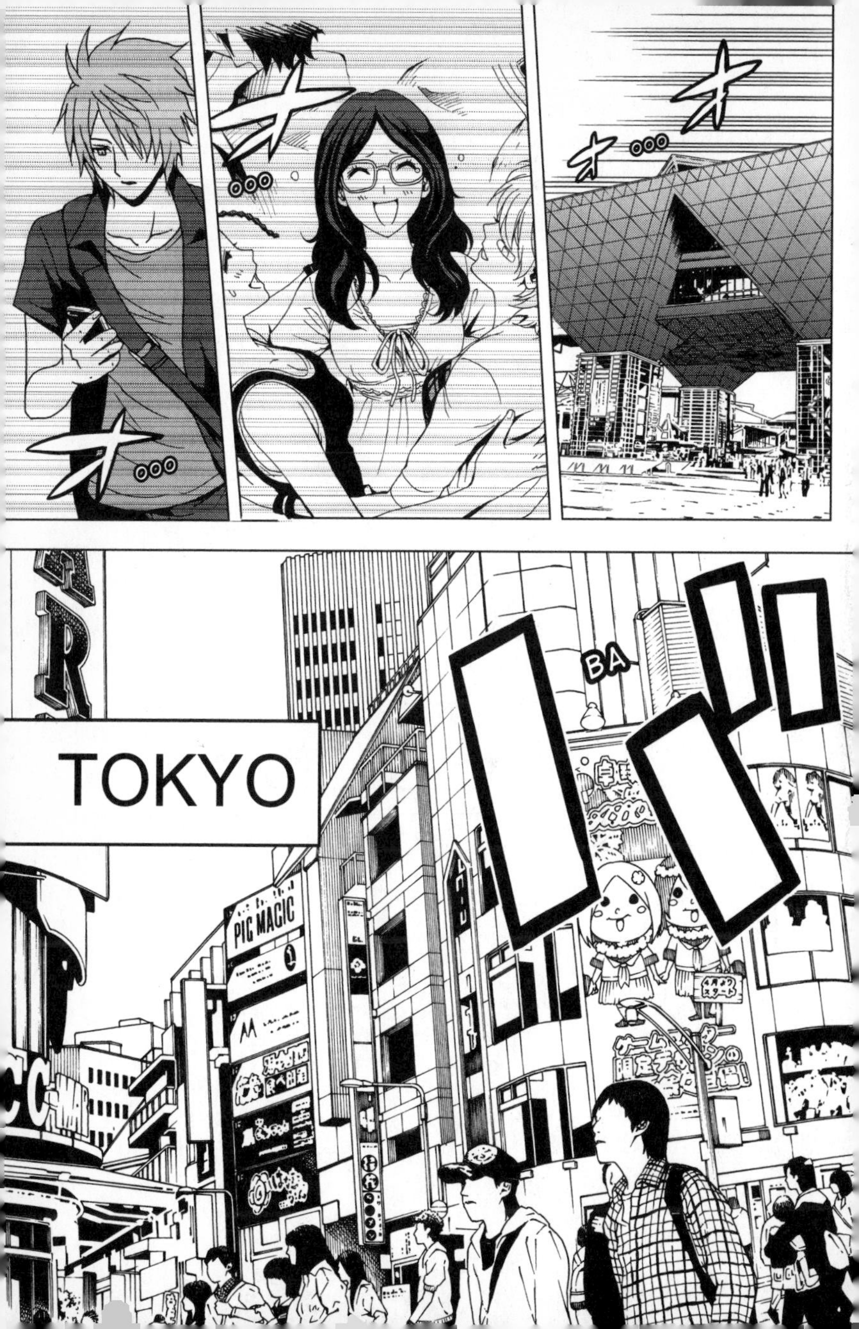

オ
オ ooo
オ ooo
オ ooo
BA
TOKYO
PIC MAGIC

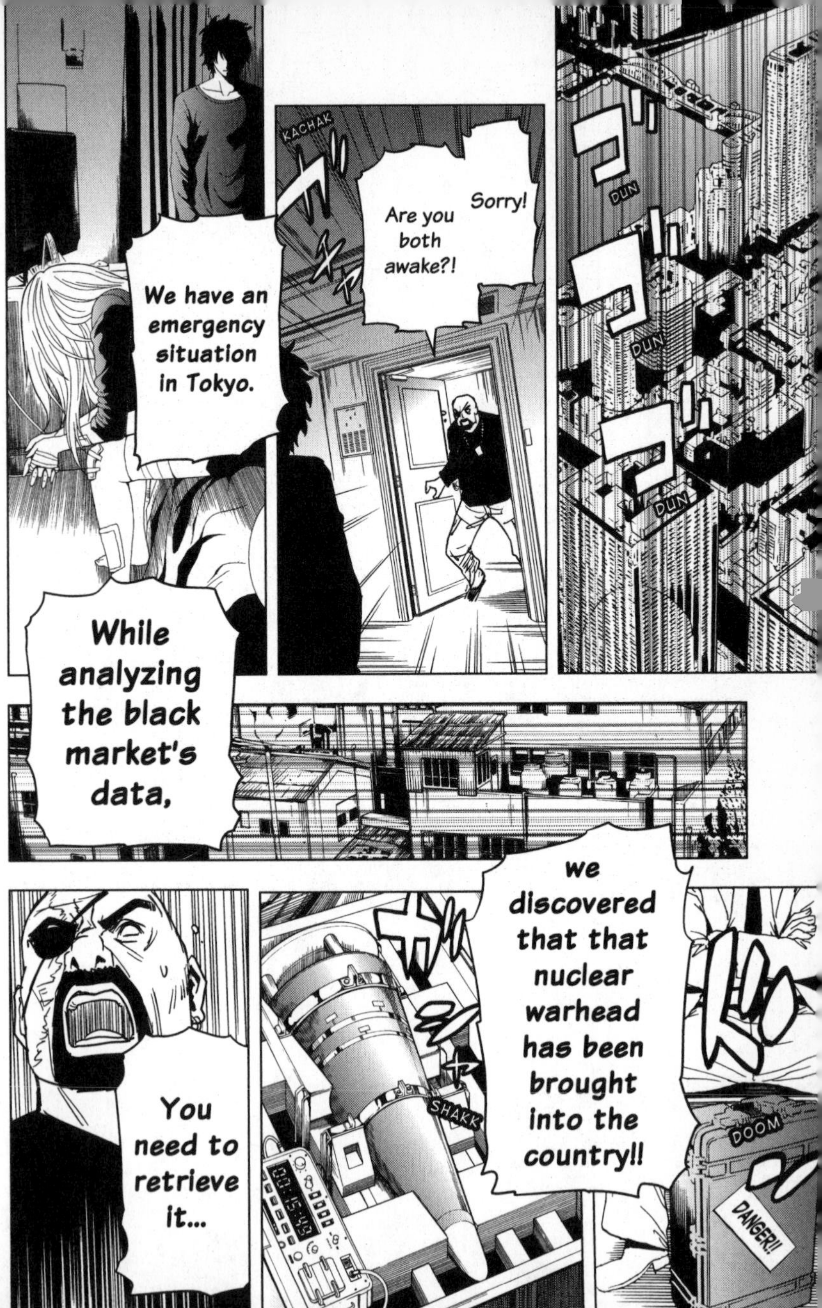
DUN
DUN
DUN
KACHAK
Sorry!
Are you both awake?!
We have an emergency situation in Tokyo.
While analyzing the black market's data,
DOOM
DANGER!!
we discovered that that nuclear warhead has been brought into the country!!
SHAKK
You need to retrieve it...

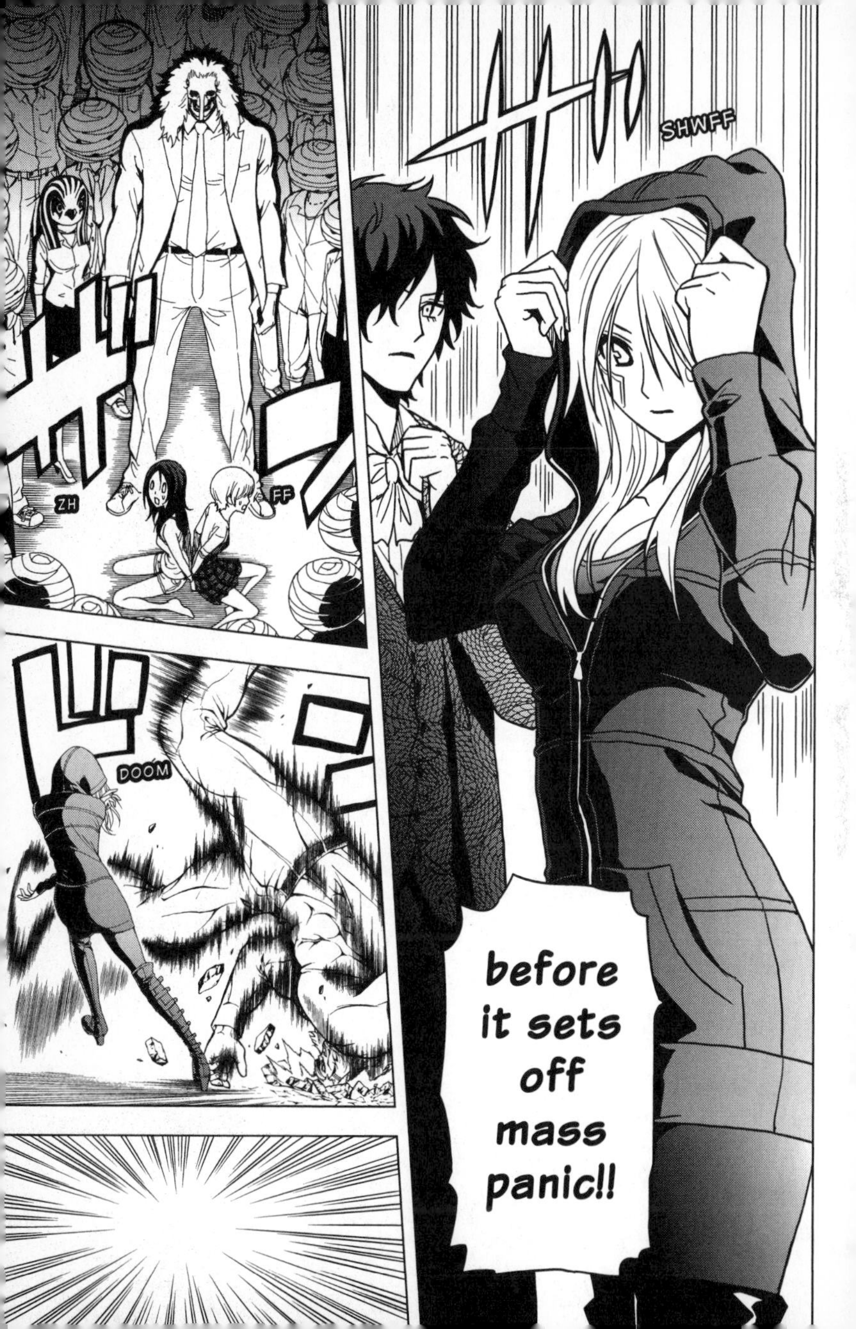
SHWFF
before it sets off mass panic!!
FF
ZH
DOOM

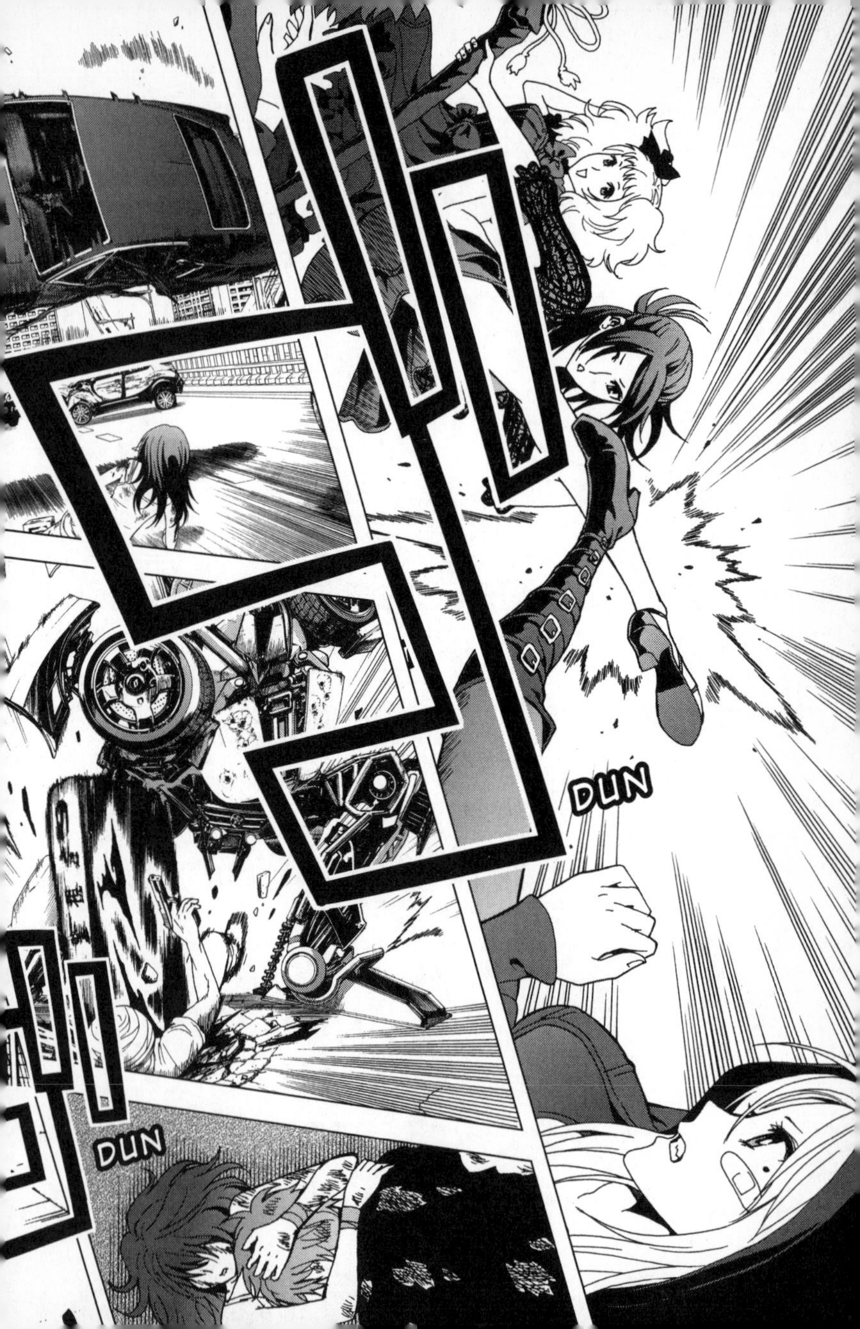
DUN
DUN

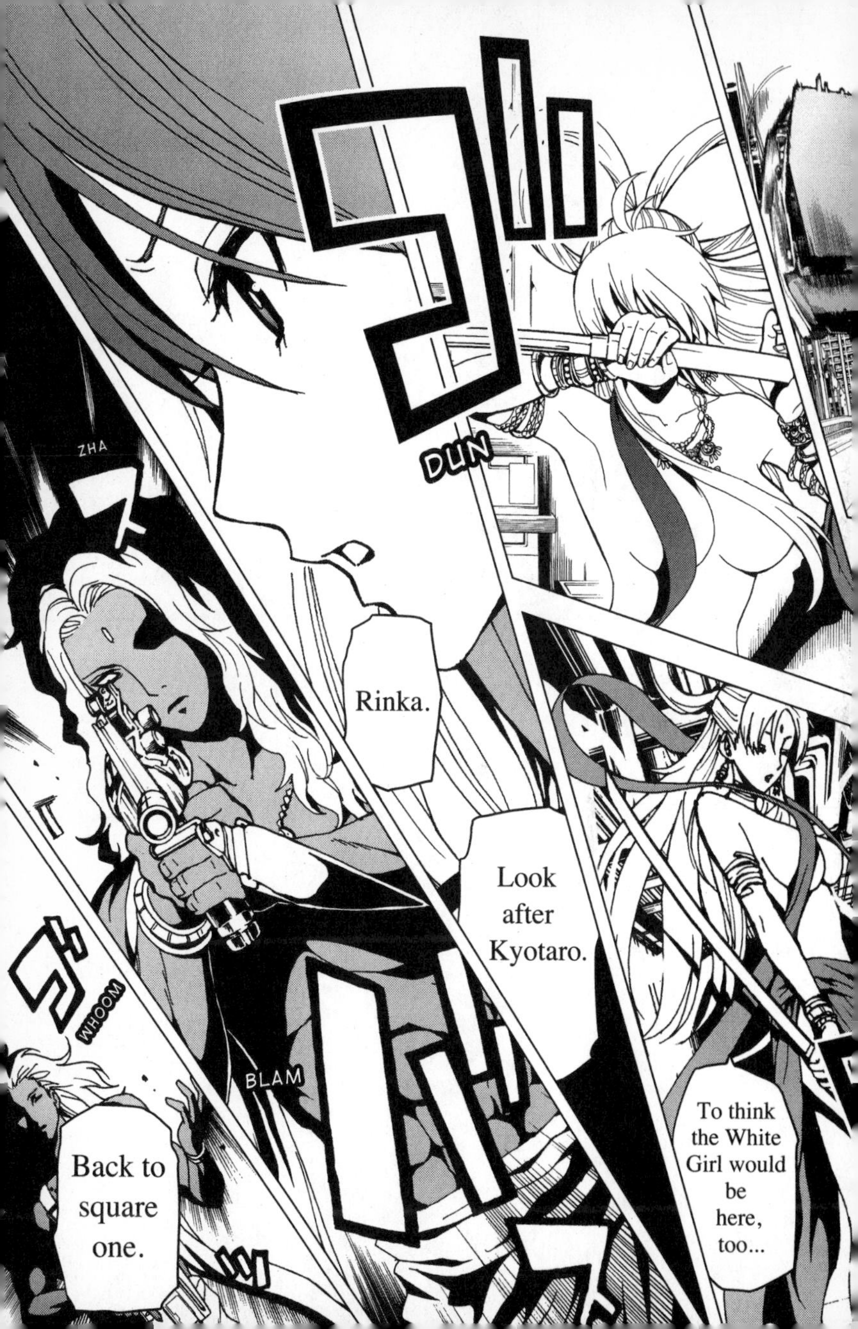
DUN
Rinka.
Look after Kyotaro.
To think the White Girl would be here, too...
ZHA
BLAM
WHOOM
Back to square one.

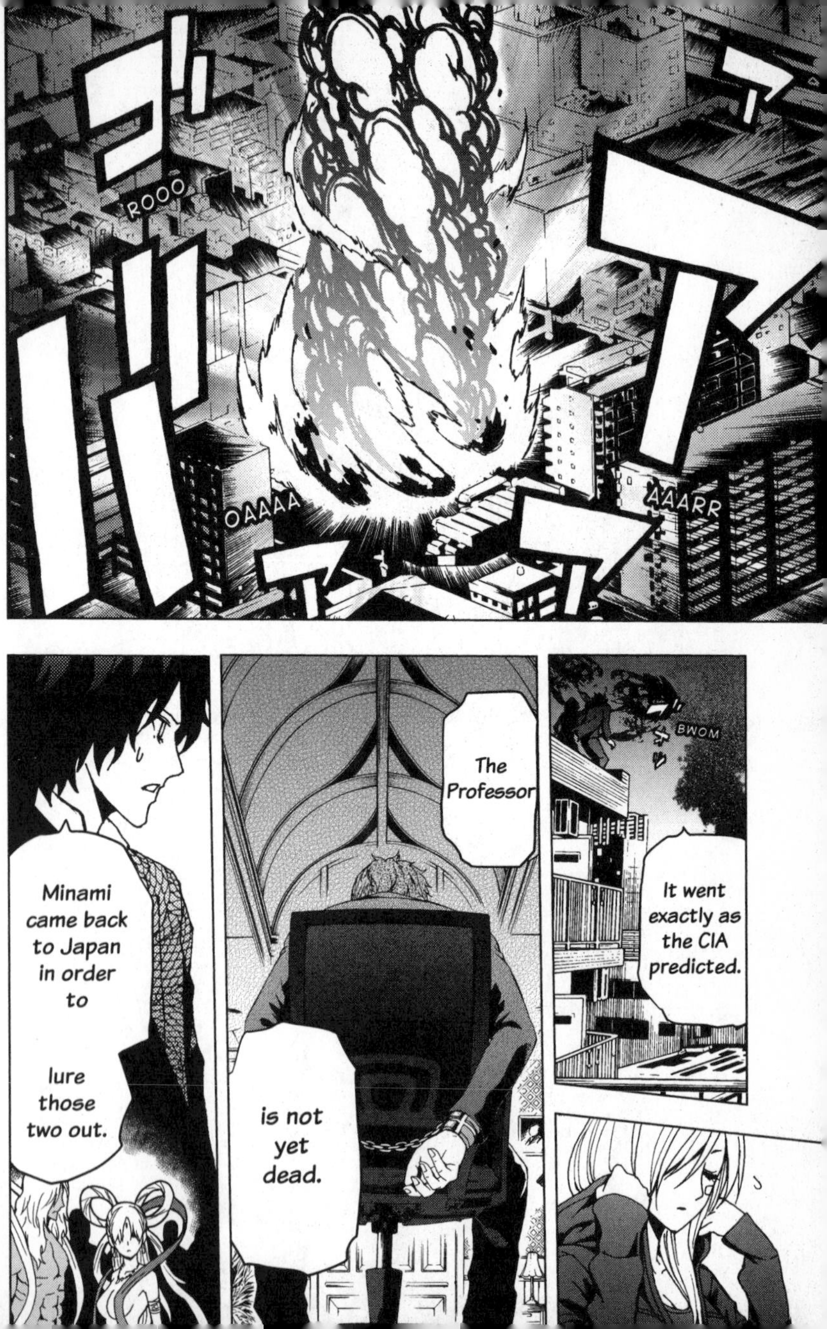
ROOO
OAAAA
AAARR
BWOM
It went exactly as the CIA predicted.
The Professor
is not yet dead.
Minami came back to Japan in order to
lure those two out.

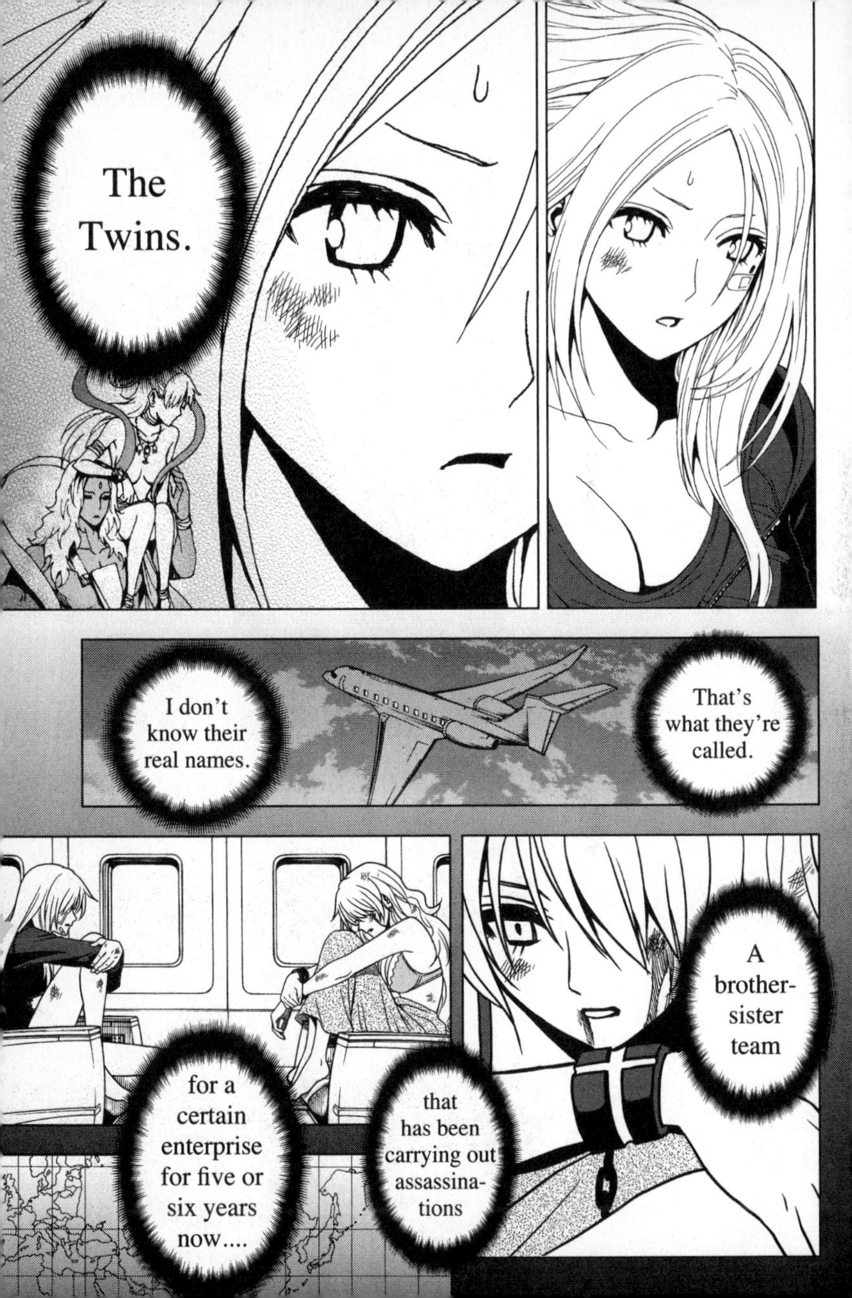
The Twins.
That's what they're called.
I don't know their real names.
A brother-sister team
that has been carrying out assassina-tions
for a certain enterprise for five or six years now....

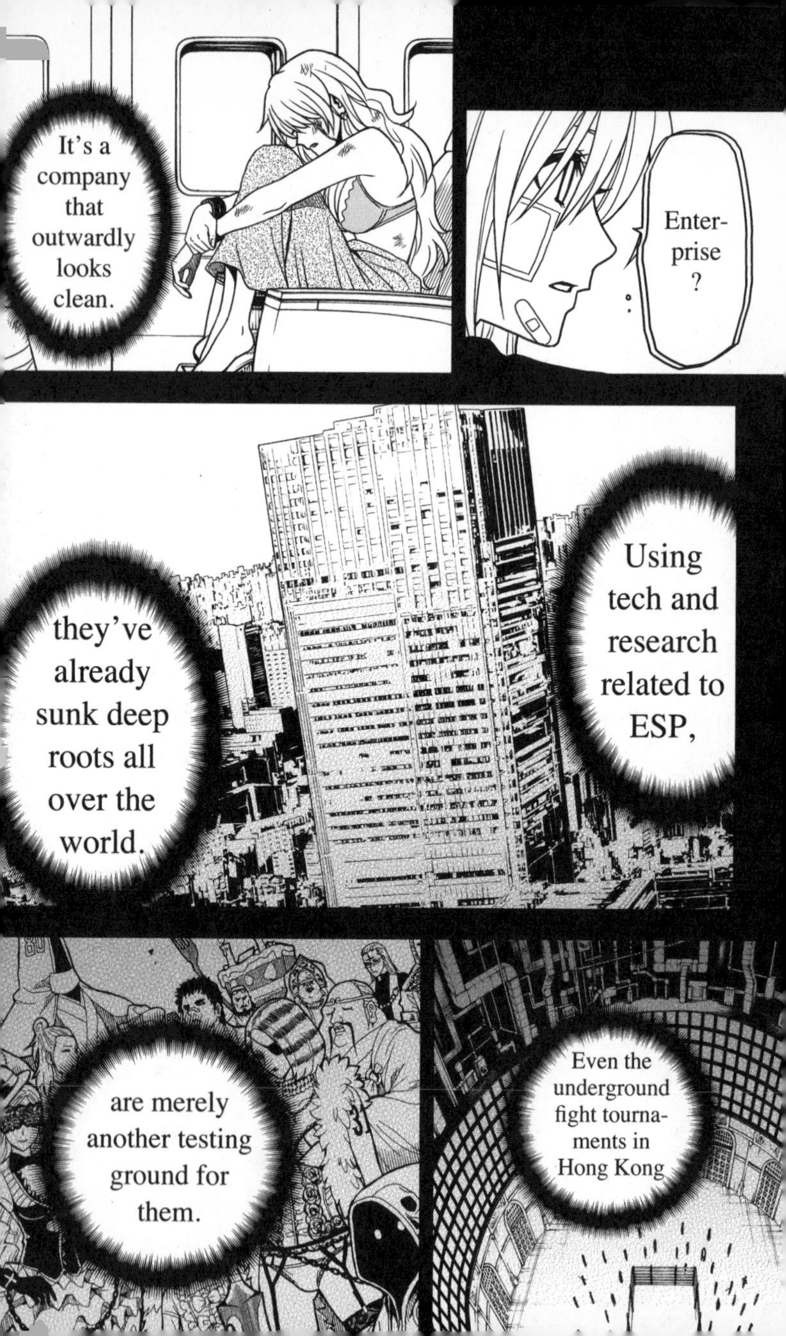
Enter-prise?
It's a company that outwardly looks clean.
Using tech and research related to ESP,
they've already sunk deep roots all over the world.
Even the underground fight tournaments in Hong Kong
are merely another testing ground for them.

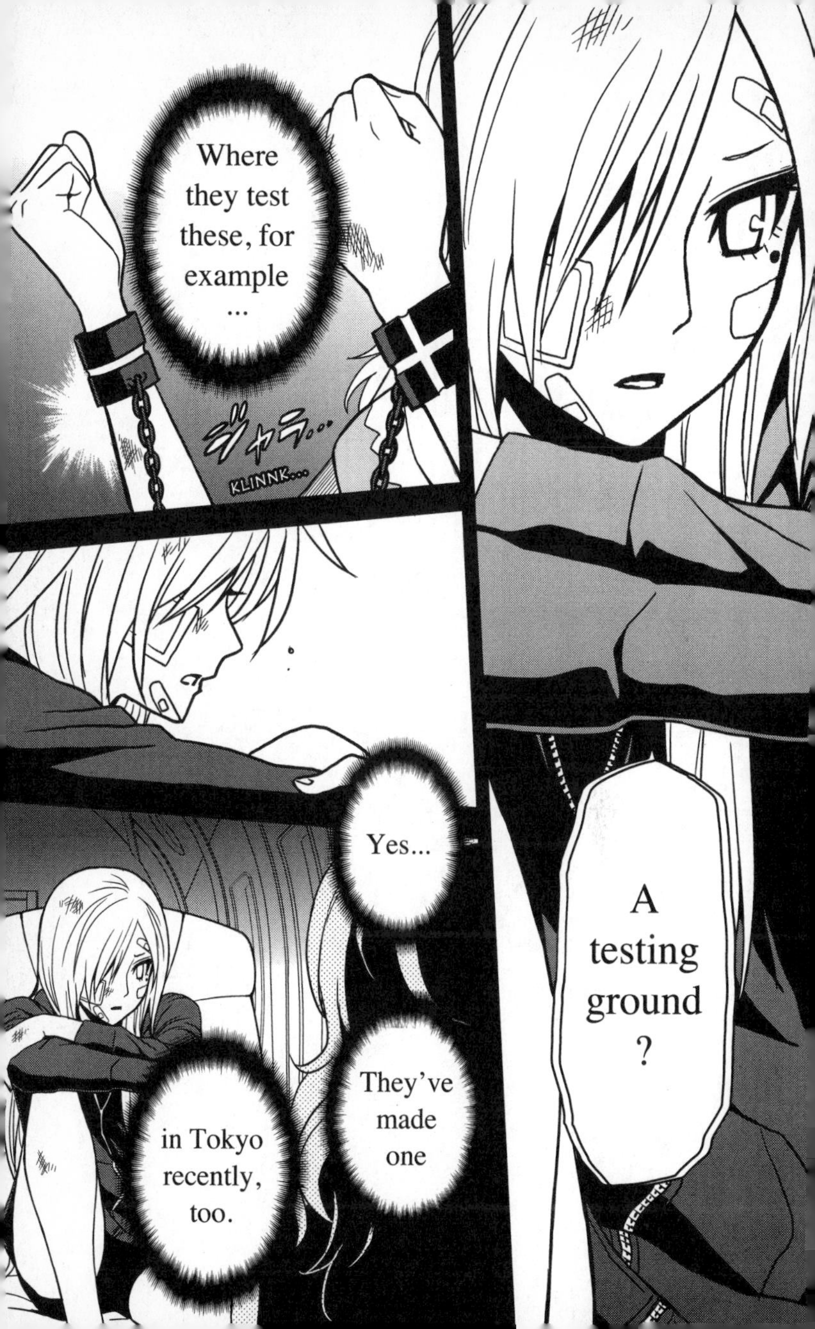
A testing ground?
Where they test these, for example...
ジャラ…
KLINNK...
Yes...
They've made one
in Tokyo recently, too.

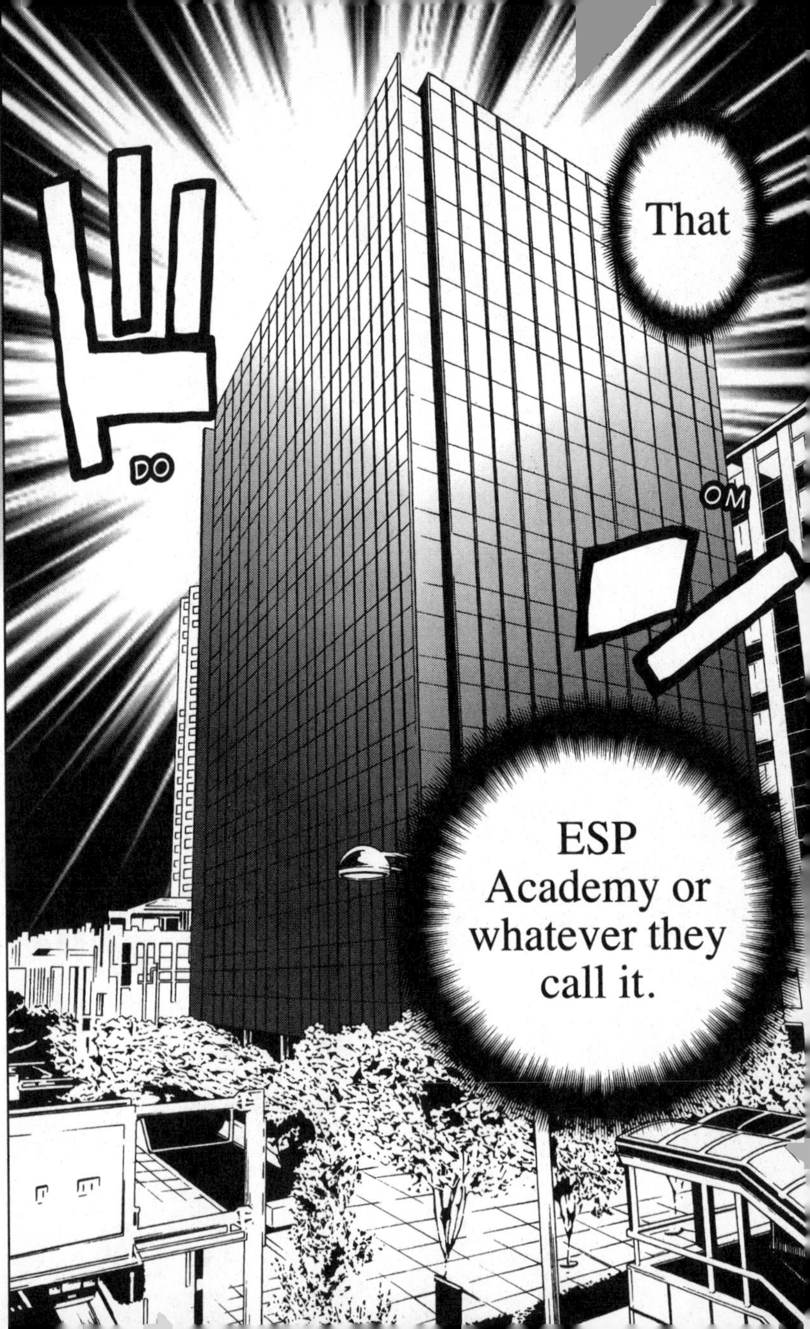
That
ESP Academy or whatever they call it.
DO
OM

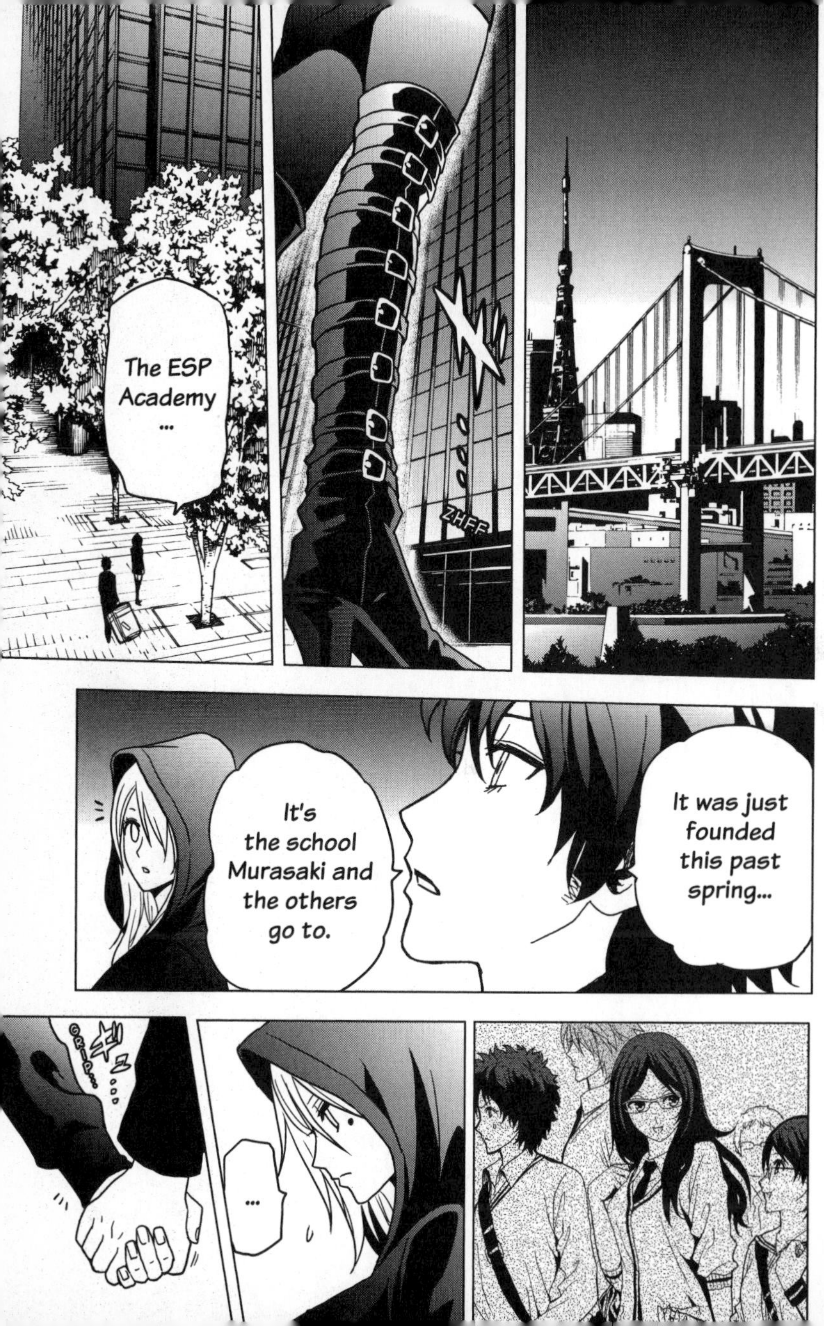
ZHFF
The ESP Academy ...
It was just founded this past spring...
It's the school Murasaki and the others go to.
...
GRIP...

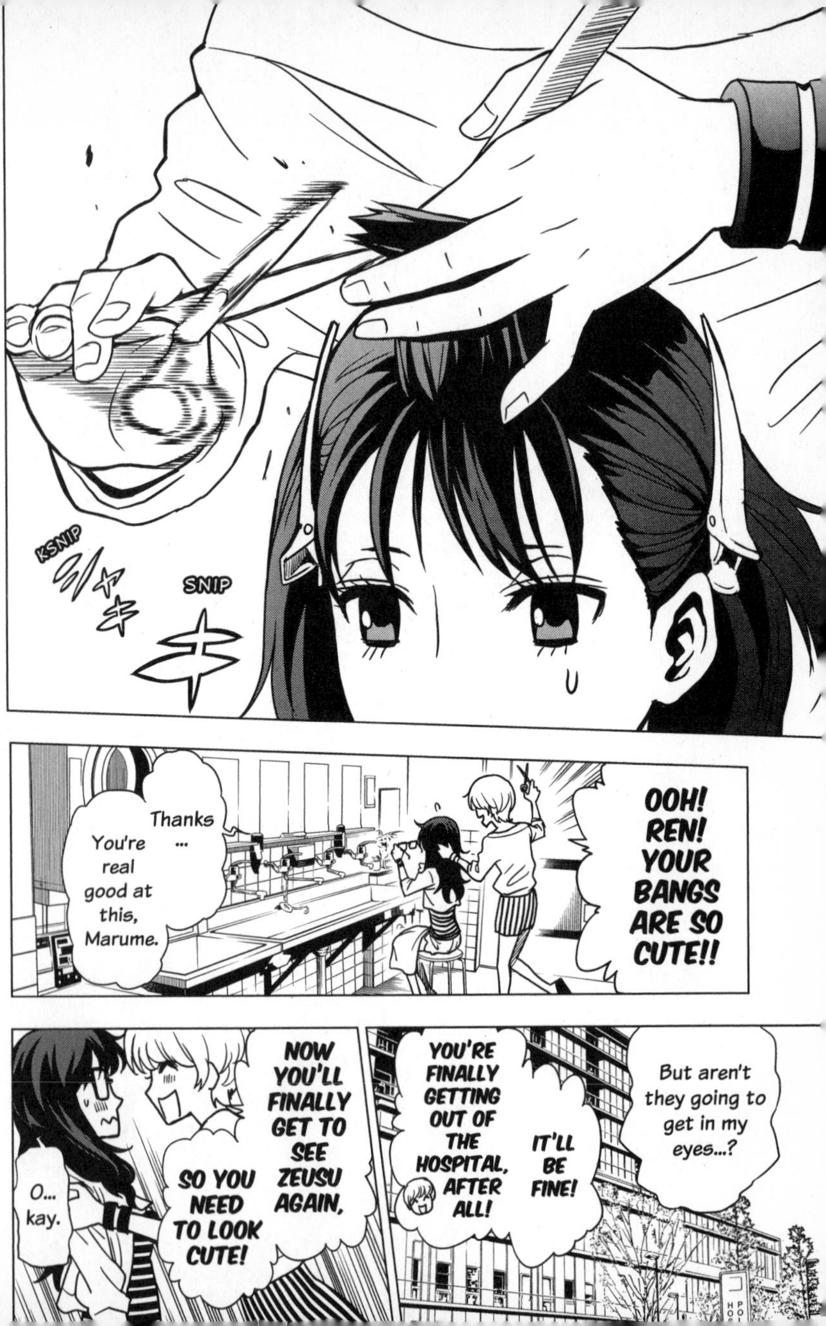
KSNIP
SNIP
OOH! REN! YOUR BANGS ARE SO CUTE!!
Thanks ... You're real good at this, Marume.
But aren't they going to get in my eyes...?
IT'LL BE FINE!
YOU'RE FINALLY GETTING OUT OF THE HOSPITAL, AFTER ALL!
NOW YOU'LL FINALLY GET TO SEE ZEUSU AGAIN,
SO YOU NEED TO LOOK CUTE!
O... kay.

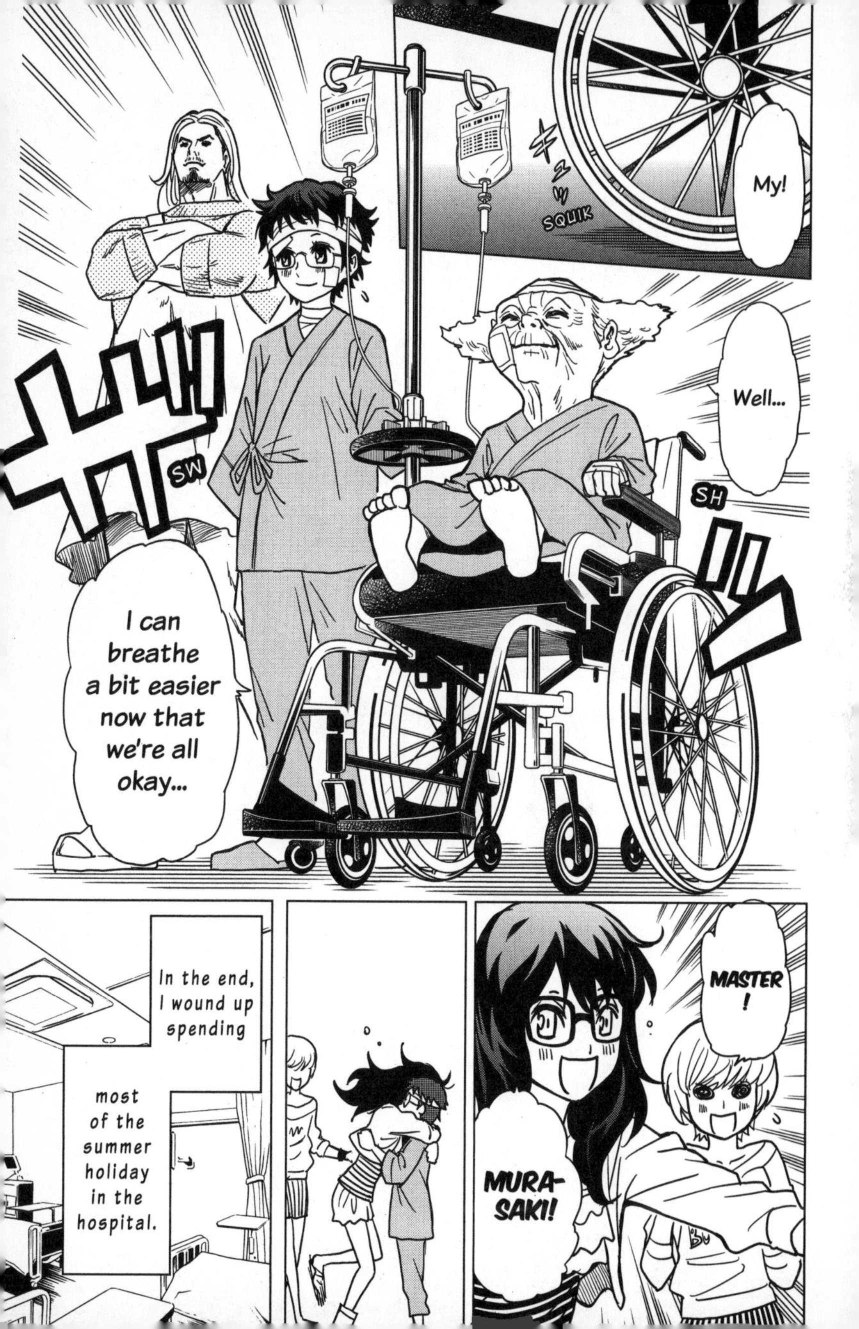
My!
SQUIK
Well...
SH
SW
I can breathe a bit easier now that we're all okay...
MASTER!
MURA-SAKI!
In the end, I wound up spending
most of the summer holiday in the hospital.

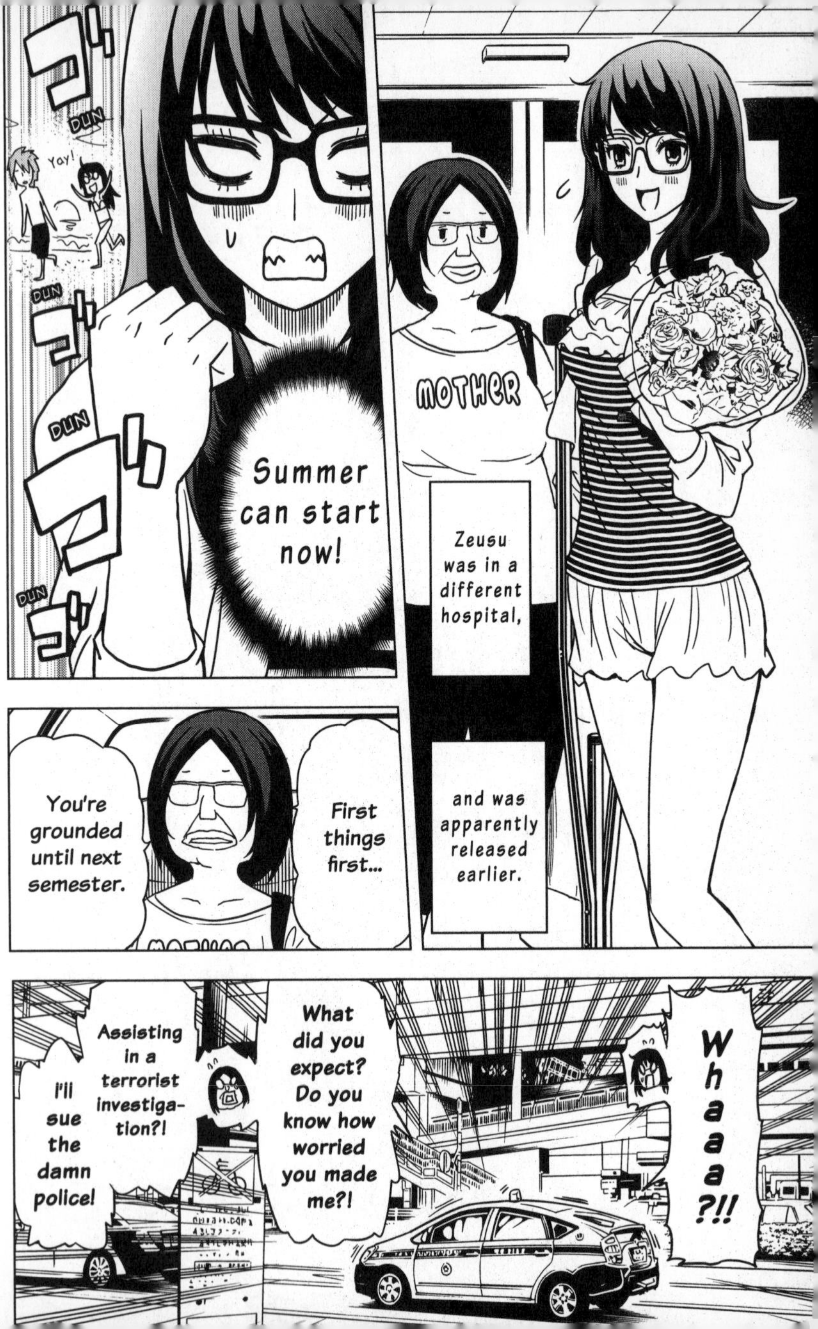
Zeusu was in a different hospital,
and was apparently released earlier.
MOTHER
DUN
Yay!
DUN
DUN
DUN
Summer can start now!
First things first...
You're grounded until next semester.
Whaaa?!!
What did you expect? Do you know how worried you made me?!
Assisting in a terrorist investigation?!
I'll sue the damn police!

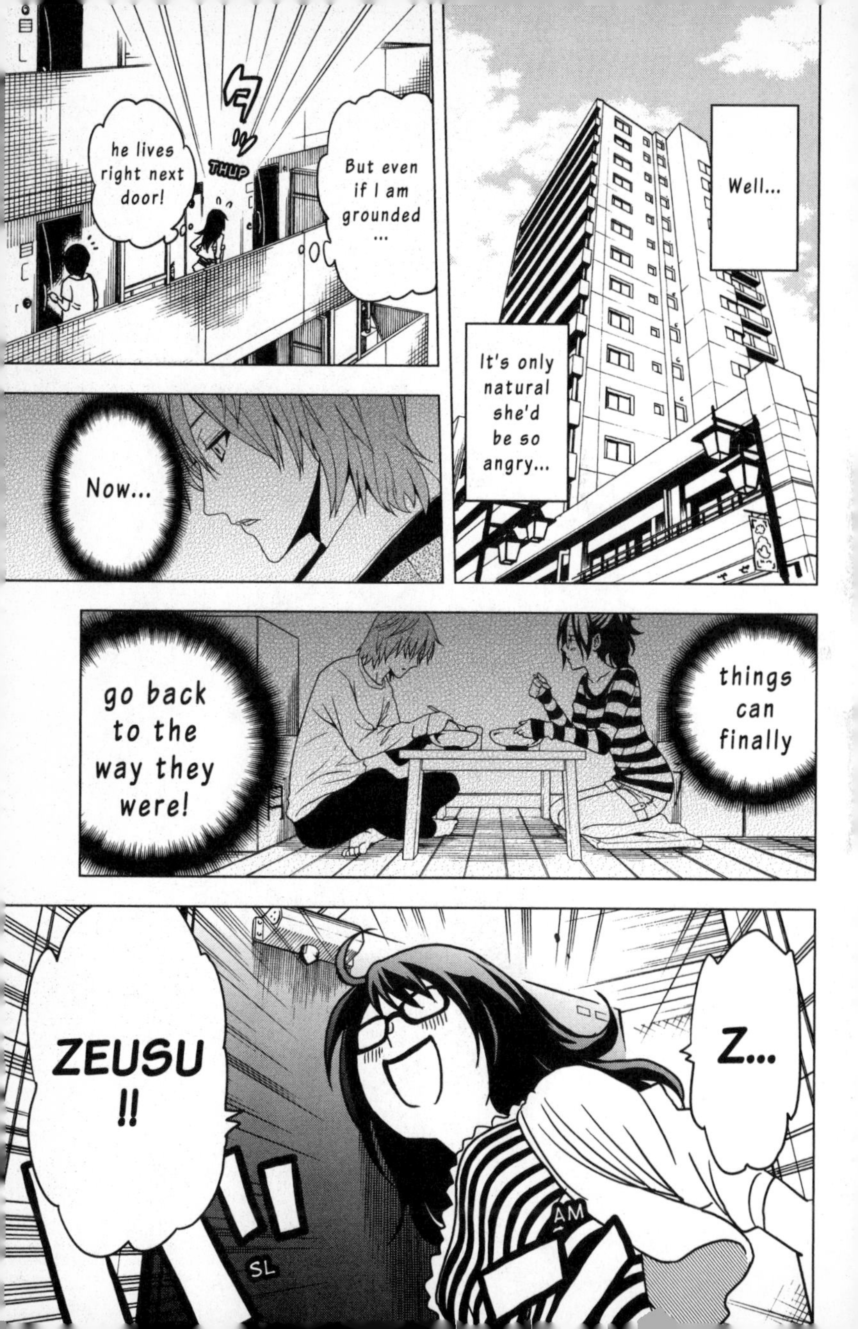
Well...
It's only natural she'd be so angry...
But even if I am grounded ...
THUP
he lives right next door!
Now...
things can finally
go back to the way they were!
Z...
AM
ZEUSU !!
SL

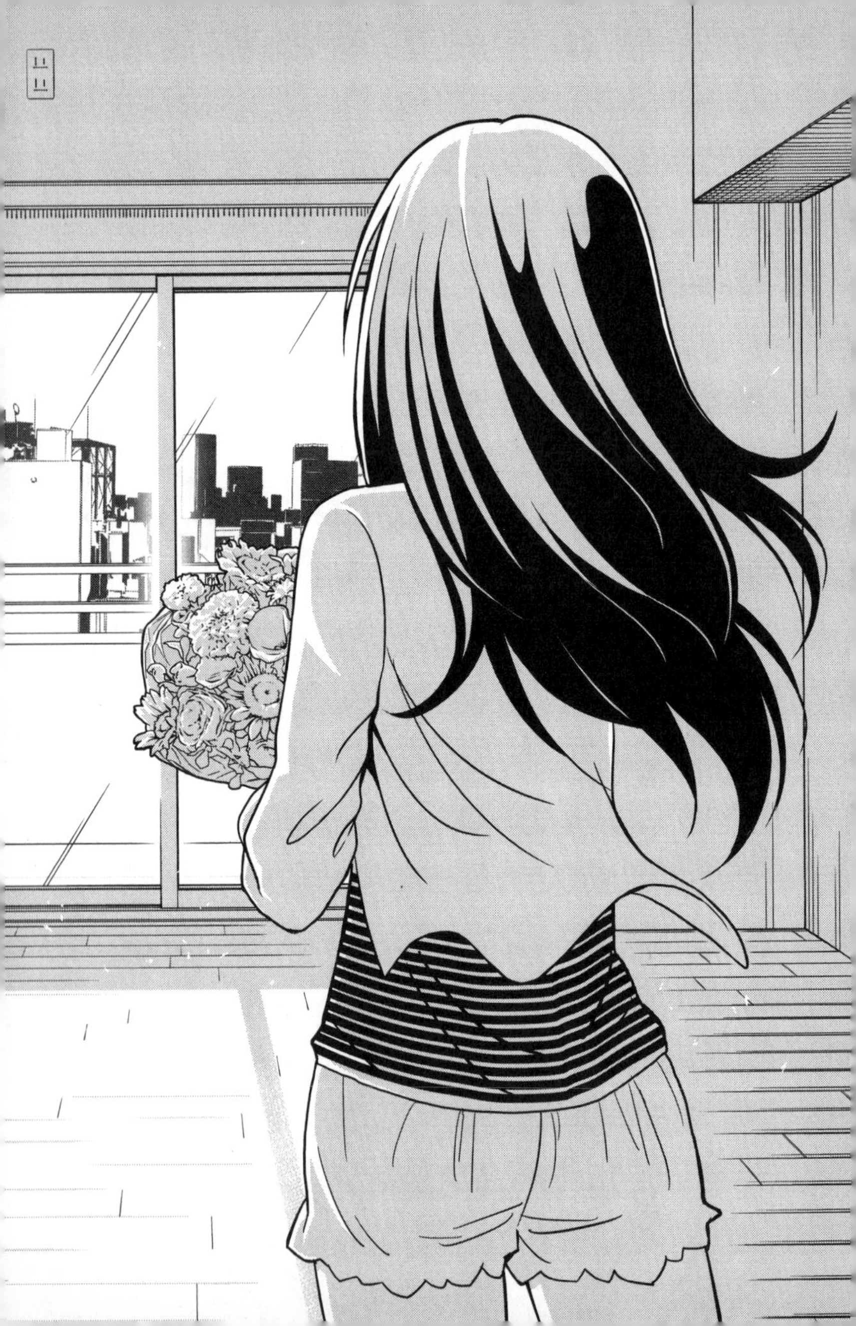

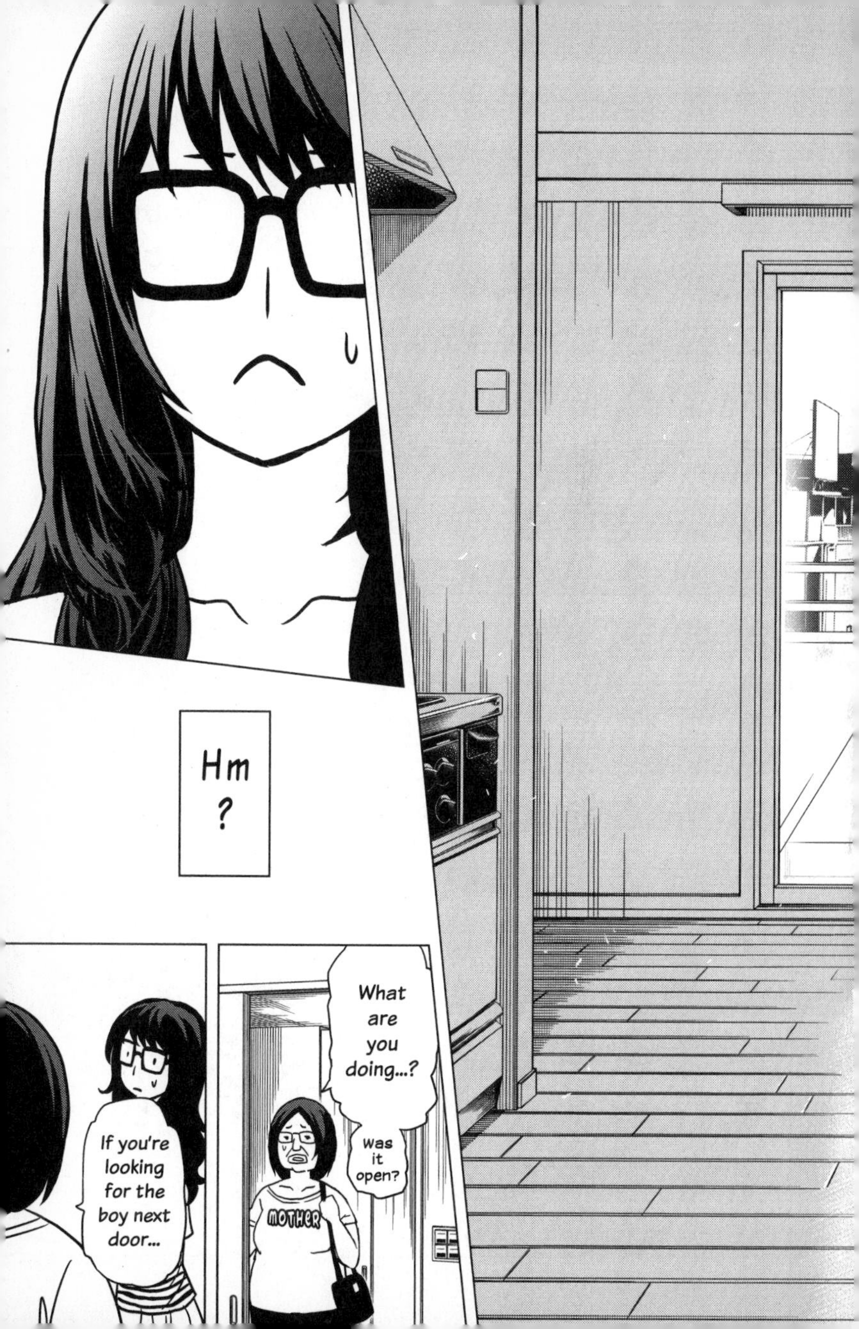
Hm ?
What are you doing...?
Was it open?
If you're looking for the boy next door...

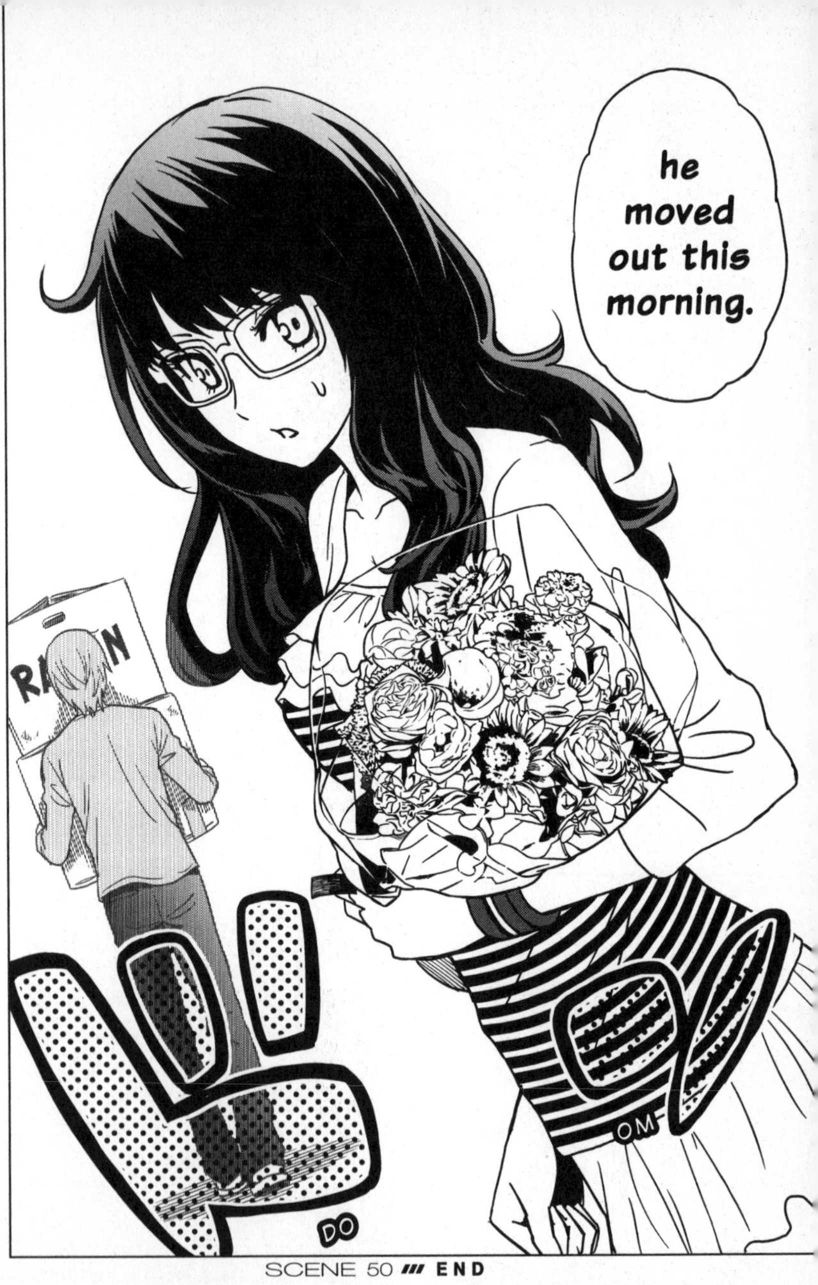
he moved out this morning.
DO
OM

SCENE 50 /// END

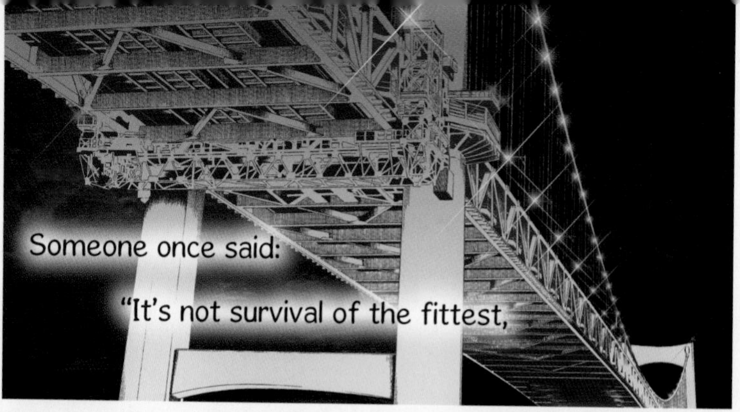
Someone once said:
"It's not survival of the fittest,

and it's not the smartest that live on.

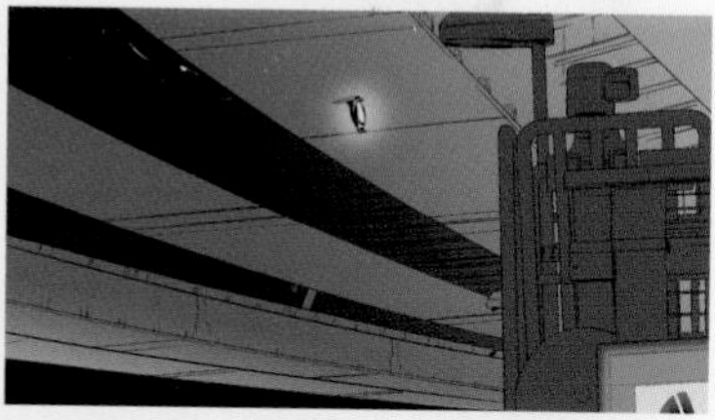

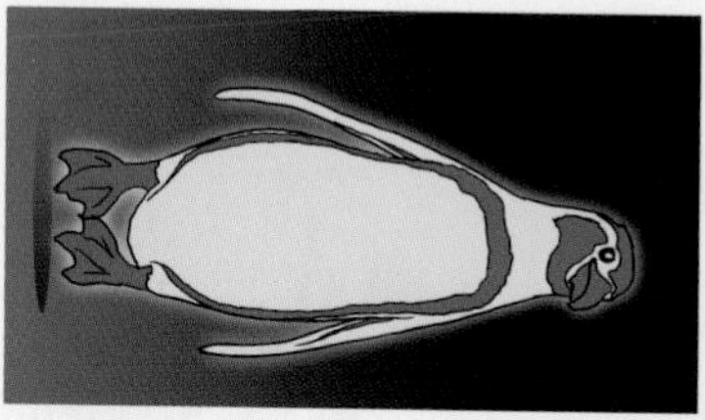

The only ones that survive are those that can change."

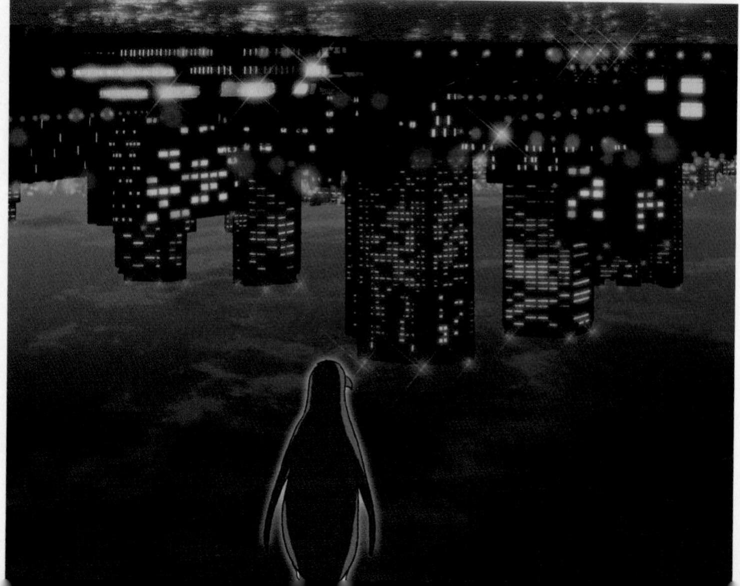

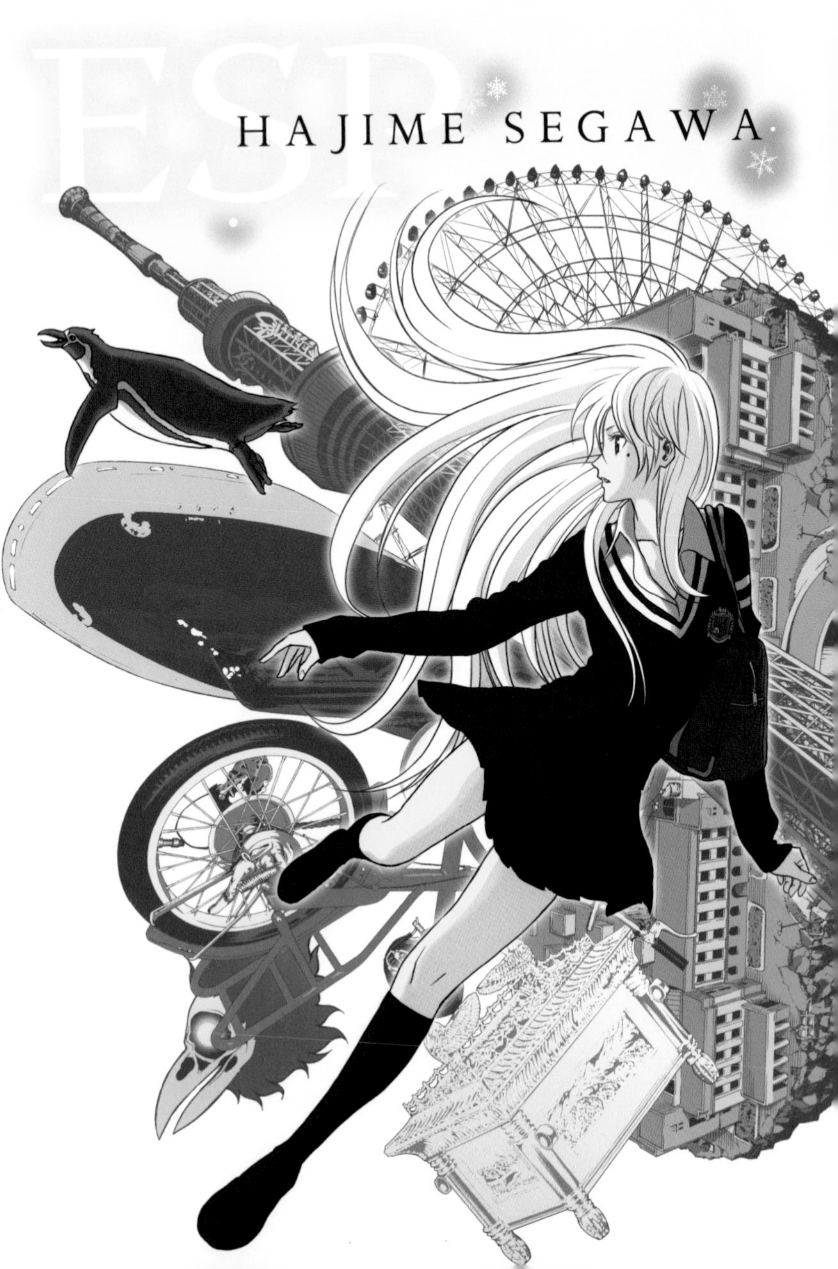
ESP
HAJIME SEGAWA

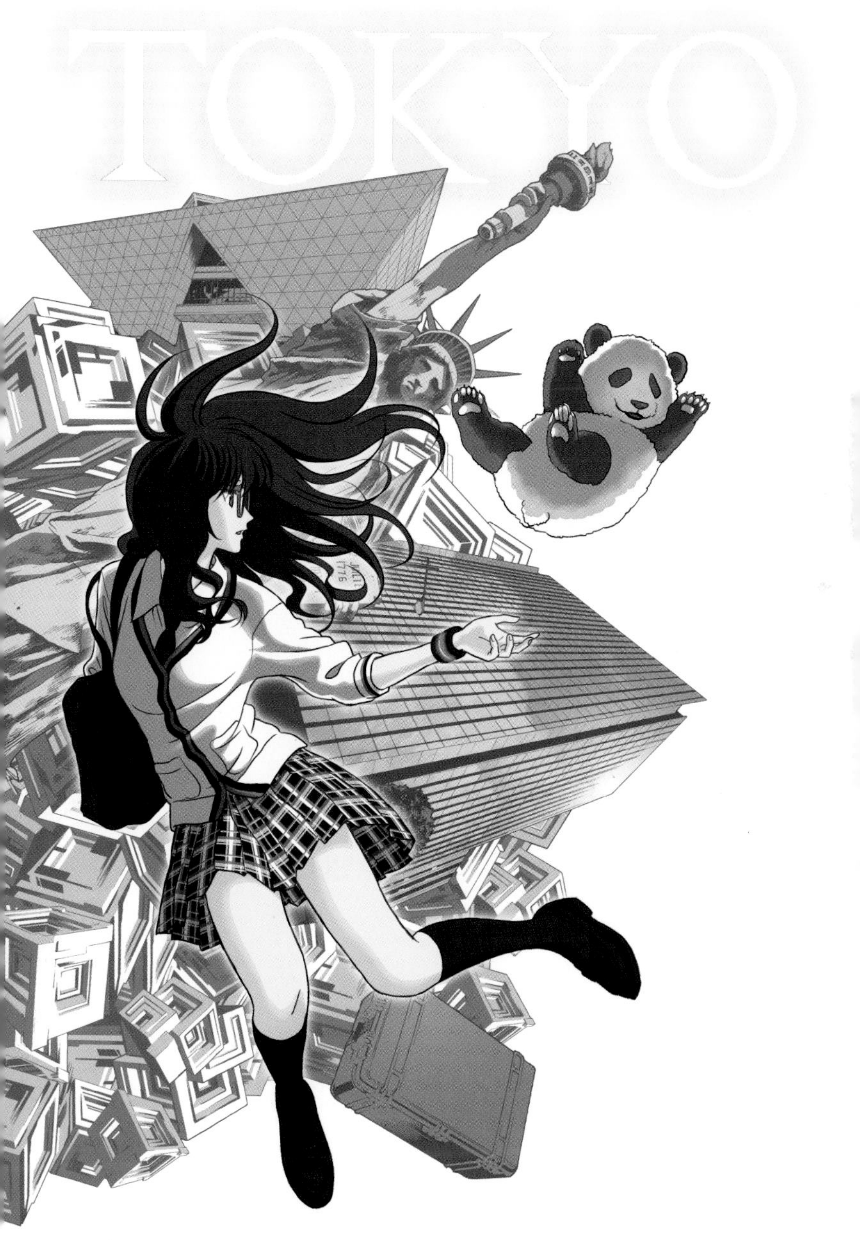
TOKYO

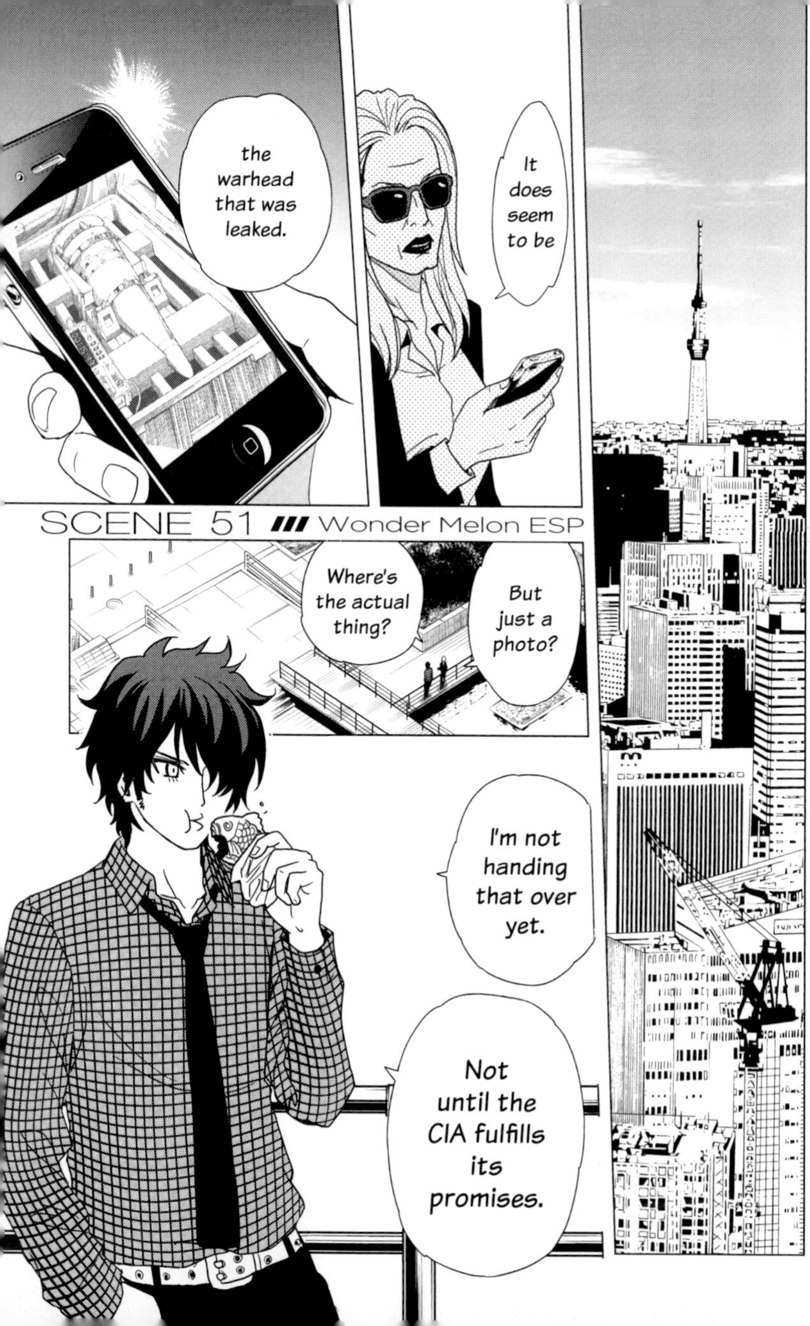
It does seem to be
the warhead that was leaked.
SCENE 51 /// Wonder Melon ESP
But just a photo?
Where's the actual thing?
I'm not handing that over yet.
Not until the CIA fulfills its promises.

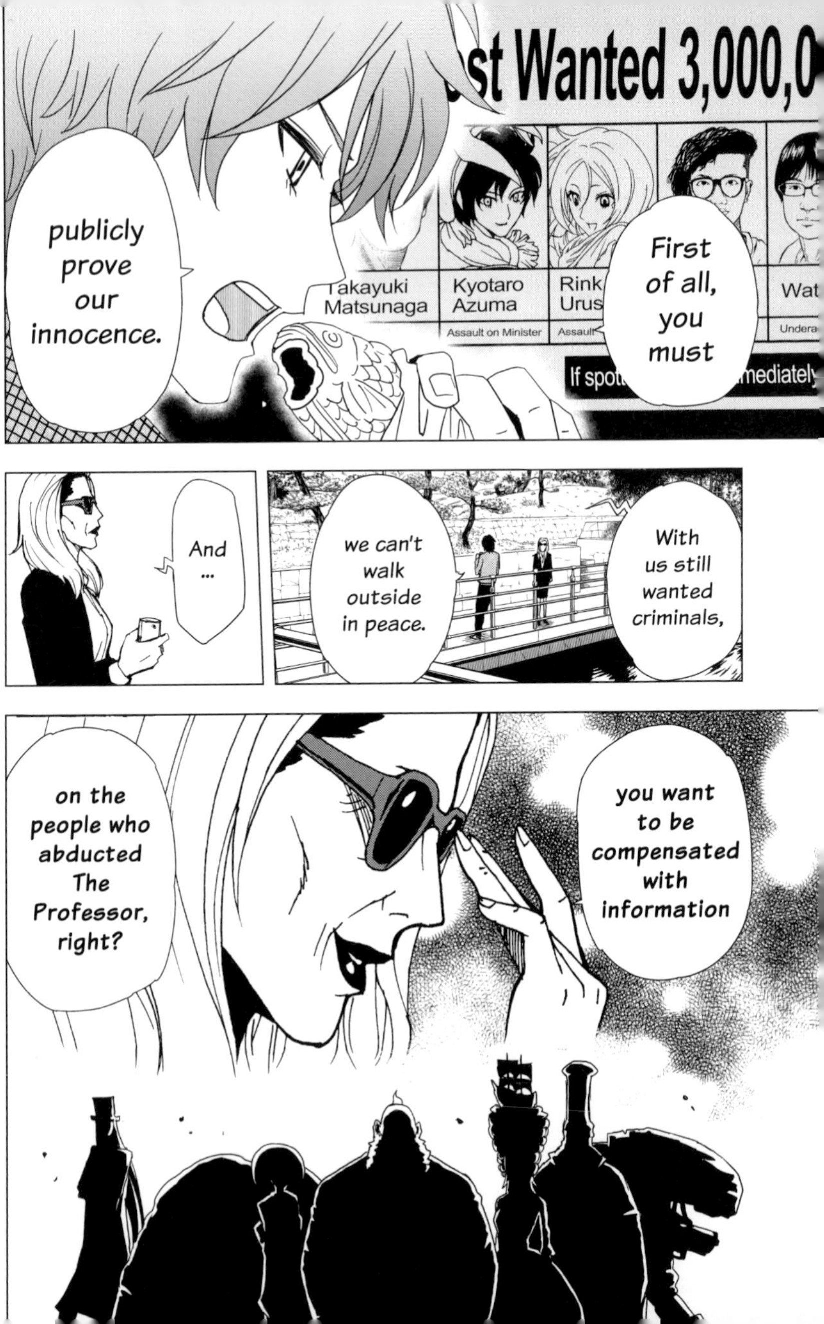
st Wanted 3,000,0
Takayuki Matsunaga
Kyotaro Azuma
Rink Urus
Wat
Assault on Minister
Assault
Undera
If spot
mediately
First of all, you must
publicly prove our innocence.
With us still wanted criminals,
we can't walk outside in peace.
And ...
you want to be compensated with information
on the people who abducted The Professor, right?

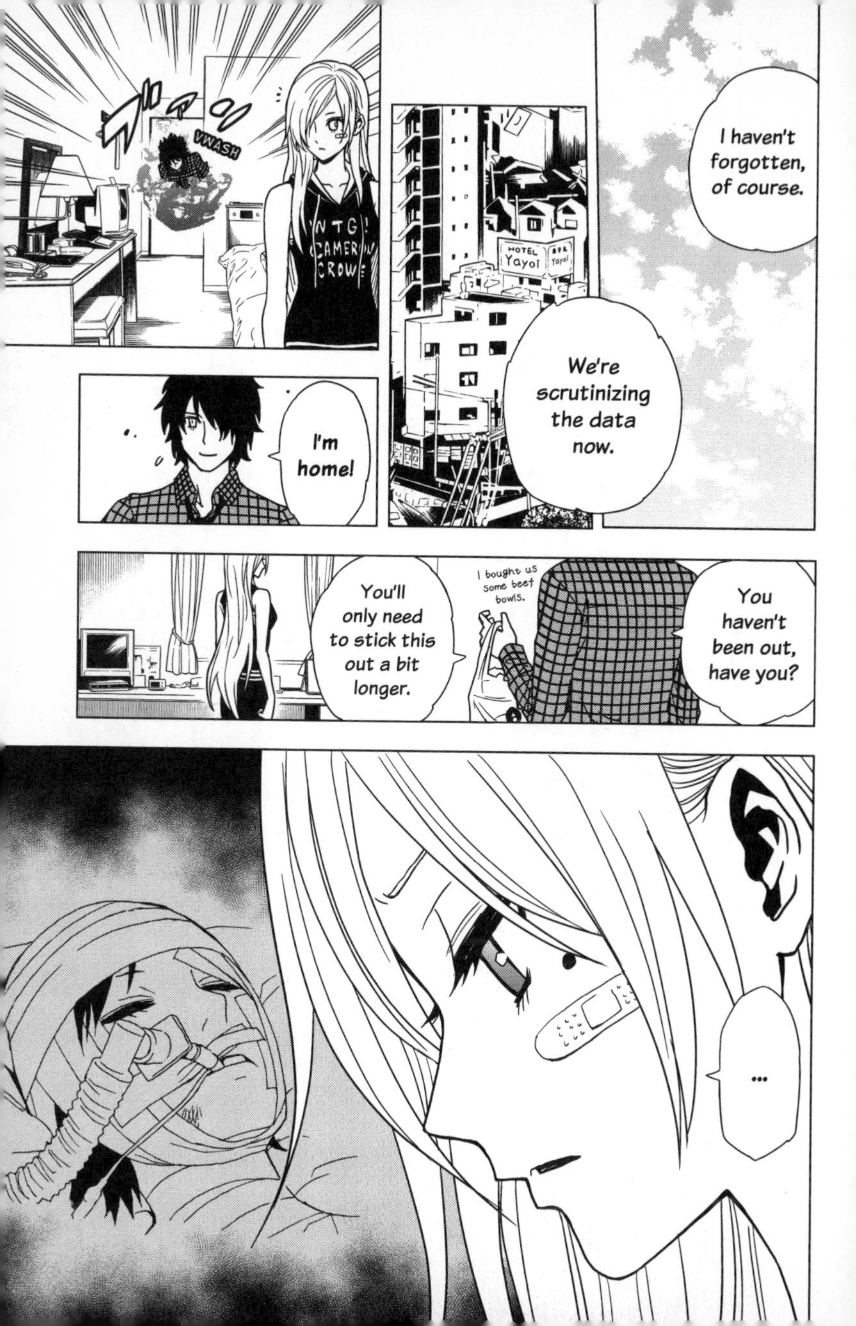
I haven't forgotten, of course.
HOTEL Yayoi
We're scrutinizing the data now.
VWASH
I'm home!
You haven't been out, have you?
I bought us some beef bowls.
You'll only need to stick this out a bit longer.
...

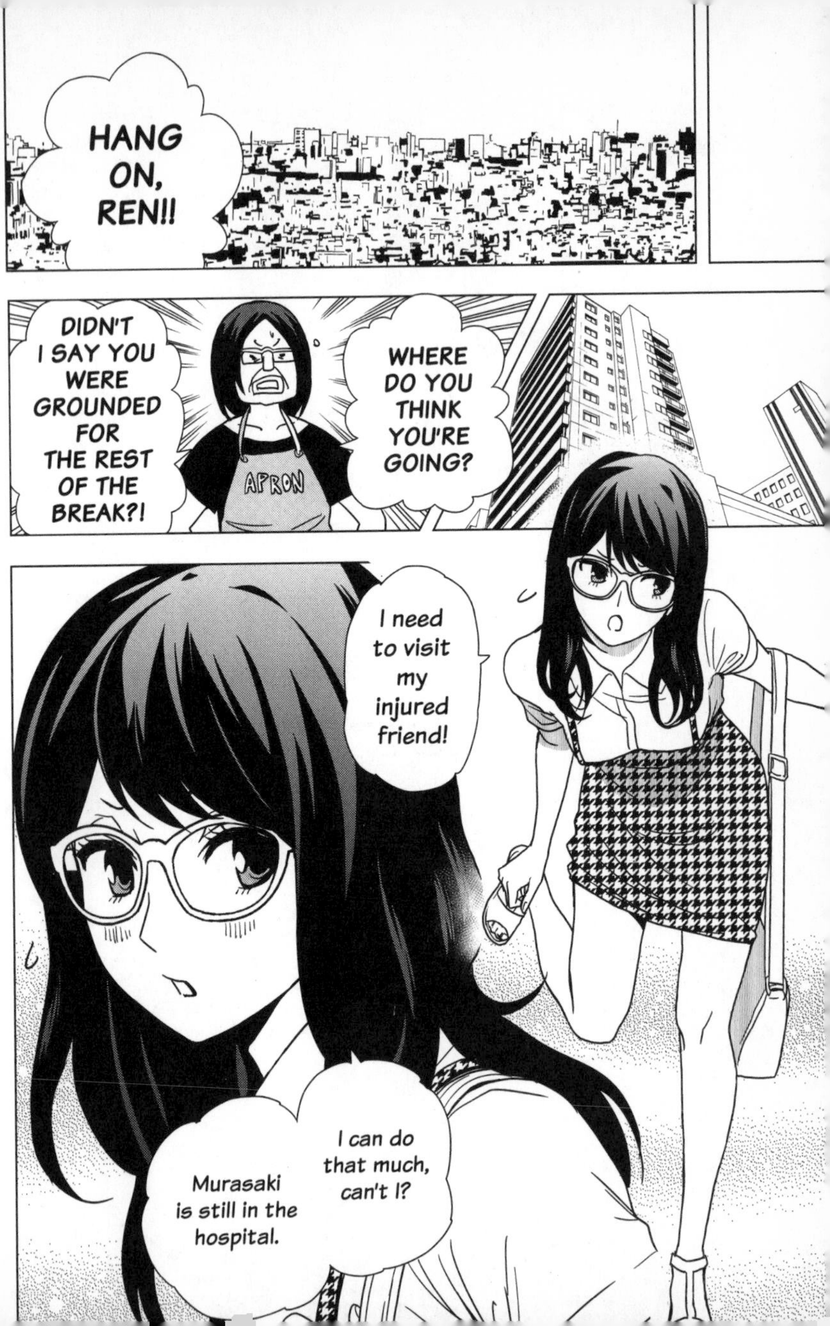
HANG ON, REN!!
WHERE DO YOU THINK YOU'RE GOING?
DIDN'T I SAY YOU WERE GROUNDED FOR THE REST OF THE BREAK?!
APRON
I need to visit my injured friend!
Murasaki is still in the hospital.
I can do that much, can't I?

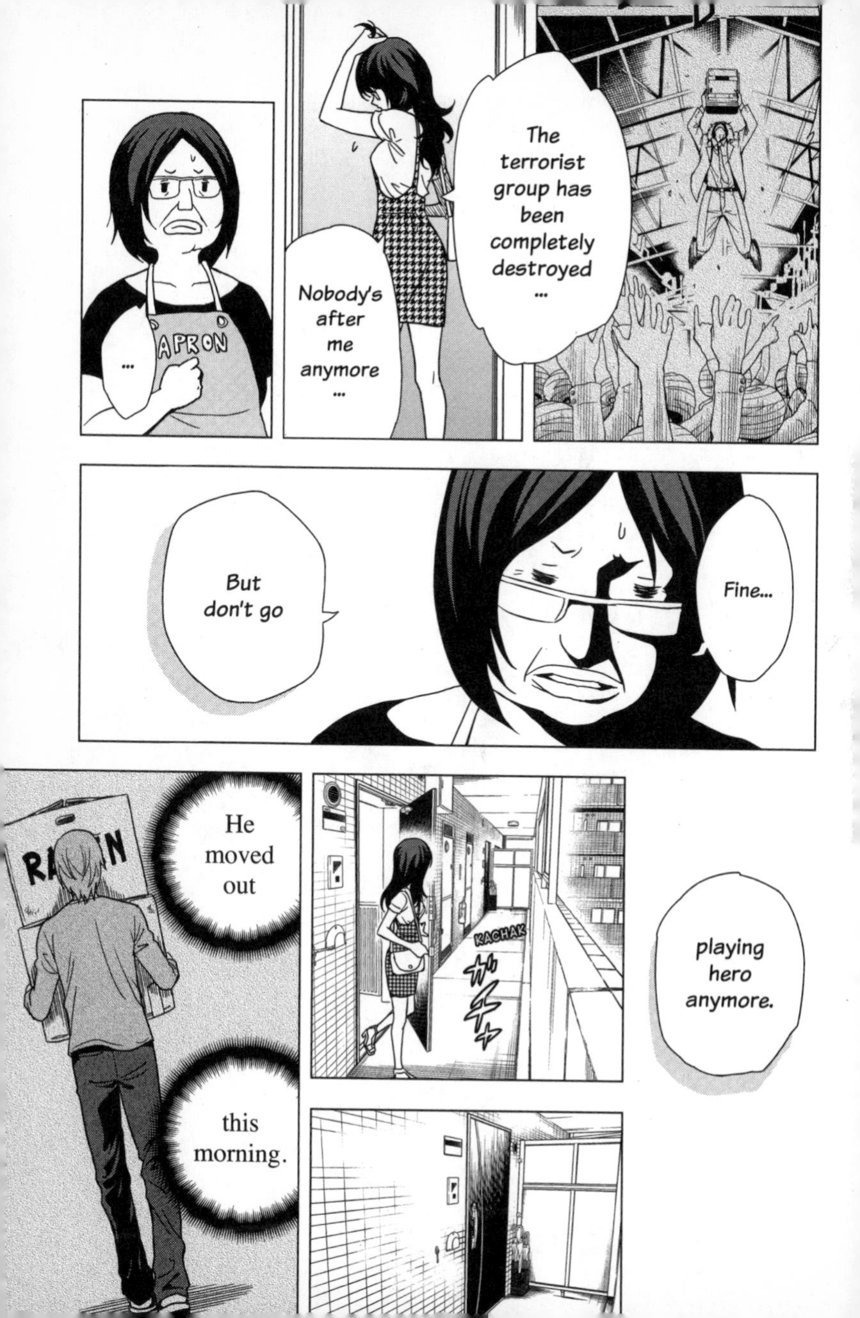
The terrorist group has been completely destroyed ...
Nobody's after me anymore ...
APRON
...
Fine...
But don't go
playing hero anymore.
KACHAK
He moved out
this morning.

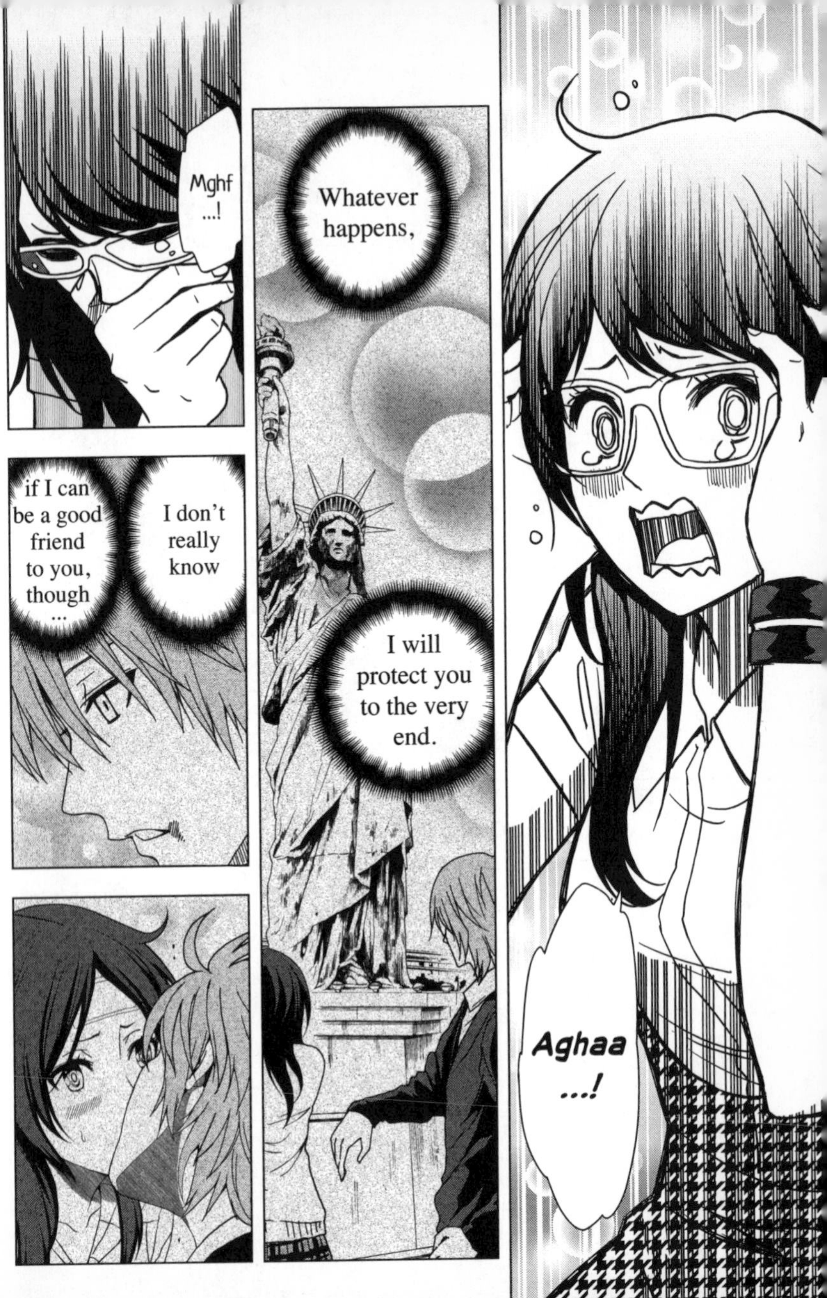
Aghaa
...!
Whatever happens,
I will protect you to the very end.
Mghf
...!
I don't really know
if I can be a good friend to you, though
...

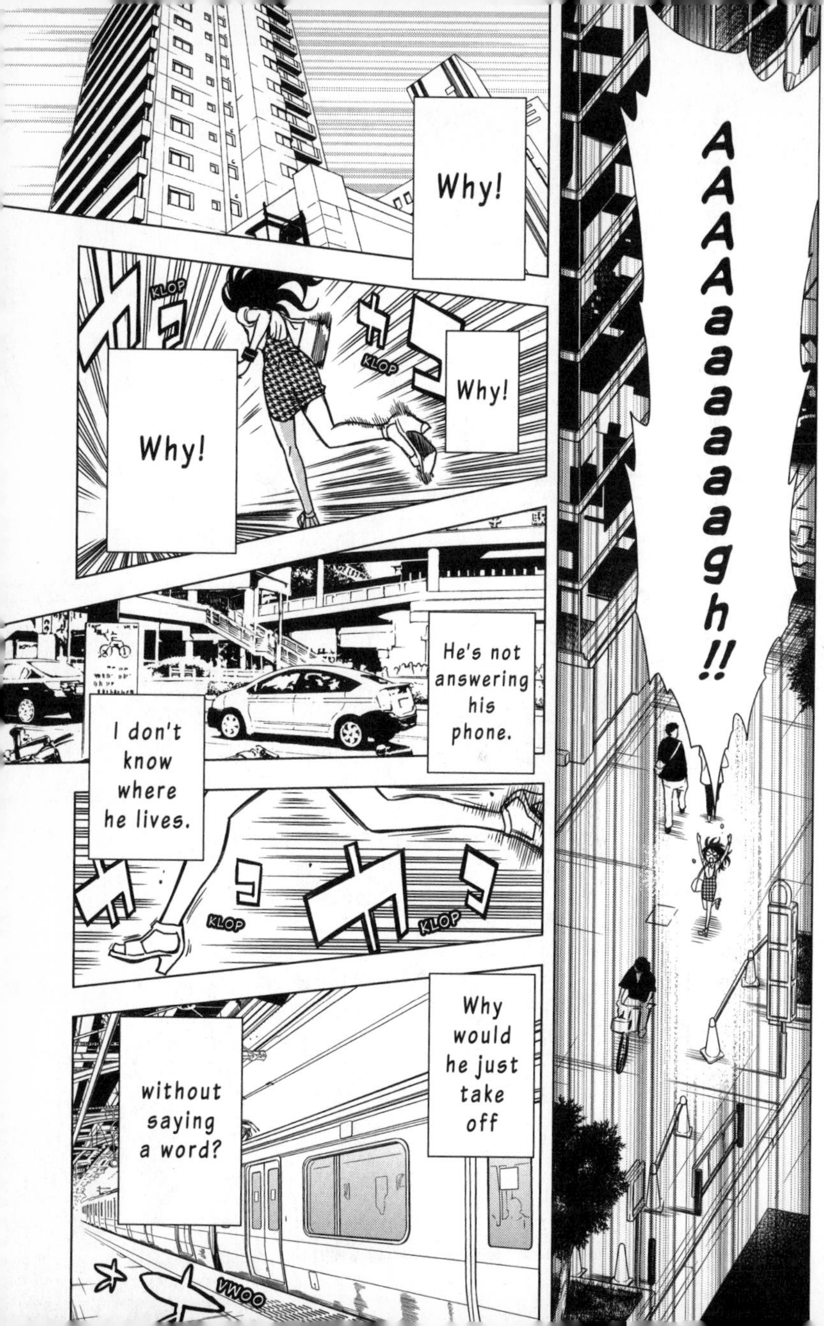
AAAAaaaaagh!!
Why!
KLOP
KLOP
Why!
Why!
He's not answering his phone.
I don't know where he lives.
KLOP
KLOP
Why would he just take off
without saying a word?
VWOO

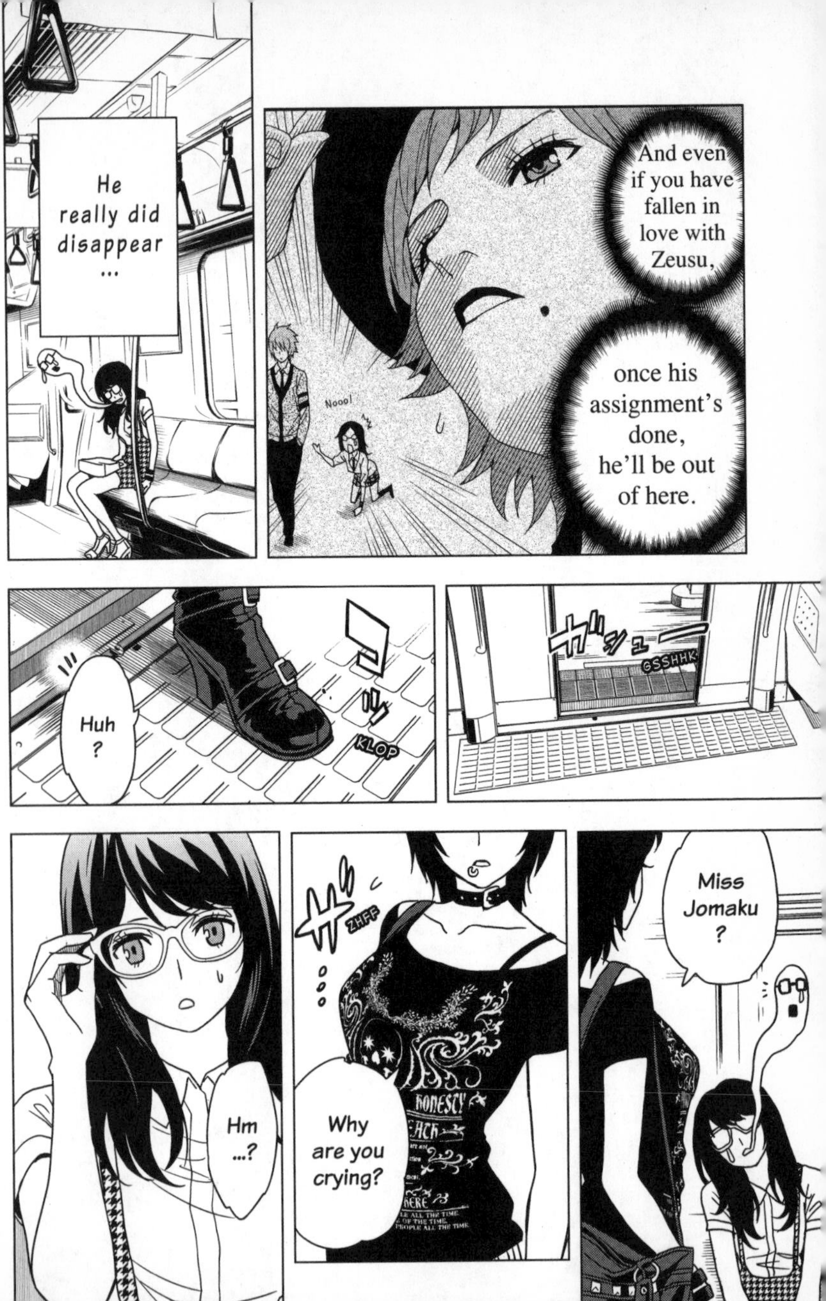
And even if you have fallen in love with Zeusu,
once his assignment's done, he'll be out of here.
Nooo!
He really did disappear ...
GSSHHK
KLOP
Huh ?
Miss Jomaku ?
ZHFF
Why are you crying?
Hm ...?

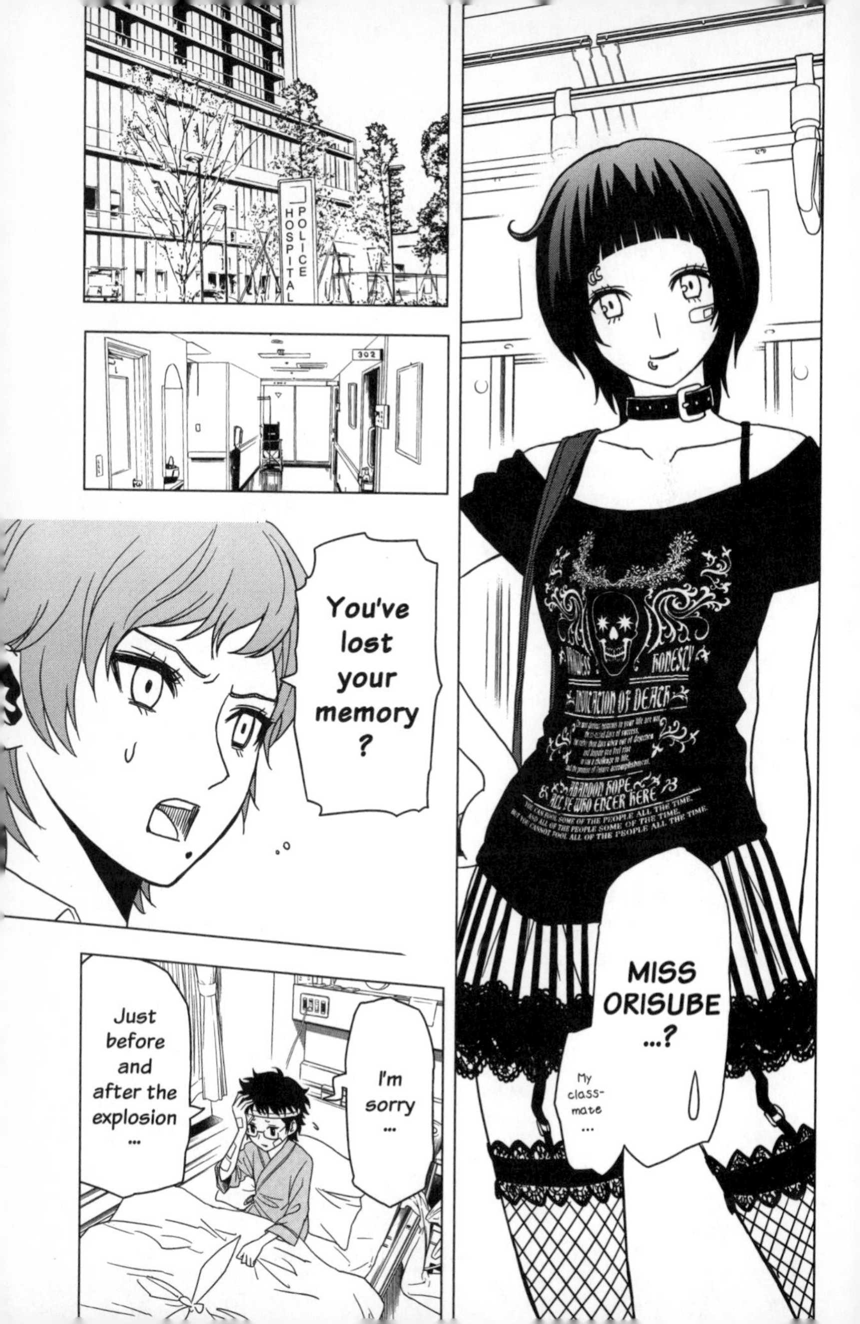
MISS ORISUBE ...?
My class-mate ...
POLICE HOSPITAL
302
You've lost your memory ?
I'm sorry ...
Just before and after the explosion ...

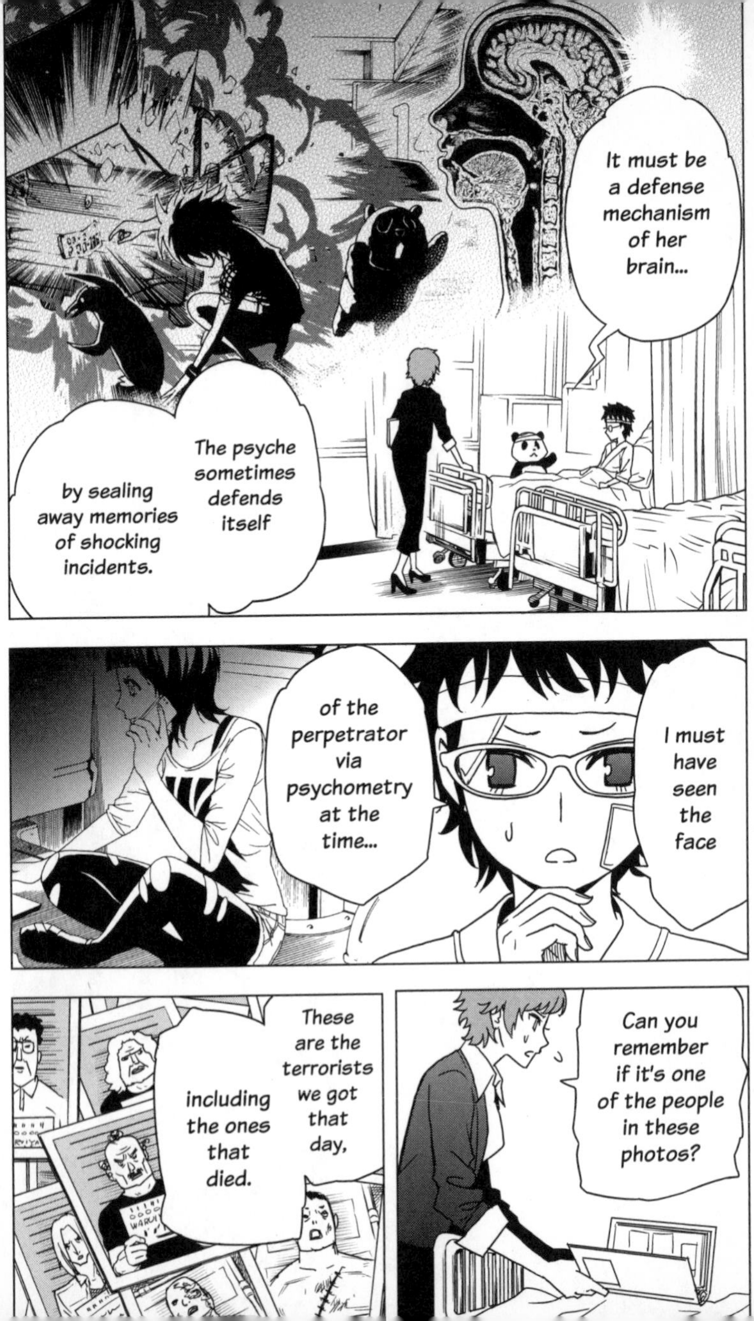
It must be a defense mechanism of her brain...
The psyche sometimes defends itself
by sealing away memories of shocking incidents.
I must have seen the face
of the perpetrator via psychometry at the time...
Can you remember if it's one of the people in these photos?
These are the terrorists we got that day,
including the ones that died.

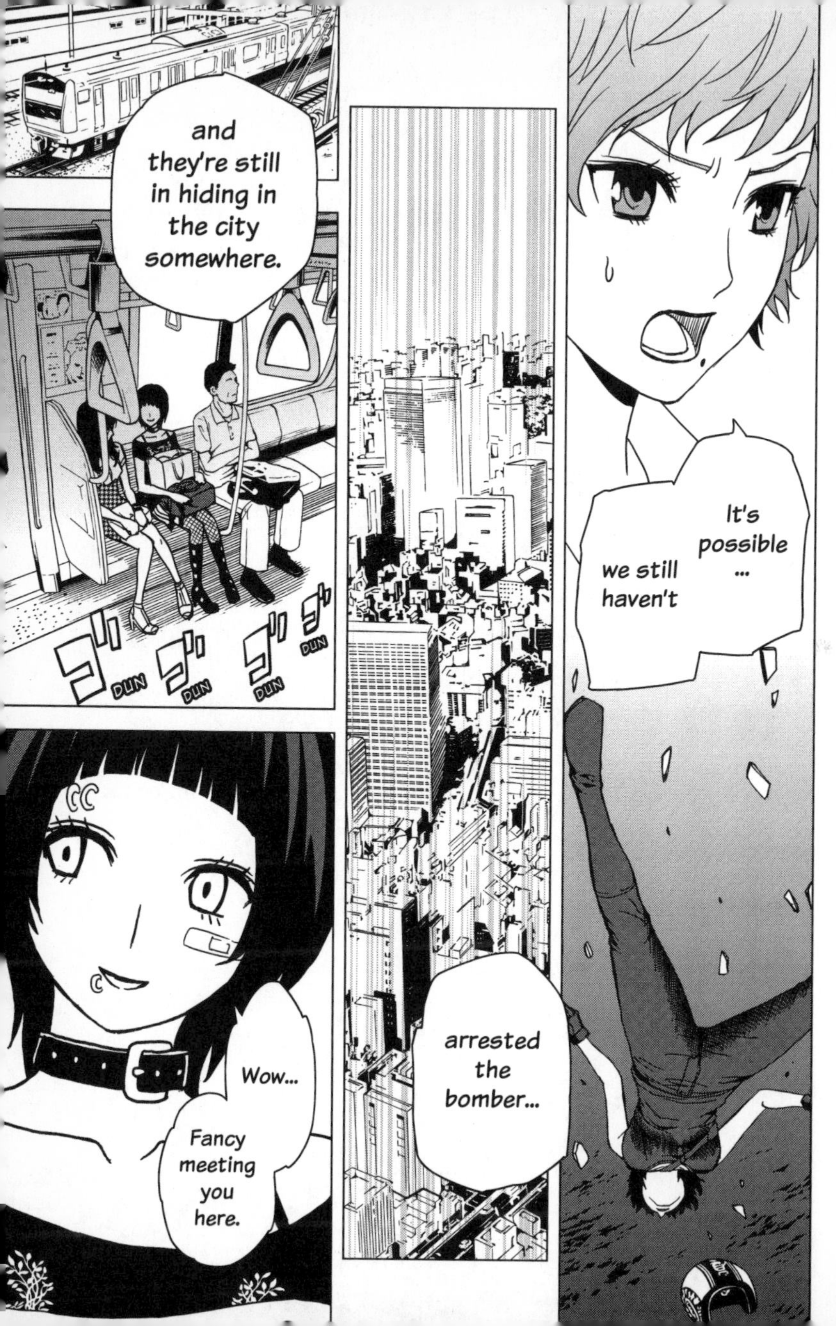
It's possible...
we still haven't
arrested the bomber...
and they're still in hiding in the city somewhere.
DUN DUN DUN DUN
Wow...
Fancy meeting you here.

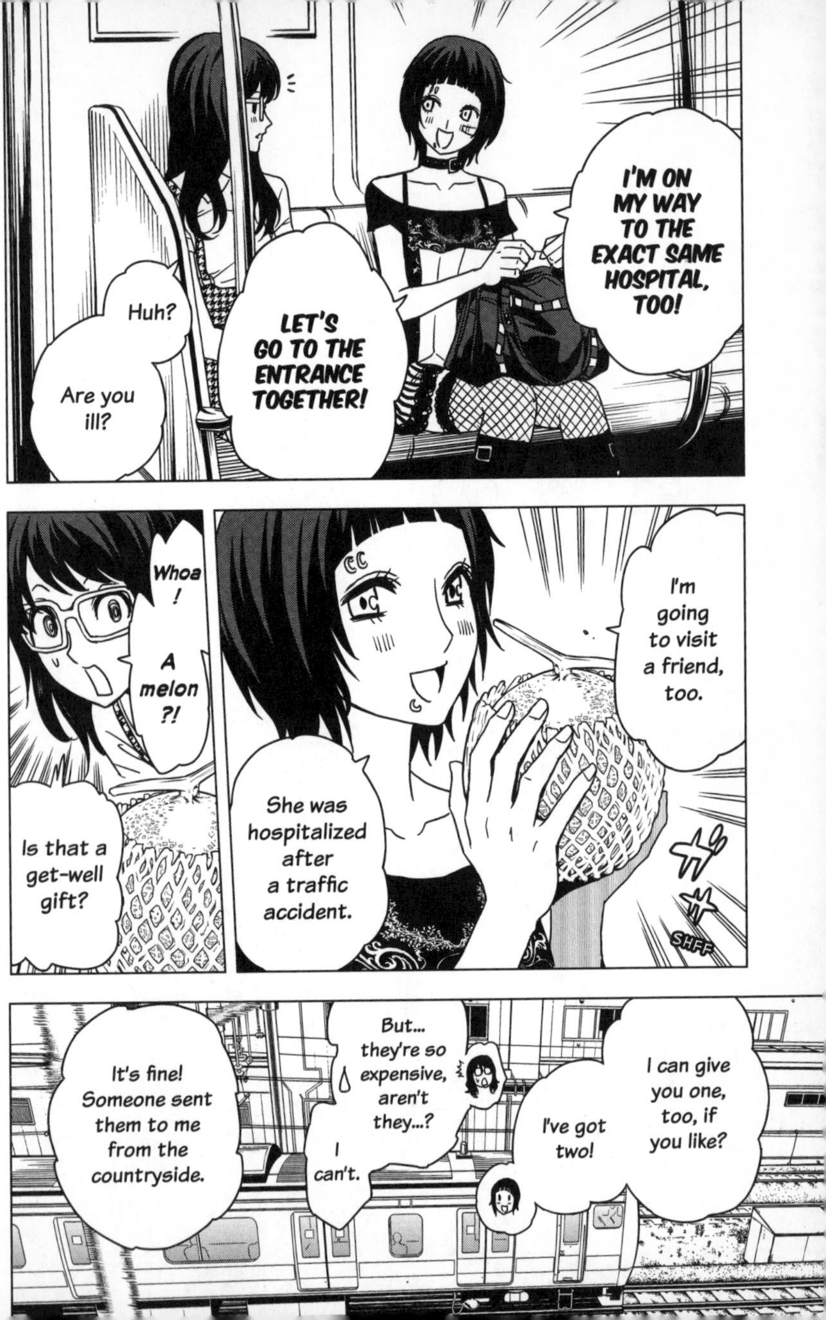

I'M ON MY WAY TO THE EXACT SAME HOSPITAL, TOO!
LET'S GO TO THE ENTRANCE TOGETHER!
Huh?
Are you ill?
I'm going to visit a friend, too.
She was hospitalized after a traffic accident.
SHFF
Whoa!
A melon ?!
Is that a get-well gift?
I can give you one, too, if you like?
I've got two!
But... they're so expensive, aren't they...?
I can't.
It's fine! Someone sent them to me from the countryside.

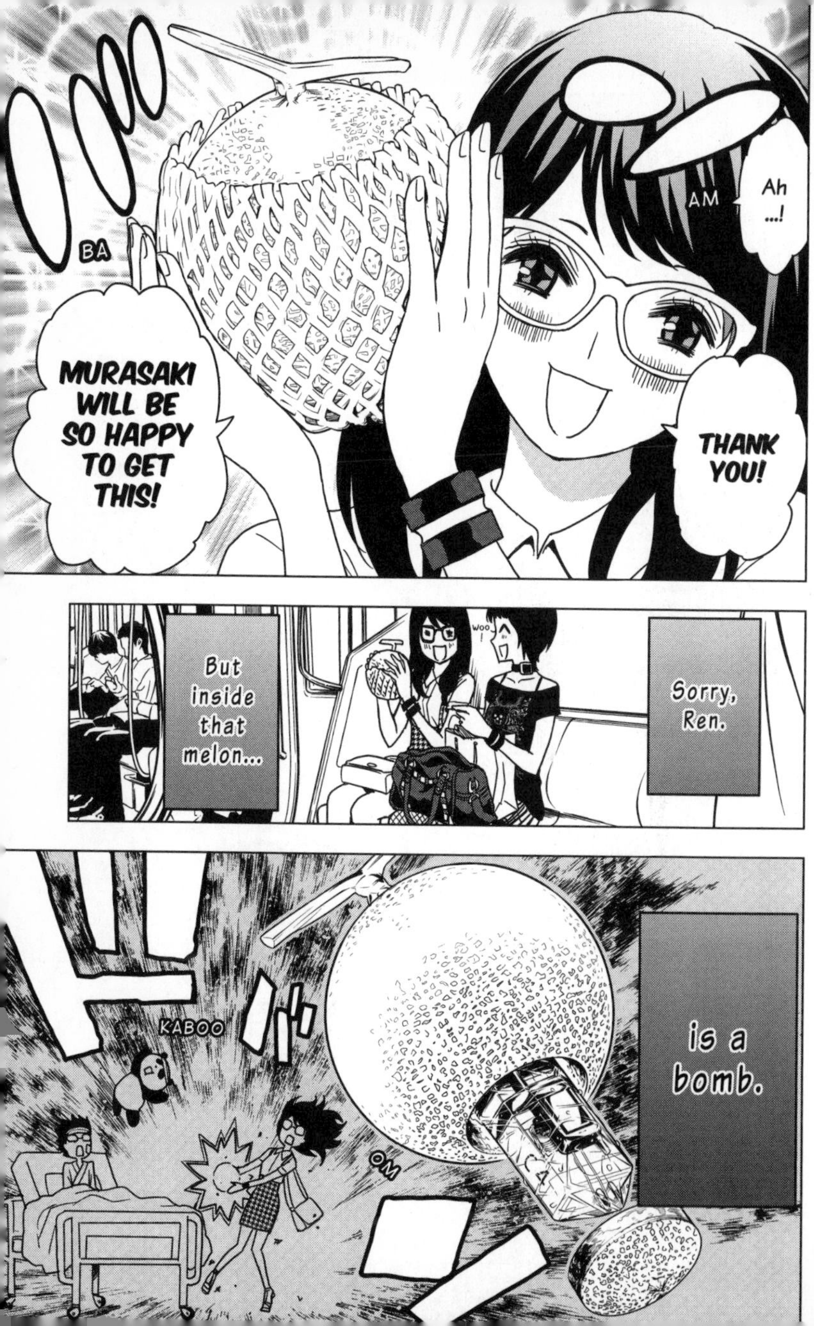
Ah
...!
AM
THANK YOU!
MURASAKI WILL BE SO HAPPY TO GET THIS!
BA
Sorry, Ren.
woo
!
But inside that melon...
is a bomb.
OM
KABOO

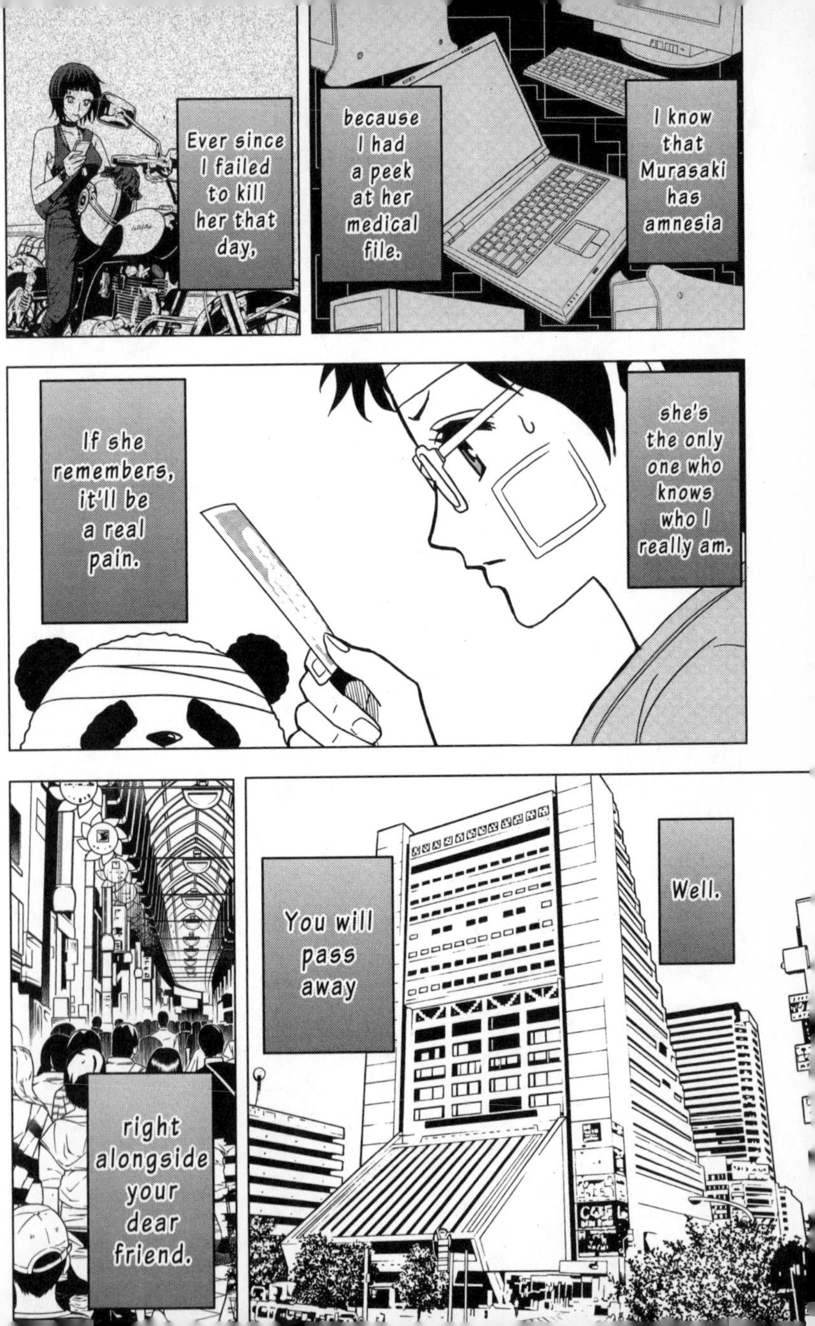
I know that Murasaki has amnesia
because I had a peek at her medical file.
Ever since I failed to kill her that day,
she's the only one who knows who I really am.
If she remembers, it'll be a real pain.
Well.
You will pass away
right alongside your dear friend.

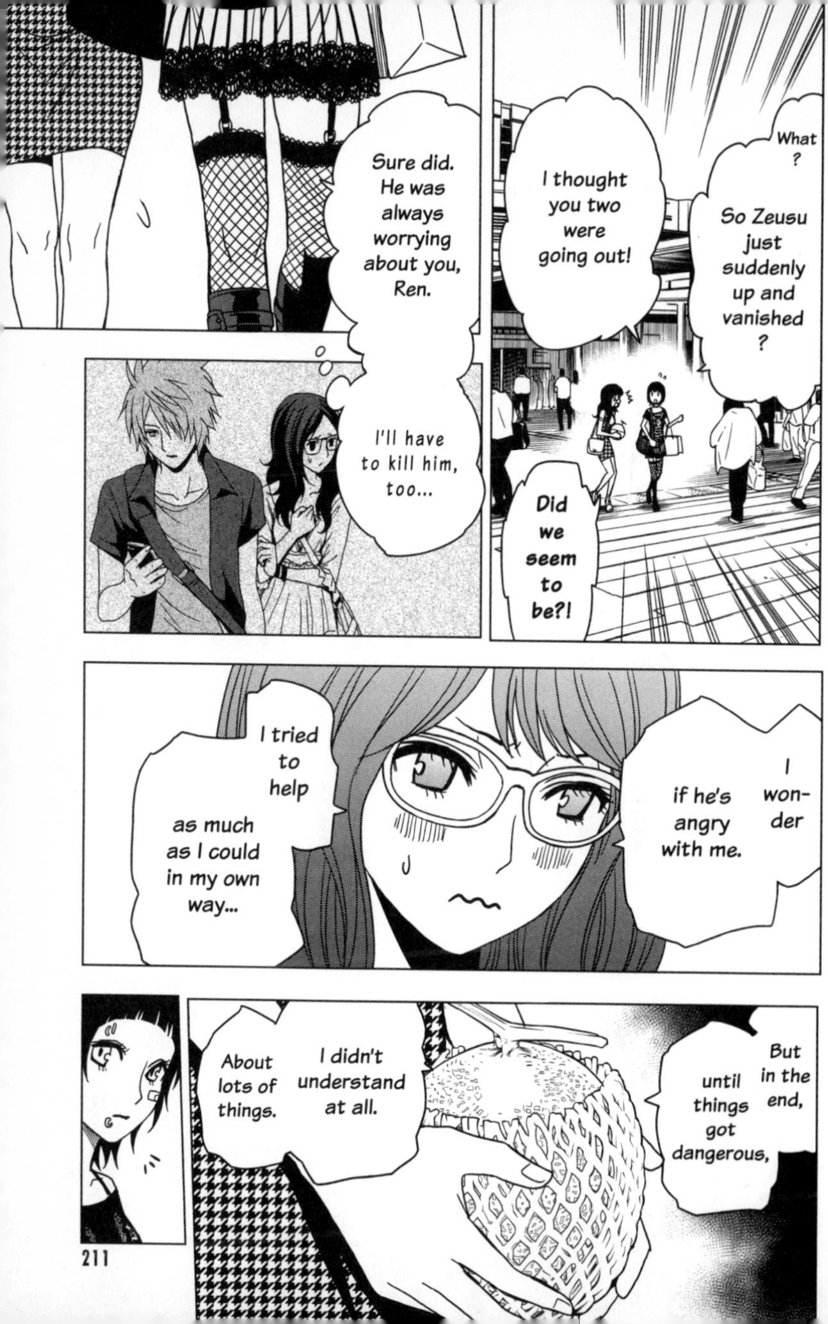
What?
So Zeusu just suddenly up and vanished?
I thought you two were going out!
Did we seem to be?!
Sure did. He was always worrying about you, Ren.
I'll have to kill him, too...
I wonder if he's angry with me.
I tried to help as much as I could in my own way...
But in the end, until things got dangerous,
I didn't understand at all.
About lots of things.

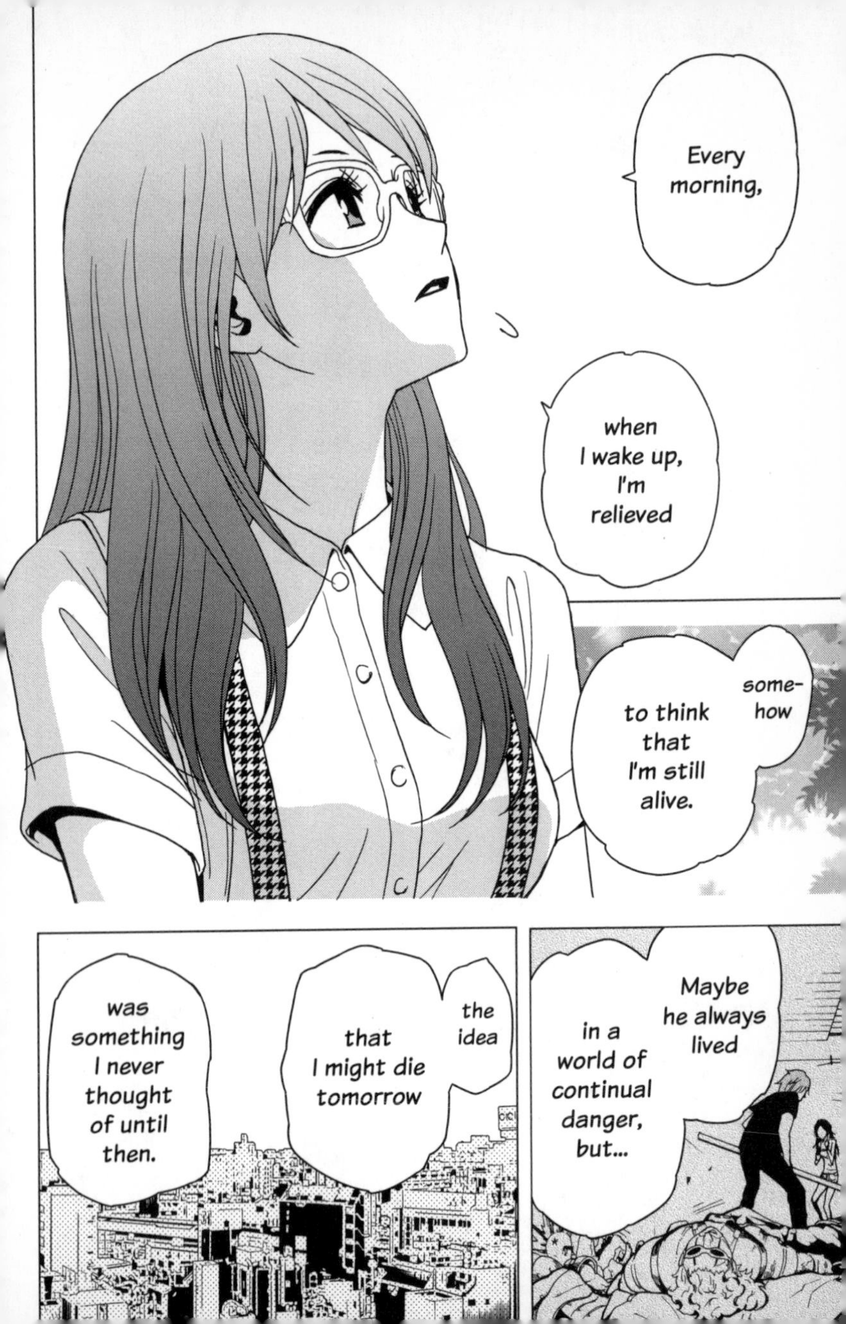
Every morning,
when I wake up, I'm relieved
some-how
to think that I'm still alive.
Maybe he always lived
in a world of continual danger, but...
the idea
that I might die tomorrow
was something I never thought of until then.

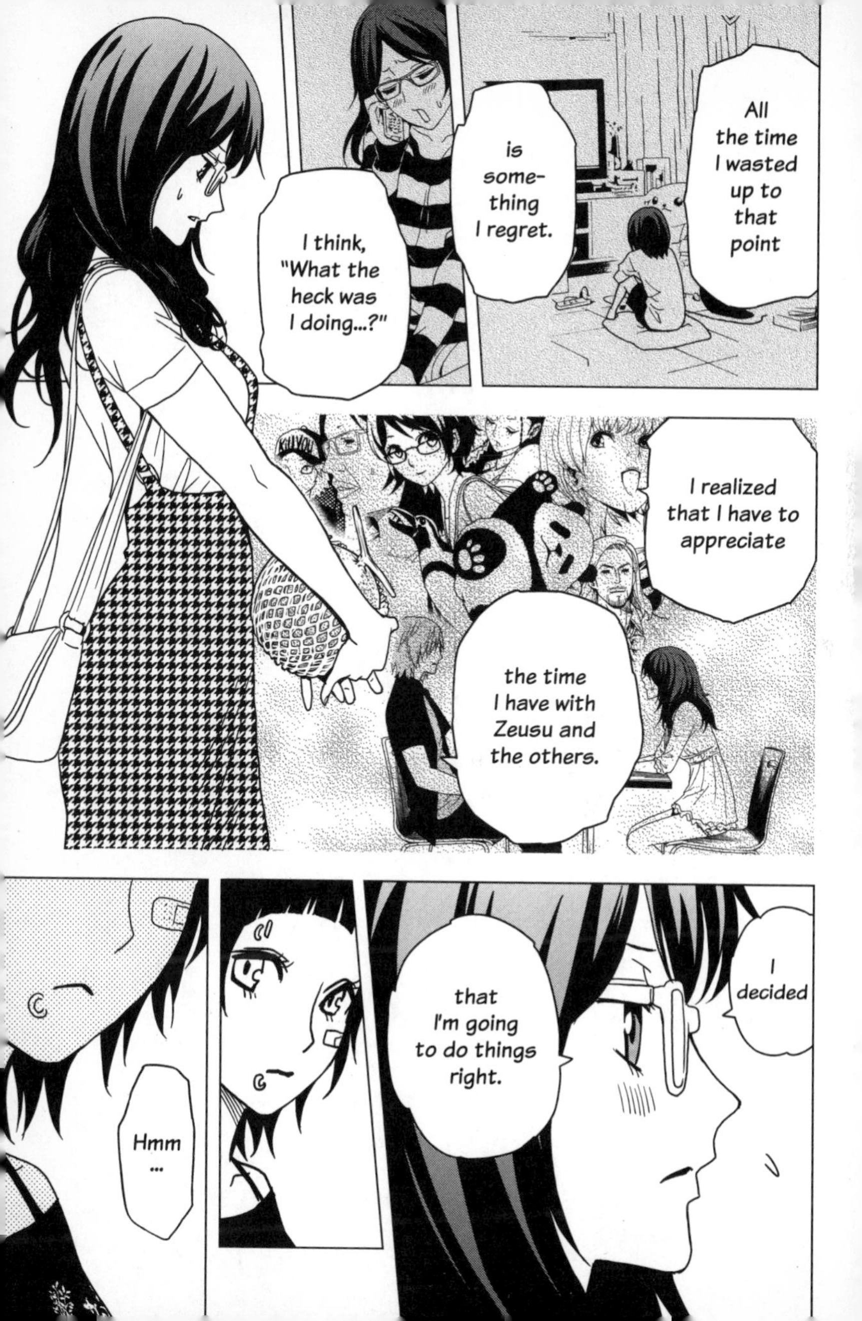
All the time I wasted up to that point
is something I regret.
I think, "What the heck was I doing...?"
I realized that I have to appreciate
the time I have with Zeusu and the others.
I decided
that I'm going to do things right.
Hmm...

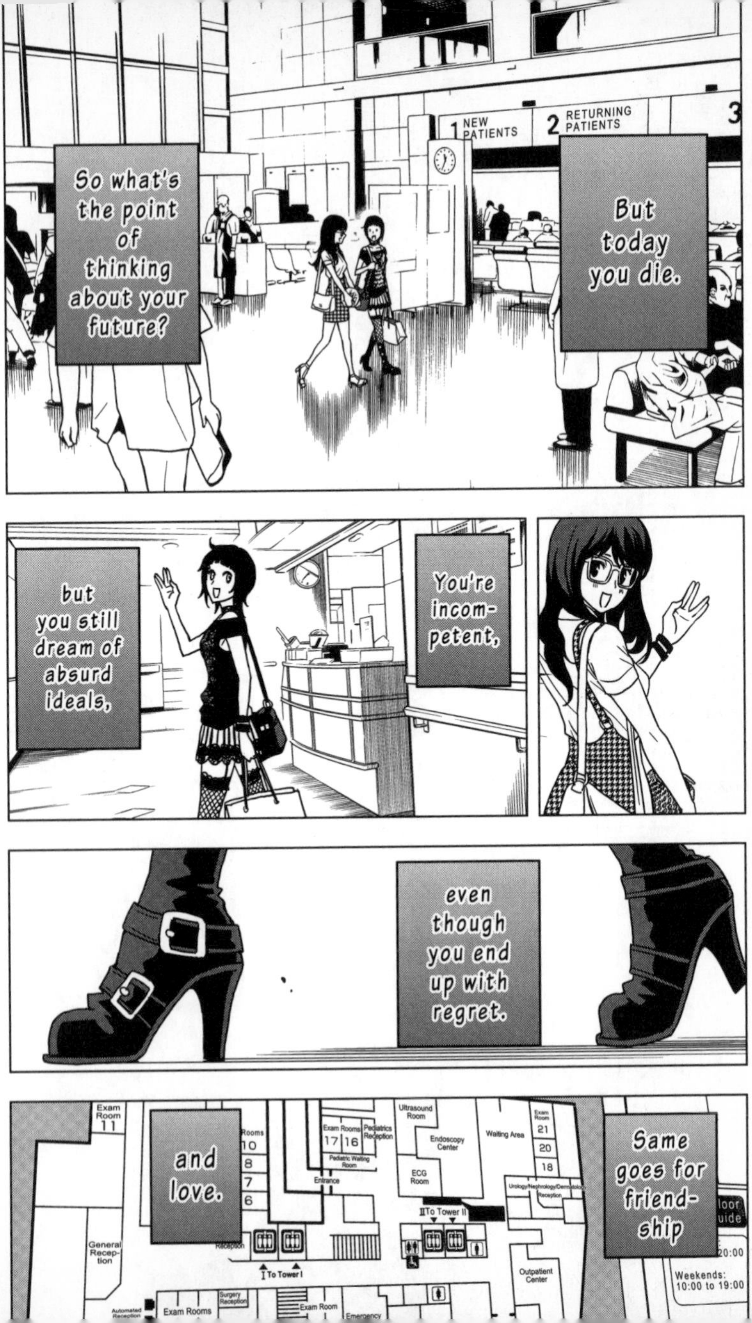
1 NEW PATIENTS
2 RETURNING PATIENTS
3
But today you die.
So what's the point of thinking about your future?
You're incom-petent,
but you still dream of absurd ideals,
even though you end up with regret.
Same goes for friend-ship
and love.
Exam Room 21
20
18
Waiting Area
Ultrasound Room
Endoscopy Center
ECG Room
Urology/Nephrology/Dermatology Reception
Exam Rooms 17 16
Pediatrics Reception
Pediatric Waiting Room
Entrance
Rooms 10
8
7
6
Exam Room 11
General Recep-tion
Reception
I To Tower I
II To Tower II
Outpatient Center
Weekends: 10:00 to 19:00
Automated Reception
Exam Rooms
Surgery Reception
Exam Room
Emergency

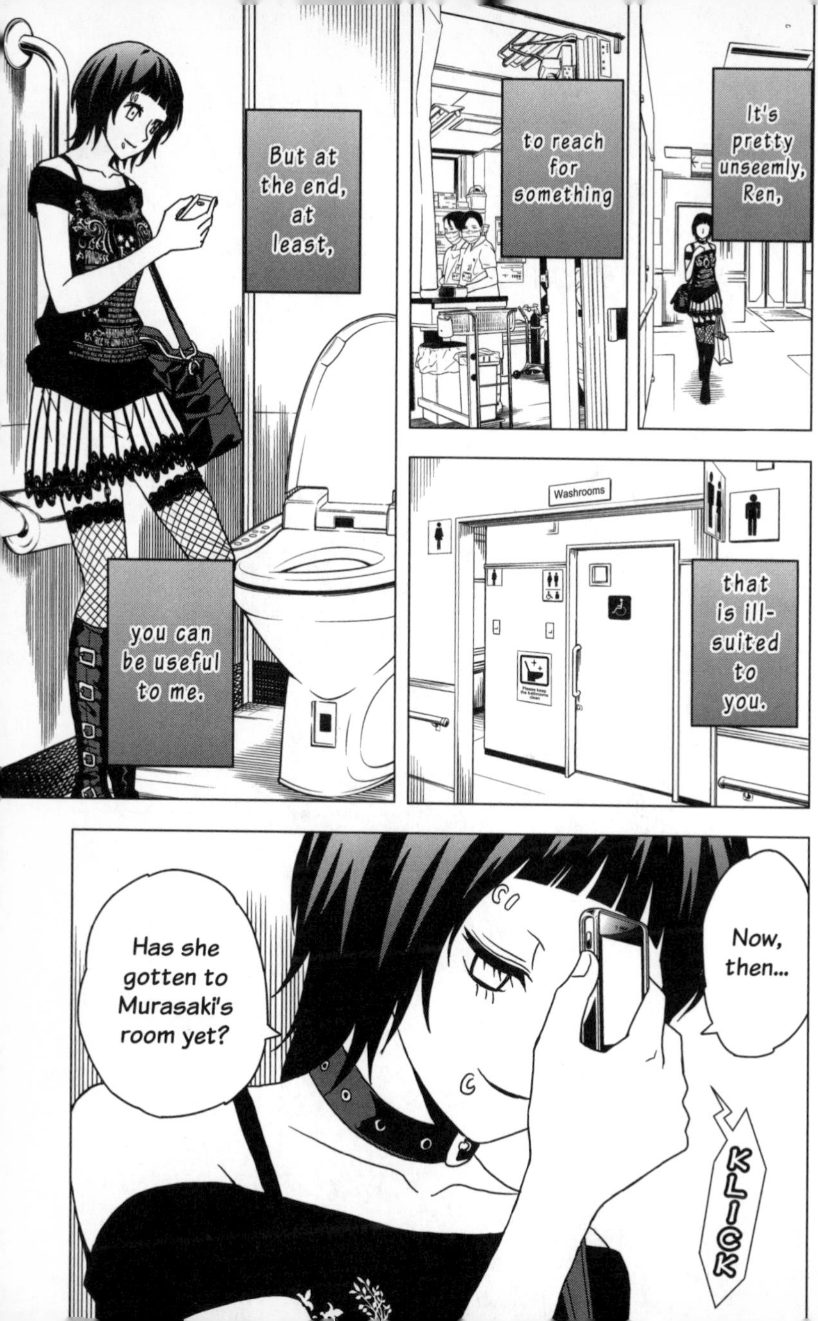
It's pretty unseemly, Ren,
to reach for something
that is ill-suited to you.
But at the end, at least,
you can be useful to me.
Washrooms
Please keep the bathrooms clean
Now, then...
KLICK
Has she gotten to Murasaki's room yet?

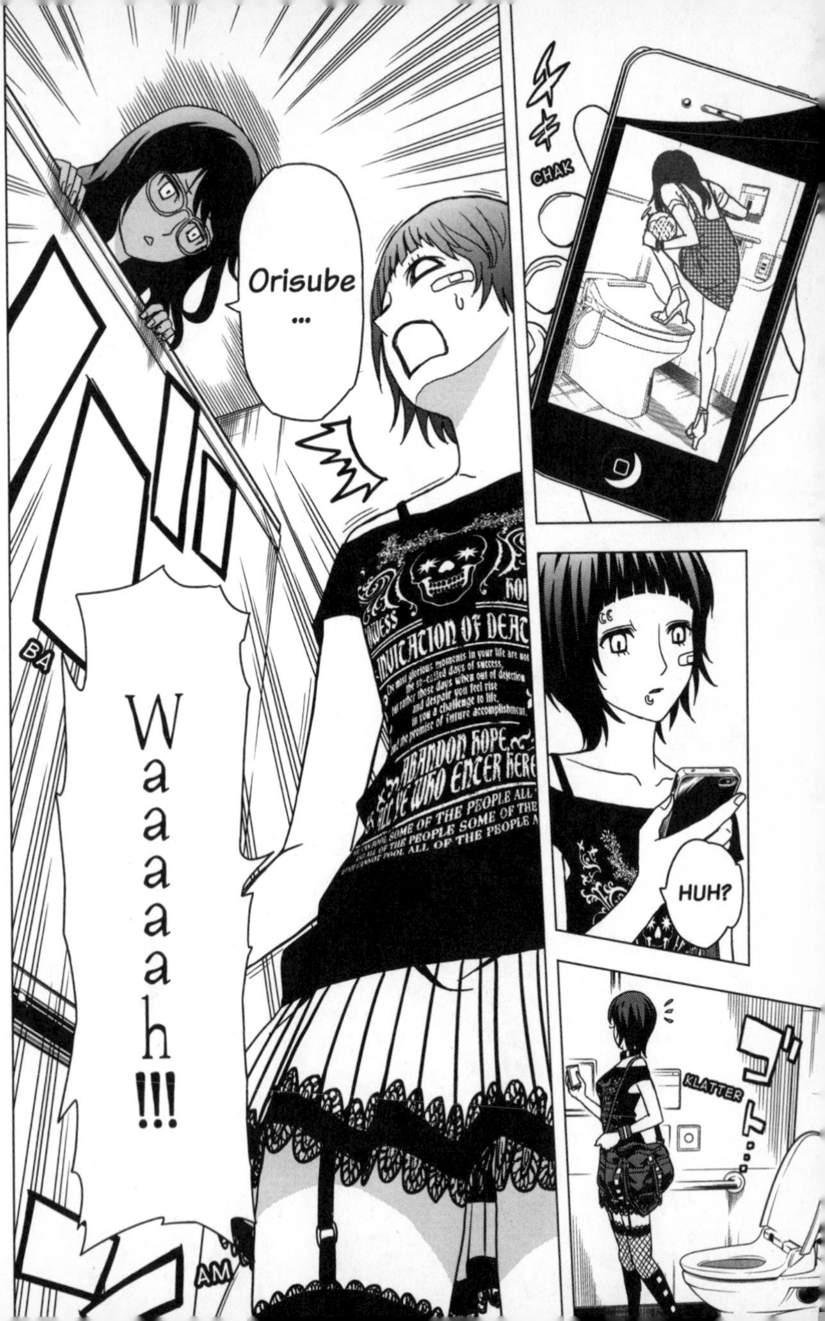
CHAK
HUH?
KLATTER
Orisube ...
BA
Waaaaaah!!!
AM

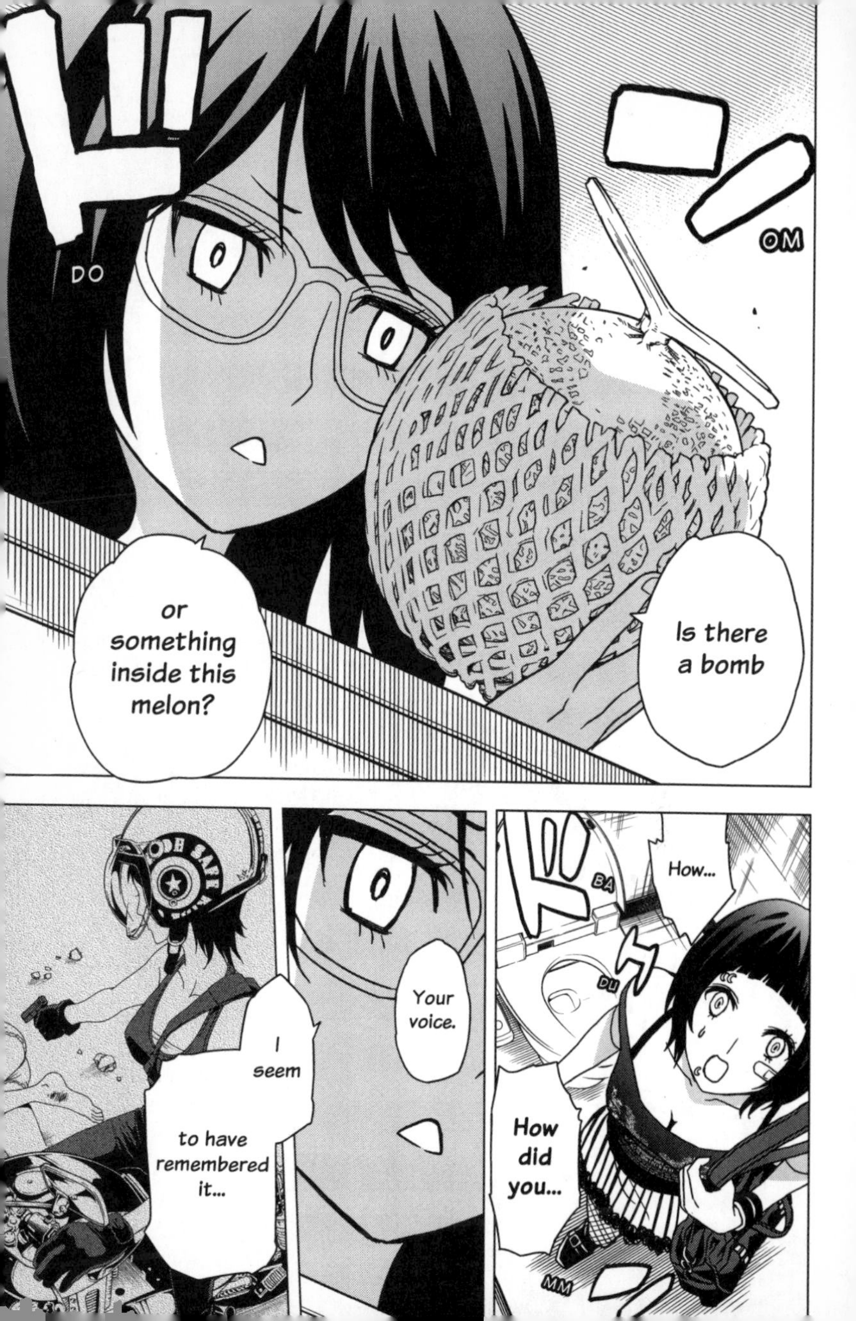
DO
OM
Is there a bomb
or something inside this melon?
How...
BA
DU
MM
How did you...
Your voice.
I seem to have remembered it...

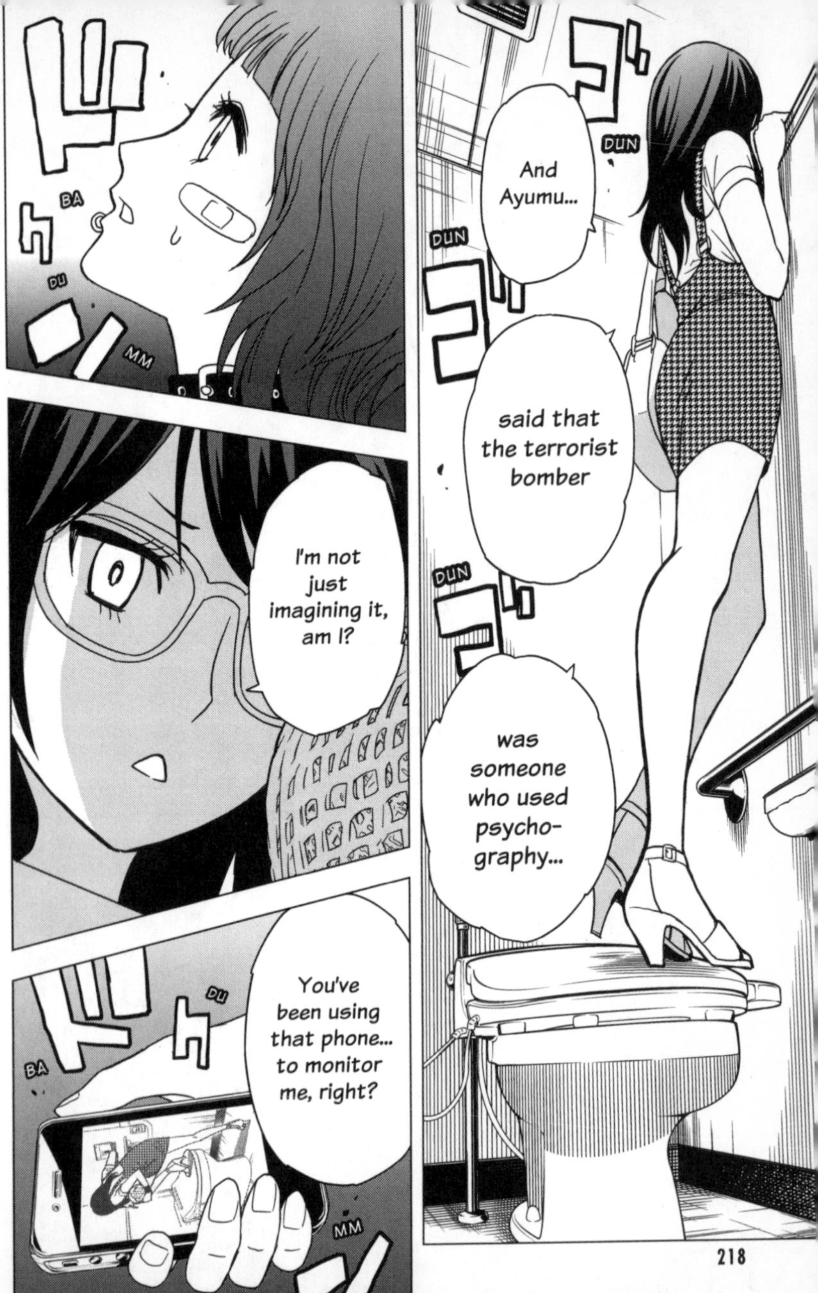
DUN
And Ayumu...
DUN
said that the terrorist bomber
DUN
was someone who used psycho-graphy...
BA
DU
MM
I'm not just imagining it, am I?
BA
DU
You've been using that phone... to monitor me, right?
MM

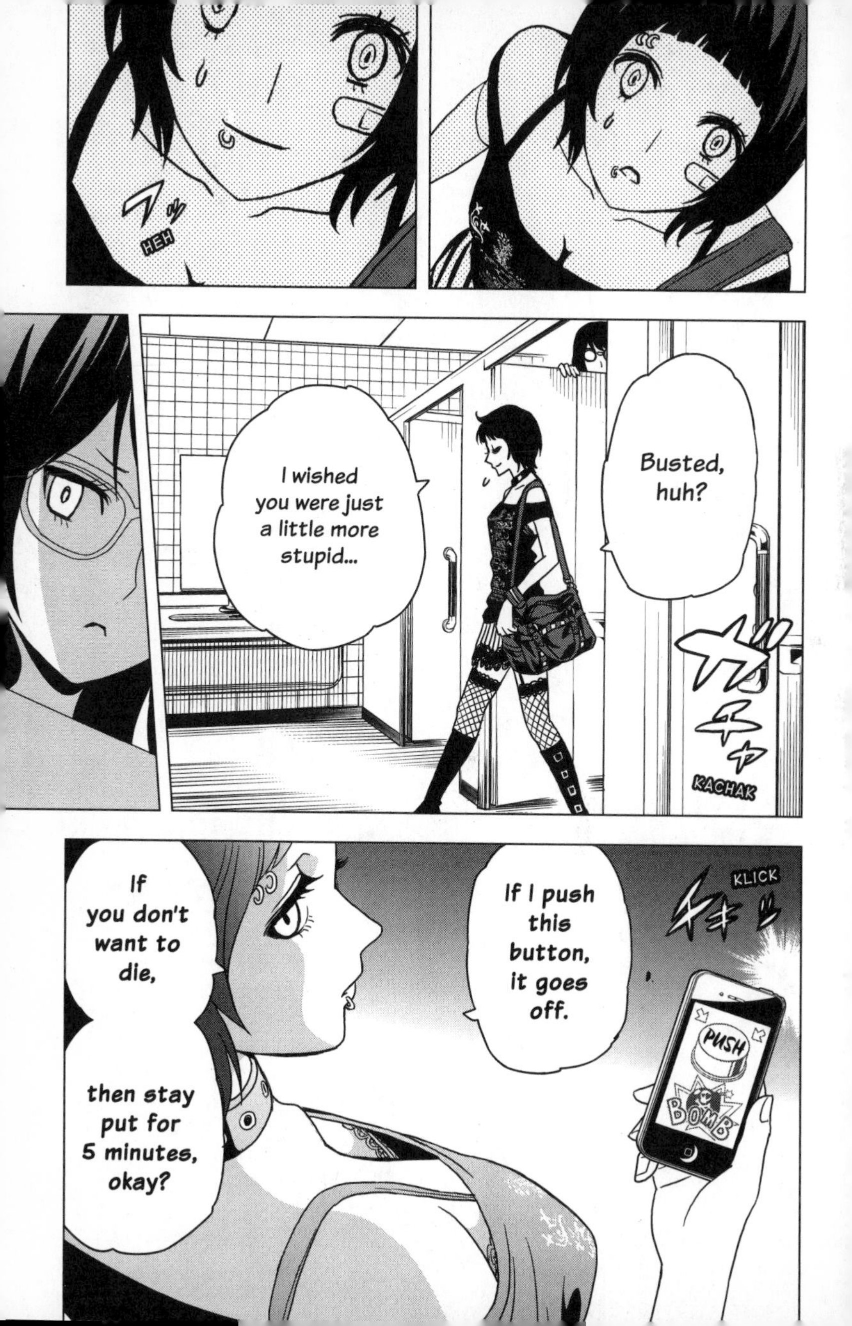
HEH
Busted, huh?
KACHAK
I wished you were just a little more stupid...
KLICK
If I push this button, it goes off.
PUSH
BOMB
If you don't want to die,
then stay put for 5 minutes, okay?

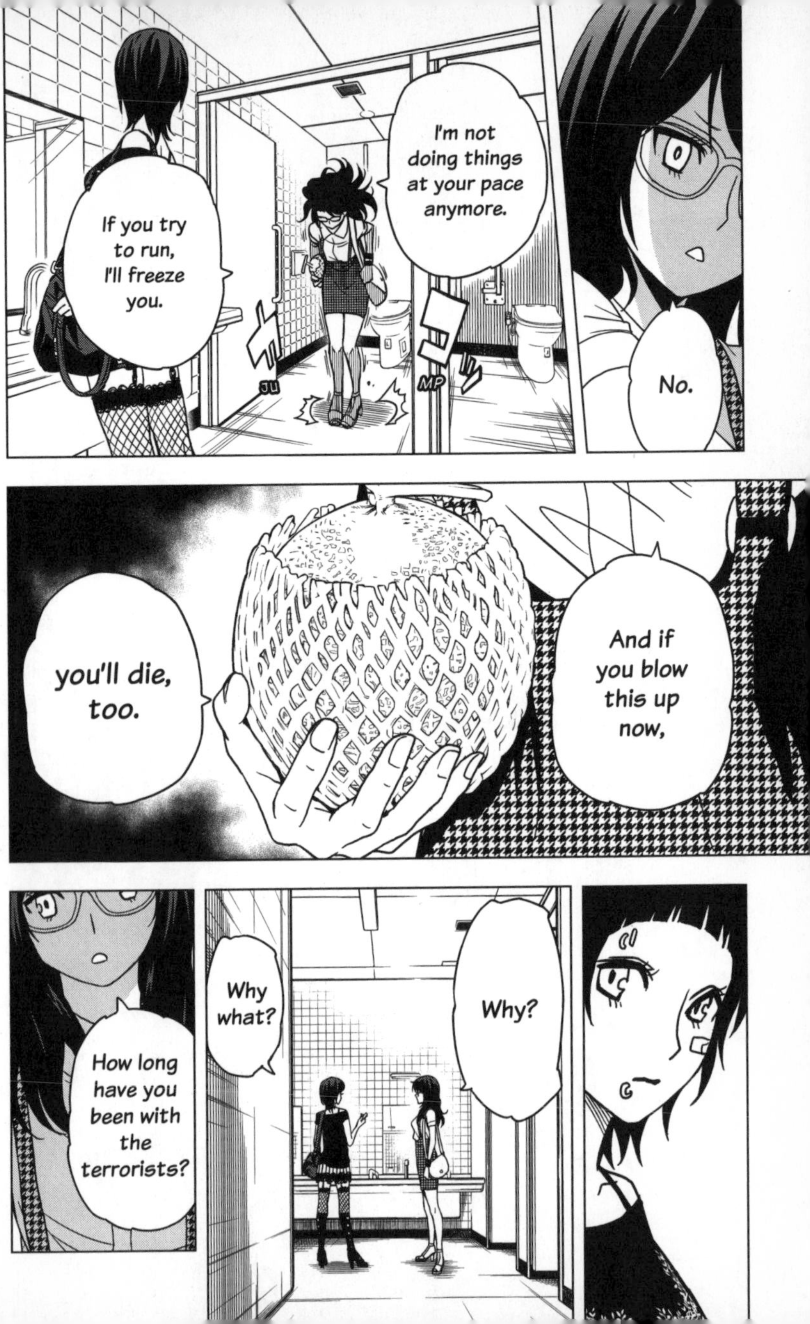
No.
I'm not doing things at your pace anymore.
MP
If you try to run, I'll freeze you.
JU
And if you blow this up now,
you'll die, too.
Why?
Why what?
How long have you been with the terrorists?

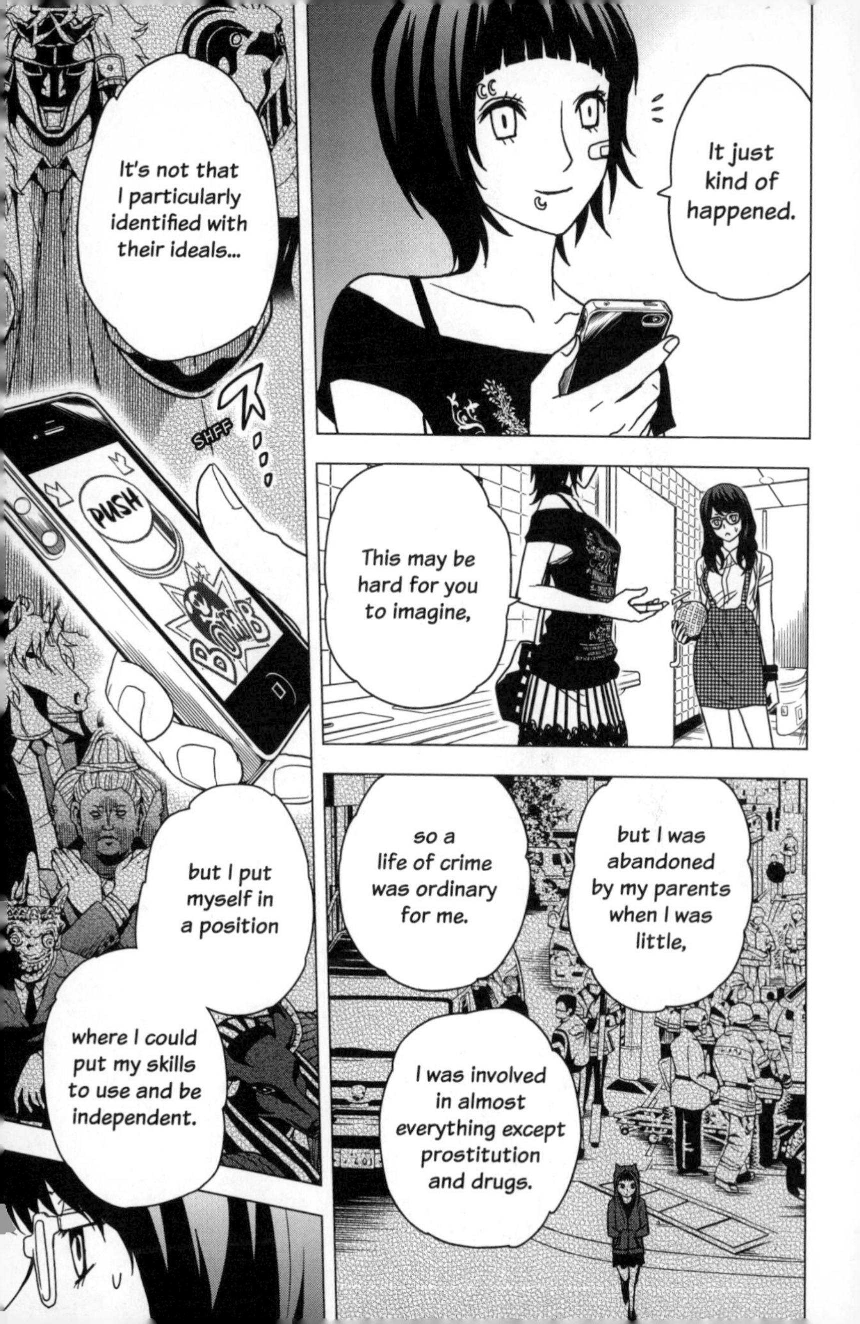
It just kind of happened.
This may be hard for you to imagine,
but I was abandoned by my parents when I was little,
so a life of crime was ordinary for me.
I was involved in almost everything except prostitution and drugs.
It's not that I particularly identified with their ideals...
SHFF
PUSH
BOMB
but I put myself in a position
where I could put my skills to use and be independent.

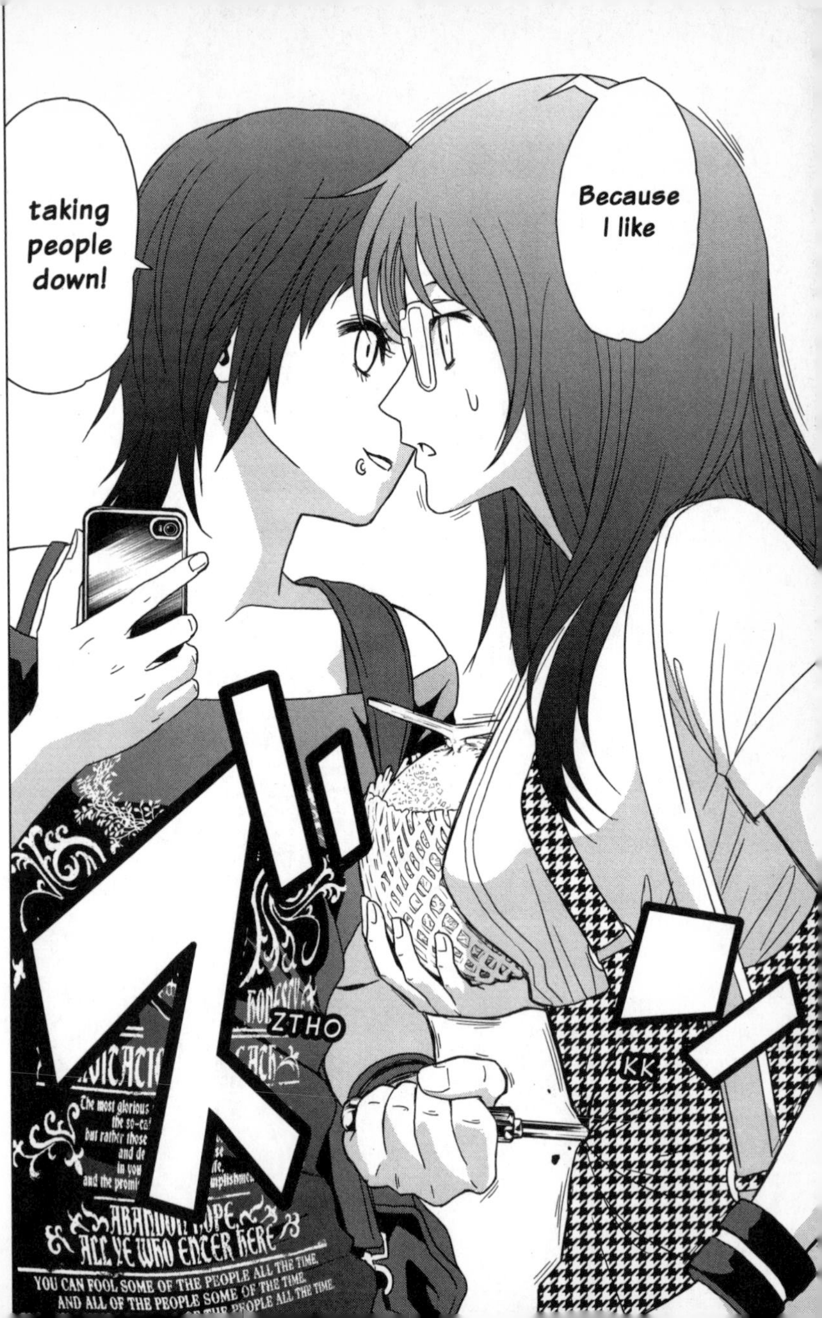
Because I like
taking people down!
ZTHO
KK
ALL YE WHO ENTER HERE
YOU CAN FOOL SOME OF THE PEOPLE ALL THE TIME
AND ALL OF THE PEOPLE SOME OF THE TIME

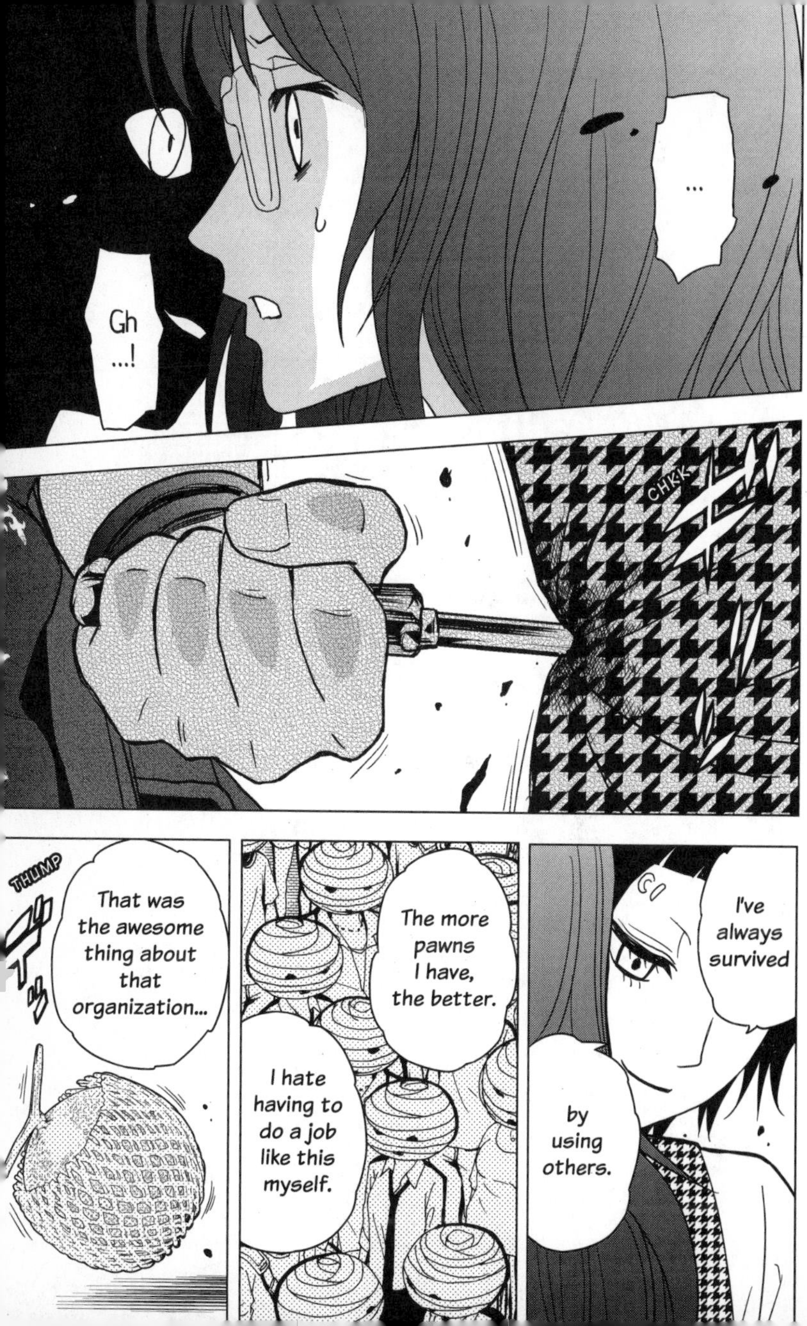
...
Gh ...!
CHKK
I've always survived
by using others.
The more pawns I have, the better.
I hate having to do a job like this myself.
THUMP
That was the awesome thing about that organization...

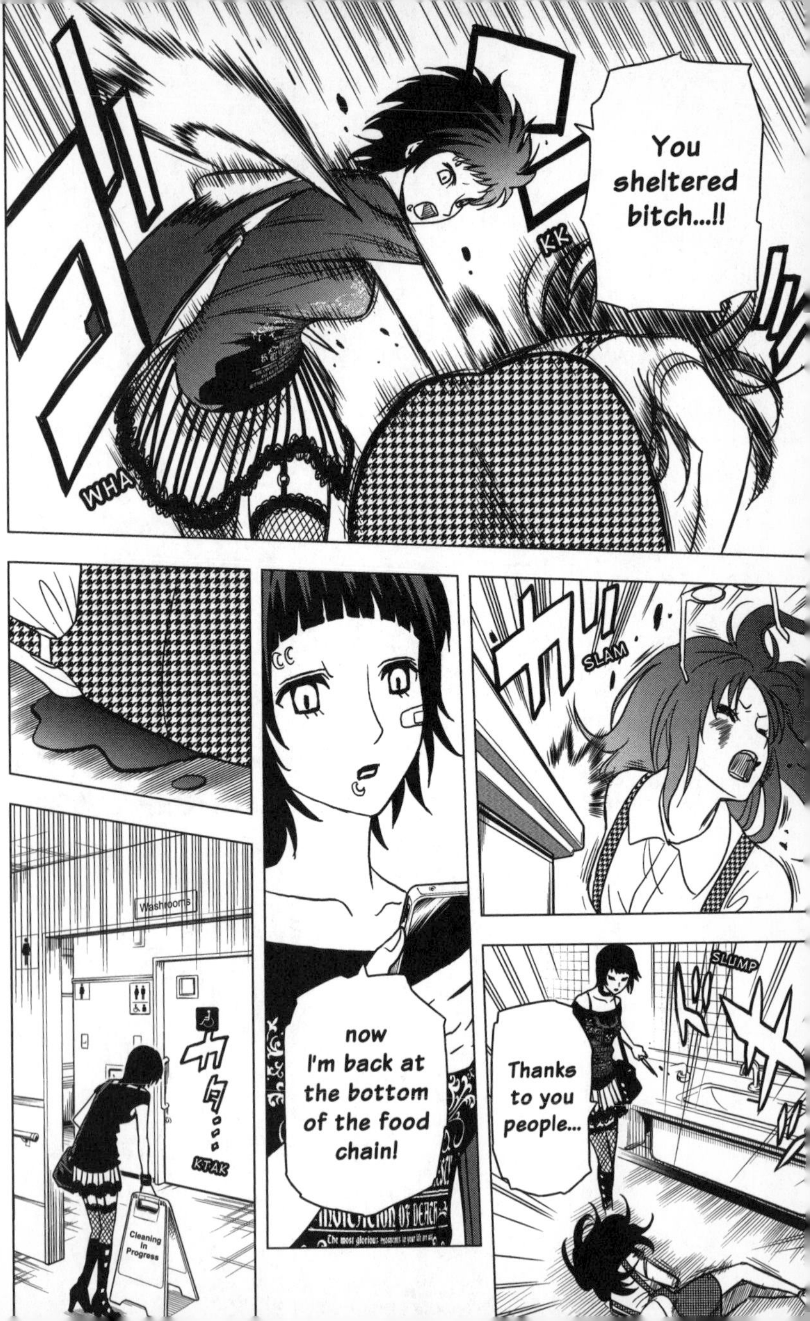
You sheltered bitch...!!
KK
WHA
SLAM
SLUMP
Thanks to you people...
now I'm back at the bottom of the food chain!
Washrooms
KTAK
Cleaning In Progress

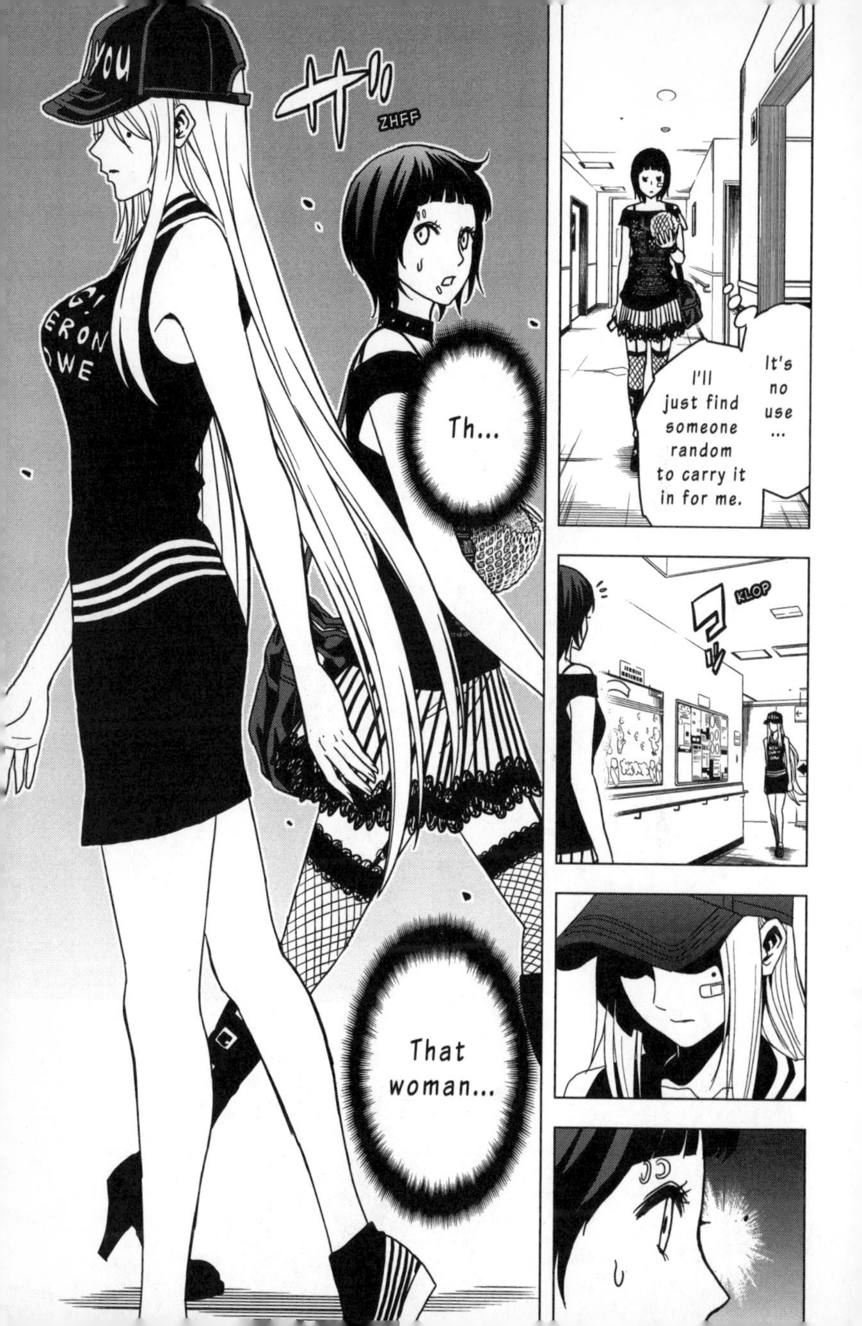
It's no use...
I'll just find someone random to carry it in for me.
KLOP
ZHFF
Th...
That woman...

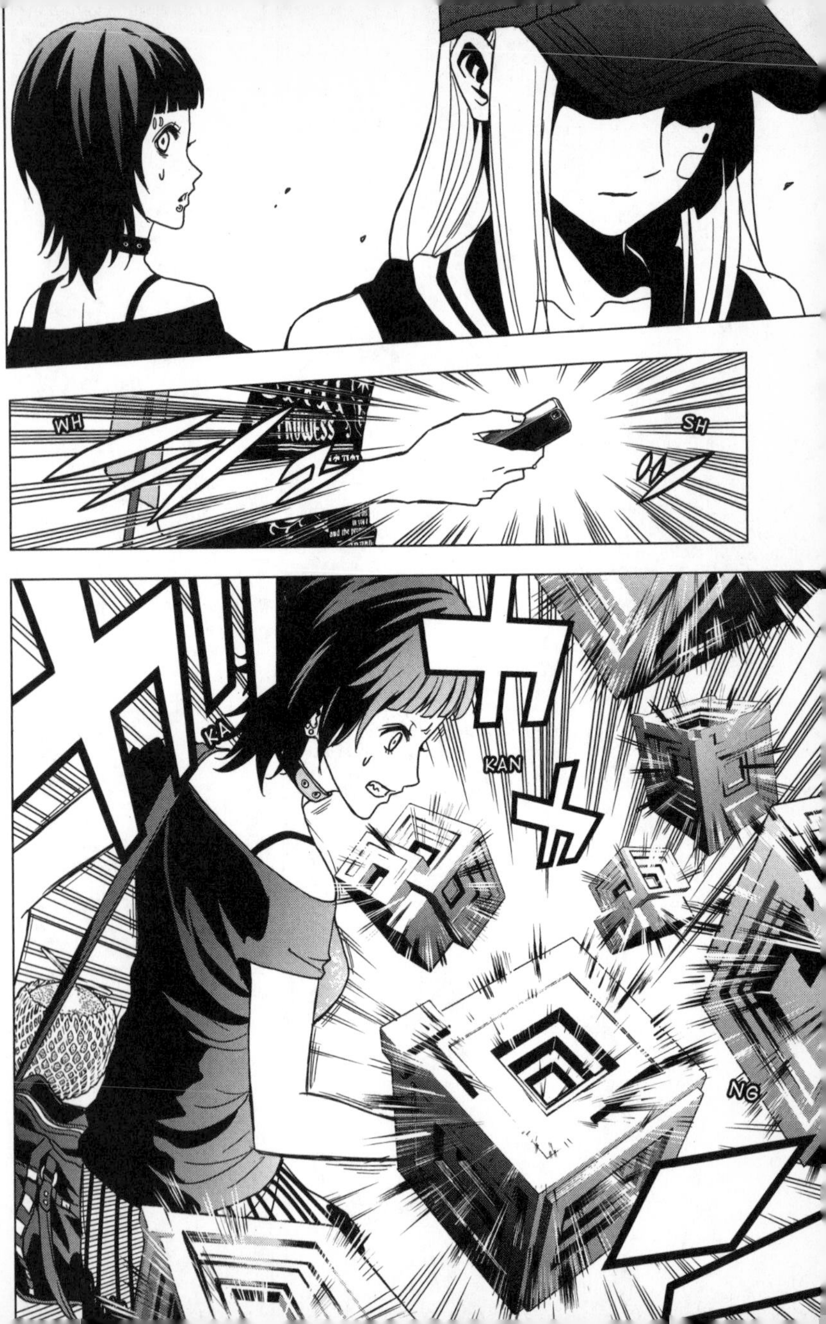
SH
WH
KA
KAN
NG

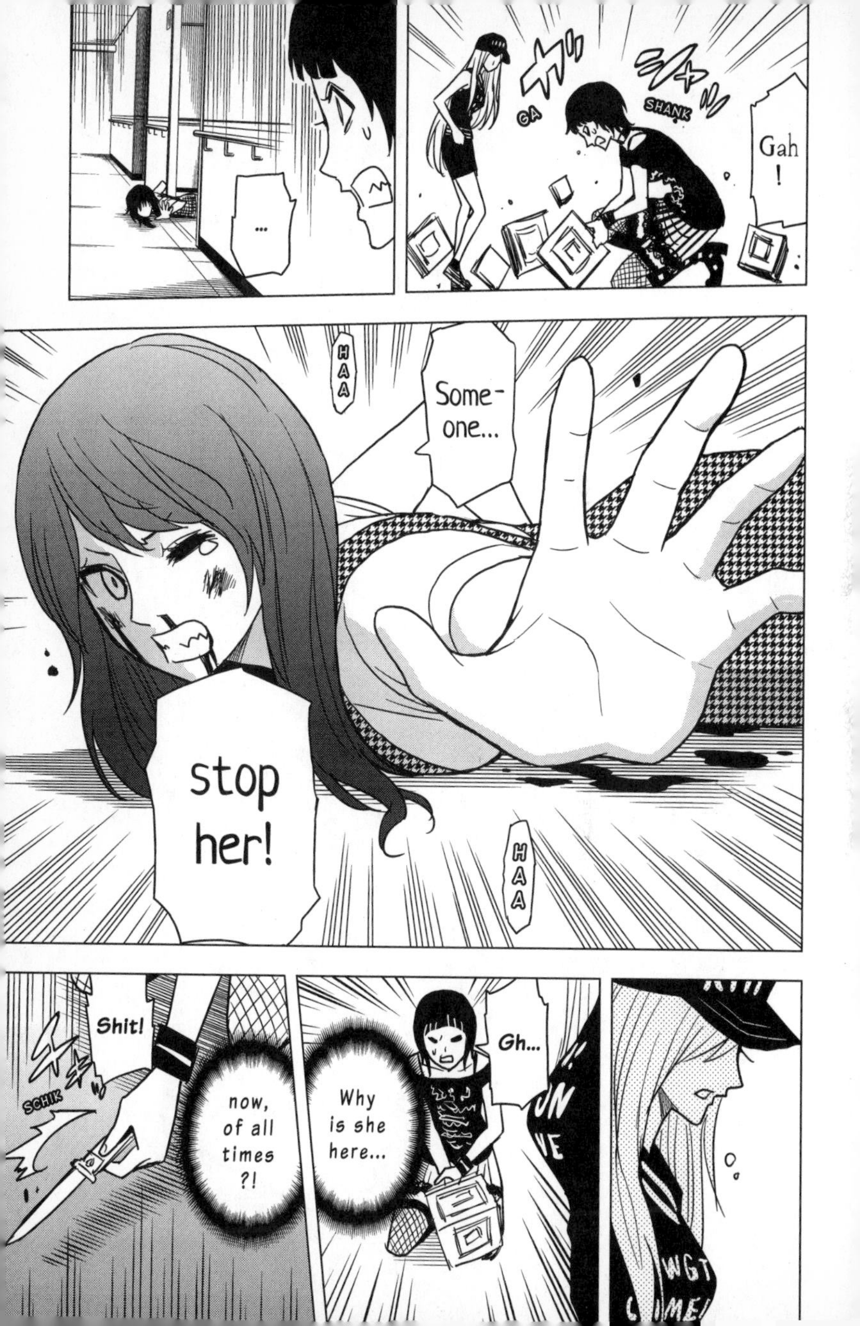
Gah!
SHANK
GA
...
Some-one...
HAA
stop her!
HAA
Gh...
Why is she here...
now, of all times ?!
Shit!
SCHIK

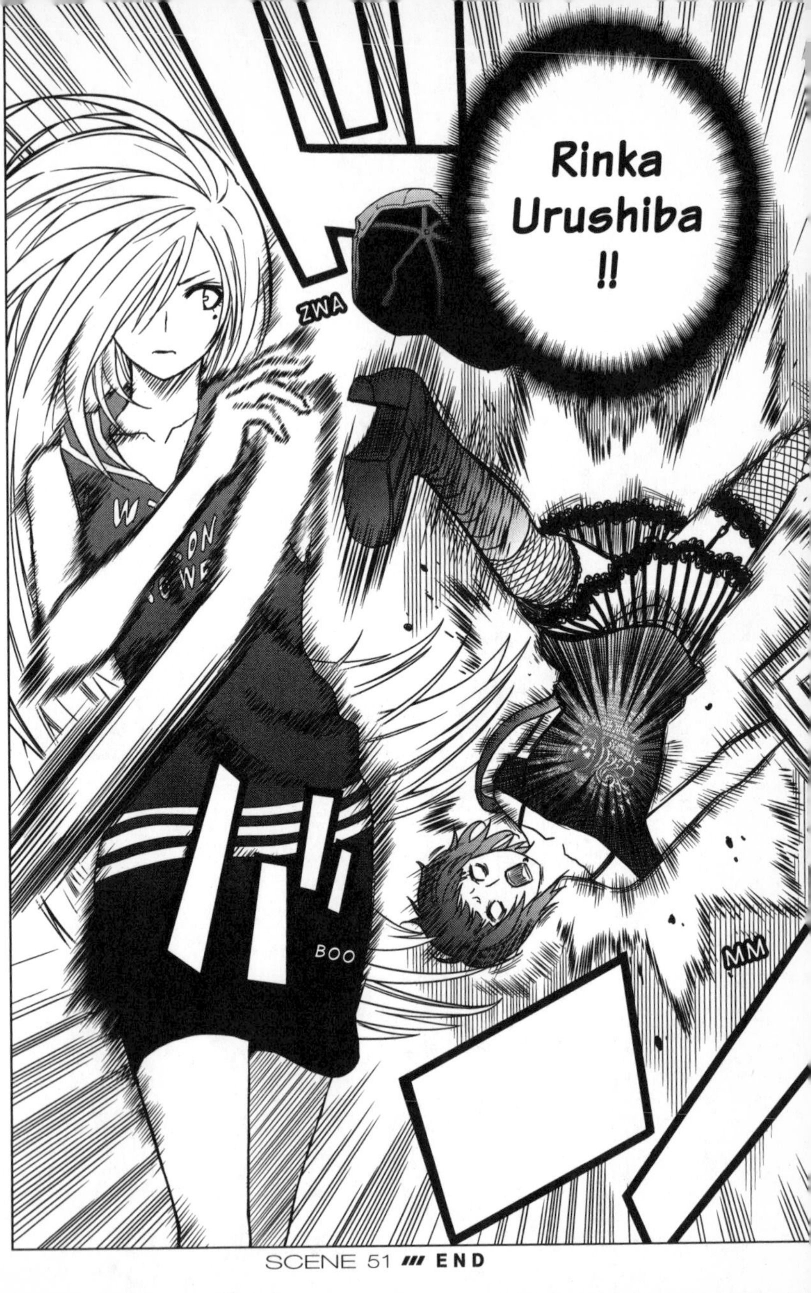
Rinka Urushiba !!
ZWA
MM
BOO

SCENE 51 /// END

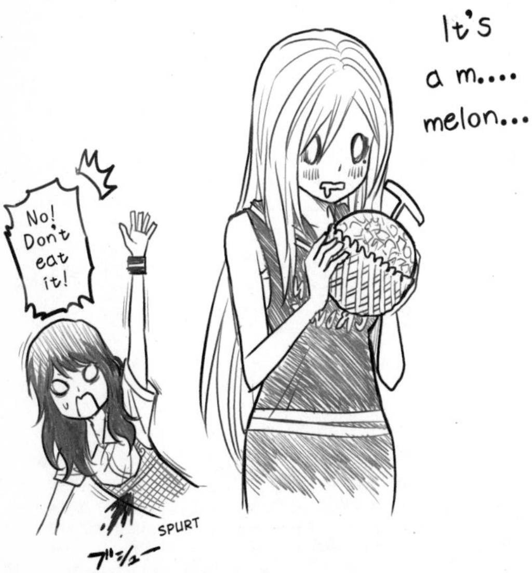
It's a m.... melon...
No! Don't eat it!
SPURT
ブシュー

TOKYO ESP

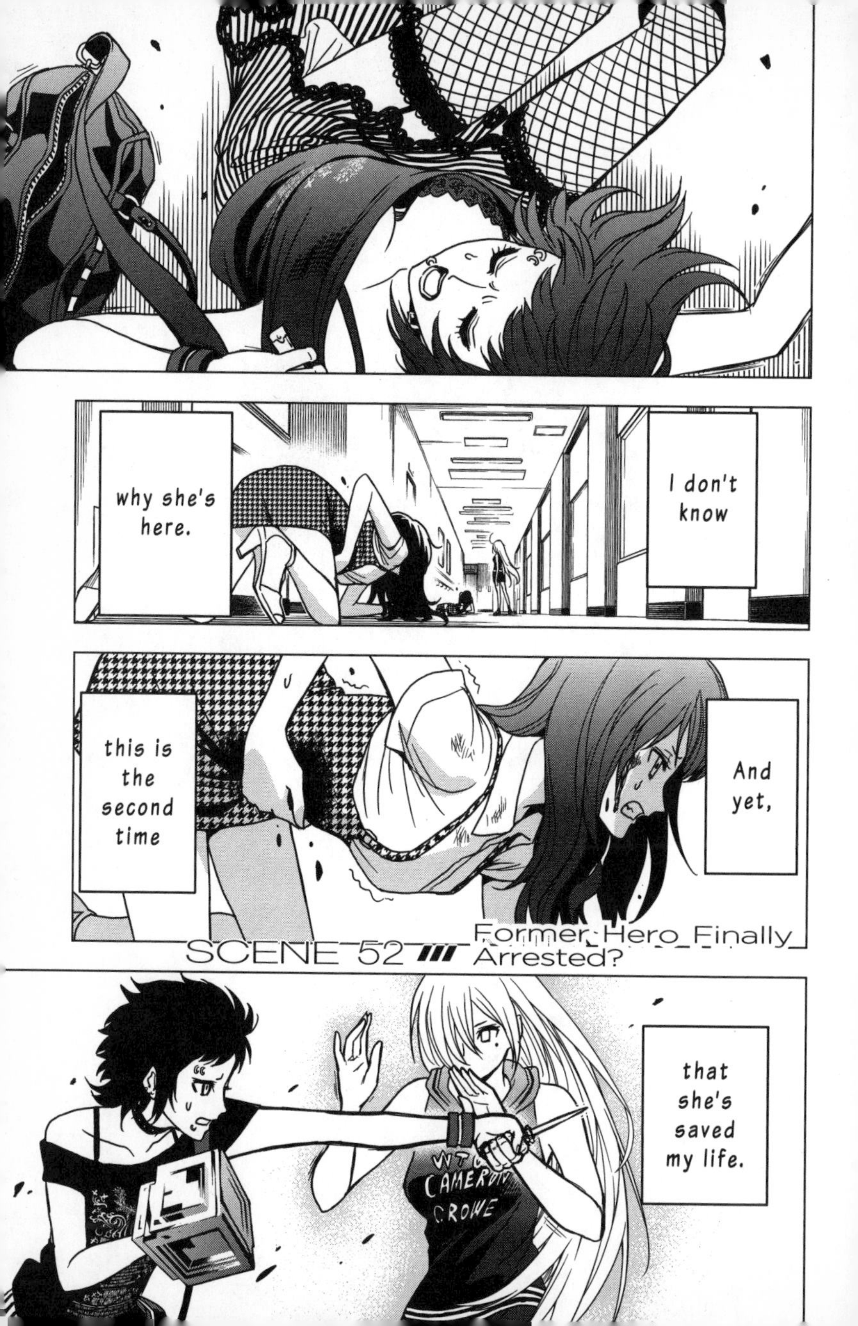
I don't know
why she's here.
And yet,
this is the second time
SCENE 52 /// Former Hero Finally Arrested?
that she's saved my life.

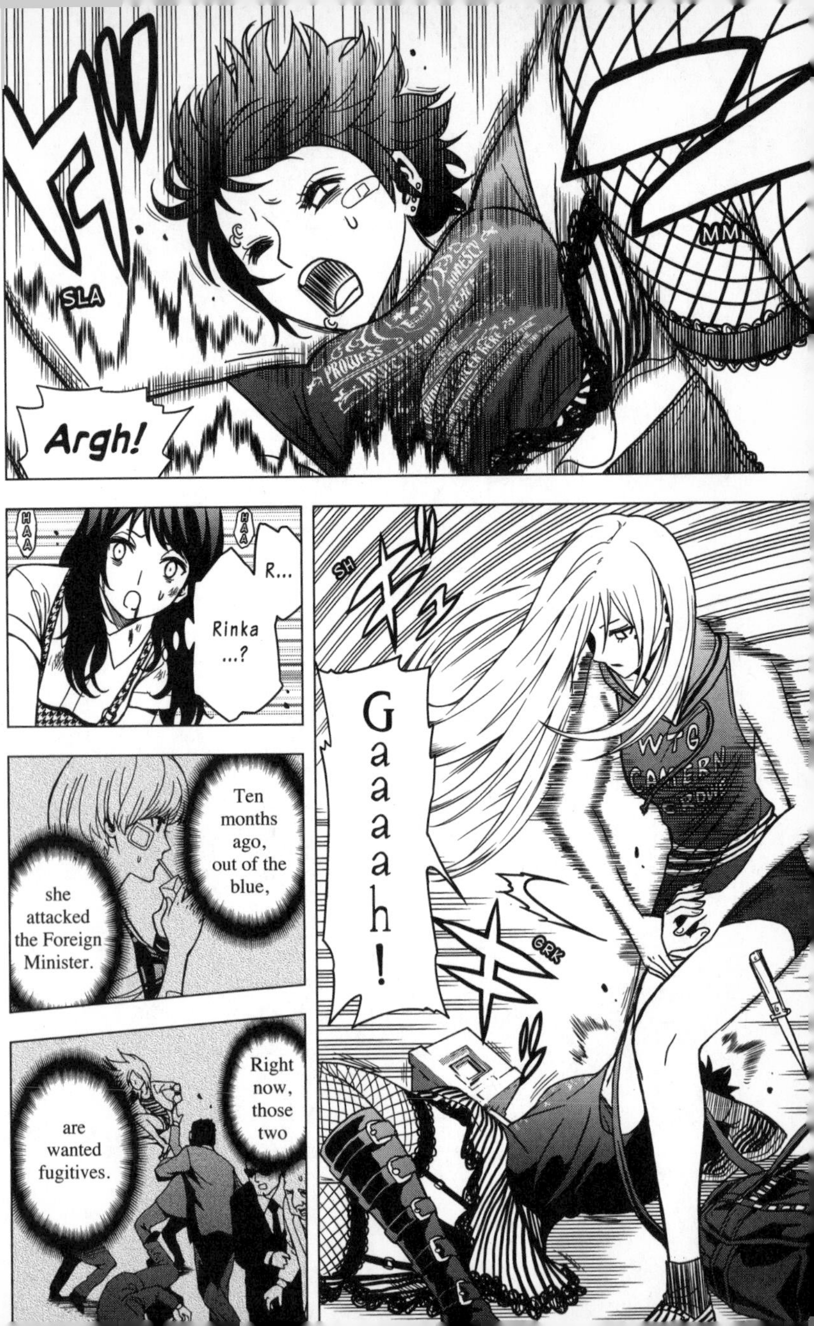
MM
SLA
Argh!
SH
Gaaaah!
GRK
HAA
HAA
R...
Rinka ...?
Ten months ago, out of the blue,
she attacked the Foreign Minister.
Right now, those two
are wanted fugitives.

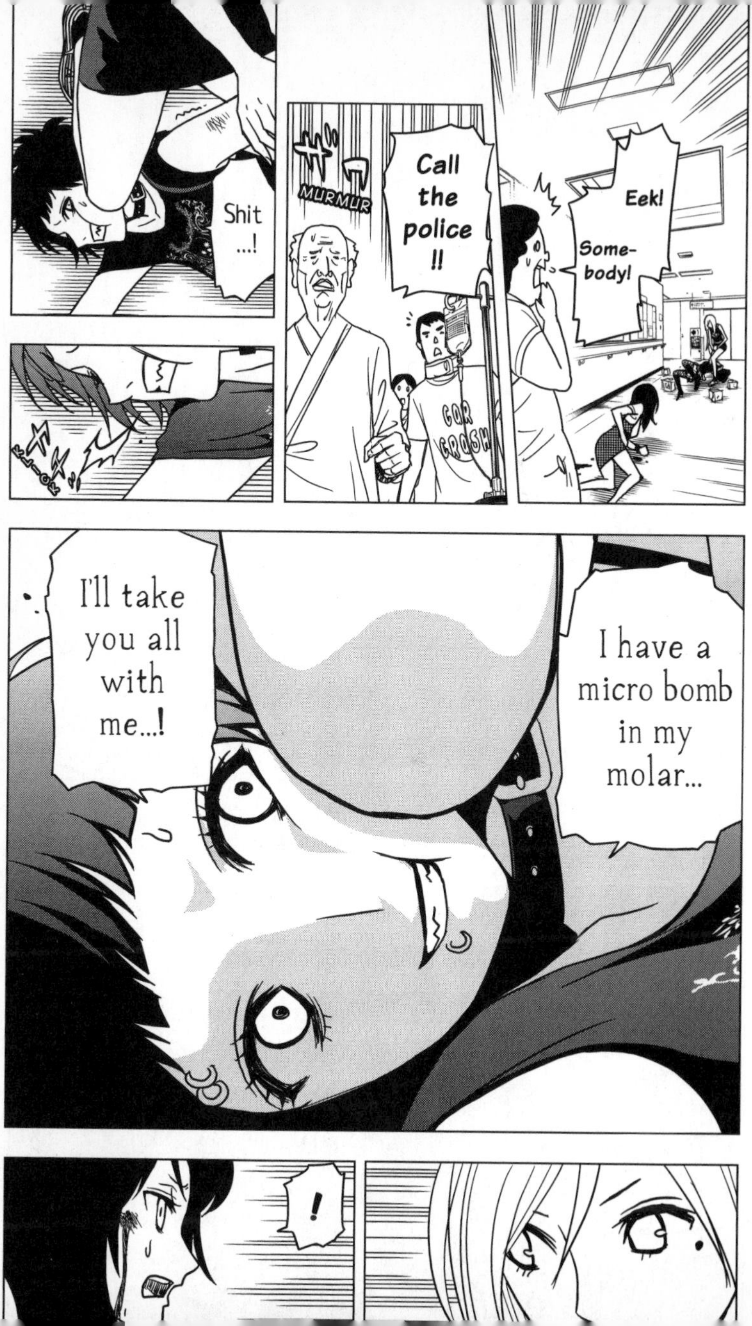
Eek!
Some-body!
MURMUR
Call the police !!
Shit ...!
I have a micro bomb in my molar...
I'll take you all with me...!
!

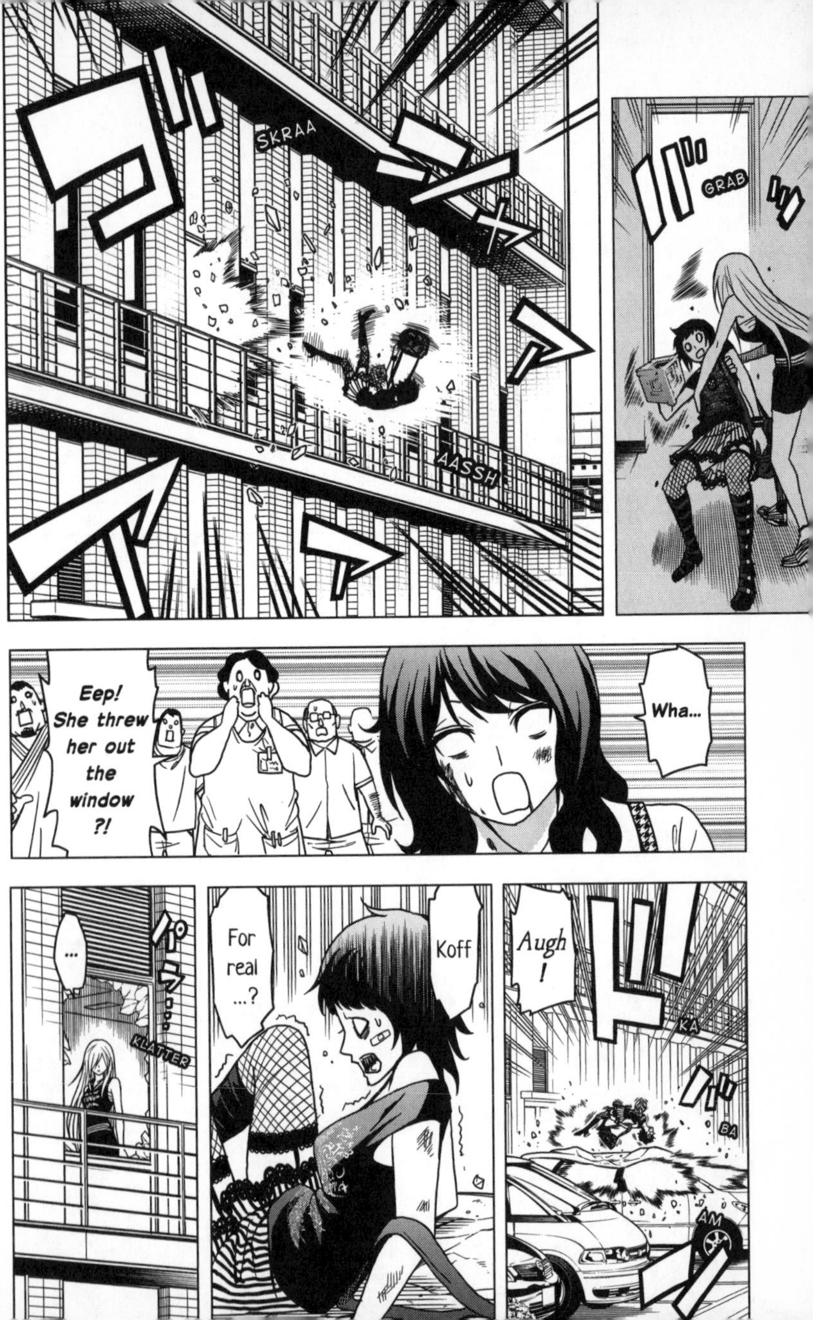
GRAB
SKRAA
AASSH
Wha...
Eep! She threw her out the window ?!
Augh !
KA
BA
AM
Koff
For real ...?
...
KLATTER

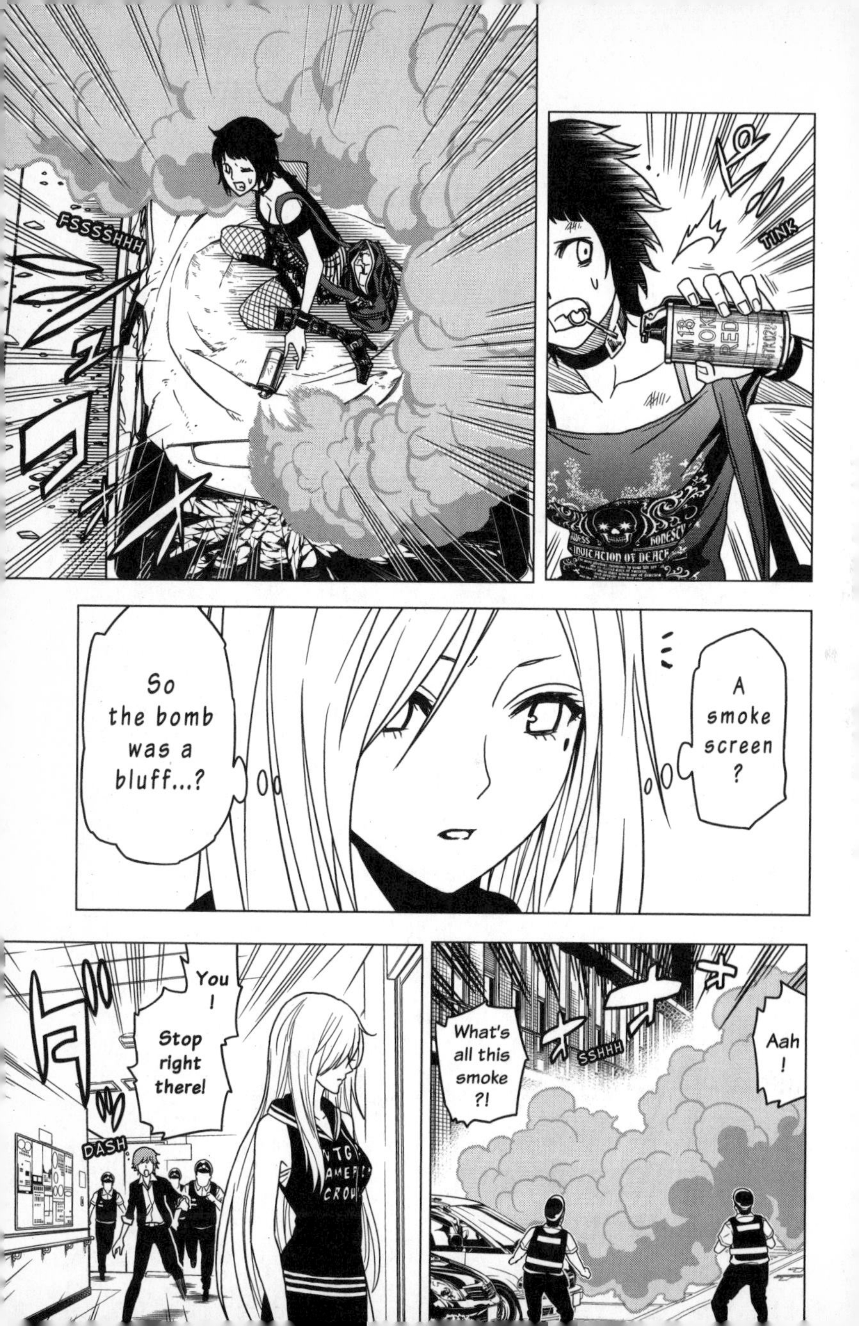
TINK
FSSSSHHH
A smoke screen?
So the bomb was a bluff...?
Aah!
SSHHH
What's all this smoke?!
You! Stop right there!
DASH

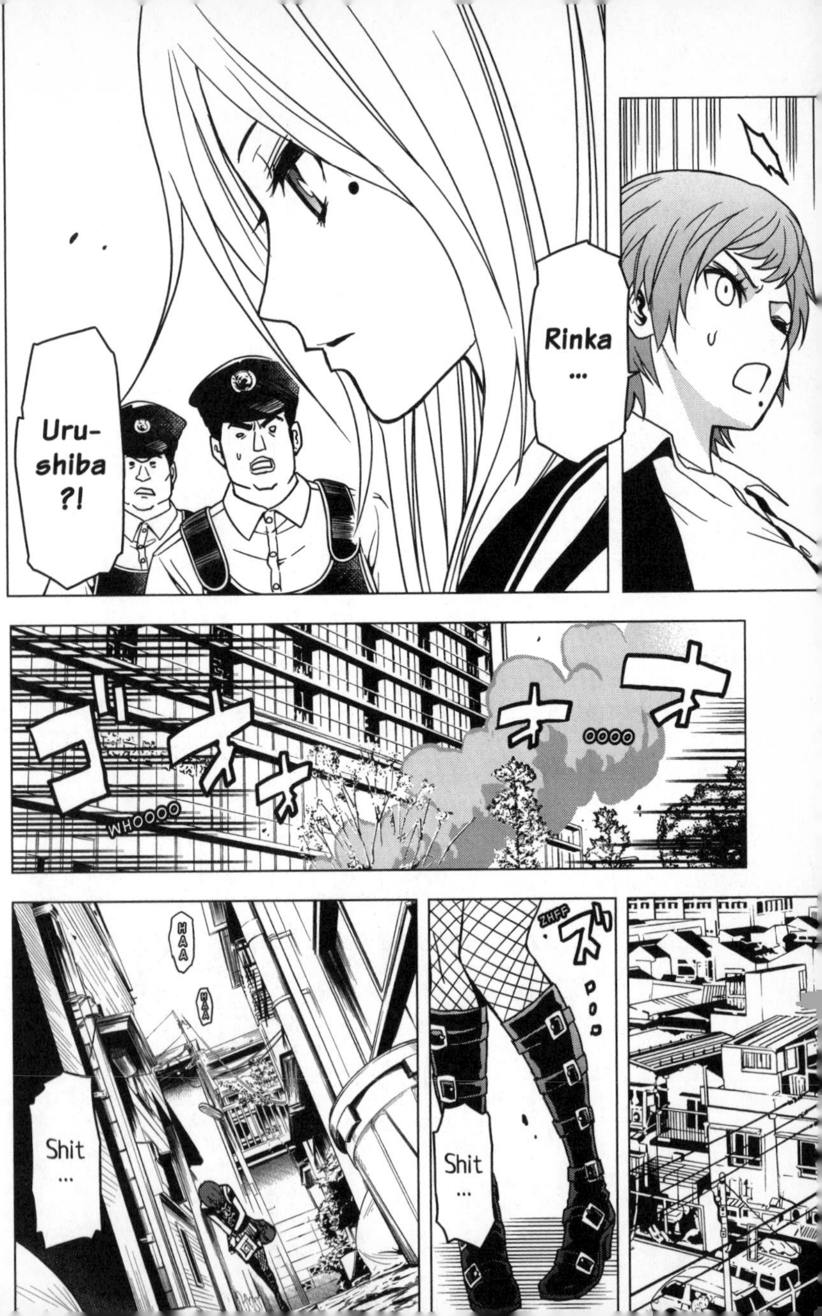
Rinka ...
Uru-shiba ?!
OOOO
WHOOOO
ZHFF
DOO
Shit ...
HAA
HAA
Shit ...

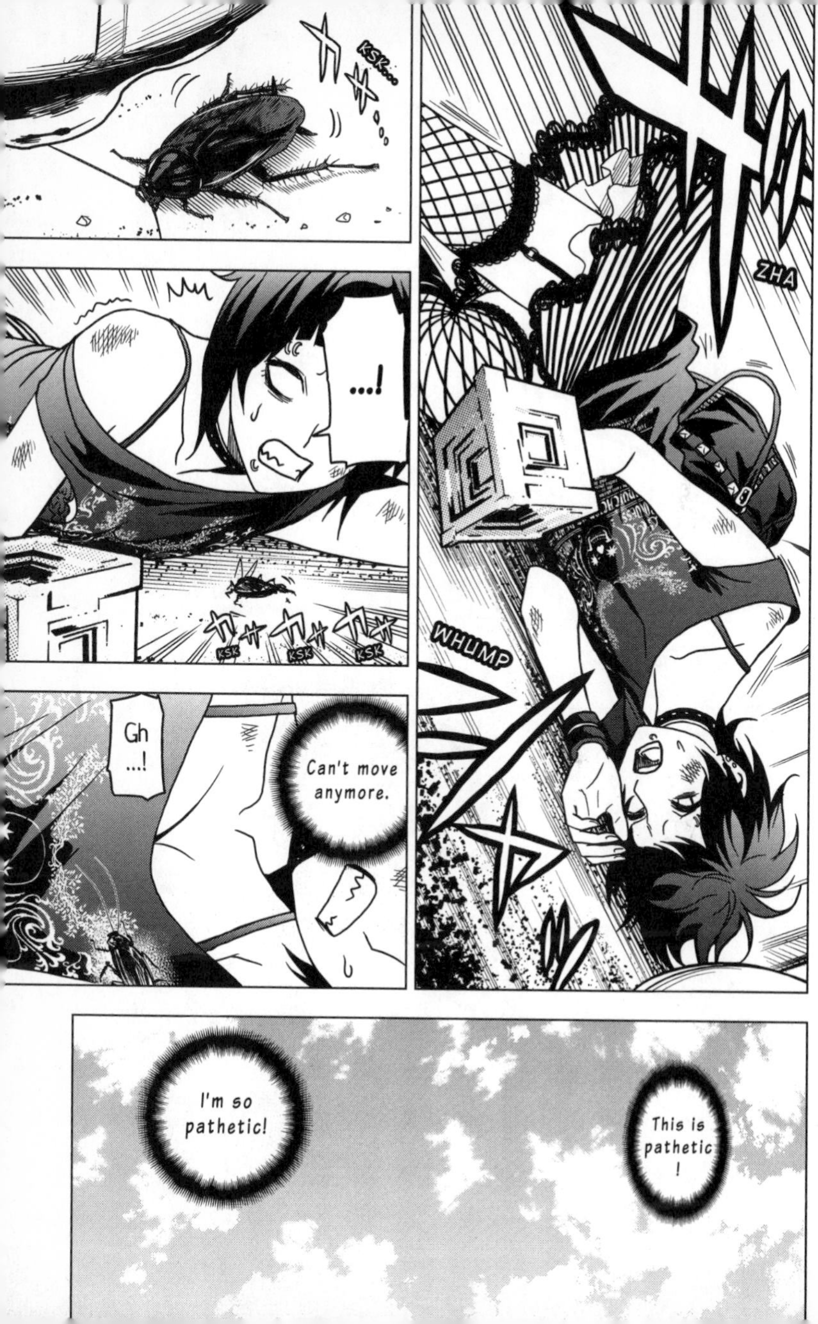
ZHA
WHUMP
KSK...
...!
KSK
KSK
KSK
Gh ...!
Can't move anymore.
This is pathetic !
I'm so pathetic!

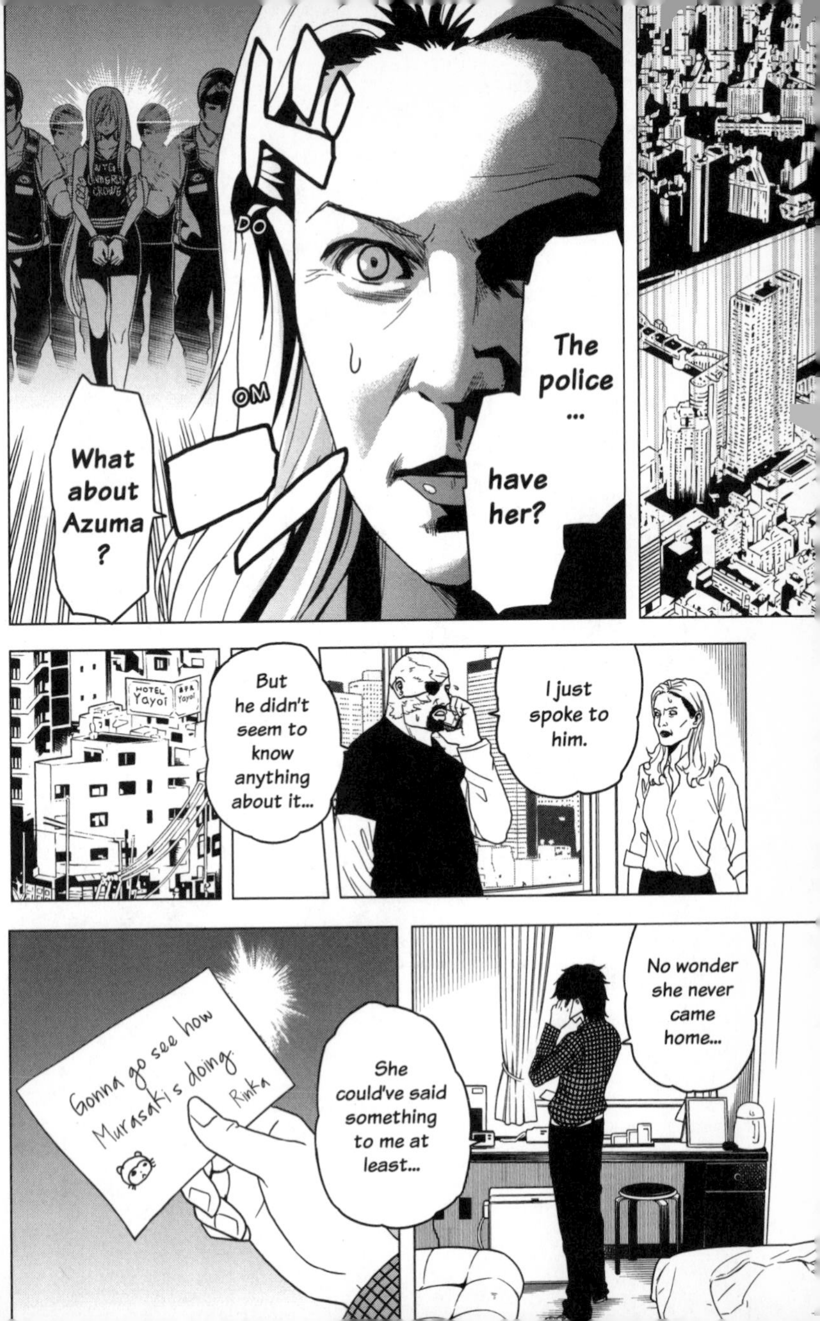

The police ... have her?
DO
OM
What about Azuma?
I just spoke to him.
But he didn't seem to know anything about it...
HOTEL Yayoi
Yayoi
No wonder she never came home...
She could've said something to me at least...
Gonna go see how Murasaki's doing.
Rinka

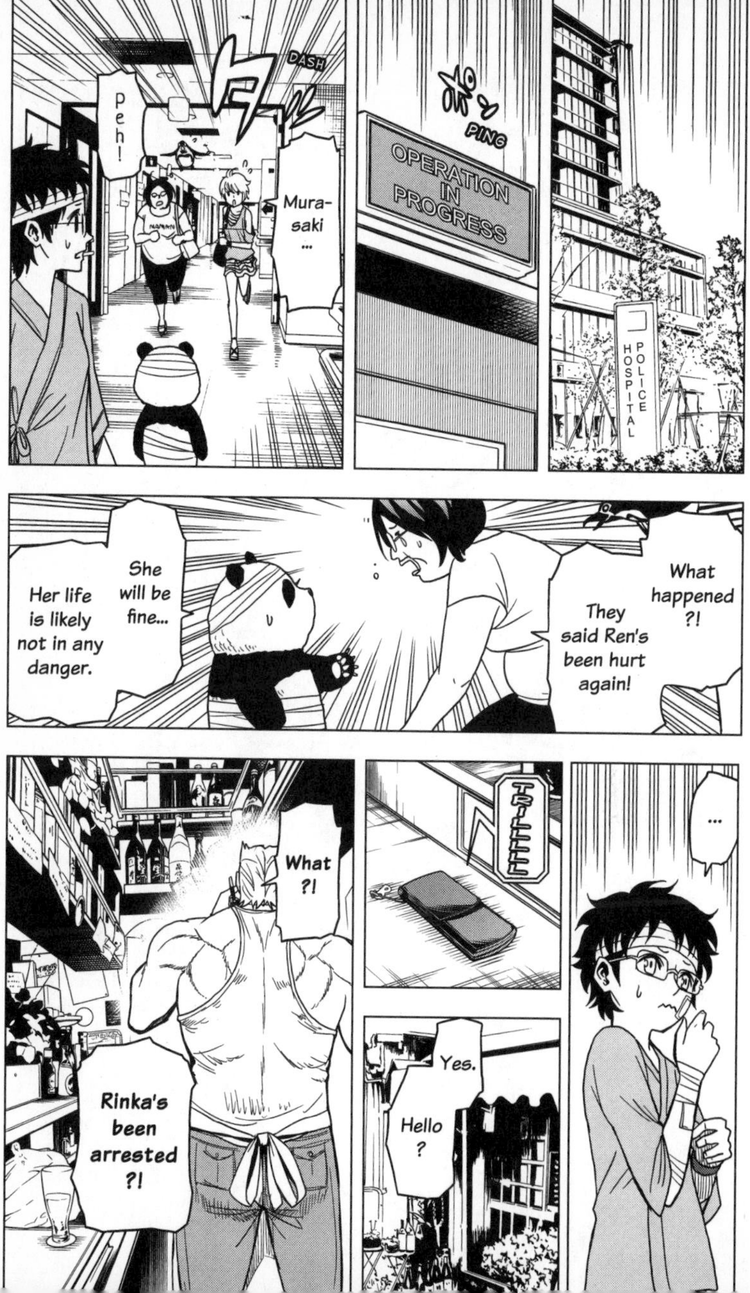
POLICE
HOSPITAL
PING
OPERATION IN PROGRESS
DASH
Peh!
Mura-saki ...
What happened ?!
They said Ren's been hurt again!
She will be fine...
Her life is likely not in any danger.
...
TRILLLL
Yes.
Hello ?
What ?!
Rinka's been arrested ?!

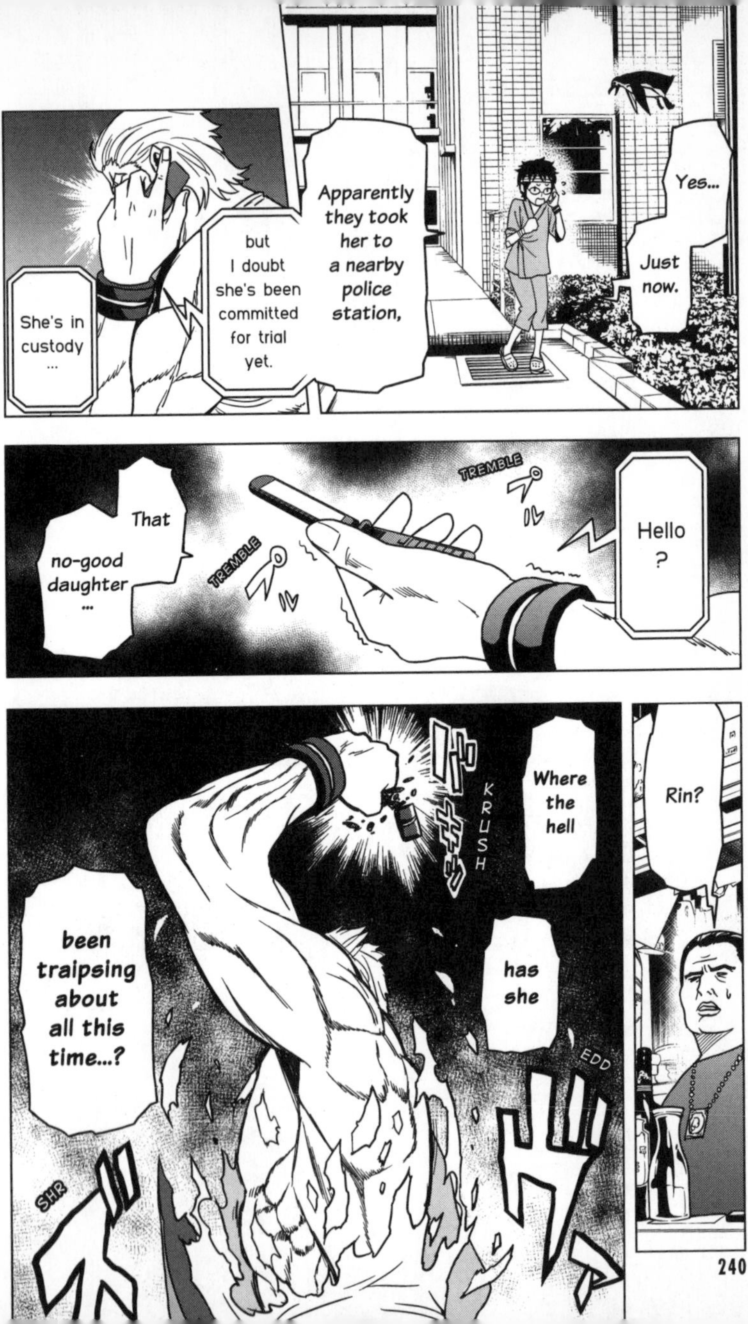
Yes...
Just now.
Apparently they took her to a nearby police station,
but I doubt she's been committed for trial yet.
She's in custody ...
Hello ?
TREMBLE
TREMBLE
That no-good daughter ...
Rin?
Where the hell
has she
been traipsing about all this time...?
KRUSH
EDD
SHR

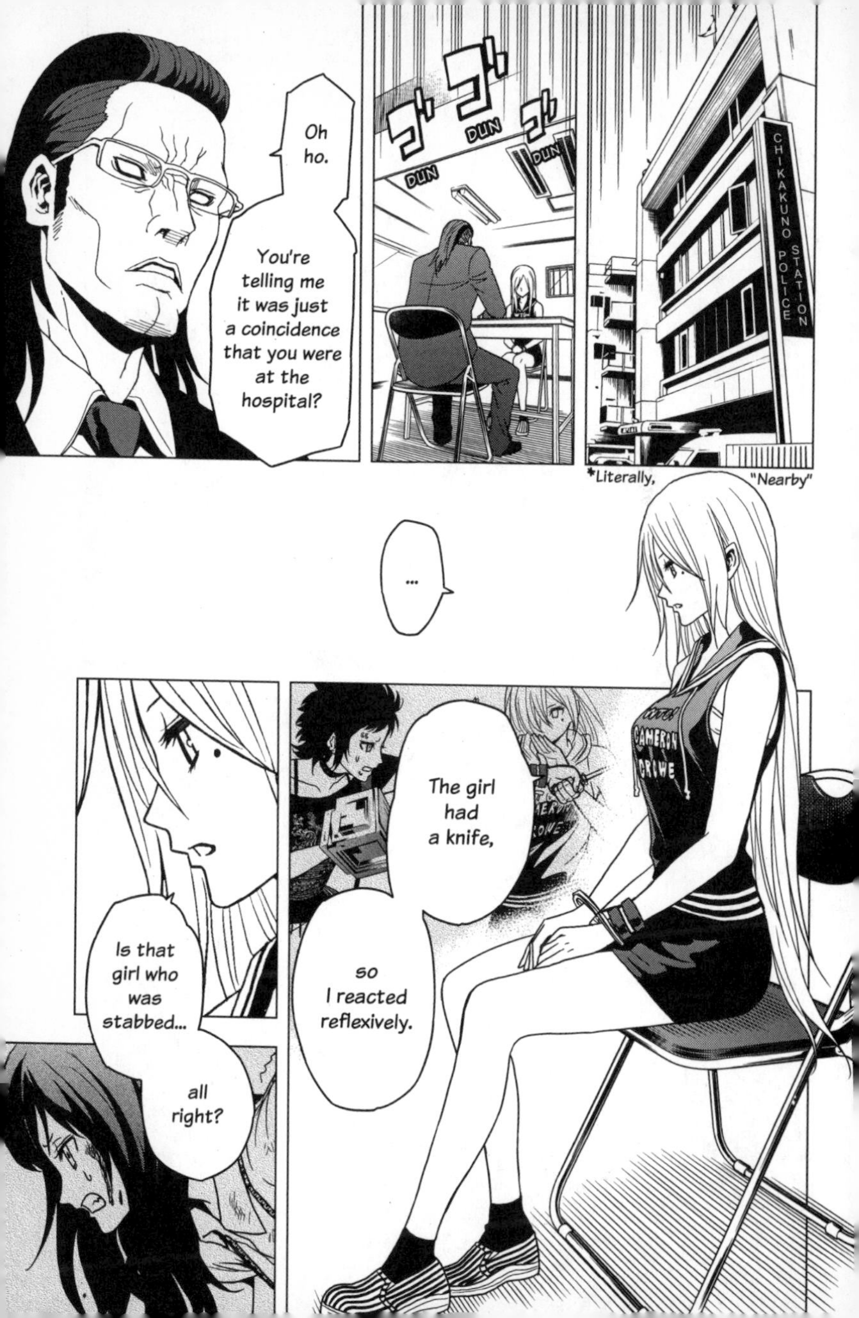
CHIKAKUNO POLICE STATION
*Literally, "Nearby"
DUN
DUN
DUN
Oh ho.
You're telling me it was just a coincidence that you were at the hospital?
...
CAMERON CROWE
The girl had a knife,
so I reacted reflexively.
Is that girl who was stabbed...
all right?

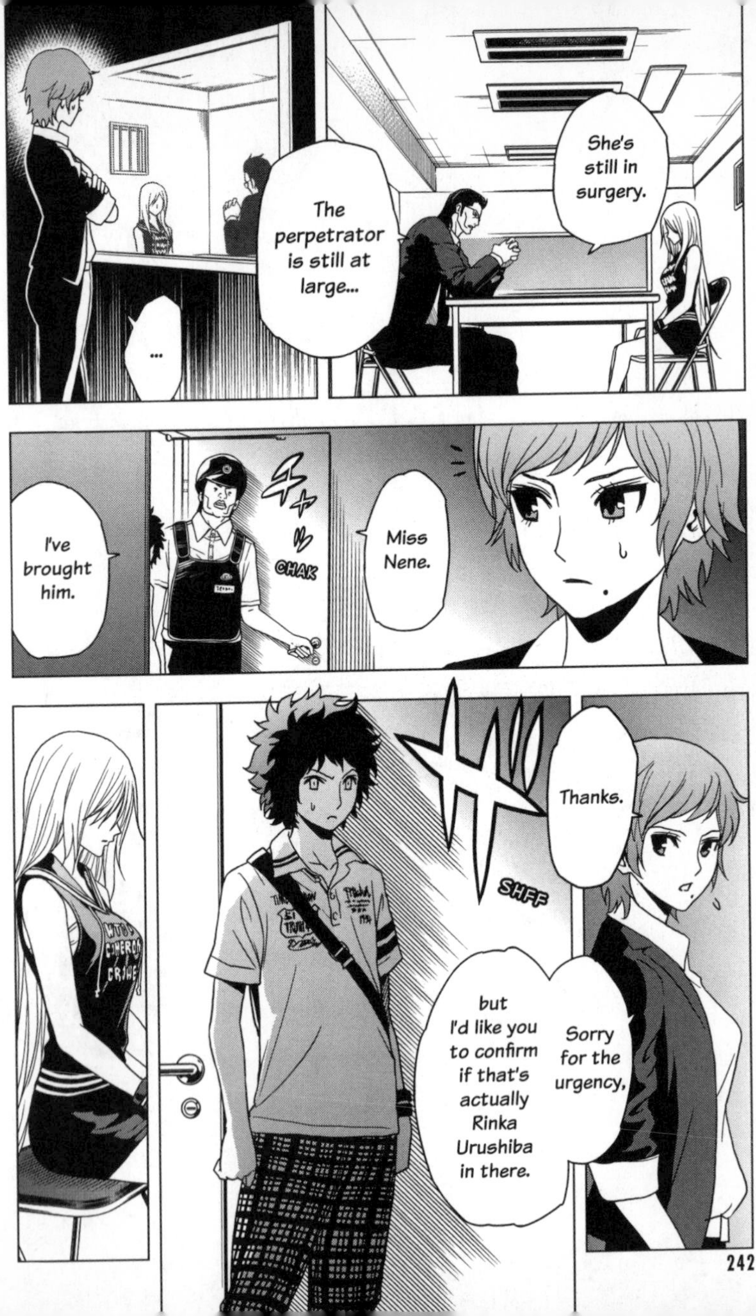
She's still in surgery.
The perpetrator is still at large...
...
Miss Nene.
CHAK
I've brought him.
Thanks.
SHFF
Sorry for the urgency,
but I'd like you to confirm if that's actually Rinka Urushiba in there.

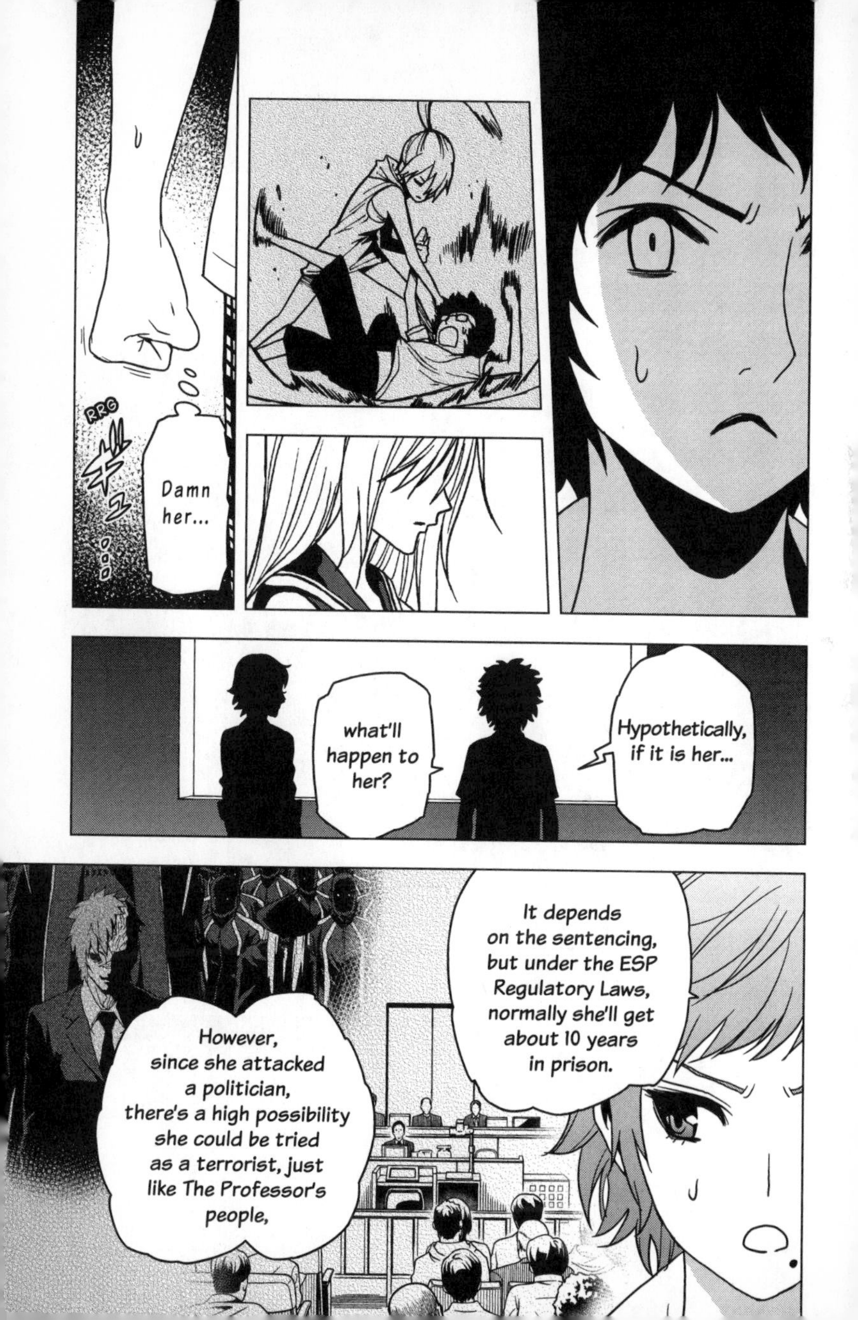
RRG
Damn her...
Hypothetically, if it is her...
what'll happen to her?
It depends on the sentencing, but under the ESP Regulatory Laws, normally she'll get about 10 years in prison.
However, since she attacked a politician, there's a high possibility she could be tried as a terrorist, just like The Professor's people,

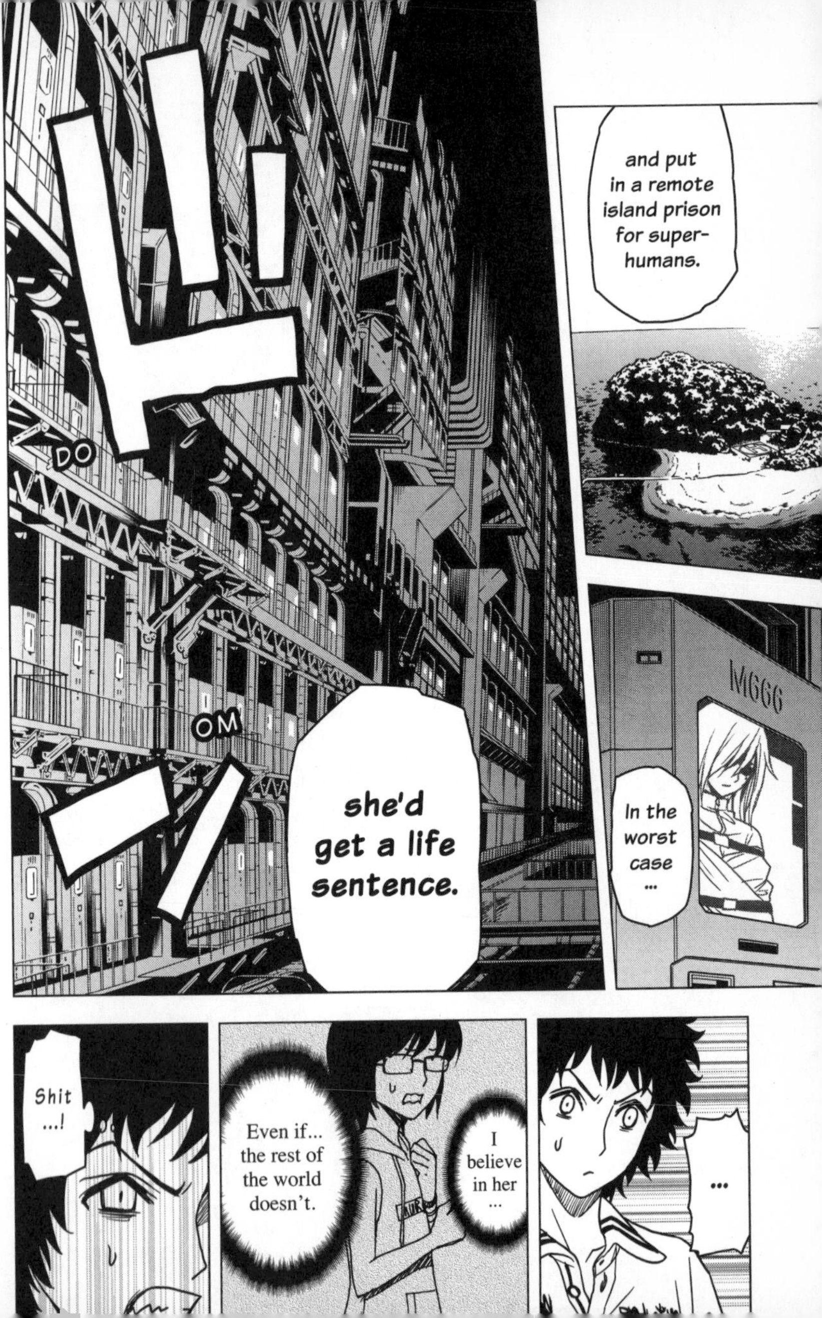
and put in a remote island prison for super-humans.
M666
In the worst case ...
DO
OM
she'd get a life sentence.
...
I believe in her ...
Even if... the rest of the world doesn't.
Shit ...!

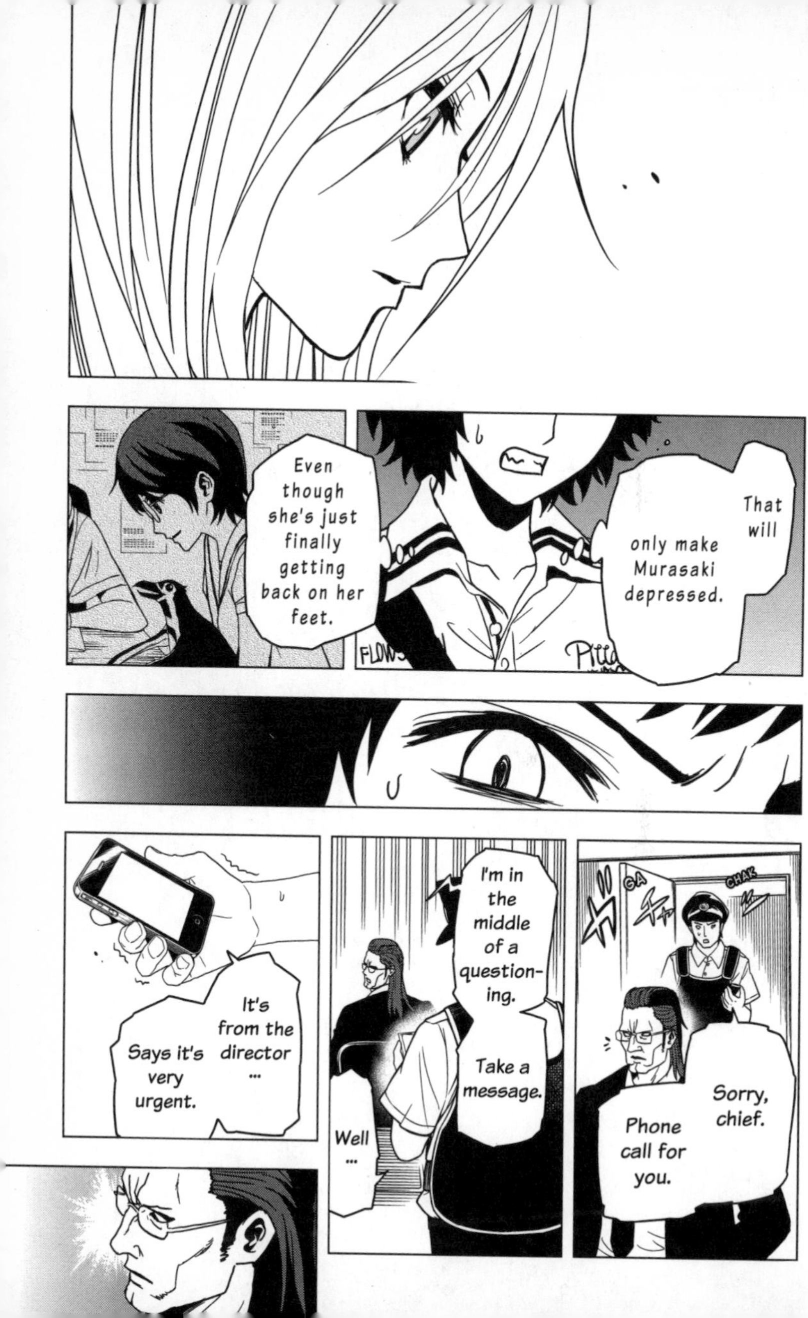
That will only make Murasaki depressed.
Even though she's just finally getting back on her feet.
GA
CHAK
Sorry, chief.
Phone call for you.
I'm in the middle of a questioning.
Take a message.
Well ...
It's from the director ...
Says it's very urgent.

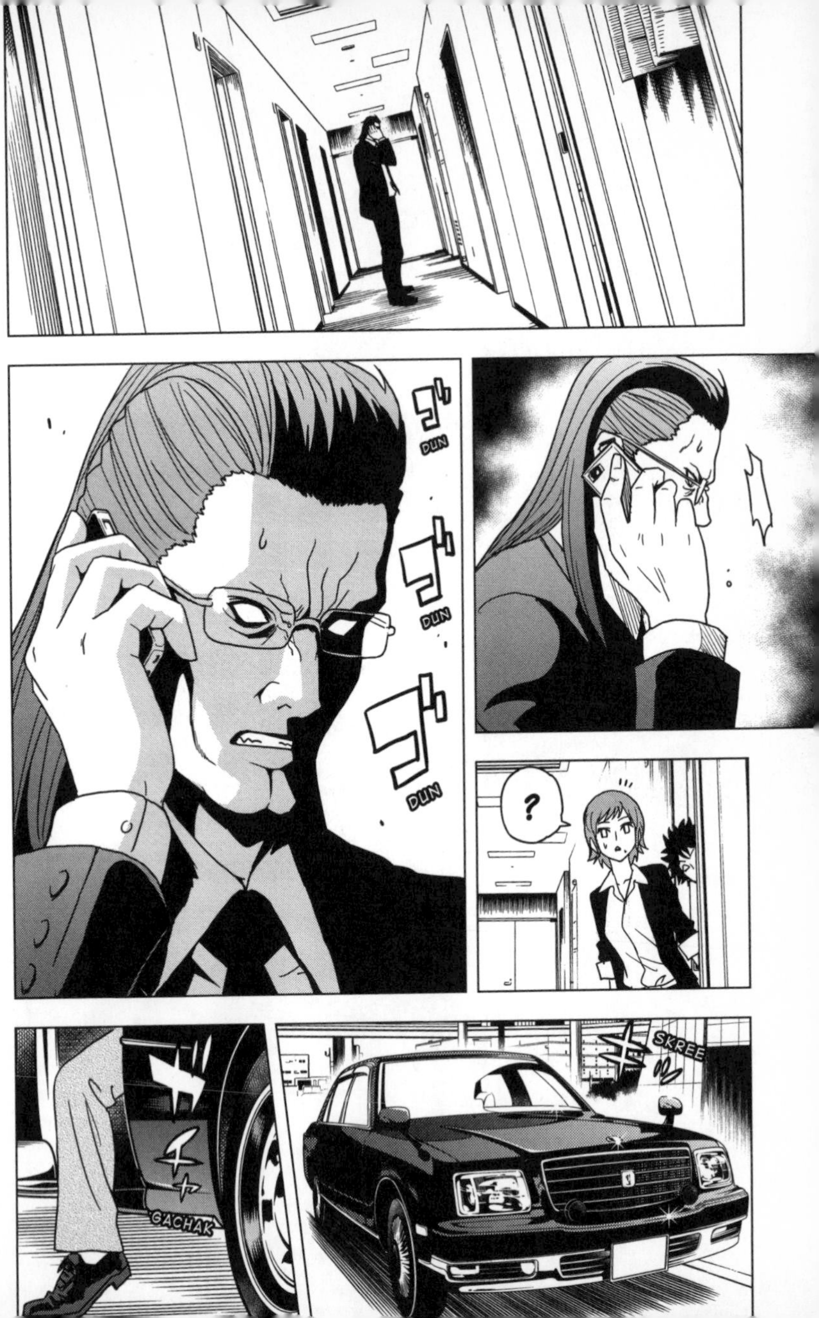
?
DUN
DUN
DUN
SKREE
GACHAK

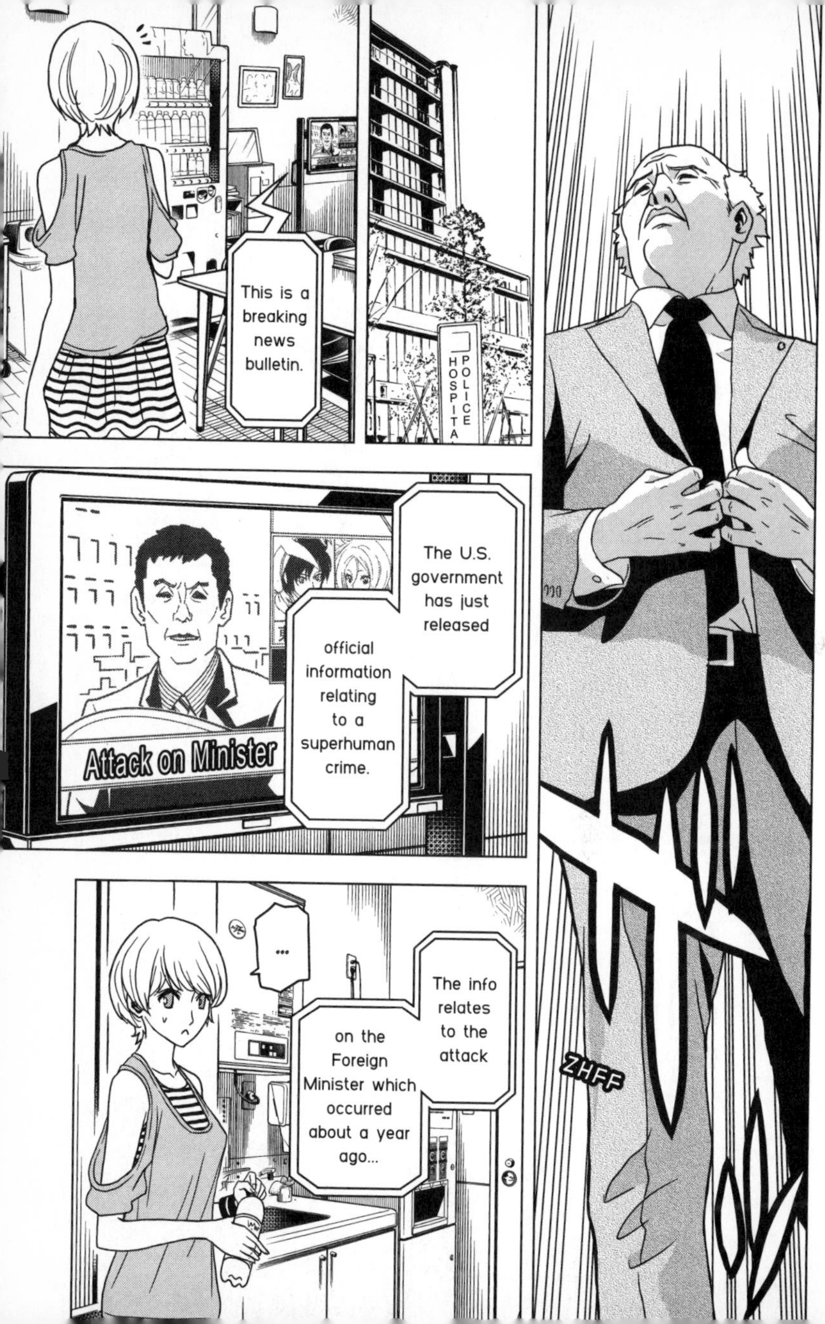
ZHFF
POLICE
HOSPITA
This is a breaking news bulletin.
The U.S. government has just released
official information relating to a superhuman crime.
Attack on Minister
The info relates to the attack
on the Foreign Minister which occurred about a year ago...
...

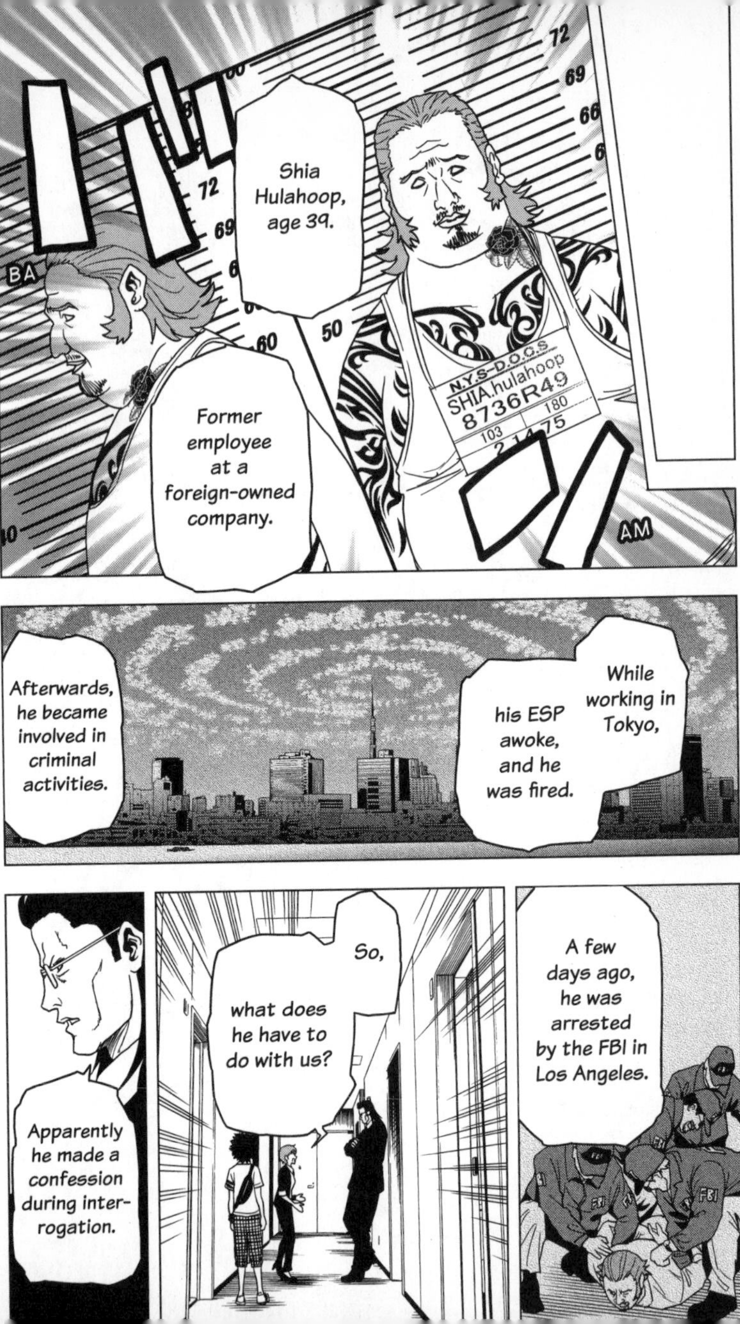
Shia Hulahoop, age 39.
Former employee at a foreign-owned company.
BA
AM
N.Y.S-D.O.C.S
SHIA.hulahoop
8736R49
While working in Tokyo,
his ESP awoke, and he was fired.
Afterwards, he became involved in criminal activities.
A few days ago, he was arrested by the FBI in Los Angeles.
So,
what does he have to do with us?
Apparently he made a confession during inter-rogation.

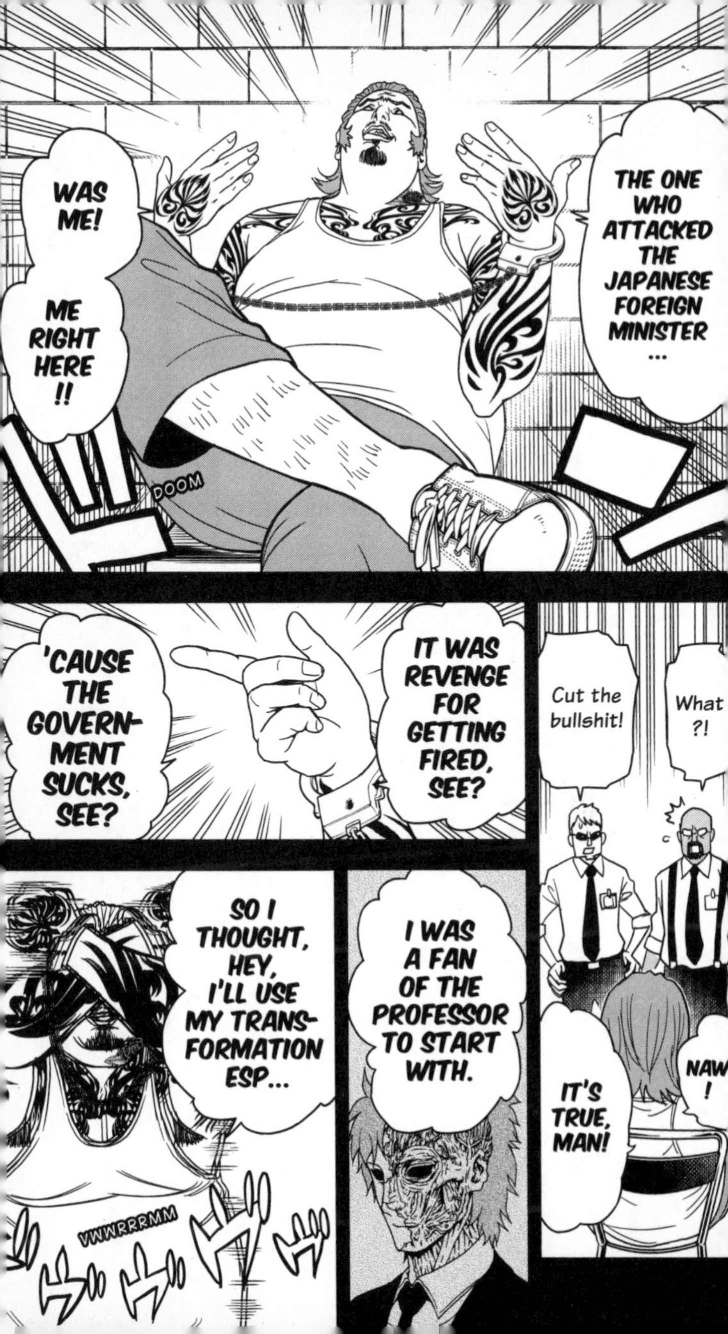
THE ONE WHO ATTACKED THE JAPANESE FOREIGN MINISTER ...
WAS ME!
ME RIGHT HERE !!
DOOM
What ?!
Cut the bullshit!
NAW !
IT'S TRUE, MAN!
IT WAS REVENGE FOR GETTING FIRED, SEE?
'CAUSE THE GOVERNMENT SUCKS, SEE?
I WAS A FAN OF THE PROFESSOR TO START WITH.
SO I THOUGHT, HEY, I'LL USE MY TRANSFORMATION ESP...
VWWRRRMM

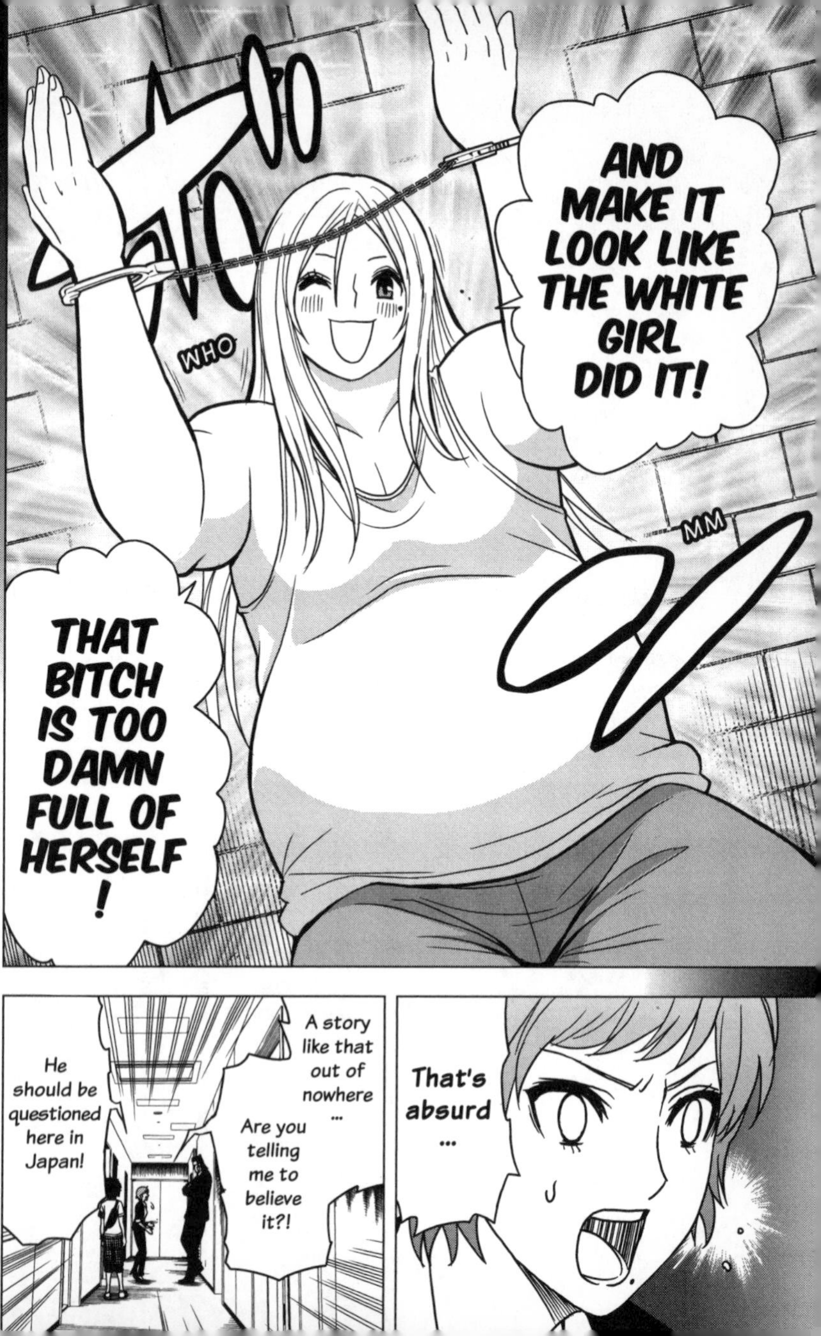
AND MAKE IT LOOK LIKE THE WHITE GIRL DID IT!
WHO
MM
THAT BITCH IS TOO DAMN FULL OF HERSELF!
That's absurd ...
A story like that out of nowhere ...
Are you telling me to believe it?!
He should be questioned here in Japan!

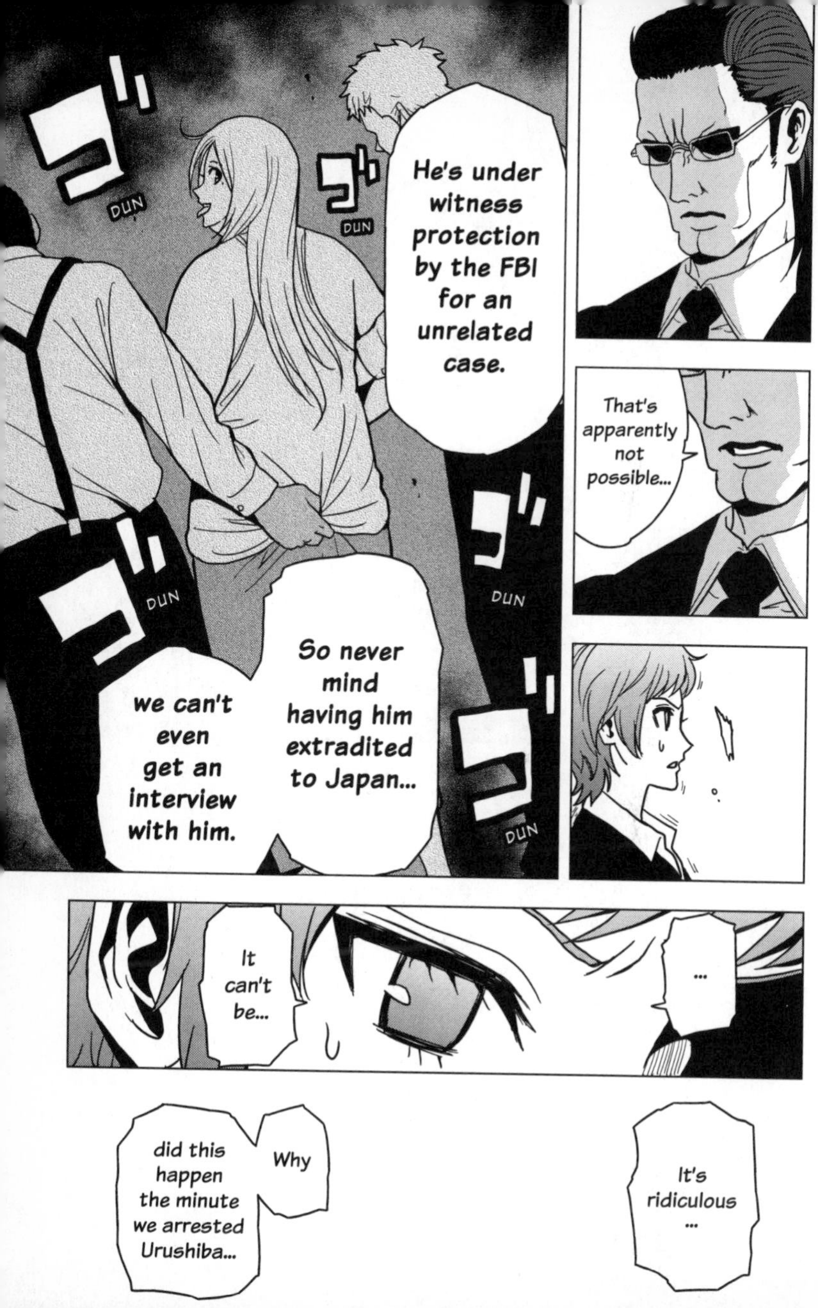
That's apparently not possible...
He's under witness protection by the FBI for an unrelated case.
DUN
DUN
So never mind having him extradited to Japan...
we can't even get an interview with him.
DUN
DUN
DUN
...
It can't be...
It's ridiculous ...
Why
did this happen the minute we arrested Urushiba...

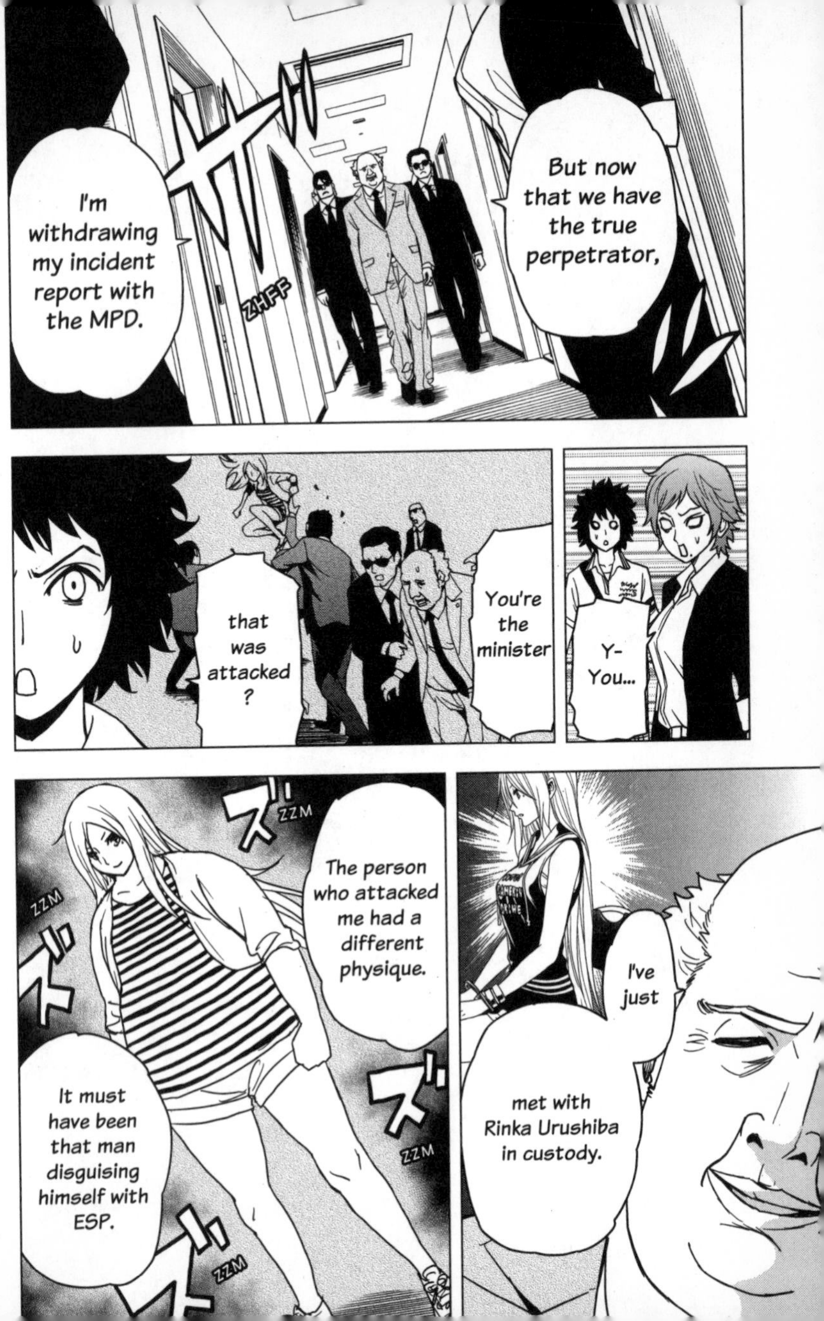
But now that we have the true perpetrator,
I'm withdrawing my incident report with the MPD.
ZHFF
Y- You...
You're the minister
that was attacked ?
I've just
met with Rinka Urushiba in custody.
The person who attacked me had a different physique.
ZZM
ZZM
It must have been that man disguising himself with ESP.
ZZM
ZZM

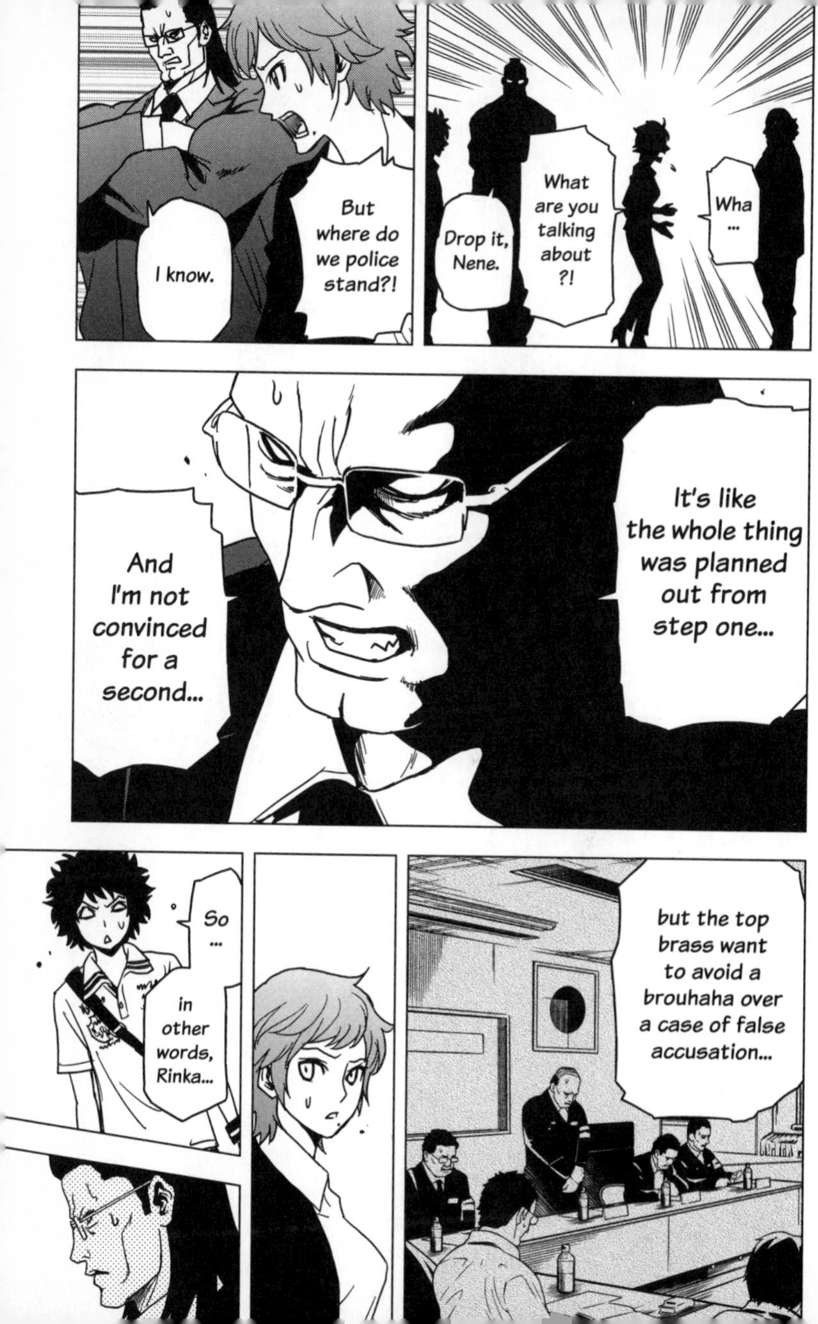
Wha ...
What are you talking about ?!
Drop it, Nene.
But where do we police stand?!
I know.
It's like the whole thing was planned out from step one...
And I'm not convinced for a second...
but the top brass want to avoid a brouhaha over a case of false accusation...
So ...
in other words, Rinka...

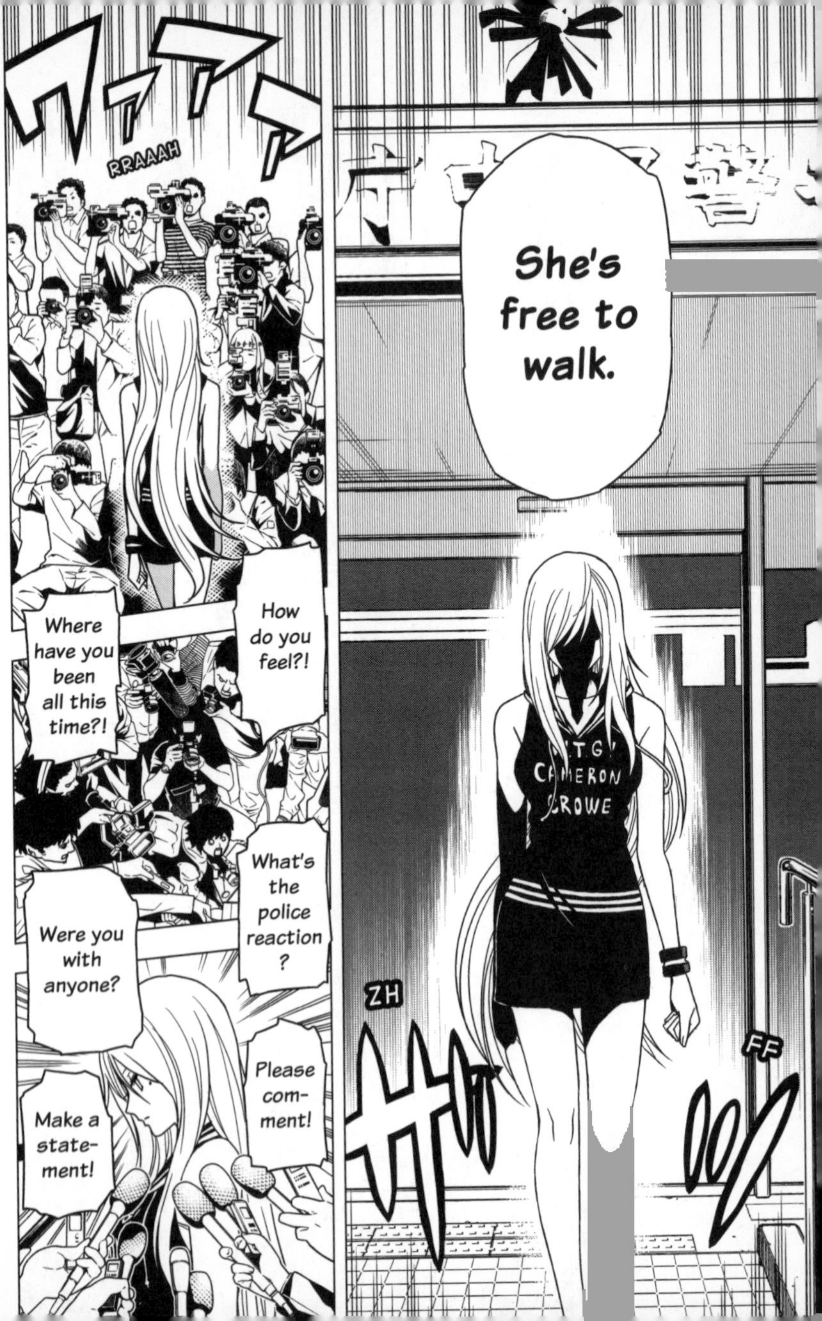
She's free to walk.
ZH
FF
ワァァァ
RRAAAH
How do you feel?!
Where have you been all this time?!
What's the police reaction?
Were you with anyone?
Please com-ment!
Make a state-ment!

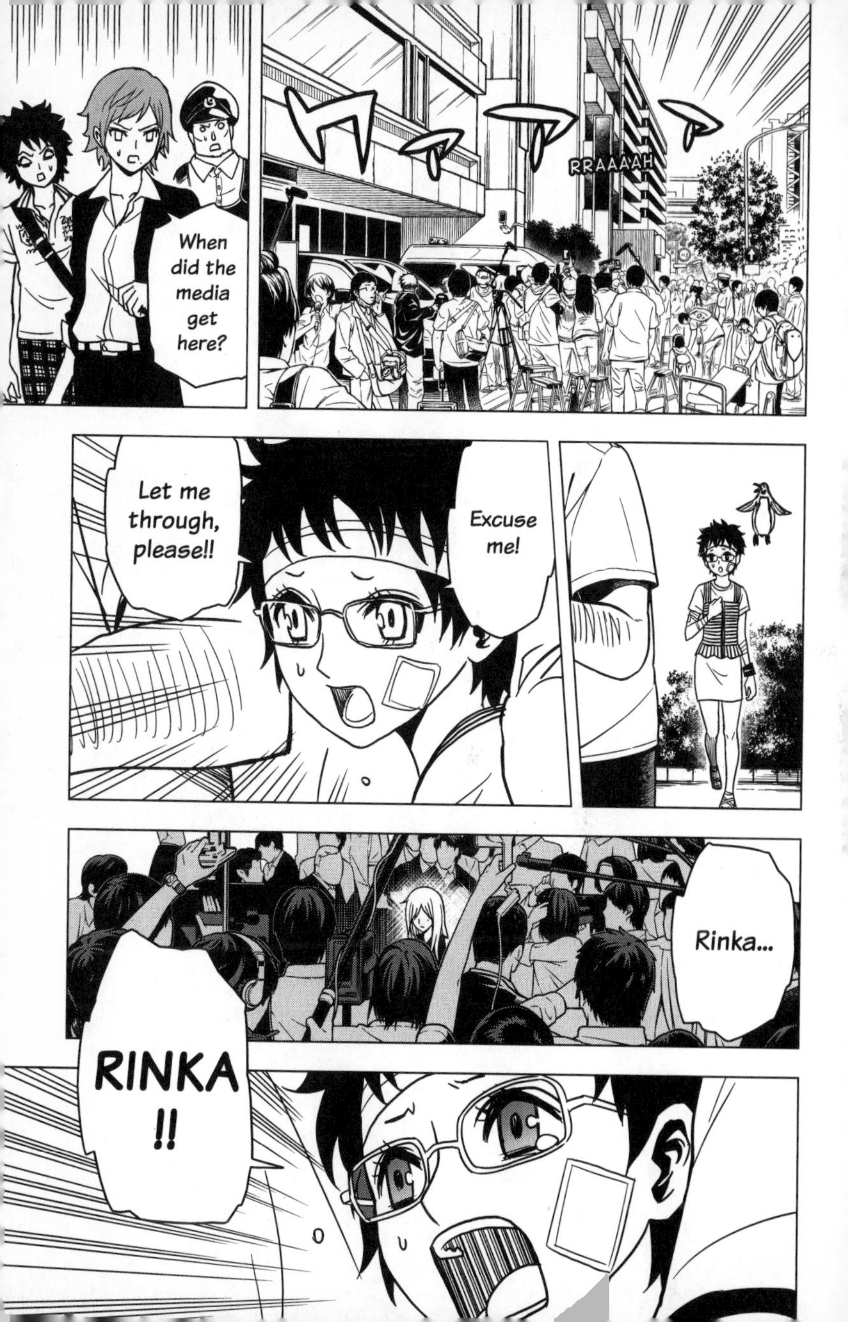
RRAAAAH
When did the media get here?
Excuse me!
Let me through, please!!
Rinka...
RINKA !!

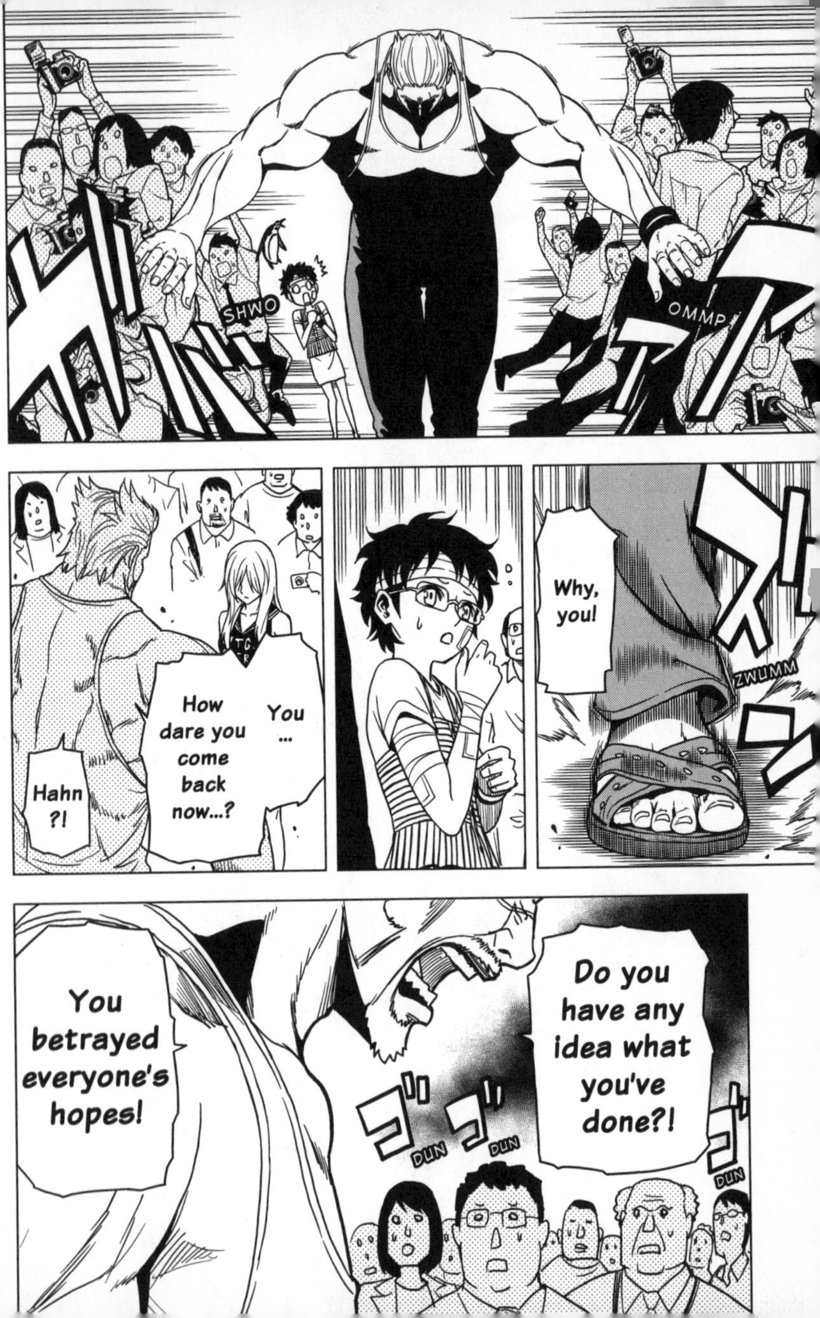
SHWO
OMMP
Why, you!
ZWUMM
You ...
How dare you come back now...?
Hahn ?!
Do you have any idea what you've done?!
DUN
DUN
DUN
You betrayed everyone's hopes!

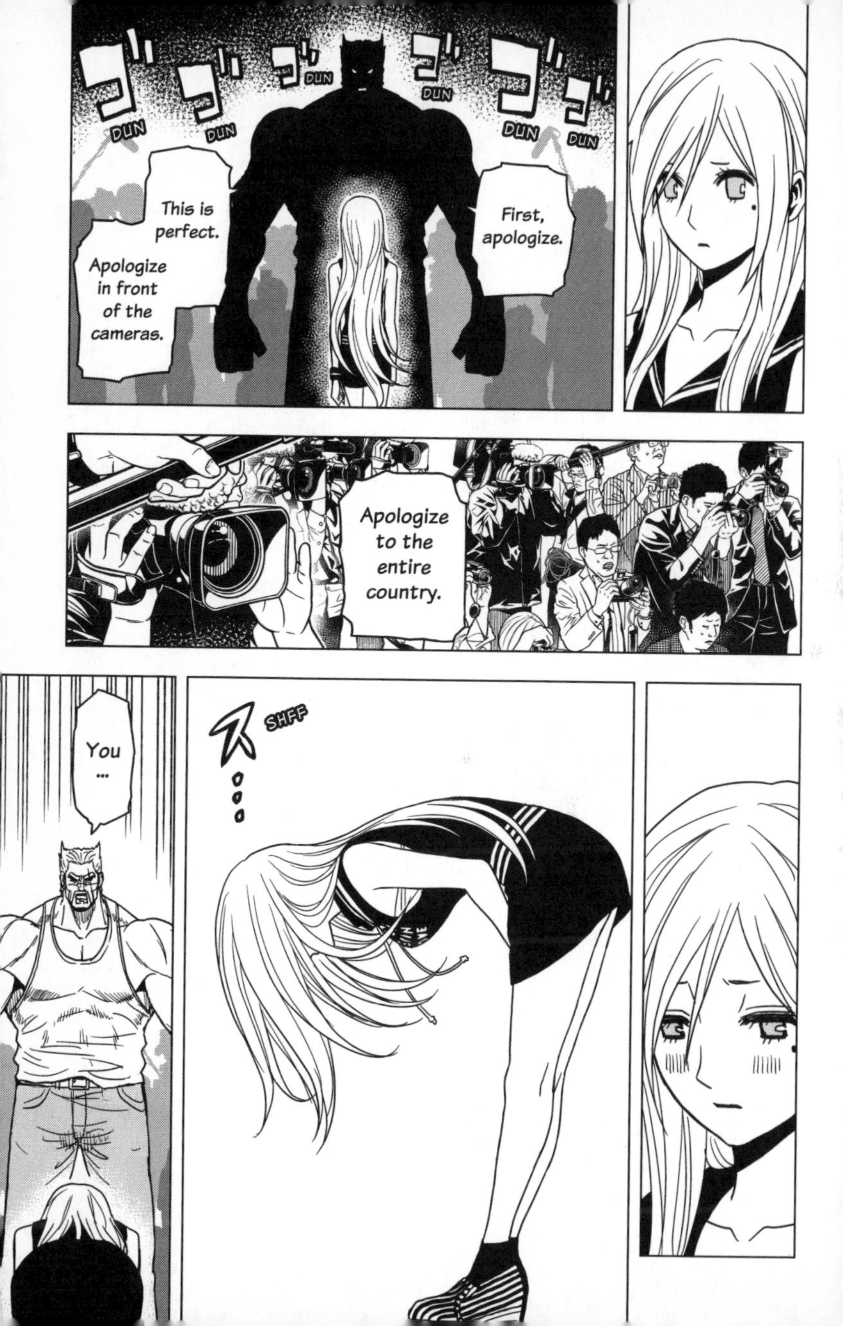
DUN DUN DUN DUN DUN DUN
First, apologize.
This is perfect.
Apologize in front of the cameras.
Apologize to the entire country.
SHFF
You ...

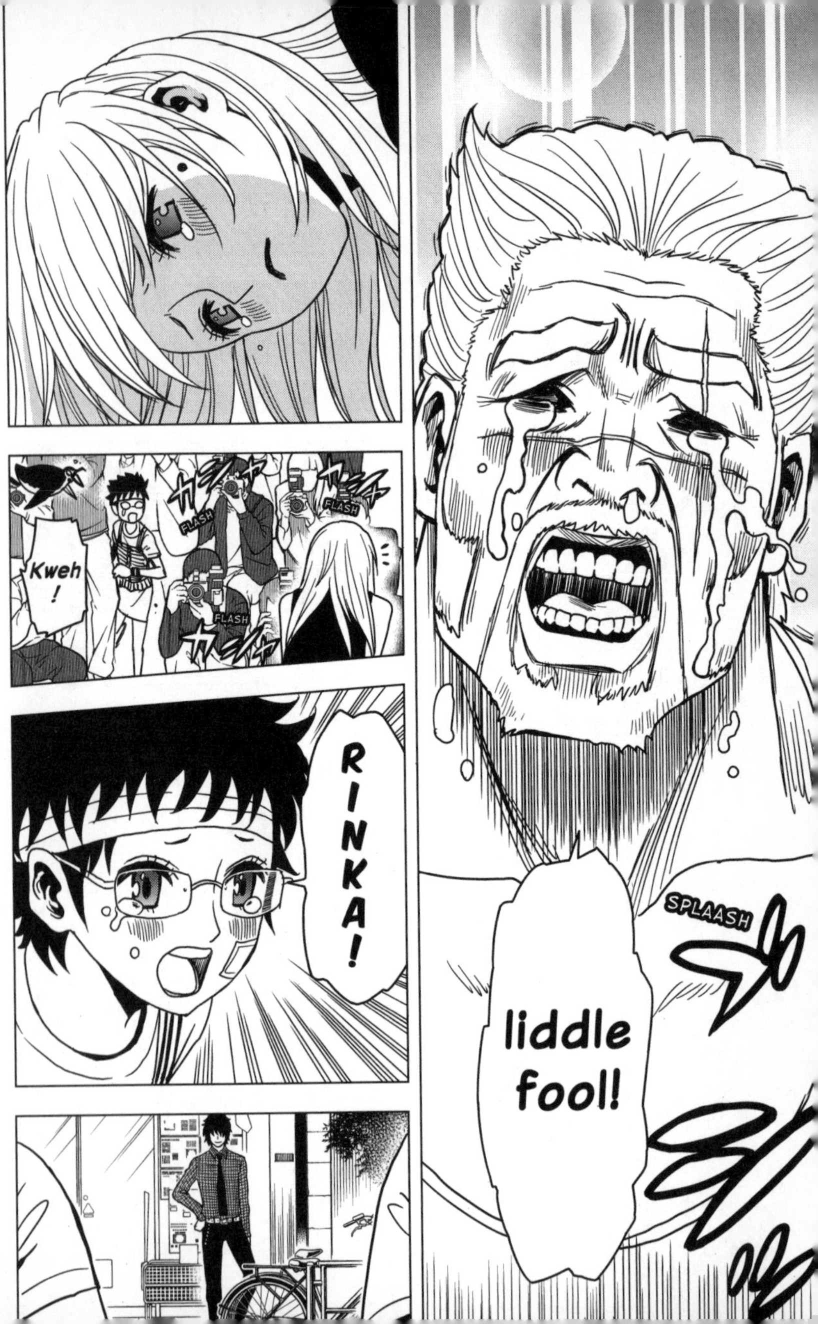
SPLAASH
liddle fool!
FLASH
FLASH
Kweh!
FLASH
RINKA!

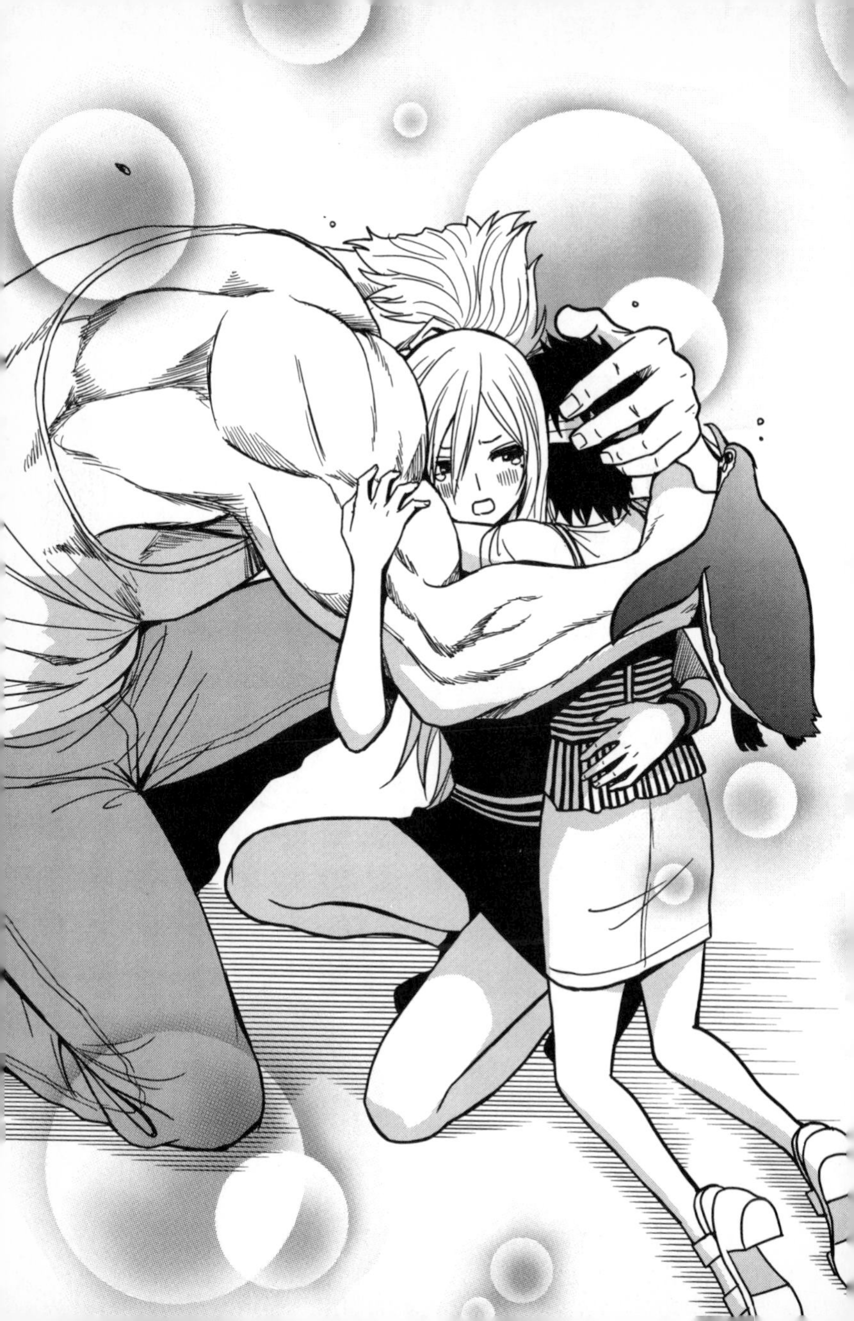

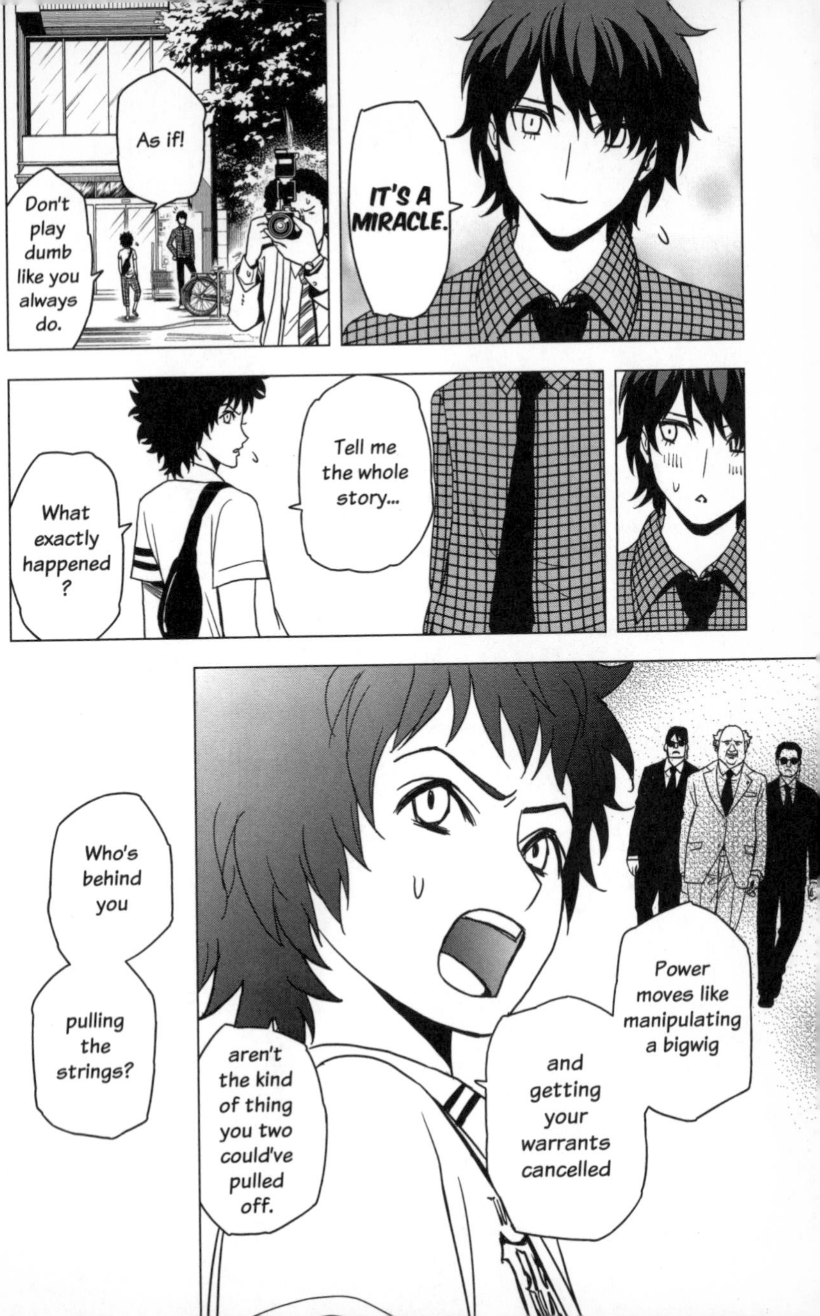
IT'S A MIRACLE.
As if!
Don't play dumb like you always do.
Tell me the whole story...
What exactly happened?
Power moves like manipulating a bigwig
and getting your warrants cancelled
aren't the kind of thing you two could've pulled off.
Who's behind you
pulling the strings?

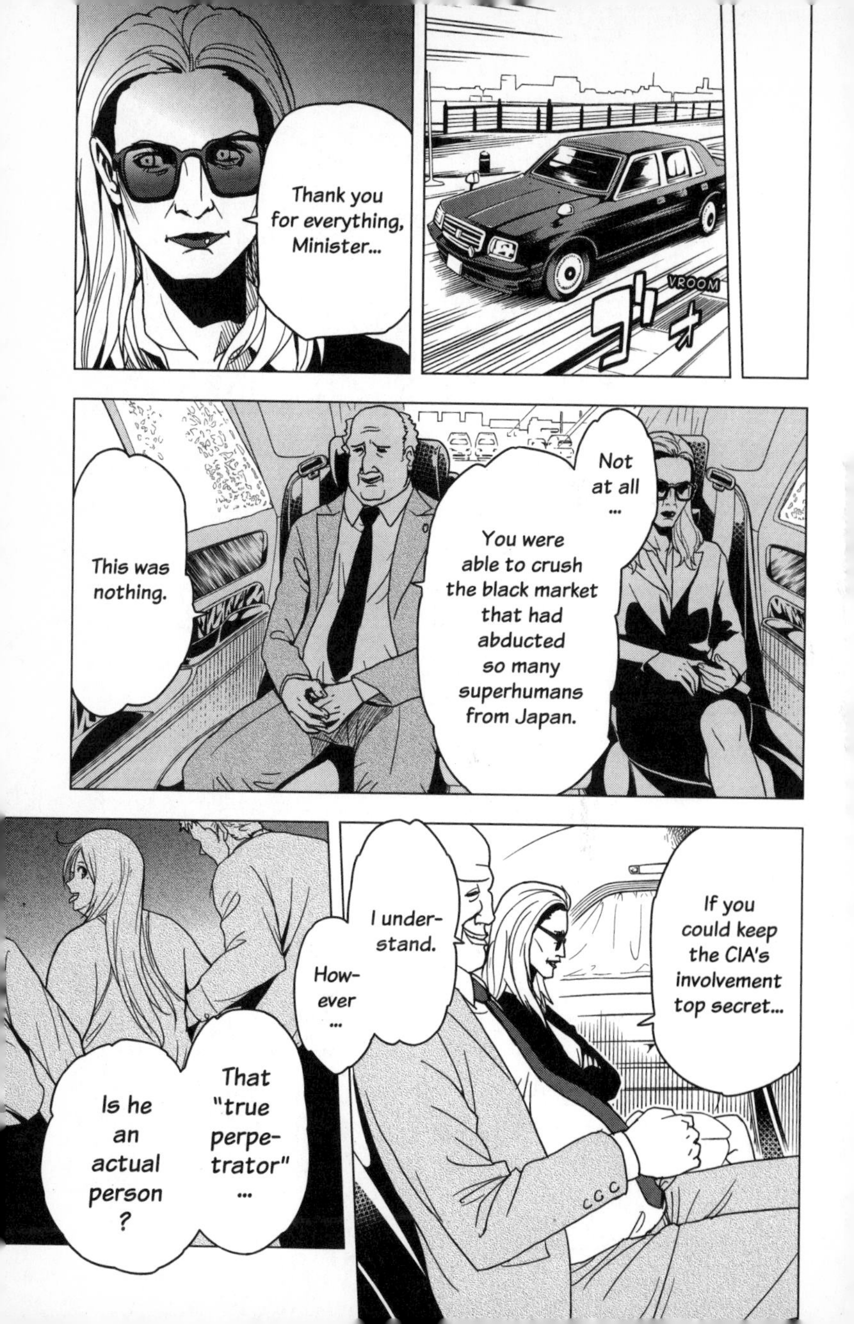
VROOM
Thank you for everything, Minister...
Not at all ...
You were able to crush the black market that had abducted so many superhumans from Japan.
This was nothing.
If you could keep the CIA's involvement top secret...
I understand.
However ...
That "true perpetrator" ...
Is he an actual person ?

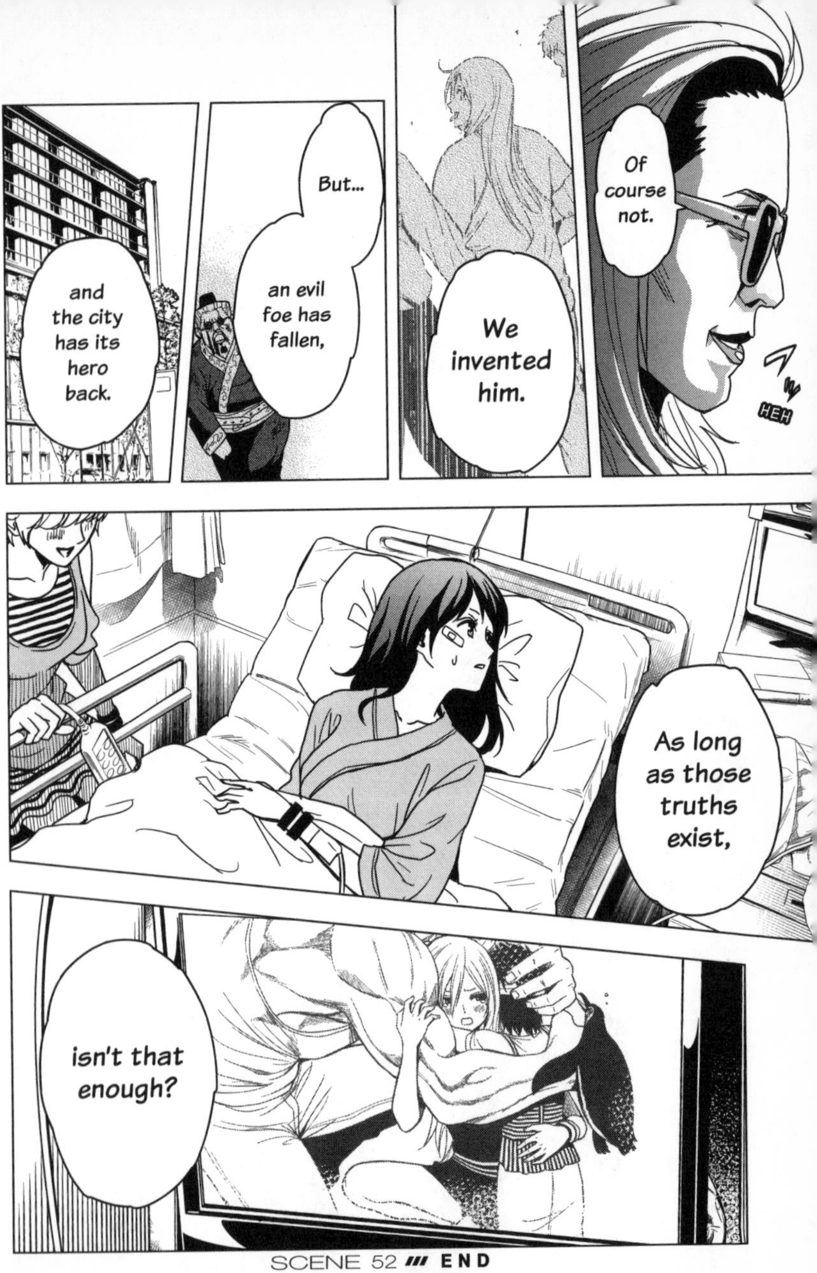
Of course not.
HEH
We invented him.
But...
an evil foe has fallen,
and the city has its hero back.
As long as those truths exist,
isn't that enough?

SCENE 52 /// END

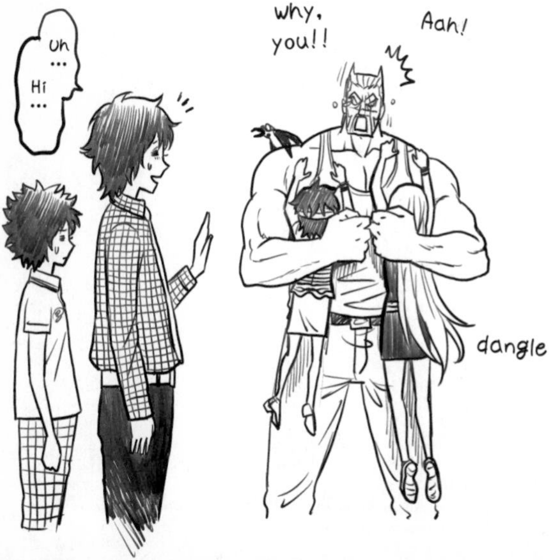
Aah!
why, you!!
dangle
Uh... Hi...

TOKYO ESP

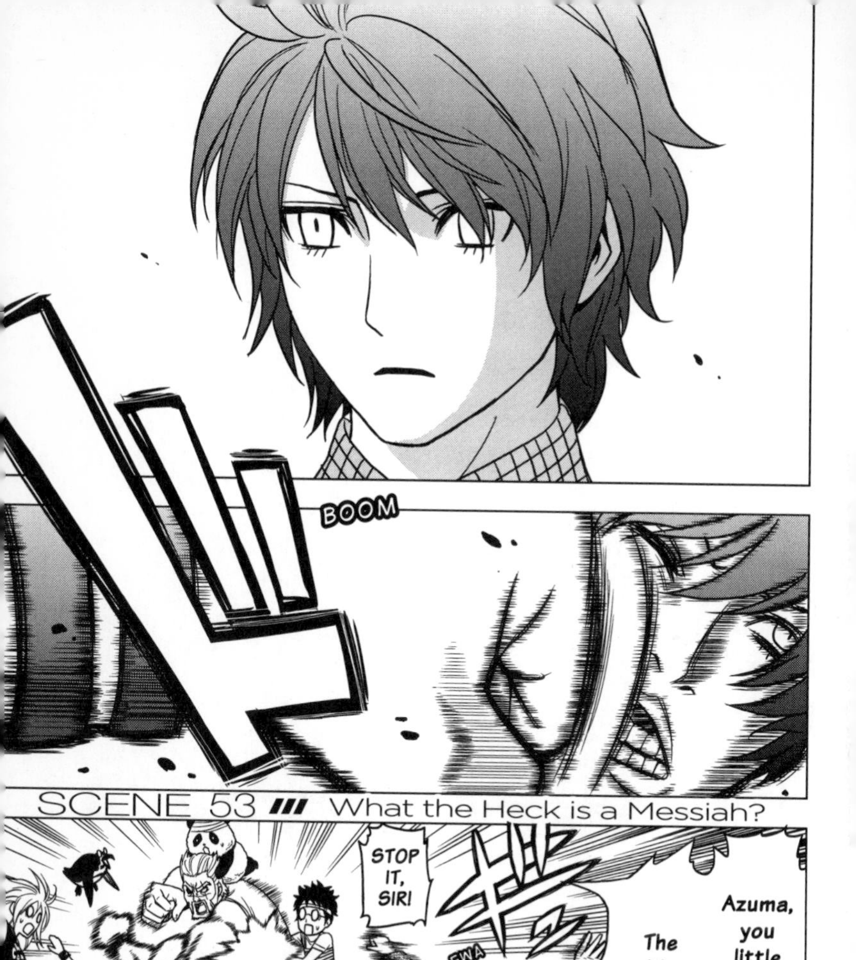
BOOM

SCENE 53 /// What the Heck is a Messiah?

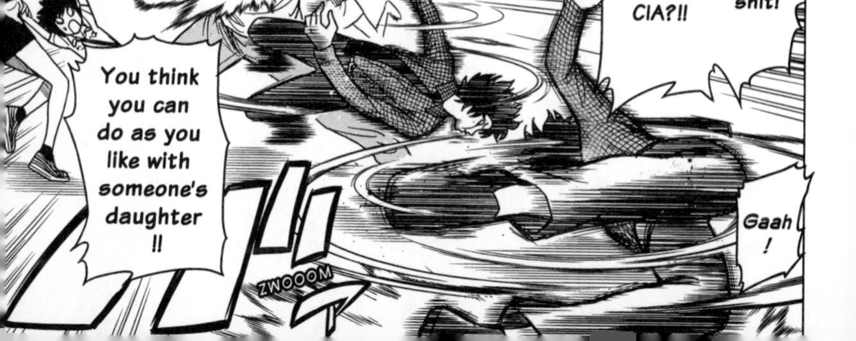
Azuma, you little shit!
The goddamn CIA?!!
STOP IT, SIR!
FWA
Gaah!
You think you can do as you like with someone's daughter!!
ZWOOOM

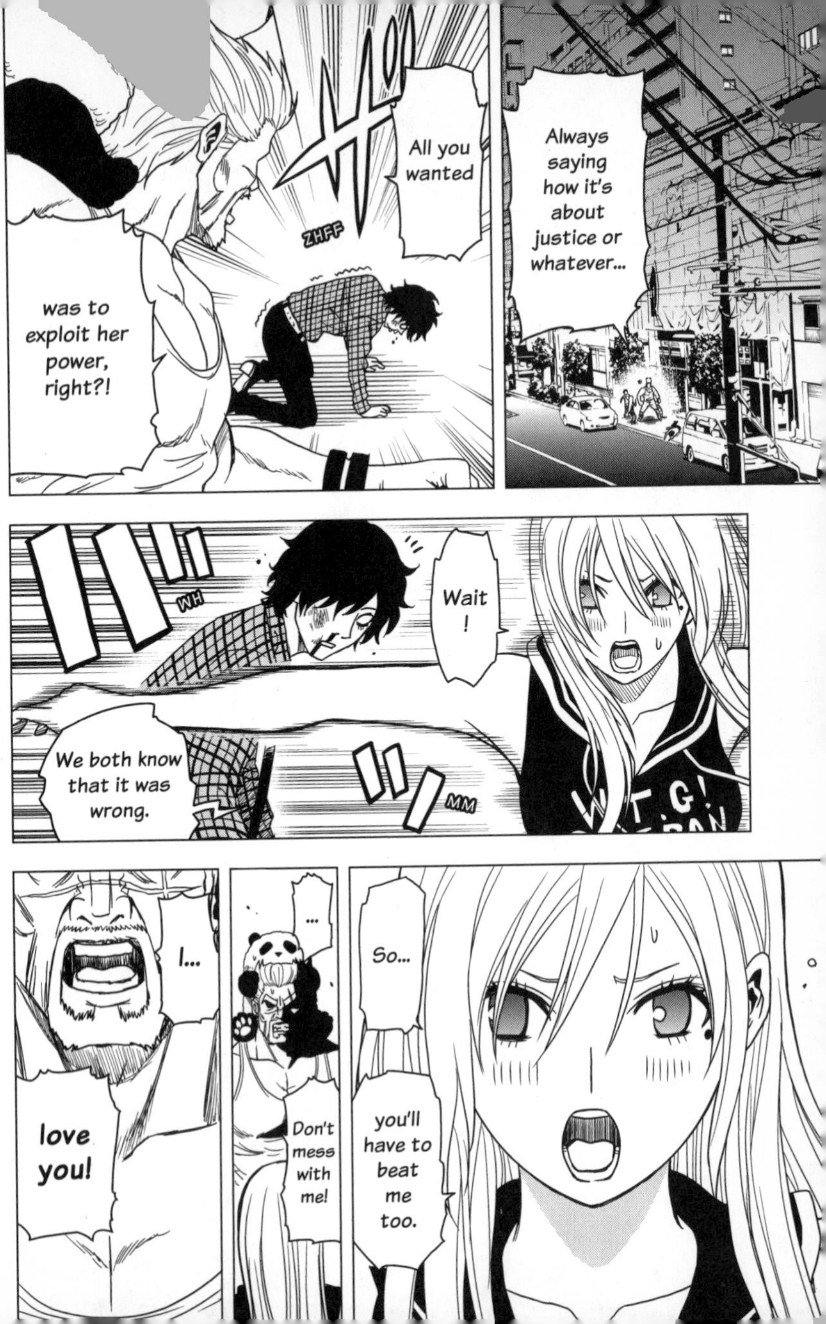
Always saying how it's about justice or whatever...
All you wanted
ZHFF
was to exploit her power, right?!
Wait!
WH
We both know that it was wrong.
MM
So...
you'll have to beat me too.
...
Don't mess with me!
I...
love you!

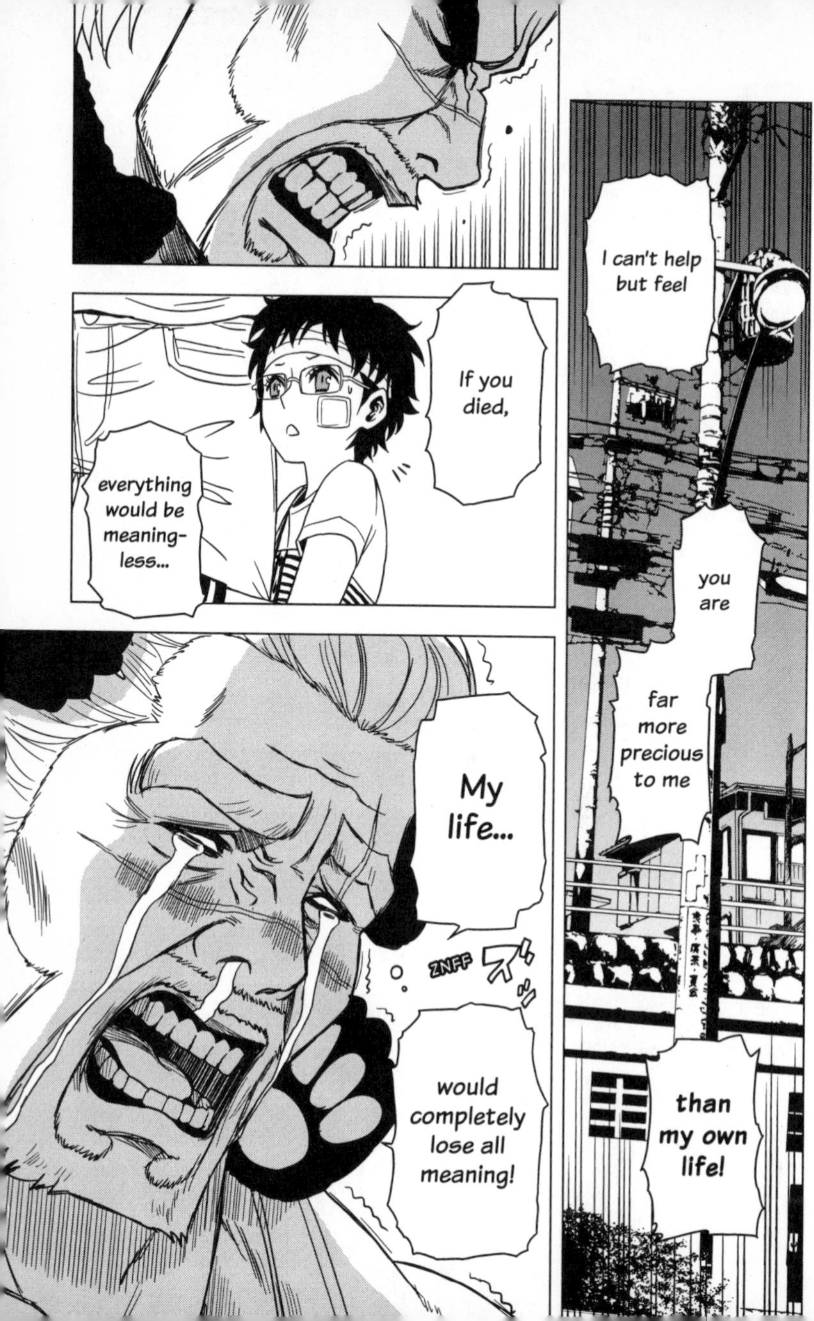

If you died,
everything would be meaning-less...
My life...
ZNFF
would completely lose all meaning!
I can't help but feel
you are
far more precious to me
than my own life!

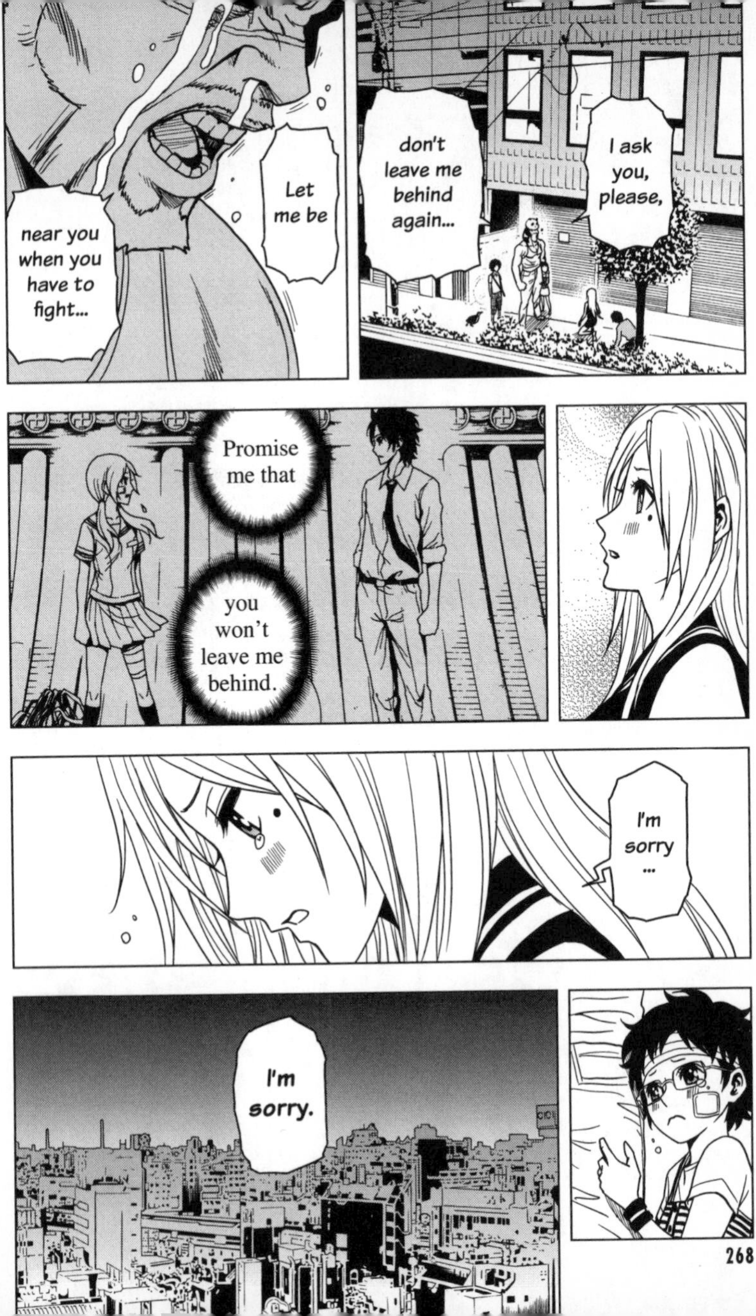
I ask you, please,
don't leave me behind again...
Let me be
near you when you have to fight...
Promise me that
you won't leave me behind.
I'm sorry ...
I'm sorry.

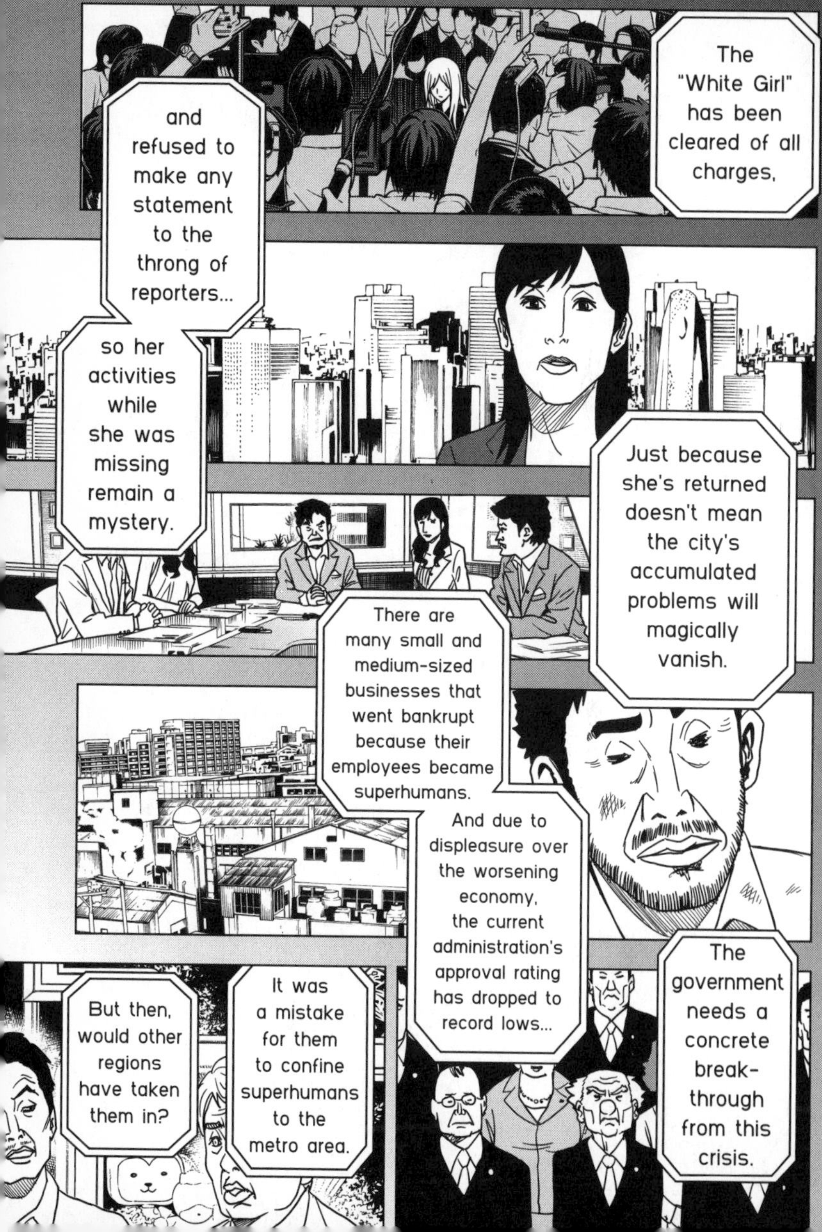
The "White Girl" has been cleared of all charges,
and refused to make any statement to the throng of reporters...
so her activities while she was missing remain a mystery.
Just because she's returned doesn't mean the city's accumulated problems will magically vanish.
There are many small and medium-sized businesses that went bankrupt because their employees became superhumans.
And due to displeasure over the worsening economy, the current administration's approval rating has dropped to record lows...
The government needs a concrete break-through from this crisis.
It was a mistake for them to confine superhumans to the metro area.
But then, would other regions have taken them in?

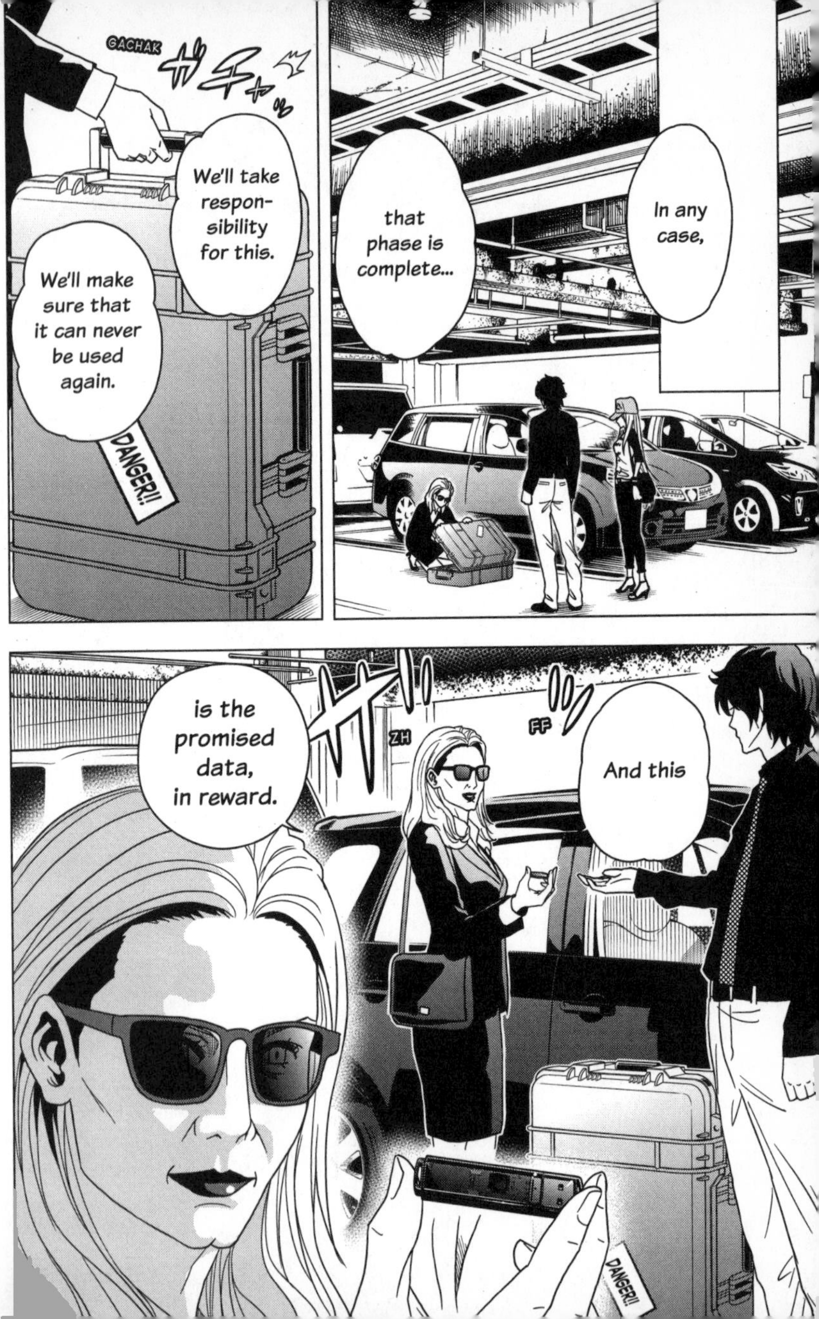
In any case,
that phase is complete...
GACHAK
We'll take respon-sibility for this.
We'll make sure that it can never be used again.
DANGER!!
FF
And this
ZH
is the promised data, in reward.
DANGER!!

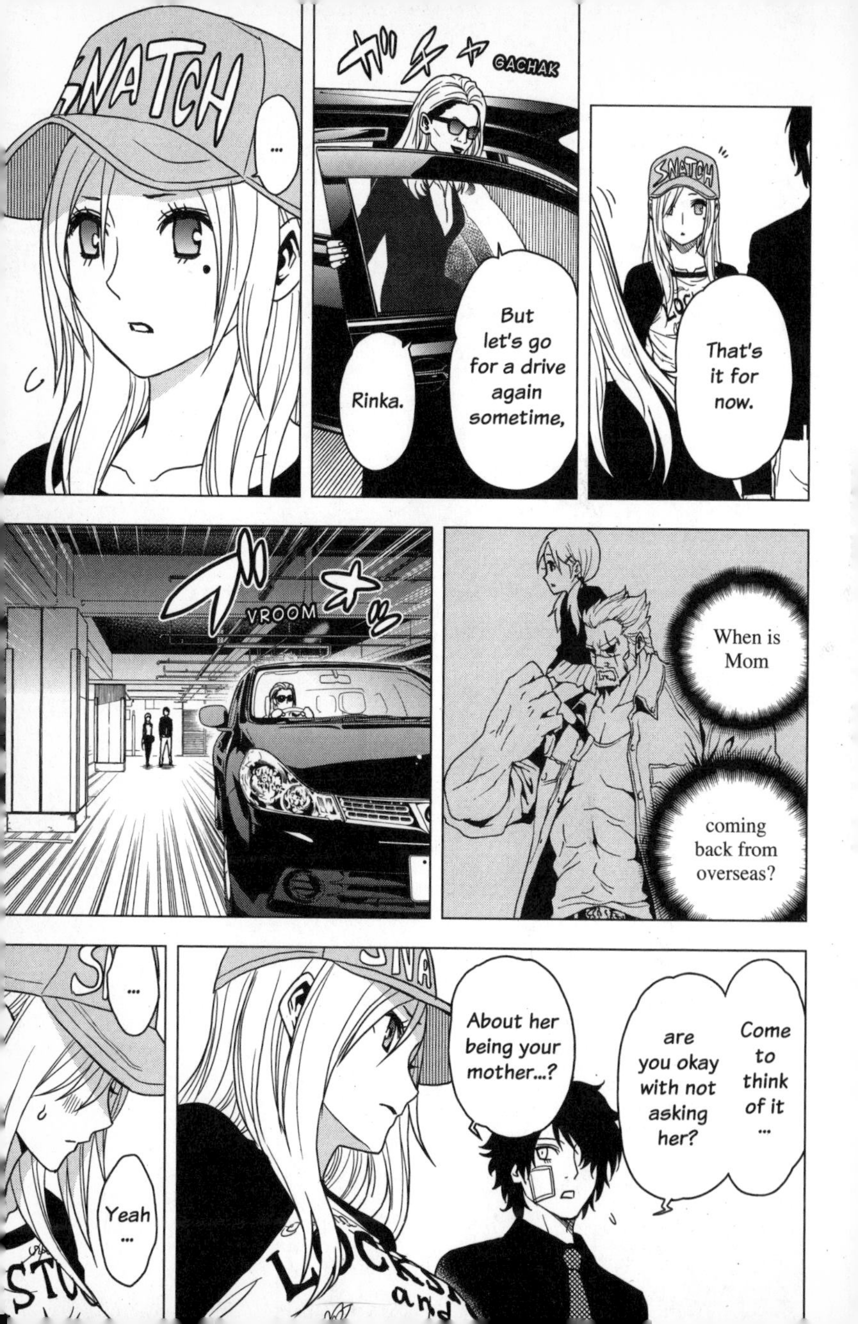
That's it for now.
GACHAK
But let's go for a drive again sometime,
Rinka.
...
When is Mom
coming back from overseas?
VROOM
Come to think of it ...
are you okay with not asking her?
About her being your mother...?
...
Yeah ...

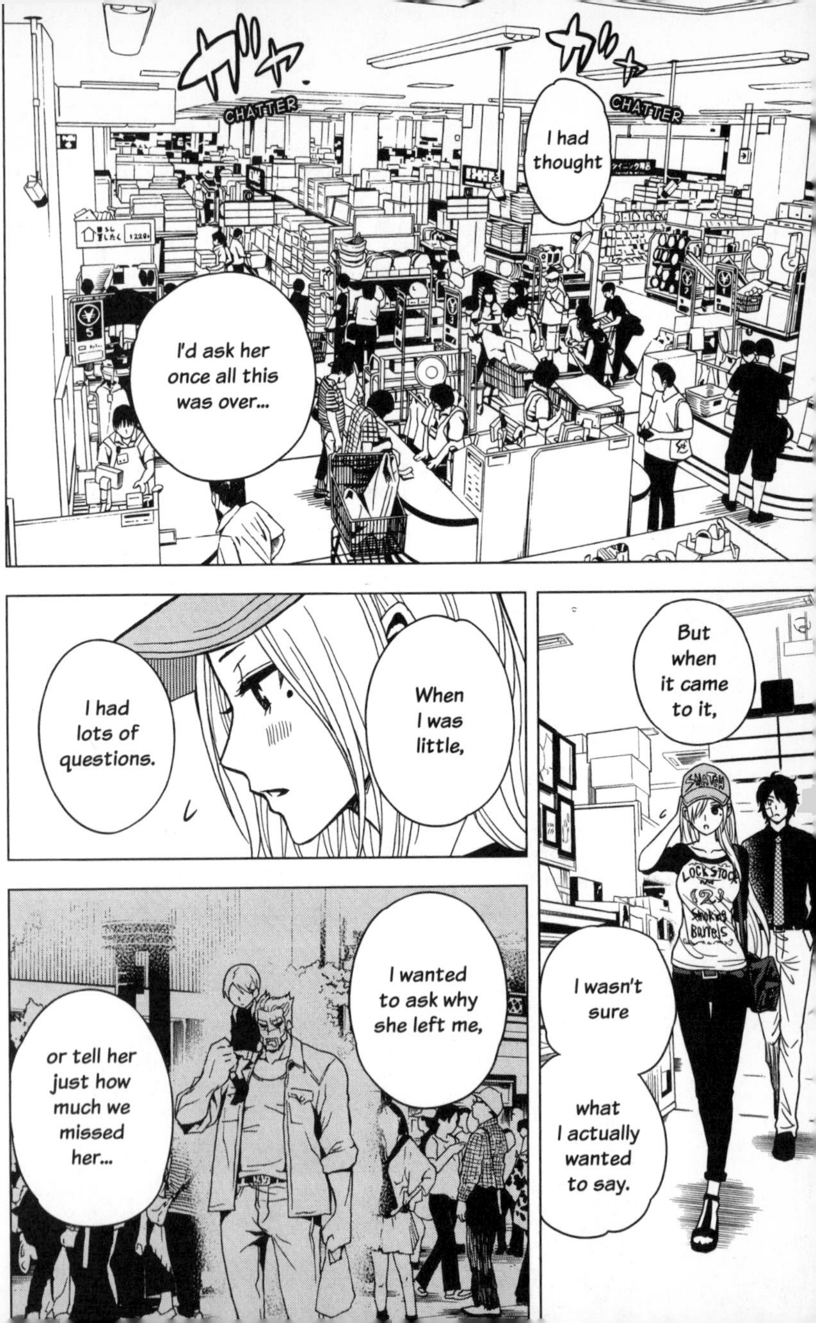

ガヤ
CHATTER
I had thought
ガヤ
CHATTER
I'd ask her once all this was over...
But when it came to it,
I wasn't sure
what I actually wanted to say.
When I was little,
I had lots of questions.
I wanted to ask why she left me,
or tell her just how much we missed her...

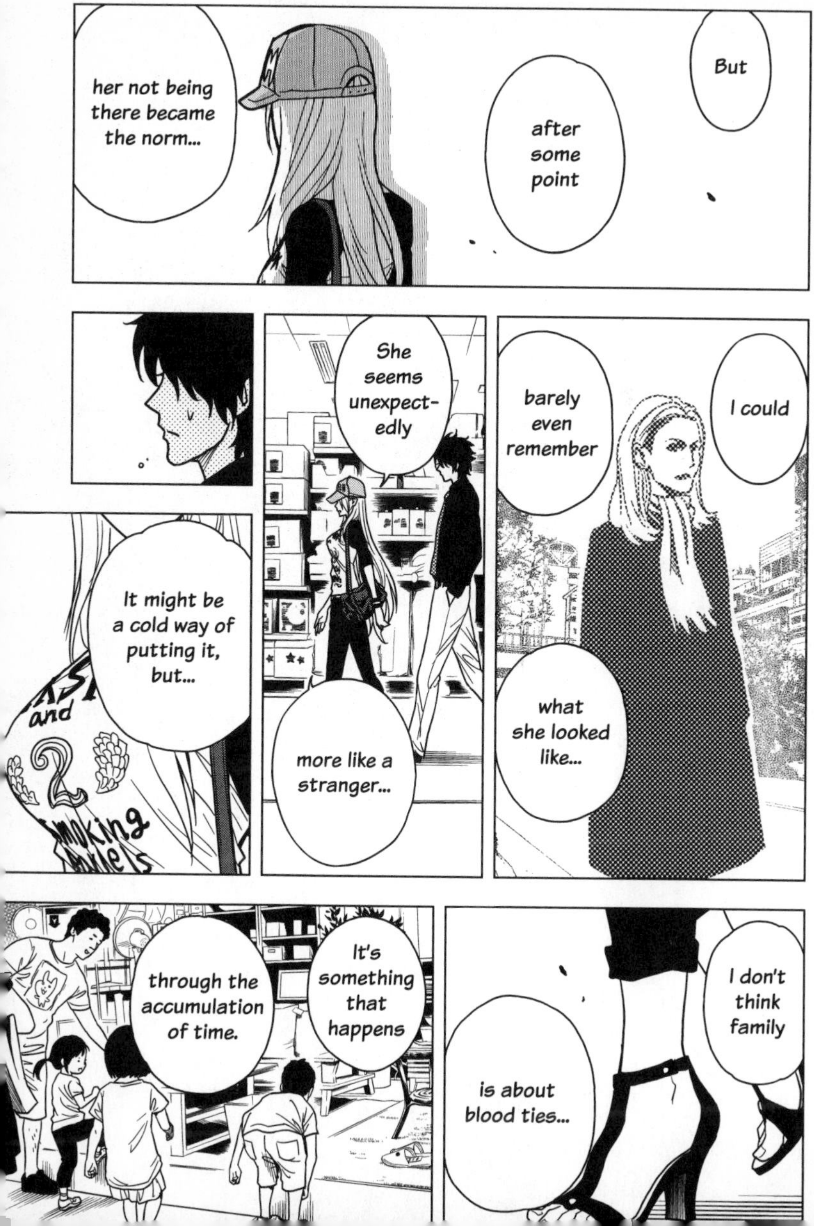

But
after some point
her not being there became the norm...
I could
barely even remember
what she looked like...
She seems unexpect-edly
more like a stranger...
It might be a cold way of putting it, but...
I don't think family
is about blood ties...
It's something that happens
through the accumulation of time.

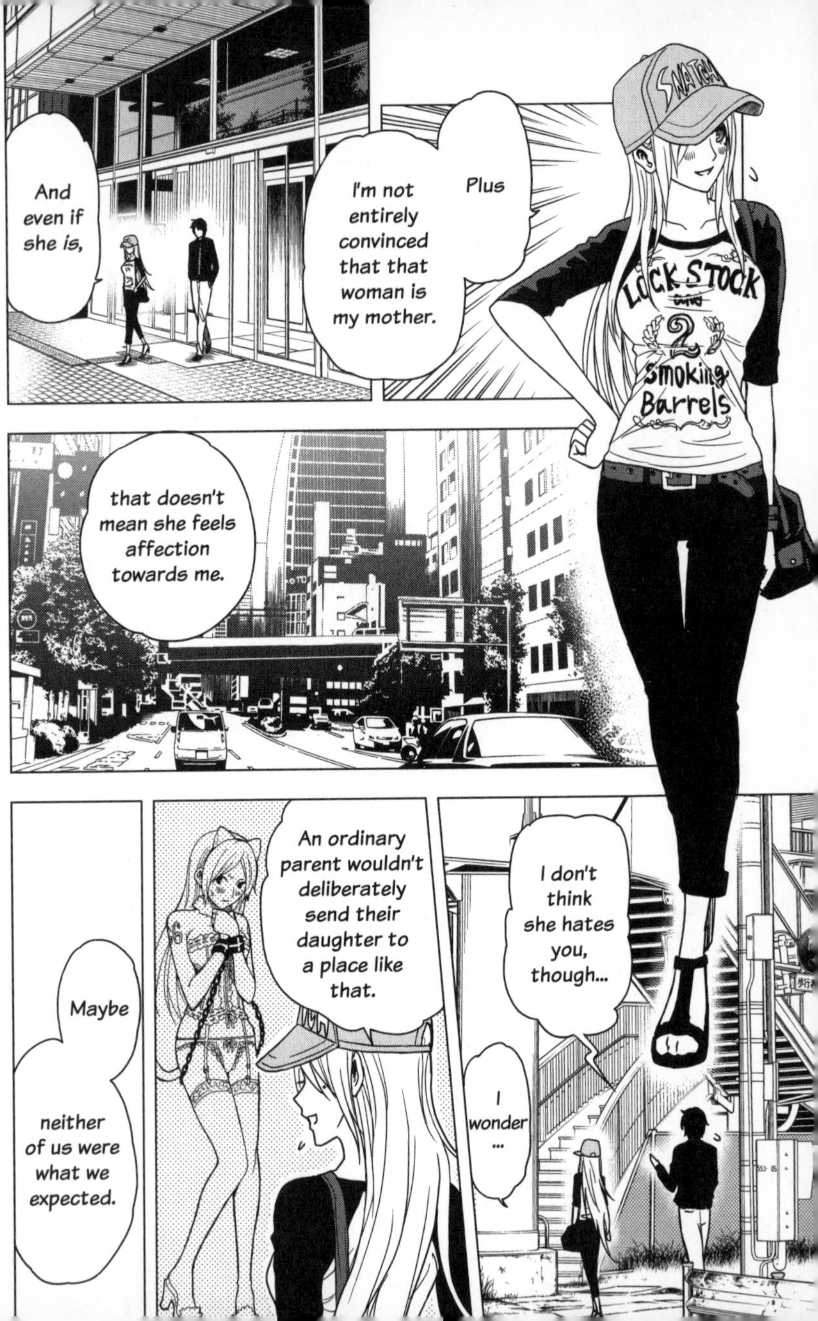
Plus
I'm not entirely convinced that that woman is my mother.
And even if she is,
that doesn't mean she feels affection towards me.
I don't think she hates you, though...
I wonder...
An ordinary parent wouldn't deliberately send their daughter to a place like that.
Maybe
neither of us were what we expected.

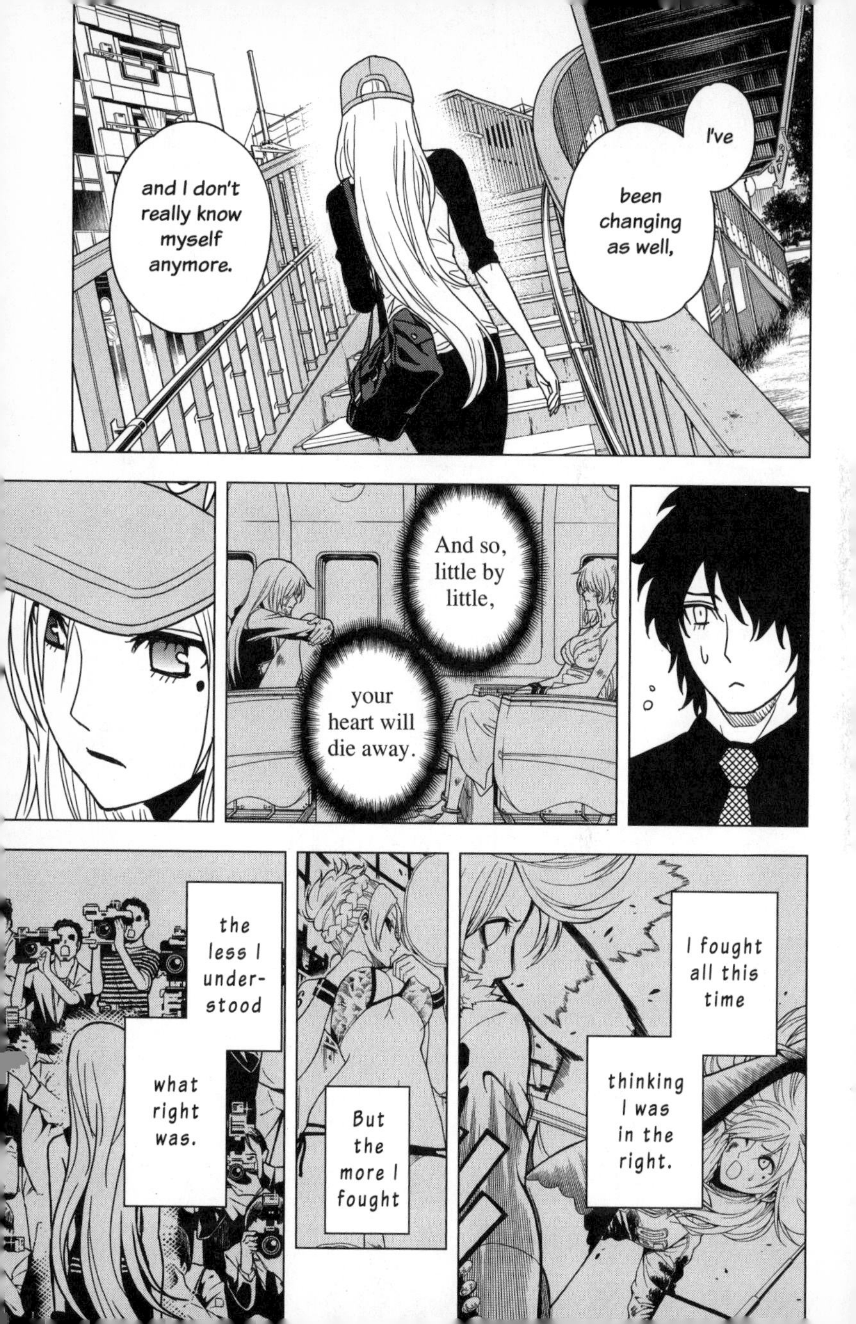
I've been changing as well,
and I don't really know myself anymore.
And so, little by little,
your heart will die away.
I fought all this time
thinking I was in the right.
But the more I fought
the less I under-stood
what right was.

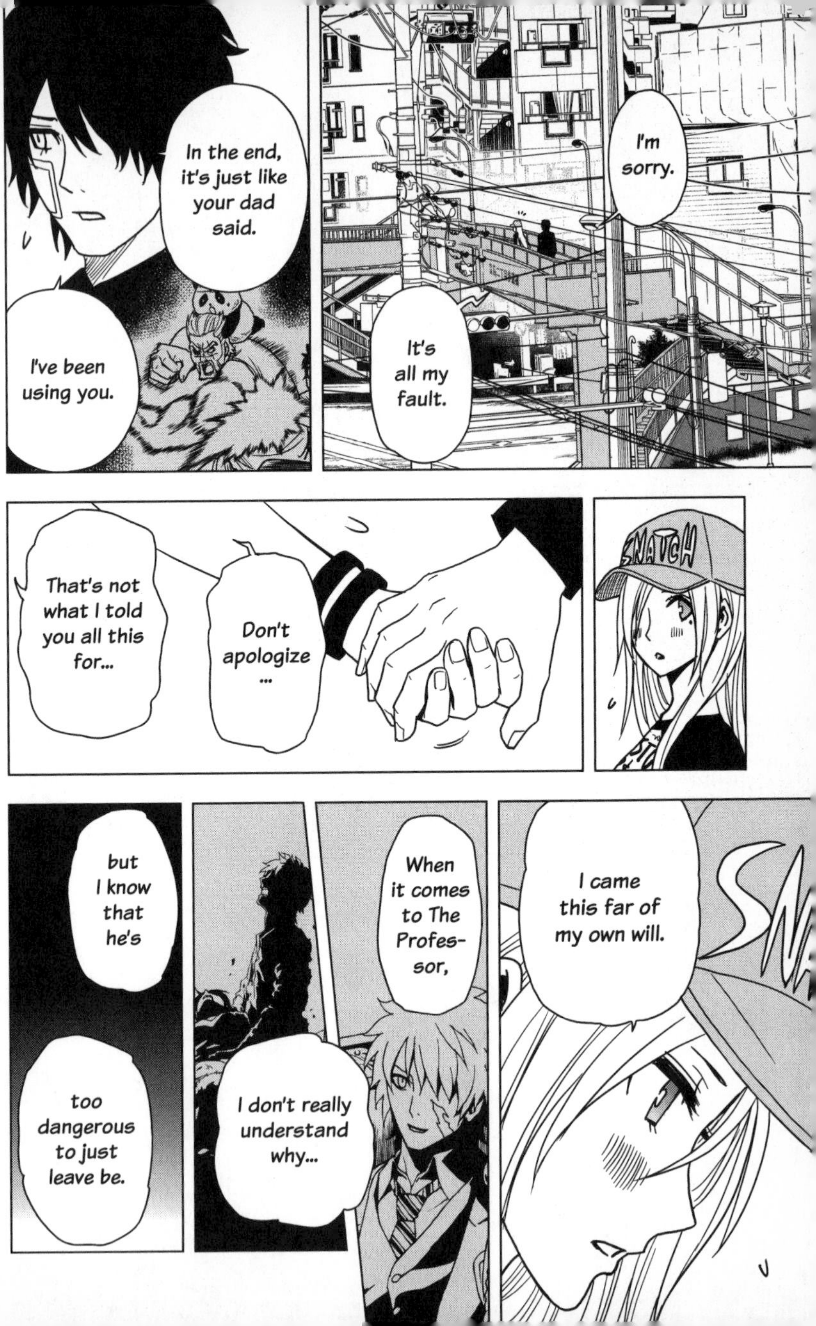
I'm sorry.
It's all my fault.
In the end, it's just like your dad said.
I've been using you.
Don't apologize...
That's not what I told you all this for...
I came this far of my own will.
When it comes to The Profes-sor,
I don't really understand why...
but I know that he's
too dangerous to just leave be.

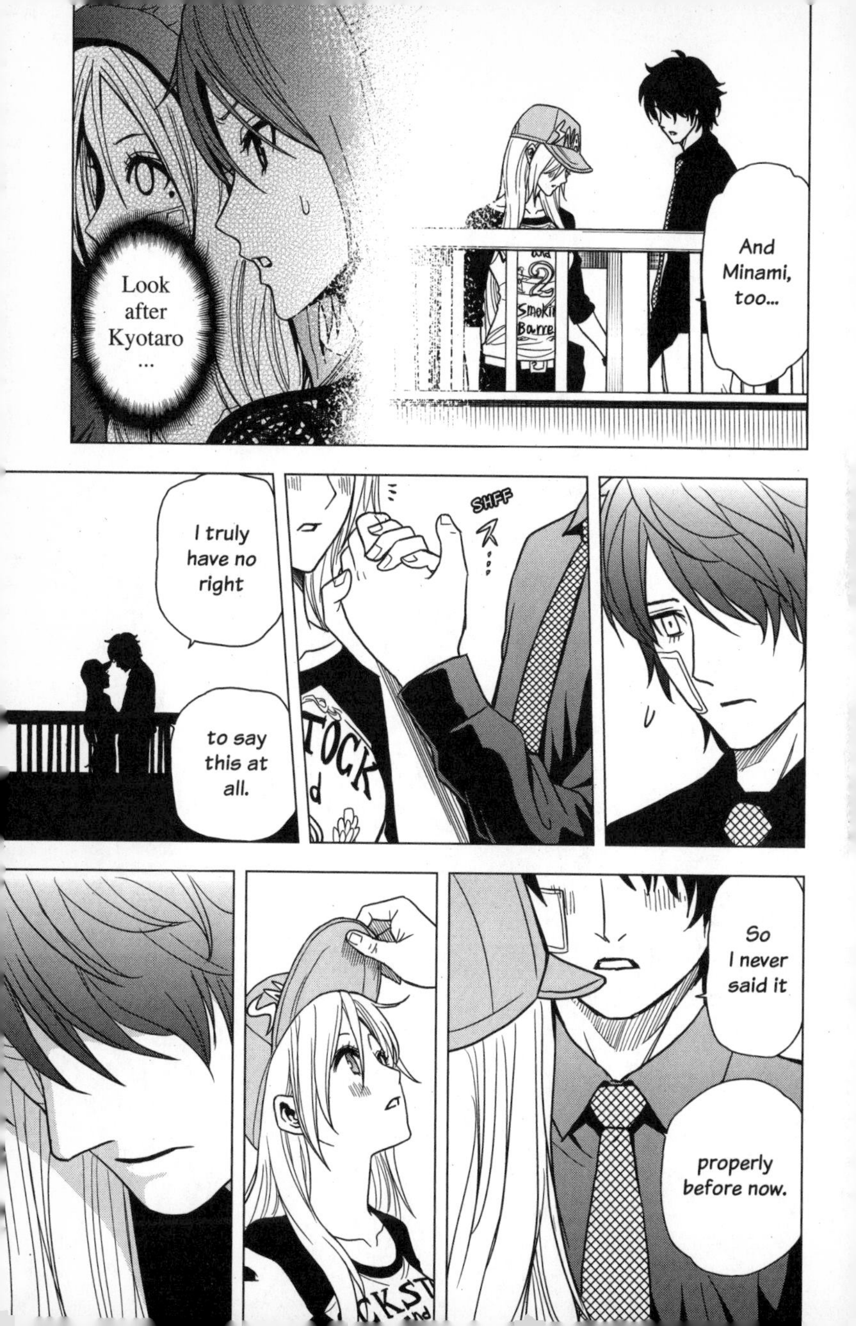
And Minami, too...
Look after Kyotaro ...
SHFF
I truly have no right
to say this at all.
So I never said it
properly before now.

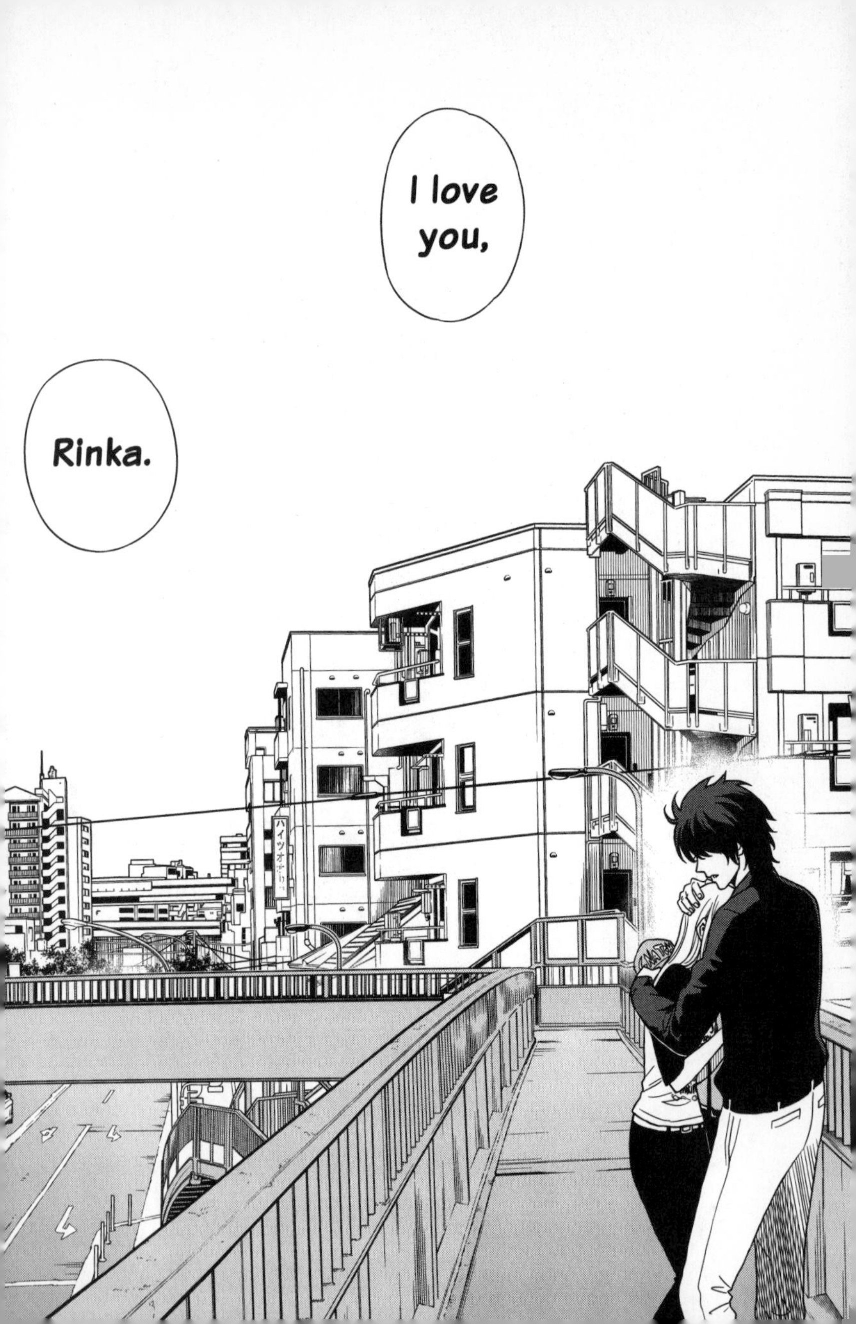
I love you,
Rinka.

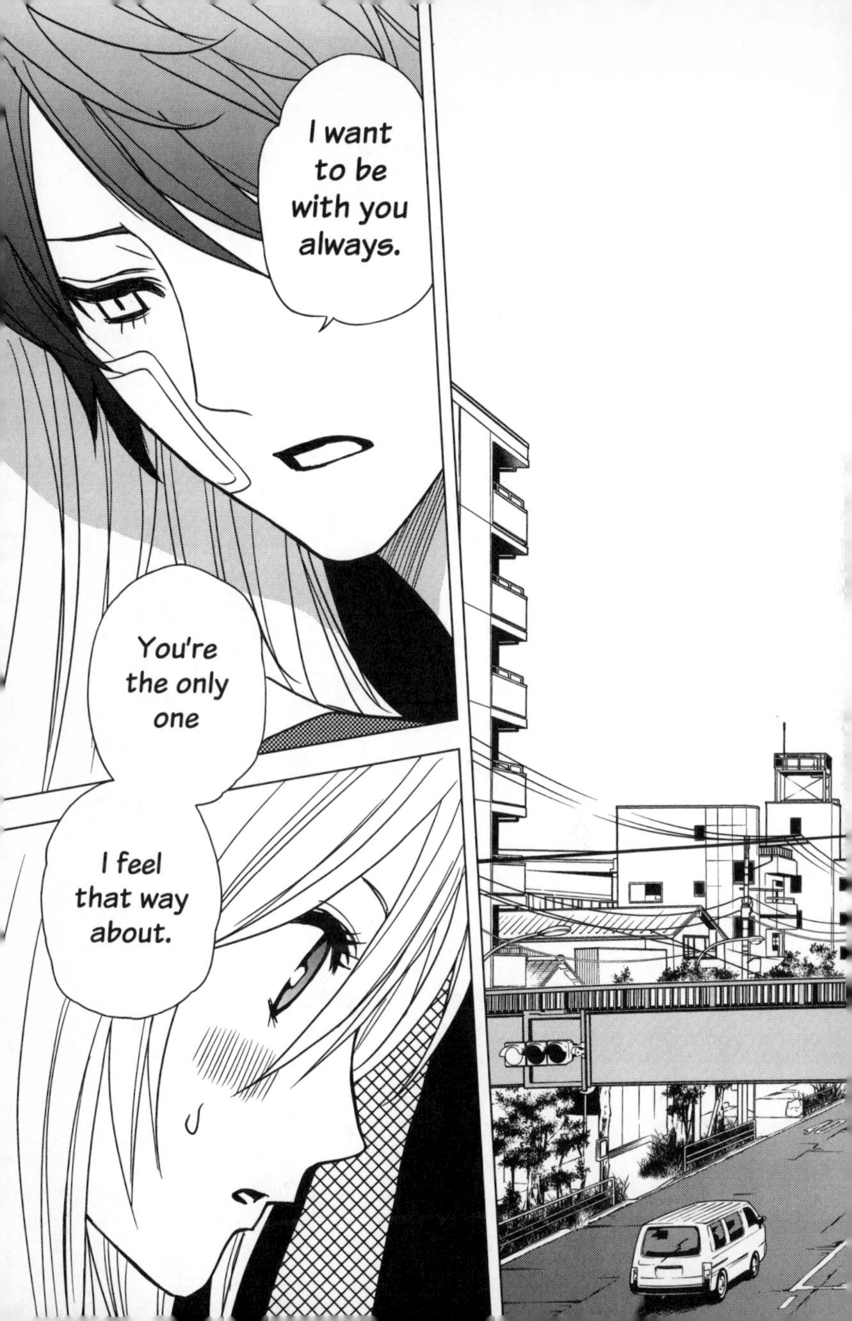
I want to be with you always.
You're the only one
I feel that way about.

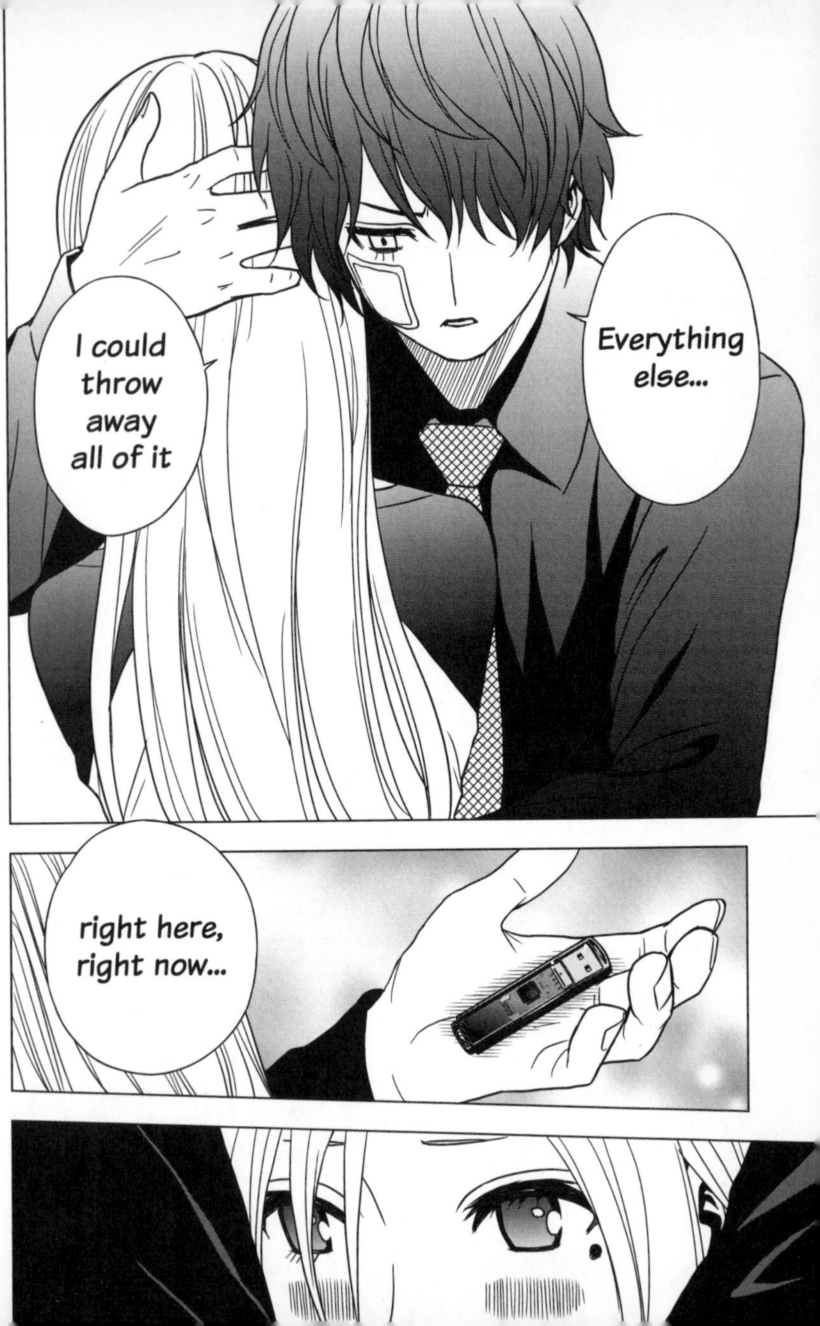
Everything else...
I could throw away all of it
right here, right now...

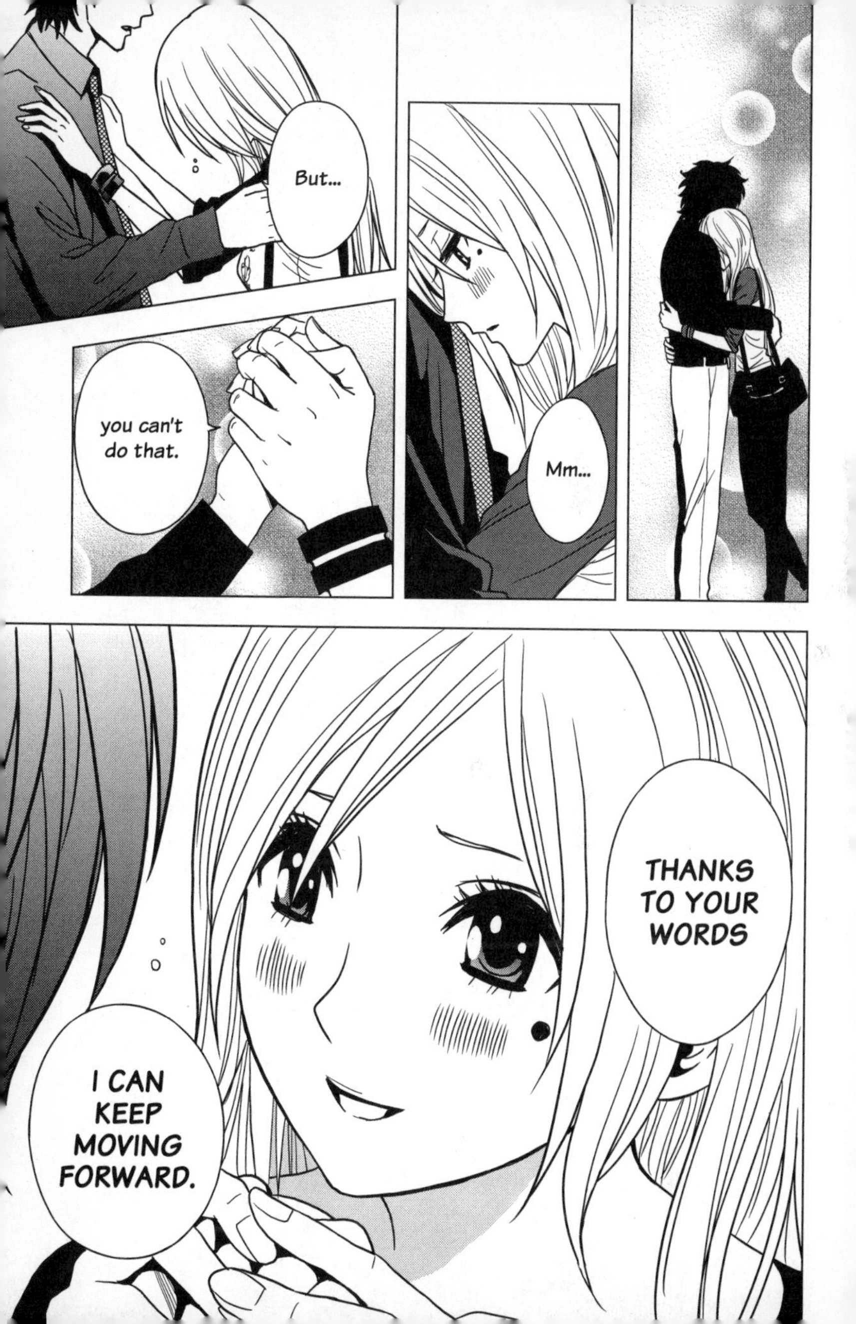

Mm...
But...
you can't do that.
THANKS TO YOUR WORDS
I CAN KEEP MOVING FORWARD.

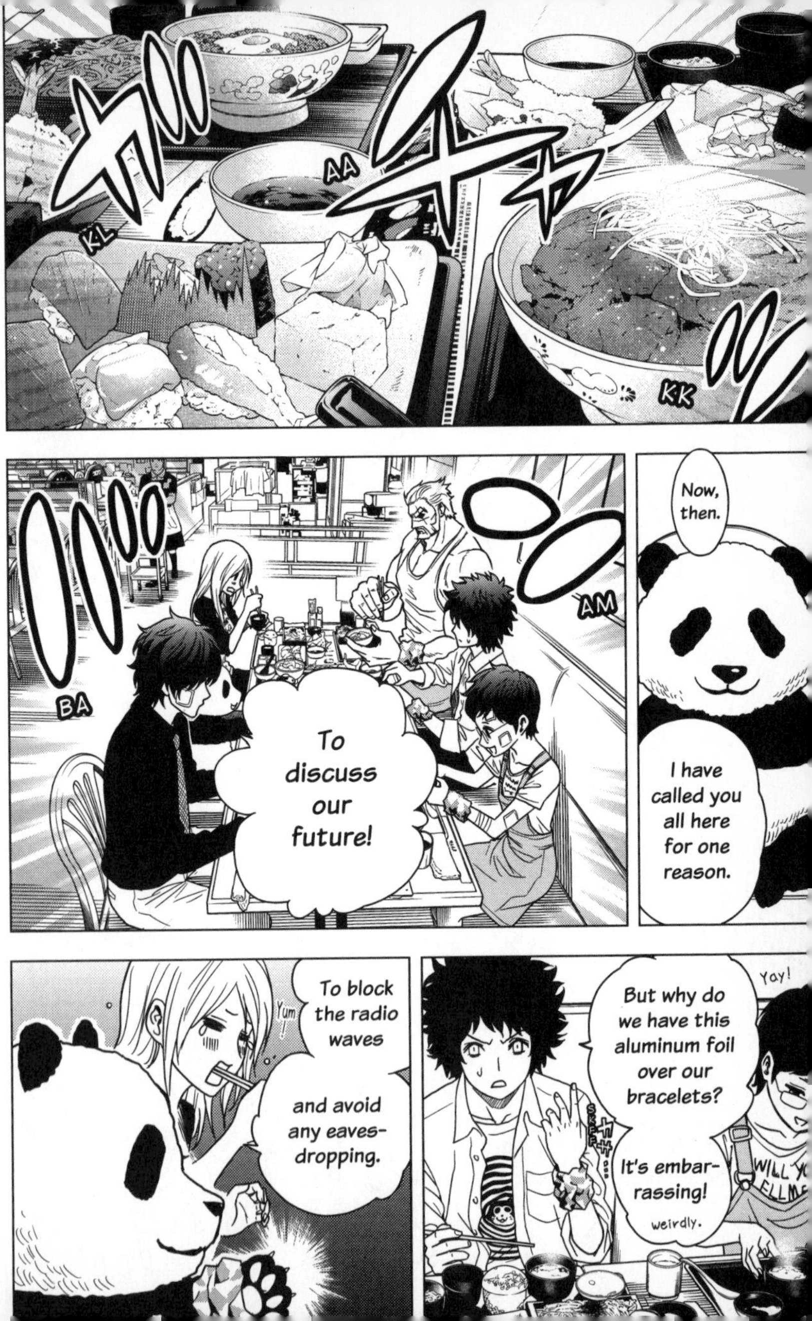
KK
AA
KL
Now, then.
I have called you all here for one reason.
AM
To discuss our future!
BA
Yay!
But why do we have this aluminum foil over our bracelets?
It's embarrassing!
weirdly.
Yum
To block the radio waves
and avoid any eaves-dropping.

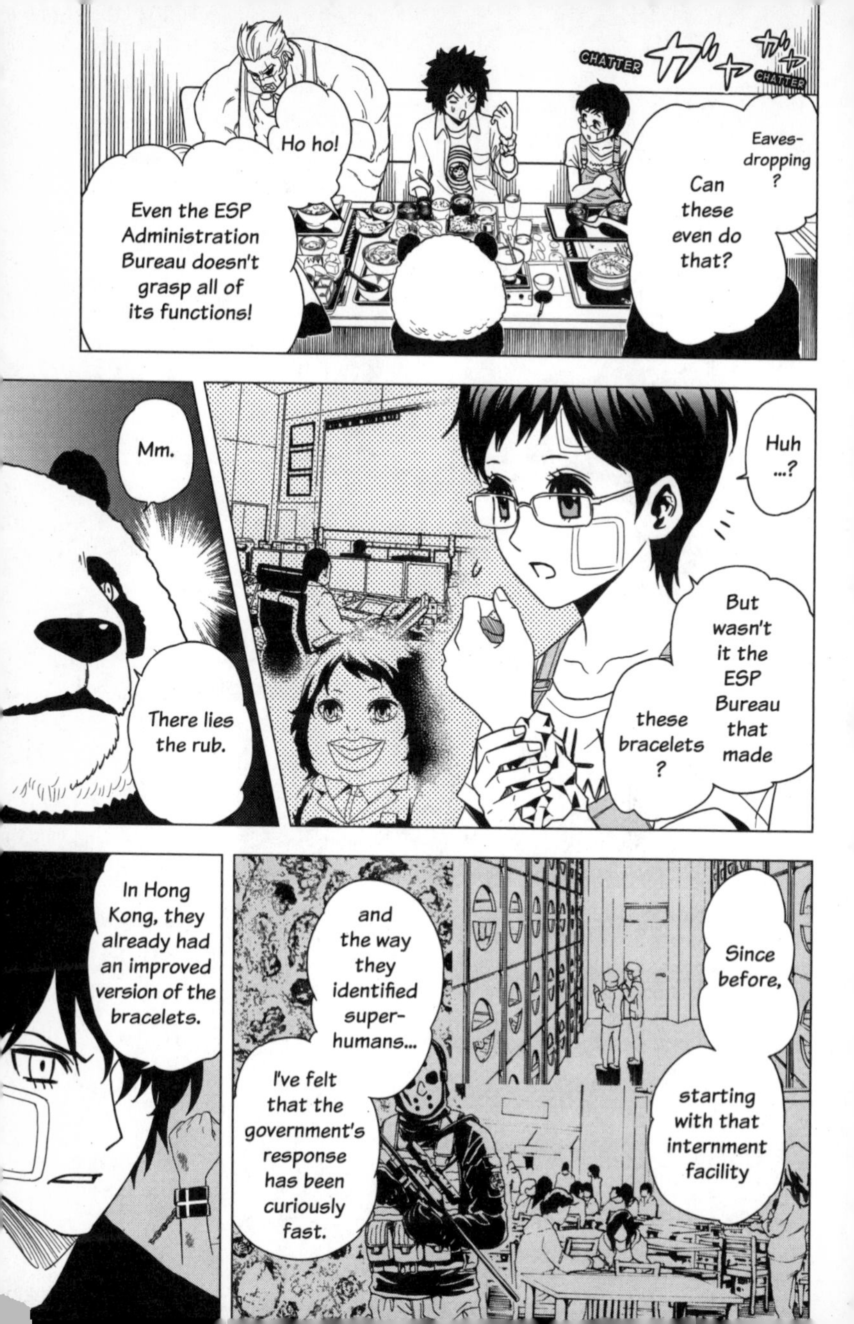
CHATTER
CHATTER
Eaves-dropping?
Can these even do that?
Ho ho!
Even the ESP Administration Bureau doesn't grasp all of its functions!
Huh...?
But wasn't it the ESP Bureau that made these bracelets?
Mm.
There lies the rub.
Since before,
starting with that internment facility
and the way they identified super-humans...
I've felt that the government's response has been curiously fast.
In Hong Kong, they already had an improved version of the bracelets.

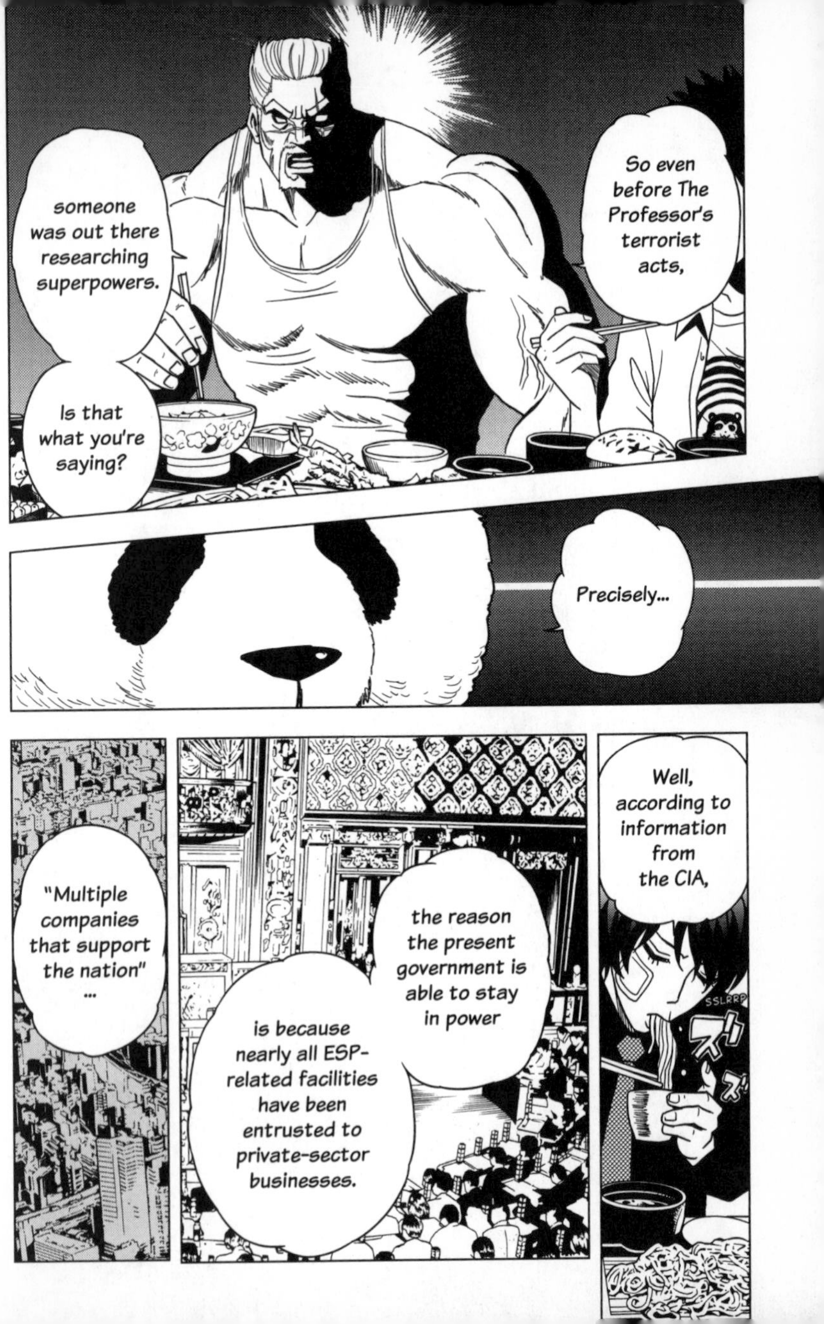
So even before The Professor's terrorist acts,
someone was out there researching superpowers.
Is that what you're saying?
Precisely...
Well, according to information from the CIA,
SSLRRP
the reason the present government is able to stay in power
is because nearly all ESP-related facilities have been entrusted to private-sector businesses.
"Multiple companies that support the nation" ...

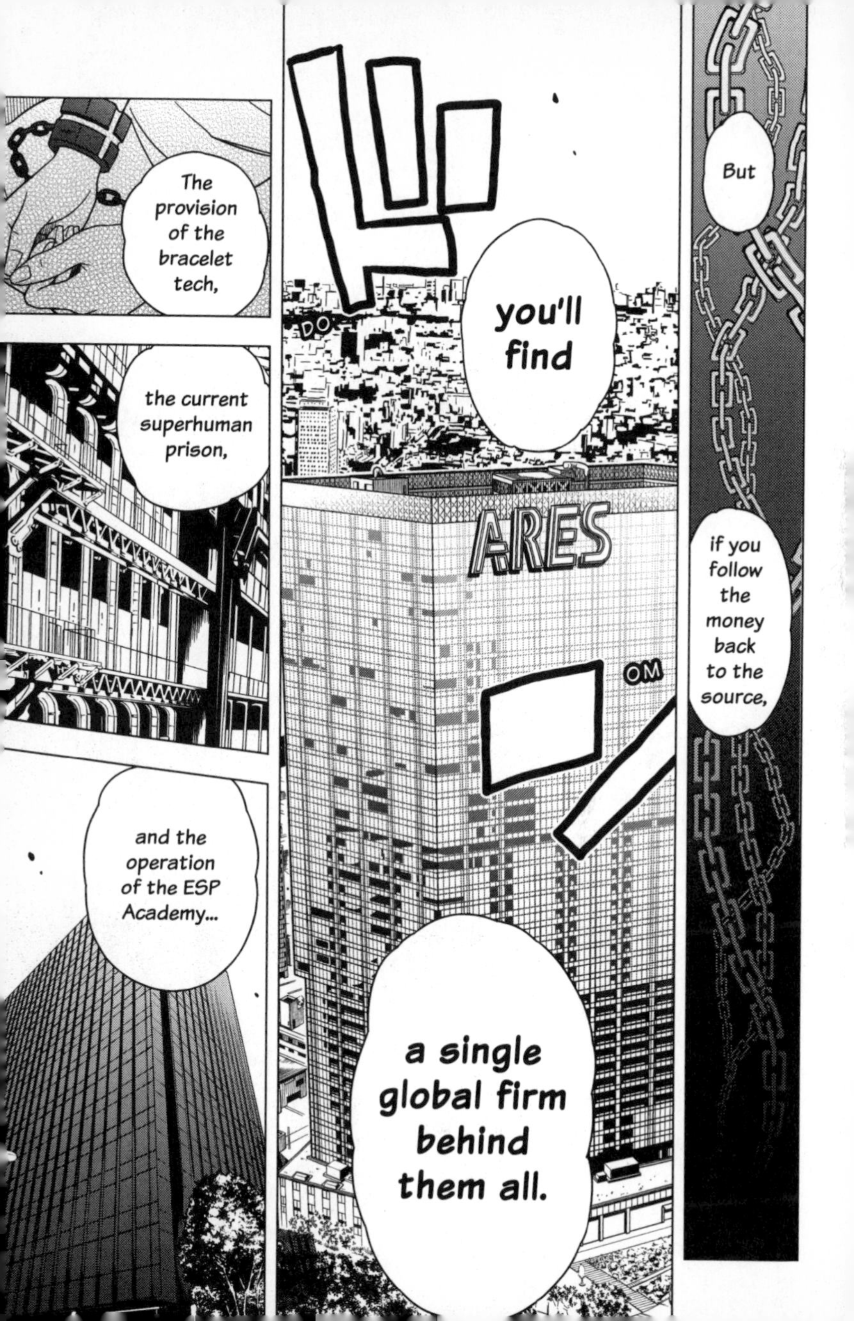

But
if you follow the money back to the source,
DO
you'll find
OM
a single global firm behind them all.
The provision of the bracelet tech,
the current superhuman prison,
and the operation of the ESP Academy...

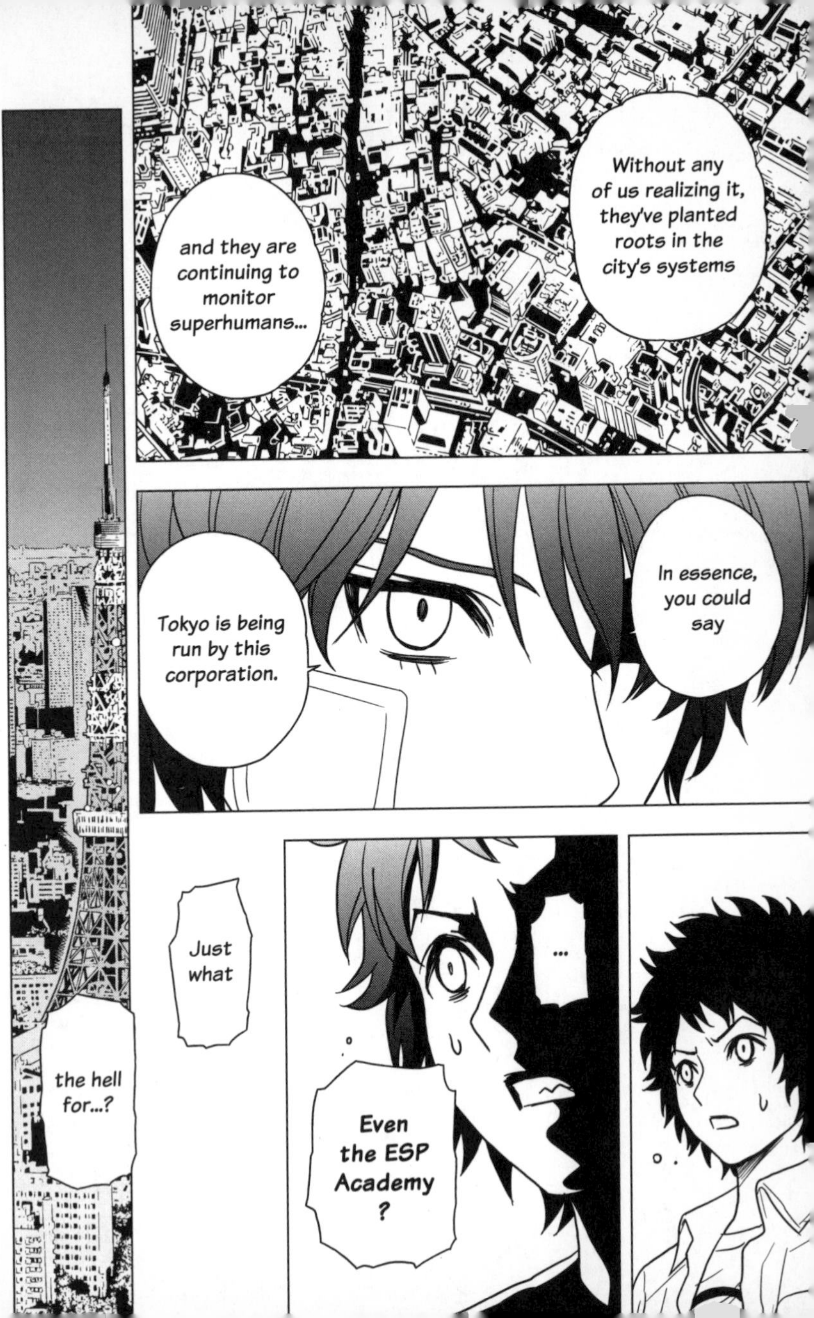

Without any of us realizing it, they've planted roots in the city's systems
and they are continuing to monitor superhumans...
In essence, you could say
Tokyo is being run by this corporation.
...
Even the ESP Academy ?
Just what
the hell for...?

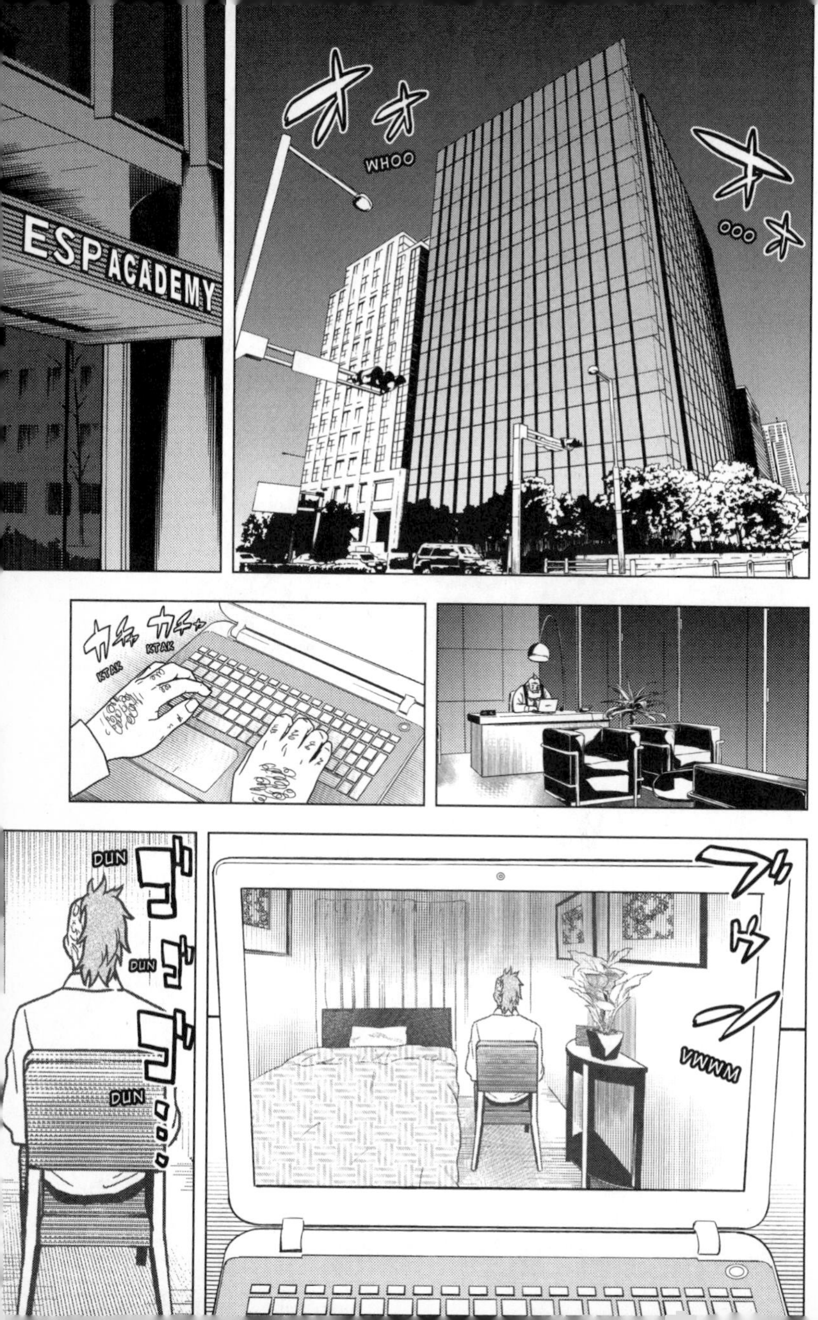

WHOO
OOO
ESP ACADEMY
KTAK
KTAK
VWWM
DUN
DUN
DUN

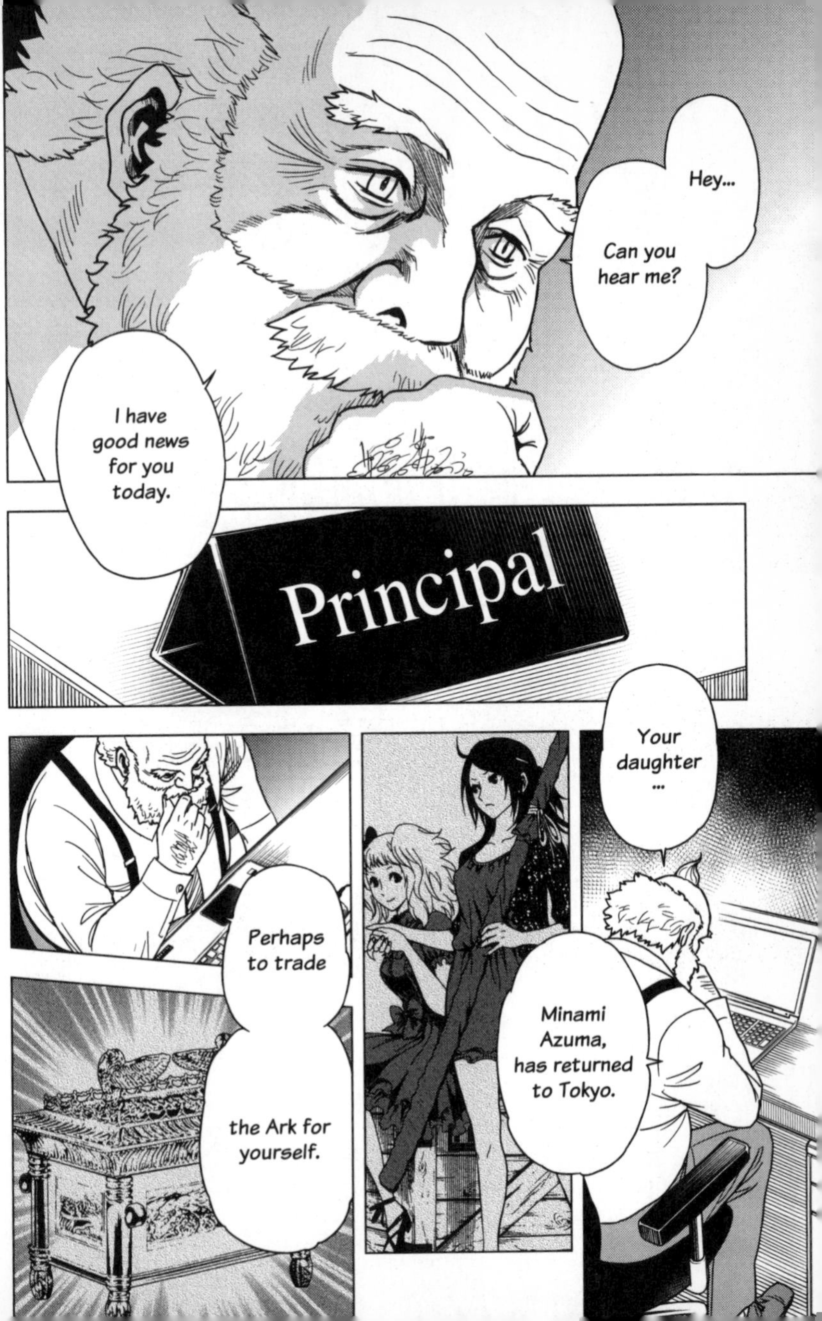
Hey...
Can you hear me?
I have good news for you today.
Principal
Your daughter ...
Minami Azuma, has returned to Tokyo.
Perhaps to trade
the Ark for yourself.

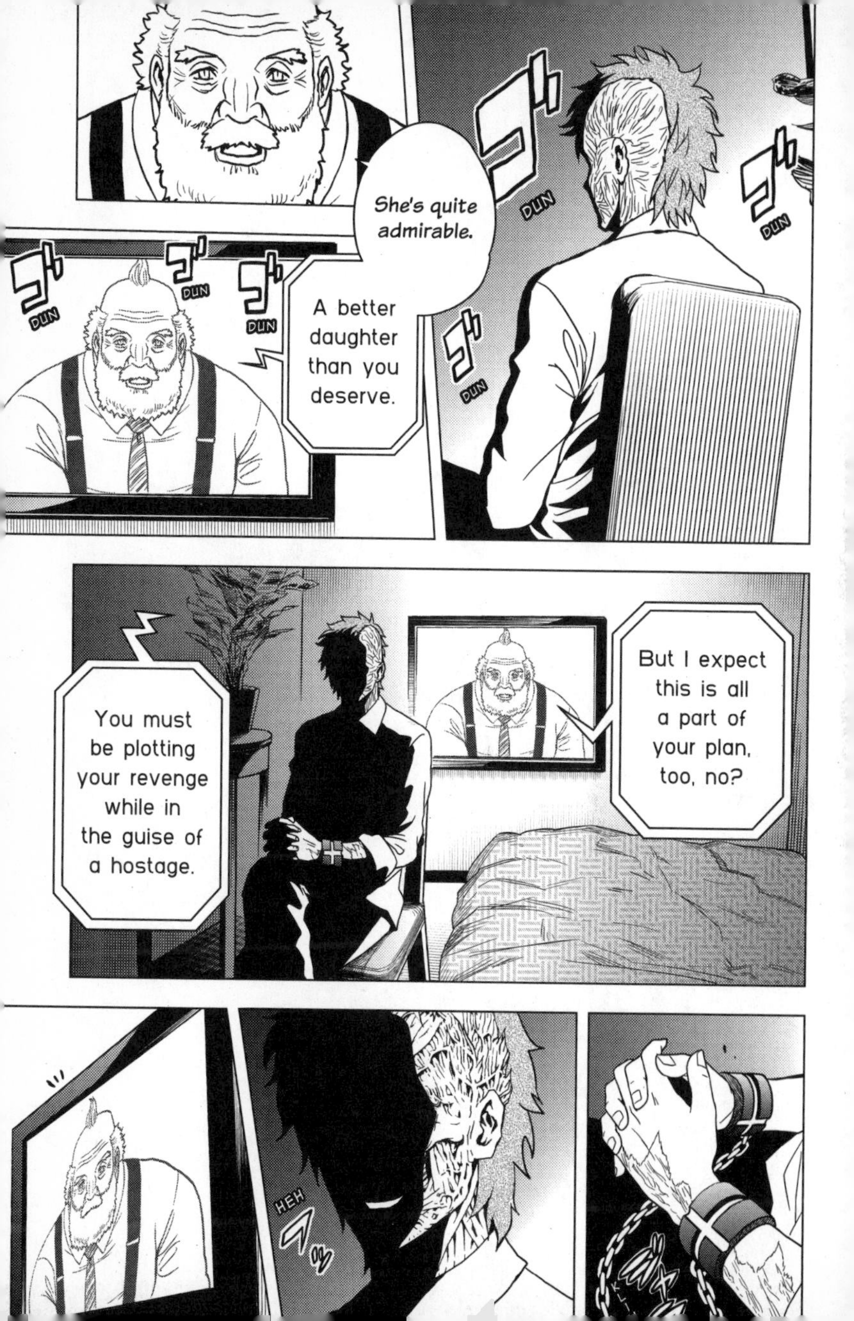
DUN
DUN
DUN
She's quite admirable.
DUN
DUN
DUN
A better daughter than you deserve.
But I expect this is all a part of your plan, too, no?
You must be plotting your revenge while in the guise of a hostage.
HEH

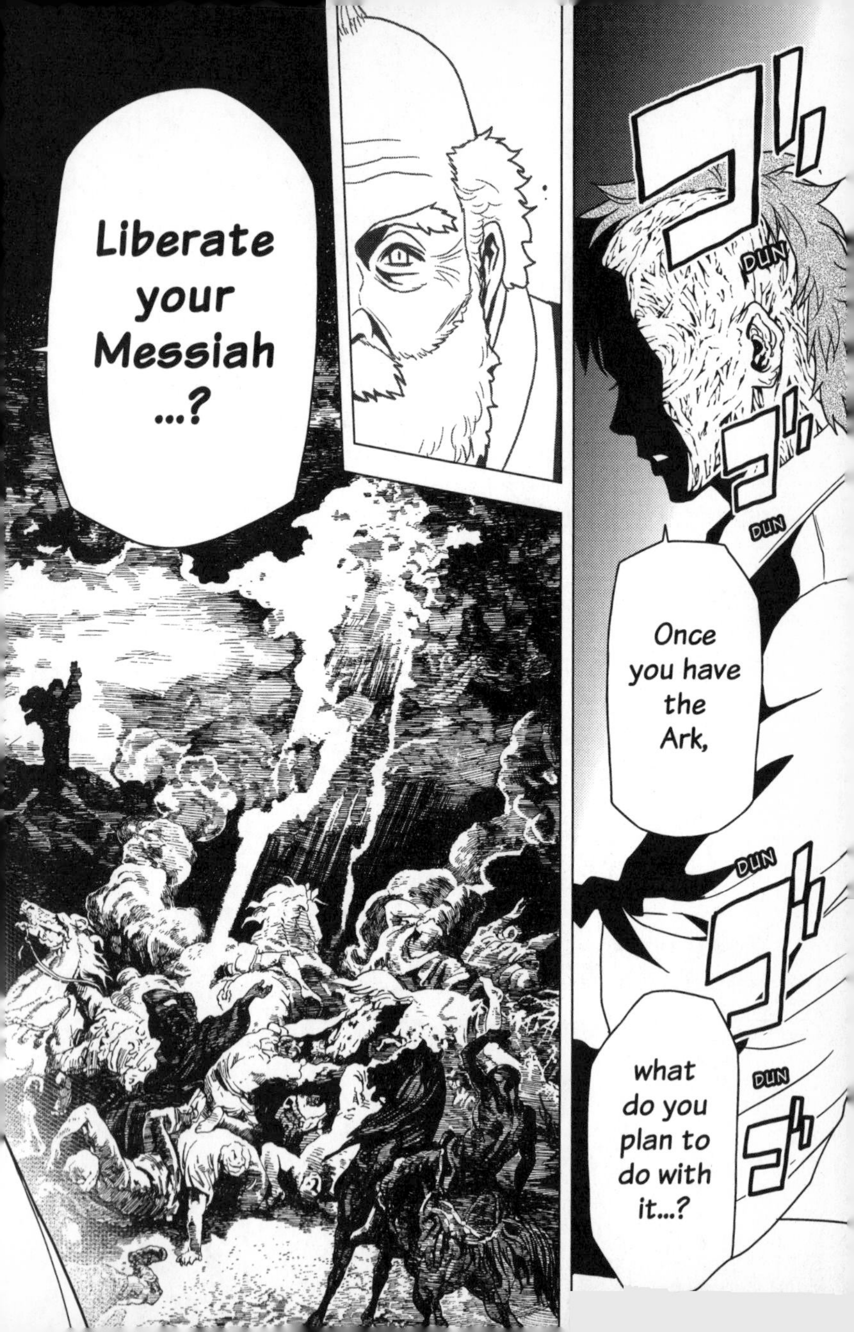
DUN
DUN
Once you have the Ark,
DUN
what do you plan to do with it...?
DUN
Liberate your Messiah ...?

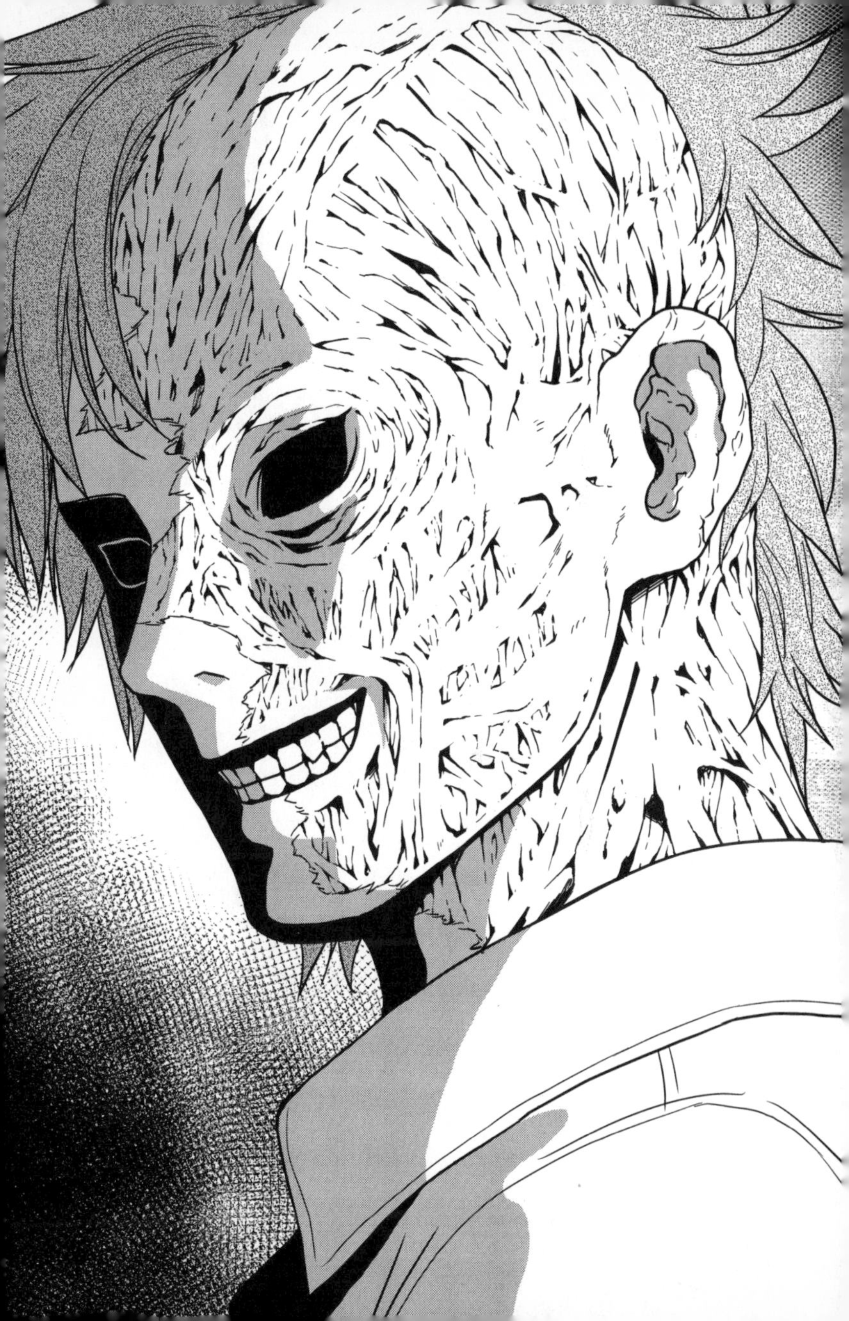

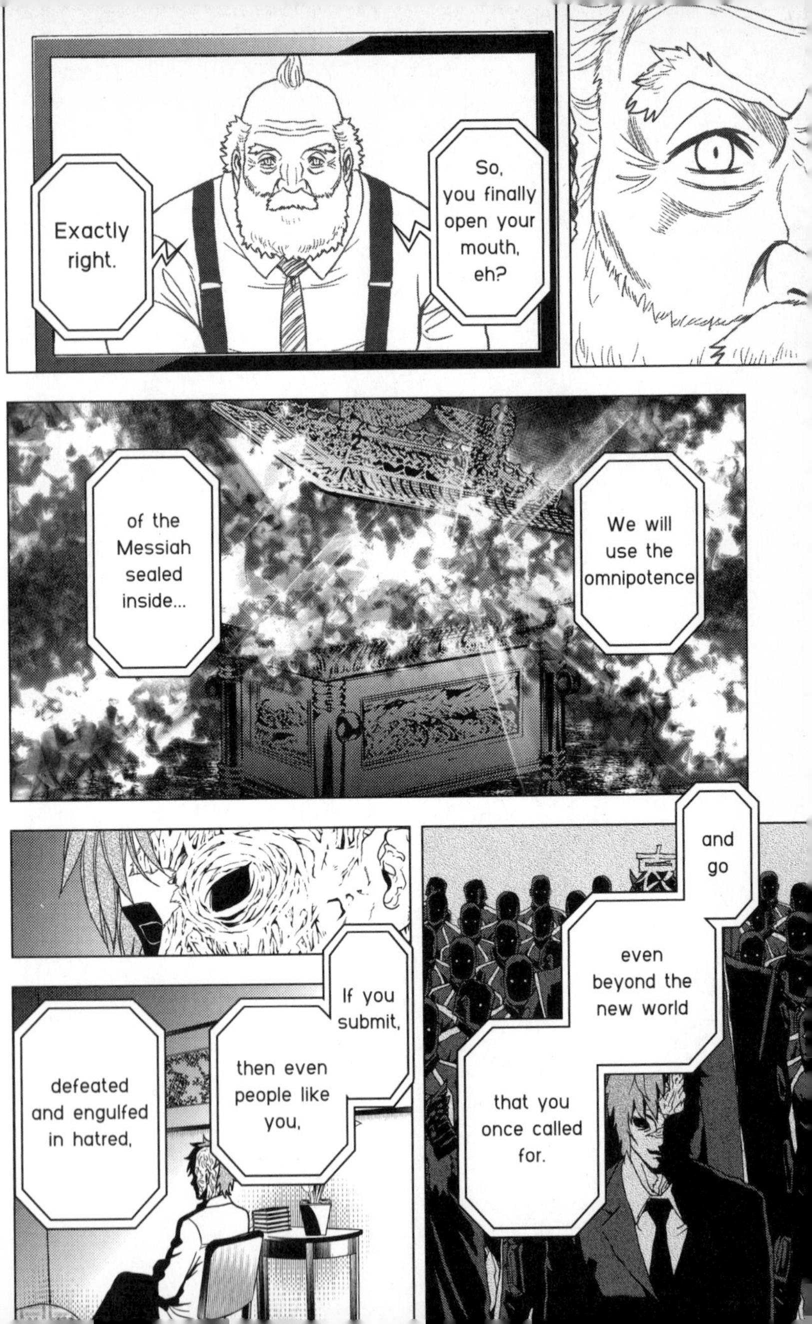
So, you finally open your mouth, eh?
Exactly right.
We will use the omnipotence
of the Messiah sealed inside...
If you submit,
then even people like you,
defeated and engulfed in hatred,
and go
even beyond the new world
that you once called for.

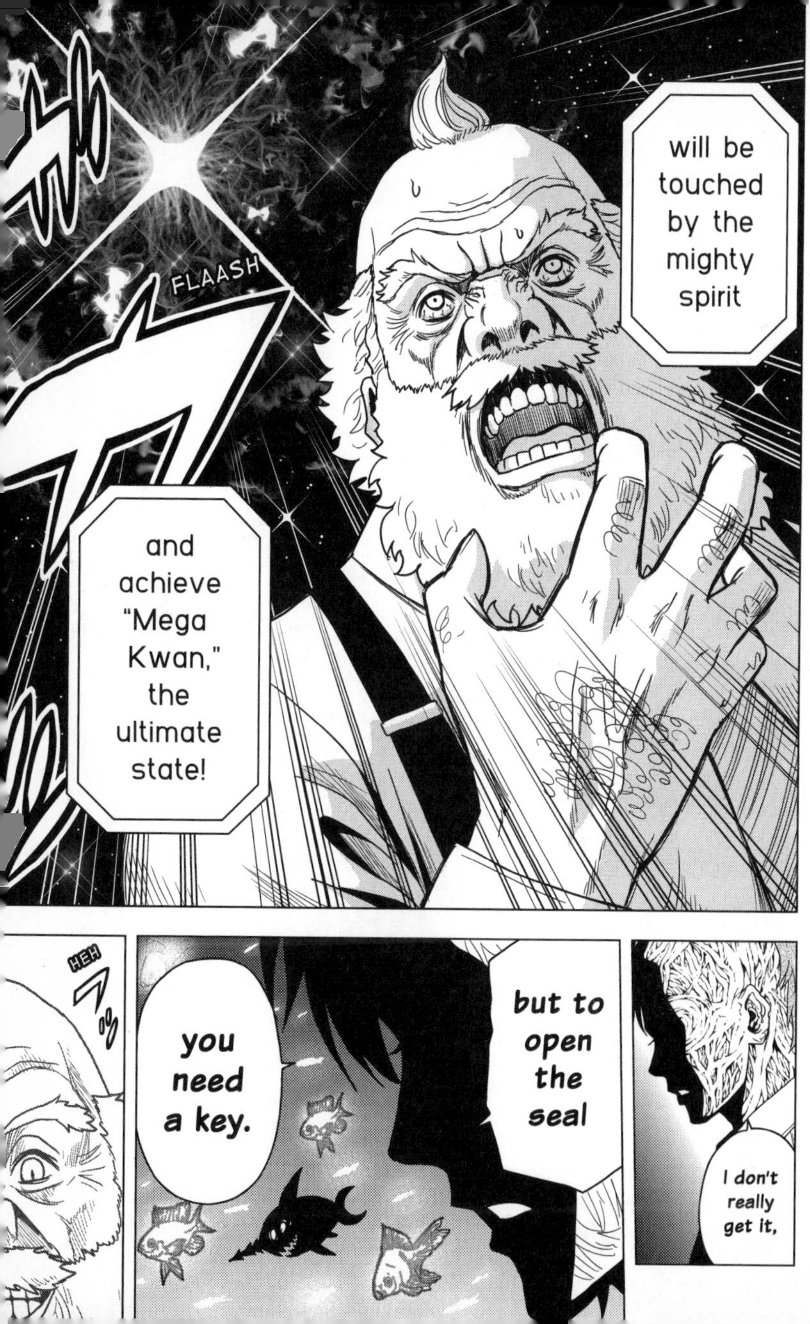
will be touched by the mighty spirit
FLAASH
and achieve "Mega Kwan," the ultimate state!
I don't really get it,
but to open the seal
you need a key.
HEH

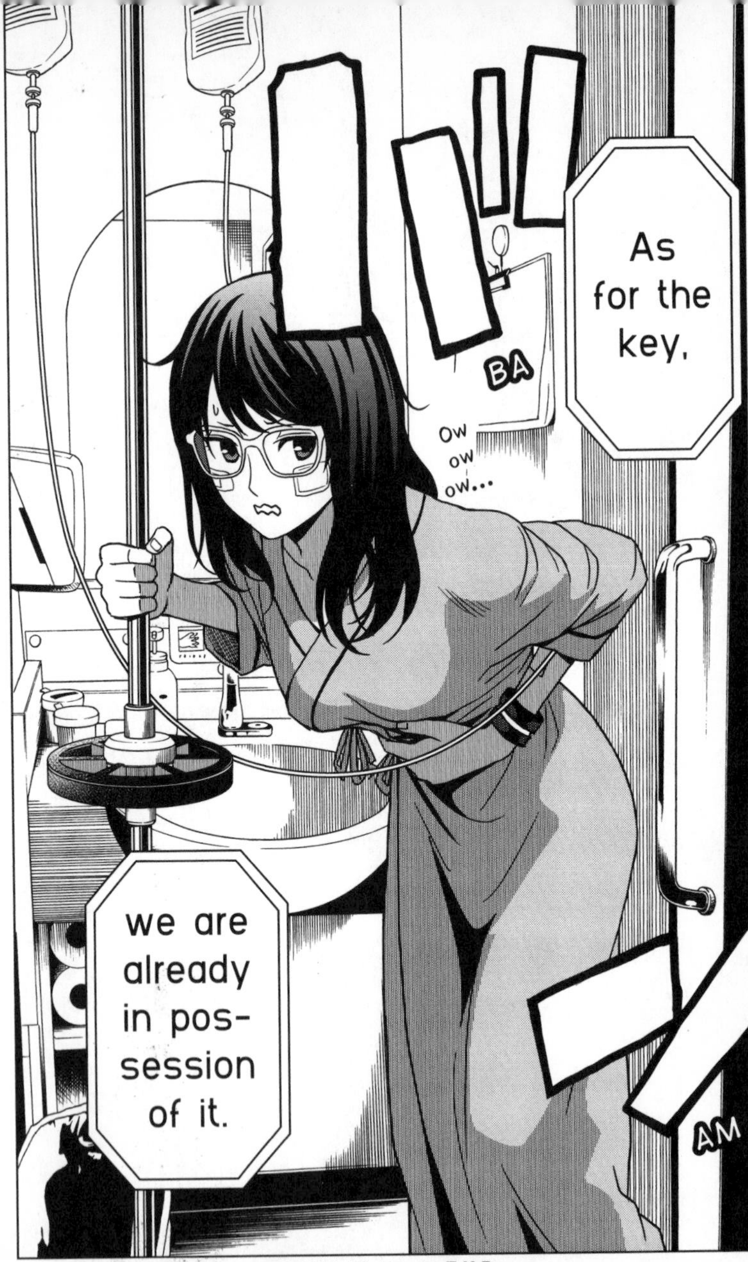
As for the key,
BA
Ow ow ow...
we are already in possession of it.
AM

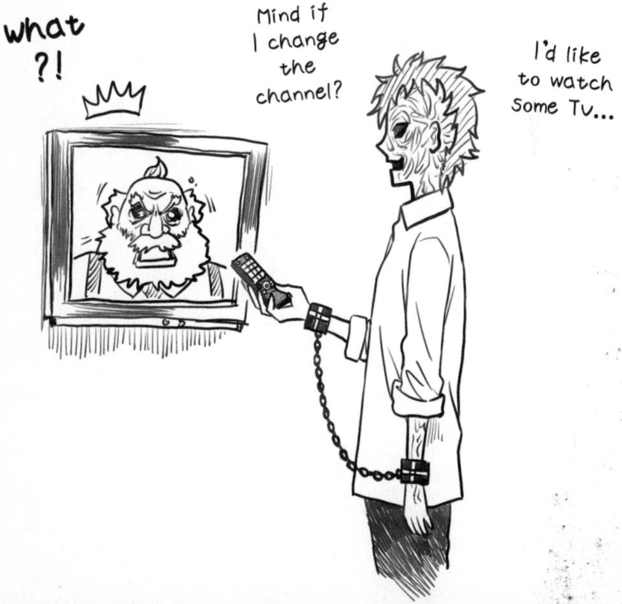
I'd like to watch Some Tv...
Mind if I change the channel?
what ?!

TOKYO ESP

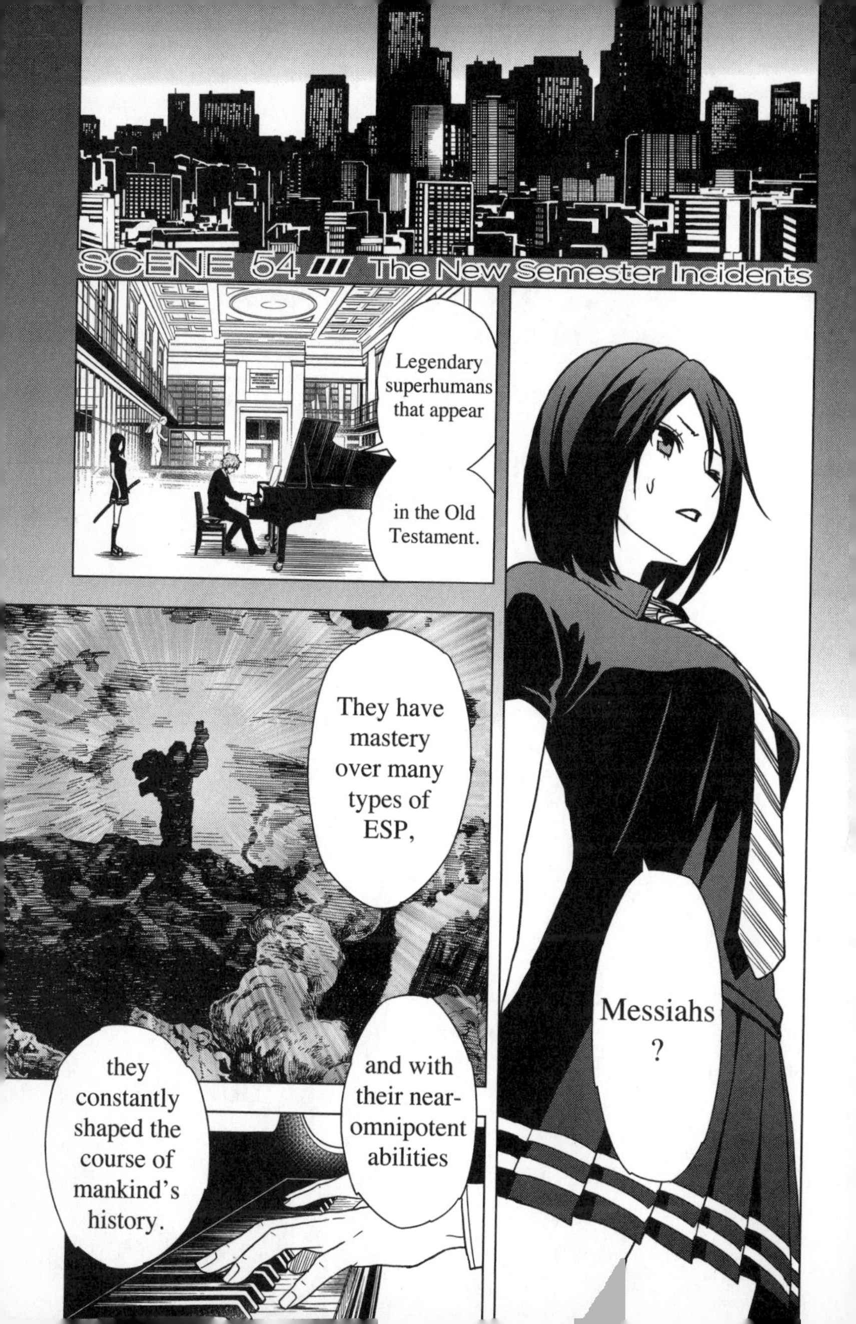
SCENE 54 /// The New Semester Incidents
Messiahs?
Legendary superhumans that appear in the Old Testament.
They have mastery over many types of ESP,
and with their near-omnipotent abilities
they constantly shaped the course of mankind's history.

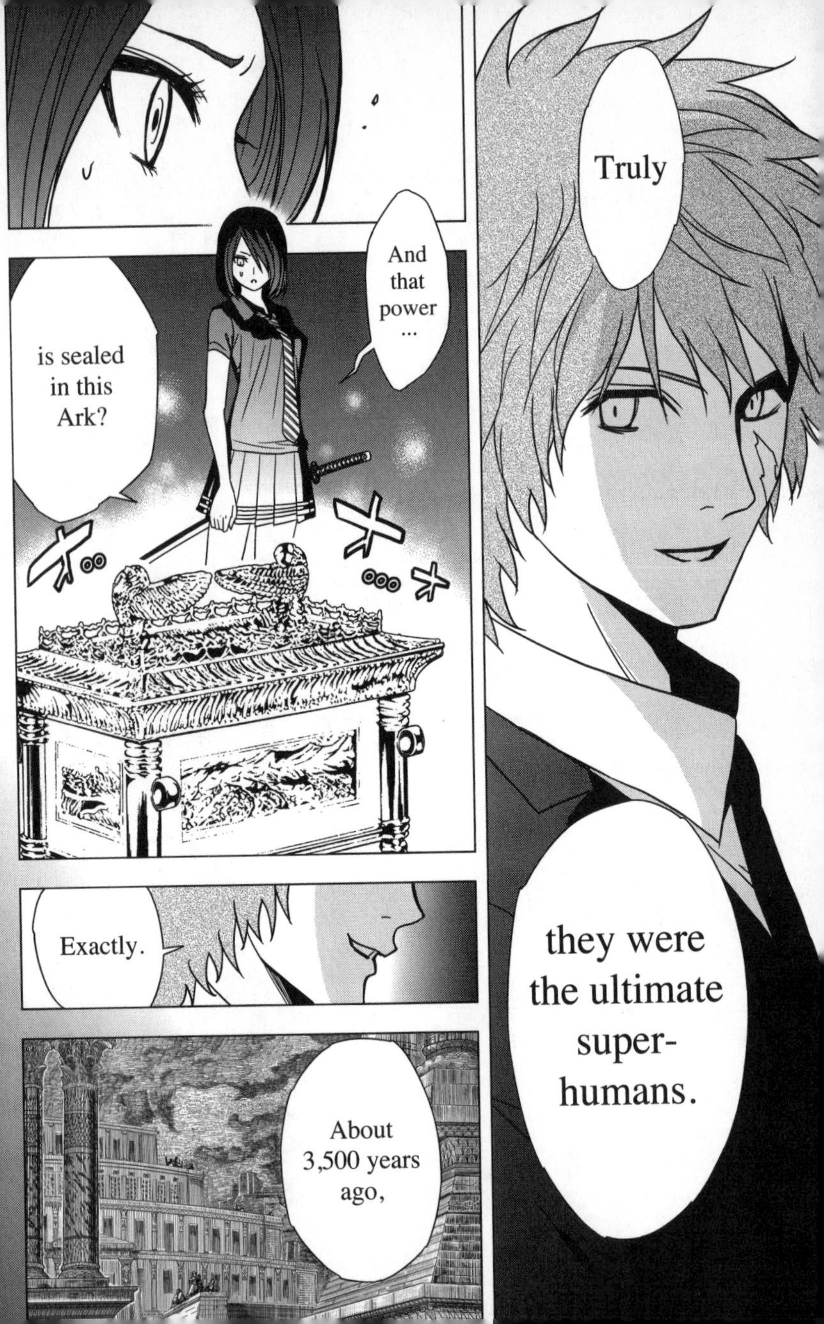
Truly
they were the ultimate super-humans.
And that power ...
is sealed in this Ark?
Exactly.
About 3,500 years ago,

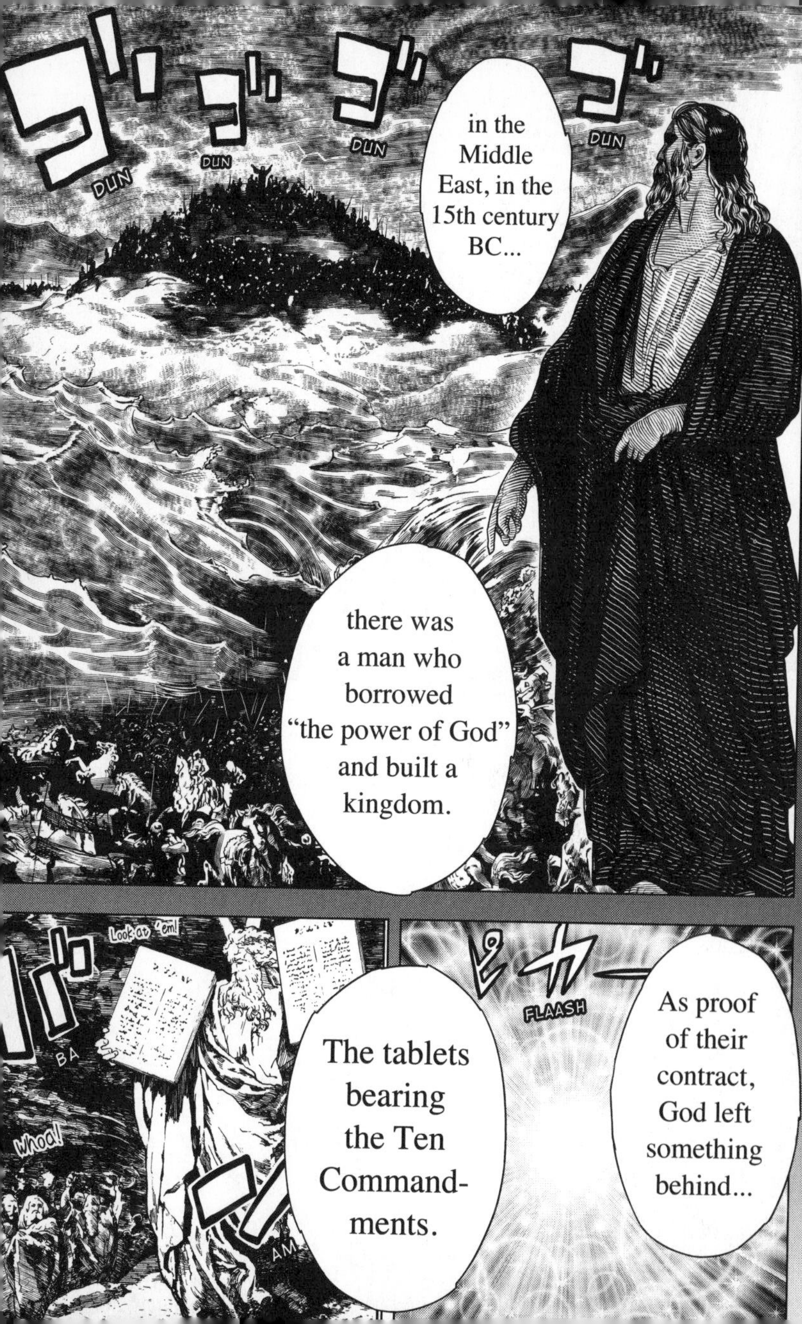
DUN
DUN
DUN
DUN
in the Middle East, in the 15th century BC...
there was a man who borrowed "the power of God" and built a kingdom.
FLAASH
As proof of their contract, God left something behind...
Look at 'em!
BA
The tablets bearing the Ten Command-ments.
whoa!
AM

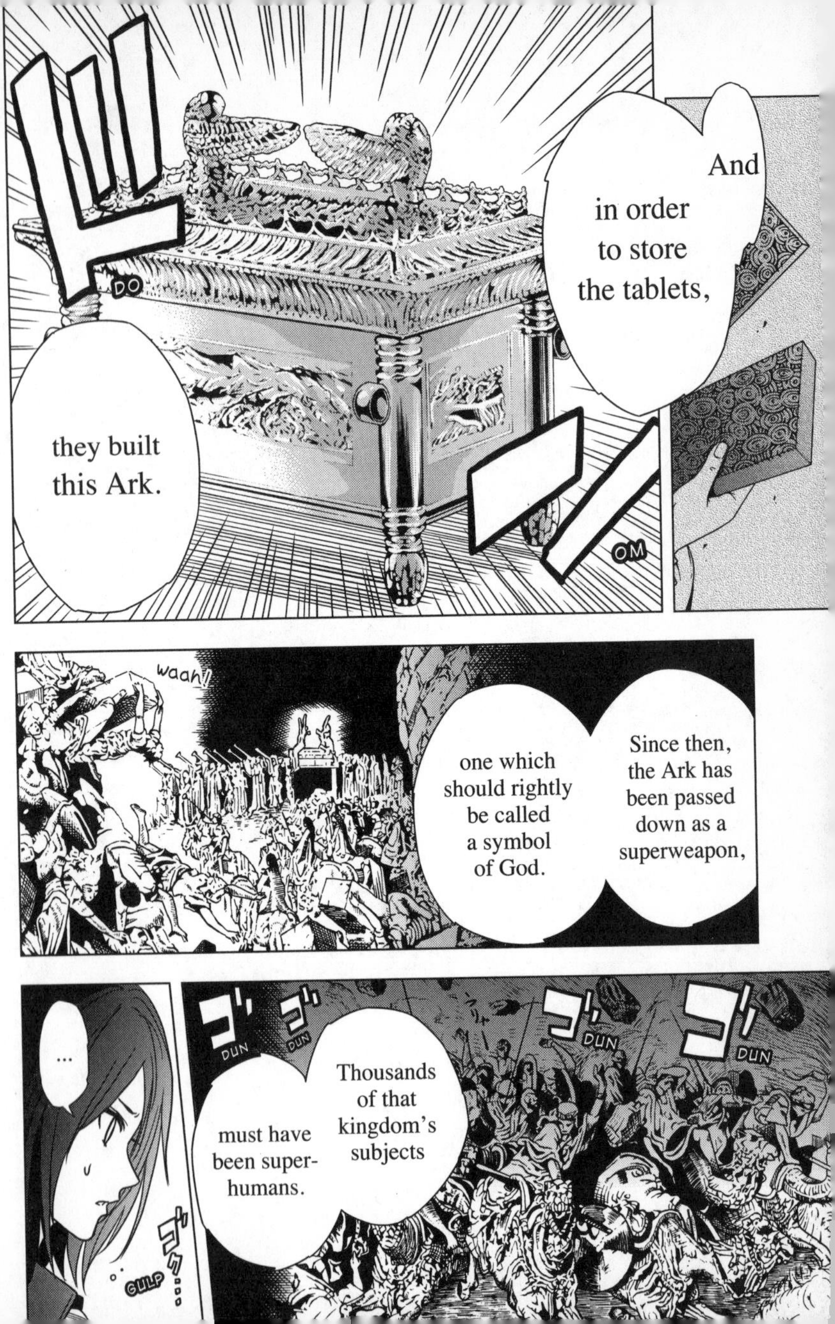
And in order to store the tablets,
DO
OM
they built this Ark.
waah!
Since then, the Ark has been passed down as a superweapon,
one which should rightly be called a symbol of God.
DUN
DUN
DUN
DUN
Thousands of that kingdom's subjects
must have been super-humans.
...
GULP

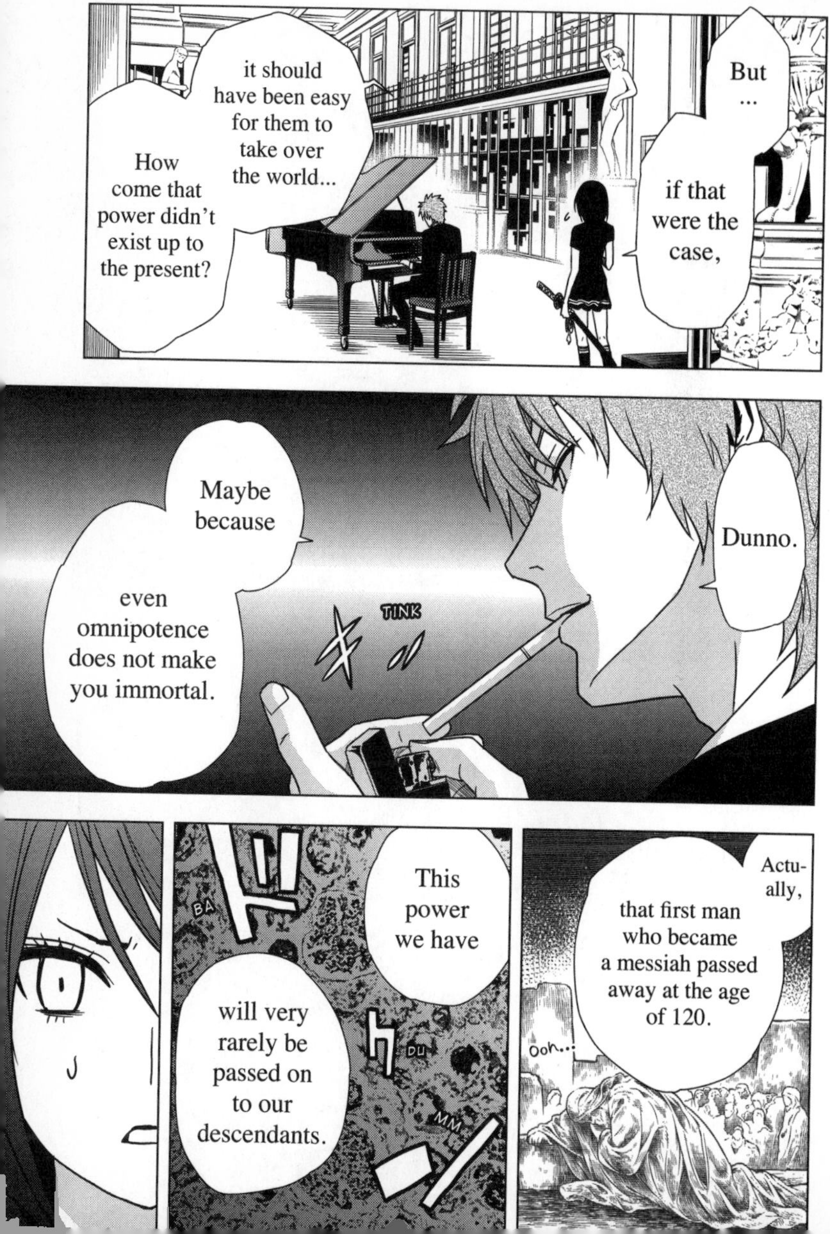
But ...
if that were the case,
it should have been easy for them to take over the world...
How come that power didn't exist up to the present?
Dunno.
TINK
Maybe because
even omnipotence does not make you immortal.
Actu-ally,
that first man who became a messiah passed away at the age of 120.
Ooh...
This power we have
will very rarely be passed on to our descendants.
BA
DU
MM

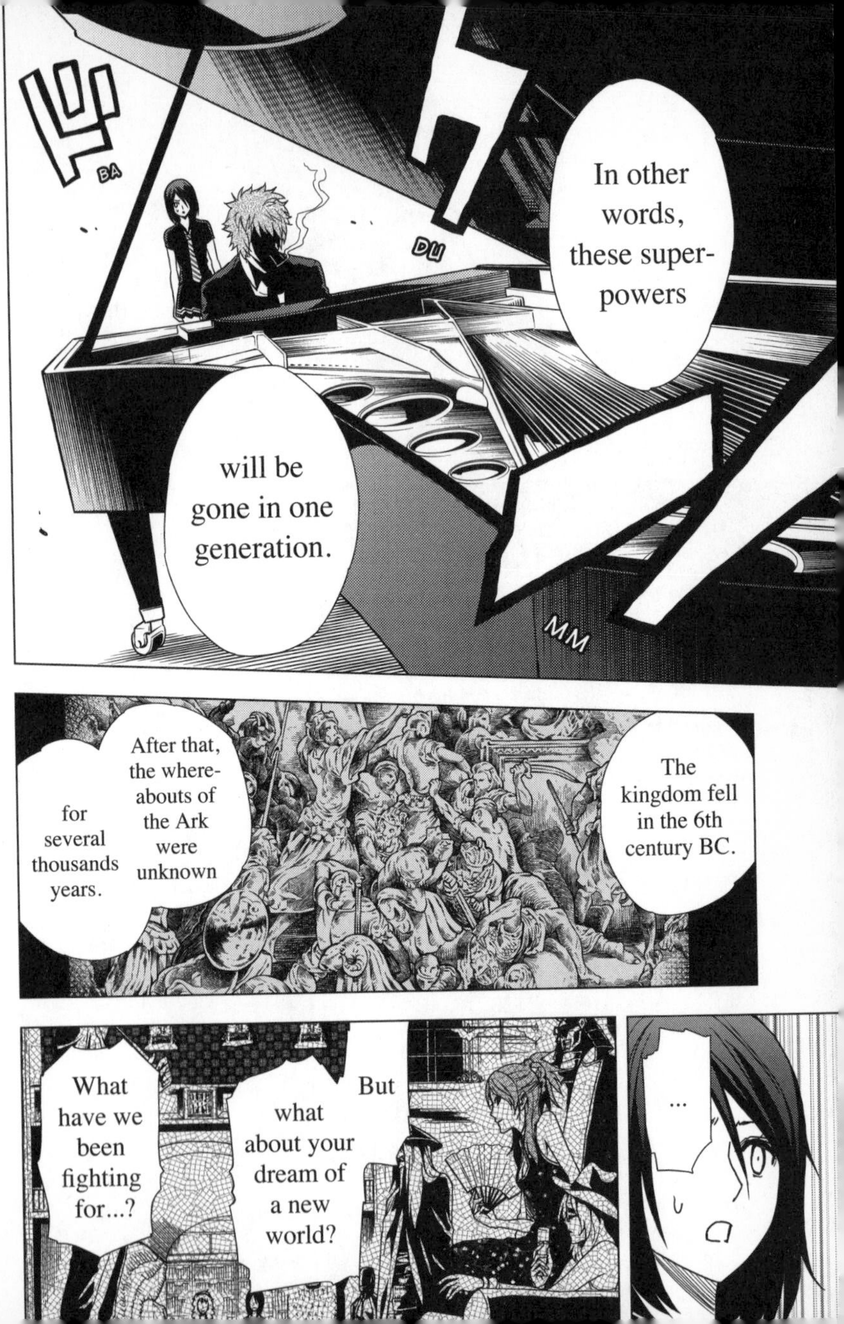
In other words, these super-powers
will be gone in one generation.
BA
DU
MM
The kingdom fell in the 6th century BC.
After that, the where-abouts of the Ark were unknown
for several thousands years.
...
But
what about your dream of a new world?
What have we been fighting for...?

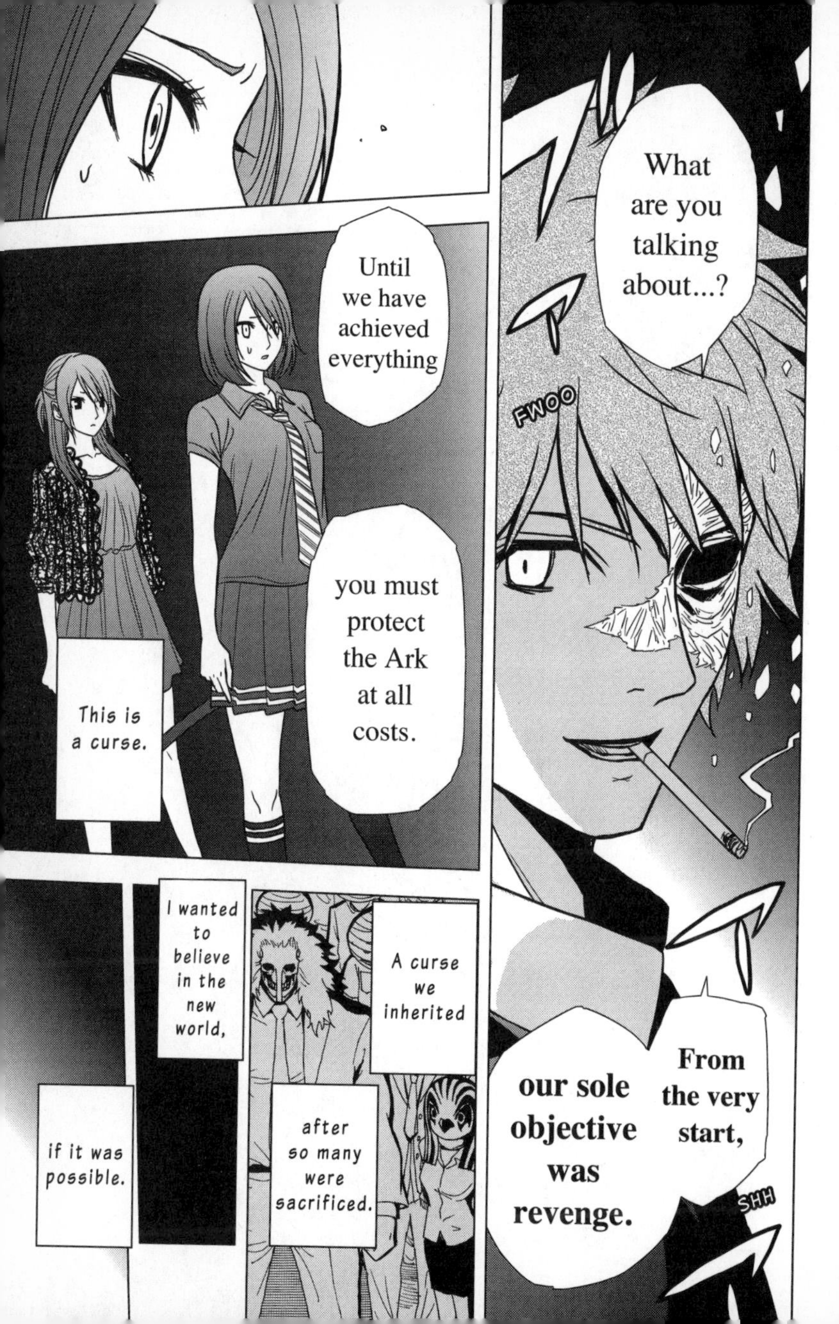
What are you talking about...?
FWOO
From the very start,
our sole objective was revenge.
SHH
Until we have achieved everything
you must protect the Ark at all costs.
This is a curse.
A curse we inherited
after so many were sacrificed.
I wanted to believe in the new world,
if it was possible.

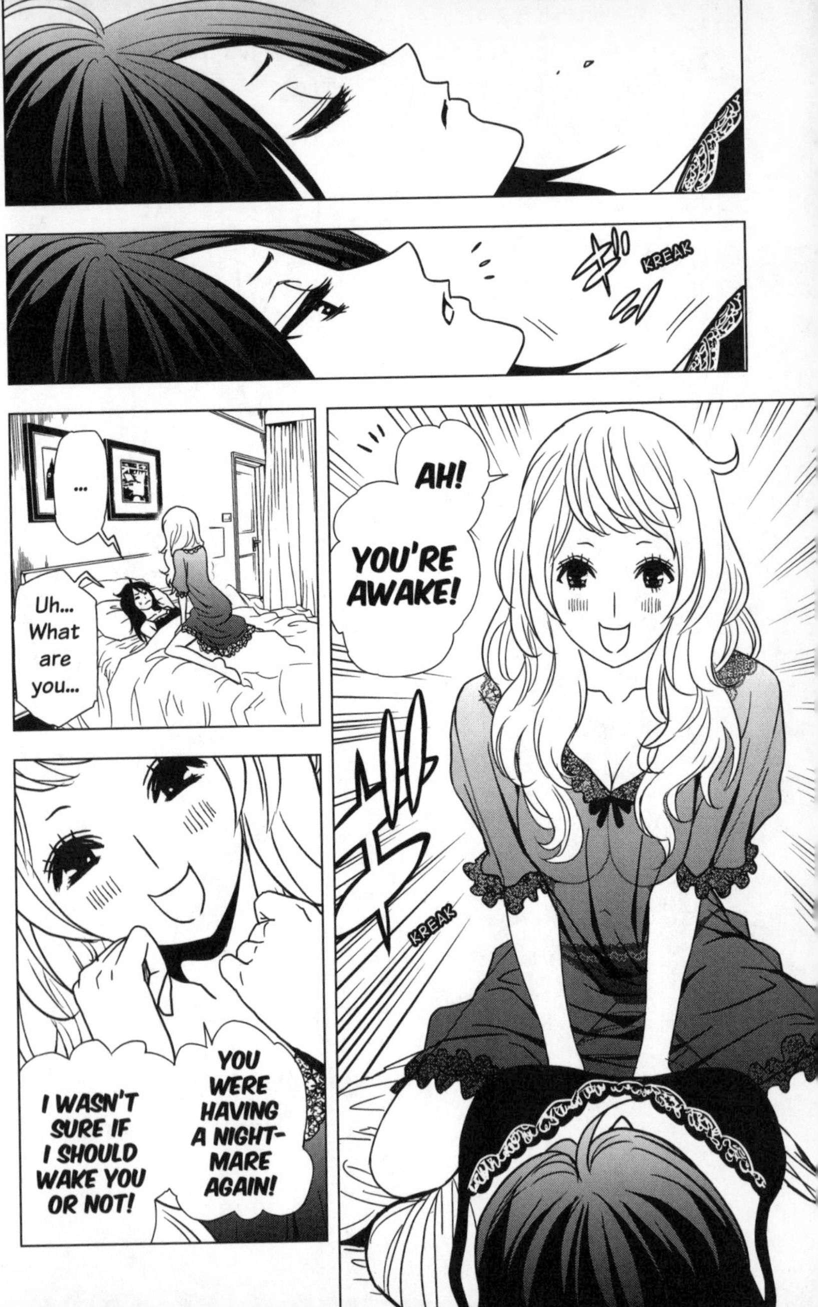
KREAK
AH!
YOU'RE AWAKE!
KREAK
...
Uh... What are you...
YOU WERE HAVING A NIGHT-MARE AGAIN!
I WASN'T SURE IF I SHOULD WAKE YOU OR NOT!

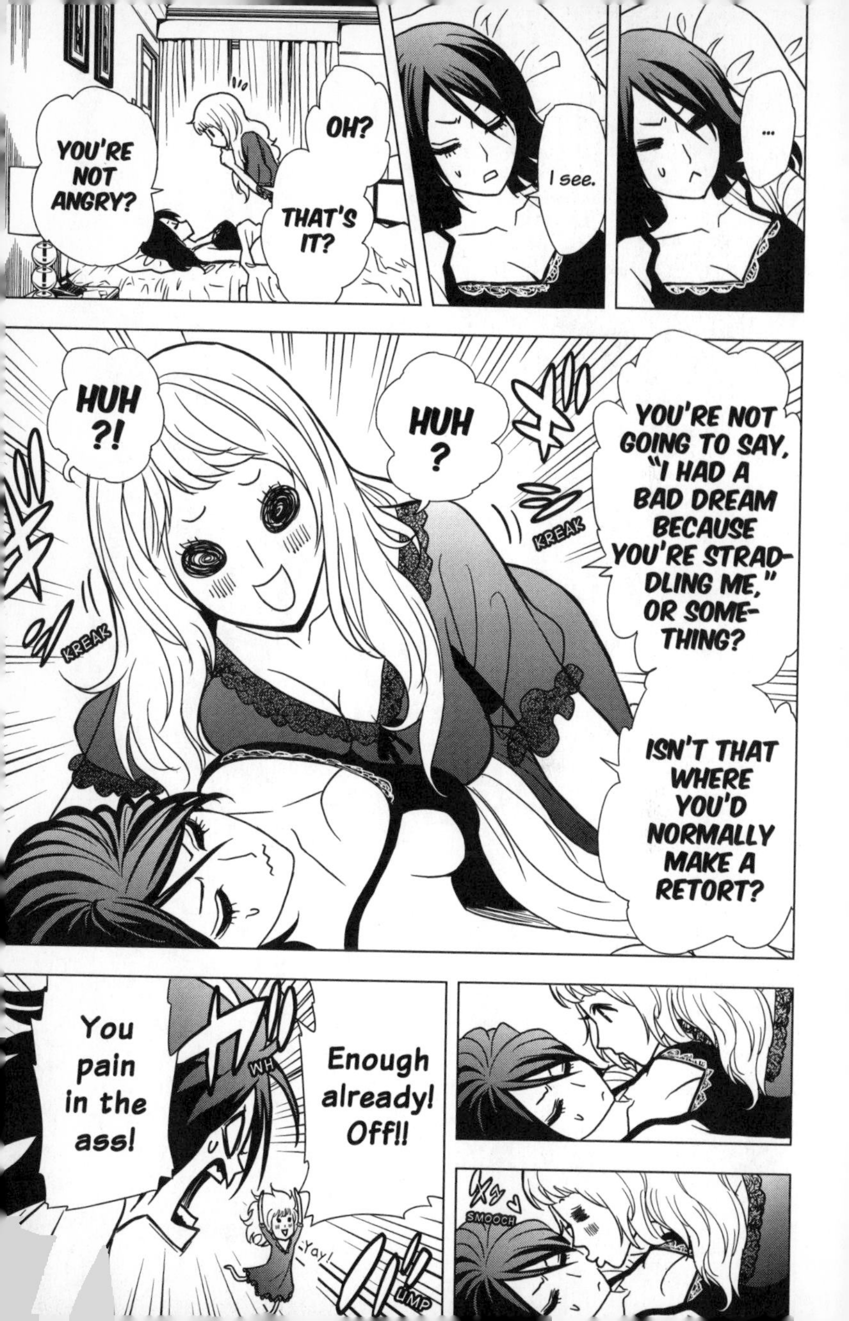
...
I see.
OH? THAT'S IT?
YOU'RE NOT ANGRY?
YOU'RE NOT GOING TO SAY, "I HAD A BAD DREAM BECAUSE YOU'RE STRADDLING ME," OR SOMETHING?
ISN'T THAT WHERE YOU'D NORMALLY MAKE A RETORT?
KREAK
HUH ?
HUH ?!
KREAK
SMOOCH
Enough already! Off!!
You pain in the ass!
WH
UMP
Yay!

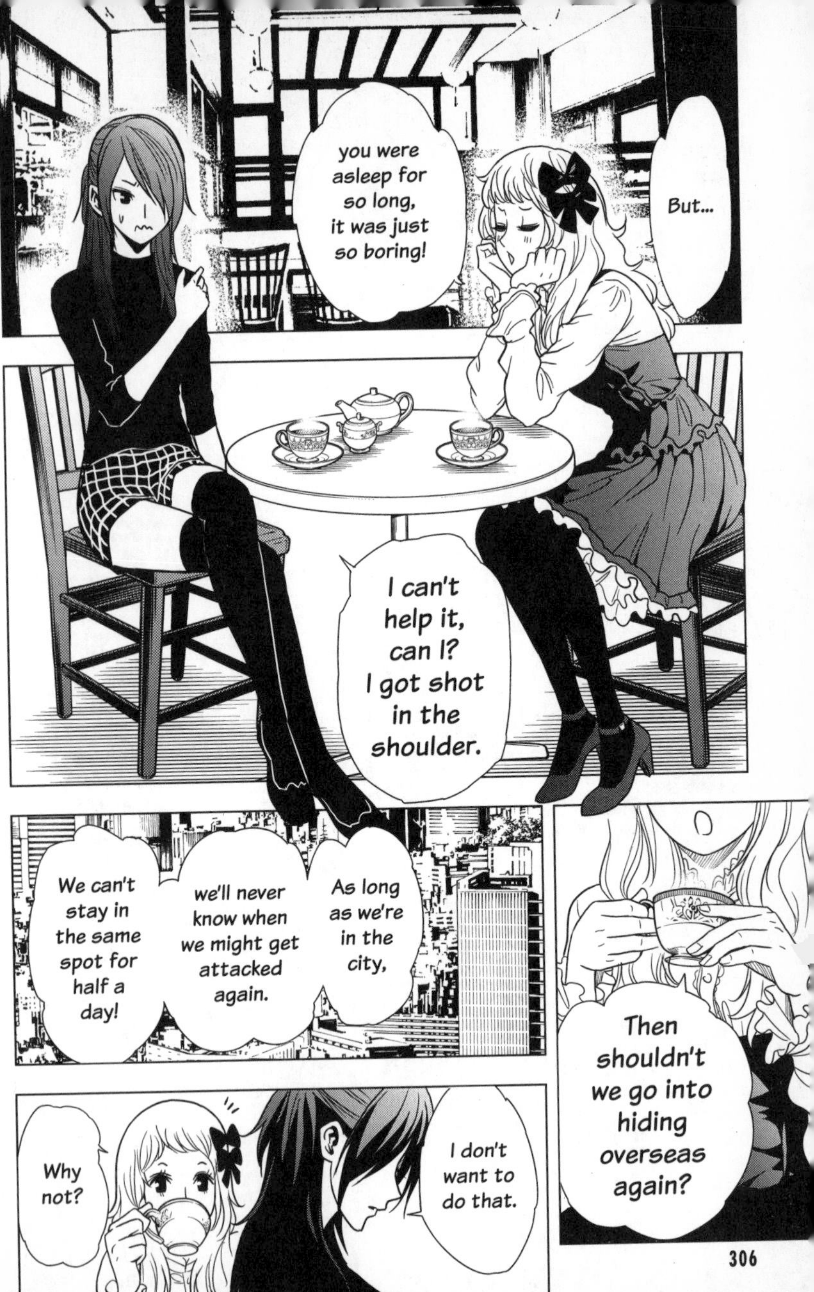

But...
you were asleep for so long, it was just so boring!
I can't help it, can I? I got shot in the shoulder.
Then shouldn't we go into hiding overseas again?
As long as we're in the city,
we'll never know when we might get attacked again.
We can't stay in the same spot for half a day!
I don't want to do that.
Why not?

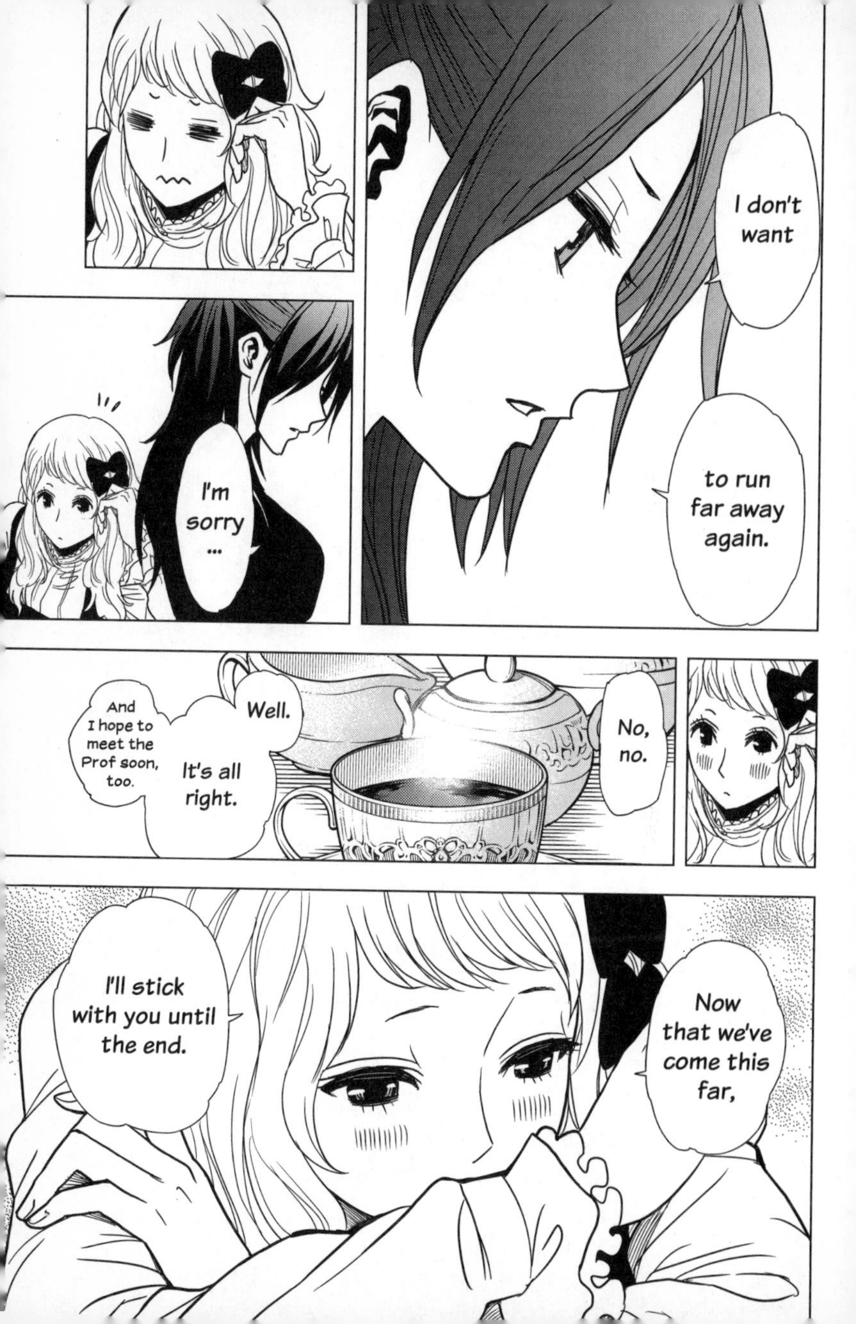
I don't want
to run far away again.
I'm sorry ...
No, no.
Well.
It's all right.
And I hope to meet the Prof soon, too.
Now that we've come this far,
I'll stick with you until the end.

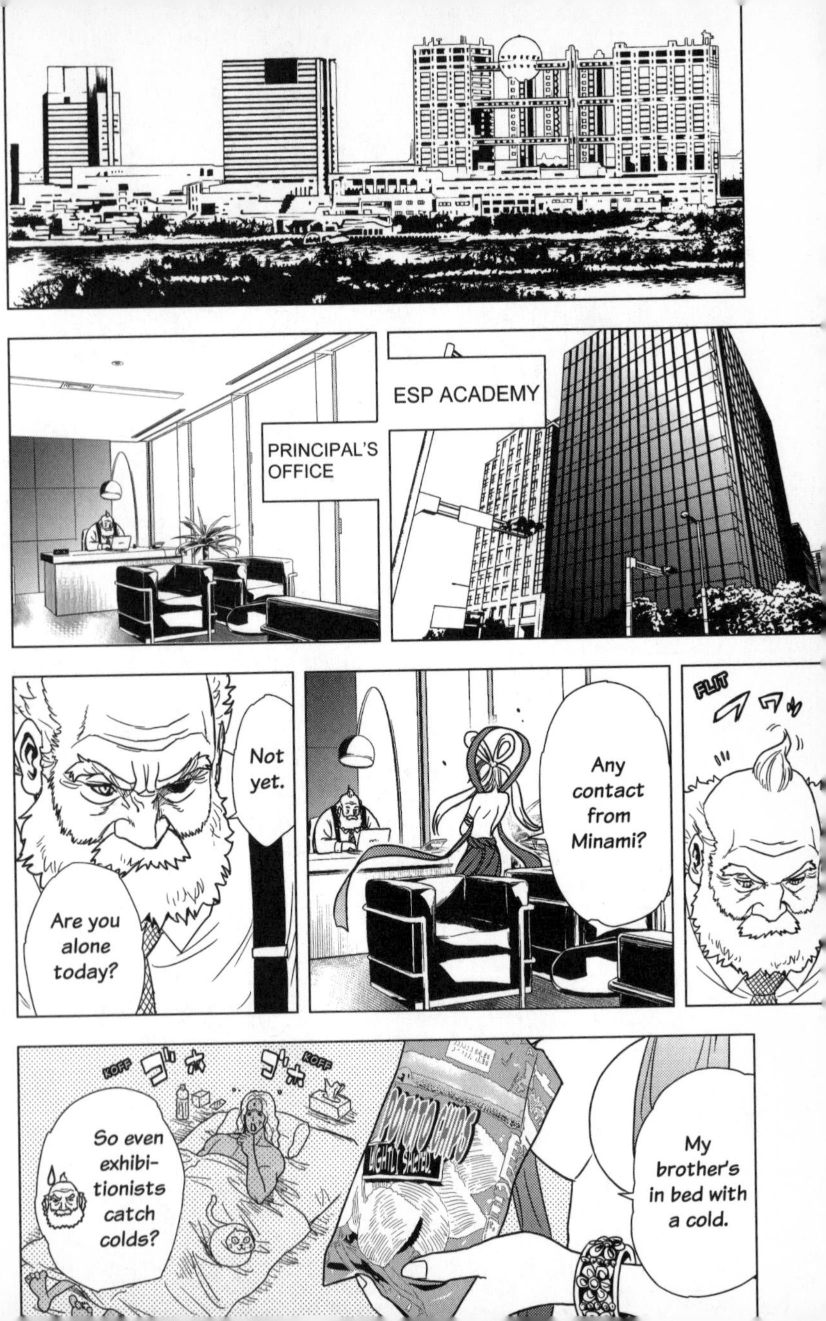
ESP ACADEMY
PRINCIPAL'S OFFICE
FLIT
Any contact from Minami?
Not yet.
Are you alone today?
My brother's in bed with a cold.
KOFF
KOFF
So even exhibi-tionists catch colds?
POTATO CHIPS
LIGHTLY SALTED

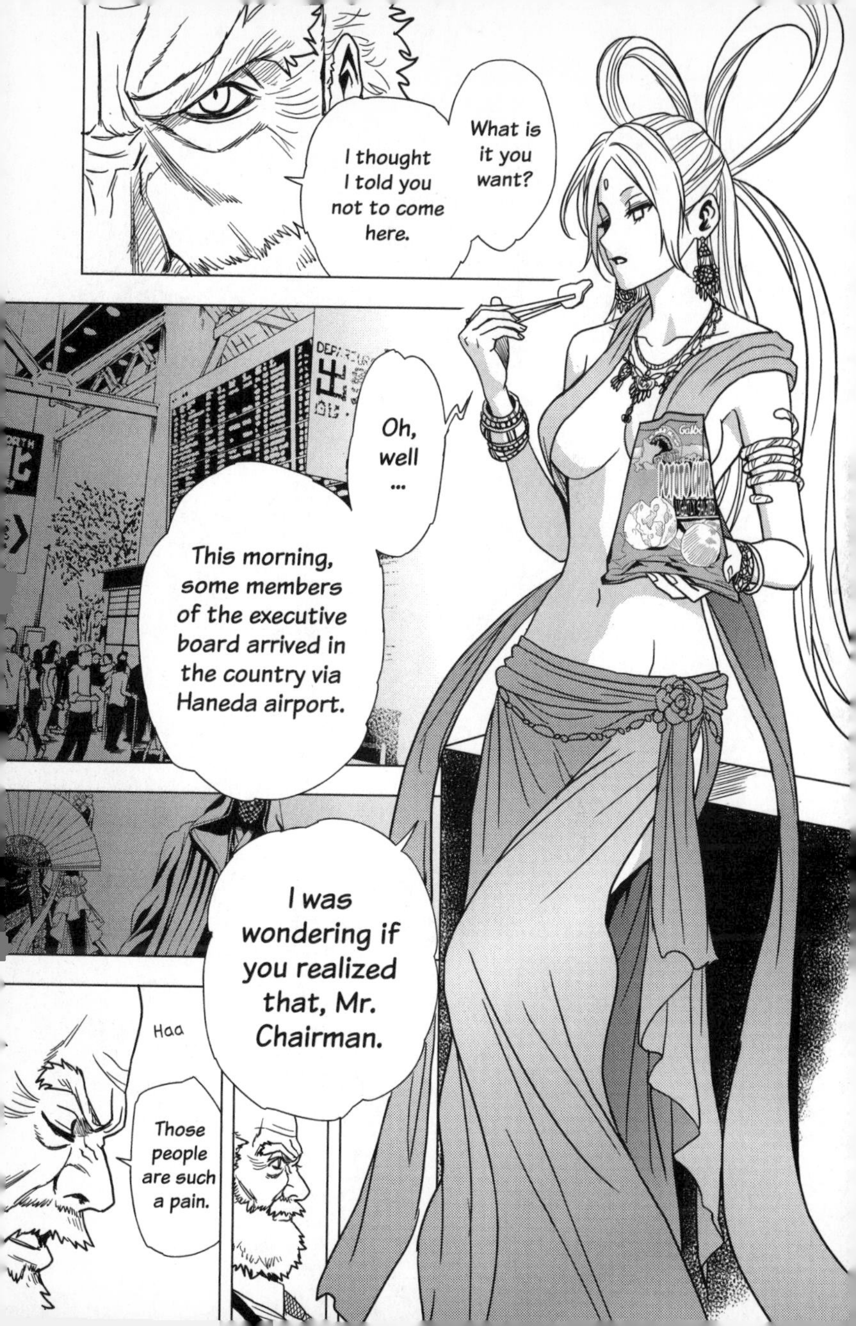
What is it you want?
I thought I told you not to come here.
Oh, well ...
This morning, some members of the executive board arrived in the country via Haneda airport.
I was wondering if you realized that, Mr. Chairman.
Haa
Those people are such a pain.

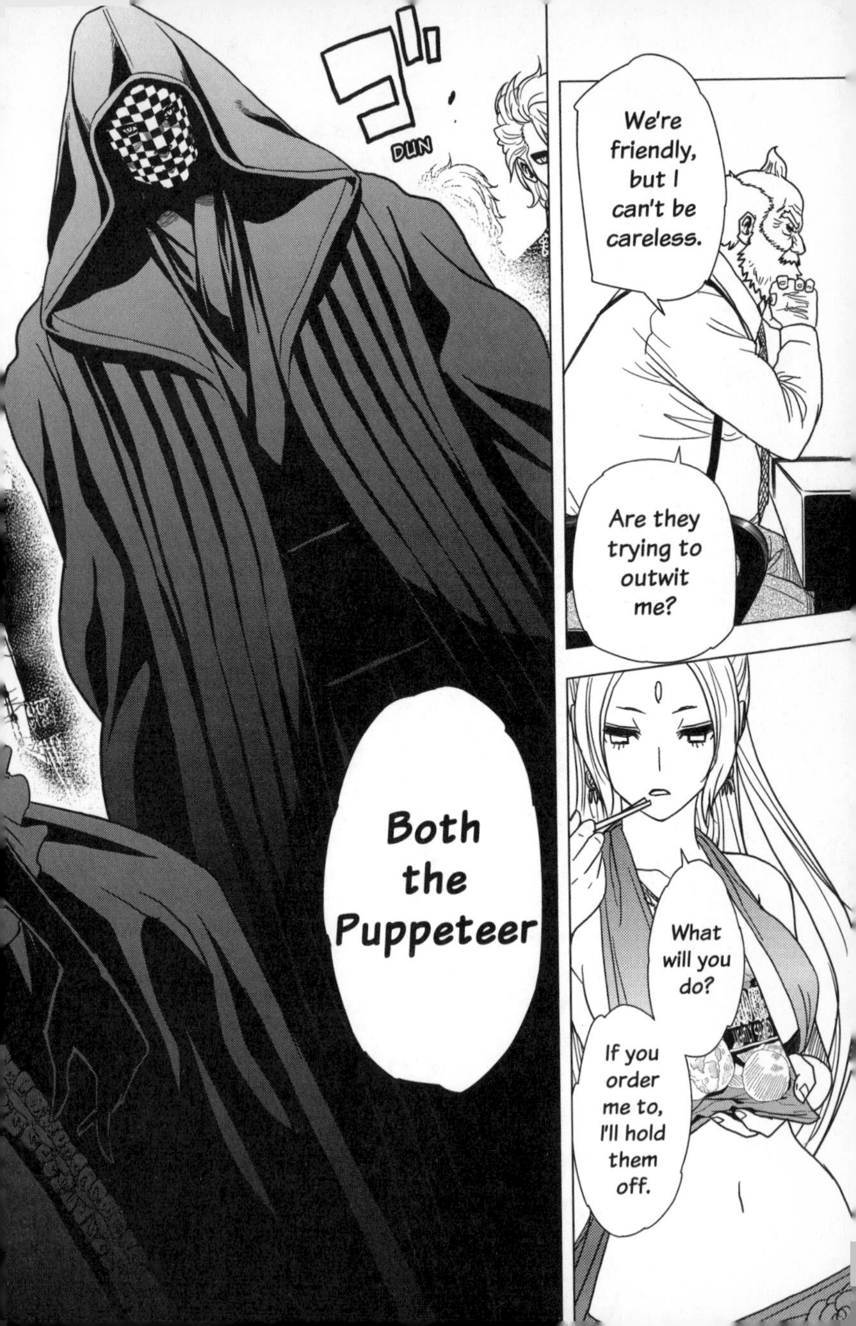
We're friendly, but I can't be careless.
Are they trying to outwit me?
What will you do?
If you order me to, I'll hold them off.
DUN
Both the Puppeteer

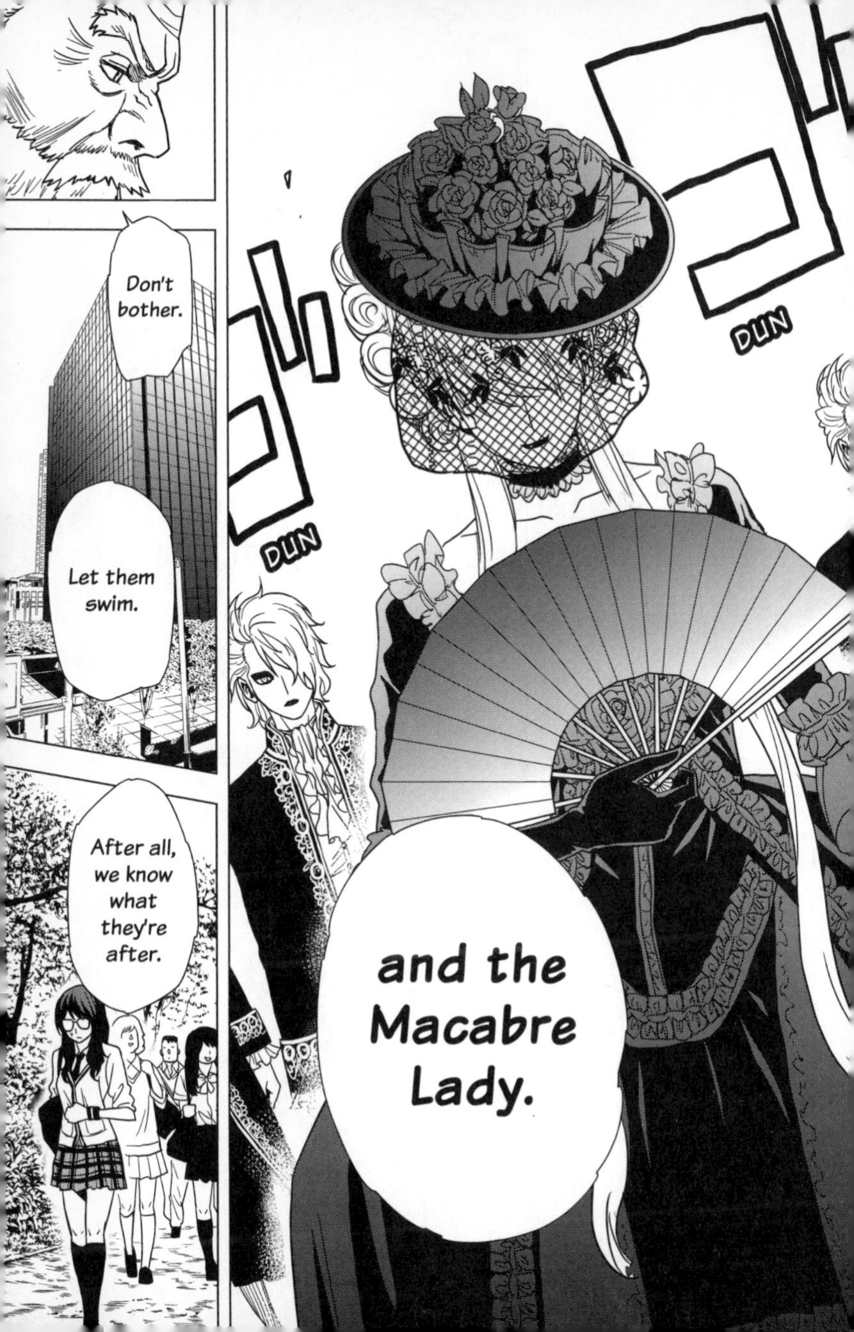
DUN
DUN
and the Macabre Lady.
Don't bother.
Let them swim.
After all, we know what they're after.

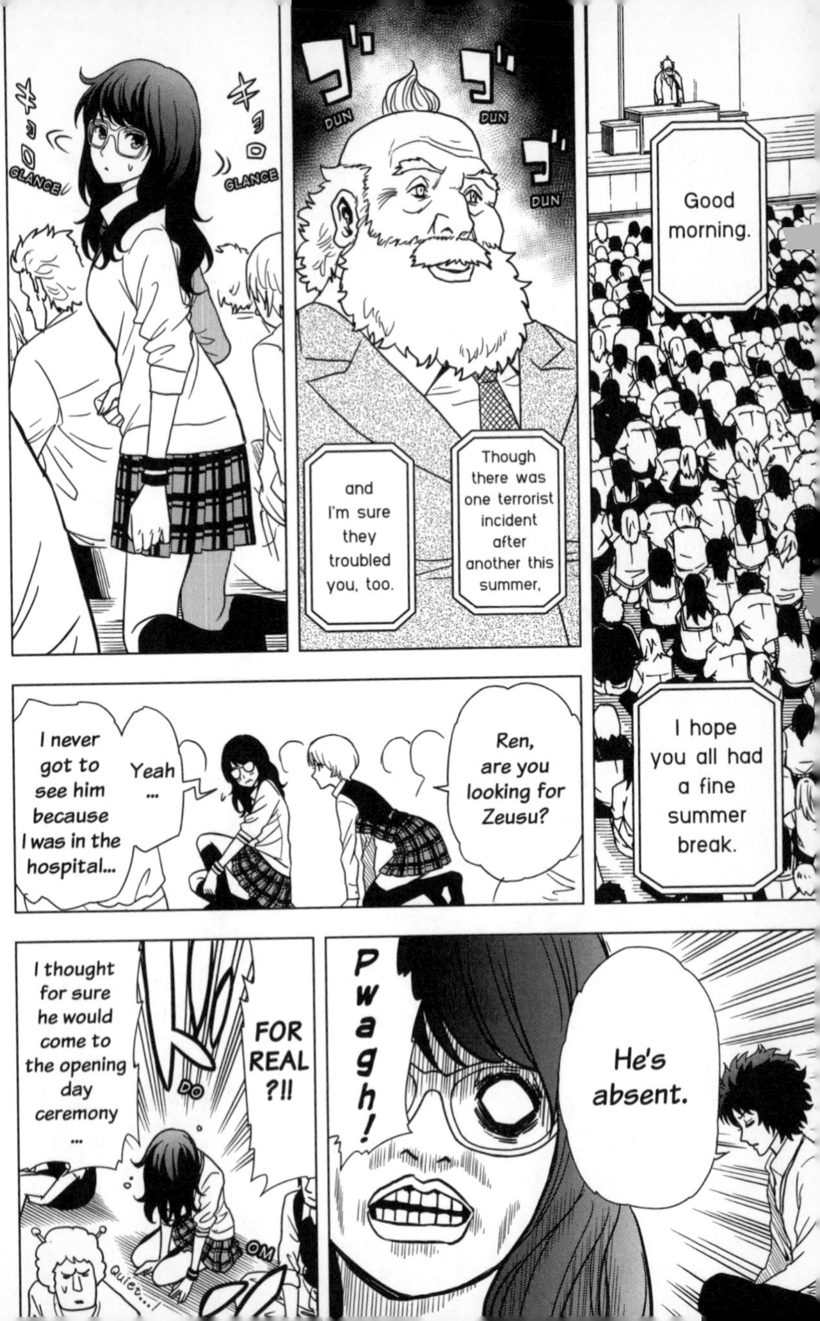
Good morning.
I hope you all had a fine summer break.
ゴ DUN
ゴ DUN
ゴ DUN
Though there was one terrorist incident after another this summer,
and I'm sure they troubled you, too.
キョロ GLANCE
キョロ GLANCE
Ren, are you looking for Zeusu?
Yeah ...
I never got to see him because I was in the hospital...
Pwagh!
He's absent.
FOR REAL?!!
DO
OM
I thought for sure he would come to the opening day ceremony ...
Quiet...!

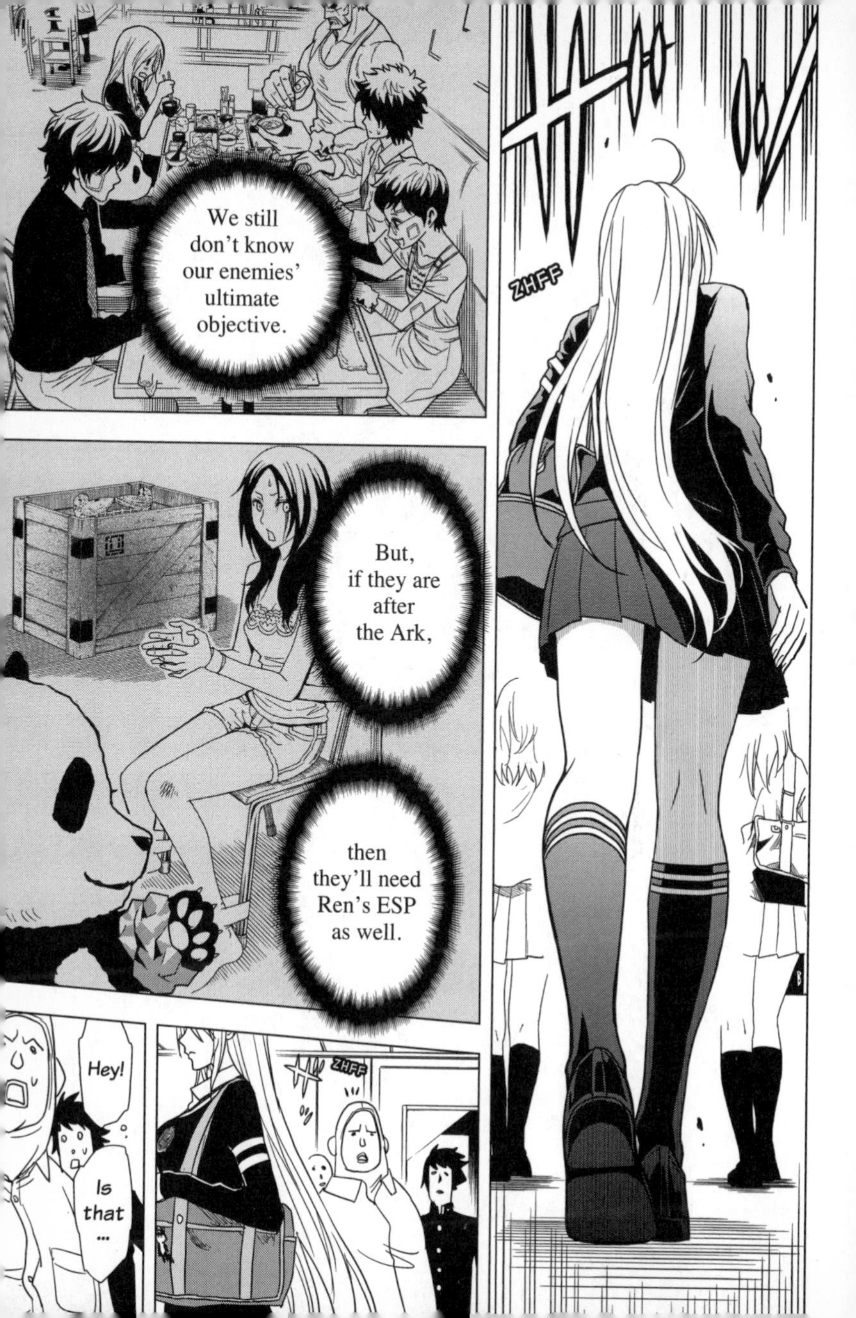
ZHFF
We still don't know our enemies' ultimate objective.
But, if they are after the Ark,
then they'll need Ren's ESP as well.
ZHFF
Hey!
Is that ...

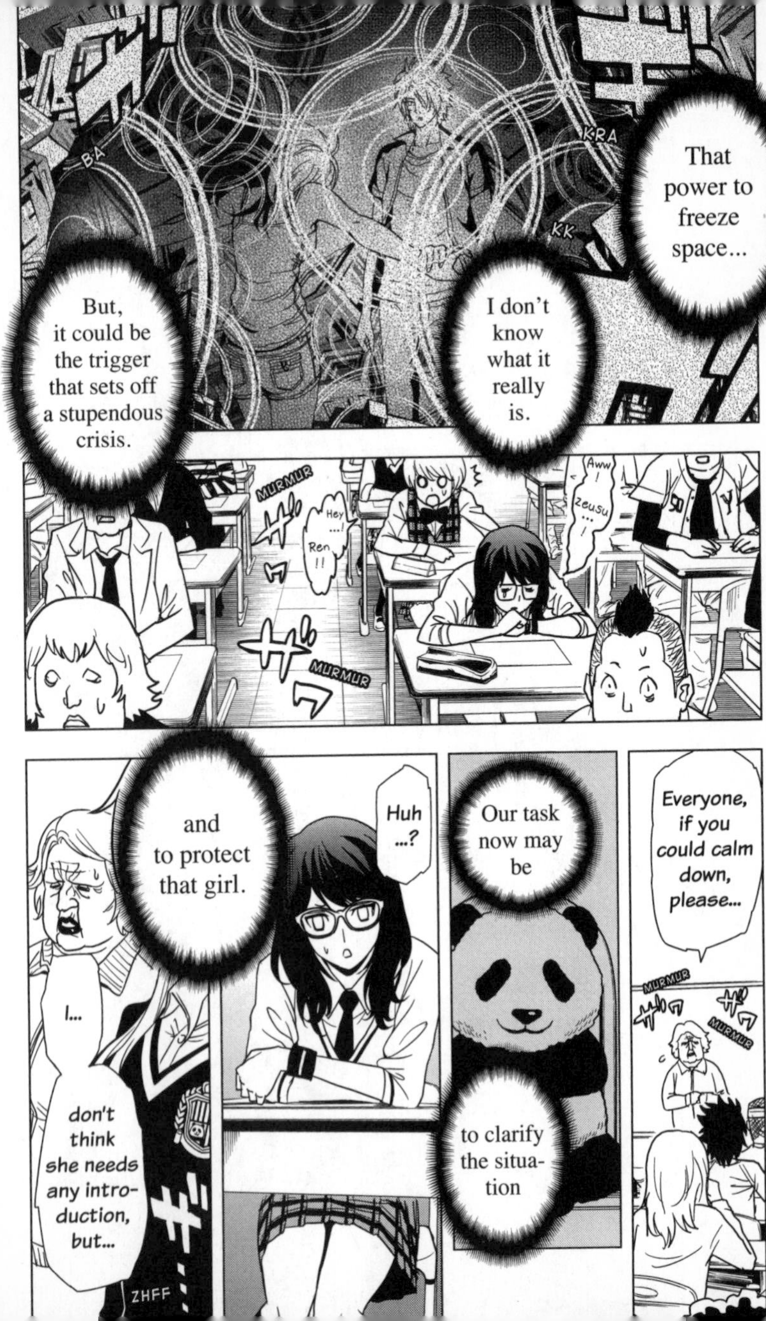
KRA
That power to freeze space...
KK
I don't know what it really is.
BA
But, it could be the trigger that sets off a stupendous crisis.
Aww! Zeusu...!
Hey...! Ren!!
MURMUR
MURMUR
Everyone, if you could calm down, please...
MURMUR
MURMUR
Our task now may be
to clarify the situation
and to protect that girl.
Huh...?
I...
don't think she needs any introduction, but...
ZHFF

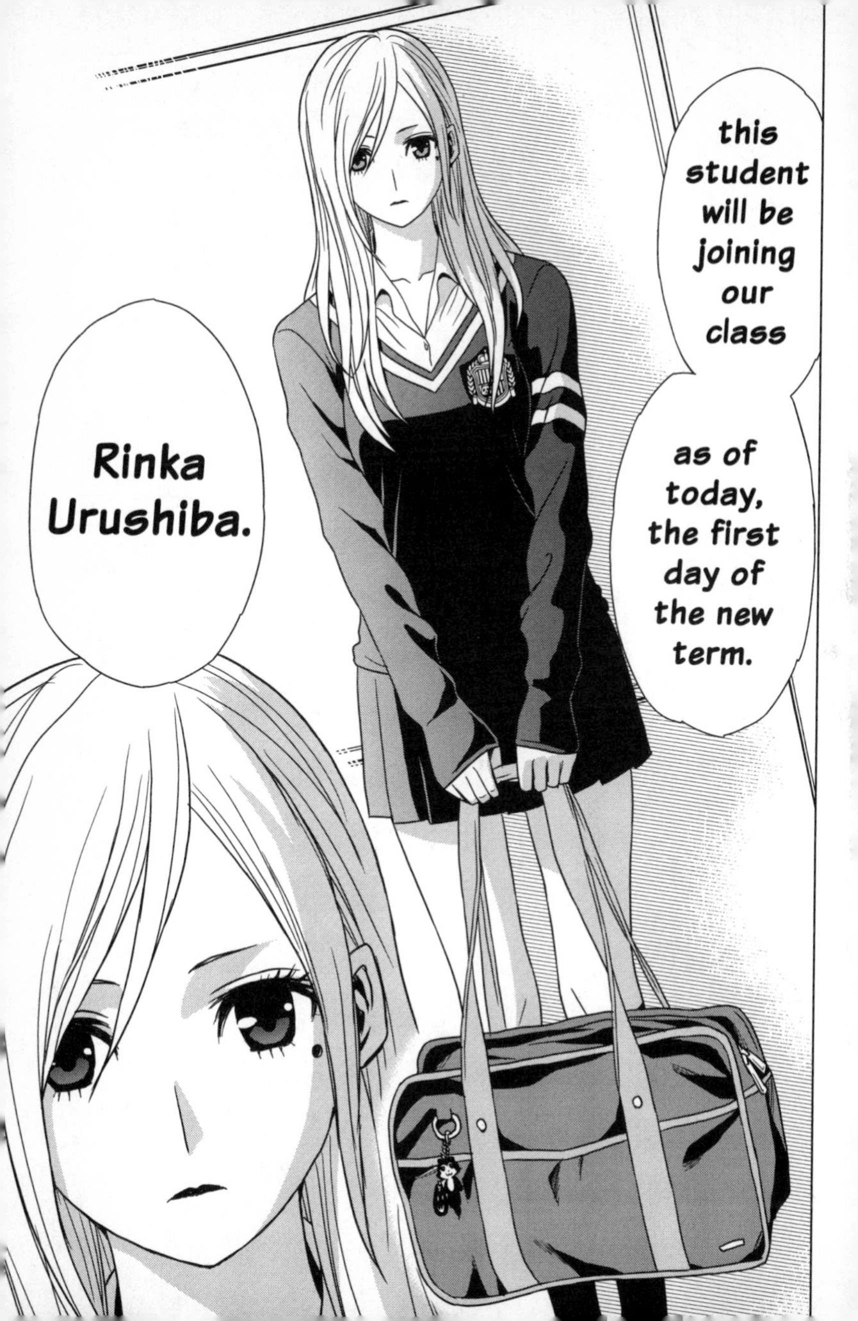
this student will be joining our class
as of today, the first day of the new term.
Rinka Urushiba.

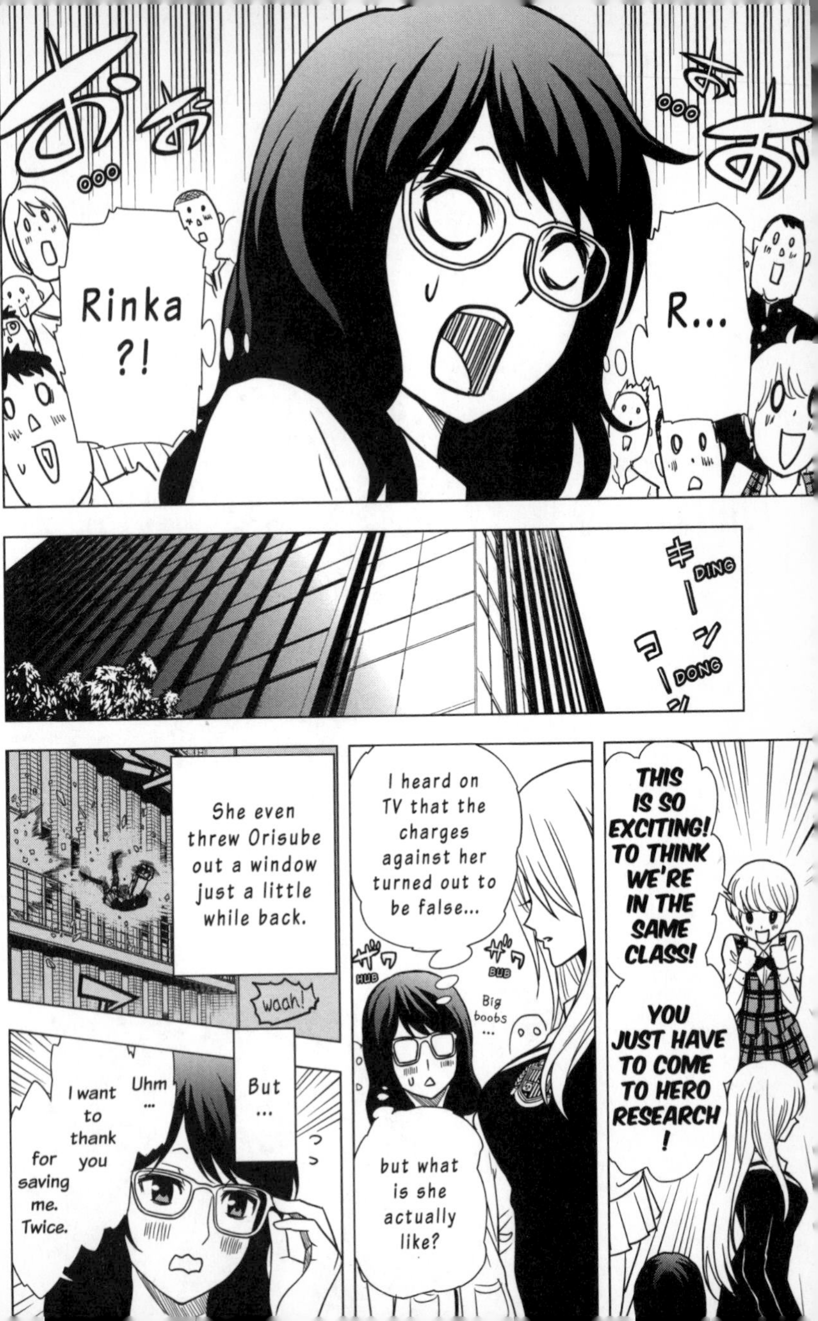

R...
Rinka ?!
キーンコーン
DING
DONG
THIS IS SO EXCITING! TO THINK WE'RE IN THE SAME CLASS!
YOU JUST HAVE TO COME TO HERO RESEARCH!
I heard on TV that the charges against her turned out to be false...
ザワ
BUB
ザワ
HUB
Big boobs ...
but what is she actually like?
She even threw Orisube out a window just a little while back.
waah!
But ...
Uhm ...
I want to thank you for saving me. Twice.

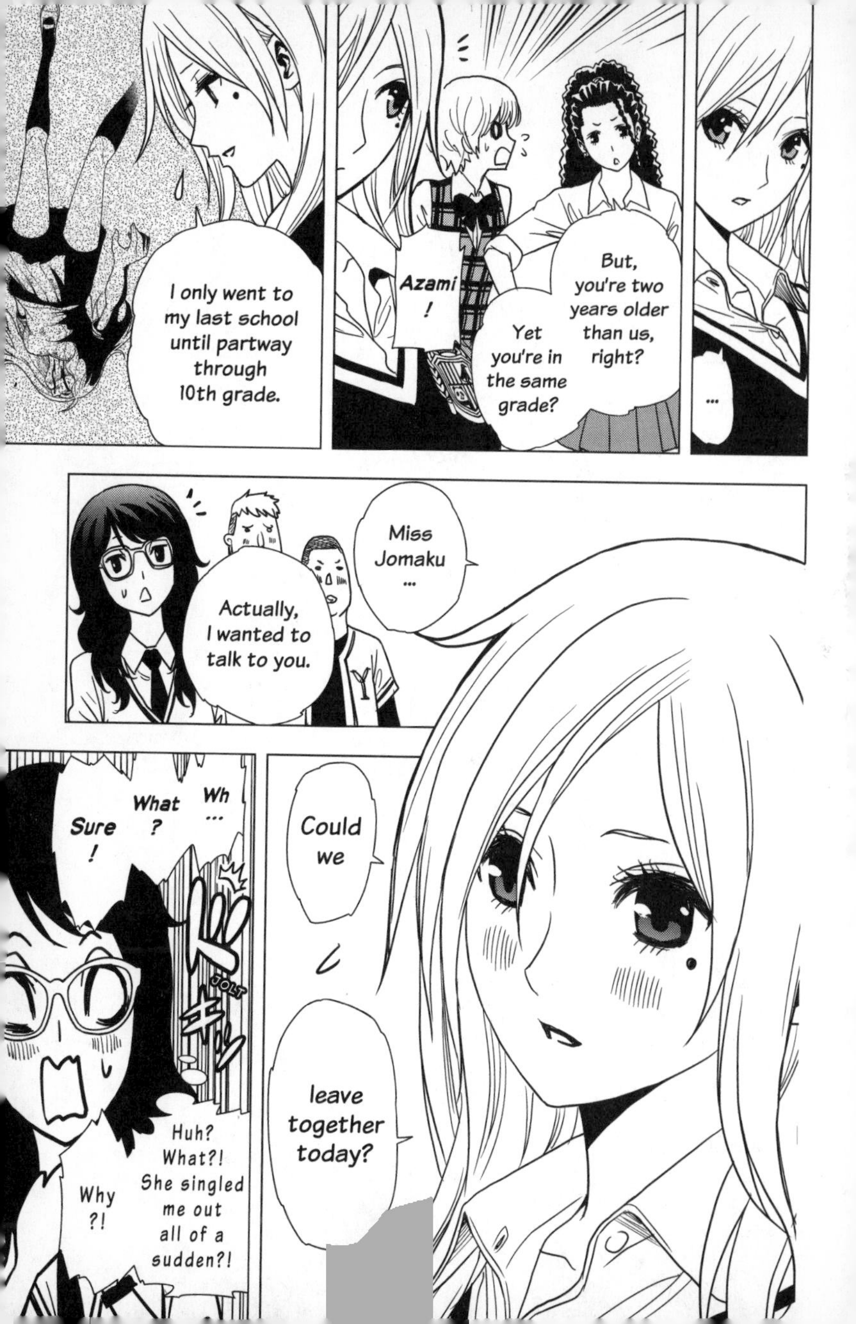
...
But, you're two years older than us, right?
Yet you're in the same grade?
Azami!
I only went to my last school until partway through 10th grade.
Miss Jomaku ...
Actually, I wanted to talk to you.
Could we
leave together today?
Wh ...
What ?
Sure !
JOLT
Huh? What?! She singled me out all of a sudden?!
Why ?!

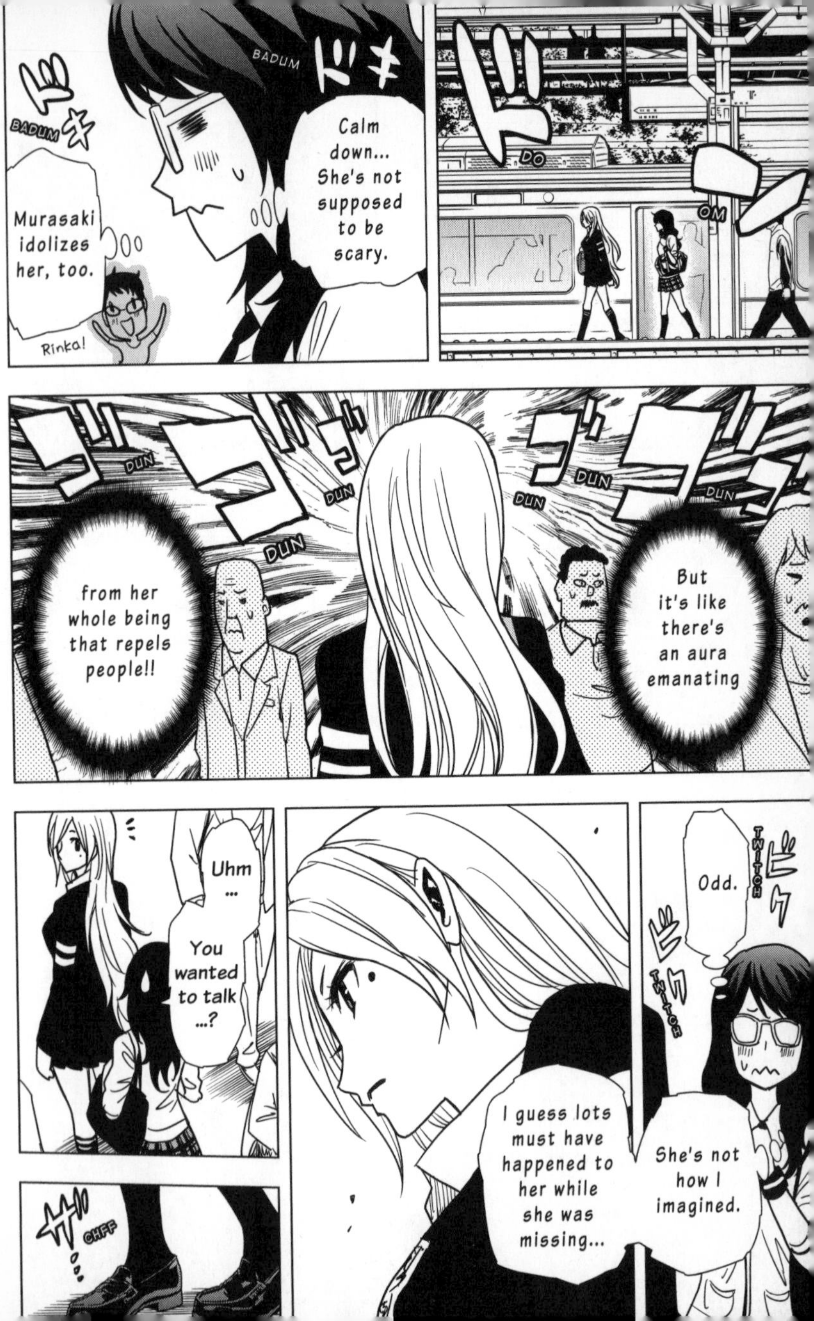
DO
OM
BADUM
Calm down... She's not supposed to be scary.
BADUM
Murasaki idolizes her, too.
Rinka!
DUN
DUN
DUN
DUN
DUN
DUN
But it's like there's an aura emanating
from her whole being that repels people!!
Odd.
TWITCH
TWITCH
She's not how I imagined.
I guess lots must have happened to her while she was missing...
Uhm ...
You wanted to talk ...?
CHFF

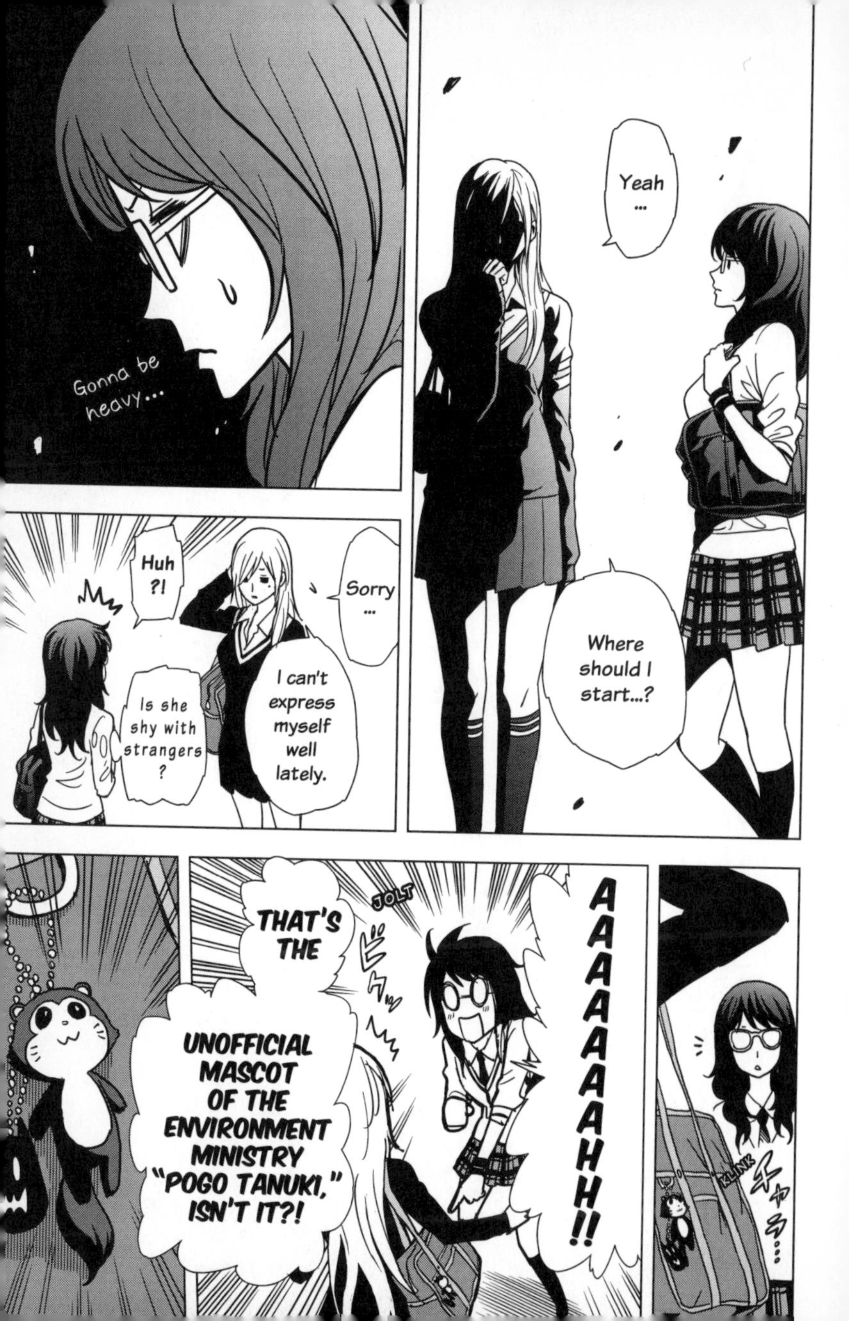
Yeah...
Where should I start...?
Gonna be heavy...
Sorry...
Huh?!
I can't express myself well lately.
Is she shy with strangers?
KLINK
AAAAAAAAAAHH!!
JOLT
THAT'S THE
UNOFFICIAL MASCOT OF THE ENVIRONMENT MINISTRY "POGO TANUKI," ISN'T IT?!

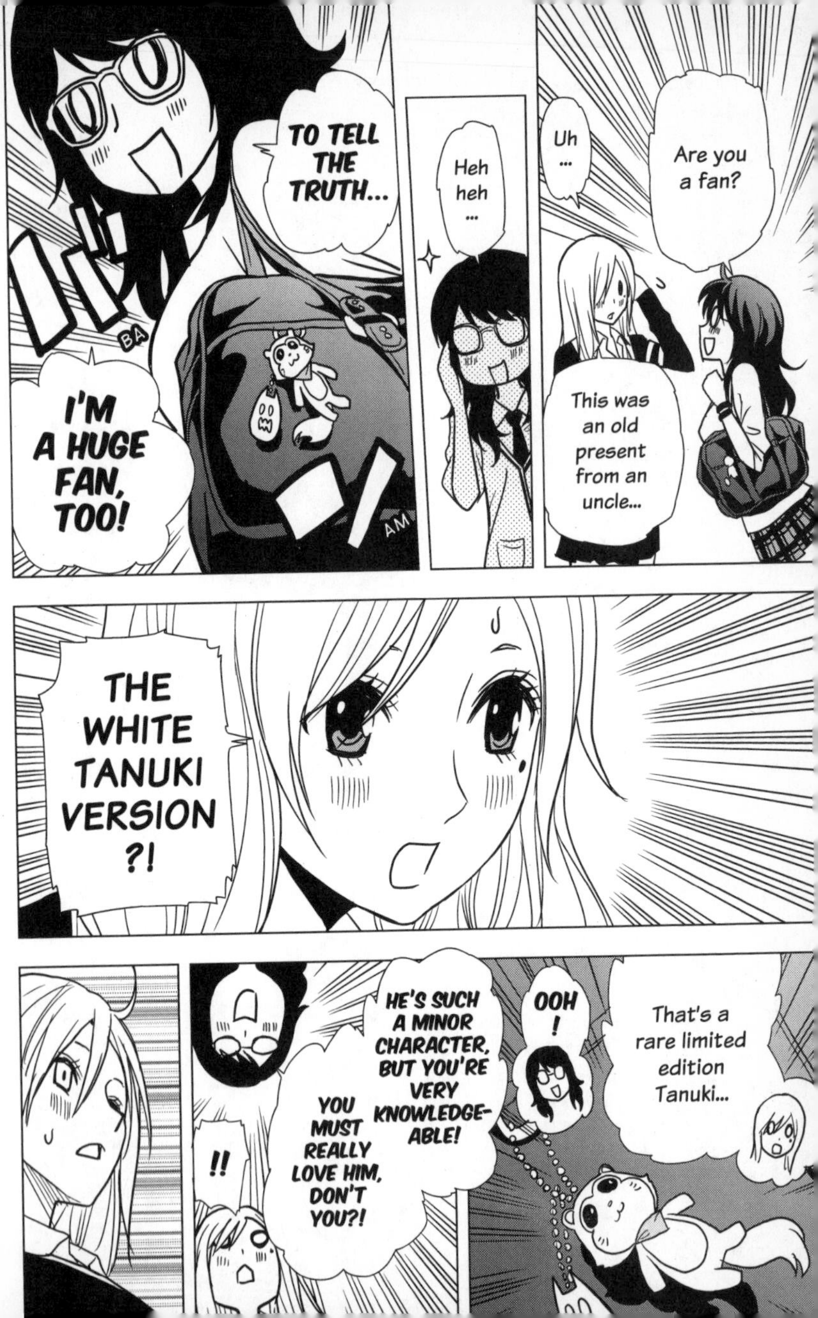
Are you a fan?
Uh ...
This was an old present from an uncle...
Heh heh ...
TO TELL THE TRUTH...
BA
AM
I'M A HUGE FAN, TOO!
THE WHITE TANUKI VERSION ?!
That's a rare limited edition Tanuki...
OOH !
HE'S SUCH A MINOR CHARACTER, BUT YOU'RE VERY KNOWLEDGE-ABLE!
YOU MUST REALLY LOVE HIM, DON'T YOU?!
!!

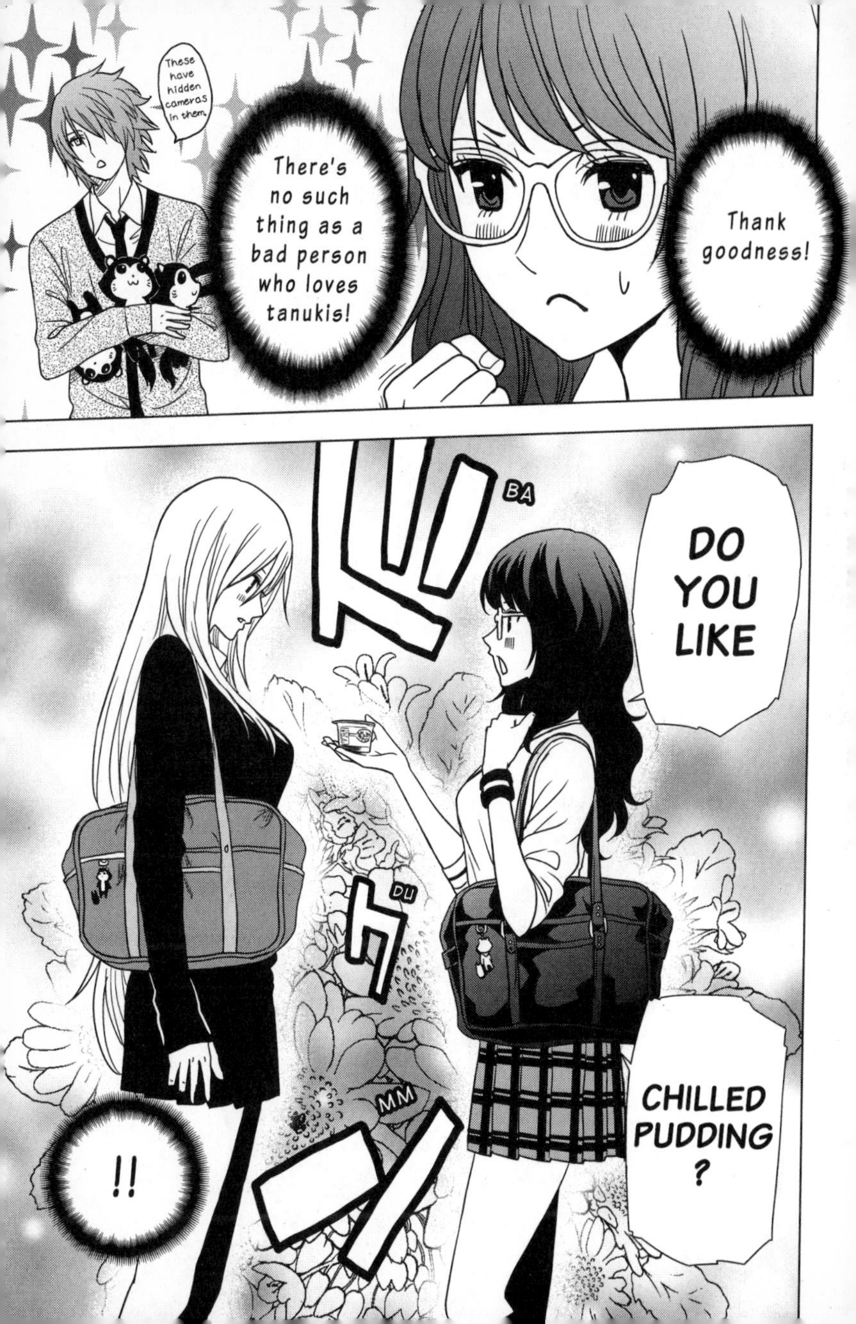
Thank goodness!
There's no such thing as a bad person who loves tanukis!
These have hidden cameras in them.
BA
DO YOU LIKE
DU
CHILLED PUDDING ?
MM
!!

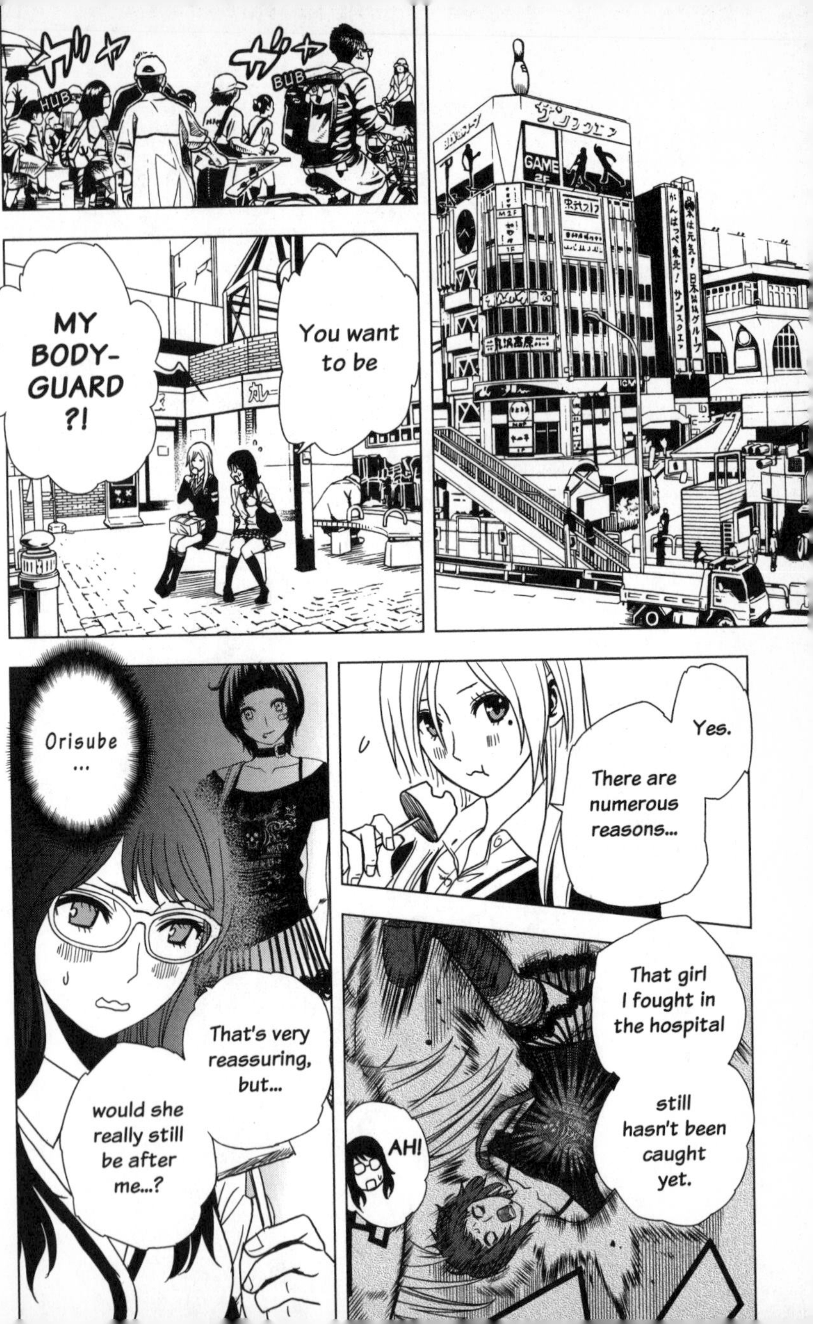
GAME
2F
HUB
BUB
You want to be
MY BODY-GUARD ?!
Yes.
There are numerous reasons...
That girl I fought in the hospital
still hasn't been caught yet.
AH!
Orisube ...
That's very reassuring, but...
would she really still be after me...?

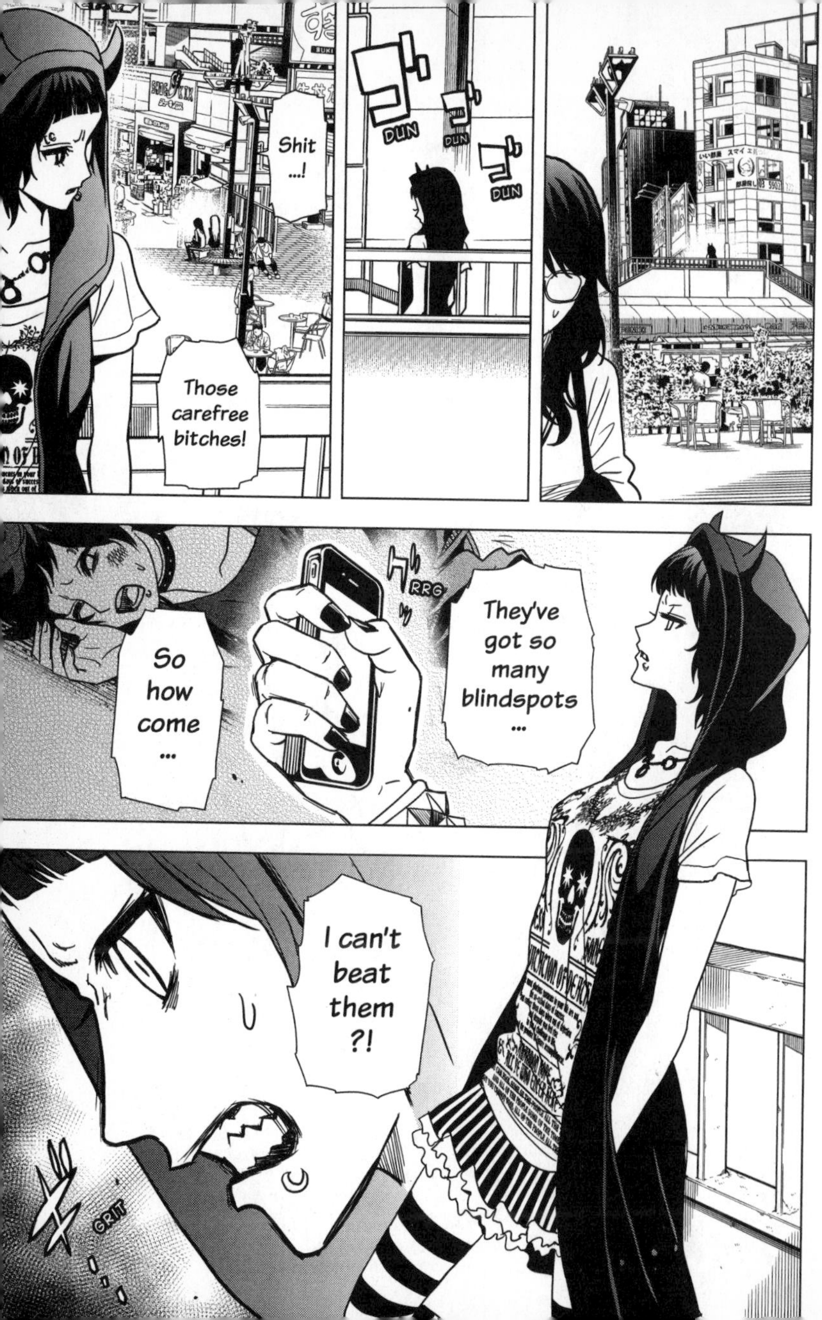
DUN
DUN
DUN
Shit ...!
Those carefree bitches!
They've got so many blindspots ...
RRG
So how come ...
I can't beat them ?!
GRIT

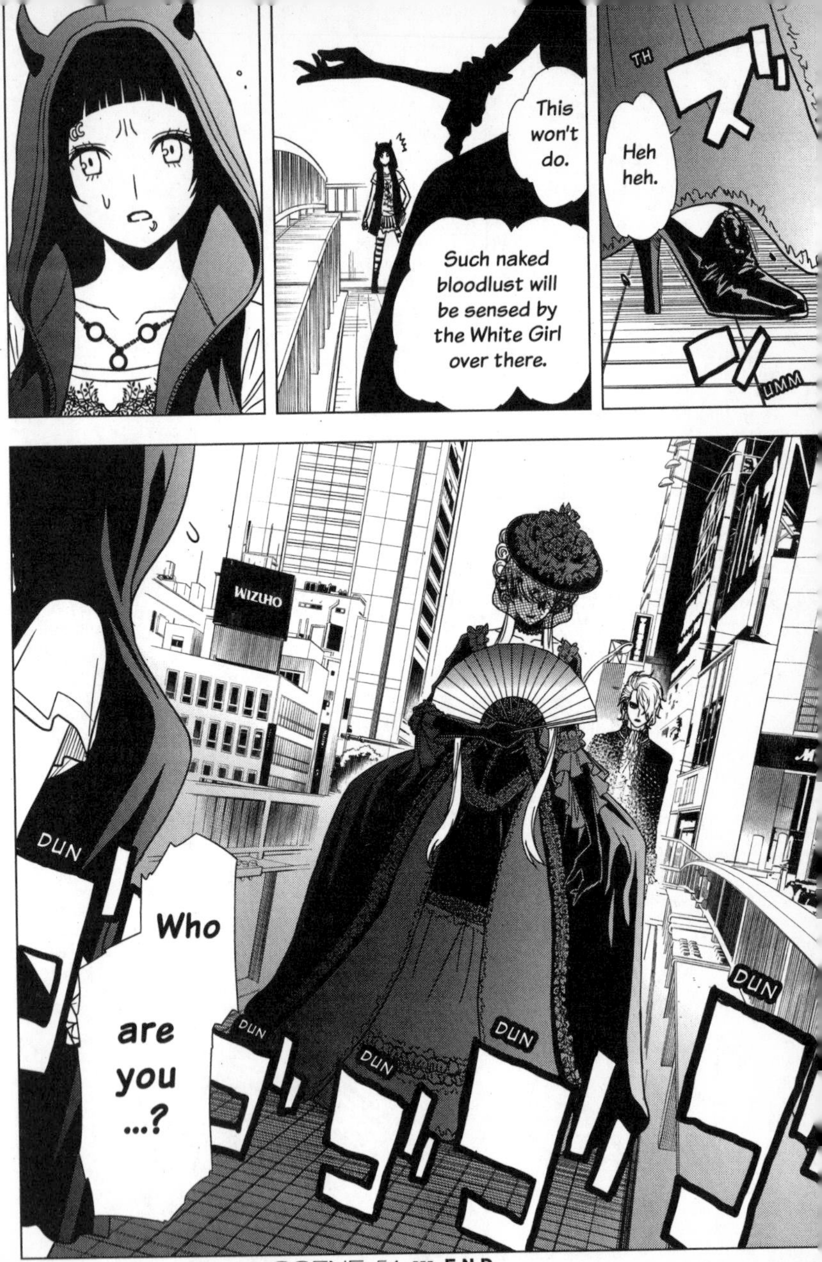
TH
Heh heh.
UMM
This won't do.
Such naked bloodlust will be sensed by the White Girl over there.
WIZHO
DUN
DUN
DUN
DUN
DUN
Who are you ...?

SCENE 54 /// END

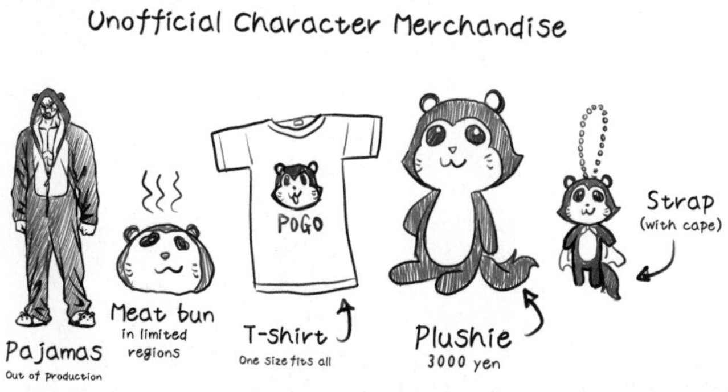
Unofficial Character Merchandise
Pajamas
Out of production
Meat bun
in limited regions
POGO
T-shirt
One size fits all
Plushie
3000 yen
Strap
(with cape)

TOKYO ESP

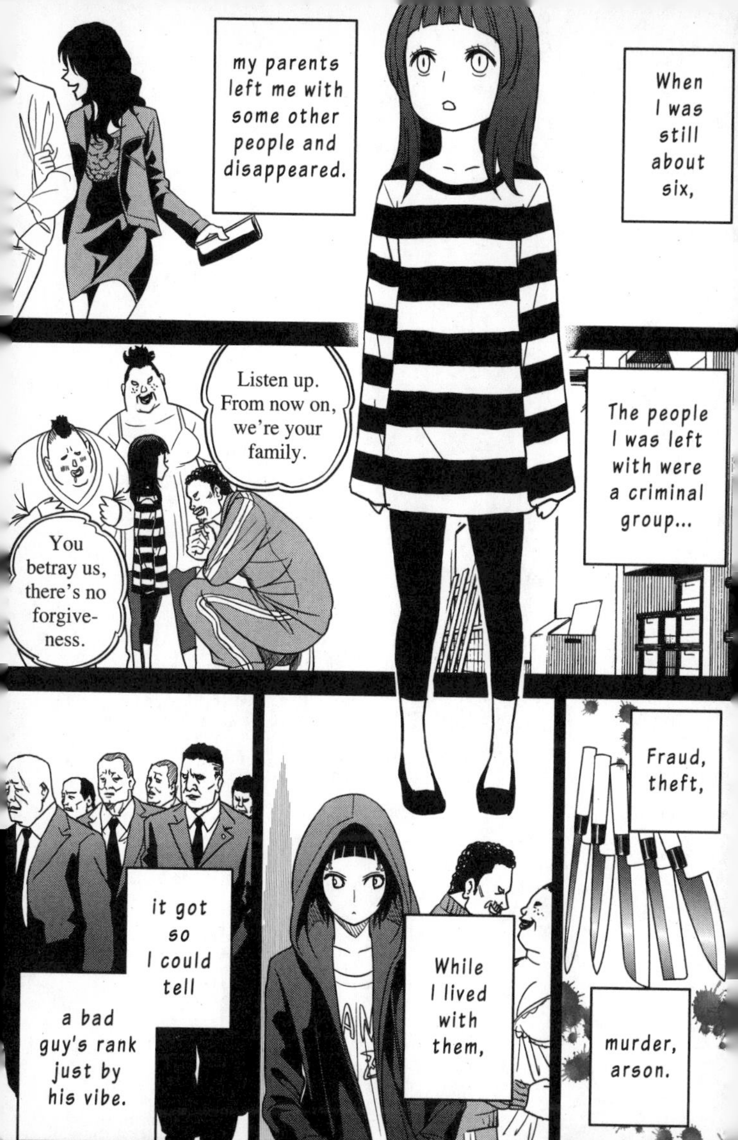
When I was still about six,
my parents left me with some other people and disappeared.
The people I was left with were a criminal group...
Listen up. From now on, we're your family.
You betray us, there's no forgive-ness.
Fraud, theft,
murder, arson.
While I lived with them,
it got so I could tell
a bad guy's rank just by his vibe.

SCENE 55 /// Greetings from the Macabre Lady

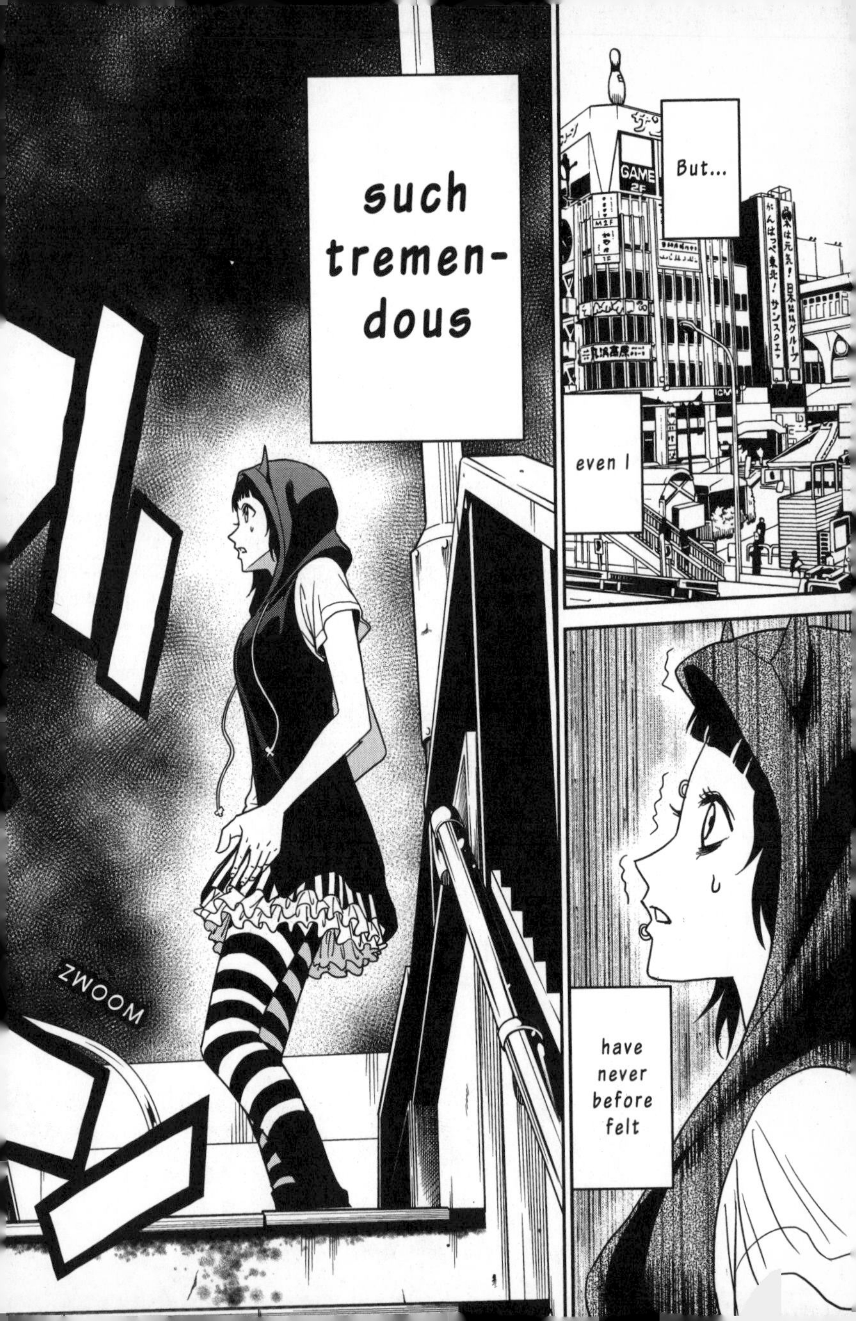
But...
even I
have never before felt
such tremendous
ZWOOM

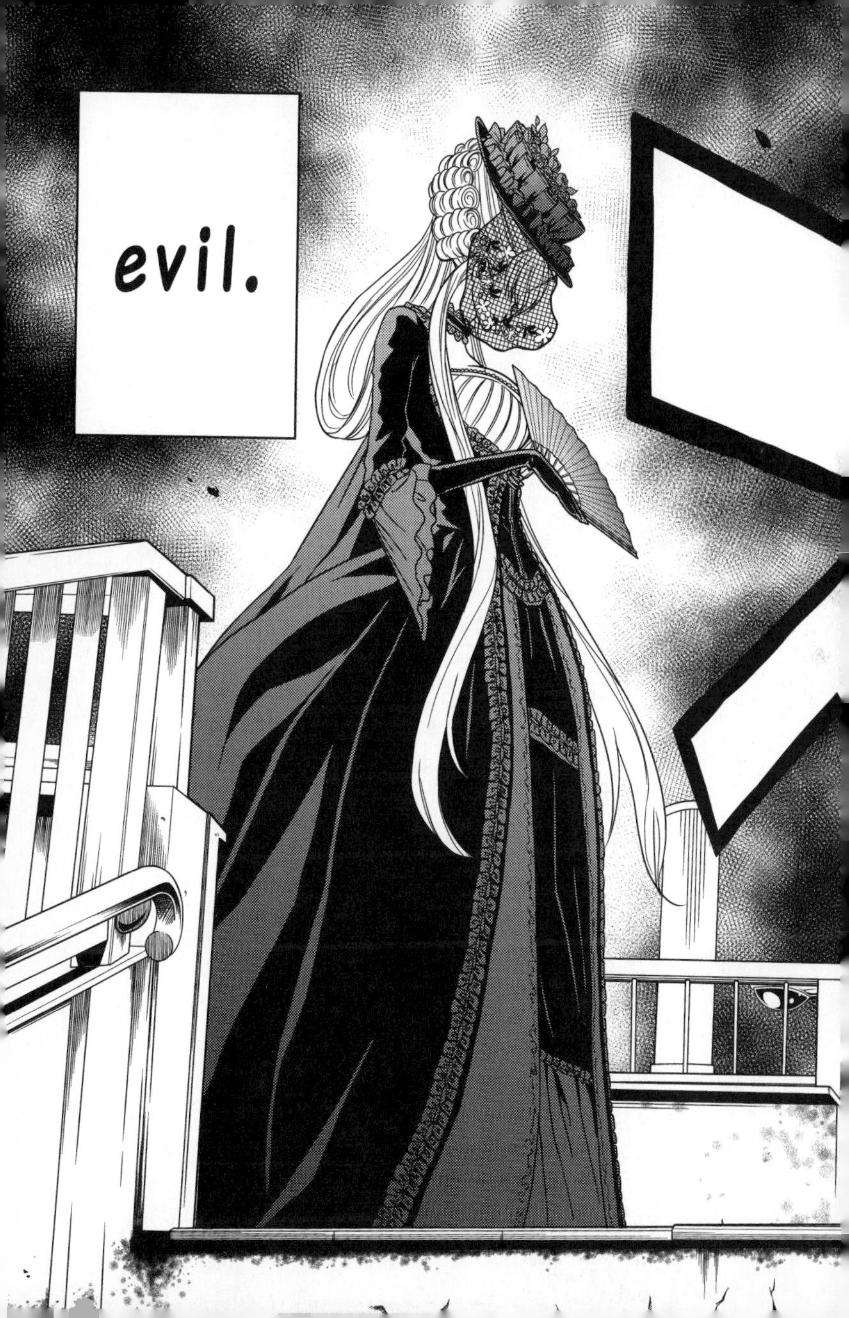
evil.

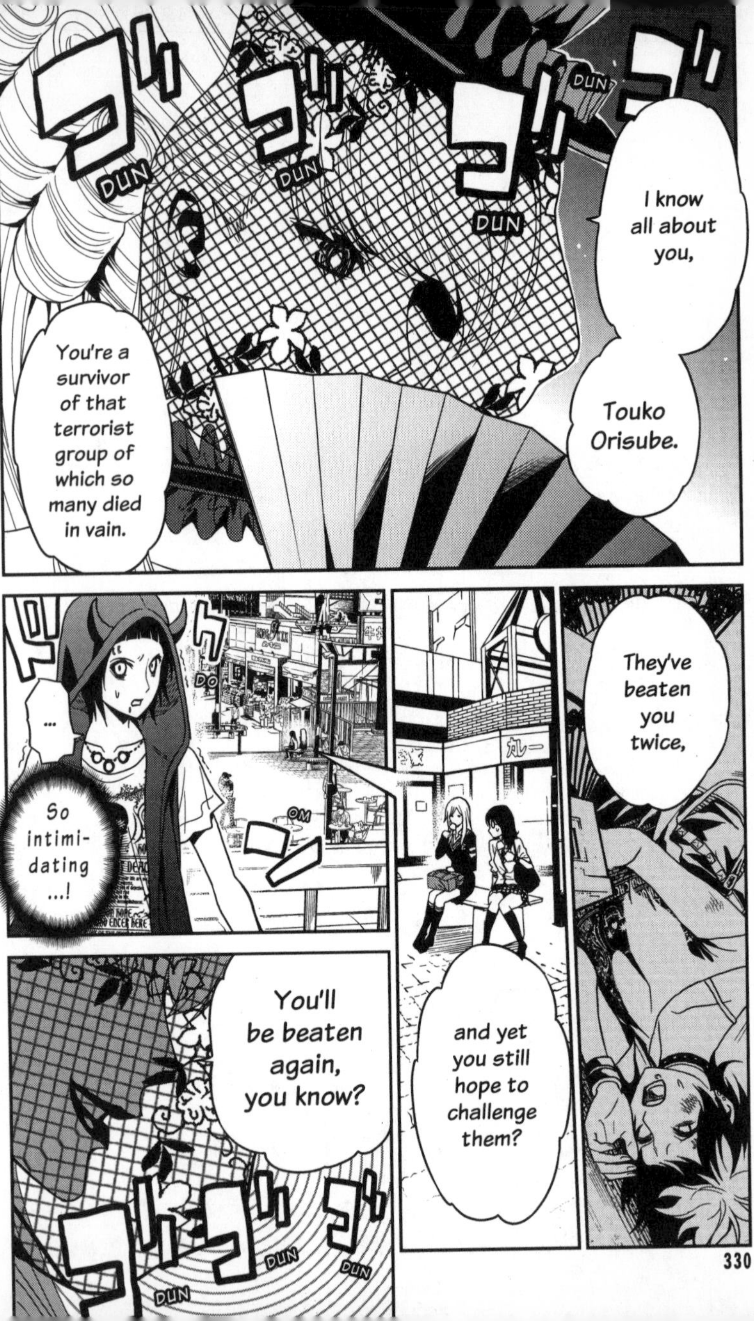
DUN
DUN
DUN
DUN
I know all about you,
Touko Orisube.
You're a survivor of that terrorist group of which so many died in vain.
They've beaten you twice,
and yet you still hope to challenge them?
DO
OM
...
So intimi-dating ...!
You'll be beaten again, you know?
DUN
DUN
DUN

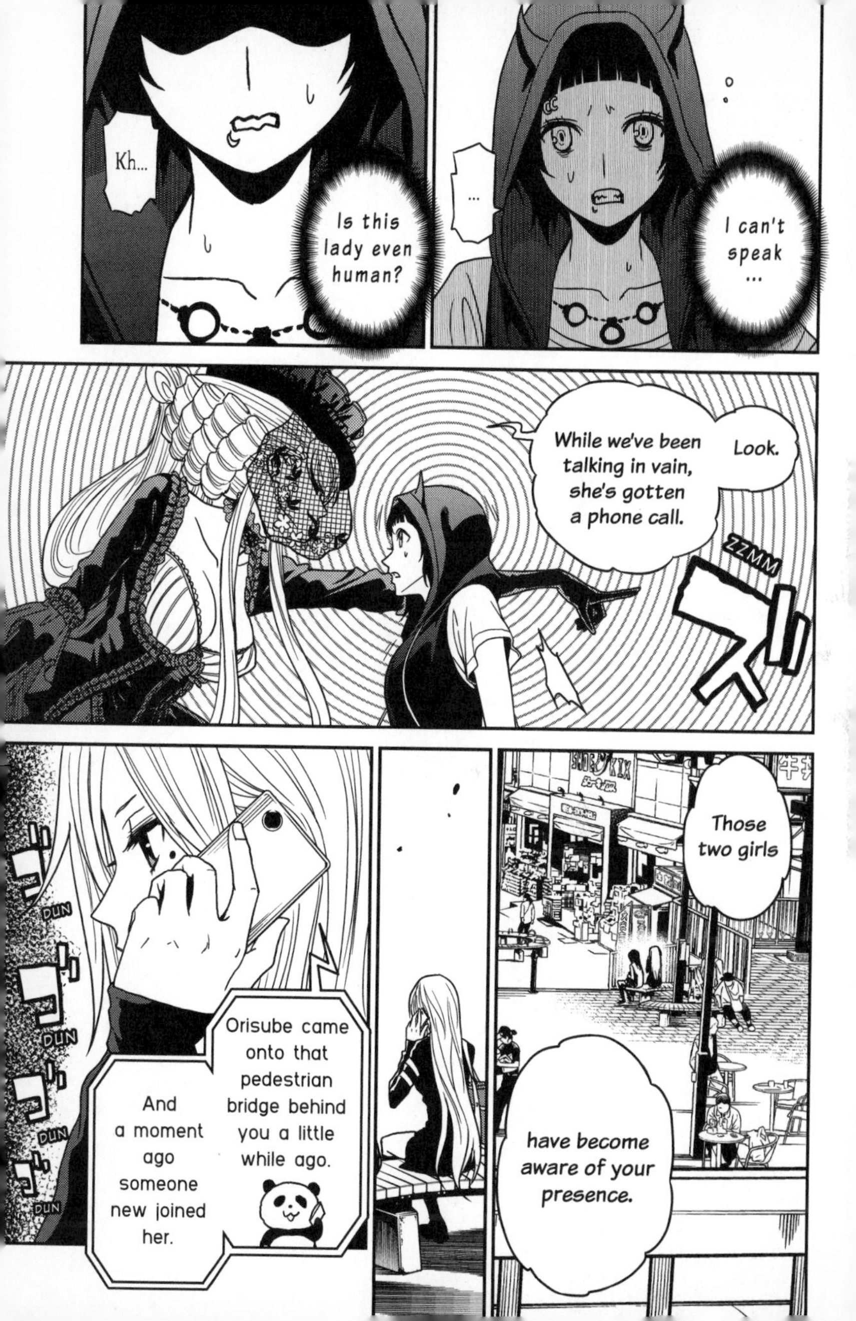
...
I can't speak ...
Kh...
Is this lady even human?
Look.
While we've been talking in vain, she's gotten a phone call.
ZZMM
Those two girls
have become aware of your presence.
Orisube came onto that pedestrian bridge behind you a little while ago.
And a moment ago someone new joined her.
DUN
DUN
DUN
DUN

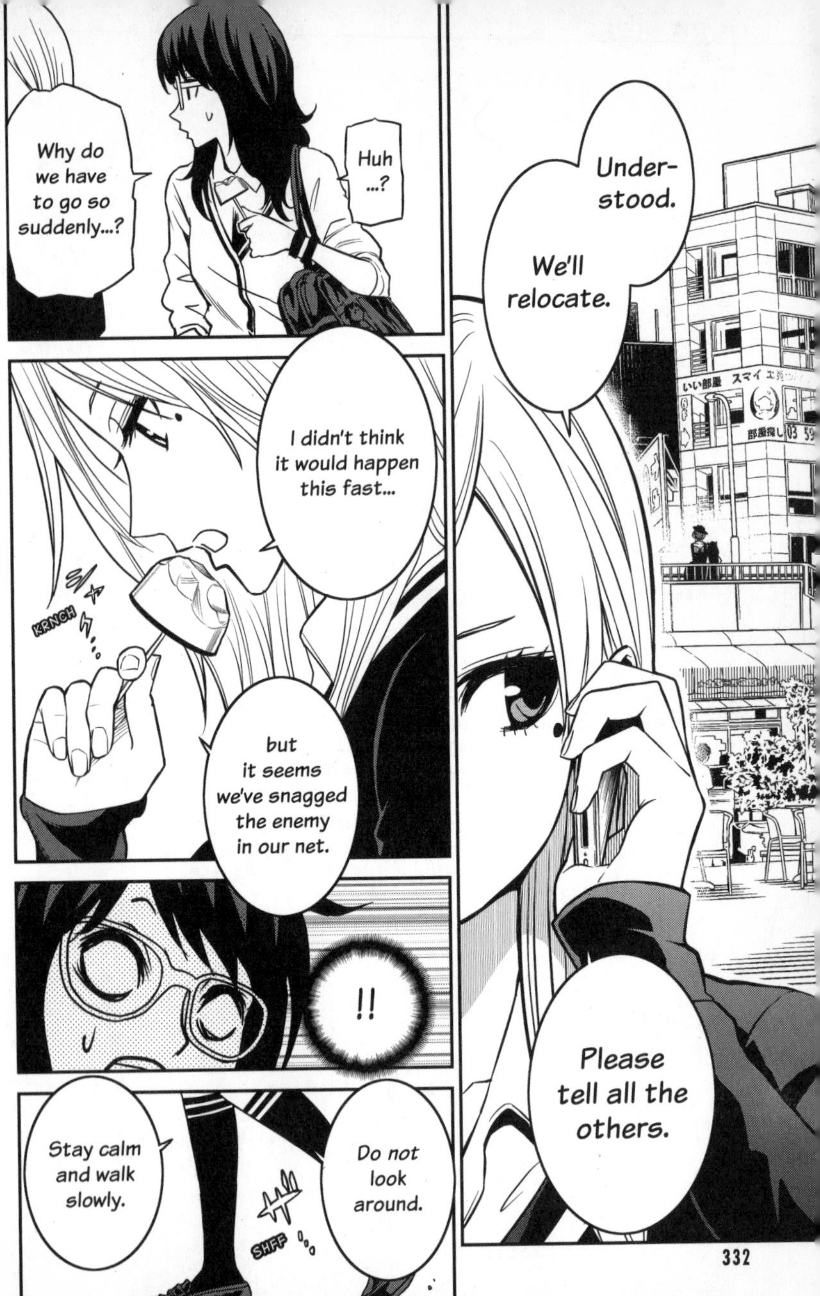

Under-stood.
We'll relocate.
いい部屋 スマイ
部屋探し
Please tell all the others.
Huh...?
Why do we have to go so suddenly...?
I didn't think it would happen this fast...
KRNCH
but it seems we've snagged the enemy in our net.
!!
Do not look around.
Stay calm and walk slowly.
SHFF

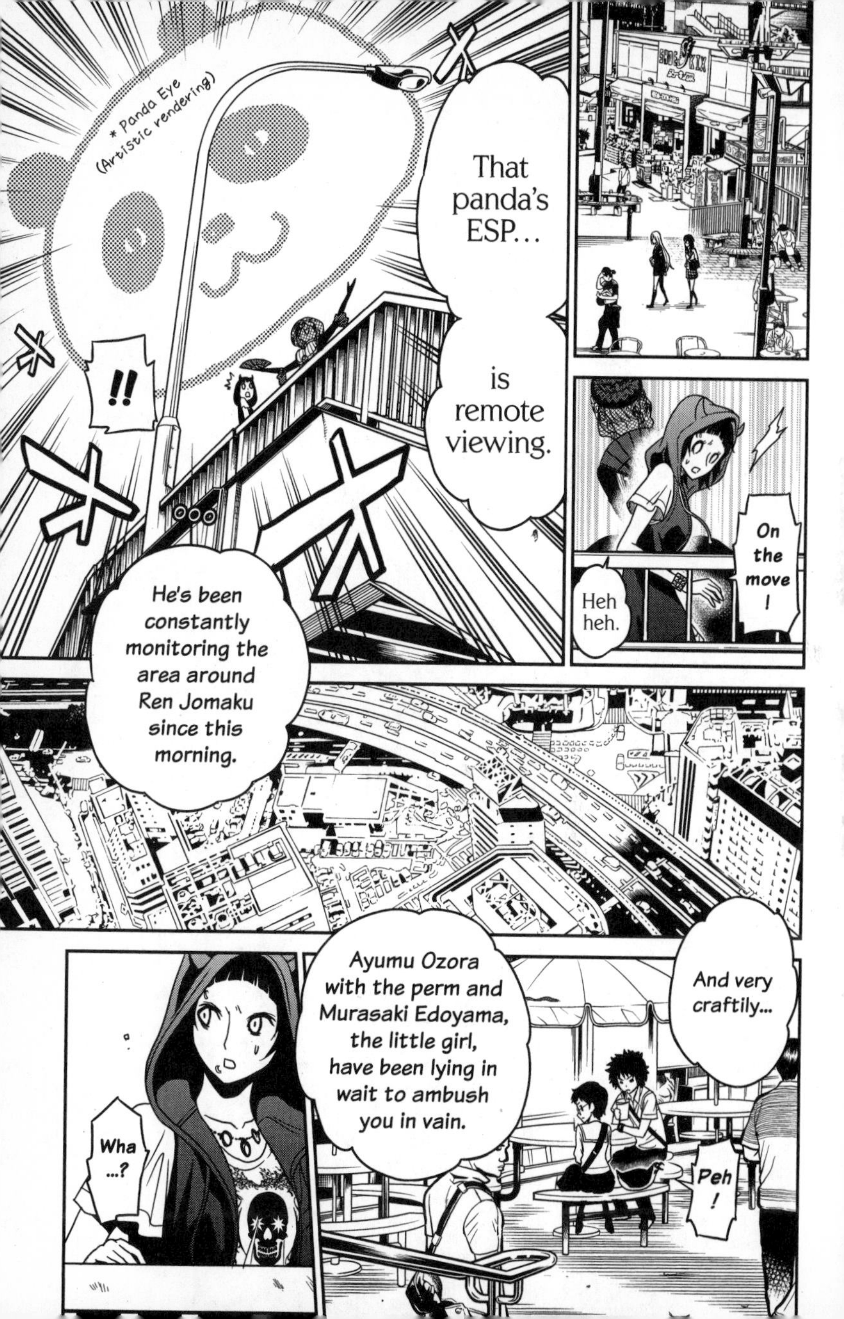
On the move!
Heh heh.
That panda's ESP…
is remote viewing.
* Panda Eye (Artistic rendering)
!!
He's been constantly monitoring the area around Ren Jomaku since this morning.
And very craftily...
Ayumu Ozora with the perm and Murasaki Edoyama, the little girl, have been lying in wait to ambush you in vain.
Peh!
Wha...?

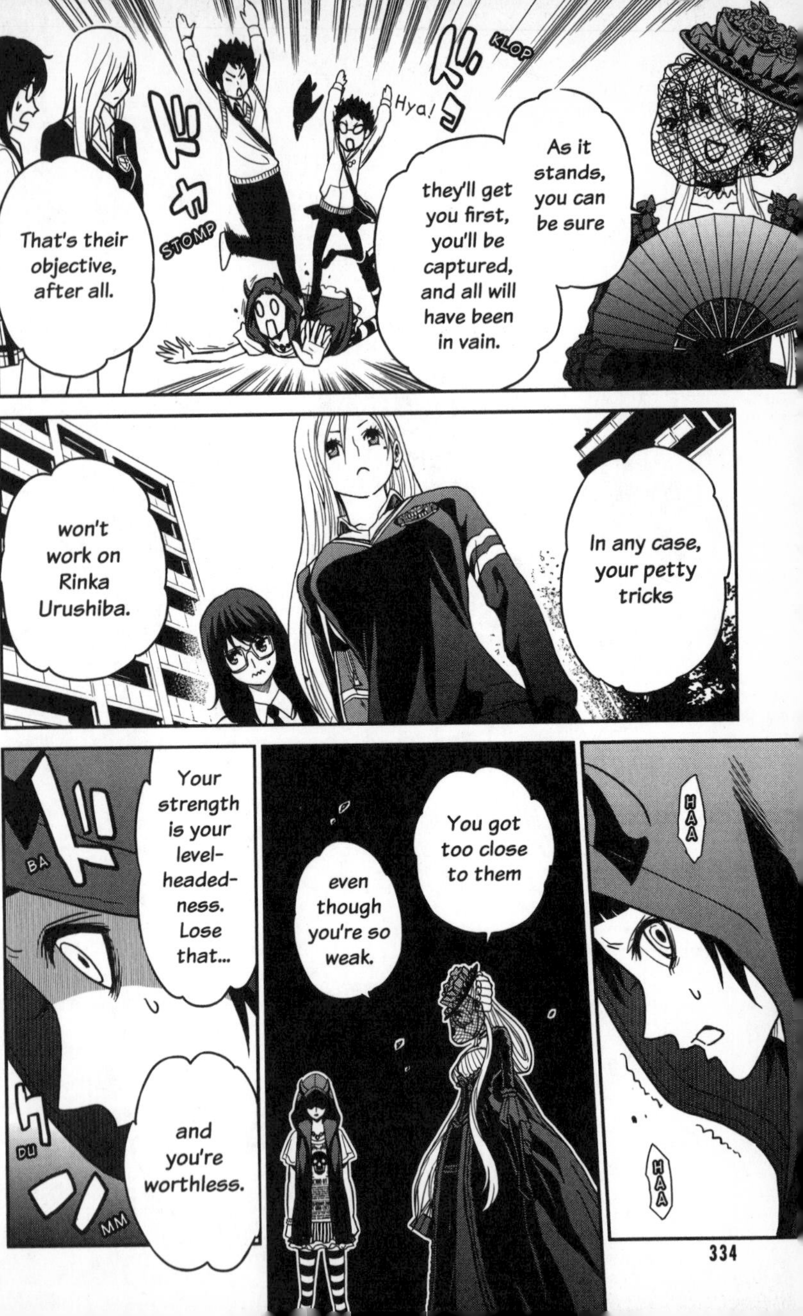
KLOP
Hya!
As it stands, you can be sure
they'll get you first, you'll be captured, and all will have been in vain.
STOMP
That's their objective, after all.
In any case, your petty tricks
won't work on Rinka Urushiba.
HAA
HAA
You got too close to them
even though you're so weak.
BA
Your strength is your level-headed-ness. Lose that...
and you're worthless.
DU
MM

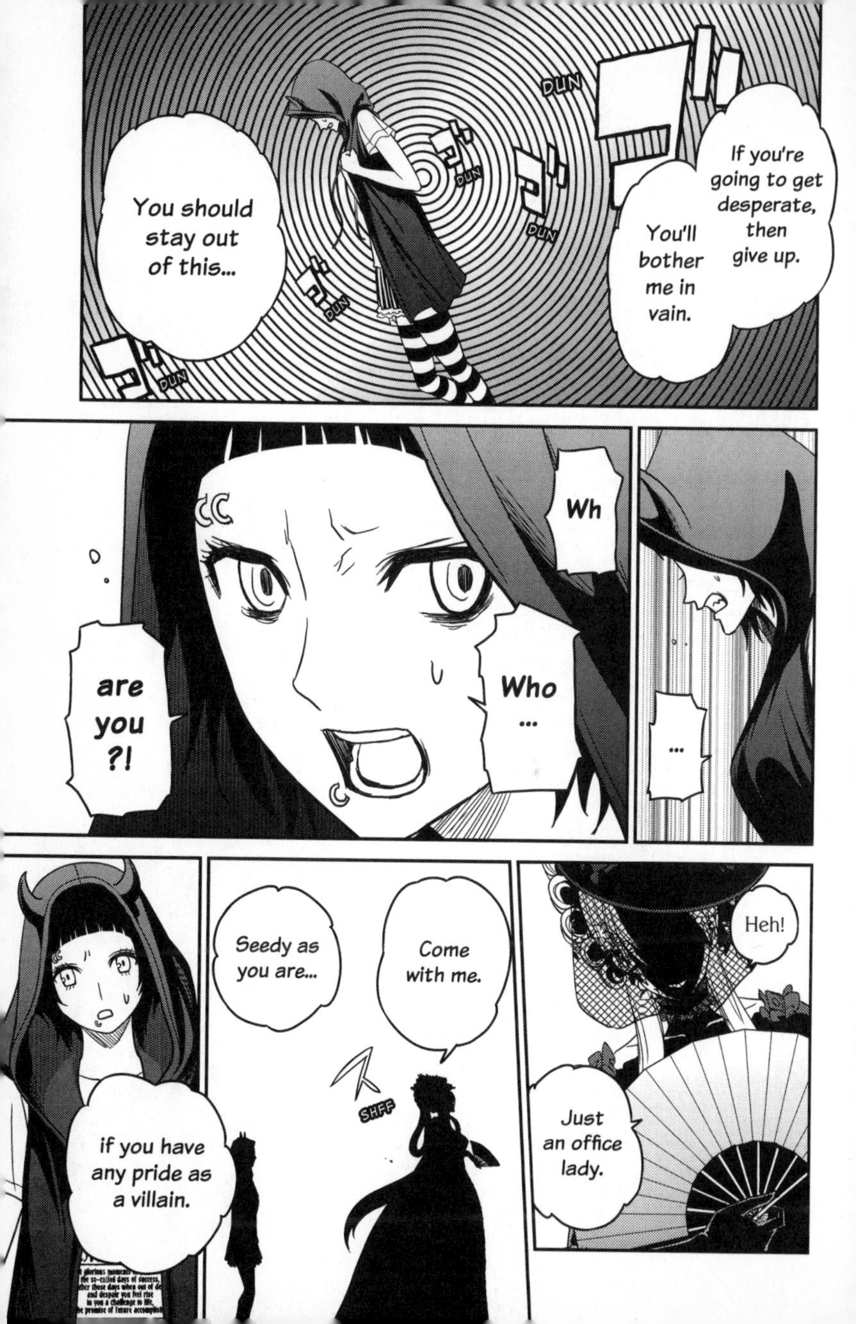
If you're going to get desperate, then give up.
You'll bother me in vain.
DUN
DUN
DUN
DUN
DUN
You should stay out of this...
...
Wh
Who ...
are you ?!
Heh!
Just an office lady.
Come with me.
Seedy as you are...
SHFF
if you have any pride as a villain.

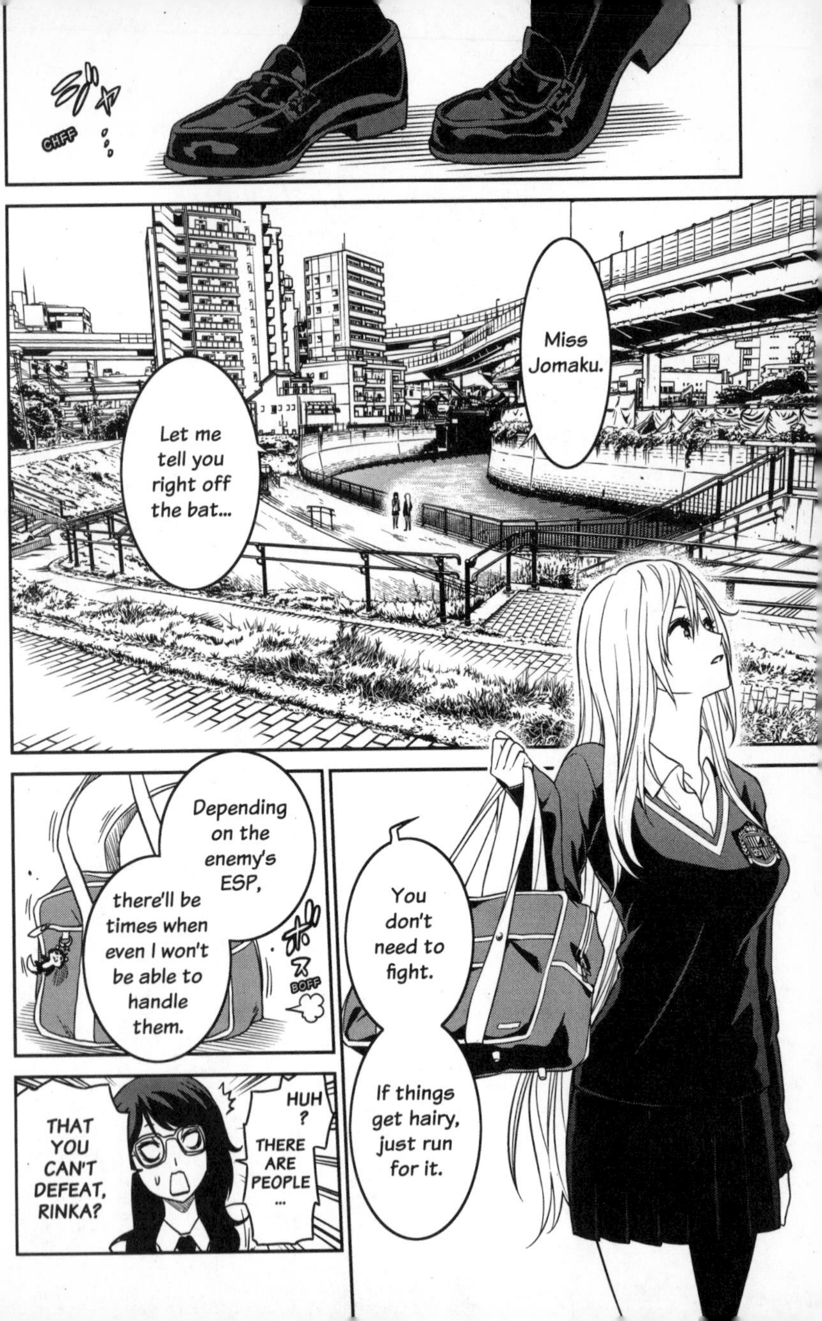
CHFF
Miss Jomaku.
Let me tell you right off the bat...
You don't need to fight.
If things get hairy, just run for it.
Depending on the enemy's ESP,
there'll be times when even I won't be able to handle them.
BOFF
HUH? THERE ARE PEOPLE ...
THAT YOU CAN'T DEFEAT, RINKA?

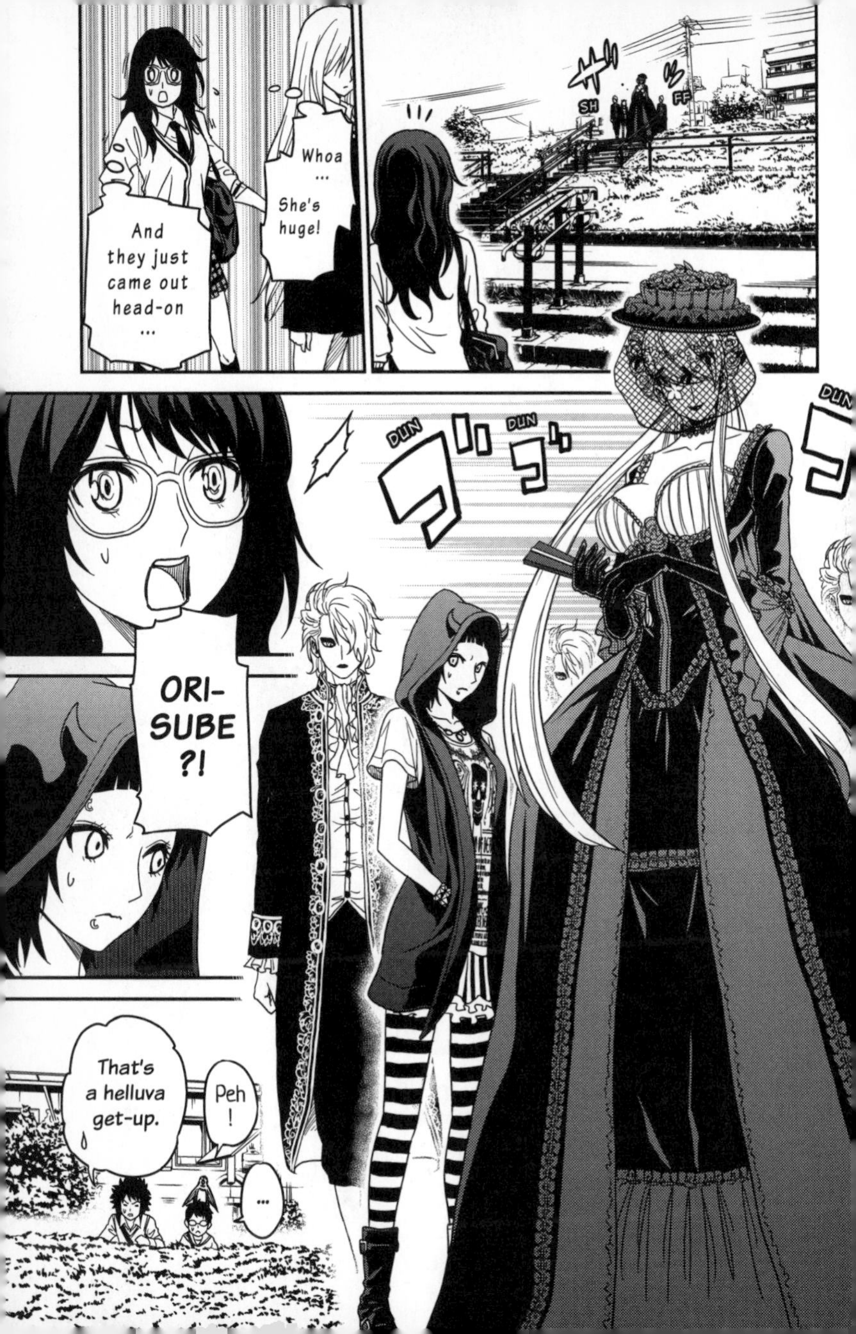
SH
FF
Whoa ... She's huge!
And they just came out head-on ...
DUN
DUN
DUN
ORI-SUBE ?!
That's a helluva get-up.
Peh !
...

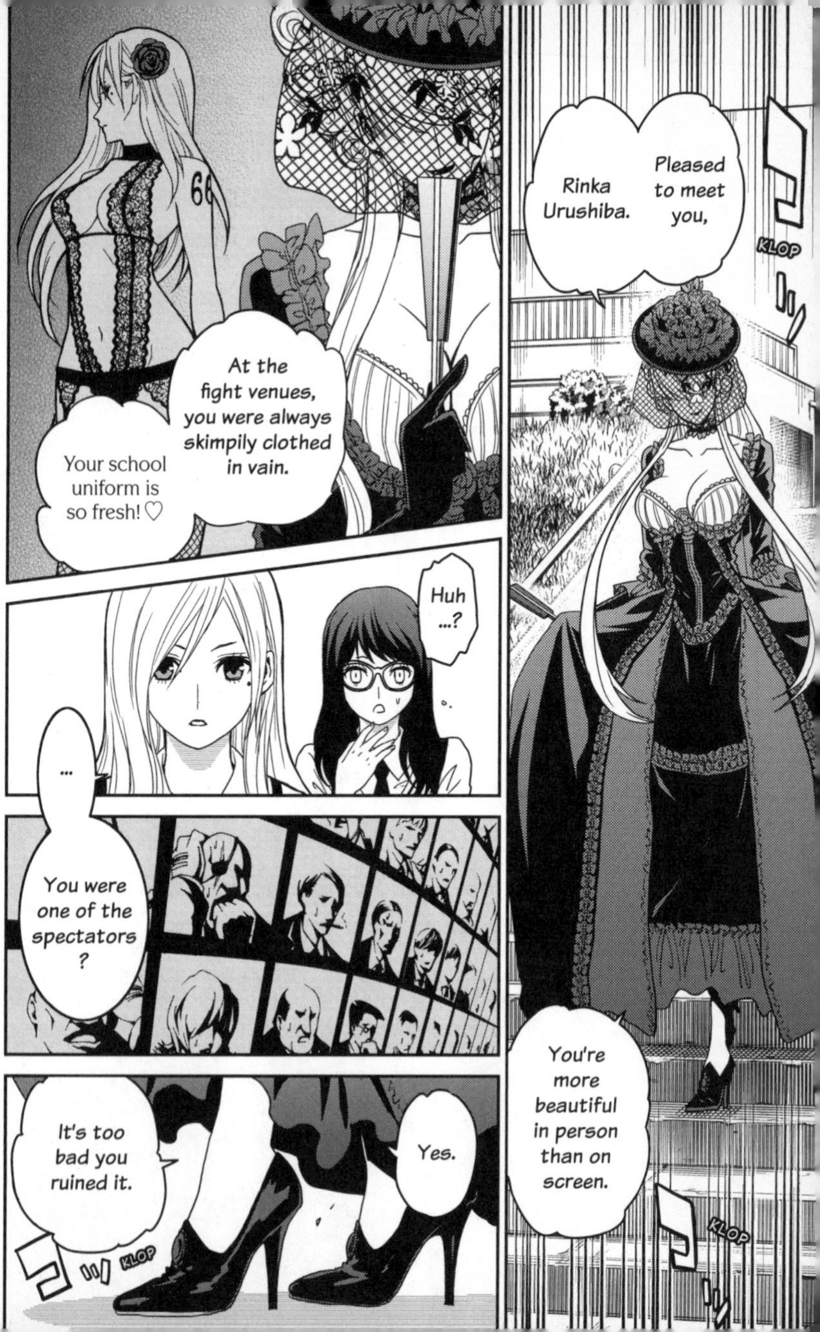
Pleased to meet you,
Rinka Urushiba.
KLOP
You're more beautiful in person than on screen.
KLOP
At the fight venues, you were always skimpily clothed in vain.
Your school uniform is so fresh! ♡
Huh ...?
...
You were one of the spectators ?
Yes.
It's too bad you ruined it.
KLOP

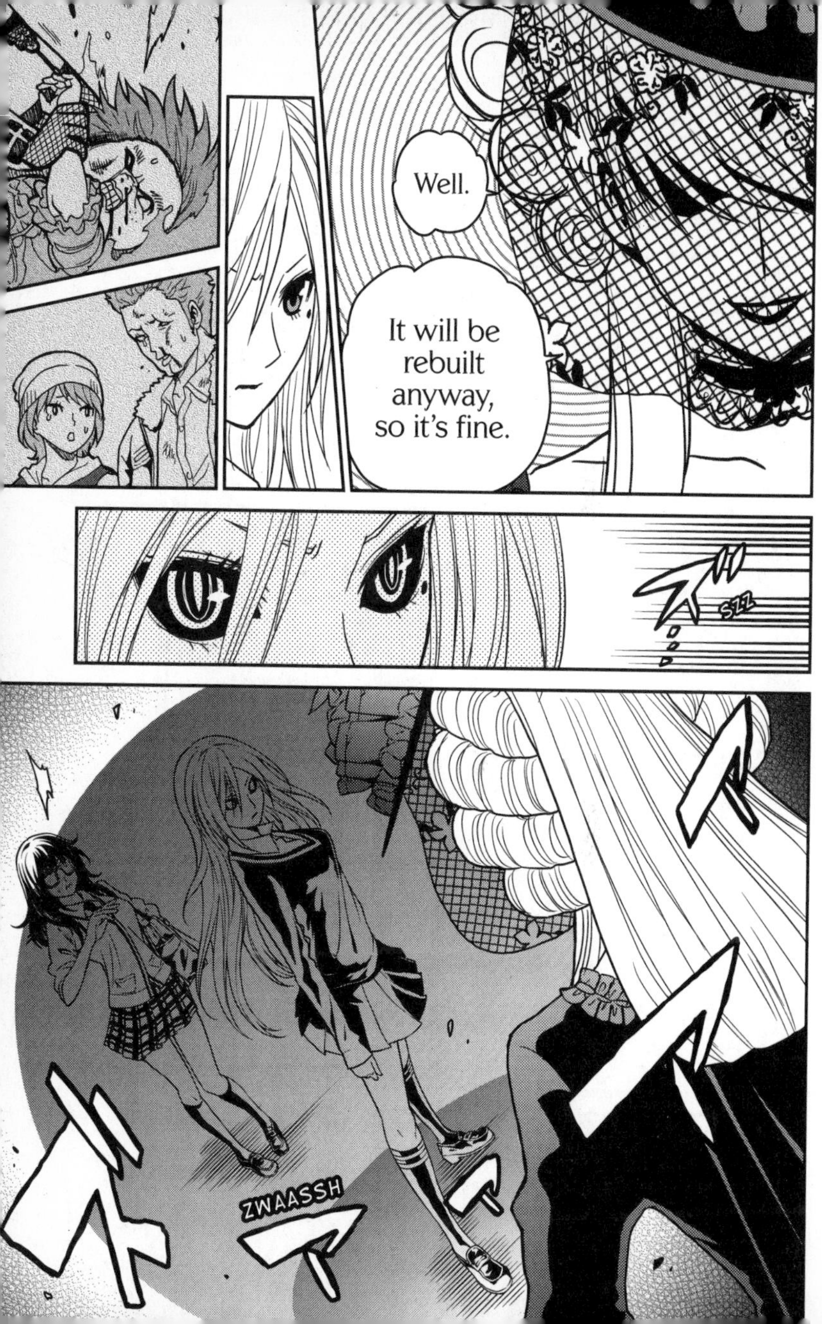
Well.
It will be rebuilt anyway, so it's fine.
SZZ
ZWAASSH

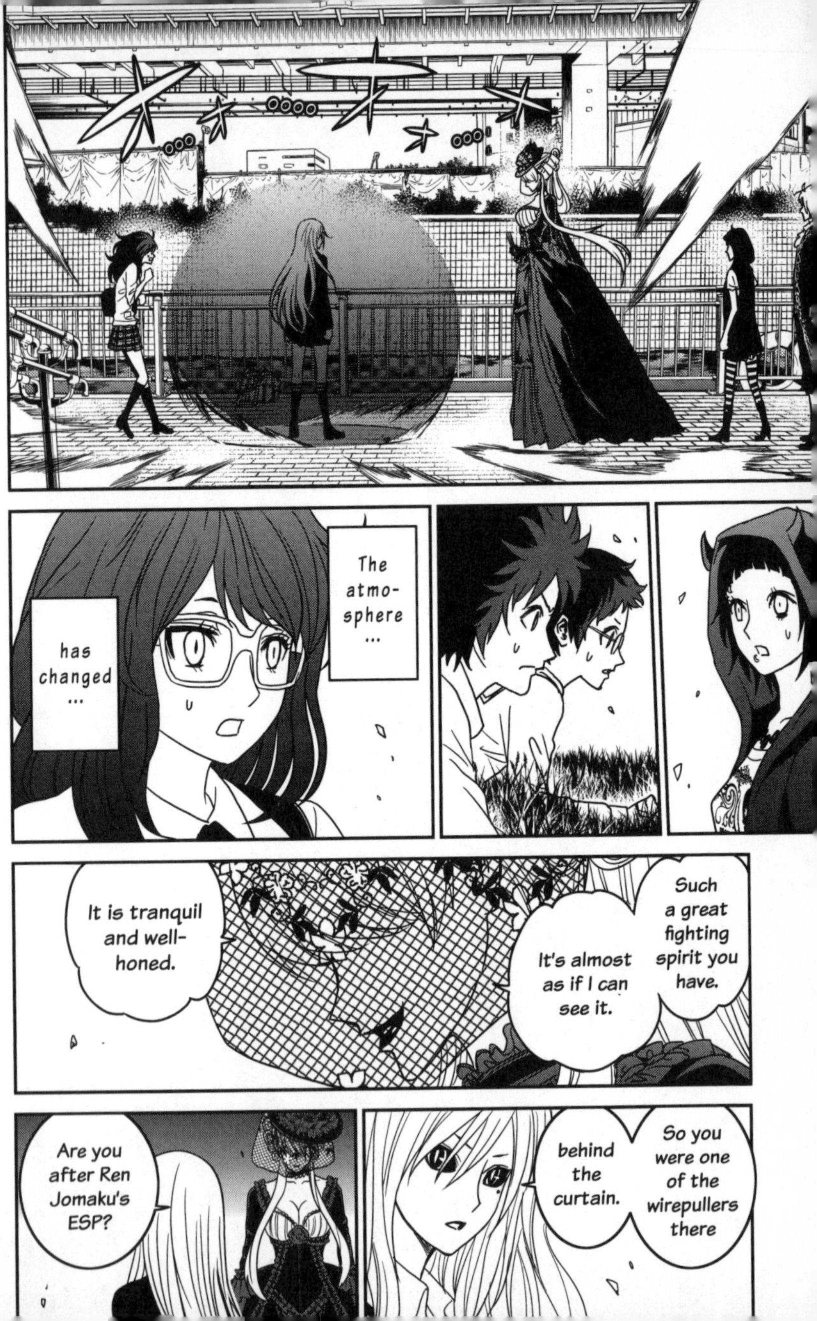
The atmosphere...
has changed...
Such a great fighting spirit you have.
It's almost as if I can see it.
It is tranquil and well-honed.
So you were one of the wirepullers there
behind the curtain.
Are you after Ren Jomaku's ESP?

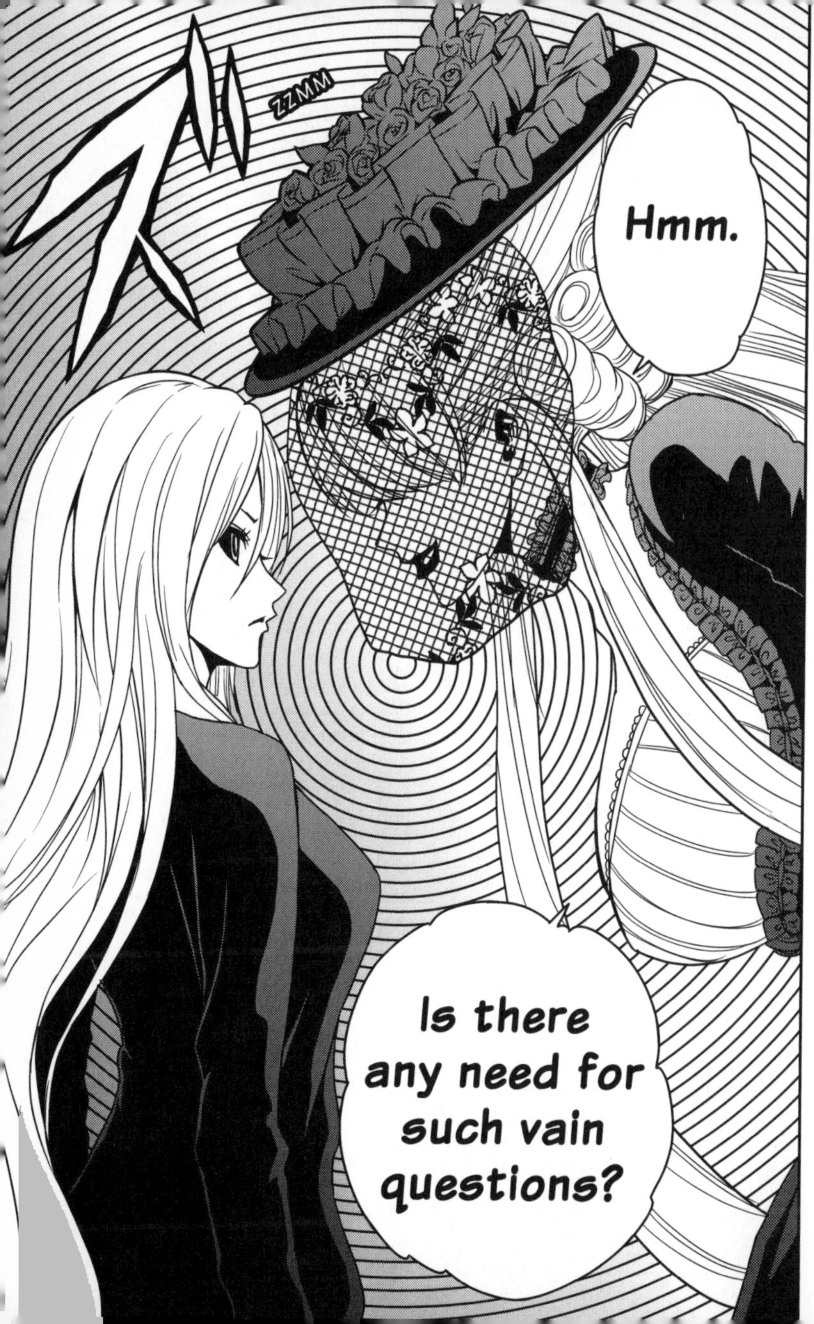
Hmm.
ZZMM
Is there any need for such vain questions?

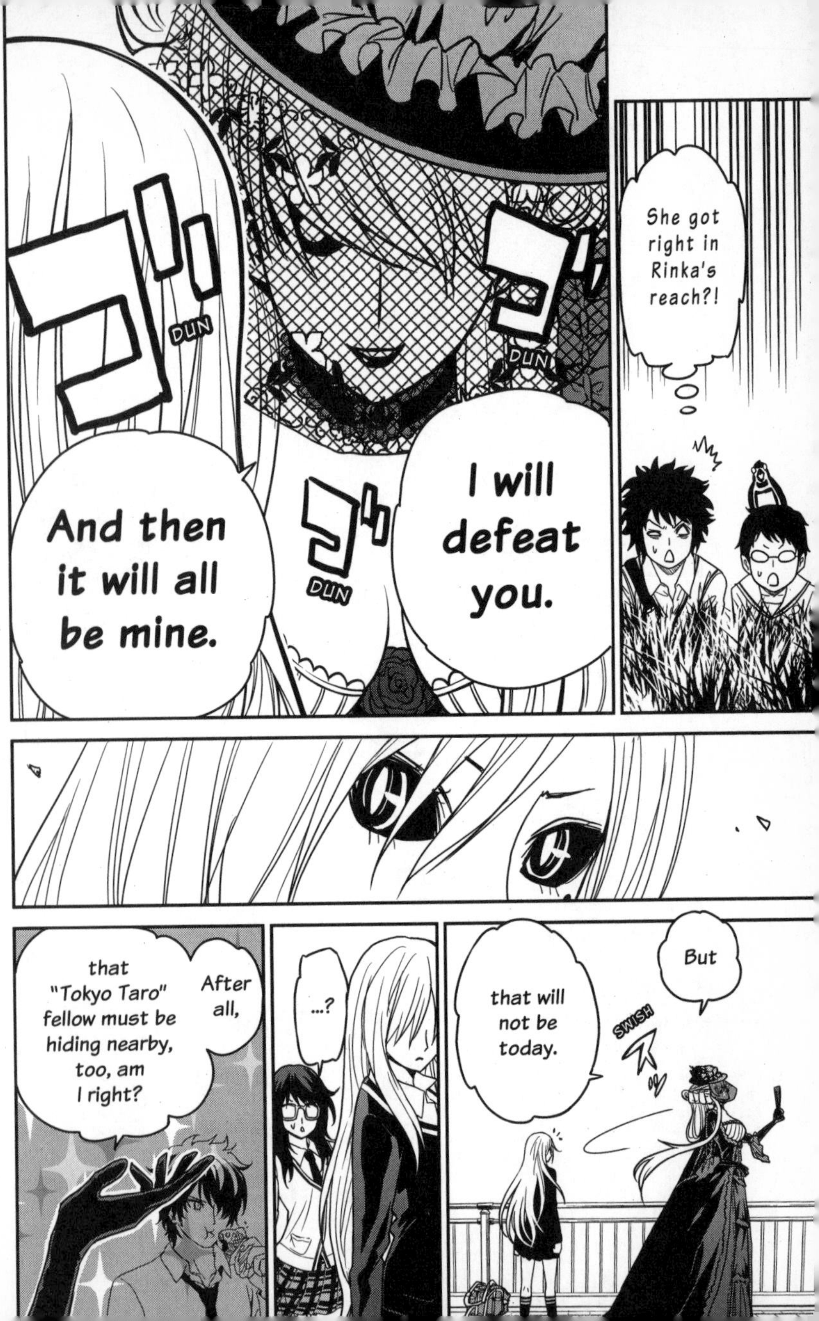
She got right in Rinka's reach?!
DUN
DUN
I will defeat you.
DUN
And then it will all be mine.
But
SWISH
that will not be today.
...?
After all,
that "Tokyo Taro" fellow must be hiding nearby, too, am I right?

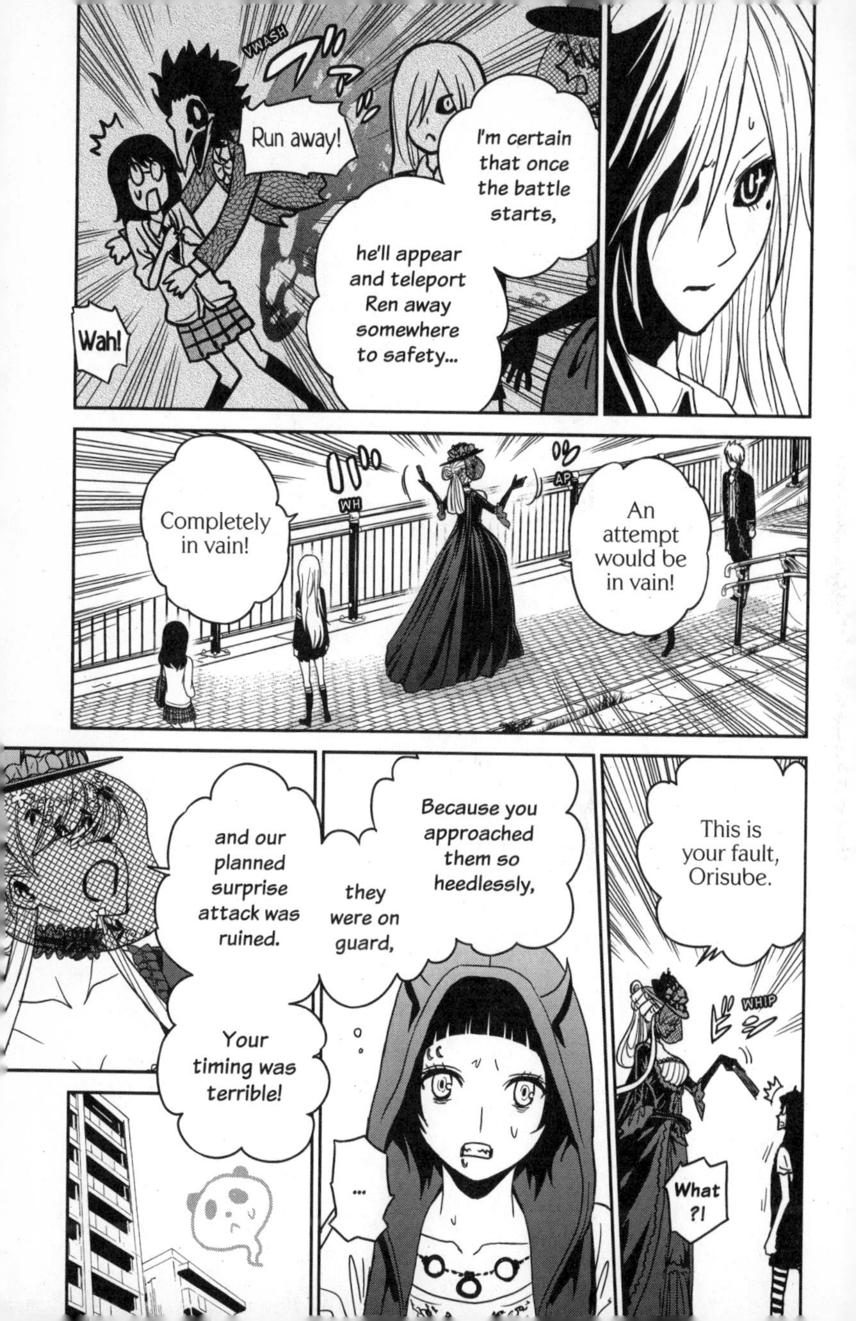
VWASH
I'm certain that once the battle starts,
Run away!
he'll appear and teleport Ren away somewhere to safety...
Wah!
An attempt would be in vain!
AP
WH
Completely in vain!
This is your fault, Orisube.
WHIP
What ?!
Because you approached them so heedlessly,
they were on guard,
and our planned surprise attack was ruined.
Your timing was terrible!
...

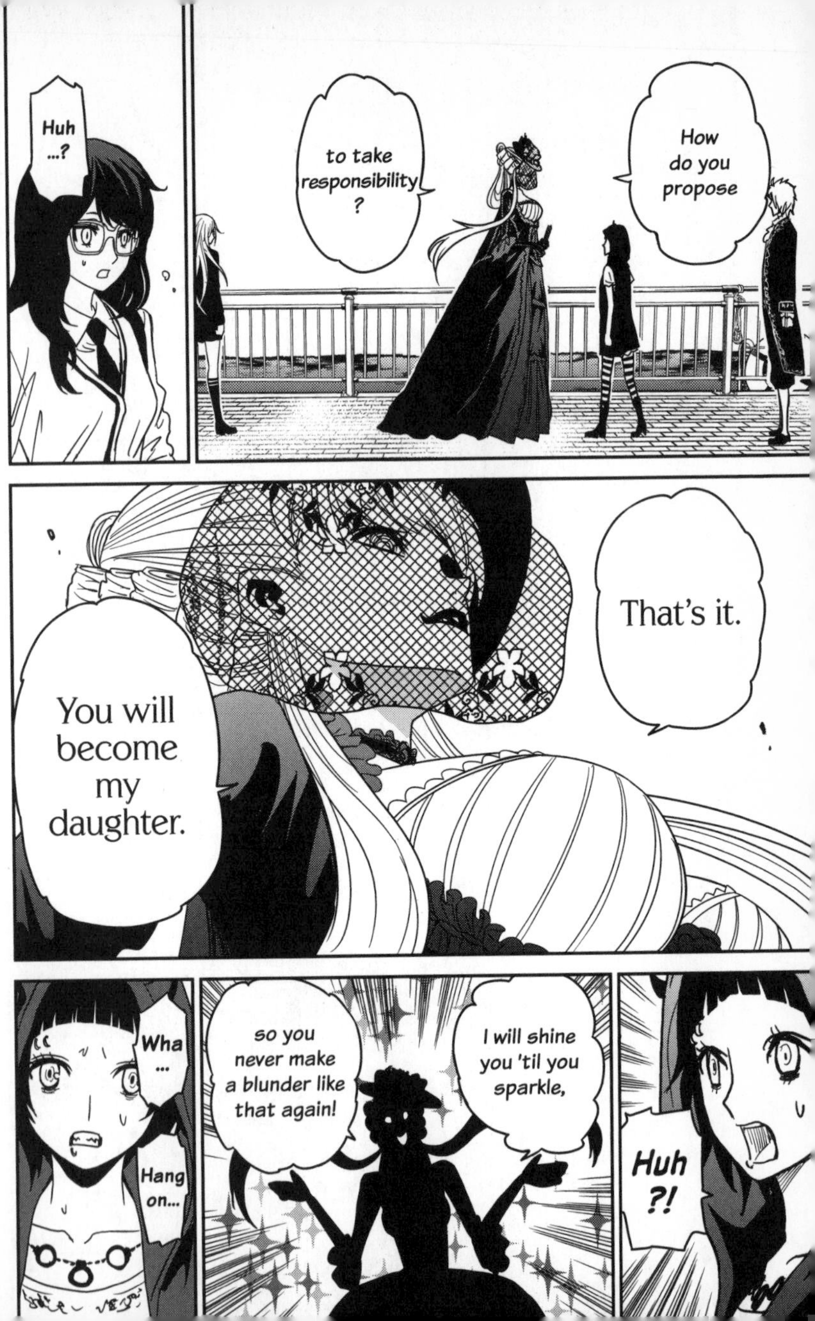
How do you propose
to take responsibility?
Huh ...?
That's it.
You will become my daughter.
Huh ?!
I will shine you 'til you sparkle,
so you never make a blunder like that again!
Wha ...
Hang on...

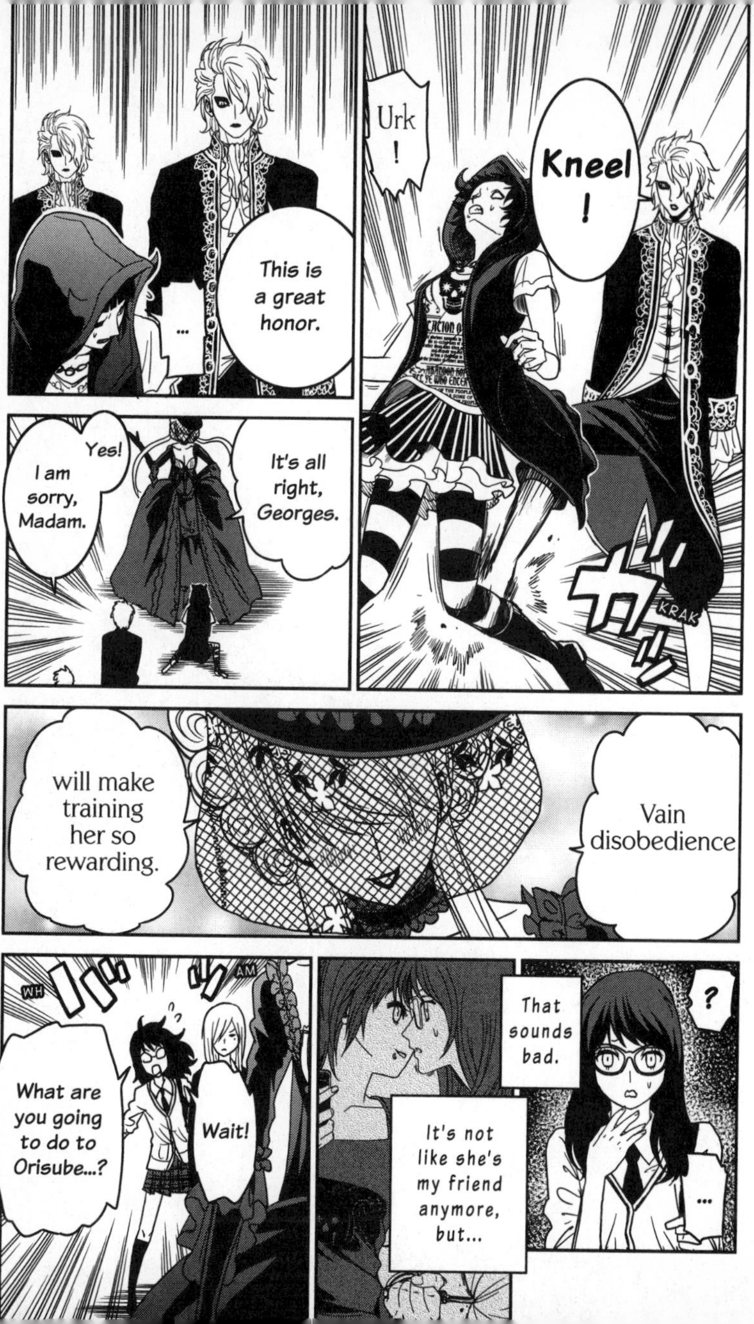

Kneel !
Urk !
KRAK
This is a great honor.
...
It's all right, Georges.
Yes! I am sorry, Madam.
Vain disobedience
will make training her so rewarding.
?
That sounds bad.
...
It's not like she's my friend anymore, but...
WH AM
Wait!
What are you going to do to Orisube...?

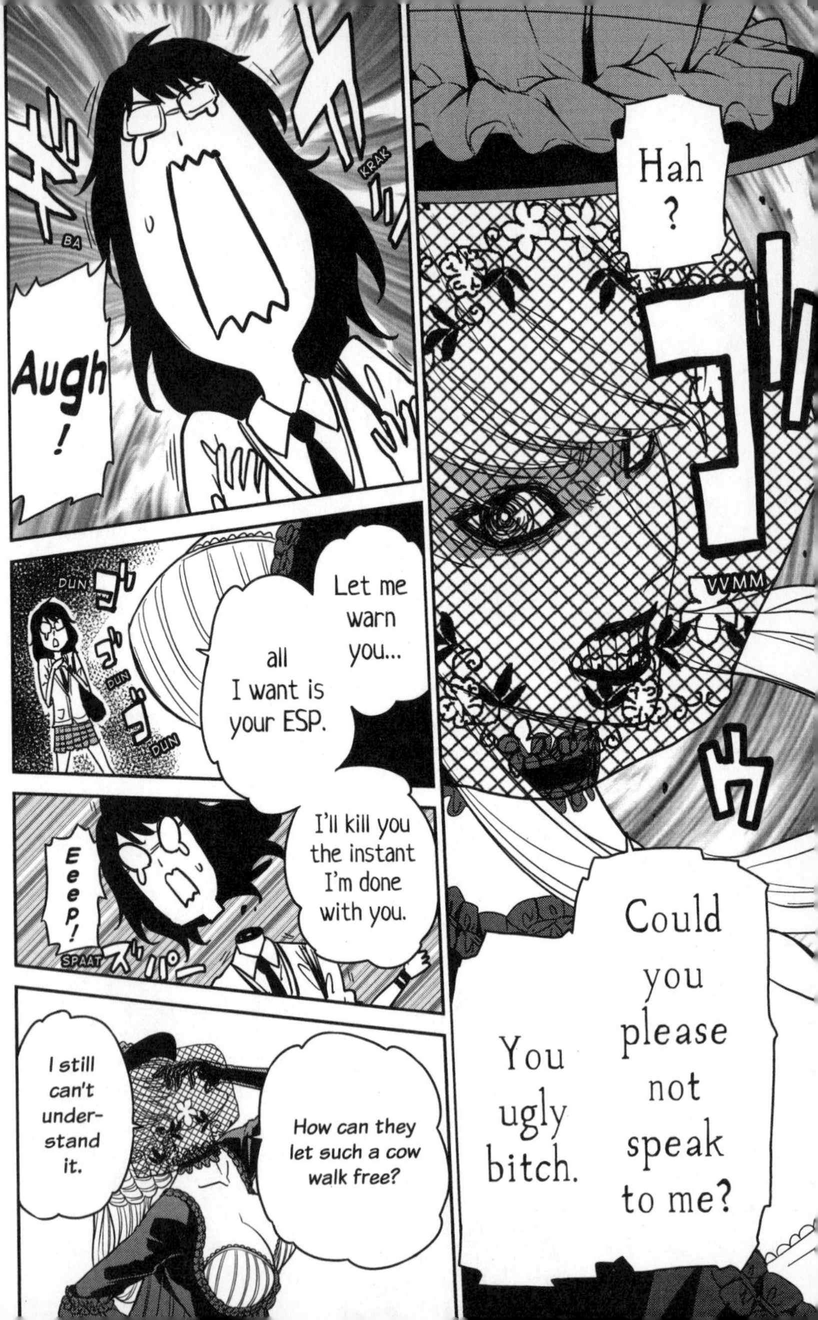
Hah?
VVMM
Could you please not speak to me?
You ugly bitch.
KRAK
BA
Augh!
DUN
DUN
DUN
Let me warn you...
all I want is your ESP.
I'll kill you the instant I'm done with you.
Eeeep!
SPAAT
How can they let such a cow walk free?
I still can't under-stand it.

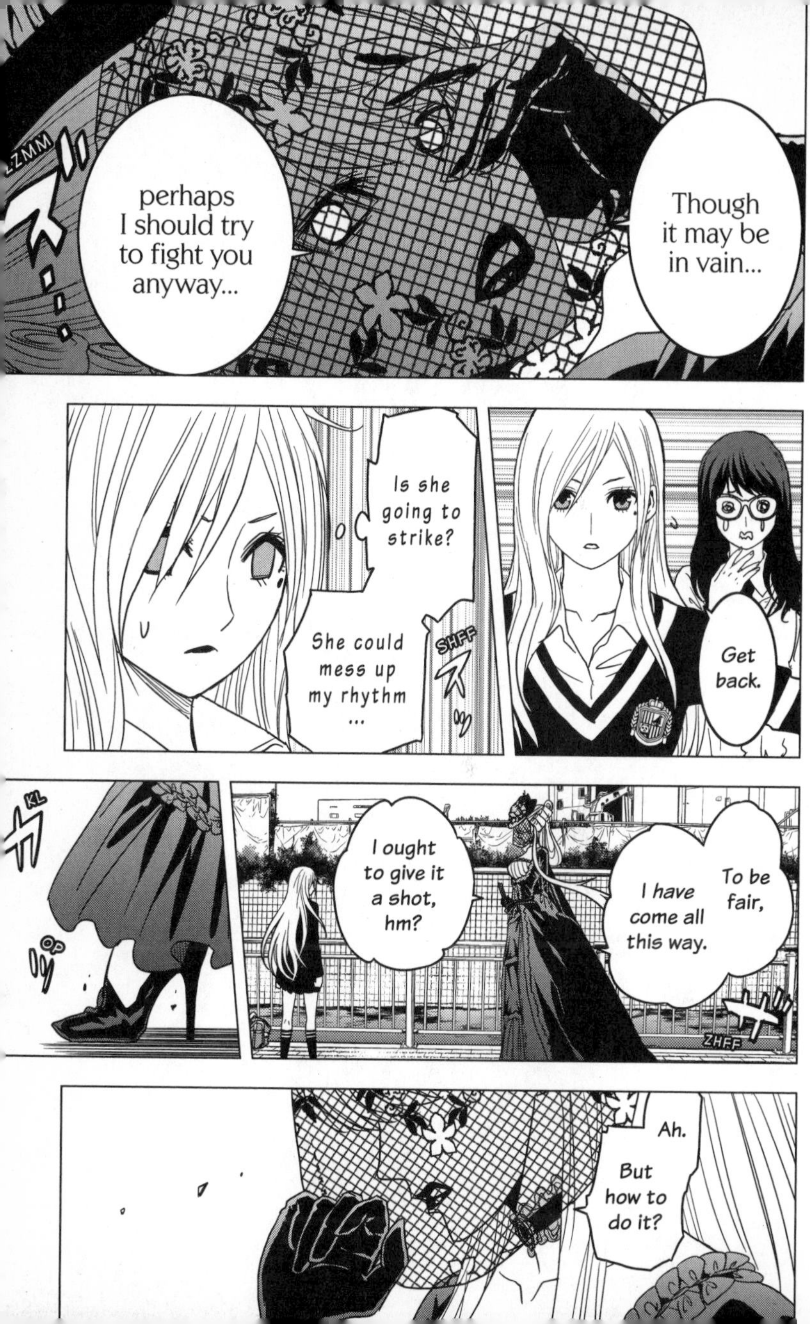
Though it may be in vain...
perhaps I should try to fight you anyway...
ZMM
Get back.
Is she going to strike?
SHFF
She could mess up my rhythm ...
To be fair,
I have come all this way.
I ought to give it a shot, hm?
ZHFF
KL
OP
Ah.
But how to do it?

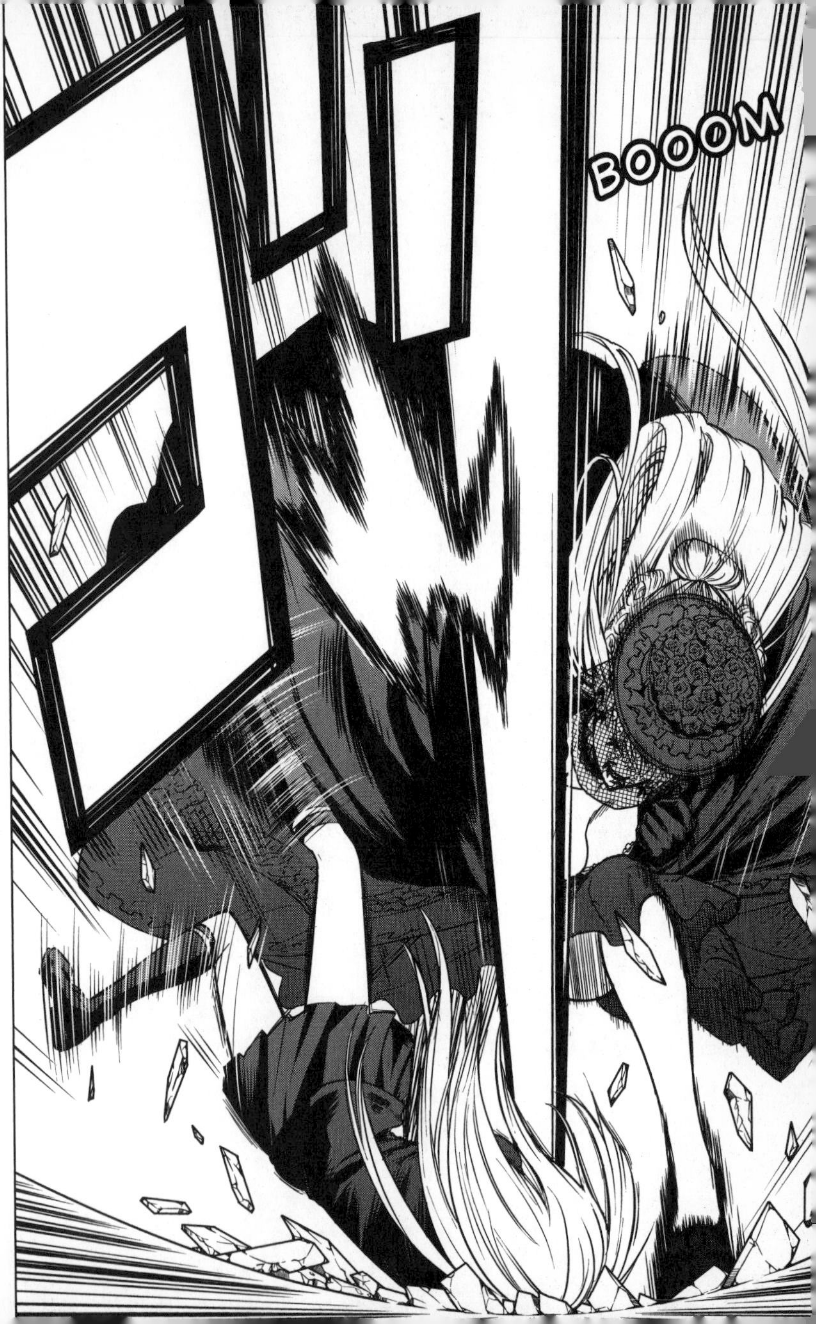
BOOOM

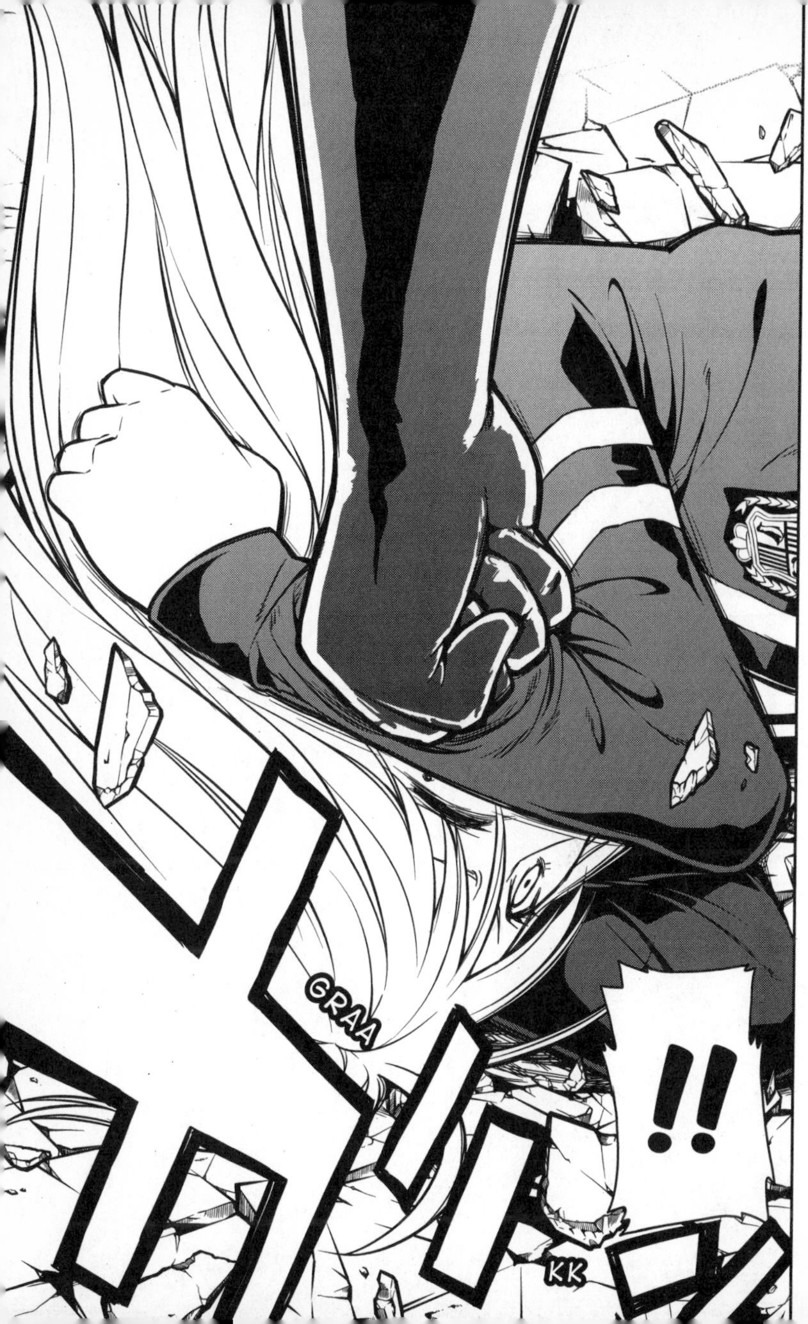
!!
GRAA
KK

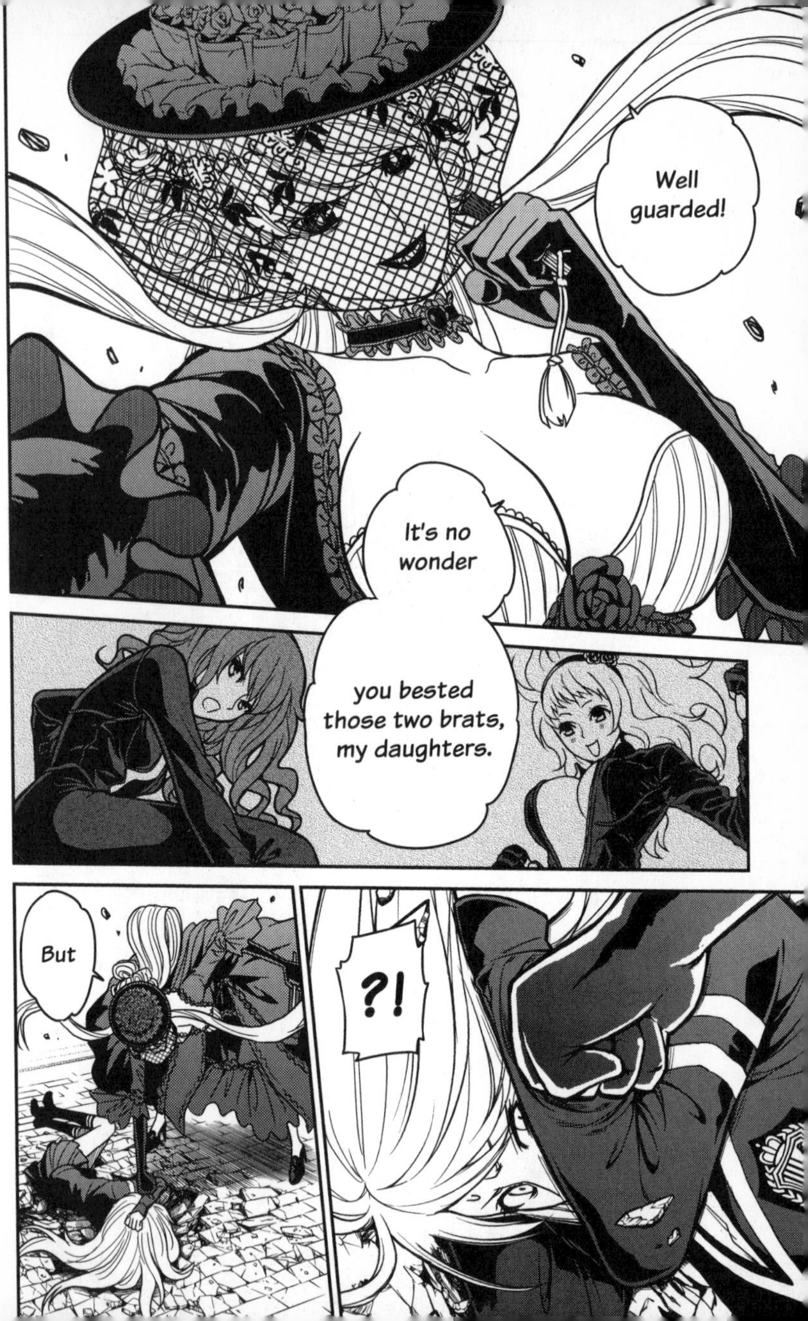
Well guarded!
It's no wonder
you bested those two brats, my daughters.
?!
But

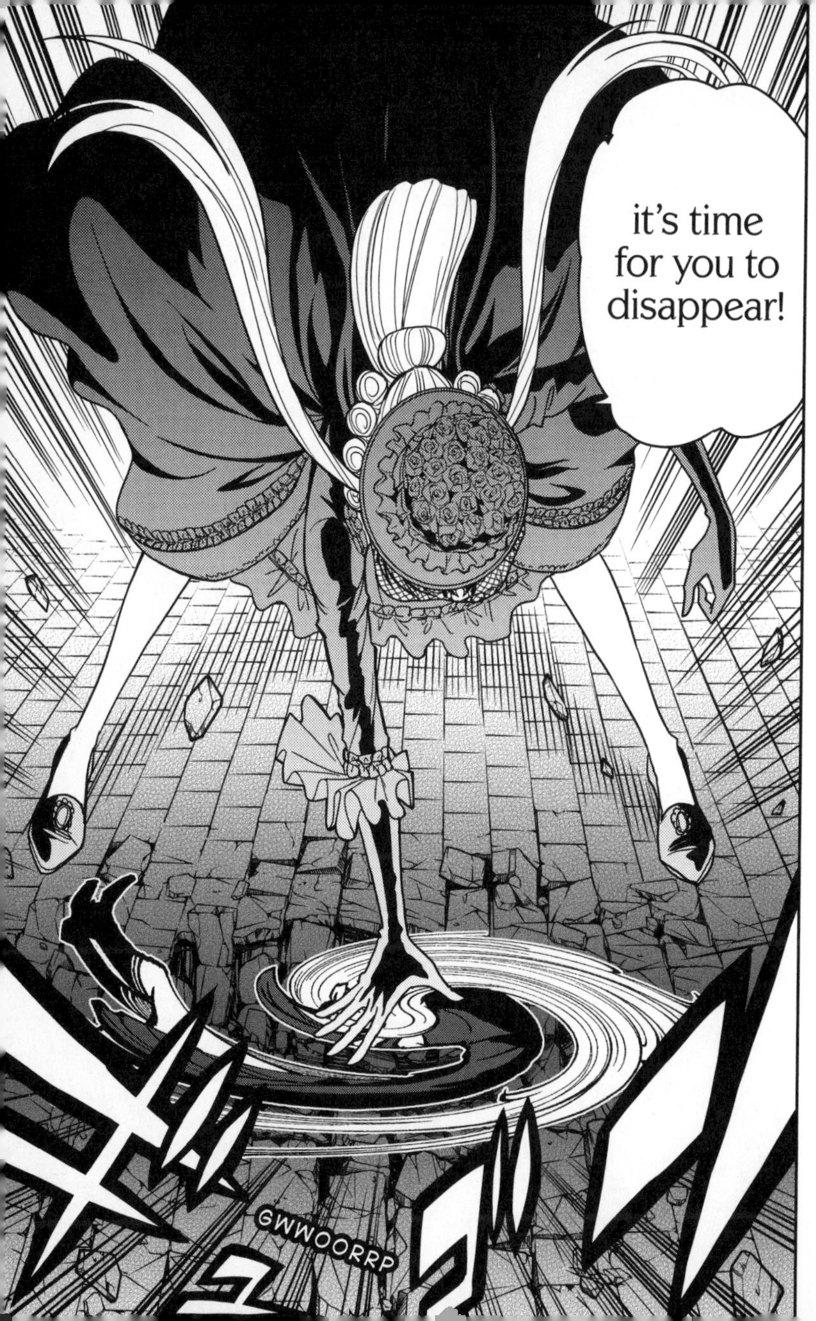
it's time for you to disappear!
GWWOORRP

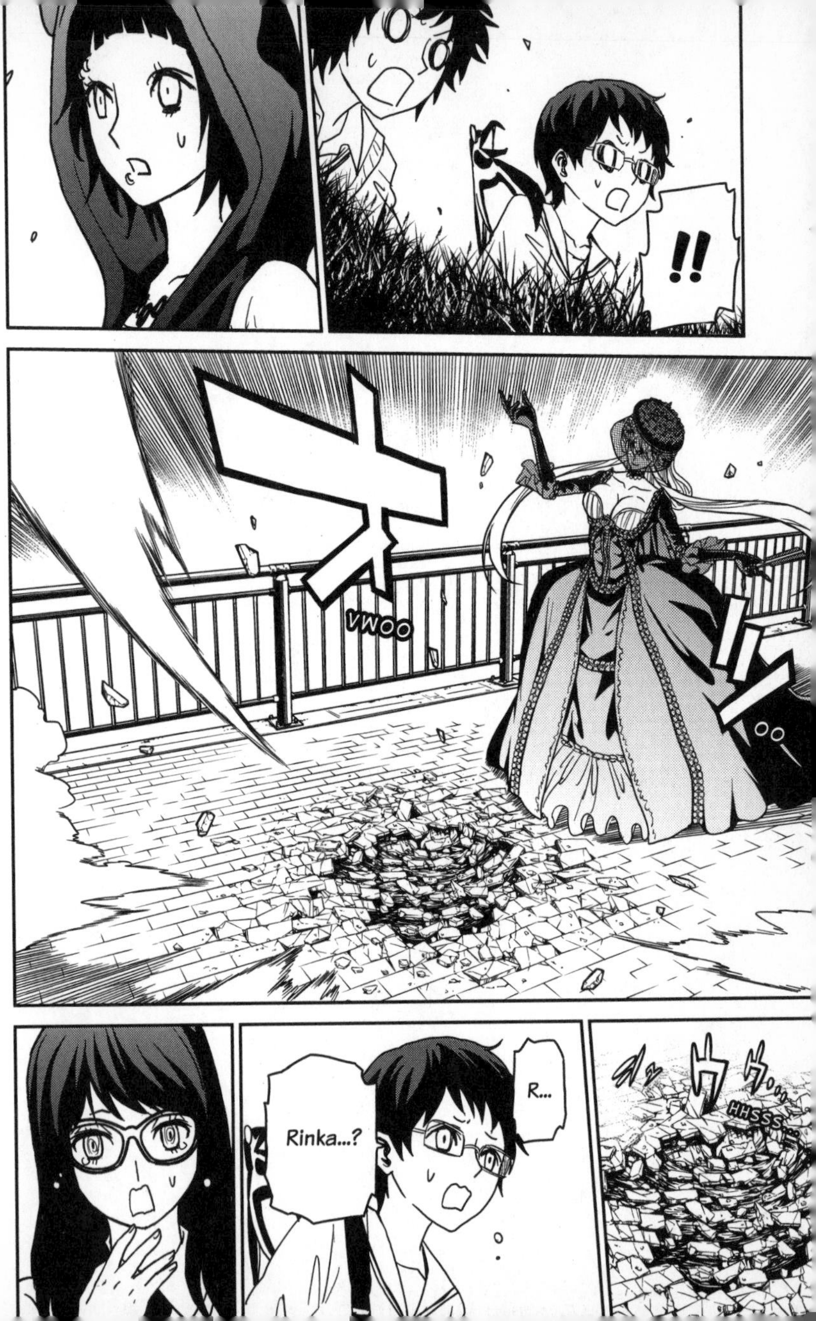
!!
VWOO
HHSSS...
R...
Rinka...?

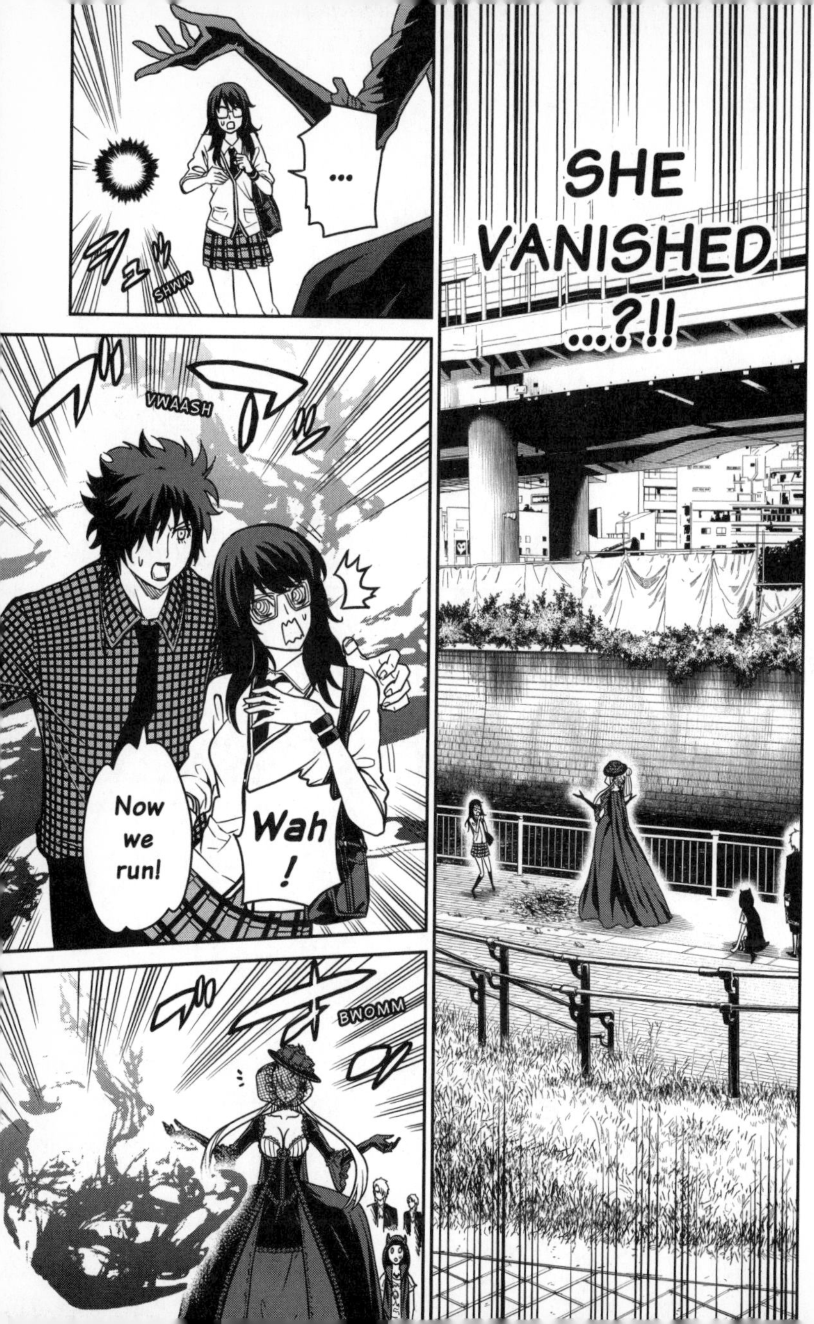
SHE VANISHED ...?!!
...
SHWW
VWAASH
Wah!
Now we run!
BWOMM

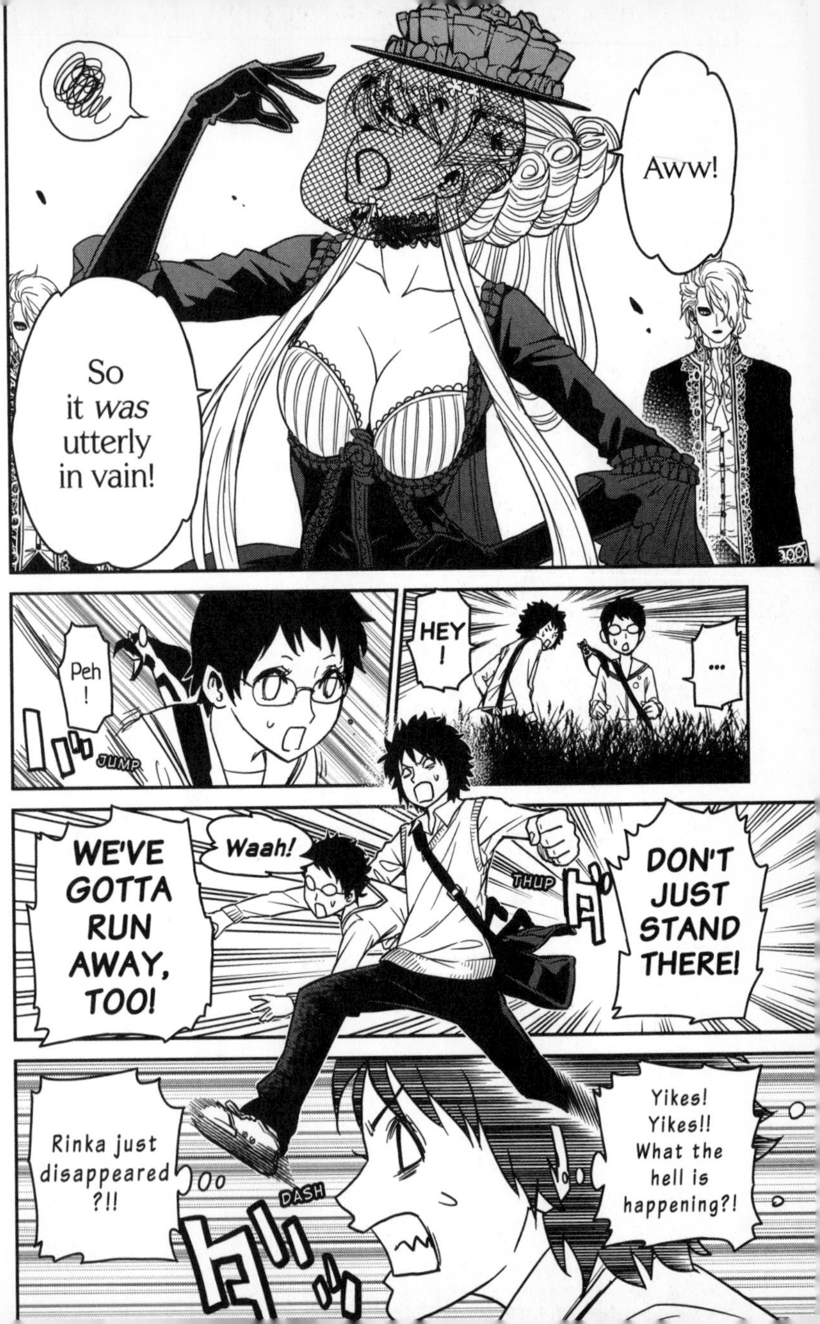
Aww!
So it *was* utterly in vain!
...
HEY!
Peh!
JUMP
DON'T JUST STAND THERE!
THUP
Waah!
WE'VE GOTTA RUN AWAY, TOO!
Yikes! Yikes!! What the hell is happening?!
DASH
Rinka just disappeared?!!

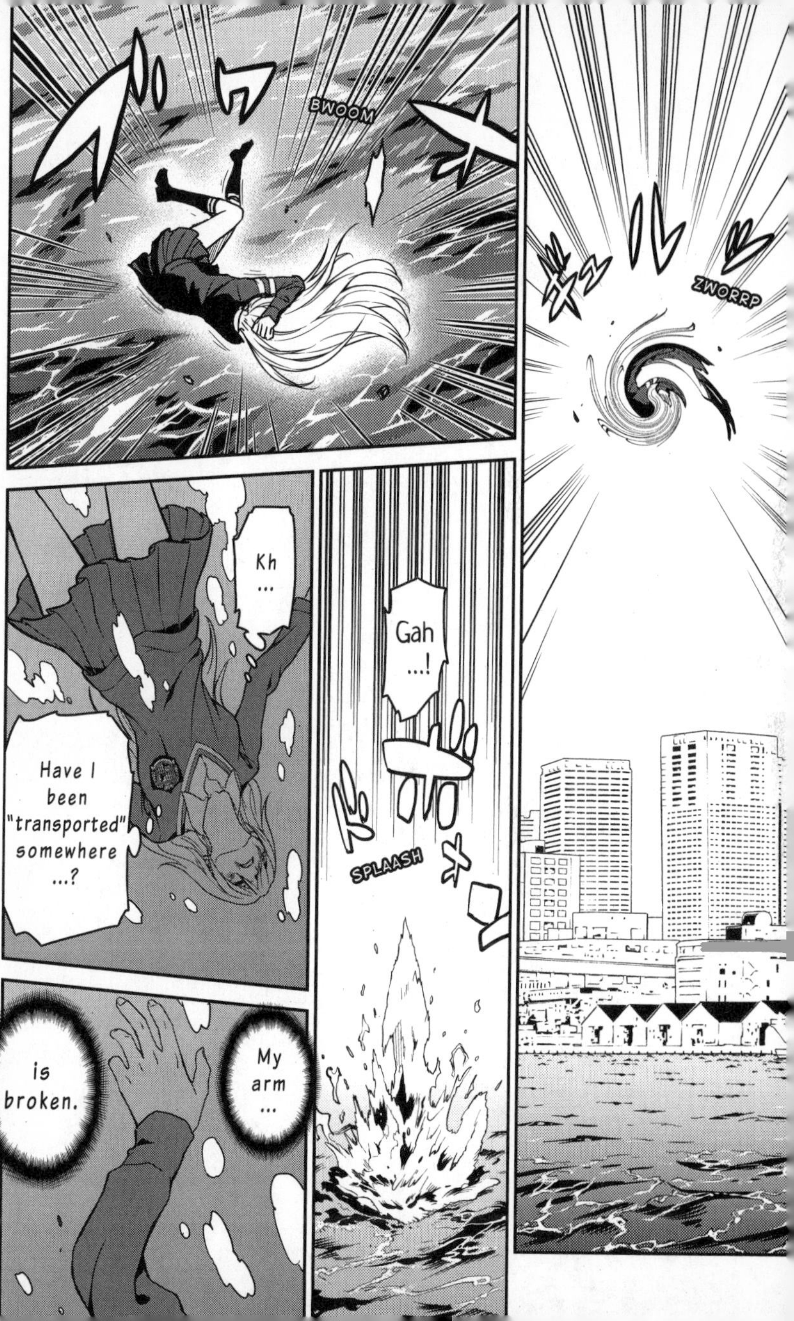
ZWORRP
BWOOM
Gah ...!
SPLAASH
Kh ...
Have I been "transported" somewhere ...?
My arm ...
is broken.

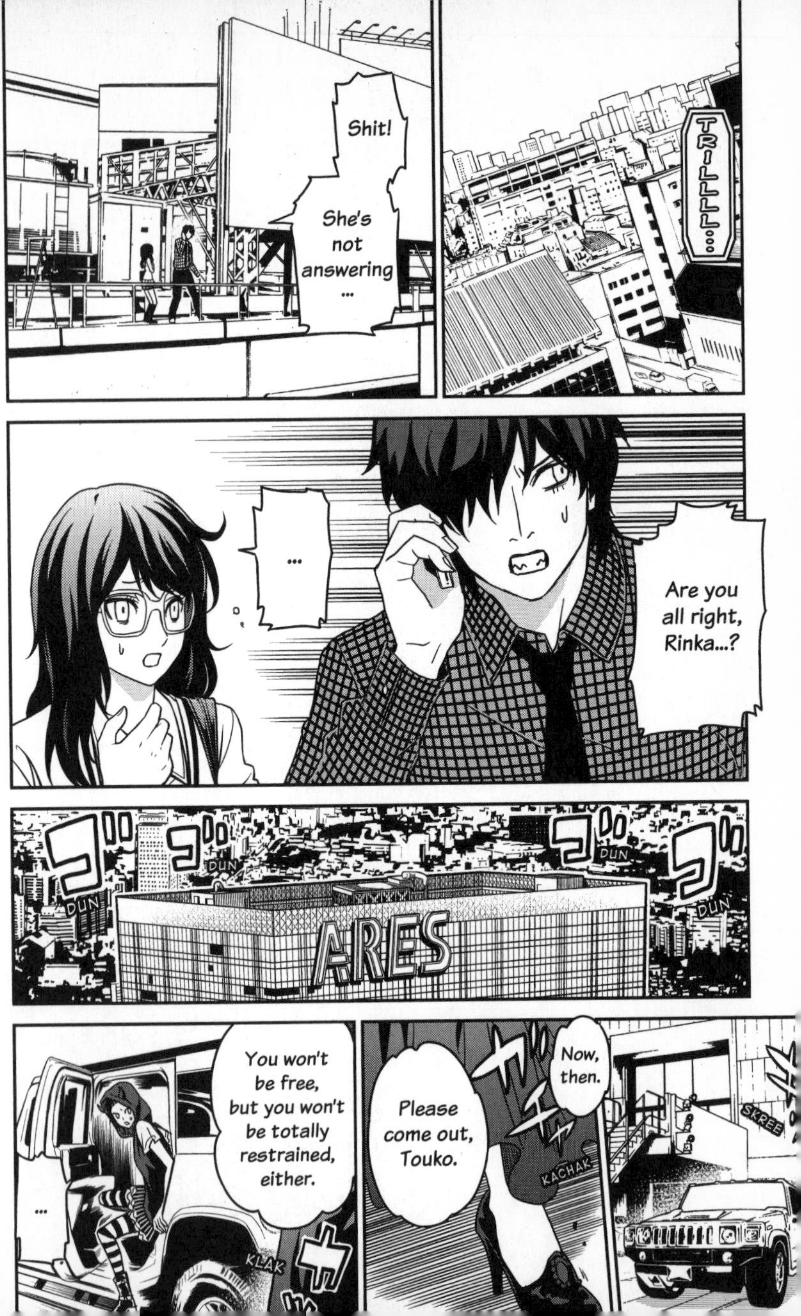
TRILLL...
Shit!
She's not answering...
Are you all right, Rinka...?
...
DUN
DUN
DUN
DUN
SKREE
Now, then.
Please come out, Touko.
KACHAK
You won't be free, but you won't be totally restrained, either.
KLAK
...

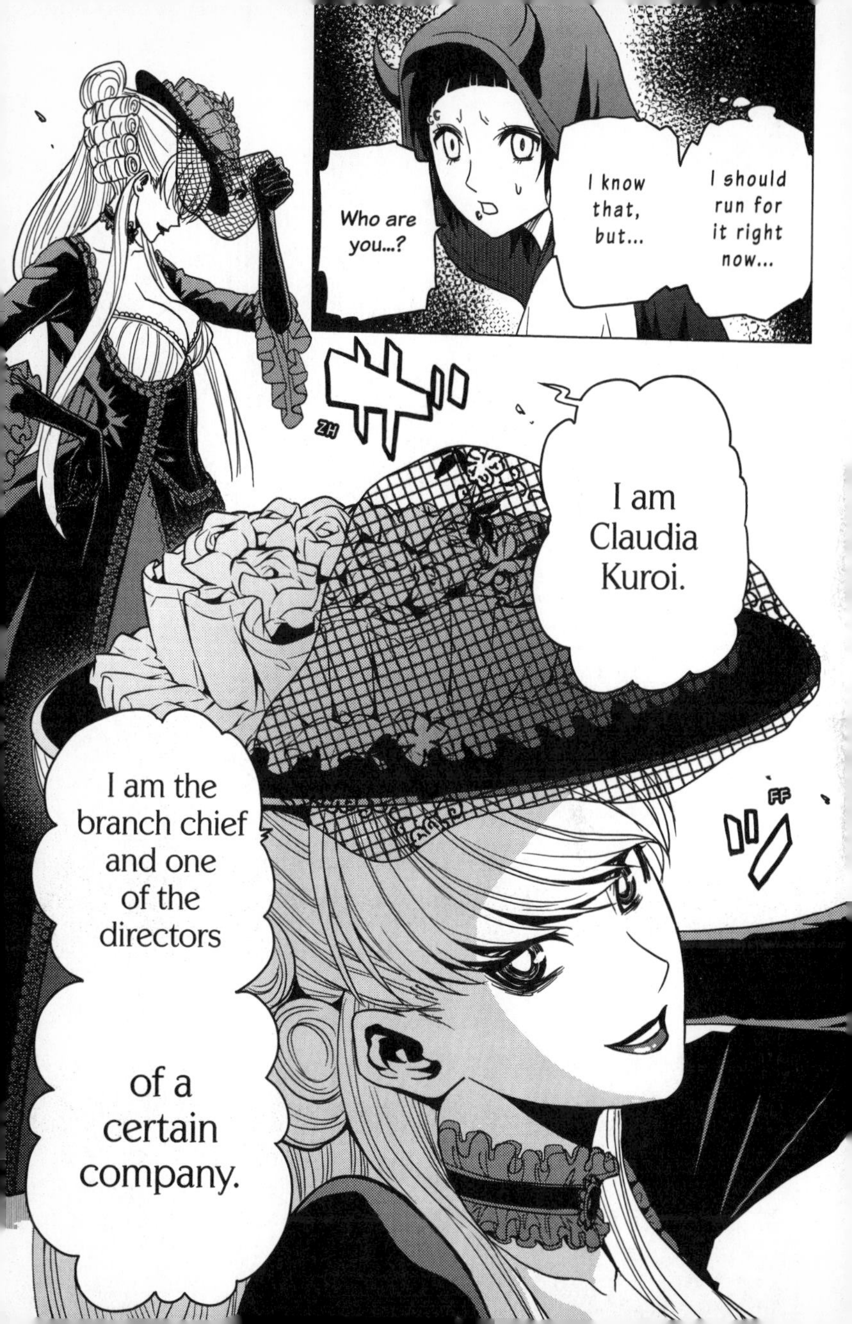
I should run for it right now...
I know that, but...
Who are you...?
ZH
I am Claudia Kuroi.
FF
I am the branch chief and one of the directors
of a certain company.

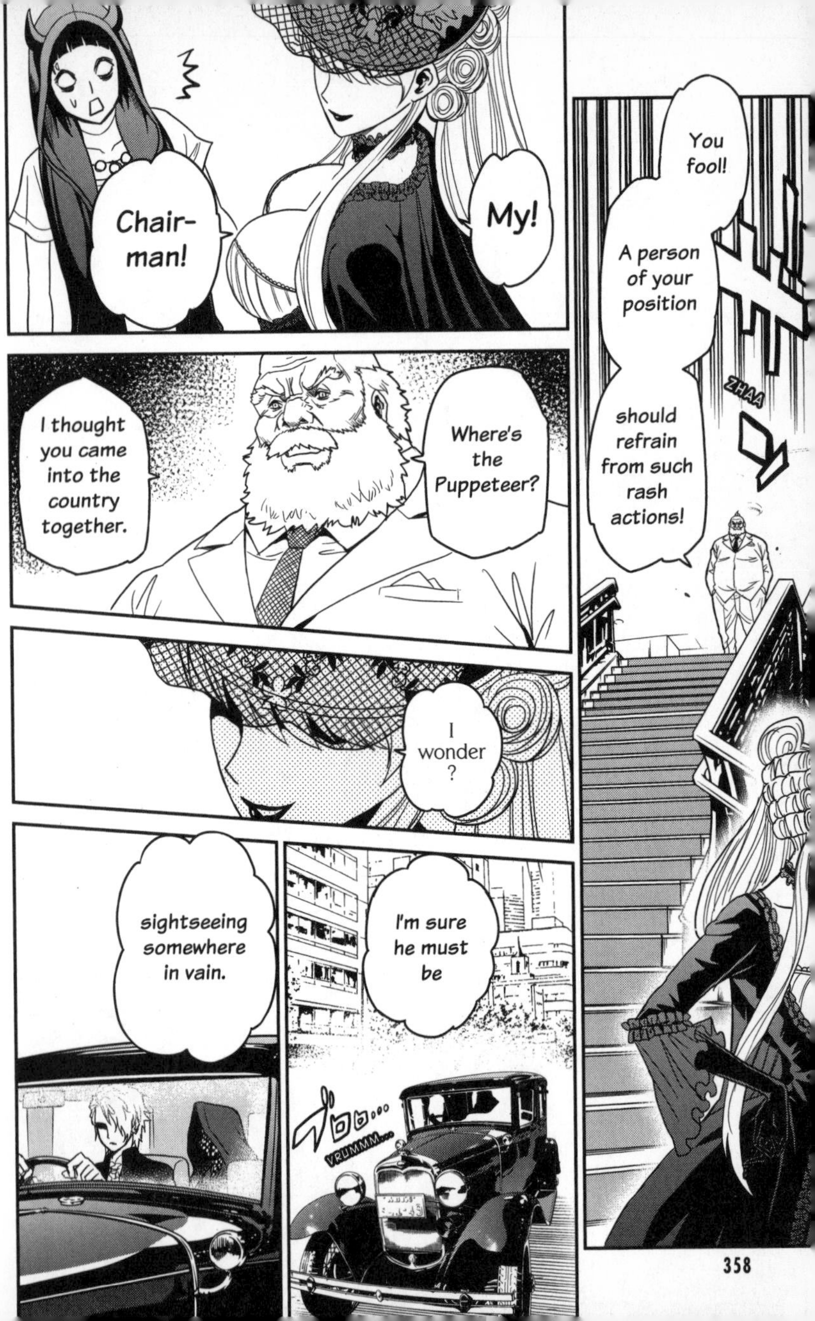
You fool!
A person of your position
should refrain from such rash actions!
ZHAA
My!
Chair-man!
Where's the Puppeteer?
I thought you came into the country together.
I wonder?
I'm sure he must be
VRUMMM...
sightseeing somewhere in vain.

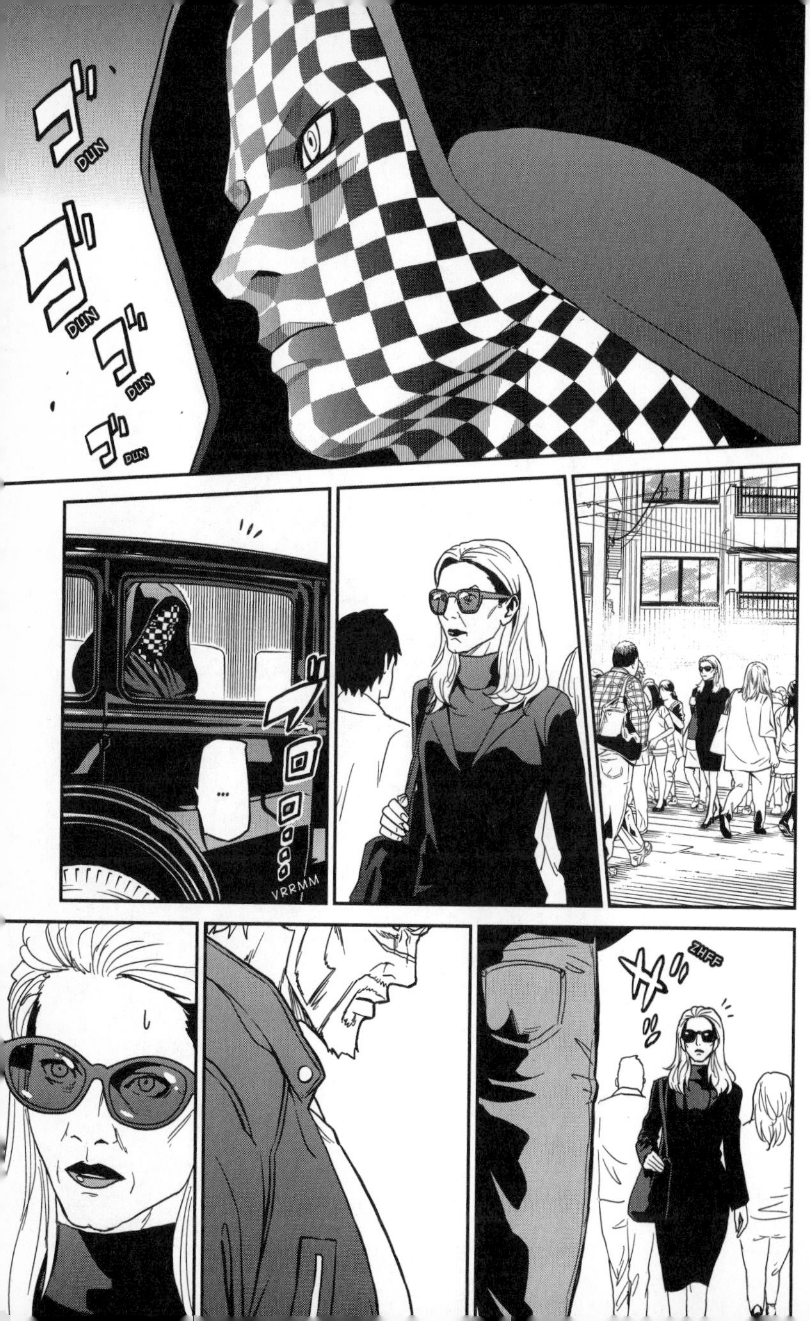
DUN
DUN
DUN
DUN
...
VRRMM
ZHFF

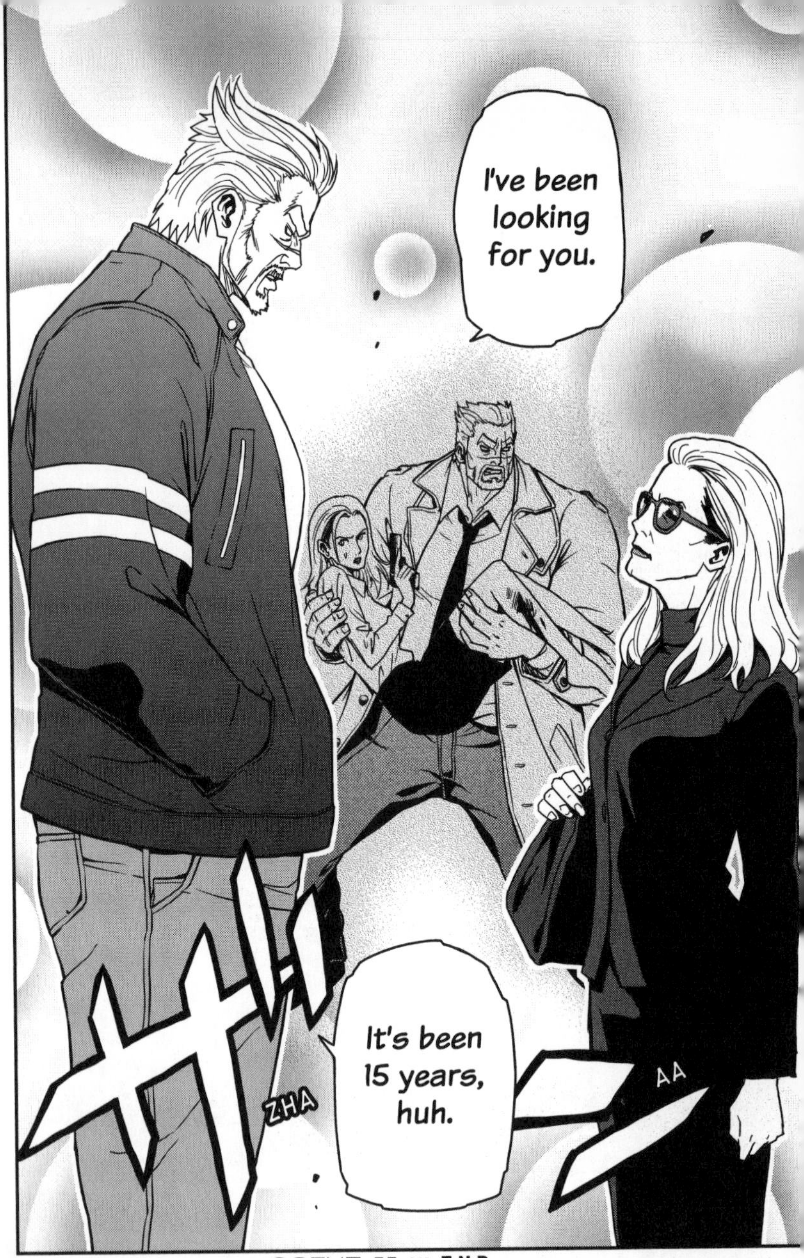
I've been looking for you.
AA
It's been 15 years, huh.
ZHA

SCENE 55 /// END

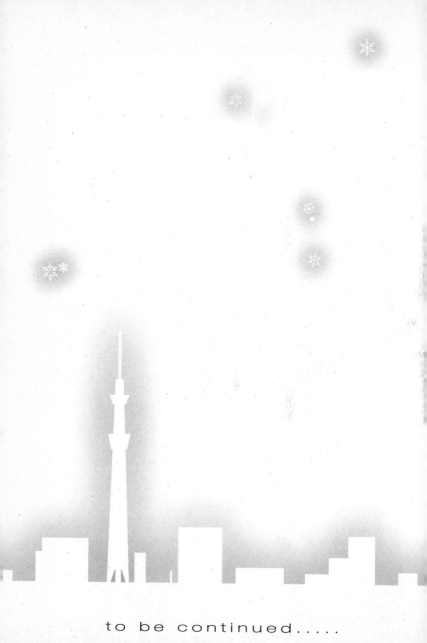

to be continued.....

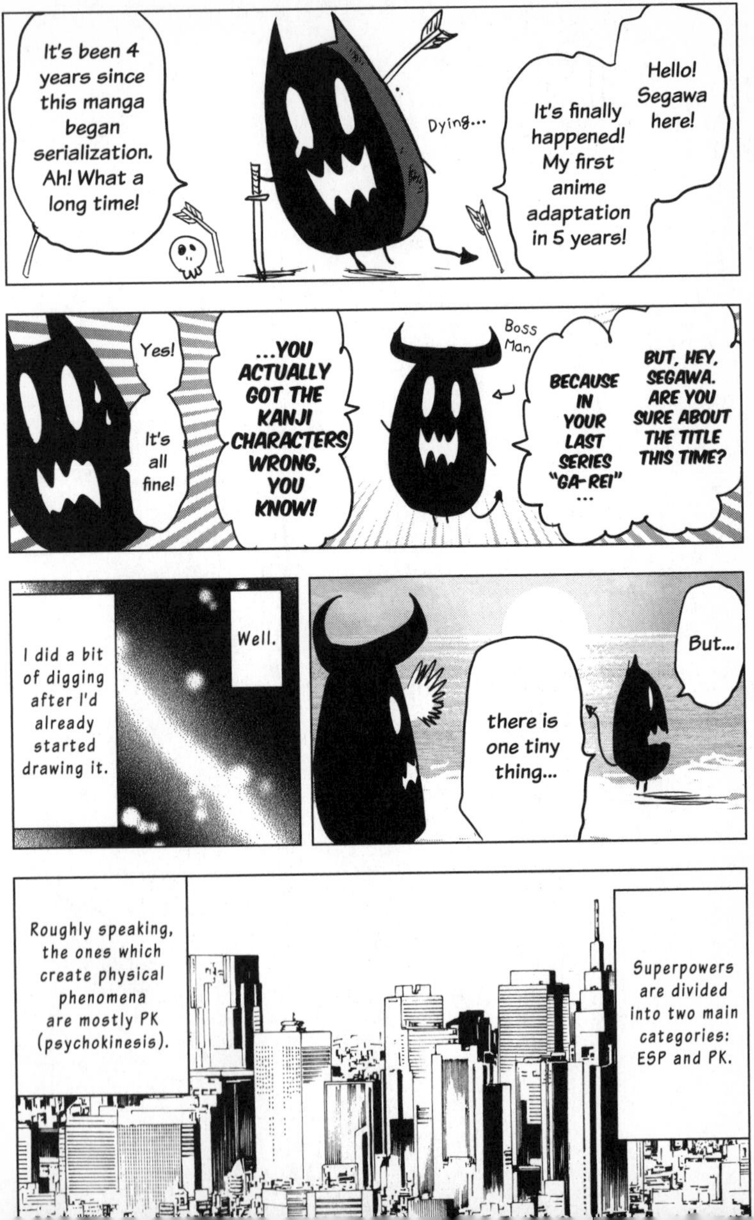
Hello! Segawa here!
It's finally happened! My first anime adaptation in 5 years!
Dying...
It's been 4 years since this manga began serialization. Ah! What a long time!
BUT, HEY, SEGAWA. ARE YOU SURE ABOUT THE TITLE THIS TIME?
BECAUSE IN YOUR LAST SERIES "GA-REI"...
Boss Man
...YOU ACTUALLY GOT THE KANJI CHARACTERS WRONG, YOU KNOW!
Yes!
It's all fine!
But...
there is one tiny thing...
Well.
I did a bit of digging after I'd already started drawing it.
Superpowers are divided into two main categories: ESP and PK.
Roughly speaking, the ones which create physical phenomena are mostly PK (psychokinesis).

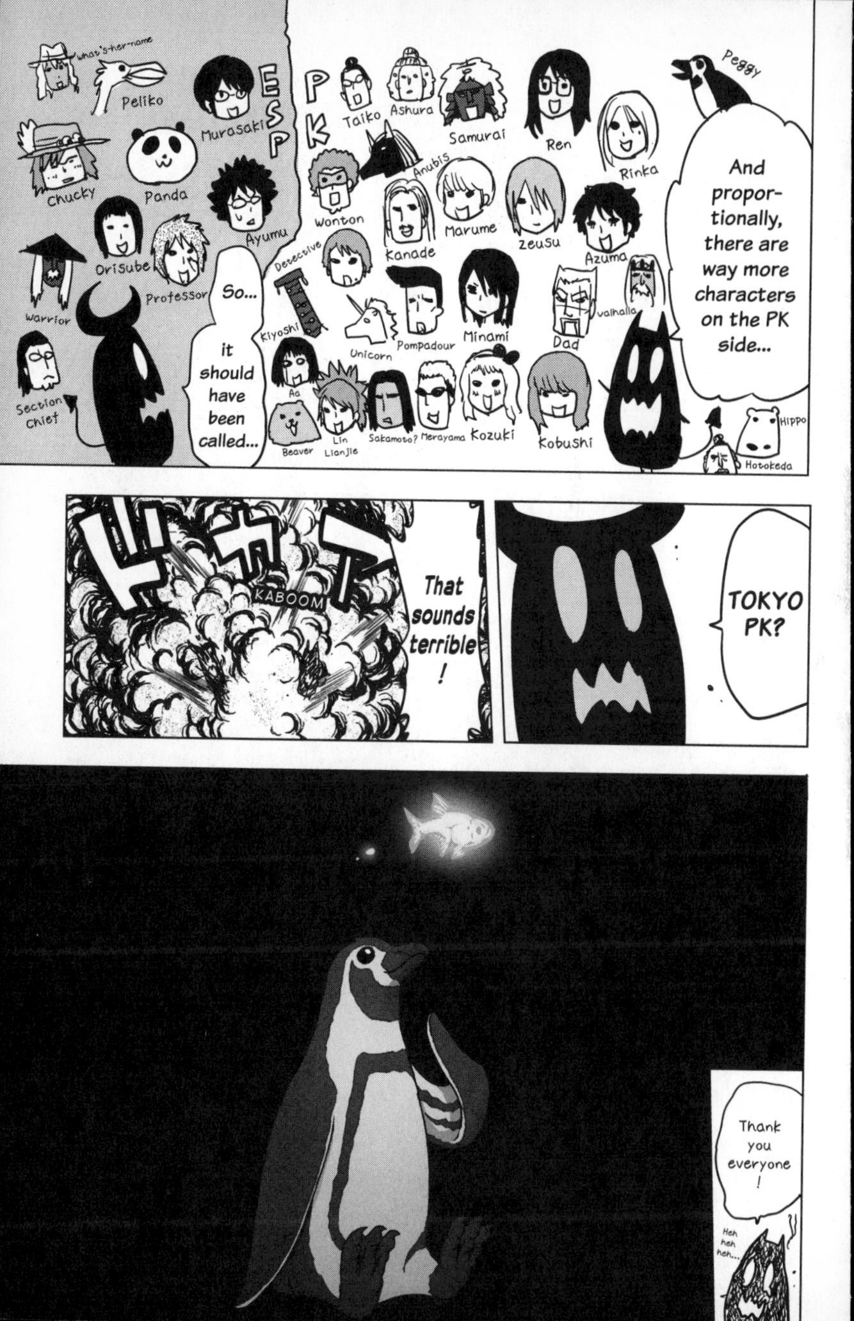
And proportionally, there are way more characters on the PK side...
So... it should have been called...
ESP
PK
Peggy
Rinka
Ren
Samurai
Ashura
Taiko
Anubis
Wonton
Marume
Kanade
zeusu
Azuma
Detective
Kiyoshi
Unicorn
Pompadour
Minami
Dad
valhalla
Aa
Beaver
Lin Lianjie
Sakamoto?
Merayama
Kozuki
Kobushi
Hippo
Hotokeda
what's-her-name
Peliko
Murasaki
Chucky
Panda
Ayumu
Orisube
Professor
warrior
Section Chief
TOKYO PK?
That sounds terrible!
KABOOM
Thank you everyone!
Heh heh heh...

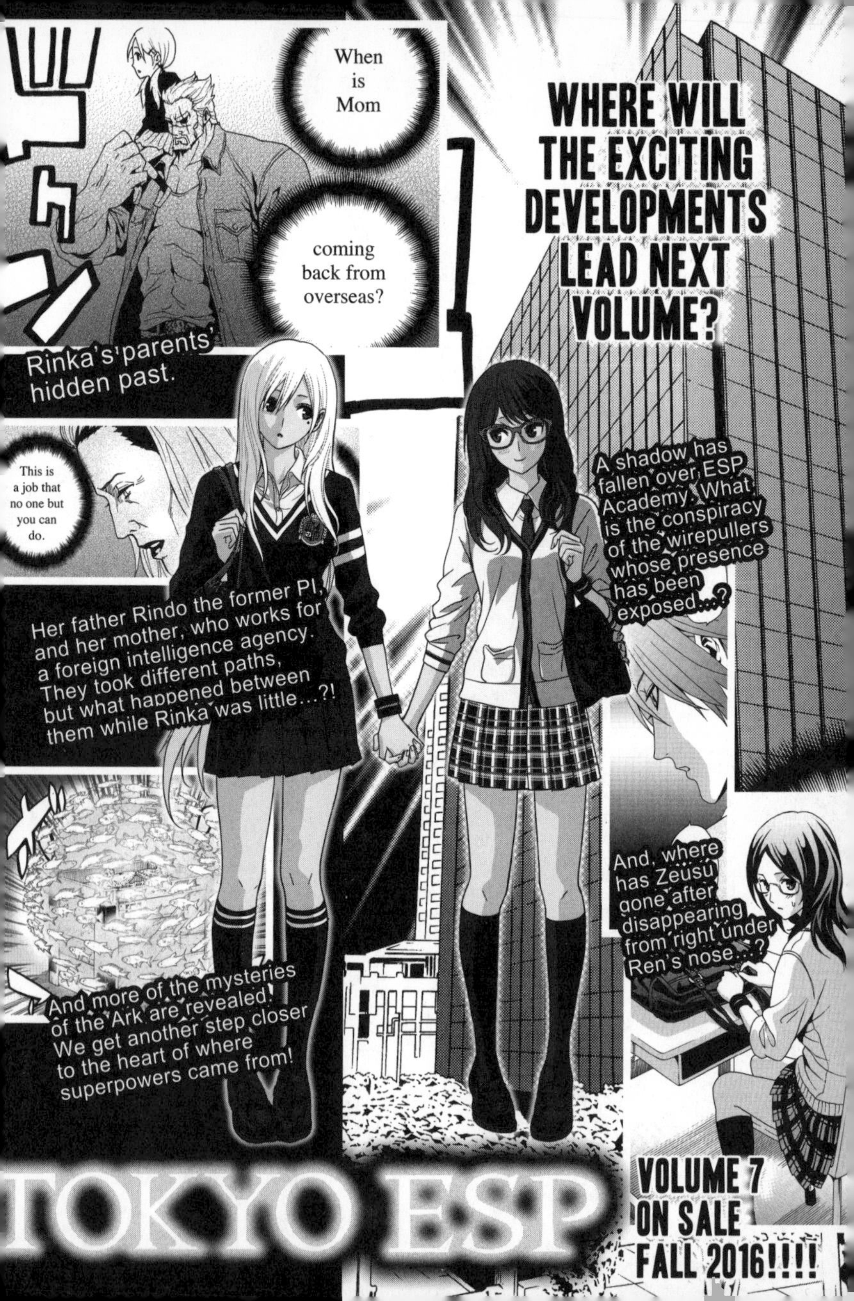
WHERE WILL THE EXCITING DEVELOPMENTS LEAD NEXT VOLUME?
When is Mom
coming back from overseas?
Rinka's parents' hidden past.
This is a job that no one but you can do.
Her father Rindo the former PI, and her mother, who works for a foreign intelligence agency. They took different paths, but what happened between them while Rinka was little...?!
A shadow has fallen over ESP Academy. What is the conspiracy of the wirepullers whose presence has been exposed...?
And, where has Zeusu gone after disappearing from right under Ren's nose...?
And more of the mysteries of the Ark are revealed! We get another step closer to the heart of where superpowers came from!
TOKYO ESP
VOLUME 7 ON SALE FALL 2016!!!!